Colorado's Historical Assets

A Research Guide for Genealogists, Local Historians and History Buffs Containing a Treasure Trove of Museums, Ghost Towns, Courthouses, Historic Homes and Hotels, along with the Libraries and Archives Holding Colorado's History

compiled by Dina C. Carson

Colorado's Historical Assets:

A Research Guide for Genealogists, Local Historians and History Buffs Containing a Treasure Trove of Museums, Maps, Ghost Towns, Courthouses, Historic Homes and Hotels, along with the Libraries and Archives Holding Colorado's History

compiled by Dina C. Carson

Published by:

Iron Gate Publishing
P.O. Box 999
Niwot, CO 80544

All rights reserved. No part of this book may be reproduced or transmitted in any form or by any means, electronic or mechanical, including photocopying, recording or any information storage and retrieval system without written permission from the publisher, except for the inclusion of brief quotations in a review.

This book is sold with the express understanding and agreement that the information and data within will be solely for internal use and will not be used for the creation or updating of mailing lists without express written permission of the publisher. For those of you who insist upon creating mailing lists anyway, *fair warning*, preference has been given to physical rather than mailing addresses.

The publisher of this directory makes no representation that it is absolutely accurate or complete. Errors and omissions, whether typographical, clerical or otherwise do sometimes occur and may occur anywhere within the body of this publication. The Publisher does not assume and hereby disclaims any liability to any party for loss or damage by errors or omissions in this publication, whether such errors or omissions result from negligence, accident or any other cause. We reserve the right not to list any group or agency that has proven difficult to work with while collecting information regarding that group or agency. *Note*: we must rely on information given to us on behalf of agencies, societies and associations herein. Information sent to us is regarded as accurate and entries are maintained until we receive word that a group has definitely disbanded.

Iron Gate Publishing has used its best efforts in collecting and preparing material for inclusion in *Colorado's Historical Assets*, but does not warrant that the information herein is complete or accurate, and does not assume, and hereby disclaims, any liability to any person for any loss or damage caused by errors or omissions in *Colorado's Historical Assets*, whether such errors or omissions result from negligence, accident or any other cause.

Copyright © 2020 by Dina C. Carson, Iron Gate Publishing
Printed in the United States of America
ISBN   1-68224-044-4   ISBN 13   978-1-68224-044-1

Dedicated to the many Colorado history nerds who love this stuff as much as I do.

Acknowledgments

To my friends at the Boulder Heritage Roundtable, thank you. You're always so supportive and the best group of history nerds I know—through and through!

To the staff at the Carnegie Library for Local History, I couldn't do half of what I love doing so much without you. Thanks a million! Most especially to Wendy Hall, who buys my books for the library's collection and hunts down anything territorial that would interest me—a huge thank you.

To the staff on the 5th Floor in the Denver Public Library whether in the genealogy collection, western history collection or archives, I may be out of your hair for awhile now that this project is done. Thanks for all of your help. Along with a special thanks to James Jeffrey, fellow genealogist and all around sage, whom I adore—sincerely. Thanks.

Thanks to my friend and fellow history nerd Carol Beam, who takes me around to see the historic properties owned by Boulder County. She's such a treasure and a help to me. Thanks for all of the fantastic road trips. I hope we're never done exploring.

To Mona Lambrecht, curator at the University of Colorado Heritage Center who loves this stuff as much as I do, and is willing to let me stick my nose into the University's upcoming sesquicentennial research, thank you!

To Silvia Pettem and Carol Taylor who write so eloquently about Boulder history, many thanks for the on-going inspiration.

A big thanks to Beth Benko for allowing me access to her study of Colorado Laws so that I could provide information on the subject in this book.

Thanks to Victoria Lopez-Terrell who gave me several days of help with state-wide grange records in the Archives and Special Collection within Morgan Library at the Colorado State University. And to Renee Caldwell, Secretary of the Colorado State Grange who got me started with a good list of active granges.

Thanks to Julie Doellingen, who created a very good list of the historic and active Masonic lodges in Colorado.

Finally, for a little housekeeping. All of the photographs are those of the author unless otherwise stated.

Contents

Introduction	7
Adams County	27
Alamosa County	41
Arapahoe County	49
Archuleta County	71
Baca County	79
Bent County	89
Boulder County	99
Broomfield County	119
Chaffee County	125
Cheyenne County	137
Clear Creek County	145
Conejos County	155
Costilla County	163
Crowley County	171
Custer County	177
Delta County	185
Denver County	195
Dolores County	227
Douglas County	235
Eagle County	247
El Paso County	257
Elbert County	281
Fremont County	291
Garfield County	303
Gilpin County	315
Grand County	325
Gunnison County	335
Hinsdale County	351
Huerfano County	359
Jackson County	369
Jefferson County	377

Kiowa County	395
Kit Carson County	403
La Plata County	413
Lake County	425
Larimer County	435
Las Animas County	453
Lincoln County	469
Logan County	477
Mesa County	487
Mineral County	499
Moffat County	507
Montezuma County	517
Montrose County	527
Morgan County	537
Otero County	545
Ouray County	555
Park County	563
Phillips County	573
Pitkin County	581
Prowers County	591
Pueblo County	601
Rio Blanco County	615
Rio Grande County	623
Routt County	631
Saguache County	643
San Juan County	653
San Miguel County	661
Sedgwick County	669
Summit County	677
Teller County	687
Washington County	697
Weld County	707
Yuma County	727
Cities & Towns Index	737
Archives & Museums Index	749

Introduction

Who Needs This Book?
Anyone who enjoys historical or genealogical research needs this book. Whether you like to go places and see them for yourself, or whether you research from afar, I've collected information you cannot find in any other single source.

What This Book is Not
This is not a history of the state of Colorado. There are many, many fine histories already out there. This book is meant to help you to discover the details of Colorado's history for yourself.

How to Use this Book
Each county has an introduction that includes when it was established, whether it was an original county or from what other county(ies) it was formed, adjacent counties, the county seat, the county government's website, population, area codes, zip codes, and a map showing where the county lies in relationship to other counties within Colorado.

Courthouses & County Government
The courthouse for each county is in the County seat, although many counties have more than one location where records are kept. Each county has contact information for:

County Commissioners. The County Commissioners are the over-arching governmental branch of elected officials at the county level. If you are researching the early settlement of a county, reading the County Commissioners minutes will give you an idea of what was going on across the county.

County Assessor. The Assessor is an elected position in Colorado and is responsible for tax assessments on property. Assessments are all electronic today, but in the past, the Assessor's card often included a photograph of the property, along with valuable information about it.

Clerk & Recorder. The Clerk & Recorder is an elected position and is responsible for recording land transactions, issuing marriage licenses and civil unions, elections and voter registration, and registers and issues titles to motor vehicles. Land records often contain valuable genealogical information.

Coroner. The Coroner or Medical Examiner is an elected position and is responsible for issuing death certificates, and issuing a determination of the cause of death in unattended deaths. In the past, the Coroner's office held inquests to determine the facts of an unattended death. These cases were often covered in the newspaper. Historical coroner's records may be found in the Coroner's office or in court records. Modern Coroner's offices do not generally deal with the general public, only the family members of someone's who is recently deceased. A few counties do not have an office of the Coroner. Those duties may be shared with another county. The Coroner's office also may be listed under the Sheriff's Department.

Elections. Many counties do not have separate offices for Elections, the responsibility for elections and voter registration may be under the Clerk & Recorder's office.

Public Health. The Public Health offices are responsible for issuing birth and death certificates. Most county offices will not release a birth or death certificate unless

Historical Assets Colorado

you are closely related to the person to whom it belongs. Older birth and death certificates can be obtained through the State Office of Vital Records. This office is also responsible for issuing marriage or divorce verifications, and registering individuals into the Colorado Voluntary Adoption Registry. Adoption records remain within the court system. Marriage certificates and divorce records remain within the counties.

Transportation (often called Public Works or Roads & Bridges). Maps can be essential to research, and often county transportation offices have the best county maps. They may also have historical road maps, and all of the petitions and reports that were generated in order to authorize a new road.

Treasurer. The Treasurer is an elected office, and they are responsible for collecting taxes for the county. Taxes, whether they be on personal or real property, are often used to establish people in place and time.

Some offices such as the coroner's office and transportation offices only list phone numbers on their websites because they're not equipped for visitors (or researchers) to stop by.

The Colorado Open Records Act (CORA) gives citizens the right to look at many documents produced by government. Many counties have a link to CORA requests on their websites. You will need to do a little bit of research before you can make a request, however, as it is difficult for staff to fill vague requests. Be specific (e.g. I'd like to see the divorce index for the year 1910).

Colorado's Defunct Counties

Arapahoe County, established on 25 Aug 1855, as a part of Kansas Territory before Colorado became a Territory still exists, although these counties were formed from Kansas Territory on 7 Feb 1859 but never organized: Broderick County, El Paso County, Fremont County, Montana County, Oro County, and Peketon County.

Jefferson Territory was formed 24 Oct 1859. It was never approved by the US Congress and it ended with the formation of Colorado Territory 28 Feb 1861. The first session of the Jefferson Territorial Legislature took place in Denver City on 7 Nov 1859. The capital of Jefferson Territory was Denver City from 24 Oct 1859 to 12 Nov 1860 and Golden City from 13 Nov 1860 to 6 June 1861, although Jefferson Territory was replaced by the official Colorado Territory on 28 Feb 1861.

The counties within Jefferson Territory are as follows with the names of the modern counties they encompassed in parentheses.

      Arrappahoe County (Arapahoe, Adams, Denver)
      Cheyenne County (Laramie County, WY)
      El Paso County (El Paso, Pueblo)
      Fountain County (SE Colorado)
      Heele or Steele County (Larimer)
      Jackson County (Boulder)
      Jefferson County (Jefferson)
      Mountain County (Gilpin, Clear Creek)
      North County (Jackson)

Introduction

> Park County (Park)
> Saratoga (County Grand, Summit)
> St Vrain County (Weld)

Guadalupe County was one of the 17 original counties established on 1 Nov 1861 but was renamed Conejos county on 7 Nov 1861.

Greenwood County was formed on 11 Feb 1870, but was split into Elbert and Bent Counties on 6 Feb 1874.

Platte County was organized from Weld County on 9 Feb 1872, but was abolished on 9 Feb 1874 when organizers failed to get voter approval. It was returned to Weld County.

Carbonate County was established on 8 Feb 1879 and renamed Lake County on 10 Feb 1879.

Uncompahgre County was formed on 27 Feb 1883 only to be renamed Ouray County on 2 Mar 1883.

South Arapahoe County was formed on 15 Nov 1902, but the name was changed back to Arapahoe County on 11 Apr 1903.

County Records

Each county has a synopsis of the types and earliest year that records were kept by the county government. The Colorado State Archives (CSA) also has vital records, and if they are earlier than what is reported in the county's holdings they will be listed with the earliest date of the records. All non-vital (birth, marriage, death) will be listed under the Colorado State Archive by the agency. County Physicians reports could include births or deaths. Remember, vital records are subject to privacy laws, so you may have to make a case for why you should have access to the records before the staff will show them to you. In some cases, you can ask the staff to confirm a birth date or death date without showing you the actual records, which may be all they are allowed to do. Having said that, find out what the rules are before you go. That way, you can make a case for a record being old enough to be open and available, for example.

County Records Held at the State Level

There are three major repositories with state-wide collections in Colorado: the Colorado State Archives, History Colorado (formerly the Colorado Historical Society) and the Denver Public Library.

The Colorado State Archives

The Colorado State Archives has records retention authority in Colorado, and is the repository of many original source materials from governmental organizations (state agencies, the legislature, cities, counties, school districts, fire protection districts, etc.) but may not have all records that have been created by these entities. With some exceptions due to records retention laws, most agencies have the final say in whether they keep their own records or send them to the Colorado State Archives.

Historical Assets Colorado

Several years ago the Colorado Council of Genealogical Societies had the finding aids for the Colorado State Archives scanned, and produced a quick guide to the holdings that would be most interesting to genealogists and local historians. You can access a copy of that quick index here: https://sites.rootsweb.com/~bgs/BGSQ/Archives_FindingAids.pdf. Because the Colorado State Archives continues to acquire material, this finding aid may not be up to date. Check with the archives for more recent acquisitions.

Your records research should include state agencies and these records are often not used for research. The following are current state agencies that may have territorial counterparts. There are also some agencies that no longer exist or agencies that have changed names over time. The agencies in bold are probably the best bet for research.

    Administration (incl state personnel, state buildings)
    Agriculture (incl records abt crops and livestock, brand books, state fair)
    Corrections (incl state penitentiary records)
    Education (incl teachers certificates and qualifications)
    FERA (Federal Emergency Relief Agency) (incl photographs)
    General Assembly (incl everything to do with the legislature)
    General Support Services (most of these records are closed, privacy)
    Governors (incl records from every governor since the territory was established)
    Health (many of these records are closed, privacy)
    Higher Education (incl the state's public college and universities)
    Human Services (incl relief agencies, youth corrections which are closed)
    Institutions (incl mental health and youth services, most records are closed)
    Judicial (incl the appeals and supreme courts)
    Labor & Employment (incl employment, workmen's compensation, closed)
    Law (incl Attorney General, legal services, litigation, mostly closed)
    Local Affairs (Local affairs helps local communities so there are some interesting records in this group, including the motion picture and television advisory committee and the Colorado Bureau of Investigation.)
    Military & Veterans Affairs (incl service records, national guard)
    Natural Resources (incl many mining records, wildlife, geology, etc.)
    Personnel (incl state employees, closed for privacy)
    Public Safety (incl state patrol, Colorado Bureau of Investigation, closed)
    Regulatory Agencies (incl licensing for doctors, dentists, nurses, etc.)
    Revenue (incl taxes, including inheritance taxes)
    Secretary of State (incl incorporation records, state-wide elections, petitions)
    Transportation (a great source for maps, early records include wagon roads, toll roads, and railroads)
    Treasury (incl records of payments to people who provided services to the state)
    Vital Records (including a state-wide birth and death index starting in 1900)

Introduction

The State of Colorado for many years was the agency that microfilmed records across the state, and the Colorado State Archives is the repository for that "master" microfilm. The master microfilm is *not* available for research (PLEASE DO NOT ASK), but should be available at the agency that holds (held) the original records. For example, if you are looking for the tax records from Adams County, you will find master film from the Adams County Treasurer's office held at the Colorado State Archives. There should be a copy of the film that is available for research at the Adams County Treasurer's office. The physical records could be held in either place.

The Colorado State Archives also has film that *is* available for research. These rolls of microfilm are copies of the master microfilms and exist in large collections such as the school district census collection from across the state. You can use these films in the main research room at the Colorado State Archives.

Two additional types of records are kept at the Colorado State Archives—publications and photographs. Publications could be anything from magazines issued by a city a group like the State Historical Society, reports by city, county or state agencies, or professional magazines such as those issued by the Colorado Medical Association, or the Colorado Stockmen's Association. The photograph collection is fairly eclectic, but includes agricultural and mining photographs from areas across the state, county courthouses, portraits of supreme court judges and legislators, and a nearly complete set of mugshots for prisoners at the state penitentiary.

Because of the sheer volume of the records held by the Colorado State Archives, each county has a listing of the agencies for which it holds physical records, film and masterfilm. You will then need to consult with the staff at the Colorado State Archives for more information about specific records during specific time periods.

Two types of records deserve special notice for genealogists: naturalizations and delayed birth certificates.

Naturalization records are mostly held within the courts for each county, and the CSA has naturalizations for many counties. In 1907, naturalizations became Federal records, although many naturalizations were filed in county courthouses even after 1907.

Many counties have deposited their delayed birth certificates at the Colorado State Archives. After Social Security began in 1935, many older people who qualified for Social Security applied for delayed birth certificates, so even if a delayed birth certificate was issued in 1940, it may belong to someone who was born 80 years earlier in 1860.

The Colorado State Archives maintains an online database of records that have been indexed, but it is in no way complete. More indexes are coming online all the time, but much of what they have has never been indexed. You can search the historical records database here: https://www.colorado.gov/pacific/archives/archives-search.

The Colorado State Archives is located at:
1313 Sherman St Rm 120, Denver, CO 80203, 303-866-2358
https://www.colorado.gov/pacific/archives/Genealogy

History Colorado

History Colorado's Hart Research Library has two online catalogs: Research Center Catalog which holds books, manuscripts, serials, maps and photography, and their Online

Historical Assets Colorado

Catalog which holds archives, artifacts and photographs (https://www.historycolorado.org/catalogs). They describe their collection highlights as: 10th Mountain Division Artifacts, Colorado's Italian Americans, Denver & Rio Grande Railroad Photographs, Firearms, Hispanic Textiles, Historical Archaeology, Mesa Verde Collections, Quilts, Spanish American War, Ute Artifacts and War Relics.

History Colorado also has one of the most extensive collections of Colorado Newspapers in the state. While some of their newspapers are searchable online at the Colorado Historic Newspapers Project (https://www.coloradohistoricnewspapers.org), many are available only at the Hart Research Library.

Long ago when the Colorado State Archives and the Colorado Historical Society became separate entities, the non-government-produced documents were to go to the Colorado Historical Society with the governmental documents remaining at the Colorado State Archives. Some items were not placed in the "correct" collection, so there is crossover between the two archives. It is worth your time to look in both catalogs to see what exists where.

The Denver Public Library

The Genealogy and Western History Collection at the Denver Public Library is one of the best genealogical and local history libraries anywhere in the country. They also maintain an archive that holds many original source materials. If there are items from the archive that are of particular interest, they will be listed. You will not find lists of books, maps, individual deeds or mining claims held at the Denver Public Library in each county's listing, as they are numerous.

Personal papers held in either the Hart Research Library or the Denver Public Library will not be listed in each county's listing. There are simply too many of them and of such diverse type that you will have to conduct that research on your own.

School Districts

The Colorado Dept of Education, has some excellent school district maps, here: https://www.cde.state.co.us/cdereval/districtmaps

School districts often do not follow county boundaries. If a school district has territory within the county, it is listed, even if a majority of the district is in a neighboring county. In the late 1940s, Colorado reorganized the hundreds of historical school districts into fewer large districts.

Historic School Districts

Colorado was early to adopt laws regarding the education of children. There are several state-wide censuses of children between the ages of 4 and 21 (or 25) who qualified to attend school. Most, but not all, of the historic school districts contained only one school. More often than not, in those small districts, the school name was the same as the district name. Around 1900, many counties established a "Union" high school for the entire county, meaning that any student from any district within the county who wished to attend high school could do so at the union school. These high schools are not listed with the historic school districts.

Introduction

Fraternal Organizations

There are many fraternal organizations throughout Colorado's history. Included in each county are the historic and current lodges for the Grange (Patrons of Husbandry), Masons, Odd Fellows, Knights of Pythias and the Benevolent Protective Order of Elks. These are not the only fraternal organizations in Colorado, but these are some of the most popular with the greatest number of chapters and members.

Most of the chapter information of these fraternal organizations came from the "Proceedings" issued after their annual state-wide meetings. "Proceedings" are not available for every fraternal organization for every year since their beginnings, but many are kept in the archives of the Denver Public Library. Much of the chapter information about the Granges can be found in the archives of the Colorado State University.

Fraternal organizations are listed in this order: name of the lodge, number, county, city and the establishment date (if known). Some lodges re-use numbers so the establishment dates may not seem in order. If you are a member of one of these lodges and have a more complete list than we have, please let us know.

Granges

The Grange movement (Patrons of Husbandry) became popular in the late 1860s in Colorado and many granges were formed. Only a few are still operational today. The state Grange office is located at 21901 East Quincy Avenue, Aurora, CO , 719-748-5008. For more information about their museum, and to make an appointment to visit: http://www.coloradograngeorg/museum/index.html. Much of the archival material relating to the historic granges are in the archives of Colorado State University in Fort Collins, CO. For more information: https://lib2.colostate.edu/archives/findingaids/agriculture/acsg.html.

Masons

Ancient Free & Accepted Masons

Even before Colorado was a Territory, there were organized Masonic lodges. The Grand Lodge of Kansas granted a charter to the Auraria Lodge in 1859, and to the Golden City Lodge on 17 Oct 1860. The Grand Lodge of Nebraska granted a charter to the Summit Lodge at Parkville in 1861, and to the Rocky Mountain Lodge at Gold Hill on 2 Aug 1861.

The Grand Lodge of Colorado is located at: 1130 Panorama Dr, Colorado Springs, CO 80904, (719) 471-9587. They have a museum as well as a library and archives. http://www.coloradofreemasons.org

Royal Arch Masons

The Royal Arch Masons are another degree of freemasonry. For more information on the Colorado Royal Arch Masons, visit their website: http://yorkrite.com/co/megrac/

Knights Templar

The Knights Templar are also an additional degree of freemasonry. The first conclave of the Knights Templar of Colorado was held in Denver in March 1876. The Grand Lodge is called the Grand Commandery, but I didn't find a website for a

Historical Assets Colorado

Grand Commandery in Colorado. There are several local Knights Templar lodges that do have websites.

Prince Hall-Affiliated Masons

The Prince Hall-Affiliated Masonic lodges are African-American lodges. The earliest lodge in this area was in Denver in 1876. While I did not find an address for a Grand Lodge here in Colorado, the website for the Grand Lodge of Colorado, Wyoming and Utah is: http://www.mwphglco.org. Within the Prince Hall-Affiliated Masons are the Knights Templar, Royal Arch Masons, Scottish Rite and Order of the Golden Circle.

Eastern Star

The Eastern Star lodges are lodges for both men and women. The organization of the Grand Chapter for the Order of the Eastern Star in Colorado was held in Colorado Springs in June 1892. For more information, see: http://www.oes-colorado.org.

Prince Hall-Affiliated Eastern Star

The Prince Hall-Affiliated Eastern Star was organized first in 1884 by African-American women. By 1900 there were Eastern Star lodges in Colorado. For more information consult the Grand Lodge of Colorado, Wyoming and Utah at their website here: http://www.mwphglco.org

Odd Fellows

The Odd Fellows are not a Masonic organization, but have a long tradition of charitable work including providing homes for orphans and the elderly. They were the first fraternal organization to accept women. The first meeting of the Odd Fellows Grand Lodge in Colorado was in 1867. The Odd Fellows Grand Lodge is located: 1545 Phelps Ave. Canon City, Colorado 81212, (719) 275-1606, http://www.ioofcolorado.org.

Rebekahs

Rebekah lodges have both male and female members. The first Rebekah lodge was established in Denver in 1865. I didn't find an address or website for the Rebekah Assembly of Colorado, but they do have a Facebook page: https://www.facebook.com/pg/Rebekah-Assembly-of-Colorado-144691148964873/posts/

Knights of Pythias

The Knights of Pythias first formed a lodge in Denver in 1872. There is no known Grand Lodge active in Colorado today. This website contains some of the history of the Colorado Lodges: http://www.kophistory.com/co/index.htm

Pythian Sisters

The Pythian Sisters are the female auxiliary to the Knights of Pythias. I didn't find any lodges listed for Colorado on the national Pythian Sisters website: https://pythiansisters.org.

Introduction

Benevolent Protective Order of Elks

The Benevolent Protective Order of Elks was organized in 1858 in NYC as a social club. Since then there have been several thousand chapters organized across the United States. The Elks number their lodges by order or admission and the Denver Lodge has the number 17 which must have been fairly early as the Boulder Lodge No. 556 was organized in 1900. For more information, https://www.elks.org.

City & Town Halls

Like county government, city and town governments produce records. There is contact information for each city hall starting with the county seat (in bold) and other cities within the county.

The following is a brief list (not a complete list) of the kinds of departments and the records you could find at departments within a city:

   Boards & Commissions (historic preservation, landmarks)
   Building (building permits)
   City Clerk (licenses)
   Court Administration (municipal court records)
   Elections (voter registration)
   Finance (taxes)
   Judicial (small claims)
   Library & Cultural Services (local history collection, historic places)
   Parks, Recreation & Open Space (cemetery, historic places)
   Planning (maps)
   Public Records (property)

Archives & Manuscript Collections

Where one exists, each county has a list of archives and manuscript collections along with a synopsis of the collection, and contact information. Archival materials are the holy grail for most genealogists and local historians. Often, some of the best gems are not the best advertised.

Local Libraries

The first library listed is the library for the county seat (in bold), followed by local libraries in smaller towns within the county. Often, local libraries will have copies of one-of-a-kind historical information written by members of the community and are worth a visit, or at least a look at the online catalog.

Historical & Genealogical Societies

Historical and genealogical societies may be the best source of local research information, and many maintain their own collections or museums. Where one exists, each county has a list of historical and genealogical societies with their contact information.

Historical Assets Colorado

Links
Each county has links to helpful websites such as the Colorado GenWeb Project, Cyndi's List, the FamilSearch Wiki, Linkpendium, the RootsWeb Wiki, and the Wikipedia page for the county.

Historic Hotels
While you are traveling, you may want to spend some time enjoying the local history outside of the courthouse, library or archives. Where there are historic hotels, they are listed with their contact information. I chose to concentrate on the hotels, but there are many lovely and historic bed & breakfast options as well. You'll have to look these up on your own, however.

Museums & Historic Sites
Each county has a list of museums and historic sites. Some museums and historic sites maintain their own archives not only of objects, but the historical provenance of the items, biographical research on the former owners of the objects, and other historical documentation. Staff libraries are often a rich source of information about specialized aspects of a museum's collection.

Special Events & Scenic Locations
Many, but not all, counties in Colorado have a county fair. Many of these have been operating for more than 100 years, which is a fine tradition. Most local communities have events that bring the community together, and scenic locations that are points of interest both to community members and travelers. Where there are events or scenic locations, each county has a list along with contact or calendar information.

Ghost Towns & Other Sparsely Populated Places
Where they exist, each county has a list of towns that have either been designated as ghost towns on popular ghost town websites such as, http://www.ghosttowns.com or Wikipedia, or they have populations under 100 in the 2010 census or in 1890, based upon Cram's *Unrivaled Atlas of the World* published in 1898 by George F Cram. Gilbert S. Bahn excerpted and re-published the atlas as *American Place Names of Long Ago* in 1998. They are both excellent sources of ghost towns and sparsely populated places, as is *Guide to the Colorado Ghost Towns and Mining Camps* by Perry Eberhart.

Newspapers
Each county has a list of newspapers in the order of earliest first publication date to the most recent, or current newspaper. The current newspaper may not be at the bottom of the list if it has been publishing a long time. It will be listed in the order that it began publishing. Remember that some counties were formed later than some of the more famous cities within them, Cripple Creek, for example. There were newspapers in Cripple Creek nearly a decade before Teller became a county. You will find those newspapers in the original county of El Paso.

Introduction

The Library of Congress's Chronicling America, http://chroniclingamerica.loc.gov has more information on where you can find extant copies or microfilm of the newspapers listed. Two of the best sources for Colorado newspapers are the Hart Library at History Colorado and the Colorado Historic Newspapers Project online at: https://www.coloradohistoricnewspapers.org. Many local libraries also have historic newspapers for their area on microfilm.

Graveyards
Because of the numbers of places for burial, and the ease of locating cemeteries on websites such as Colorado Gravestones (www.coloradogravestones.org), FindAGrave (www.findagrave.com) or Billion Graves (www.billiongraves.com), graveyards or cemeteries have not been listed.

Places on the National Register
Each county has a list of buildings on the National Register of Historic Places along with the city where they are located, and the address. The National Register of Historic Places (NRHP) is the federal government's official list of "districts, sites, buildings, structures and objects deemed worthy of preservation for their historical significance." [Wikipedia]. For more information on the criteria to be included on the National Register, see https://www.nps.gov/subjects/nationalregister/what-is-the-national-register.htm.

USGS Historic Places
The US Geological Survey maintains a database of places that have been listed as "historical" which, in many cases, means that they no longer exist. This list includes the name of the historical place, the city it is in or is nearest to (or its topo map name equivalent), and the GPS coordinates for its location. The nearest city may be in another county.

Grand Army of the Republic (GAR) Posts
Shortly after the end of the Civil War, the Grand Army of the Republic formed to give Union veterans of the war a place for camaraderie but also to exert political pressure on Congress to grant Civil War veterans pensions. The motto of the GAR was "Fraternity, Charity, Loyalty." It held a National Encampment every year from 1866 to 1949. The GAR peaked in the 1890s with over 400,000 members. Eventually the GAR named the Sons of Union Veterans as its successor, and the GAR ceased to exist in 1956 with the death of its last member.

There were many GAR posts in Colorado within the Colorado-Wyoming Department. Local Posts were organized underneath the larger departments. Most of the local posts have left records of their meetings, many held at the Denver Public Library, the Carnegie Library for Local History in Boulder, and other locations. A good catalog of records for the GAR in Colorado is here: https://www.suvcw.org/garrecords/garposts/co.htm.

USGS Historic Military Places
Where there is an historic military place in the USGS database, it is listed along with the city where it is (or was) located, along with the GPS coordinates.

Historical Assets Colorado

Historic Forts
Rather than list these by county which did not apply to most of these forts, they are being listed here.

Camp Alva Adams
East of Colorado Blvd, Denver
Established Apr 1898, abandoned May 1898
2nd US Volunteer Cavalry Regiment

Fort Bent
Bent's Old Fort (Fort Williams), 35110 Hwy 194 E, La Junta, CO 81050, 719-383-5010

Established in 1833 by William and Charles Bent, along with Ceran St Vrain as a trading post. Living history museum run by the National Park Service, https://www.nps.gov/beol/index.htm

Fort Crawford
Established 21 July 1880 on the west bank of the Uncompahgre River, 8 miles south of Montrose.

Fort Garland
Established in 1858 in the San Luis Valley during the gold rush. Also home of the 9th Cavalry Buffalo Soldiers. Fort Garland Museum (run by History Colorado), 29477 Hwy 159, Fort Garland, CO 81133, 719-379-3512

Fort Lewis
18683 Hwy 140, Hesperus, CO 81326, 970-385-4574

Established in 1878 in Pagosa Springs, it was moved to Hesperus in 1880 and decommissioned in 1891. Now known as the San Juan Basin Research Center

Fort Logan
Established in Oct 1887 eight miles southwest of Denver at the time. It was used as a prisoner of war camp in 1943-1944 and closed in 1946 following WWII. The buildings were used as a soldier's home for a time in the 1950s and in 1960 the Fort Logan Mental Health Center was established. The Field Officers Quarters is now a historic museum (Building 10), located at 3742 W Princeton Cr. Friends of Historic Fort Logan have more history here: http://www.friendsofhistoricfortlogan.org/history/

Fort Lupton
Established around 1835 by Lancaster Platt Lupton on the Platte River as a fur trading post. The town of Fort Lupton grew up around the area.

Fort Lyon
The fort from which Colonel John Chivington launched the attack on the Cheyenne and Arapahoe at Sand Creek in 1864.

Introduction

Fort Massachusetts

Established on the west bank of Ute Creek for the protection of settlers in the San Luis Valley. Built in 1852, it was abandoned in 1858.

Fort Morgan

Established in 1865 as Camp Wardwell, along the Overland Trail for the protection of wagons headed to Denver and the mining districts. The fort closed in 1868. Fort Morgan Museum, 414 Main St, Fort Morgan, CO 80701, 970-542-4010

Fort Pueblo

Established in the 1840s as a military fort and trading center. It was abandoned after the Christmas massacre of 1854 by the Utes and Apache. There is a museum that has artifacts and a replica trading post. El Pueblo History Museum, 301 N Union, Pueblo, CO 81001, 719-583-0453

Fort Sedgwick

Originally called Camp Rankin, it was built in the summer of 1864. It was a place of shelter when Julesburg was attacked in 1865. It was abandoned in May 1871.

Fort St Vrain

One of the Platte River forts, it was established in the 1830s as a fur trading fort by Ceran St Vrain.

Fort Uncompahgre

Established as a military fort and trading outpost in the 1820s by Antione Robidoux, it is now an interpretative museum. Fort Uncompahgre Museum, 440 N Palmer St, Delta, CO 81416, 970-874-8349

Fort Vasquez

Established in 1830s by Louis Vasquez along the Platte River as a fur trapping post. It was abandoned by the time the gold rush came to Colorado in 1859. Fort Vasquez Museum, 13412 US Hwy 85, Platteville, CO 80651, 970-785-2832

Military Bases

Military bases often have their own libraries and museums. Active military bases are often restricted, so you may need to make an appointment to visit, and requesting personnel records is not possible due to privacy issues. Historic personnel (service or pension) records will be found at either the National Archives in Washington, D.C. or at the National Personnel Records Center in St. Louis, MO. You may be able to locate unit or regimental histories at an active military base. There are only six active military bases in Colorado, located in Arapahoe, El Paso and Pueblo counties.

Historical Assets Colorado

Post Offices
Many Federal census records include a post office location on the sheet. These post office locations include the city where it is or was located, the date it was established (if known), the date it was discontinued (if known), and the zip code if it is an active post office. If a discontinuation date has an asterisk, it means that the post office operated between the establishment date and discontinuation date but not continuously. If a post office has a 2 behind its name, it is usually because there was a post office in that county with the same name that was discontinued, and a new post office with that name was established either in a different location in the county, or it is still open.

Many post offices operated in more than one county due to county boundaries changing and not necessarily that the physical post office moved. The best source to determine the history of Colorado post offices is: Bauer, William H., James L. Ozment, and John H. Willard. *Colorado Post Offices, 1859–1989: A Comprehensive Listing of Post Offices, Stations, and Branches.* Golden: Colorado Railroad Museum, 1971; second revised edition, 1990.

Online, the US Postal Service has a Postmaster Finder that is very helpful in locating postmasters as well as post offices, https://about.usps.com/who-we-are/postmaster-finder/welcome.htm. There are also some interesting historical documents to read from that site including *Post Offices in Antarctica,* and *Ladies Delivery Windows.* Another website where you can search for postal locations is: www.postallocations.com/co/.

The National Archives and Records Administration has the following types of records about post offices, some of which have been indexed and are online: Records of Postmasters, Records of Post Office Locations and Post Office Names.

Topo Quads
Topographical maps are useful for identifying geographical features such as mountains, rivers and lakes, but also man-made features such as wells, mines, buildings, roads, cemeteries, churches, schools, canals and railroads.

Topographical maps have been made by public agencies such as the General Land Office, the War Department, the Coast Survey and beginning in 1879, the US Geological Survey (USGS).

The Geographic Names Information System (GNIS) is the official database for place names. It is maintained by the USGS and contains the names of places that exist today and those that no longer exist.

USGS Topo Map Coordinates
The combination of the four coordinates given will give the latitude and longitude of the four corners of the map. For example, the coordinates for Dalkan Mountain in Douglas county are: 391500N, 390730N, 1050000W, and 1050730W. When you combine these coordinates you get:

    391500N, 1050000W
    391500N, 1050730W
    390730N, 1050000W
    390730N, 1050730W

Introduction

Dates
You may find dates written in the conventional genealogical way, for example 24 May 1876, or reversed as 1876 May 24. The meaning is the same, it may be the collection method that is different. Collecting dates in an Microsoft Excel spreadsheet is more reliable when reversed so that Excel does not try to re-make the dates into a non-genealogical, but more standard format such as 24-May-76.

Statewide Research
State Capitol
200 E Colfax, Denver, CO 80203, https://www.colorado.gov/capitol
Historical tours are offered free daily which include a self-guided tour of the 3rd floor museum.

State Archives
1313 Sherman St, Denver, CO 80203, 303-866-2358
https://www.colorado.gov/archives
Historical Records Index Search
https://www.colorado.gov/pacific/archives/archives-search

The Colorado State Archives is the primary repository for government-generated records for the state, counties, cities and special districts. It also has records for Federal projects such as the Civilian Conservation Corps and the Historical Records Survey by the Works Progress Administration.

Colorado Vital Records Office
Colorado Department of Health
4300 Cherry Creek Drive S, Denver CO 80222, 303-756-4464
https://www.colorado.gov/pacific/cdphe/searching-vital-records

State-Wide Records Research
The first **censuses** in the area were the census of the four territories that covered the area: Kansas (listed in Arapahoe County), Nebraska (listed under unorganized territory), New Mexico (listed in Taos and Mora Counties), and Utah (not settled in the area that would become Colorado). Colorado also conducted a **state census** in 1885 that included a mortality schedule.

Birth and Death records were kept by the clerks in towns and counties until 1907. The Colorado State Archives has birth, delayed birth and death records for some counties. Check with the Vital Records Office of the Colorado Department of Health for birth and death records after 1907. Marriage and Divorce records are kept in the counties.

Land records are kept in a variety of places. **Spanish land grants** prior to 1862 were processed in the New Mexico Office. The U.S. Surveyor processes **land claims** from 1855 to 1890. The first **general land office** opened in Colorado in 1863. Most land office records are at the National Archives, Denver Branch. County Clerks & Recorders keep **private land records**.

Historical Assets Colorado

National Archives at Denver
17101 Huron St, Broomfield, CO 80023, (303) 604-4740
denver.archives@nara.gov; https://www.archives.gov/denver
US District Courts (bankruptcy, civil & criminal cases, naturalizations, 1860-1960)
Bureau of Land Management (homestead records, township survey plats, Civilian Conservation Corps)
Bureau of Indian Affairs (Indian agents, treaties, annuity goods, land allotments)
Denver Mint (assaying records, deposits of bullion)
IRS (tax assessments from 1873-1917)
Forest Service (Forest Service Civilian Conservation Corps)

Bureau of Land Management, Colorado Office
2850 Youngfield St, Lakewood, CO 80215, (303) 239-3600
https://www.blm.gov/colorado

Colorado State Library
Colorado Virtual Library Collection
https://www.coloradovirtuallibrary.org

Researching the Law

Often, if you want to know why records are kept and where to look for them, you need to understand the law.

You will find the Territorial Session General Laws General Laws, Joint Resolutions, Memorials and Private Acts published in 1861, 1864, 1865, 1866, 1867 (plus Revised Statues), 1870, 1872 and 1874 digitized on Google Books (books.google.com). The same is true for the Session Laws once Colorado became a state, published every other year from 1879 to 1921. There were extraordinary sessions in 1894, 1902, 1914, and 1922. More recent volumes of the Colorado Revised Statutes can be found here: http://lawcollections.colorado.edu/colorado-session-laws/.

You will find a map of the judicial districts here: http://www.courts.state.co.us/Courts/Map.cfm.

Colorado Courts At a Glance here: https://www.courts.state.co.us/userfiles/file/Media/Brochures/2020webglance.pdf

And, the Colorado Judicial Learning Center, here: https://cjlc.colorado.gov/

Colorado Supreme Court
2 E 14th Avenue, Denver, CO 80203, 720-625-5150
https://www.coloradosupremecourt.com

U.S. District Court
Alfred A Arraj Courthouse, 901 19th St, Denver, CO 80294
Clerk's Office 303-844-3433
http://www.cod.uscourts.gov

Introduction

10th Circuit Court of Appeals

Byron Rogers Courthouse, 1929 Stout St, Denver, Colorado 80294, 303-844-3591
https://www.ca10.uscourts.gov/library

Water Courts

Division One, South Platte River Basin (based at the Weld County Courthouse in Greeley)

Division Two, Arkansas River Basin (based at the Pueblo County Judicial Building in Pueblo)

Division Three, Rio Grande River Basin (based at the Alamosa County Courthouse in Alamosa)

Division Four, Gunnison River Basin (based at the Montrose County Courthouse in Montrose)

Division Five, Colorado River Basin (based at the Garfield County Courthouse in Glenwood Springs, CO)

Division Six, White River Basin (based at the Routt County Justice Center in Steamboat Springs)

Division Seven, San Juan River Basin (based at La Plata Combined Courts in Durango)

National Indian Law Library

1522 Broadway, Boulder, CO 80302, 303-447-8760
https://www.narf.org/nill/

State-Wide Genealogical & Historical Societies

History Colorado
Museum; Hart Library & Archives
1200 N Broadway, Denver, CO 80203, 303-447-8679
https://www.historycolorado.org

Other History Colorado Sites:
Center for Colorado Women's History at Byers-Evans House, Denver
El Pueblo History Museum, pueblo
Fort Garland Museum & Cultural Center, Fort Garland
Fort Vasquez, Platteville
Georgetown Loop Historic Mining & Railroad Park, Georgetown
Healy House Museum & Dexter Cabin, Leadville
Trinidad History Museum, Trinidad
Ute Indian Museum, Montrose

Colorado Council of Genealogical Societies
P.O. Box 40270, Denver, CO 80204-0270
https://cocouncil.org

Historical Assets Colorado

Colorado Genealogical Society
P.O. Box 9218, Denver, CO 80209-0218
https://cogensoc.us

Colorado Historic Cemetery Association
P.O. Box 924, Castle Rock, CO 80104
https://www.coloradohistoriccemeteries.org

Colorado Society of Hispanic Genealogy
c/o Christ the King Lutheran Church, 2300 S Patton Ct, Denver, CO 80219
http://www.hispanicgen.org
Research Library: http://www.hispanicgen.org/RESEARCH.HTM

Online Research

There is quite a lot available to the genealogist or historian online, however, I would remind you that much more is available in local archives, city halls and courthouses than is may ever be online.

The Library of Congress

The Library of Congress has one of the best collections of original source material in the entire world, and unfortunately, it often goes under used by genealogists and local historians. At https://www.loc.gov you can search the catalog of physical items, digital images, and look through the changing collections. A search for Colorado yielded more than 92,000 items in its catalog.

Genealogical Websites

Ancestry.com is a subscription website that caters to genealogists and those who want to build family trees or see DNA results online. A search of the card catalog yielded more than 100 databases of information about Colorado.

FamilySearch.org is a free website supported by the Church of Jesus Christ of Latter Day Saints. The church has microfilmed records all over the world and is working to digitize its microfilm so that much of its collection will become available online. Unfortunately, the church has not microfilmed as much in Colorado as it has in other states.

GenealogyBank.org is a subscription website that has a good collection of newspapers, historical books, and government publications. A search showed 157 Colorado newspapers in their collection along with more than 28,000 government reports.

MyHeritage.org is a subscription website with a strength in Eastern European research. It has the 1885 Colorado Census, along with a database of marriage records, and a few historical books about Colorado.

FindmyPast.org is a subscription website with a strength in British Isles research. It also has the 1885 Colorado census, along with a few historical books, and a database of Denver obituaries.

Introduction

Online Books

There are many good online sources for books to help with your research. Many of these sources have digitized and made available good historical works such as county or local histories that are no longer under copyright protection. Often you can find good historical information about a community in these books. Here are a few places to find online books:

Google Books, https://books.google.com

Hathi Trust, https://www.hathitrust.org

Internet Archive, https://archive.org [also the home of the WayBack Machine]

Open Library, https://openlibrary.org

Links

Colorado GenWeb
https://cogenweb.com

FamilySearch Wiki
https://www.familysearch.org/wiki/en/Colorado,_United_States_Genealogy

Linkpendium Colorado
http://www.linkpendium.com/co-genealogy/

Random Acts of Genealogical Kindness
https://www.raogk.org/lookups/region/colorado/

RootsWeb Wiki
https://wiki.rootsweb.com/wiki/inex.php/Colorado_Family_History_Research

US Maps Colorado
https://www.mapofus.org/colorado/

Recommended Books

Abbott, Carl, Stephen J. Leonard, and David McComb. *Colorado: A History of the Centennial State*. Niwot, CO: University Press of Colorado, 1994.

Arps, Louisa Ward. *Denver in Slices*. Denver: Sage Books, 1959.

Athearn, Robert G. *The Coloradoans*. Albuquerque, NM: University of New Mexico Press, 1982.

Babb, Sanora. *An Owl on Every Post: A Personal Recollection of Life on the Plains*. New York: The McCall Publishing Co., 1970.

Baca, Vincent Z. C. de, ed. *La Gente: Hispano History and Life in Colorado*. Denver: Colorado Historical Society, 1999.

Baker, James H, ed.; LeRoy R Hafen, assoc. ed. *History of Colorado* (5 Vols). Denver: State Historical and Natural History Society of Colorado and Linderman Co., 1927.

Historical Assets Colorado

Bauer, William H., James L. Ozment, and John H. Willard. *Colorado Post Offices, 1859–1989: A Comprehensive Listing of Post Offices, Stations, and Branches*. Golden: Colorado Railroad Museum, 1971; second revised edition, 1990.

Coel, Margaret Speas. *Chief Left Hand: Southern Arapaho*. Norman, OK: University of Oklahoma Press, 1981.

Crossen, Forest. *The Switzerland trail of America*. Boulder, CO: Pruett Press, 1978.

Danilov, Victor J. *Colorado Museums and Historic Sites: A Colorado Guide Book*. Niwot, CO: University Press of Colorado, 2000.

Eberhart, Perry. *Guide to the Colorado Ghost Towns and Mining Camps*. Athens, GA: Swallow Press, 1969.

Hall, Frank. *History of the State of Colorado...from 1858 to 1890* (4 Vols). Chicago: The Blakely Printing Co., 1889–1895.

Mangan, Terry William. *Colorado on Glass: Colorado's First Half Century as Seen by the Camera*. Denver: Sundance Ltd., 1975.

Michener, James A.*Centennial*. New York: Random House, 1974.

Noel, Thomas J. *Guide to Colorado Historic Places: Sites Supported by the Colorado Historical Society's State Historical Fund*. Englewood, CO: Westcliffe Pub, 2007.

Noel, Thomas J., Paul F. Mahoney, and Richard E. Stevens. *Historical Atlas of Colorado*. Norman, OK: University of Oklahoma Press, 1994. Latest edition, 2000.

Steinel, Alvin Theodore. *History of Agriculture in Colorado: A Chronological Record of Progress in the Development of General Farming, Livestock Production, and Agricultural Education and Investigation...1858 to 1926*. Fort Collins, CO.: The State Agricultural College (Colorado State University), 1926.

Smith, Duane A. *The Birth of Colorado: A Civil War Perspective*. Norman, OK: University of Oklahoma Press, 1989.

Smith, Duane A. *The Trail of Gold and Silver: Mining in Colorado, 1859-2009*. Niwot, CO: University Press of Colorado, 2011.

Wiatrowski, Claude. *Railroads of Colorado: Your Guide to Colorado's Historic Trains and Railway Sites*. Helena, MT: Farcountry Press, 2012.

Wolle, Muriel Sibell. *Stampede to Timberline: The Ghost Towns and Mining Camps of Colorado*. Boulder, CO: Sage Books, 1949.

Wyckoff, William. *Creating Colorado: The Making of a Western American Landscape, 1860–1940*. New Haven, CT: Yale University Press, 1999.

Zamonsky, Teddy and Stanley W Keller. *The Fifty-Niners: Roaring Denver in the Gold Rush Days*. New York: Stanza-Yarp, 1967.

Please Help Us Make this Research Guide Better

If you find errors or omissions, or find that something needs to be clarified, please contact us at alert@irongate.com. Thank you for your help and support.

Adams County

Introduction

Established: 1901   Population: 503,167

Formed from: Arapahoe County

Adjacent Counties: Weld, Morgan, Washington, Arapahoe, Denver, Jefferson, Broomfield

County Seat: Brighton
  Other Communities: Aurora, Bennett, Brighton, Commerce City, Federal Heights, Northglenn, Westminster

Website, http://www.adcogov.org

Area Codes: 303

Zip Codes: 80019, 80022, 80024, 80030, 80031, 80035, 80036, 80037, 80040, 80042, 80045, 80102, 80136, 80137, 80221, 80229, 80233, 80234, 80241, 80260, 80601, 80602, 80614, 80640

Historical Assets Colorado

Adams County Courthouse ca 1906
Courtesy History Colorado

Adams County Courthouse after the 1939 remodel, now the Brighton City Hall

Present Adams County Justice Center

Courthouses & County Government

Adams County
  http://www.adcogov.org/
Adams County Courthouse (Justice Center) (17th Judicial District), 1100 Judicial Center Dr, Brighton, CO 80601, 303-659-1161;http://www.courts.state.co.us/Courts/District/Index.cfm?District_ID=17
Assessor, 4430 S Adams County Pkwy, Brighton, CO 80601, 720-523-6038; http://co-adamscounty.civicplus.com/index.aspx?nid=93
Board of County Commissioners, 4430 S Adams County Pkwy, Brighton, CO 80601, 720-523-6100, http://www.adcogov.org/bocc

Adams County

Clerk & Recorder, 4430 S Adams County Pkwy, Brighton, CO 80601, 720-523-6020; http://www.co.adams.co.us/index.aspx?NID=140

Coroner, 330 N 19th Ave, Brighton, CO 80601, 303-659-1027; http://www.adcogov.org/coroner

Elections, 4430 S Adams County Pkwy, 1st Fl, Brighton, CO 80601, 720-523-6500; https://www.adamsvotes.com

Public Health, 6162 S Willow Dr, Ste 100, Greenwood Village, CO 80111, 303-220-9200; http://www.tchd.org/

Transportation (Public Works), 4430 S Adams County Pkwy, Brighton, CO 80601, 970-523-6875; http://www.adcogov.org/public-works

Treasurer, 4430 S Adams County Pkwy, Brighton, CO 80601, 720-523-6160; http://co-adamscounty.civicplus.com/index.aspx?NID=812

County Records

Birth 1902   Marriage 1901   Death 1902
Land 1901 (some land records from Arapahoe County before 1901)
Probate 1902   Court 1902 (17th Judicial District)
Burial records (some)   CSA Coroner 1903

County & Municipal Records Held at the State Level

The Colorado State Archives

Physical Records
Assessor
Clerk & Recorder
Coroner
County Commissioners
    County Court
District Court
Justice Court
Public Trustee
Treasurer
WPA Historical Records
WPA Religious Institutions Survey
Cities
    Aurora
    Commerce City
    Northglenn
    Westminster

Records on Film
Clerk & Recorder
County Court
District Court
Cities
    Aurora
    Commerce City
    Northglenn
    Westminster

Records on Master Film
Clerk & Recorder
Coroner
County Commissioners
County Court
District Court
Finance
Public Trustee
School Districts
Sheriff
Social Services
Treasurer
Cities
    Aurora
    Brighton
    Commerce City
    Northglenn
    Thornton
    Westminster

The Denver Public Library

Adams County Colorado Marriage Records, 1859-1901
Colorado Theatre Program Collection, 1900-
Treasurer's Certificates of Purchase, 1894-1939 [delinquent taxes]
WWI Draft Registration Cards (microfilm)

Historical Assets Colorado

School Districts

School Districts, http://www.adcogov.org/local-school-districts

District 1, Mapleton, 7350 N Broadway, Denver, CO 80221, 303-853-1100; https://www.mapleton.us/

District 12 Five Star Schools, 1500 E 128th Ave, Thornton, CO 80241, 720-972-4000; https://www.adams12.org/

District 14, Commerce City, 5291 E 60th Ave, Commerce City, CO 80022, 303-853-3333; https://www.adams14.org/

District 26J, Deer Trail, 350 2nd Ave, Deer Trail, CO 80105, 303-769-4421; https://www.facebook.com/pages/category/Public-School/Deer-Trail-School-District-26J-1420878648165572/

District 27J, Brighton, 18551 E 160th Ave, Brighton, Co 80601, 303-544, 2900; https://www.sd27j.org/

District 28J, Aurora, 15701 E 1st Ave, Aurora, CO 80011, 303-344-8060; https://aurorak12.org/

District 29J, Bennett, 615 7th St, Bennett, CO 80102, 303-644-3234; https://www.bsd29j.com/

District 31J, Strasburg, P.O. Box 207, Strasburg, CO 80136, 303-622-9211; http://www.strasburg31j.com/

District 32J, Byers, 444 E Front St, Byers, CO 80103, 303-822-5292; https://www.byers32j.k12.co.us/

Westminster Public Schools, 6933 Raleigh St, Westminster, CO 80030, 303-428-3511; https://www.westminsterpublicschools.org/

District RE3J, Keenesburg, 99 W Broadway, St, Keenesburg, CO 80643, 303-536-2000; https://re3j.com/

District RE-50J, Wiggins, 320 Chapman St, Wiggins, CO 80654, 970-483-7762; http://wiggins50.k12.co.us/

Historic School Districts

1. Mapleton, Retreat Park
2. Berkoutz
3. Riverdale
4. Utah Junction
5. Chicago, Mountain View, Shamrock
6. Burn Lee
7. Derby
8. Brantner (1867)
9. Westminster
10. Pleasant Plains
11. Hazeltine
12. Eastlake
13.
14. Adams City
15. Pleasant Valley, Leader, Valley Center
16. Welby
17. Living Springs, Roper, Comanche
18. Goldnrod, Westpoint, Badger, Columbine
19.
20. Hurry Back Valley, Hutchinson
21. Central Valley
22. Sunnydale
23. Long Branch
24. Sable
25. Baker
26. Potty Brown, Roseland, Evergreen, Moore
27. Brighton
28. Aurora
29. Bennett
30. Arcadia, Whittier, Friendship
31. Strasburg
32. Busy Bee, Lone Tree, Opportunity, Hopewell, Bijou
33. Watkins
34. Westlake
35.
36.
37. First Creek
38. Barr Lake
39. [1903]
40. [1903]
41. [1903]
42.
43.

Adams County

44.
45.
46.
47.
48.
49.
50. Westminster
51.
52. Box Elder
53. Pleasant View
54. [1903]
55. Watkins
56. Cactus Ridge
57.
58.
59. [1903]
60. [1903]
61. Rose Hill
62. Duff, Clyde Miller
63. [1903]
64. [1903]
65. [1903]
66. [1903] (in Yuma Co)
67. [1903] (in Yuma Co)
68. [1903] (in Yuma Co)
69.
70. [1903] (in Yuma Co)
71. Webster
72. [1903] (in Yuma Co)
73. [1903]
74. [1903] (in Yuma Co)
75. [1903] (in Yuma Co)
76. [1903] (in Yuma Co)
77. [1903] (in Yuma Co)
78. [1903] (in Yuma Co)
79. [1903] (in Yuma Co)
80.
81. Moreland
82. [1903] (in Yuma Co)
83. [1903] (in Yuma Co)
84. [1903]
85. (in Yuma Co)
86. [1903] (in Yuma Co)
87. [1903] (in Yuma Co)
88. [1903] (in Yuma Co)
89. [1903] (in Yuma Co)
90. [1903] (in Yuma Co)
91. [1903] (in Yuma Co)
92. [1903] (in Yuma Co)
93. [1903] (in Yuma Co)
94. [1903] (in Yuma Co)
95. Henderson
96. [1903] (in Yuma Co)
97. Irondale
98. Berkley Gardens
99. [1903] (in Yuma Co)
100. [1903] (Yuma Co)
101. [1903] (Yuma Co)

U1. Adams City
U3. Westminster

Fraternal Organizations

Granges
Henderson, No. 96, Adams, Island Station/Henderson, 11 Feb 1890
Success, No. 132, Adams, Brighton, 17 Jan 1894
Barr, No. 133, Adams, Barr, 13 Feb 1894
Westminster, No. 184, Adams, Westminster, 5 Feb 1910
Riverdale, No. 187, Adams, Brighton, 5 Mar 1910
Horse Creek, No. 190, Adams, Bashor/Brighton, 25 June 1910
Central Valley, No. 200, Adams, Bennett, 29 Apr 1911
Simpson, No. 238, Adams, Simpson, 13 Mar 1915
Antelope Flat, No. 240, Adams, Byers, 8 Mar 1915
Meadow Lark, No. 245, Adams, Strasburg, 27 Mar 1915
Rose Hill, No. 256, Adams, Commerce City, 7 July 1915
Sunnydale, No. 273, Adams, Keenesburg, 25 Mar 1916
United Farmers, No. 288, Adams, Leader, 20 May 1916
Saw Arroyo, No. 331, Adams, Adena, 24 Mar 1917
Windy Point, No. 352, Adams, Deer Trail/Alewin, 21 Apr 1917
Nestor, No. 410, Adams, Bennett, 1 Dec 1931
Green Valley, No. 441, Adams, Brighton/Commerce City, 23 Oct 1936
Tri-Valley, No. 458, Adams, Strasburg, 24 May 1945

Masons

Ancient Free & Accepted Masons
Brighton No. 78, Adams, Brighton, 16 Sept 1890
Paul Revere, No. 130, Adams, Westminster, 24 Jan 2009
Westminster, No. 176, Adams, Westminster, 23 Jan 1952
Miracle, No. 182, Adams, Eastlake, 28 Jan 1959

Historical Assets Colorado

    Mosaic, No. 184, Adams, Eastlake, 27 Jan 1960
    Tri-Lumina, No. 189, Adams, Commerce City, 25 Jan 1961
    Northglenn, No. 194, Adams, Eastlake, 28 Jan 1974

Royal Arch Masons
    none

Knights Templar
    none

Eastern Star
    Lorraine, No. 52, Adams, Brighton
    Dawn, No. 125, Adams, Aurora
    Stardust, No. 149, Adams, Adams City

Prince Hall Masons
    Centennial Lodge No. 4, Adams, Aurora, 1898
    Daniel "Chappie" James Military Lodge No. 27, Adams, Aurora, 1978

Prince Hall Order of the Eastern Star
    Queen of the South Chapter No. 11, Adams, Aurora

Prince Hall Holy Royal Arch Masons
    Nathaniel Spencer Chapter No. 4, Adams, Aurora

Prince Hall Knights Templar
    William B S Harris Commandery No. 3, Adams, Aurora

Odd Fellows
    Fidelity, No. 20, Adams, Brighton

Rebekahs
    Lily, No. 140, Adams, Commerce City

Knights of Pythias
    Eureka, No. 56, Adams, Brighton

Pythian Sisters
    Harmony, No. 15, Adams, Brighton

Benevolent Protective Order of Elks
    Brighton, No. 1586, Adams, Brighton
    Northglenn, No. 2438, Adams, Northglenn

City & Town Halls

Brighton, 50 S 4th Ave, Brighton, CO 80601, 303-655-2000; https://www.brightonco.gov/

Aurora, 15151 E Alameda Pky, Aurora, CO 80012, 303-739-7000; https://www.auroragov.org/

Bennett, 207 Muegge Wy, Bennett, CO 80102, 303-644-3249; https://www.colorado.gov/townofbennett

Commerce City, 7887 E 60th Ave, Commerce City, CO 80222, 303-289-3600; https://www.c3gov.com/

Federal Heights, 2380 W 90th Ave, Federal Heights, CO 80260, 303-428-3526; https://www.fedheights.org/

Adams County

Northglenn, 11701 Community Center Dr, Northglenn, CO 80233, 303-451-8326; https://www.northglenn.org/government/city_hall/
Westminster, 4800 W 92nd Ave, Westminster, CO 80031, 303-658-2400; https://www.cityofwestminster.us/

Archives & Manuscript Collections

Dayton Memorial Library, Archives & Special Collections • Regis University, 3333 Regis Blvd • Denver, CO 80221-1099 • (303) 458-4030 • http://libguides.regis.edu/archives

Historical & Genealogical Societies

Adams County Genealogical Society, P.O. Box 1254, East Lake, CO 80614, https://sites.google.com/site/adamscountygenealogysociety/
Adams County Historical Society, Historical Museum, 9601 Henderson Rd, Brighton, CO 80601, (303) 659-7103, https://www.adamscountymuseum.com
Brighton Genealogical Society, 343 S 21st Ave, P.O. Box 1005, Brighton, CO 80601-2525
Brighton Historic Preservation Commission, Brighton City Museum & Research Room, Historic City Hall, 500 W 4th Ave, Brighton, CO 80601, (303) 655-2042, https://www.brightonco.gov/1072/Historic-Preservation
Comanche Crossing Historical Society, Historical Museum, 56060 E Colfax Ave, Strasburg, CO 80136-0647, (303) 622-4690, https://www.facebook.com/pages/Comanche-Crossing-Historical-Society-Museum/1470971483229878
Northglenn Historical Preservation Foundation, 10950 Fox Run Pkwy, Northglenn, CO 80233, (720) 232-4402, http://www.northglennhistory.com
Westminster Historical Society, Westminster History Center, 7200 Lowell St, P.O. Box 492, Westminster, CO 80036, (303) 428-3993, https://www.westminstercohistory.com
Westminster Historical Society, Bowles House Museum, 3924 W 72nd Ave, P.O. Box 492, Westminster, CO 80036, (303) 430-7929, https://www.westminstercohistory.com

Local Libraries

Brighton
Anythink Brighton Branch, 327 E Bridge St , Brighton, CO 80601, (303) 405-3230, https://www.anythinklibraries.org/location/anythink-brighton
Aurora Public Library, 14949 E Alameda Pkwy, Aurora, CO 80012, (303) 739-6630, http://www.auroralibrary.org
Anythink Library-Bennett Branch, 495 7th Ave , Bennett, CO 80102, (303) 405-3231 https://www.anythinklibraries.org/location/anythink-bennett
Anythink Commerce City Library, 7185 Monaco, Commerce City, CO 80022, (303) 287-0063, http://www.anythinklibraries.org
Anythink Huron St Library, 9417 Huron St, Thornton, CO 80260, (303) 432-7534, https://www.anythinklibraries.org/location/anythink-huron-street
Westminster Public Library, 3705 W 112th Ave, Westminster, CO 80031, (303) 658-2400, https://www.cityofwestminster.us/Libraries/LocationsandHours

Historical Assets Colorado

Links
CO GenWeb
http://cogenweb.com/adams/

Cyndi's List
https://www.cyndislist.com/us/co/counties/adams/

FamilySearch Wiki
https://www.familysearch.org/wiki/en/Adams_County,_Colorado_Genealogy

Linkpendium
http://www.linkpendium.com/adams-co-genealogy/

RootsWeb Wiki
https://wiki.rootsweb.com/wiki/index.php/Adams_County,_Colorado

Wikipedia
https://en.wikipedia.org/wiki/Adams_County,_Colorado

Historic Hotels
None

Museums & Historic Sites
Adams County Historical Society, Historical Museum, 9601 Henderson Rd, Brighton, CO 80601, (303) 659-7103, https://www.adamscountymuseum.com

Bowles House Museum, 3924 W 72nd Ave, P.O. Box 492, Westminster, CO 80036, (303) 430-7929, https://www.westminstercohistory.com

Brighton City Museum & Research Room, Historic City Hall, 500 W 4th Ave, Brighton, CO 80601, (303) 655-2042, https://www.brightonco.gov/1072/Historic-Preservation

Comanche Crossing Historical Society, Historical Museum, 56060 E Colfax Ave, Strasburg, CO 80136-0647, (303) 622-4690, https://www.facebook.com/pages/Comanche-Crossing-Historical-Society-Museum/1470971483229878

Westminster Historical Society, Westminster History Center, 7200 Lowell St, P.O. Box 492, Westminster, CO 80036, (303) 428-3993, https://www.westminstercohistory.com

Special Events & Scenic Locations
Adams County Fair, 9755 Henderson Rd, Brighton, CO 80601, 303-637-8000, Early August (tomato-throwing contest, live music); http://adamscountyfair.com

Barr Lake State Park, 13401 Picadilly Rd, Brighton, CO 80603; Bald Eagle Festival in February; https://cpw.state.co.us/placestogo/parks/barrlake

Berry Patch Farm, 13785 Potomac St, Brighton, CO 80601-7278; (pick your own strawberries, flowers); https://www.berrypatchfarms.com

Rocky Mountain Arsenal National Wildlife Refuge, 6550 Gateway Rd, Commerce City, CO 80022; https://www.fws.gov/refuge/rocky_mountain_arsenal/

Ghost Towns & Other Sparsely Populated Places
None

Adams County

Newspapers

The Brighton Register. (Brighton, Colo.) 1885-19??
The Brighton Standard. ([Brighton, Colo.) 19??-????
Han'guk ilbo, Tenbŏ = The Korea Times Denver edition. (Aurora, CO) 19??-current | Languages: Korean
Commerce City News. (Commerce City, Colo.) 19??-1978
Northglenn-Thornton Sentinel. (Thornton, Colo.) 19??-current
Colorado Weekly News. (Deer Trail, Colo.) 19??-current
The Eastern Colorado News. (Strasburg, Adams County, Colo.) 19??-current
The Brighton Blade. and G.A.R. Guardian. (Brighton, Adams County, Colo.) 1902-1903
The Brighton Blade. (Brighton, Adams County, Colo.) 1902-current
The Adams County News. (Aurora, Colo.) 1909-195?
The Aurora Democrat. (Aurora, Colo.) 1909-19??
The Adams County Republican. (Brighton, Adams County, Colo.) 1924-1953
Aurora-Fitzsimons Sun. (Aurora, Adams County, Colo.) 1928-19??
The Aurora Advocate. (Aurora, Colo.) 194?-1972
Westminster Journal. (Westminster, Colo.) 1947-1972
Aurora Upstart. (Aurora, Colo.) 1947-19??
The Aurora Star and Adams County News. (Aurora, Colo.) 195?-196?
The Adams County Sentinel. (Brighton, Adams County, Colo.) 1953-1955
The Adams County Sentinel formerly the Adams County republican. (Brighton, Adams County, Colo.) 1953-1954
The Booster. ([Aurora] Adams County, Colo.) 1954-19??
Hoffman Heights Mirror. (Hoffman Heights, Colo.) 1954-????
The Brighton Explorer. (Brighton, Colo.) 1959-19??
Northglenn Tribune. (Thorton, CO) 1960-1961
Northglenn News. (Northglenn, Colo.) 1960-19??
The Aurora Times. (Aurora, Colo.) 1960-19??
The Aurora Star Sentinel. (Aurora, Colo.) 196?-1972
North Valley World. (Thornton, Adams County, Colo.) 196?-1970
Free Dispatch. (Northglenn, Colo.) 1965-1972
Northglenn Impressions. (Northglenn, Adams County, Colo.) 1968-1972
Independent Tribune. ([Aurora, Colo.]) 1970-19??
The North Valley World Sentinel. (Westminster, Colo.) 1970-1971
Thornton-North Valley Sentinel. (Westminster, Colo.) 1971-1972
Dispatch-Sentinel. (Denver, Colo.) 1972-1980
Aurora Advocate Sentinel. (Aurora, Colo.) 1972-1979
Journal-Sentinel. (Denver, Colo.) 1972-1977
The Aurora Sun. (Aurora, Colo.) 1972-19??
Westminster Journal Sentinel. (Denver, Colo.) 1977-1979
Adams-Weld Market Place. (Brighton, Colo.) 1978-1979
Commerce City News/Almanac. (Commerce City, Colo.) 1978-1979
Westminster Window. (Westminster, Colo.) 1978-1991
Aurora Sentinel. (Denver, Colo.) 1979-2018
Commerce City Sentinel. (Commerce City, Colo.) 1979-current

Historical Assets Colorado

Westminster Sentinel. (Denver, Colo.) 1979-1991
Gateway Gazette. (Aurora, Colo.) 1983-current
Aurora Independent. (Denver, Colo.) 1985-1985
Community Accent. (Aurora, Colo.) 1990-current
The Aurora Villager. (Englewood, Colo.) 1990-current
Westminster Window. (Westminster, CO) 199?-current
Olde Towner: Arvada's Community Newspaper. (Arvada, CO) 199?-1999
Westminster Window and Westminster Sentinel. (Westminster, Colo.) 1991-199?
Sentinel. (Aurora, Colo.) 2018-current

Places on the National Register

Aurora, Fuller, Granville, House, 2027 Galena St.
Aurora, Robidoux, M.J. Lavina, House, 1615 Galena St.
Aurora, Wilson, Blanche A., House, 1671 Galena St.
Brighton, Adams County Courthouse, 22 S 4th Ave.
Brighton, Brighton High School, 830 E. Bridge St
Brighton, Bromley Farm—Koizuma Hishinuma Farm,15820 E. 152nd Ave.
Denver, Brannan Sand and Gravel Pit #8—Lake Sangraco Boathouse Complex, Address Restricted
Denver, Riverside Cemetery, 5201 Brighton Blvd.
Northglenn, Thede Farmhouse, 3190 W. 112th Ave.
Strasburg, Engelbrecht Farm, 2024 Strasburg Rd.
Thornton, Eastlake Farmers Co-Operative Elevator Co, 126th Ave & Claude Ct
Westminster, Gregory, William J., House, 8140 Lowell Blvd.
Westminster, Harris Park School, 7200 Lowell Blvd.
Westminster, Gregory, William J., House, 8140 Lowell Blvd.
Westminster, Harris Park School, 7200 Lowell Blvd.
Westminster, Metzger Farm, 12080 Lowell Blvd.
Westminster, Union High School, 3455 W. 72nd Ave.
Westminster, Westminster University, 3455 W. 83rd Ave.

USGS Historic Places

Arvada, Berkeley Gardens Elementary School, 39.79339, -105.03518
Arvada, Iver C Ranum High School, 39.8430415, -105.0166483
Arvada, Junction School, 39.7980419, -105.0060928
Arvada, Marycrest School, 39.7933197, -105.0244267
Arvada, Orchard Court School, 39.8324861, -105.0377602
Arvada, Roush School, 39.8402637, -105.0058147
Arvada, Southwest Adams County Fire Rescue Station 13, 39.7980265, -105.0162573
Arvada, Vista Grande Elementary School, 39.85735, -105.0489
Arvada, Westminster Hills Elementary School, 39.84355, -105.0422
Brighton, Henderson Airport, 39.9163739, -104.8674751
Brighton, Reasoner Airport, 39.9163738, -104.8055282
Brighton, Vaile Reservoir, 39.9292085, -104.7954663
Commerce City, Alternative No 1 High School, 39.8377637, -104.9744246
Commerce City, Derby School, 39.8269305, -104.9119221

Adams County

Commerce City, Holy Cross School, 39.8674856, -104.9538679
Commerce City, Hutton High School, 39.8658189, -104.9769245
Commerce City, Mapleton High School, 39.8133195, -104.9808139
Commerce City, Oneida School, 39.8299861, -104.9074774
Commerce City, Open Door Fellowship of Commerce City, 39.8183333, -104.9125
Commerce City, Saint Catherine School, 39.826375, -104.9102553
Commerce City, Sunhealth Speciality Hospital For Denver, 39.8505414, -104.980258
Denver International Airport, Box Elder School, 39.8560965, -104.6296882
Denver International Airport, First Creek School, 39.7552652, -104.7341376
Denver International Airport, Sky Ranch Airport, 39.7594318, -104.7455268
Fitzsimons, Fitzsimons Army Medical Center, 39.7452651, -104.8371974
Horse Creek, Horth Strip, 39.9783171, -104.5938515
Leader, Plainview School, 39.8991496, -104.0941198
Leader NW, Range View School, 39.9713723, -104.2452302
Leader NW, Sunrise School, 39.8841494, -104.1496762
Leader SE, Busy Bee School, 39.8130372, -104.075511
Leader SW, Opportunity School, 39.7691479, -104.1335679
Leader SW, Singleton Ranch Airport, 39.871927, -104.1535654
Mile High Lakes, Heckendorf Ranches Airport, 39.9630397, -104.7494144
Mile High Lakes, Stevens Airport, 39.9663729, -104.6507988
Montbello, Rocky Mountain Arsenal, 39.8336111, -104.8419444
Roper School, Bowen Farms Number 2 Airport, 39.7997053, -104.3285692
Roper School, Comanche Livestock Airport, 39.8353203, -104.3259947
Watkins, Watkins Fire Department, 39.7444973, -104.6051663

Grand Army of the Republic Posts
None

USGS Historic Military Places
Montbello, Rocky Mountain Arsenal, 39.8336111, -104.8419444

Military Bases
None

Post Offices

Abbott	1887 Aug 6	1926 Apr 15	
Adams City	1923 Sept 26	1963 Oct 11	
Arikaree	1888 June 9	1961 June 23	
Aurora	1908 Jan 15	1939 Dec 31	
Aurora	1962 Apr 28		80010
Barr	1883 Mar 15	1914 Oct 17	
Barr Lake	1914 Oct 17	1952 Aug 31	
Bashor	1909 Mar 5	1918 July 31	
Beecher	1902 Aug 12	1905 Nov 3	
Bennet	1877 Mar 16	1907 June 1	
Bennett	1907 June 1		80102

Historical Assets Colorado

Brighton	1879 Aug 4		80601
Bunell	1919 Feb 14	1921 Nov 2	
Camp Speer	1918 Dec 5	1919 Feb 14	
Comanche	1911 July 6	1923 Oct 31	
Commerce City	1963 Feb 1		80022
Cope	1888 Apr 23		80812
Derby	1910 Jan 27	1963 Jan 31	
Dupont	1926 June 19		80024
Eastlake	1912 June 8		80614
Eskdale	1911 July 11	1933 Aug 15	
Fitzsimons	1921 Nov 2	1923 Apr 30	
Fox	1890 May 17	1912 Dec 15	
Hale	1890 May 17	1984 June 1*	
Harris	1890 Apr 21	1908 June 5	
Harrisburg	1908 Oct 29	1955 Mar 31	
Hazeltine	1893 Jan 7	1907 Jan 15	
Idalia	1888 Sept 18		80735
Kirk	1887 Nov 18		80824
Landsman	1883 Mar 27	1918 May 31	
Lansing	1886 Sept 17	1910 Feb 28	
Leader	1910 Mar 26	1940 Dec 31	
Lindon	1888 Sept 21		80740
Newton	1889 Aug 6	1918 Apr 15	
Oleson	1916 July 18	1931 July 7	
Sigman	1926 June 25	1935 Jan 31	
Simpson	1910 June 24	1943 Aug 31	
Strasburg	1908 May 25		80136
Swinford	1912 May 28	1913 Oct 15	
Thedalund	1917 July 17	1926 July 31	
Thurman	1888 July 6	1955 Mar 31	
Vernon	1888 June 26		80755
Watkins	1878 Jan 31	1893 Oct 14	
Watkins	1894 Nov 6		80137
Welby	1910 Dec 19	1911 Mar 31	
Westminster	1908 June 5		80030

Topo Quads

Arvada	395230N	394500N	1050000W	1050730W
Bennett	395230N	394500N	1042230W	1043000W
Brighton	400000N	395230N	1044500W	1045230W
Byers	394500N	393730N	1040730W	1041500W
Coal Creek	394500N	393730N	1043730W	1044500W
Commerce City	395230N	394500N	1045230W	1050000W
Cottonwood Valley North	394500N	393730N	1034500W	1035230W

Adams County

Denver International Airport	395230N	394500N	1043730W	1044500W
Englewood	394500N	393730N	1045230W	1050000W
Fitzsimons	394500N	393730N	1044500W	1045230W
Horse Creek	400000N	395230N	1043000W	1043730W
Leader	400000N	395230N	1040000W	1040730W
Leader NW	400000N	395230N	1040730W	1041500W
Leader SE	395230N	394500N	1040000W	1040730W
Leader SW	395230N	394500N	1040730W	1041500W
Living Springs	400000N	395230N	1041500W	1042230W
Manila	395230N	394500N	1043000W	1043730W
Mile High Lakes	400000N	395230N	1043730W	1044500W
Montbello	395230N	394500N	1044500W	1045230W
Noonen Reservoir	394500N	393730N	1035230W	1040000W
Peoria	394500N	393730N	1040000W	1040730W
Poison Springs	395230N	394500N	1035230W	1040000W
Potty Brown Creek	400000N	395230N	1035230W	1040000W
Roper School	395230N	394500N	1041500W	1042230W
Shamrock	400000N	395230N	1034500W	1035230W
Shamrock SE	395230N	394500N	1034500W	1035230W
Strasburg	394500N	393730N	1041500W	1042230W
Strasburg NW	394500N	393730N	1042230W	1043000W
Sunnydale	400000N	395230N	1042230W	1043000W
Watkins	394500N	393730N	1043000W	1043730W

Suggested Reading

Dorr, W Carl. *History of Adams County, Brighton and Fort Lupton, Colorado*. Brighton, CO: NP, 1959.

Dorr, W Carl. *Looking Back: A Historical Account of the Development of Brighton and Surrounding Community from 1859-1976*. Brighton, CO: Brighton Centennial-BiCentennial Committee, 1976.

Shaffer, Ray. *A Guide to Places in Colorado, Adams County*. NL: NP, 1990.

Wagner, Albin. *Adams County, Colorado: A Centennial History, 1902-2002*. Virginia Beach, VA: Donning Co. Publishers, 2002.

Wagner, Albin. *Adams County: Crossroads of the West*. Brighton, CO: Board of County Commissioners, Adams County, 1977.

Historical Assets Colorado

Alamosa County

Introduction
Established: 1913   Population: 15,445
Formed from: Costilla
Adjacent Counties: Saguache, Huerfano, Costilla, Conejos, Rio Grande
County Seat: Alamosa
  Other Communities: Hooper, Mosca, Waverly
Website, https://www.colorado.gov/pacific/alamosacounty/
Area Codes: 719
Zip Codes: 81101, 81102, 81136, 81146

Historical Assets Colorado

Alamosa County Courthouse

Courthouses & County Government

Alamosa County
   https://www.colorado.gov/pacific/alamosacounty/
Alamosa County Courthouse (12th Judicial District), 702 4th St, Alamosa, CO 81101, 719-589-4996; http://www.courts.state.co.us/Courts/County/Index.cfm?County_ID=32
Assessor, 402 Edison Ave, Alamosa, CO 81101, 719-589-6365; http://www.alamosacounty.org/
Board of County Commissioners, 8900A Independence Wy, Alamosa, CO 81101, 719-589-4848, https://www.colorado.gov/pacific/alamosacounty/board-county-commissioners-0
Clerk & Recorder, 402 Edison Ave, Alamosa, CO 81101, 719-689-5581; http://www.alamosacounty.org/
Coroner, 205 State Ave, Alamosa, CO 81101, 719-589-4271; https://www.colorado.gov/pacific/alamosacounty/coroner-4
Courts (Alamosa Combined Court), 8955 Independence Wy, Alamosa, CO 81101, 719-589-4996; Elections (in the Clerk & Recorder's office); https://www.colorado.gov/pacific/alamosacounty/voter-information-1
Public Health, 8900-B Independence Wy, Alamosa, CO 81101, 719-589-6639; http://www.alamosacounty.org/
Treasurer, 402 Edison Ave, Alamosa, CO 81101, 719-589-3626; http://www.alamosacounty.org

County Records

Birth 1870	Marriage 1914	Divorce 1914
Death 1902	Land 1914	Probate 1914
Court 1914		

Some marriage records for Costilla and Conejos counties for the late 1800s.
CSA naturalizations 1915-1991

Alamosa County

County & Municipal Records Held at the State Level

The Colorado State Archives

Physical Records
County Court
District Court
WPA Historical Records
WPA Religious Institutions
  Survey
Cities
  Alamosa

Records on Film
None

Records on Master Film
Clerk & Recorder
County Court
District Court
School Districts
San Luis Valley Historical
  Society (cemetery)

The Denver Public Library
WPA Historical Records Survey
WWI Draft Registration Cards (microfilm)

School Districts

School Districts, http://www.adcogov.org/local-school-districts
Alamosa School District RE-11J, 209 Victoria Ave, Alamosa, CO 81101, 719-587-1600; https://www.alamosa.k12.co.us/
Sangre de Christo School District 22J, 8751 Lane 7 N, Mosca, CO 81146, 719-378-2321; http://sdc.schooldesk.net/

Historic School Districts

1. Mt Pleasant
2. Waverly
3. Alamosa
4. Henry
5. East Alamosa/Maddox
6.
7.
8. Newsom/Becker
9. Uracca/Airdale
10.
11.
12.
13.
14. McGinty
15. Excelsior
16.
17. Carmel
18.
19.
20.
21.
22.
23.
24. Star

C1. Mosca
C2. Stanley
JtC 23. Sangre de Christo/
  Hooper

Fraternal Organizations

Granges
Mosca, No. 404, Alamosa, Mosca, 8 Feb 1927
Hooper, No. 405, Alamosa, Hooper, 9 Feb 1927
Rocky Mountain Hi, No. 494, Alamosa, Alamosa, 1963

Masons

Ancient Free & Accepted Masons
Alamosa, No. 44, Alamosa, Alamosa, 21 Sept 1881

Royal Arch Masons
San Luis Valley, No. 18, Alamosa, Alamosa

Knights Templar
Rio Grande Del Norte Commandery, No. 15, Alamosa, Alamosa, 1889 Apr 4

Historical Assets Colorado

Eastern Star
Sierra Blanca, No. 43, Alamosa, Alamosa
Ruth, No. 46, Alamosa, Hooper

Odd Fellows
Hooper, No. 44, Alamosa, Hooper
Alamosa, No. 63, Alamosa, Alamosa, 1884 Dec 13
Friendship, No. 134, Alamosa, Alamosa
Mosca, No. 137, Alamosa, Mosca

Rebekahs
Hooper, No. 17, Alamosa, Hooper
Rio Grande, No. 117, Alamosa, Alamosa

Knights of Pythias
Alamosa, No. 96, Alamosa, Alamosa
Hooper, No. 109, Alamosa, Hooper

Pythian Sisters
None

Benevolent Protective Order of Elks
Alamosa, No. 1297, Alamosa, Alamosa

City & Town Halls

Alamosa, 300 Hunt Ave, Alamosa, CO 81101, 719-589-2593, https://cityofalamosa.org

Hooper, 8660 Main St, Hooper, CO 81136, 719-378-2204, https://www.colorado.gov/pacific/alamosacounty/town-hooper

Archives & Manuscript Collections

None

Historical & Genealogical Societies

San Luis Valley Historical Society, P.O. Box 982, Alamosa, CO 81101-0982, (719) 589-9217, http://slvhistoricalsociety.org

Local Libraries

Alamosa Public Library, 300 Hunt Ave, Alamosa, CO 81101, (719) 589-6592, https://www.alamosalibrary.org

Nielsen Library, Adams State University, 1701 1st St, Alamosa, CO 81101, (719) 587-7781, https://www.adams.edu/library/

Links

CO GenWeb
http://cogenweb.com/alamosa/

Cyndi's List
https://www.cyndislist.com/us/co/counties/alamosa/

Alamosa County

FamilySearch Wiki
https://www.familysearch.org/wiki/en/Alamosa_County,_Colorado_Genealogy

Linkpendium
http://www.linkpendium.com/alamosa-co-genealogy/

RootsWeb Wiki
https://wiki.rootsweb.com/wiki/index.php/Alamosa_County,_Colorado

Wikipedia
https://en.wikipedia.org/wiki/Alamosa_County,_Colorado

Historic Hotels

None

Museums & Historic Sites

Luther Bean Museum, Adams State University, Richardson Hall 2-600, 208 Edgemont Blvd, Alamosa, CO 81102, (719) 587-7151, https://www.adams.edu/luther-bean/

San Luis Valley History Museum, 401 Hunt Ave, P.O. Box 1593, Alamosa, CO 81101, (719) 587-0667, https://www.museumtrail.org/san-luis-valley-museum.html

Special Events & Scenic Locations

In January look for the Rio Frio Ice Fest featuring ice carving.

Alamosa Roundup features a rodeo, an old west cattle drive and a demolition derby. It takes place in June every year. http://www.alamosaroundup.com. Alamosa County Fair & Rodeo Grounds, 8784 Old Sanford Rd, Alamosa, CO 81101

The Alamosa County Fair takes place in July most years. Alamosa County Fair, Fair & Rodeo Grounds, 8784 Old Sanford Rd, Alamosa, CO 81101, https://www.facebook.com/pages/Alamosa-Fair-Grounds/182066985175648.

Summerfest on the Rio takes place in June and features live music and food booths. http://www.summerfestontherio.org.

Sundays at Six runs every Sunday from June through August featuring live music.

Weekends on the Rio runs every weekend from June through August featuring outdoor activities in Cole Park.

Beat the Heat BBQ, Brews & Chili Challenge takes place in July with food booths and games. https://www.slvbeattheheat.com.

Enjoy the Early Iron Club's Car Show during Labor Day weekend featuring hot rods and classic cars.

Chalk-a-Walk takes place in September challenging chalk artists of all ages.

Alamosa National Wildlife Refuge Visitor Center, 9383 El Rancho Ln, Alamosa, CO 81101, 719-589-4021, https://www.fws.gov/refuge/alamosa/

Great Sand Dunes Wilderness Visitor Center, 11999 CO-150, Mosca, CO 81146, 719-378-695, https://www.nps.gov/grsa/index.htm

Los Caminos Antiguos Scenic and Historic Byway, https://www.codot.gov/travel/scenic-byways/south-central/los-caminos

Monte Vista National Wildlife Refuge

Historical Assets Colorado

Old Spanish National Historic Trail
Rio Grande National Forest
San Luis State Park
Sangre de Cristo Wilderness

Ghost Towns & Other Sparsely Populated Places
Hooper

Newspapers
The Colorado Independent. (Alamosa, Colo.) 18??-1???
The Hooper Tribune. (Hooper, Colo.) 18??-1914
The Mosca Herald. (Mosca, Costilla County, Colo.) 18??-19??
The Expositor. (Alamosa, Colo.) 1883-1???
Alamosa Journal. (Alamosa, Colo.) 1884-1885
San Luis Valley Gazette. (Henry, Rio Grande County, Colo.) 1884-1???
The Alamosa Independent-Journal. (Alamosa, Colo.) 1885-1914
The Sentinel. (Alamosa, Colo.) 1885-1???
San Luis Valley Courier. (Alamosa, Colo.) 1889-1900
The Garrison Tribune. (Garrison, Colo.) 1891-1???
Alamosa Daily Evening Courier. (Alamosa, Colo.) 1894-1894
The Weekly Lance. (Alamosa, Colo.) 1895-1???
The Alamosa News combined with The Morning News. (Alamosa, Colo.) 19??-19??
The Alamosa News. (Alamosa, Colo.) 19??-19??
San Luis Valley Crier. (Alamosa, Colo.) 19??-19??
The Alamosa Courier. (Alamosa, Conejos County, Colo.) 1901-1917
The Alamosa Empire. (Alamosa, Colo.) 1909-19??
Alamosa Journal. (Alamosa, Alamosa County, Colo.) 1914-19??
The Hooper-Mosca Tribune. (Hooper, Alamosa County, Colo.) 1914-19??
The Alamosa Courier The Alamosa Leader. (Alamosa, Colo.) 1917-1926
The Daily Courier. (Alamosa, Colo.) 192?-1936
Alamosa Courier. (Alamosa, Alamosa County, Colo.) 1926-192?
The Alamosa Daily Courier. (Alamosa, Colo.) 1936-1952
Alamosa Sun. (Alamosa, Colo.) 1950-19??
The Valley Shopper. (Alamosa, Colo.) 1952-1953
The Daily Courier. (Alamosa, Colo.) 1952-1955
The Valley Sun. (Alamosa, Colo.) 1953-19??
The San Luis Valley Courier. (Alamosa, Colo.) 1955-1955
The Valley Courier. (Alamosa, Colo.) 1955-Current

Places on the National Register
Alamosa, Alamosa County Courthouse, 702 Fourth St.
Alamosa, Alamosa Post Office, 703 4th St.
Alamosa, American National Bank Building, 500 State Ave.
Alamosa, Denver and Rio Grande Railroad Depot, 610 State St.
Alamosa, Denver and Rio Grande Railroad Locomotive No.169, Along Chamber Dr. within Cole Park

Alamosa County

Alamosa, First Baptist Church, 408 State Ave.
Alamosa, Husung Hardware, 625 Main St.
Alamosa, Mt. Pleasant School, Jct. of Cty Rd. 3 S and Rd. 103 S
Alamosa, Sacred Heart Catholic Church, 727 4th St.
Alamosa, St. Thomas Episcopal Church, 607 Fourth St.
Hooper, Howard Store, 8681 Main St.
Hooper, Trujillo Homesteads, Address Restricted
Mosca, Medano Ranch Headquarters, 2.6 mi. N of 6N Ln.
Mosca, Superintendent's Residence, Great Sand Dunes National Monument, CO 150, SW of Mosca
Mosca, Trujillo Homestead, Unnamed two-track road, 9.3 mi. NE of MOsca
Mosca, Zapata Ranch Headquarters, 5303 CO 150

USGS Historic Places
None

Grand Army of the Republic Posts
Pfeiffer, No. 36, Alamosa, Alamosa
Osterhaus, No. 101, Alamosa, Hooper

USGS Historic Military Places
Alamosa West, Waverly School, 37.4336159, -105.9833575

Military Bases
None

Post Offices

Alamosa	1878 Mar 12		81101
Garnett	1888 Mar 3	1921 Sept 30	
Hooper	1896 July 17		81136
Mosca	1890 Dec 30		81146

Topo Quads

Alamosa East	373000N	372230N	1054500W	1055230W
Alamosa West	373000N	372230N	1055230W	1060000W
Baldy	373000N	372230N	1053730W	1054500W
Blanca	373000N	372230N	1053000W	1053730W
Capulin	372230N	371500N	1060000W	1060730W
Dry Lakes	373730N	373000N	1053730W	1054500W
Hooper SE	373730N	373000N	1054500W	1055230W
La Jara	372230N	371500N	1055230W	1060000W
Lasauses	372230N	371500N	1053730W	1054500W
Medano Ranch	374500N	373730N	1053730W	1054500W
Mount Pleasant School	373730N	373000N	1055230W	1060000W

Historical Assets Colorado

Pikes Stockade	372230N	371500N	1054500W	1055230W
Zapata Ranch	374500N	373730N	1053000W	1053730W

Suggested Reading

Colorado: the San Luis Valley. Denver: Bradford-Robinson Printing Co, 1930.

Feitz, Leland. *Alamosa: The City and County.* Colorado Springs, CO: Little London Press, 1976.

Gibson, C E. *History of the Alamosa Town Site.* Denver: Civil Works Administration, 1933.

Inventory of the County Archives of Colorado. No.2. Alamosa County. Denver: Historical Records Survey, 1942.

Little Bits Here and There of the History of RE-11J Schools. Alamosa, CO: Ye Olde Print Shoppe, 1983.

McAllister, Melvin. *Life in Hooper, Colorado.* Tehachapi, CA: M McAllister, 1998.

Arapahoe County

Introduction

Established: 1861   Population: 643,052

Formed from: Original County

Adjacent Counties: Denver, Adams, Washington, Lincoln, Elbert, Douglas, Jefferson

County Seat: Littleton

Other Communities: Aurora, Centennial, Cherry Hills Village, Englewood, Glendale, Greenwood Village, Sheridan, Bennett, Bow Mar, Columbine Valley, Deer Trail, Foxfield, Castlewood, Southglenn, Aetna Estates, Brick Center, Byers, Cherry Creek, Columbine, Comanche Creek, Dove Valley, Holly Hills, Inverness, Peoria, Strasburg, Watkins

Website, http://www.co.arapahoe.co.us

Area Codes: 303, 719

Zip Codes: 80010, 80011, 80012, 80013, 80014, 80015, 80016, 80017, 80018, 8001, 80044, 80046, 80047, 80103, 80105, 80110, 80110, 80111, 80112, 80113, 80120, 80121, 80122, 80150, 80151, 80155, 80160, 80161, 80165, 80166, 80247

Historical Assets Colorado

Arapahoe County Courthouse

Courthouses & County Government

Arapahoe County
http://www.co.arapahoe.co.us

Arapahoe County Courthouse (Littleton), 1790 W Littleton Blvd, Littleton, CO 80120, 303-798-4591; http://www.courts.state.co.us/Courts/County/Index.cfm?County_ID=57

Arapahoe County Courthouse (Justice Center)(18th Judicial District), 7325 S Potomac St, Centennial, CO 80112, 303-649-6355; http://www.courts.state.co.us/Courts/County/Index.cfm?County_ID=57

Historic Arapahoe County Courthouse

Assessor, 5334 S Prince St, Littleton, CO 80120, 303-795-4600; http://www.co.arapahoe.co.us/Departments/CR/index.asp

Board of County Commissioners, 5334 S Prince St, Littleton, CO 80120, 303-795-4630, http://www.co.arapahoe.co.us/204/Assessor

Clerk & Recorder, 5534 S Prince St, Littleton, CO 80120, 303-795-4520; http://www.co.arapahoe.co.us/Departments/CR/index.asp

Coroner, 13101 E Broncos Pkwy, Centennial, CO 80112, 720-874-3625; http://www.co.arapahoe.co.us/369/Coroner

Elections, 5334 S Prince St, Littleton, CO 80120, 303-795-4511; https://www.arapahoevotes.com/

Public Health, 6162 S Willow Dr, Ste 100, Greenwood Village, CO 80111, 303-220-9200; http://www.tchd.org/

Arapahoe County

Transportation, Lima Plaza, 6924 S Lima St, Centennial, CO 80112, 720-874-6500; http://www.co.arapahoe.co.us/946/Transportation-Planning-and-Studies

Treasurer, 5334 S Prince St, Littleton, CO 80120, 303-795-4550; http://www.co.arapahoe.co.us/departments/tr/

County Records

Birth 1876	Marriage 1902	Divorce 1903
Death 1907	Probate 1903	Court 1903

Land 1902 (incomplete from 1860s Arapahoe County, Kansas Territory)
CSA County Physician 1889
CSA Death 1894
CSA Delayed Birth Certificates 1941

County & Municipal Records Held at the State Level

The Colorado State Archives

Physical Records
Building
Civilian Conservation Corps
Clerk & Recorder
Coroner
County Commissioners
County Court
District Court
Justice Court
Public Trustee
Sheriff
Social Services
Treasurer
WPA Historical Records
WPA Religious Institutions Survey
Cities
Cherry Hills Village
Columbine Valley
Englewood
Glendale
Greenwood Village
Littleton

Records on Film
1885 Census
Clerk & Recorder
County Commissioners
District Court
School Districts
Treasurer
Cities
Cherry Hills Village
Englewood
Glendale
Greenwood Village

Records on Master Film
Clerk & Recorder
County Court
District Court
District Attorney
Record & Map Division
School Districts
Sheriff
Treasurer
Cities
Englewood
Glendale
Greenwood Village

The Denver Public Library

1861 Quit Claim Deeds
1885 Colorado Census
Acadia Cemetery Deed (Masonic), 1867
Alps Gold Mining Company Records, 1889-1907
Arapahoe County Coroner's Ledger 1879-1891
Arapahoe County Courthouse Corner Stone Records, 1881
Arapahoe County Justice Court Records, 1861-1867

Historical Assets Colorado

Arapahoe County Marriage Records, 1859-1901
Ash Grove Parent Teacher Association Records, 1929-1982
Clayton College Records, 1851-1999
Colorado Deeds, 1868-1911
Colorado Genealogical Society Records, 1849-2017
Colorado National Guard, Routt Rifles Muster Roll, 1881
Colorado Theatre Program Collection, 1900-
Columbine Genealogical and Historical Society Records, 1861-2019
Declarations of Intention (Naturalization) 1880-1906
Denver & Arapahoe County Real Estate Records, 1886-1974
Denver, Abstracts of Title, 1860-1969
Denver, Auditor's Office Records, 1922-1984
Denver, Building Department Records, 1893-1960
Denver, Building Permits 1889-1955
Denver, Board of Park Commissioners Records, 1893-1916
Denver, Board of Water Commissioners, Water Tap Papers, 1872-1987
Denver, City Council Records, 1859-2011
Denver, Department of Finance, Treasury Division Records, 1864-1978
Denver, Department of Finance, Assessment Division Records, 1863-1985
Denver, Department of Improvement and Parks Records, 1895-1959
Denver, Department of Public Works Records, 1890-2003
Denver, Department of Revenue Assessment, Lot Indexes, 1860
Denver, Public School Records, 1890-2018
Denver, Street Department Letters, 1894-1916
Denver Public School Records, 1890-2018 [photographs]
Denver Tramway Corporation Records, 1888-1975
Development Engineering Services Records, 1893-1995
George Tritch Hardware Company Records, 1886-1930
Greenwood Village Records, 1982-1090
Kansas-Burroughs Consolidated Mining Company Records, 1870-1906
LaCrosse Gold Mining Company Records, 1877-1905
Marriage Records, 1859-1901
Mission Viejo Homeowners Association Records, 1972-2007
New York-Central Gold Mining Company Records, 1896-1909
Presbyterian-St Luke's Medical Center Records, 1890-2009
Prudential Insurance Company of America Records, 1915
Real Estate Analysis Company Records, 1949-1990s
Town of Sheridan Ordinances, 1890-1919
Treasurer's Certificates of Purchase, 1894-1939
West Arapahoe Conservation District Records, 1945-2006
Whale Mining & Milling Company Correspondence, 1894
WPA Historical Records Survey
WWI Draft Registration Cards (microfilm)

Arapahoe County

School Districts

School Districts, http://www.adcogov.org/local-school-districts

Aurora Public Schools, 15701 E 1st Ave, Aurora, CO 80011, 303-344-8060; https://aurorak12.org/

Bennett School District 29J, 615 7th St, Bennett, CO 80102, 303-644-3234; https://www.bsd29j.com/

Byers School District, 444 E Front St, Byers, CO 80103, 303-822-5292; https://www.byers32j.k12.co.us/

Cherry Creek Schools, 4700 S Yosemite St, Greenwood Village, CO 80111, 303-773-1184; https://www.cherrycreekschools.org

Deer Trail School District 26J, 350 2nd Ave, Deer Trail, CO 80105, 303-769-4421; https://www.dt26j.com/

Englewood School District, 4101 S Bannock St, Englewood, CO 80110, 303-761-7050; https://www.englewoodschools.net/

Littleton Public Schools, 5776 S Crocker St, Littleton, CO 80120, 303-347-3300; https://littletonpublicschools.net/

Sheridan School District No. 2, 4150 S Hazel Ct, Englewood, CO 80110, 720-833-9991; https://www.ssd2.org/

Strasburg School District 31J, 56729 E Colorado Ave, Strasburg, CO 80136, 303-622-9211; http://www.strasburg31j.com/

Historic School Districts

1. Englewood
2. Sheridan
3. [1878]
4. Melvin
5. Castlewood/Cherry Creek
6. Littleton
7. Englewood
8. Brantner (1867)
9. [1878]
10. [1878]
11. [1878]
12. Sullivan
13. Fort Logan
14. [1878]
15. Pine Ridge
16. College View
17. [1878]
18. Garden Home/Westwood
19. Cherry Creek
20. [1878]
21. [1878]
22. Englewood
23. Petersburg
24. Winnview/Opal/Green Street
25. Toll Gate
26. Deer Trail
27. [1884]
28. Aurora [Joint Adams]
29. Bennett [Joint Adams]
30. Sunnyside (Sunnydale)
31. Strasburg [Joint Adams]
32. Byers
33. Windy Point/Nestor
34. Brick Center
35. Ash Grove
36. Cherry Hills/Breen Avenue
37. Curtis
38. [1887]
39. [1887]
40. [1887]
41. [1887]
42. [1887]
43. [1887]
44. [1887]
45. [1887]
46. [1887]
47. [1887]
48. [1887]
49. [1887]
50. [1887]
51. Coal Creek
52. [1887]
53. [1887]
54. Mountain View
55. Watkins
56. [1888]
57. [1888]
58. Denver
59. [1888]
60. [1888]
61. [1888]
62. Day/Altura
63. [1888]
64. [1888]
65. [1888]
66. [1888]
67. [1888]
68. [1888]
69. Maple Grove
70. [1888]
71. [1888]
72. Belleview
73. Wolf Creek
74. Nestor

Historical Assets Colorado

75. Fort Logan >1941	84. [1889]	93. [1890]
76. [1889]	85. [1889]	94. [1891]
77. [1889]	86. [1890]	95. [1891]
78. [1889]	87. [1890]	96. [1891]
79. [1889]	88. [1890]	97. [1891]
80. [1889]	89. [1890]	98. [1892]
81. [1889]	90. [1890]	99. [1892]
82. [1889]	91. [1890]	100. [1892]
83. [1889]	92. [1890]	101. [1892]

Fraternal Organizations

Granges
Ceres, No. 1, Arapahoe, Denver, Mar 1873
Platte Canyon, No. 11, Arapahoe, Littleton/Lower Platte, 16 Dec 1873
Plum Creek, No. 12, Arapahoe, Platte, 17 Dec 1873
Platte Valley, No. 13, Arapahoe, Denver/Lower Platte, 19 Dec 1873
Littleton, No. 19, Arapahoe, Littleton, 29 Dec 1873
Union, No. 26, Arapahoe, Denver, 17 Jan 1874
59er, No. 34, Arapahoe, Island Station/Denver, 15 Jan 1874
Denver, No. 37, Arapahoe, Denver, 21 Jan 1874
Cherry Creek, No. 58, Arapahoe, Cherry Creek/Denver, 11 Apr 1874
Capital, No. 75, Arapahoe, Denver, 25 Feb 1887
Glenn Dale, No. 77, Arapahoe, Littleton, 23 Jan 1888
Garden, No. 78, Arapahoe, South Denver, 18 Feb 1888
Glendale, No. 135, Arapahoe, Denver/Harmon, 19 Dec 1896
Breen Ave, No. 151, Arapahoe, Littleton, 8 Jan 1905
Columbine, No. 153, Arapahoe, Littleton, 3 Dec 1906
Pleasant Park, No. 156, Arapahoe, Littleton, 30 Mar 1907
Castlewood, No. 159, Arapahoe, Englewood, 9 Oct 1907
Running Creek, No. 169, Arapahoe, Watkins, 10 Apr 1909
Prairie Gem, No. 193, Arapahoe, Byers, 11 Feb 1911
Bijou Valley, No. 208, Arapahoe, Byers, 18 May 1912
Box Elder, No. 232, Arapahoe, Watkins, 26 Dec 1914
Pine View, No. 236, Arapahoe, Deer Trail, 6 Mar 1915
Rocky Mountain, No. 294, Arapahoe, Englewood, 29 June 1916
Deer Trail, No. 412, Arapahoe, Deer Trail, 6 Mar 194
Victory, No. 452, Arapahoe, Aurora, 8 May 1942
Castlewood, No. 469, Arapahoe, Littleton/Centennial, 24 Mar 1948

Masons

Ancient Free & Accepted Masons
Denver, No. 5, Arapahoe, Denver, 10 Dec 1861
Union, No. 7, Arapahoe, Dener, 3 Nov 1863
Weston, No. 22, Arapahoe, Litleton, 24 Sept 1872
Schiller, No. 41, Arapahoe, Denver, 21 Sept 1881
Harmony, No. 61, Arapahoe, Denver, 17 Sept 1884
Temple, No. 84, Arapahoe, Denver, 16 Sept 1890

Arapahoe County

    Emulation, No. 84, Arapahoe, Centennial, 25 Jan 1993
    Centennial, No. 84, Arapahoe, Centennial, 26 Jan 2002
    Acadia, No. 85, Arapahoe, Denver, 15 Sept 1891
    Highlands, No. 86, Arapahoe, Denver, 16 Sept 1891
    Oriental, No. 87, Arapahoe, Denver, 15 Sept 1891
    Rob Morris, No. 92, Arapahoe, Denver, 20 Sept 1893
    South Denver, No. 93, Arapahoe, Denver, 20 Sept 1893
    Byers, No. 152, Arapahoe, Byers, 8 Oct 1919
    Aurora, No. 156, Arapahoe, Aurora, 20 Sept 1922
    Englewood, No. 166, Arapahoe, Englewood, 22 Sept 1926
    Revelation, No. 180, Arapahoe, Aurora, 25 Jan 1955

Royal Arch Masons
    Denver, No. 2, Arapahoe, Denver
    Colorado, No. 29, Arapahoe, Denver

Knights Templar
    Colorado Commandery, No. 1, Arapahoe, Denver, 1866 Jan 13
    Denver Commandery, No. 25, Arapahoe, Denver, 1892 Dec 29

Eastern Star
    Queen City, No. 4, Arapahoe, Denver
    Queen City, No. 6, Arapahoe, Denver
    Manzanita, No. 85, Arapahoe, Littleton
    Grace, No. 121, Arapahoe, Byers
    Hope, No. 122, Arapahoe, Bennett
    Englewood, No. 128, Arapahoe, Englewood

Odd Fellows
    Union, No. 1, Arapahoe, Denver, 1864 Aug 18
    Denver, No. 4, Arapahoe, Denver, 1866 Sept 29
    United, No. 4, Arapahoe, Denver, 1906 Oct 17
    Germania, No. 14, Arapahoe, Denver, 1872 Apr 26
    Arapahoe, No. 24, Arapahoe, Denver
    Rowland, No. 31, Arapahoe, Denver
    Tri-County, No. 33, Arapahoe, Englewood
    Anchor, No. 66, Arapahoe, Denver
    Littleton, No. 90, Arapahoe, Littleton
    Byers, No. 126, Arapahoe, Byers
    Englewood, No. 138, Arapahoe, Englewood

Rebekahs
    Enterprise, No. 1, Arapahoe, Denver
    Colfax, No. 11, Arapahoe, Denver
    Martha, No. 12, Arapahoe, Denver
    Engelwood, No. 19, Arapahoe, Englewood
    Columbine, No. 34, Arapahoe, Columbine
    Bijou Valley, No. 36, Arapahoe, Byers
    Littleton, No. 56, Arapahoe, Littleton
    Pearl, No. 68, Arapahoe, Englewood
    Aurora, No. 120, Arapahoe, Aurora

Historical Assets Colorado

Knights of Pythias
    Colorado, No. 1, Arapahoe, Denver
    Damon, No. 2, Arapahoe, Denver
    Inter Ocean, No. 6, Arapahoe, Denver, 1875 Aug 26
    Centennial, No. 8, Arapahoe, Denver
    Washington, No. 32, Arapahoe, Denver
    Denver, No. 41, Arapahoe, Denver
    Capitol, No. 44, Arapahoe, Denver
    Arapahoe, No. 45, Arapahoe, Denver, 1888 Nov 28
    Rathbone, No. 59, Arapahoe, Denver
    Linne, No. 63, Arapahoe, Denver, 1890 Nov 22
    Silver State, No. 65, Arapahoe, Denver
    South Denver, No. 74, Arapahoe, South Denver, 1891 Dec 16
    Enterprise, No. 81, Arapahoe, Denver
    Dunham, No. 85, Arapahoe, Denver, 1892 Nov 1

Pythian Sisters
    Denver, No. 11, Arapahoe, Denver

Benevolent Protective Order of Elks
    Denver, No. 17, Arapahoe, Denver
    Littleton, No. 1650, Arapahoe, Littleton
    Aurora, No. 1921, Arapahoe, Aurora
    Englewood, No. 2122, Arapahoe, Englewood
    Deer Trail, No. 2307, Arapahoe, Deer Trail

City & Town Halls

Littleton, 2255 W Berry Ave, Littleton, CO 80120, 303-795-3700, https://www.littletongov.org

Aurora, 15151 E Alameda Pkwy, Aurora, CO 80012, 303-739-7160, https://www.auroragov.org

Centennial, 13133 E Arapahoe Rd, Centennial, CO 80112, 303-325-8000, https://www.centennialco.gov/Home

Cherry Hills Village, 2450 E Quincy Ave, Cherry Hills Village, CO 80113, 303-789-2541, https://www.cherryhillsvillage.com

Englewood, 1000 Englewood Pkwy, Englewood, CO 80110, 303-762-2310, https://www.englewoodco.gov

Glendale, 950 S Birch St, Glendale, CO 80246, 303-759-1513, https://www.glendale.co.us

Greenwood Village, 6060 S Quebec St, Greenwood Village, CO 80111, 303-773-0252, https://www.greenwoodvillage.com

Sheridan, 4101 S Federal Blvd, Sheridan, CO 80110, 303-762-2200, http://www.ci.sheridan.co.us

Bennett, 207 Muegge Wy, Bennett, CO 80102, 303-644-3249, https://www.colorado.gov/townofbennett

Columbine Valley, 2 Middlefield, Columbine Valley, CO 80123, 303-795-1434, https://columbinevalley.org

Deer Trail, 555 2nd Ave, Deer Trail, CO 80105, 303-769-4464, http://www.deertrail-colorado.org

Arapahoe County

Archives & Manuscript Collections
Arapahoe County Colorado Archive Center (digital), https://www.arapahoegov.com/Archive.aspx

Englewood Public Library & City Archive, 1000 Englewood Pkwy, Englewood, CO 80110, (303) 762-2555, https://englewood.marmot.org

Historical & Genealogical Societies
Aurora Genealogical Society of Colorado, c/o Aurora Central Library Genealogy Collection, 14949 E Alameda Pkwy, P.O. Box 31732, Aurora, CO 80041-0732, http://www.freewebs.com/auroragenealogysociety/

Aurora Historical Society, Aurora History Museum, 15051 E Alameda Dr, Aurora, CO 80012-1546, (303) 360-8545, http://www.auroramuseum.org

Cherry Creek Valley Historical Society, Melvin Schoolhouse Museum & Library, 4950 S Laredo St, Aurora, CO 80015, (303) 699-5145, https://www.ccvhsco.com

Columbine Genealogical & Historical Society, P.O. Box 2074, Centennial, CO 80161-2074, (303) 770-7164, http://columbinegenealogy.com

International Society for British Genealogy and Family History, P.O. Box 3345, Centennial, CO 80161, http://isbgfh.org

Littleton Historical Society, Historical Museum, 6028 S Gallup St, Littleton, CO 80120-2703, (303) 795-3950, https://www.littletongov.org/city-services/city-departments/museum

Sheridan Historical Society, 4101 S Federal Blvd, Sheridan, CO 80110-5399, http://www.shs-co.org

Society of Mayflower Descendants in the State of Colorado, 7129 W Arlington Wy, Littleton, CO 80123, http://wp.coloradomayflowersociety.org

Local Libraries
Edwin A Bemis Library, 6014 S Datura St, Littleton, CO, 80161, (303) 795-3961, https://bemis.marmot.org

Anythink Bennett, 495 7th St, Bennett, CO 80102, (303) 405-3231, https://www.anythinklibraries.org/location/anythink-bennett

Aurora Public Library, 14949 E Alameda Pkwy, Aurora, CO 80012, (303) 739-6630, http://www.auroralibrary.org

Englewood Public Library & City Archive, 1000 Englewood Pkwy, Englewood, CO 80110, (303) 762-2555, https://englewood.marmot.org

Koelbel Library, 5955 S Holly St, Centennial, CO 80121, (303) 542-7279, https://arapahoelibraries.org

Lutheran Church-Missouri Synod Rocky Mountain District Library, 14334 E Evans Ave, Aurora, CO 80014, (303) 695-8001, http://rm.lcms.org

Sheridan Library, 3425 W Oxford Ave, Sheridan, CO 80236, (303) 542-7279, https://arapahoelibraries.org/locations/SH/

Historical Assets Colorado

Links
CO GenWeb
http://cogenweb.com/arapahoe/
Cyndi's List
https://www.cyndislist.com/us/co/counties/arapahoe/
FamilySearch Wiki
https://www.familysearch.org/wiki/en/Arapahoe_County,_Colorado_Genealogy
Linkpendium
http://www.linkpendium.com/arapahoe-co-genealogy/
RootsWeb Wiki
https://wiki.rootsweb.com/wiki/index.php/Arapahoe_County,_Colorado
Wikipedia
https://en.wikipedia.org/wiki/Arapahoe_County,_Colorado

Historic Hotels
None

Museums & Historic Sites
17 Mile House Farm Park, 8181 S Parker Rd, Centennial, CO 80016, (720) 874-6540, http://www.co.arapahoe.co.us/Facilities/Facility/Details/17-Mile-House-Farm-Park-23

Aurora Historical Society, Aurora History Museum, 15051 E Alameda Dr, Aurora, CO 80012-1546, (303) 360-8545, http://www.auroramuseum.org

Centennial House Museum, 1671 Galena St, Aurora, CO 80010, (303) 739-6666, http://www.auroragov.org

Cherry Creek School House Museum, 9300 E Union Ave, Englewood, CO 80111, (303) 693-1500, https://www.historycolorado.org/location/cherry-creek-schoolhouse

Cherry Creek Valley Historical Society, Melvin Schoolhouse Museum & Library, 4950 S Laredo St, Aurora, CO 80015, (303) 699-5145, https://www.ccvhsco.com

Colorado Grange Museum, 21901 E Hampden Ave, Aurora, CO 80013, (303) 693-3621, http://coloradogrange.org/museum/index.html

John Gully Homestead Museum, 200 S Chambers Rd, Aurora, CO 80017, (303) 739-6666, http://auroracohistoricalsociety.org/116/

Littleton Historical Society, Historical Museum, 6028 S Gallup St, Littleton, CO 80120-2703, (303) 795-3950, https://www.littletongov.org/city-services/city-departments/museum

Plains Conservation Center, 21901 E Hampden Ave, Aurora, CO 80013, (303) 693-3621, http://www.plainsconservationcenter.org

Special Events & Scenic Locations
The Arapahoe County Fair takes places in July most years. Arapahoe County Fair, Fairgrounds & Events Center, 25690 E Quincy Ave, Aurora, CO 80016, 303-795-4955, https://www.arapahoecountyfair.com

Arapahoe County

There are dozens of walking history tours offered throughout the year. https://www.denver.org/events/history-heritage/

Cherry Creek State Park
Smoky Hill Trail
South Platte Trail
Highline Canal National Recreation Trail
Platte River Greenway National Recreation Trail

Ghost Towns & Other Sparsely Populated Places

Abbott, Argo Junction, Argo Park, Arickaree, Avoca, Badger, Barr, Berkeley, Berlin, Burnham, Circle Crossing, Colorado Central Cut Off, Condon, Cope, Corcoran, Coronado, Denver Mills, Derby, Duff, Ebert, Fort Logan, Fox, Friend, Globeville, Hale, Harris, Harrisburg, Hatchery, Henderson, Idalia, Independence, Irondale, Island Station, Jersey, Kenwood, Lansing, Lindon, Logan, Loretto, Lyman, Magnolia, Melvin, Military Junction, Military Post, Mooreville, Newton, Oakes, Overland Park, Petersburgh, Scranton, Sheridan Junction, Shields, South Denver, Strasburg, Thurman, Townsend, University Park, Utah Junction, Valverde, Villa Park, Washburn, Watkins, West Denver

Newspapers

The Denver Democrat And National Standard. (Denver, Colo.) 1???-1905
The Denver Citizen. (Denver, Colo.) 1???-19??
The Highland Chief. (Denver, Colo.) 18??-19??
The Daily Colorado Price Current and Livestock Journal. (Denver, Colo.) 18??-1897
Colorado Farm and Livestock Journal. (Denver, Colo.) 18??-1???
The Colorado Farmer. (Denver, Colo.) 18??-1???
The Colorado Evening Sun. (Denver, Colo.) 18??-1???
Rocky Mountain Illustrated Weekly. (Denver, Colo.) 18??-1897
The Denver Examiner. (Denver, Colo.) 18??-1916
The Elite. ([Denver, Colo.]) 18??-1885
Daily Fair Programme. (Denver, Colo.) 18??-1???
Denver Hotel Bulletin. (Denver, Colo.) 18??-19??
The Evening Star. (Denver, Colo.) 18??-1???
Rocky Mountain Cricket. (Denver, Colo.) 18??-1???
The Silver Age. (Denver, Colo.) 18??-1???
The State Mining Journal. (Denver, Colo.) 18??-1???
Rocky Mountain News. (Cherry Creek, Kan. Terr. [Denver, Colo.]) 1859-1864
Rocky Mountain Herald. (Denver, Colo.) 1860-1861
Denver Weekly Mountaineer. (Denver, Colo.) 1860-1861
Daily Denver Mountaineer. (Denver, Colo. Terr. [Colo.]) 1860-1861
The Daily Herald And Rocky Mountain Advertiser. (Denver, Colo.) 1860-1861
Daily Rocky Mountain News. (Denver, Jefferson [Colo.]) 1860-1879
The Daily Colorado Republican and Rocky Mountain Herald. (Denver City, Colorado Territory [Denver, Colo.]) 1861-1862

Historical Assets Colorado

The Weekly Colorado Republican and Rocky Mountain Herald. (Denver City, Colorado Territory. [Denver, Colo.]) 1861-1862
The Weekly Commonwealth and Republican. (Denver City, Colo. Territory [Denver, Colo.]) 1862-1863
The Daily Commonwealth. (Denver City, Colorado Territory [Denver, Colo.]) 1863-1864
The Weekly Commonwealth. (Denver City, Colorado Territory [Denver, Colo.]) 1863-1864
The Weekly Denver Gazette. (Denver, Colo.) 1865-1???
The Daily Denver Gazette. (Denver, Colo.) 1865-1869
The Denver Daily. (Denver, Colo.) 1867-1867
The Weekly Colorado Tribune. (Denver, Colo.) 1867-1868
The Colorado Tribune. (Denver, Colo.) 1867-1867
The Rocky Mountain Herald. (Denver, Colo.) 1868-1976
The Colorado Tribune. (Denver, Colo.) 1869-18??
The Daily Gazette and Commercial Advertiser. (Denver, Colo.) 1869-1???
Denver Daily Democrat. (Denver, Colo.) 187?-18??
The Colorado Weekly Republican. (Denver, Colo.) 187?-1???
Colorado Journal. (Denver, Colo.) 187?-1??? | Languages: German
The Denver Press. (Denver, Colo.) 1871-1901
The Denver Tribune. (Denver, Colo.) 1871-1884
Colorado Journal. (Denver, Colo.) 1872-1901 | Languages: German
Colorado Agriculturalist and Stock Journal. (Denver, Colo.) 1873-1???
Denver Mirror. (Denver, Colo.) 1873-1879
Colorado Democrat. (Denver, Colo.) 1874-1???
Daily Colorado Transcript. (Denver, Colo.) 1875-1???
Denver Daily Times. (Denver, Colo.) 1875-1886
Denver Daily Tribune. (Denver, Colo.) 1875-1879
The Daily Democrat. (Denver, Colo.) 1876-18??
The Weekly Democrat. (Denver, Colo.) 1876-18??
Kansas and Colorado Illustrated Monthly Newspaper. (Kansas City, Mo. and Denver, Colo.) 1878-1???
Weekly Republican. (Denver, Colo.) 1878-1884
The Denver Republican. (Denver, Colo.) 1879-1884
Colorado Post. (Denver, Colo.) 1879-1??? | Languages: German
The Daily Hotel Reporter. (Denver, Colo.) 1879-1???
The Colorado Antelope. (Denver, Colo.) 1879-1879
Hello. (Denver, Colo.) 188?-????
Inter-Ocean. (Denver, Colo.) 1880-1???
The Great West. (Denver, Colo.) 1880-1882
Pomeroy's Democrat. (Denver, Colo.) 1880-1???
Montclair Mirror. (Denver, Colo.) 188?-19??
The Denver Detective. (Denver, Colo.) 188?-1???
Denver Argus. (Denver, Colo.) 188?-1???
Railway And Mining Gazette. (Denver, Colo.) 1881-1881
Hanson's Mining Gazette. (Denver, Colo.) 1881-????

Arapahoe County

The Rocky Mountain Celt. (Denver, Colo.) 1881-1???
Sunday Morning Paragraph. (Denver, Colo.) 1881-188?
Our Opinion. (Denver, Colo.) 1881-18??
Evening Truth. (West Denver, Colo.) 1881-1882
The Truth. (West Denver, Colo.) 1881-1881
Denver Evening Press. (Denver, Colo.) 1881-1???
Die Sonntags-Post. (Denver, Colo.) 1881-1??? | Languages: German
Pomeroy's Great West. (Denver, Colo.) 1882-????
The Denver World. (Denver, Colo.) 1882-1???
The Silver State. (Denver, Colo.) 1882-????
Republican Journal. (Denver, Colo.) 1882-1???
The Denver Mercury. (Denver, Colo.) 1882-1???
Denver Evening World. (Denver, Colo.) 1882-1???
Evening Telegram. (Denver, Colo.) 1882-1???
The Denver Star. (Denver, Colo.) 1882-18??
Denver Weekly World. (Denver, Colo.) 1882-1???
North Denver Villa Park Telephone. (Denver, Colo.) 1883-18??
Home Journal. (Denver, Colo.) 1883-18??
Opinion. (Denver, Colo.) 1884-1???
The Vidette. (Denver, Colo.) 1884-1???
Western Sport and Theatrical Record. (Denver, Colo.) 1884-????
Denver Tribune-Republican. (Denver, Colo.) 1884-1886
Weekly Tribune-Republican. (Denver, Colo.) 1884-1886
Denver Herold. (Denver, Colo.) 1884-1??? | Languages: German
Colorado Catholic. (Denver, Colo.) 1884-1899
La Stella. (Denver, Colo.) 1885-1??? | Languages: English, Italian
The Brighton Register. (Brighton, Colo.) 1885-19??
The Colorado Graphic. (Denver, Colo.) 1886-19??
Field and Farm. (Denver, Colo.) 1886-1920
Denver Evening Telegram. (Denver, Colo.) 1886-1887
Home Journal. (North Denver and Highlands [Colo.]) 1887-1???
North Denver and Highlands Home Journal. (North Denver and Highlands, Colo.) 1887-1887
The Denver Exchange Journal. (Denver, Colo.) 1887-1888
The Road. (Denver, Colo.) 1887-1896
The Weekly Republican. (Denver, Colo.) 1887-1913
Rocky Mountain Sentinel. (Denver, Colo.) 1887-19??
Denver Afternoon. (Denver, Colo.) 1887-1???
The Denver Republican. (Denver, Colo.) 1887-1913
Colorado Exchange Journal. (Denver, Colo.) 1888-1891
The Mountain Mirror. (Denver, Colo.) 1888-1???
The Littleton Gazette. (Littleton, Arapahoe County, Colo.) 1888-1891
The Western Standard. (Denver, Colo.) 1888-1???
The Arbitrator. (Denver, Colo.) 1889-1???
The West Side Citizen. (Villa Park, Colo.) 1889-????
Denver Fidibus. (Denver, Colo.) 1889-189? | Languages: German

Historical Assets Colorado

The Mining Exchange Journal. (Denver, Colo.) 1889-1892
The Cow-Boy Roundup. (Denver, Colo.) 1889-1???
The Golden Perhaps. (Denver, Colo.) 1889-1???
Barr City Gazette. (Barr City, Arapahoe County, Colo.) 1889-1???
The Rocky Mountain Post: Weekly Edition of The Denver Evening Post. (Denver, Colo.) 189?-????
Denver Fidibus-Herold. (Denver, Colo.) 189?-1901 | Languages: German
The Denver Dispatch. (Denver, Colo.) 1890-1???
The Illustrated Rocky Mountain Globe. (Denver, Colo.) 189?-1901
The Colorado Democrat. (Denver, Colo.) 189?-1???
La Patria. (Denver, Colo.) 189?-1??? | Languages: Italian
Denver Commercial Review. (Denver, Colo.) 1890-1???
Colorado State Capital. (Denver, Colo.) 1890-1???
Cheely's Democrat. (Denver, Colo.) 1890-1???
The African Advocate. (Denver, Colo.) 1890-1???
The Denver Financial News. (Denver, Colo.) 1890-1???
The Tomahawk. (Denver, Colo.) 1890-1???
The Lindon Sun. (Lindon, Arapahoe County, Colo.) 1890-18??
The Colorado Sun. (Denver, Colo.) 1891-1???
The People. (Denver, Colo.) 1891-1???
Littleton Independent. (Littleton, Colo.) 1891-1918
Next. (Denver, Colo.) 1892-1???
The Western Irishman. (Denver, Colo.) 1892-1???
The Evening Post. (Denver, Colo.) 1892-1895
Littleton Republican. (Littleton, Colo.) 1892-1???
Progress. (Denver, Colo.) 1893-1???
The Daily Mining Record. (Denver, Colo.) 1893-1913
Industrial Advocate. (Denver, Colo.) 1893-1900
The Colorado Weekly Sun. (Denver, Colo.) 1893-1895
Rocky Mountain American. (Denver, Colo.) 1893-1???
The Daily State Mining Journal. (Denver, Colo.) 1893-1893
The Prohibition Globe. (Denver, Colo.) 1893-1???
The Democratic Record. (Denver, Colo.) 1893-1???
National Populist. (Denver, Colo.) 1893-1???
The Altrurian. (Denver [Colo.]) 1894-1901
Co-Operation. (University Park, Colo.) 1894-1???
The Bi-Metallist. (Denver, Colo.) 1894-1???
The Daily Populist. (Denver, Colo.) 1894-1???
Our Nation's Crisis. (Denver, Colo.) 1895-????
The Denver Weekly Times-Sun. (Denver, Colo.) 1895-1901
The Colorado Statesman. (Denver, Colo.) 1895-1961
The New Road. (Denver, Colo.) 1896-1898
The Grip of Gold. (Denver, Colo.) 1896-1???
The National Standard. (Denver, Colo.) 1897-19??
Daily Denver Stockman. (Denver, Colo.) 1897-1900
Illustrated Sentinel. (Denver, Colo.) 1897-1898

Arapahoe County

The Daily Journal. (Denver, Colo.) 1897-Current
Illustrated Sentinel Weekly. (Denver, Colo.) 1898-1899
George's Weekly (The New Road). (Denver, Colo.) 1898-1898
George's Weekly (The Road). (Denver, Colo.) 1898-1900
Clay's Review. (Denver, Colo.) 1898-19??
The Denver Democrat. (Denver, Colo.) 1899-19??
Der Unterhaltungs-Bote. ([Denver, Colo.]) 1899-1899 | Languages: German
Illustrated Weekly. (Denver, Colo.) 1899-1908
South Side Citizen. (Denver, Colo.) 1899-1???
The Woman's Crier and Illustrated Free-Thinker. (Denver, Colo.) 1899-1???
Rocky Mountain World and The Denver Press. (Denver, Colo.) 1900-????
The Arapahoe Democrat with which is consolidated The Englewood Tribune and Arapahoe Republican. (Englewood, Colo.) 19??-19??
The Englewood Tribune and The Arapahoe Republican. (Englewood, Colo.) 19??-19??
Englewood News. (Englewood [Colo.]) 19??-19??
Englewood Monitor. (Englewood, Arapahoe County, Colo.) 19??-19??
Arapahoe Republican. (Englewood, Colo.) 19??-1910
The Englewood Herald and Enterprise. (Englewood, Arapahoe County, Colo.) 19??-1935
South Jefferson Times. (Littleton, Colo.) 19??-1991
Equality. (Denver, Colo.) 1900-19??
Colorado Weekly News. (Deer Trail, Colo.) 19??-Current
The Englewood Enterprise. (Englewood, Arapahoe County, Colo.) 19??-1956
Littleton's Arapahoe Herald. (Littleton, Colo.) 19??-1972
The Eastern Colorado News. (Strasburg, Adams County, Colo.) 19??-Current
Life At Ken-Caryl. (Littleton, Colo.) 19??-Current
The Denver Citizen and "Business." (Denver, Colo.) 1900-1901
George's Weekly. (Denver, Colo.) 1900-1907
Daily Edition Denver Record-Stockman. (Denver, Colo.) 1901-19??
Denver Record-Stockman. (Denver, Colo.) 1901-1919
Svensk Amerikanska Western Svenska Korrespondenten. (Denver, Colo.) 1901-1913 | Languages: English, Swedish
Columbia. (Denver, Colo.) 1901-19?? | Languages: Swedish
The Rocky Mountain Miner. (Denver, Colo.) 1901-19??
Colorado Chronicle. (Denver, Colo.) 1901-1903
Arapahoe Herald and South Arapahoe Herald. (Littleton, Arapahoe County, Colo.) 1902-1903
Arapahoe Herald. (Littleton, Arapahoe County, Colo.) 1903-1918
The Englewood Great West. (Englewood, Colo.) 1904-19??
The Englewood Tribune. (Englewood, Colo.) 1906-1909
Englewood Tribune and Arapahoe County News. (Englewood, Colo.) 1909-1909
Englewood Tribune and Sheridan News. (Englewood, Colo.) 1909-1910
The Adams County News. (Aurora, Colo.) 1909-195?
The Aurora Democrat. (Aurora, Colo.) 1909-19??
Englewood Tribune and Arapahoe County News. (Englewood, Colo.) 1910-1910
Arapahoe Republican and The Englewood Tribune. (Englewood, Colo.) 1910-191?

Historical Assets Colorado

Englewood Enterprise. (Englewood, Colo.) 1911-1916
Englewood Enterprise and Deer Trail Tribune. (Deer Trail, Colo.) 1913-19??
Deer Trail Tribune. (Deer Trail, Colo.) 1913-1953
Englewood Advertiser. (Englewood, Arapahoe County, Colo.) 1915-1916
Englewood Enterprise and Englewood Advertiser. (Englewood, Colo.) 1916-19??
The Tabloid. (Englewood, Colo.) 1918-19??
Littleton Independent and The Arapahoe Herald. (Littleton, Arapahoe County, Colo.) 1918-1956
The Englewood Herald. (Englewood, Colo.) 192?-19??
The Englewood Messenger. (Englewood, Arapahoe County, Colo.) 1924-19??
Aurora-Fitzsimons Sun. (Aurora, Adams County, Colo.) 1928-19??
The Monitor. (Englewood, Colo.) 193?-1938
The Independent Press. (Englewood, Arapahoe County, Colo.) 1931-19??
The Liberty Press. (Englewood, Arapahoe County, Colo.) 1932-19??
The Englewood Press. (Englewood, Colo.) 1933-1957
The Englewood Herald. (Englewood, Arapahoe County, Colo.) 1935-1938
The Englewood Herald and The Monitor. (Englewood, Arapahoe County, Colo.) 1938-1941
Garden Home News. (Garden Home, Colo.) 1938-19??
The Aurora Advocate. (Aurora, Colo.) 194?-1972
The Shopper. (Englewood, Colo.) 194?-19??
The Englewood Herald. (Englewood, Arapahoe County, Colo.) 1941-1956
Fort Logan News and Views. (Fort Logan, Colo.) 1942-19??
Aurora Upstart. (Aurora, Colo.) 1947-19??
New Views. (Littleton, Colo.) 1948-19??
The Aurora Star and Adams County News. (Aurora, Colo.) 195?-196?
Tri-County Tribune. (Deer Trail, Arapahoe County, Colo.) 1954-1973
Hoffman Heights Mirror. (Hoffman Heights, Colo.) 1954-????
The Englewood Herald and Enterprise. (Englewood, Arapahoe County, Colo.) 1956-1957
Littleton Independent. (Littleton, Colo.) 1956-1982
The Independent American. (New Orleans, La.) 1957-1991
The Englewood Herald and Enterprise and The Press. (Englewood, Arapahoe County, Colo.) 1957-1968
The Aurora Star Sentinel. (Aurora, Colo.) 196?-1972
Englewood Shopping News. (Englewood, Colo.) 1966-19??
The Englewood Herald. (Englewood, Colo.) 1968-1970
The Suburban Sun News. (Englewood, Colo.) 1970-19??
The Englewood Herald Sentinel. (Englewood, Colo.) 1970-1979
Aurora Advocate Sentinel. (Aurora, Colo.) 1972-1979
Arapahoe Herald. (Littleton, Colo.) 1972-1974
Columbine Independent. (Littleton, Colo.) 1973-1982
Tri-County Tribune and Ledger. (Deer Trail, Arapahoe County, Colo.) 1973-1979
The Englewood News. (Englewood, Colo.) 1974-1974
The Englewood Newspaper. (Englewood, Colo.) 1974-19??
Ken-Caryl Ranch News. ([Littleton, Colo.]) 1974-19??

Arapahoe County

Arapahoe Herald Independent. (Littleton, Colo.) 1975-1976
Arapahoe Independent. (Littleton, Colo.) 1976-19??
Englewood Independent. (Englewood, Colo.) 1978-1979
Aurora Sentinel. (Denver, Colo.) 1979-2018
Tri-County Tribune. (Deer Trail, Colo.) 1979-Current
Englewood Sentinel. (Englewood, Colo.) 1979-1991
The Villager. (Englewood, Colo.) 198?-Current
Littleton Times. (Littleton, Colo.) 198?-Current
Highlands Ranch Herald. (Littleton, Co) 198?-Current
The Independent. (Littleton, Colo.) 1982-1986
Aurora Independent. (Denver, Colo.) 1985-1985
Aurora Edition. (Aurora, Colo.) 1985-1985
The Littleton Sentinel Independent. (Littleton, Colo.) 1986-1991
The Aurora Villager. (Englewood, Colo.) 1990-Current
The I-70 Scout. (Strasburg, Colo.) 199?-Current
Littleton Independent. (Littleton, Colo.) 1991-Current
The Englewood Herald. (Littleton, Colo.) 1991-Current
Zhong Mei You Bao = Chinese American Post. (Littleton, Co) 1994-Current | Languages: Chinese
Sentinel. (Aurora, Colo.) 2018-Current

Places on the National Register

Aurora, Commandant of Cadets Building, US Air Force Academy, 1016 Boston St.
Aurora, DeLaney Barn, 200 S. Chambers Rd.
Aurora, Gully Homestead, 200 S. Chambers Rd.
Aurora, Melvin School, 4950 S. Laredo St.
Aurora, Smith, William, House, 412 Oswego Ct.
Cherry Hills Village, Foster—Buell Estate, 2700 E. Hampden Ave.
Cherry Hills Village, Little Estate, 1 Littleridge Ln.
Cherry Hills Village, Maitland Estate, 9 Sunset Dr.
Cherry Hills Village, Owen Estate, 3901 S. Gilpin St.
Englewood, Arapahoe Acres, Roughly bounded by W. Bates and Dartmouth Aves., and S. Marion and Franklin Sts.
Englewood, Brown, David W., House, 2303 E. Dartmouth Ave.
Englewood, Englewood Post Office, 3332 S. Broadway
Englewood, Hopkins Farm, 4400 E. Quincy Ave.
Greenwood Village, Curtis School, 2349 E. Orchard Rd.
Littleton, Arapaho Hills, Bounded by Arrowhead, W. Berry, & S. Manitou Rds., S. Lowell Blvd.
Littleton, Geneva Home, 2305 W. Berry Ave.
Littleton, Knight—Wood House, 1860 W. Littleton Blvd.
Littleton, Littleton Main Street, Roughly along W. Main St., from S. Curtice St. to S. Sycamore St.
Littleton, Littleton Town Hall, 2450 W. Main St.
Parker, Seventeen Mile House, 8181 S. Parker Rd.
Strasburg, Comanche Crossing of the Kansas Pacific Railroad, On Union Pacific Railroad tracks E of the Strasburg depot

Historical Assets Colorado

USGS Historic Places
Coal Creek, Aurora Airpark, 39.7358203, -104.6549683
Coal Creek, Washington School, 39.659154, -104.6463579
Englewood, Cherry Hills Full Gospel Center, 39.6283333, -104.9780556
Englewood, Cunningham School, 39.6972097, -104.876366
Englewood, Duncan School, 39.6288766, -104.9813707
Englewood, Grace Evangelical Lutheran Church, 39.6302778, -104.9780556
Englewood, Laredo School, 39.7372092, -104.9666471
Englewood, Lowell School, 39.6483208, -104.9816484
Englewood, Paradise Valley Country Club, 39.6255435, -104.90359
Englewood, Saint George's Episcopal Church, 39.6511111, -104.9780556
Englewood, Village Heights School, 39.6502655, -104.9424801
Fitzsimons, Burns Memorial School, 39.7324874, -104.8538648
Fitzsimons, Cherry Creek Airport, 39.6547101, -104.8399761
Fitzsimons, Peoria School, 39.7299874, -104.8477534
Fort Logan, Oliver School, 39.6452654, -105.0338724
Fort Logan, Petersburg School, 39.6499875, -105.0035937
Fort Logan, Sheridan Fire Department Station 1, 39.65468, -105.01156
Highlands Ranch, Castlewood Census Designated Place, 39.585938, -104.904539
Highlands Ranch, Cherry Creek Mine, 39.5880438, -104.9130351
Highlands Ranch, Curtis School, 39.6099879, -104.9602589
Highlands Ranch, Southglenn Census Designated Place, 39.591735, -104.956963
Littleton, Grant Junior High School, 39.6116544, -105.0088718
Littleton, Littleton Historical Museum, 39.6066667, -105.0011111
Littleton, West School, 39.60971, -105.0183166

Grand Army of the Republic Posts
Abraham Lincoln, No. 4, Arapahoe, Denver, Oct 1879
Phil Kearney, No. 19, Arapahoe, Denver, 1882
Reno, No. 39, Arapahoe, Denver, 1883
Veteran, No. 42, Arapahoe, Denver, 1883
Farragut, No. 46, Arapahoe, Denver, 1883
George G Meade, No. 47, Arapahoe, Denver, 1883
Hamey/Broadway, No. 50, Arapahoe, Denver, 1885
M M Crocker, No. 81, Arapahoe, North Denver, 1890
John C Fremont, No. 83, Arapahoe, Littleton
George Washington, No. 85, Arapahoe, Denver, 1891
J H Platt, No. 99, Arapahoe, Denver, 1896

USGS Historic Military Places
Fitzsimons, Buckley Air Force Base, 39.7111872, -104.76259

Arapahoe County

Military Bases
Buckley Air Force Base
18500 E 6th Ave, Aurora, CO 80011, 720-847-5613
Home of the 460th Space Wing, Colorado Air National Guard, Colorado Army National Guard

Post Offices

Abbott	1887 Aug 6	1926 Apr 15	
Alcott	1896 May 18	1904 June 30	
Alva	1887 Aug 6	1888 Sept 18	
Arapahoe	1906 May 5		80802
Argo	1881 Apr 11	1911 Sept 15	
Arikaree	1888 June 9	1961 June 23	
Athens	1892 July 20	1896 May 13	
Aurora	1908 Jan 15	1939 Dec 31	
Avoca	1889 June 10	1891 Oct 27	
Badger	1890 Jan 1	1894 July 20*	
Barnum	1892 Feb 5	1901 June 30	
Barr	1883 Mar 15	1914 Oct 17	
Beaver Creek	1915 Feb 9	1916 Feb 15	
Beecher	1902 Aug 12	1905 Nov 3	
Bennet	1877 Mar 16	1907 June 1	
Berkeley	1890 Oct 24	1896 May 18	
Bird	1880 Aug 4	1880 Nov 22*	
Bolton	1900 May 1	1901 Sept 9	
Brighton	1879 Aug 4		80601
Byers	1873 Feb 27		80103
Cary	1888 Apr 23	1890 Feb 28	
Cherrelyn	1894 June 6	1916 Feb 29	
Cherry Creek	1869 July 26	1886	
College View	1946 Aug 7	1948 Mar 31	
Condon	1888 June 7	1892 May 23	
Cope	1888 Apr 23		80812
Coraville	1859 Mar 22	1859 June 25	
Corcoran	1889 Sept 11	1894 Apr 19	
Deer Trail	1875 June 3	1895 May 17	
Deer Trail 2	1950 Oct 1		80105
Deertrail	1894 May 17	1950 Oct 1	
Denver	1866 Feb 13		80202
Denver City	1859 Jan 18	1866 Feb 13	
Denver Mills	1892 Jan 20	1918 Sept 30*	
Derblay	1892 July 13	1892 Dec 22	
Duff	1884 May 19	1896 July 28*	
Elyria	1895 Feb 15	1904 Jan 15	
Englewood	1903 Oct 24	1913 Nov 30	
Englewood 2	1930 Sept 15		80110

67

Historical Assets Colorado

Fort Logan	1889 May 3	1971 Aug 31	
Fox	1890 May 17	1912 Dec 15	
Friend	1887 June 27	1901 July 31	
Frost	1899 July 15	1901 Aug 15	
Fulton	1866 Mar 27	1867 Aug 22	
Globeville	1890 Mar 4	1900 June 16	
Gray	1888 Apr 23	1889 July 16	
Hale	1890 May 17	1984 June 1*	
Harman	1887 Aug 16	1904 Jan 16	
Harris	1890 Apr 21	1908 June 5	
Harrisburg	1887 Feb 19	1906 Aug 31*	
Hazeltine	1893 Jan 7	1907 Jan 15	
Heritage	1976 Jan 1	1978 Sept 23	
Highlands	1884 Oct 15	1897 Nov 13	
Highlandtown	1883 June 29	1884 Oct 15	
Hughes	1871 Apr 13	1879 Aug 4	
Idalia	1888 Sept 18		80735
Inche	1891 Sept 14	1891 Dec 10	
Irondale	1889 Dec 11	1895 Sept 19	
Island Station	1872 Aug 29	1894 Mar 1	
Jefferson	1860 Jan 18	1860 Dec 6	
Kirk	1887 Nov 18		80824
Landsman	1883 Mar 27	1918 May 31	
Lansing	1886 Sept 17	1910 Feb 28	
Lena	1895 Oct 4	1896 June 17	
Lindon	1888 Sept 21		80740
Littleton	1869 Apr 8		80120
Living Springs	1865 July 5	1867 Nov 27	
Logan	1887 May 14	1901 July 31	
Loretto	1896 Sept 28	1966 Mar 11	
Lyman	1885 Mar 2	1895 Feb 15	
Melvin	1888 May 4	1895 Dec 26	
Montana	1859 Jan 18	1859 Oct 1	
Montclair	1888 July 3	1912 Mar 31	
Newton	1889 Aug 6	1918 Apr 15	
Oakes	1890 June 9	1905 May 31	
Overland	1892 Apr 12	1920 Feb 14	
Peoria	1906 Mar 3	1914 Jan 15	
Petersburgh	1876 May 4	1907 June 12*	
Quimby	1895 Oct 8	1900 Oct 20	
Rogers	1886 Mar 24	1888 Sept 21	
Salem	1894 Aug 28	1919 Jan 15	
Scranton	1887 Aug 12	1888 July 25	
Sheffield	1891 Feb 25	1892 Jan 20	
Shields	1887 Aug 6	1894 Sept 22*	
South Denver	1889 Nov 20	1896 May 13	

Arapahoe County

Stockyards	1898 Apr 16	1904 Jan 15		
Strasburg	1908 May 25		80136	
Taclamur	1888 Aug 20	1890 Apr 11		
Thurman	1888 July 6	1955 Mar 31		
Townsend	1890 Jan 14	1893 Sept 29		
University Park	1890 June 19	1915 Dec 31*		
Valverde	1889 Oct 14	1908 Feb 29		
Vernon	1888 June 26		80755	
Villa Park	1890 Feb 15	1895 May 6		
Villapark	1895 May 6	1920 Apr 20		
Wales	1887 Aug 6	1888 Sept 21		
Washburn	1889 Sept 12	1893 Jan 7*		
Watkins	1878 Jan 31	1893 Oct 14		
Watkins	1894 Nov 6		80137	
Winnview	1933 Aug 14	1942 Oct 3		

Topo Quads

Byers SW	393730N	393000N	1040730W	1041500W
Cottonwood Valley South	393730N	393000N	1034500W	1035230W
Deer Trail	393730N	393000N	1040000W	1040730W
Noonen Reservoir SW	393730N	393000N	1035230W	1040000W
Piney Creek	393730N	393000N	1043730W	1044500W
Strasburg SE	393730N	393000N	1041500W	1042230W
Strasburg SW	393730N	393000N	1042230W	1043000W
Watkins SE	393730N	393000N	1043000W	1043730W

Suggested Reading

Arapahoe County: *Community of Contrast and Change*. NL: Arapahoe County, CO, 1983.

Arapahoe County Portrait: Past and Present. Littleton, CO: The District, 1981.

Arapahoe County Sheriff's Office: History 1855-2006. Evansville, IN: M.T. Pub Co., 2006.

Boldt, Richard O. *The Story of Littleton, Denver's Best Suburb 1888-1938*. Littleton, CO: Littleton Independent and Arapahoe Herald, 1938.

Deer Trail Rodeo Centennial, 1869-1969: Colorado Past Lives. Deer Trail, CO" Deer Trail Colorado Pioneer Historical Society, 1969.

Inventory of the County Archives of Colorado, No. 3. Arapahoe County (Littleton). Denver:, Historical Records Survey, 1939.

Vickers, W B and O L Baskin & Co. *History of the City of Denver, Arapahoe County, and Colorado*. Evansville, IN: Unigraphic, 1977.

Historical Assets Colorado

Archuleta County

Introduction

Established: 1885   Population: 12,854

Formed from: Conejos

Adjacent Counties: Mineral, Rio Grande, Conejos, La Plata, Hinsdale

County Seat: Pagosa Springs

  Other Communities: Arboles, Chimney Rock, Chromo, Juanita

Website, https://www.archuletacounty.org

Area Codes: 970

Zip Codes: 81121, 81128, 81147, 81157

Historical Assets Colorado

Archuletta County Courthouse

Courthouses & County Government

Archuleta County
https://www.archuletacounty.org

Archuleta County Courthouse (6th Judicial District), 449 San Juan St, Pagosa Springs, CO 81147, 970-264-8160; http://www.courts.state.co.us/Courts/County/Index.cfm?County_ID=12

Assessor, 449 San Juan St, Pagosa Springs, CO 81147, 970-264-8310; http://www.archuletacounty.org/index.aspx?nid=84

Board of County Commissioners, 449 San Juan Dr, Pagosa Springs, CO 81147, 970-264-8300, https://www.archuletacounty.org/86/Commissioners

Clerk & Recorder, 449 San Juan St, Pagosa Springs, CO 81147, 970-264-8350; http://www.archuletacounty.org/index.aspx?nid=84

Coroner, 970-731-2160; https://www.archuletacounty.org/85/Coroner

Elections, 449 San Juan St, Pagosa Springs, CO 81147, 970-264-8331; https://www.archuletacounty.org/192/Elections

Public Health, 281 Sawyer Dr, Durango, CO 81302, 970-247-5702; http://sjbhd.org/

Transportation, 970-264-2250; https://www.archuletacounty.org/520/Transportation

Treasurer, 449 San Juan St, Pagosa Springs, CO 81147, 970-264-8325; http://www.archuletacounty.org/?nid=96

County Records

Birth 1880	Marriage 1886	Marriage 1886
Divorce 1885	Death 1907	Land 1886
Probate 1886	Court 1885	

Archuleta County

County & Municipal Records Held at the State Level

The Colorado State Archives

Physical Records	Records on Film	Records on Master Film
WPA Historical Records	None	Clerk & Recorder
WPA Religious Institutions Survey		County Court
		District Court
WPA Pagosa Springs		Combined Courts
		School Districts

The Denver Public Library
WWI Draft Registration Cards (microfilm)

School Districts

School Districts, http://www.adcogov.org/local-school-districts
Archuleta School District 50JT, 309 Lewis St, Pagosa Springs, CO 81147, 970-264-2794; https://www.mypagosaschools.com/

Historic School Districts

1. Pagosa Springs
2. Chromo
3. Edith, Montezuma
4. Yellow Jacket
5. Little Blanco, Marquez, Lower Blanco, Upper Blanco
6. Blanco Basin
7. Trujillo
8. Pagosa Junction
9. Duke, Stollsteimer
10. Arboles
11. O'Neal Park
12. Echo Glade, Echo Lake
13. Kearns
14. Piedra
15. Pargin
16. Bayles
17. Russell, Coyote Park
18. Deer Creek, Kohler
19. Juanita
20. Lone Tree
21. Mile, Hayden
22.
23.
24.
Jt 25. Allison, Arboles

Fraternal Organizations

Granges
None

Masons

Ancient Free & Accepted Masons
Pagosa, No. 114, Archuleta, Pagosa Springs, 16 Sept 1902

Royal Arch Masons
None

Knights Templar
None

Eastern Star
Harmony, No. 84, Archuleta, Pagosa Springs

Odd Fellows
Pagosa, No. 122, Archuleta, Pagosa Springs
Piedra, No. 183, Archuleta, Chimney Rock

Historical Assets Colorado

Rebekahs
Pagosa, No. 134, Archuleta, Pagosa Springs

Knights of Pythias
Edith, No. 118, Archuleta, Edith
Pagosa, No. 126, Archuleta, Pagosa Springs

Pythian Sisters
None

Benevolent Protective Order of Elks
None

City & Town Halls
Pagosa Springs, 551 Hot Springs Blvd, Pagosa Springs, CO 81147, 970-264-4151, https://www.pagosasprings.co.gov

Archives & Manuscript Collections
Archuleta County Archive (digital); https://www.archuletacounty.org/Archive.aspx

Historical & Genealogical Societies
San Juan Historical Society, Pagosa Springs History Museum, 96 Pagosa St, Pagosa Springs, CO 81147, (970) 264-4424, http://www.pagosamuseum.org

Local Libraries
Ruby M Sisson Memorial Library, 811 San Juan, P.O. Box 849, Pagosa Springs, CO 81147-0849, (970) 264-2209, https://pagosalibrary.org

Links
CO GenWeb
http://cogenweb.com/archuleta/

Cyndi's List
https://www.cyndislist.com/us/co/counties/archuleta/

FamilySearch Wiki
https://www.familysearch.org/wiki/en/Archuleta_County,_Colorado_Genealogy

Linkpendium
http://www.linkpendium.com/archuleta-co-genealogy/

RootsWeb Wiki
https://wiki.rootsweb.com/wiki/index.php/Archuleta_County,_Colorado

Wikipedia
https://en.wikipedia.org/wiki/Archuleta_County,_Colorado

Historic Hotels
None

Archuleta County

Museums & Historic Sites
Chimney Rock National Monument, 3179 CO 151, Chimney Rock, CO 81121, (970) 883-5359, http://www.chimneyrockco.org
San Juan Historical Society, Pagosa Springs History Museum, 96 Pagosa St, Pagosa Springs, CO 81147, (970) 264-4424, http://www.pagosamuseum.org

Special Events & Scenic Locations
The Archuleta County Fair takes place in July and August most years. Archuleta County Fair, 344 US Hwy 84, Pagosa Springs, CO 81147, 970-264-5931, https://www.archuletacountyfair.com.
The Pagosa Springs Area Chamber of Commerce keeps a full calendar of events, https://web.pagosachamber.com/events

Rio Grande National Forest
San Juan National Forest
Chimney Rock National Monument
South San Juan Wilderness
Navajo State Park
Continental Divide National Scenic Trail
Old Spanish National Historic Trail

Ghost Towns & Other Sparsely Populated Places
Carracas, Chromo, Juanita, Pagosa Junction, Piedra

Newspapers
Pagosa Springs Herald. (Pagosa Springs, Colo.) 1889-1???
The Pagosa Springs News. (Pagosa Springs, Archuleta County, Colo.) 1890-19??
The Elwood Weekly Mining Herald. (Elwood, Colo.) 1896-1???
The Weekly Times. (Pagosa Springs, Archuleta County, Colo.) 1899-1904
Pagosa Springs New Era. (Pagosa Springs, Colo.) 1905-1915
The Times-Observer. (Pagosa Springs, Archuleta County, Colo.) 1905-190?
Pagosa Springs Observer. (Pagosa Springs, Colo.) 1906-19??
The Pagosa Springs Sun. (Pagosa Springs, Archuleta County, Colo.) 1909-Current
The Pagosa Journal. (Pagosa Springs, Colo.) 1916-19??

Places on the National Register
Antonito, Denver & Rio Grande Railroad San Juan Extension, Between Antonito and Chama, NM via Cumbres Pass
Arboles, Labo Del Rio Bridge, Cty. Rd. F40 over Piedra River
Chimney Rock, Chimney Rock Archeological Site, Address Restricted

USGS Historic Places
Allison, Navajo Landing Strip, 37.0013942, -107.4233815

Historical Assets Colorado

Grand Army of the Republic Posts
Gen E Hatch, No. 104, Archuleta, Pagosa Springs

USGS Historic Military Places
None

Military Bases
None

Post Offices

Arboles	1882 Dec 13		81121
Carracas	1909 Mar 3	1911 Jan 31	
Chimney Rock	1950 Nov 1		
Chromo	1885 Oct 30		81128
Dyke	1901 Apr 10	1950 Oct 31*	
Edith	1895 Oct 28	1917 Oct 31*	
Gladwyn	1885 Aug 2	1890 Apr 14	
Juanita	1904 May 2	1912 June 15	
Kearns	1913 Aug 15	1925 Oct 31*	
Pagosa Junction	1899 July 25	1954 Nov 30	
Pagosa Springs	1878 June 7		81147
Piedra	1879 May 16	1927 June 30*	
Squaretop	1917 June 11	1918 Aug 15	
Trujillo	1900 Feb 20	1905 Sept 30	

Topo Quads

Archuleta Creek	370730N	370000N	1063000W	1063730W
Blackhead Peak	372230N	371500N	1064500W	1065230W
Carracas	370730N	370000N	1071500W	1072230W
Chama Peak	370730N	370000N	1063730W	1064500W
Chimney Rock	371500N	370730N	1071500W	1072230W
Chris Mountain	372230N	371500N	1070730W	1071500W
Chromo	370730N	370000N	1064500W	1065230W
Cumbres	370730N	370000N	1062230W	1063000W
Devil Mountain	372230N	371500N	1071500W	1072230W
Edith	370730N	370000N	1065230W	1070000W
Elephant Head Rock	371500N	370730N	1063730W	1064500W
Harris Lake	371500N	370730N	1064500W	1065230W
Jackson Mountain	372230N	371500N	1065230W	1070000W
Lonetree Canyon	371500N	370730N	1070730W	1071500W
Oakbrush Hill	371500N	370730N	1070000W	1070730W
Pagosa Junction	370730N	370000N	1070730W	1071500W
Pagosa Springs	372230N	371500N	1070000W	1070730W
Serviceberry Mtn	371500N	370730N	1065230W	1070000W
Summit Peak	372230N	371500N	1063730W	1064500W

Archuleta County

Tiffany	370730N	370000N	1073000W	1073730W
Trujillo	370730N	370000N	1070000W	1070730W
Victoria Lake	371500N	370730N	1063000W	1063730W

Suggested Reading

Corman, Larry S. *A History of Ranching Families in La Plata and Archuleta Counties*. NL: NP, 2017.

Motter, John M. *Pagosa Country: The First Fifty Years: A Pioneer History of Archuleta County*. Pagosa Springs, CO: J M Motter, 1984.

Pierce, Shari and Glenn Raby. *Pagosa Springs, Colorado: A Brief History*. Pagosa Springs, CO: San Juan Historical Society, 2003.

Remembrances: The Bride of the Silver San Juan. Pagosa Springs, CO: San Juan County Historical Society, 1997.

Remembrances: Voices from the Past. Pagosa Springs, CO: San Juan Historical Society, 2005.

Remembrances, Volume 1: Founding Families. Pagosa Springs, CO: San Juan Historical Society 1996.

Vail, E E. *An Interesting Story of Pagosa Hot Springs (the Carlsbad of America), Archuleta County, Colorado*. Pagosa Springs, CO: Pagosa Springs Herald, 1896.

Historical Assets Colorado

Baca County

Introduction
Established: 1889 Population: 3,568

Formed from: Las Animas

Adjacent Counties: Prowers, Las Animas, Bent

County Seat: Springfield

Other Communities: Campo, Pritchett, Two Buttes, Vilas, Walsh, Deora, Lycan, Utleyville

Website, https://www.bacacountyco.gov

Area Codes: 719

Zip Codes: 81029, 81064, 81073, 81084, 81087, 81090

Historical Assets Colorado

Baca County Courthouse

Courthouses & County Government

Baca County
   https://www.bacacountyco.gov
Baca County Courthouse (15th Judicial District), 741 Main St, Springfield, CO 81073, 719-523-4555; http://www.courts.state.co.us/Courts/County/Index.cfm?County_ID=48
Assessor, 741 Main St, Springfield, CO 81073, 719-523-4332; http://www.springfieldcolorado.com/bacacountygov.html
Board of County Commissioners, 741 Main St, Springfield, CO 81073, 719-523-6532, https://www.bacacountyco.gov/government/county-commissioners/
Clerk & Recorder, 741 Main St, Springfield, CO 81073, 719-523-4372; http://www.springfieldcolorado.com/bacacountygov.html
Coroner, P.O. Box 70, Walsh, CO 81090, 719-324-5251
Elections, 741 Main St, Springfield, CO 81073, 719-523-4881; https://www.bacacountyco.gov/government/clerk-and-recorder/elections/
Public Health, 741 Main St, Ste 4, Springfield, CO 81073, 719-523-6621; http://www.bacadem.com/BC%20Nursing.htm
Treasurer, 741 Main St, Springfield, CO 81073, 719-523-4262; http://www.springfieldcolorado.com/bacacountygov.html

County Records

Birth 1910	Marriage 1889	Divorce 1918
Death 1911	Land 1889	Probate 1918
Court 1918	Naturalization (some)	

Baca County

County & Municipal Records Held at the State Level

The Colorado State Archives

Physical Records
Clerk & Recorder
WPA Historical Records
WPA Religious Institutions
 Survey

Records on Film
Clerk & Recorder

Records on Master Film
Clerk & Recorder
County Court
District Court
School Districts
Sheriff

The Denver Public Library
WWI Draft Registration Cards (microfilm)

School Districts

School Districts, http://www.adcogov.org/local-school-districts
Campo Re-6, 480 Maple St, Campo, CO 80129, 719-787-2226; http://www.campok12.org/Home
Pritchett School District, P.O. Box 7, Pritchett, CO 81064, 719-523-4045; http://www.pritchettre3.org/
Springfield School District RE-4, 389 Tipton St, Springfield, CO 81073, 719-523-6654; http://www.spre4.org/
Vilas School District RE-5, 202 N Collingwood Ave, Vilas, CO 81087, 719-523-6738; http://www.vilasre5.us/
Walsh RE-1, 301 W Poplar, Walsh, CO 81090, 719-324-5632; http://www.walsheagles.com/

Historic School Districts

1. Blaine
2. Two Buttes
3. Carrizo, Furnish
4. Springfield
5. Vilas
6. Bartlett
7. Boston
8. Lewisville, Prairie View
9. Pleasant Ridge
10. Echo
11. West Floemont
12. Bray
13. East Floemont
14. Big Rock, Pilot Point
15. East Liberty
16. East Wentworth
17. North Fork
18. Riverside
19. Richards
20. Independence
21. Beulah
22. Grandview
23. North Liberty
24. Prairie Dell
25. Eagle Center
26. Konantz
27. Liberty
28. Lone Star
29. [1889]
30. Mitchell
31. Stonington
32. Oklarado
33. Valley View
34. [1890]
35. North Lone Star
36. [1890]
37. Walnut Grove
38. Campo
39. Maddox
40. Bethel
41. Pleasant Valley
42. Sandy Soil
43. New Hope
44. Bubbling Springs, Frontier
45. Mystic Dell
46. Edler
47. Short Grass
48. Big Float
49.
50. Walsh
51. Maxey
52. Sunderland
53. Pritchett
54. Prairie Queen
55. Diamond Ridge, Butcher
56. Prairie Ridge, Prairie Center
57. Sunnyside
58. Mesa View
59. Mountain View
60. Bear
61. Bluemound, Friendship
62. Crescent

Historical Assets Colorado

63. Glendale
64. Ute Valley
65. Rock Crossing
66. Northeast Corner
67. Lycan
68. McKinley
69. Murray
70. Buffalo
71. Buena Vista, Liberty Bell
72. Big Rock
73. East Floemont

Fraternal Organizations

Granges
Stonington, No. 322, Baca, Stonington, 23 Feb 1917
Pretty Prairie, No. 323, Baca, Stonington, 14 Feb 1917
Progressive, No. 324, Baca, Konatz,
Lamport, No. 333, Baca, Lamport, 4 Apr 1917
Big Flat, No. 342, Baca, Vilars, 4 May 1917
Big Rock, No. 408, Baca, Springfield, 29 July 1930
Lycan, No. 413, Baca, Lycan, 14 May 1934
Stonington, No. 419, Baca, Stonington, 6 Sept 1935
Edler, No. 426, Baca, Springfield, 9 Jan 1936
Campo, No. 442, Baca, Campo, 23 Oct 1936
Villas Grande, No. 443, Baca, Vilas, 14 May 1937
Two Buttes, No. 444, Baca, Two Buttes, 1 Apr 1938
Pritchett, No. 449, Baca, Pritchett, 14 Mar 1940
State Line, No. 460, Baca, Walsh, 22 June 1945

Masons
Ancient Free & Accepted Masons
Springfield, No. 158, Baca, Springfield, 20 Sept 1922

Royal Arch Masons
None

Knights Templar
None

Eastern Star
Springfield, No. 131, Baca, Springfield

Odd Fellows
Baca, No. 63, Baca, Springfield
Two Buttes, No. 169, Baca, Two Buttes

Rebekahs
Two Buttes, No. 26, Baca, Two Buttes
Royal, No. 109, Baca, Springfield

Knights of Pythias
None

Pythian Sisters
None

Benevolent Protective Order of Elks
None

Baca County

City & Town Halls
Springfield, 748 Main St, Springfield, CO 81073, 719-523-4528, https://www.springfieldcolorado.com

Pritchett, 300 Randolph St, Pritchett, CO 81064, 719-523-4710, https://www.bacacountyco.gov/towns/pritchett-colorado/

Two Buttes, https://www.bacacountyco.gov/towns/two-buttes/

Walsh, 401 N Colorado St, Walsh, CO 81090, 719-324-5411, https://townofwalsh.colorado.gov

Archives & Manuscript Collections
None

Historical & Genealogical Societies
Baca County History; https://bacacountyhistory.com

Local Libraries
Baca County Library, 1260 Main St #1, Springfield, CO 81073, (719) 523-6962, http://www.springfieldcolorado.com/library.html

Walsh Library, 409 N Colorado St, Walsh, CO 81090, (719) 324-5411

Links
CO GenWeb
http://cogenweb.com/baca/

Cyndi's List
https://www.cyndislist.com/us/co/counties/baca/

FamilySearch Wiki
https://www.familysearch.org/wiki/en/Baca_County,_Colorado_Genealogy

Linkpendium
http://www.linkpendium.com/baca-co-genealogy/

RootsWeb Wiki
https://wiki.rootsweb.com/wiki/index.php/Baca_County,_Colorado

Wikipedia
https://en.wikipedia.org/wiki/Baca_County,_Colorado

Historic Hotels
None

Museums & Historic Sites
Springfield Museum, 1260 Main St, Springfield, CO 81073, (719) 523-6962, http://www.springfieldcolorado.com/history.html

Two Buttes-Dr Verity Museum, 500 Main St, Two Buttes, CO 81084

Historical Assets Colorado

Special Events & Scenic Locations
The Baca County Fair & Rodeo takes place in July or August each year. Baca County Fair Grounds, 28500 Cty Rd 24.6, Springfield, CO 81073, https://www.facebook.com/BacaFairAndRodeoInc

Santa Fe National Historic Trail

Ghost Towns & Other Sparsely Populated Places
Atlanta, Boston, Brookfield, Campo, Carrizo City (Carriso), Carrizo Springs, Copper City, Decatur, Lycan, Maxey, Minneapolis, Progress, Ruff, Springfield, Stonington, Two Buttes, Vilas

Newspapers
Springfield Republican. (Springfield, Colo.) 18??-1???
Minneapolis Chico. (Minneapolis, Colo.) 18??-1???
The Baca County Journal. (Boston, Baca County, Colo.) 18??-1???
The Springfield Beacon. (Springfield, Colo.) 1887-1???
The Springfield Herald. (Springfield, Baca County, Colo.) 1887-1919
The Boston Banner. (Boston, Las Animas County, Colo.) 1887-1???
Carrizo Weekly Miner. (Carrizo, Colo.) 1900-19??
Carrizo Weekly Miner and Stockmen's Range Journal. (Carrizo, Colo.) 190?-19??
The-Campo-Enterprise. (Campo, Baca County, Colo.) 19??-19??
The Baca County Republican. (Springfield, Colo.) 19??-1937
Walsh Topic. (Walsh, Baca County, Colo.) 19??-19??
The Two Buttes Sentinel. (Two Buttes, Baca County, Colo.) 1910-19??
Artesian News : Stonington News. (Stonington, Colo.) 1917-????
The Democrat-Herald. (Springfield, Baca County, Colo.) 1919-19??
The Walsh Tab. (Walsh, Baca County, Colo.) 192?-19??
Springfield Plainsman. (Springfield, Baca County, Colo.) 1937-1939
Plainsman-Herald. (Springfield, Colo.) 1939-Current
The Baca County Banner. (Springfield, Colo.) 1940-19??

Places on the National Register
Ruxton, Colorado Millennial Site, Address Restricted
Springfield, Springfield Schoolhouse, 281 W. 7th Ave.
Stonington, Stonington First Methodist—Episcopal Church, 48854 Co. Rd. X
Two Buttes, Two Buttes Gymnasium, 5th and C Sts.

USGS Historic Places
McEndree Ranch, Brookfield, 37.5939008, -102.8421447

Grand Army of the Republic Posts
Mulligan, No. 79, Baca, Springfield

Baca County

USGS Historic Military Places
None

Military Bases
None

Post Offices

Atlanda	1887 Dec 13	1899 Aug 31	
Baker	1915 Feb 27	1921 June 30	
Bartlett	1929 Sept 5	1938 Mar 31	
Boston	1887 Apr 14	1893 June 16	
Brookfield	1887 Aug 30	1902 July 15	
Buster	1916 July 28	1927 July 30	
Campo	1913 Apr 10		81029
Carriso	1887 June 2	1895 July 11*	
Carriso Springs	1888 Aug 27	1890 May 17	
Carrizo	1907 Sept 21	1916 Jan 31*	
Clyde	1889 Feb 18	1920 June 15*	
Corrizo	1899 Dec 13	1907 Dec 14	
Decatur	1888 July 25	1891 Aug 8	
Deora	1920 Apr 21	1974 Mar 1	
Edler	1916 Feb 16	1947 Dec 31	
Estelene	1910 Apr 8	1927 Aug 10	
Graft	1916 Aug 12	1934 Dec 31	
Joycoy	1915 Aug 13	1927 Mar 15	
Kirkwell	1917 June 1	1921 Dec 24	
Konantz	1895 Jan 4	1924 Apr 30*	
Lamport	1908 June 8	1927 May 31	
Lycan	1913 June 27	1975 Sept 12	
Maxey	1889 Jan 19	1920 July 31*	
Minneapolis	1887 Aug 12	1899 Nov 15	
Monon	1901 Nov 1	1918 Apr 15	
Nowlinsville	1916 May 29	1919 June 14	
Oklarado	1916 May 12	1935 June 29	
Onine	1918 June 6	1921 June 30	
Pride	1914 Dec 18	1920 June 15	
Pritchett	1927 Mar 15		81064
Progress	1888 Sept 26	1895 Nov 19	
Regnier	1900 Sept 25		
Richards	1912 Jan 27	1938 Feb 28	
Rodley	1910 May 21	1937 Sept 30	
Ruff	1889 Sept 16	1896 May 18	
San Arroyo	1915 Oct 20	1917 Dec 31	
Seton	1915 June 3	1916 Jan 22	
Setonsburg	1916 Jan 22	1920 May 31	
Springfield	1887 June 2		81073

Historical Assets Colorado

Stonington	1888 Jan 20		81075	
Townsite	1900 Mar 18	1902 Dec 31		
Tuck	1916 Feb 16	1917 June 9		
Two Buttes	1910 Mar 1		81084	
Utleyville	1917 June 9	1973 Jan 5		
Vilas	1887 June 20		81087	
Walsh	1926 Dec 23		81909	
Wentworth	1911 June 15	1921 June 30		
Westola	1914 Aug 20	1917 May 31		

Topo Quads

Bartlett	373000N	372230N	1020730W	1021500W
Big Hole Canyon	370730N	370000N	1025230W	1030000W
Big Rock Grange	373730N	373000N	1023730W	1024500W
Bisonte	372230N	371500N	1023000W	1023730W
Campo	370730N	370000N	1023000W	1023730W
Campo NE	371500N	370730N	1023000W	1023730W
Campo NW	371500N	370730N	1023730W	1024500W
Campo SW	370730N	370000N	1023730W	1024500W
Deora	373730N	373000N	1025230W	1030000W
Edler	371500N	370730N	1024500W	1025230W
Furnish Canyon East	370730N	370000N	1030000W	1030730W
Furnish Canyon West	370730N	370000N	1030730W	1031500W
Harbord	373000N	372230N	1024500W	1025230W
Horse Creek Springs	373730N	373000N	1023000W	1023730W
Lone Rock	372230N	371500N	1025230W	1030000W
Lycan	373730N	373000N	1020730W	1021500W
McEndree Ranch	373730N	373000N	1024500W	1025230W
Midway	371500N	370730N	1020730W	1021500W
Midway SW	370730N	370000N	1020730W	1021500W
Moore Draw NE	371500N	370730N	1021500W	1022230W
Moore Draw NW	371500N	370730N	1022230W	1023000W
Moore Draw SE	370730N	370000N	1021500W	1022230W
Moore Draw SW	370730N	370000N	1022230W	1023000W
Pritchett	372230N	371500N	1024500W	1025230W
Pritchett NW	373000N	372230N	1025230W	1030000W
Reader Lake	371500N	370730N	1025230W	1030000W
Springfield East	373000N	372230N	1023000W	1023730W
Springfield SW	372230N	371500N	1023730W	1024500W
Springfield West	373000N	372230N	1023730W	1024500W
Stonington	372230N	371500N	1020730W	1021500W
Two Buttes	373730N	373000N	1022230W	1023000W
Two Buttes SE	373730N	373000N	1021500W	1022230W
Vilas North	373000N	372230N	1022230W	1023000W

Baca County

Vilas South	372230N	371500N	1022230W	1023000W
Walsh	373000N	372230N	1021500W	1022230W
Walsh SE	372230N	371500N	1021500W	1022230W

Suggested Reading

Austin, J R. *A History of Early Baca County*. Westminster, CO: J R Austin, 1936.

Baca County, Colorado. Lubbock, TX: Baca County Historical Society, 1983.

Brooks, Kent. *Old Boston: As Wild as They Come*. Casper, WY: Lonesome Prairie Publications, 2018.

Grant, Clarence G. *The Covered Wagon Rests on the Hill*. San Diego: Dimension-Four Unlimited, 1987.

Harper, Thomas Alan. *The Development of a High Plains Community: A History of Baca County, Colorado*. Thesis, University of Denver, 1967.

Hill, James Henderson. *A History of Baca County*. Thesis, Colorado State Collee of Education, 1941.

Historic Baca County: Southeast Colorado's Finest Land. Denver: Colorado Preservation, Inc., 2010.

Woodward, N E. *Brief History of Baca County, Colorado*. NL: Federal Emergency Relief Administration, 1934.

Historical Assets Colorado

Bent County

Introduction

Established: 1870   Population: 5,861

Formed from: Pueblo, Greenwood

Adjacent Counties: Kiowa, Prowers, Baca, Las Animas, Otero

County Seat: Las Animas

  Other Communities: Hasty, Able, Boggsville, Caddoa, Fort Lyon, Marlman, Mc-Clave, Melina, Ninaview

Website, http://www.bentcounty.net/

Area Codes: 719

Zip Codes: 81038, 81044, 81054, 81057

Historical Assets Colorado

Bent County Courthouse

Courthouses & County Government

Bent County
http://www.bentcounty.net

Bent County Courthouse (16th Judicial District), 725 Bent Ave, Las Animas, CO 81054, 719-456-1353; http://www.courts.state.co.us/Courts/County/Index.cfm?County_ID=52

Assessor, 725 Bent Ave, Las Animas, CO 81054, 719-456-2010; http://bentcounty.org/contacts/

Board of County Commissioners, 725 Bent Ave, Las Animas, CO 81054, 719-456-1600, http://www.bentcounty.net/government/commissioners.php

Clerk & Recorder, 725 Bent Ave, Las Animas, CO 81054, 719-456-1600; http://bent-county.org/contacts/

Coroner, P.O. Box 350, Las Animas, CO 81054, 719-456-1600; http://www.bentcounty.net/government/coroner.php#.XOS5vqR7mUk

Public Health, 701 Park Ave, Las Animas, CO 81054, 719-456-0517; http://bentcounty.org/2010/11/bent-county-public-health/

Treasurer, 725 Bent Ave, Las Animas, CO 81054, 719-456-0796; http://bentcounty.org/contacts/

County Records

Birth 1905	Marriage 1888	Divorce 1888
Death 1908	Land 1888	Probate 1888
Court 1888		

Early birth and death records were kept by the Nursing Service

Bent County

County & Municipal Records Held at the State Level
The Colorado State Archives

Physical Records	Records on Film	Records on Master Film
Clerk & Recorder	Clerk & Recorder	Clerk & Recorder
County Court	Combined Courts	County Court
District Court	Treasurer	District Court
Combined Courts		Combined Court
WPA Historical Records		Hospital Register 1885
WPA Religious Institutions Survey		School Districts
WPA Las Animas		

The Denver Public Library
Arkansas Valley Land and Cattle Company Records, 1882-1883
Bent County Stock Association Records, 1874-1902
WPA Historical Records Survey
WWI Draft Registration Cards (microfilm)

School Districts
School Districts, http://www.adcogov.org/local-school-districts
Las Animas District RE-1, 1021 2nd St, Las Animas, CO 81054, 719-456-0161; https://www.la-schools.com/
McClave District RE-2, 308 Lincoln St, McClave, CO 81057, 719-829-4517; http://www.mcclaveschool.org/
Wiley District RE-13 JT, 510 Ward St, Wiley, CO 719-829-4806; http://www.wileyschool.org/

Historic School Districts

1. Las Animas, District No One
2. Horse Creek
3. Cornelia, Closson
4. North Gageby
5. McClave
6. Rixey, Crosley
7. Melonfield
8. Enterprise, Lake View
9. Huey, Sunnyside
10. One-Hundred-One, Big Bend
11. Star
12. Cloverleaf
13. Wiley
14. White, Muddy Valley
15. Prairie View, Good Intent
16. Caddoa, Lone Tree, Indian Rock
17. Keller, Dayton
18. Woodrow, Shamrock
19. Prairie Dale
20. Antelope
21. Valley Springs, Center View
22. Mount Hope
23. Prairie Home
24. Bethel
25. West Riverview
26. Hughes
27. Prowers, Dayton, Eads, Bungalow, Little Kansas, Riverview, North Riverview
28. Pearl, Pine Hill, Galatea
29. Prairie Hill
30. [1900]
31. Lone Cedar
32. Pipe Springs
33. Penrose
34. Pioneer
35. Rule
36. Prairie Flower
37. Hopewell
38. Kreybill
39. Red Rock
40. [1901]
41.
42.
43.
44.
45. Hasty
46.
47.
48.
49. [1898]

Historical Assets Colorado

Fraternal Organizations

Granges
Golden Rule, No. 137, Bent, Caddoa, 17 Mar 1899
Prairie Flower, No. 233, Bent, McClane, 6 Feb 1915
Indian Rock, No. 283, Bent, Caddoa, 13 May 1916
Little Kansas, No. 295, Bent, Mud Creek, 26 June 1916
Mud Creek, No. 393, Bent, Mud Creek, 6 May 1920

Masons

Ancient Free & Accepted Masons
King Solomon, No. 30, Bent, Las Animas, 20 Sept 1876

Royal Arch Masons
Las Animas, No. 49, Bent, Las Animas

Knights Templar
None

Eastern Star
Alamo, No. 33, Bent, Las Animas

Odd Fellows
Elders, No. 11, Bent, Las Animas, 1870 Sept 3

Rebekahs
Faith, No. 64, Bent, Las Animas

Knights of Pythias
Las Animas, No. 120, Bent, Las Animas

Pythian Sisters
None

Benevolent Protective Order of Elks
None

City & Town Halls
Las Animas, https://www.colorado.gov/cityoflasanimas

Archives & Manuscript Collections
None

Historical & Genealogical Societies
Bent County Historical Society, John W Rawlins Heritage Center, 560 Bent Ave, P.O. Box 68, Las Animas, CO 81054, (719) 456-6066, http://www.bentcountyheritage.org

Local Libraries
Las Animas-Bent County Public Library, 306 5th St, Las Animas, CO 81054, (719) 456-0111, https://www.labclibrary.com

Bent County

Links
CO GenWeb
http://cogenweb.com/bent/
Cyndi's List
https://www.cyndislist.com/us/co/counties/bent/
FamilySearch Wiki
https://www.familysearch.org/wiki/en/Bent_County,_Colorado_Genealogy
Linkpendium
http://www.linkpendium.com/bent-co-genealogy/
RootsWeb Wiki
https://wiki.rootsweb.com/wiki/index.php/Bent_County,_Colorado
Wikipedia
https://en.wikipedia.org/wiki/Bent_County,_Colorado

Historic Hotels
None

Museums & Historic Sites
Bent County Historical Society, John W Rawlins Heritage Center, 560 Bent Ave, P.O. Box 68, Las Animas, CO 81054, (719) 456-6066, http://www.bentcountyheritage.org

Special Events & Scenic Locations
The Bent County Fair takes places in July or August each year. Bent County Fair, Bent County Fairgrounds, 1499 Ambassador Thompson Blvd, Las Animas, CO 81054, 719-456-0764, https://www.facebook.com/BentCountyFair/

The Bent County Harvest Show takes place in October, https://www.facebook.com/events/714-elm-ave-las-animas-co-81054-1738-united-states/bent-county-harvest-show/426451717979486/

The local newspaper, the Bent County Democrat, keeps a good calendar of events, https://www.bcdemocratonline.com/news/20180417/bent-county-democrat-calendar-of-events

John Martin Reservoir State Park
American Discovery Trail
Santa Fe National Historic Trail
Santa Fe Trail National Scenic Byway

Ghost Towns & Other Sparsely Populated Places
Boggsville, Caddoa, Hilton, Prowers, Robinson, Toonerville, Trail City

Newspapers
Las Animas, Col., Leader. (Las Animas, Colo.) 1873-1877
Las Animas, Col. Leader. (Las Animas, Colo.) 1873-19??

Historical Assets Colorado

Las Animas Leader. (West Las Animas, Colo.) 1877-19??
La Junta Tribune. (La Junta, Bent County, Colo.) 1881-1939
La Junta Tribune. (La Junta, Otero County, Colo.) 1881-1939
Bent County Democrat. (Las Animas, Colo.) 1886-Current
Lamar Leader. (Lamar, Bent County, Colo.) 1886-1???
Bent County Register. (Lamar, Colo.) 1886-1889
Bent County Register. (Lamar, Colorado) 1886-1889
The Water Valley Clarion. (Water Valley, Bent County, Colo.) 1887-1???
Cheyenne Wells Gazette. (Cheyenne Wells, Bent County, Colo.) 1887-1???
The Stuart Chronicle. (Stuart, Kiowa Co., Colo.) 1888-1889
Las Animas Populist. (Las Animas, Colo.) 1894-1???
The Hasty Herald. (Hasty, Bent County, Colo.) 1939-19??

Places on the National Register

Las Animas, Bent County Courthouse and Jail, 725 Carson Ave.
Las Animas, Bent County High School, 1214 Ambassador Thompson Blvd
Las Animas, Boggsville, S of Las Animas on CO 101
Las Animas, Fort Lyon, Jct. of Bent Cty. Rd. 15 and Fort Lyon Gate Rd.
Las Animas, Las Animas Post Office, 513 6th St.
Prowers, Prowers Bridge, Cty. Rd. 34

USGS Historic Places

Las Animas, Fort Lyon Veterans Hospital, 38.0763957, -103.1324277

Grand Army of the Republic Posts

Richardson, No. 69, Bent, West Las Animas

USGS Historic Military Places

None

Military Bases

None

Post Offices

Albany	1887 July 21	1905 Sept 30*
Alkali	1874 June 24	1875 June 14
Arden	1888 June 22	1888 Nov 5
Arlington	1887 Aug 16	2011 Oct 15
Ayr	1888 July 25	1893 Sept 4
Bee	1887 Aug 16	1887 Oct 27*
Bents Fort	1863 June 4	1873 Dec 2
Blackwell	1881 July 7	1886 May 11*
Brandon	1888 May 19	1893 May 3
Caddoa	1881 Nov 7	1958 Mar 7*
Catlin	1879 Nov 6	1895 Nov 4

Bent County

Cheyenne Wells 2	1876 May 8	1895 Aug 21	
Chivington	1887 Oct 24	1991 Jan 1	
Dayton	1887 June 1	1887 Dec 8	
Eads	1887 Nov 18		81036
Ella	1873 May 14	1876 Feb 2	
Fergus	1888 June 7	1890 Sept 2	
Fort Lyon	1862 Aug 2	1889 Dec 26	
Fort Lyon 2	1919 Oct 25	1924	
Fort Lyon 3		2002 Sept 20	
Fredonia	1892 May 27	1900 Sept 29	
Galatea	1887 Dec 22	1948 July 31	
Gem	1907 Aug 30	1913 May 31	
Granada	1873 July 10		81041
Harbourdale	1915 Sept 20	1925 June 15	
Hasty	1910 Dec 7		81044
Higbee	1872 Apr 25	1925 Feb 28	
Holly	1880 Nov 26		81047
Kit Carson	1869 Dec 29	1881 May 17	
Kit Carson	1882 Feb 14		80825
La Junta	1876 Jan 26	1877 July 27	
La Junta	1878 Sept 20		81050
Lamar	1886 July 16		81052
Las Animas	1871 Apr 4	1883 June 8*	
Las Animas 2	1886 Sept 4		81054
Lavender	1873 June 20	1874 Apr 6	
Maine Ranch	1872 Mar 5	1875 Dec 22	
McClave	1908 Oct 20		81057
McMillin	1886 May 1	1887 Apr 16	
Medford Springs	1916 Nov 8	1922 May 31	
Mud Creek	1911 Sept 4	1918 Mar 30	
Mulvane	1888 June 8	1893 Feb 20	
New Fort Lyon	1908 Jan 17	1908 May 31	
Ninaview	1915 Sept 20	1965 July 30	
Opal	1913 Oct 28	1923 July 31	
Oxford	1882 Apr 27	1890 Sept 6	
Pinnacle	1898 Apr 22	1949 Apr 15*	
Prowers	1881 Mar 11	1933 May 15*	
Rawlings	1886 Apr 24	1887 July 7	
Rocky Ford	1871 Dec 1		81067
Rule	1909 Mar 12	1921 June 30	
Sanborn	1878 May 17	1905 June 3	
Sheridan Lake	1887 Sept 20		81071
South Side	1869 Feb 22	1877 Sept 12	
Stewart	1888 Apr 23	1899 Apr 25	
Stockade	1873 Mar 21	1874 Jan 30	
Texas Ranch	1871 Dec 19	1873 June 16	

Historical Assets Colorado

The Meadows	1873 Apr 10	1876 Oct 2		
Toledo	1887 Apr 16	1889 Sept 16		
Towner	1888 Feb 20	1992 May 9		
Water Valley	1887 Sept 9	1894 Sept 12		
West Las Animas	1873 Nov 3	1886 Sept 4		
Wild Horse	1877 Jan 5	1877 May 25		
Wild Horse 2	1904 Apr 13		80862	
Wilde	1887 Aug 6	1893 June 10		

Topo Quads

Bishop Ranch	381500N	380730N	1030730W	1031500W
Clay Ranch	374500N	373730N	1030000W	1030730W
Corbin Canyon	374500N	373730N	1032230W	1033000W
Cornelia	380730N	380000N	1031500W	1032230W
Denny Lake	380000N	375230N	1024500W	1025230W
Dripping Spring	375230N	374500N	1024500W	1025230W
Floating W Ranch	374500N	373730N	1024500W	1025230W
Gilpin	380000N	375230N	1030730W	1031500W
Hackamore Ranch	380000N	375230N	1031500W	1032230W
Hadley	380730N	380000N	1032230W	1033000W
Hand Springs	375230N	374500N	1025230W	1030000W
Hasty	380730N	380000N	1025230W	1030000W
Higbee	375230N	374500N	1032230W	1033000W
High Rock	380000N	375230N	1025230W	1030000W
Kreybill	380730N	380000N	1030000W	1030730W
Las Animas	380730N	380000N	1030730W	1031500W
Lewis Ranch	381500N	380730N	1032230W	1033000W
Lubers	381500N	380730N	1025230W	1030000W
McClave	381500N	380730N	1024500W	1025230W
McIntosh Ranch	381500N	380730N	1031500W	1032230W
Ninaview	374500N	373730N	1030730W	1031500W
Pipe Spring	374500N	373730N	1025230W	1030000W
Prowers	380730N	380000N	1024500W	1025230W
Rock Canyon	374500N	373730N	1031500W	1032230W
Thompson Arroyo	380000N	375230N	1032230W	1033000W
Toonerville	375230N	374500N	1030730W	1031500W
Toonerville NE	380000N	375230N	1030000W	1030730W
Toonerville SE	375230N	374500N	1030000W	1030730W
Tree Top Ranch	381500N	380730N	1030000W	1030730W
Turkey Canyon	375230N	374500N	1031500W	1032230W

Suggested Reading

A Pictorial History of Bent County, Colorado: Marceline, MO: Heritage House Pub, 1992.

Bent County (Colorado) History. Las Animas, CO: Bent County History Book Committee and Holly Pub. Co., 1986.

Bent County

Directory and History of Bent County, Colorado: of which Las Animas is the County Seat and Leading City. NL: NP, 1928.

Gimeno, Emil. *The Adobe Castle of the Santa Fe Trail: the History and Reconstruction of Bent's Old Fort.* NL: NP, 2004.

Hurd, C W. Boggsville: *Cradle of the Colorado Cattle Industry.* Grand Junction, CO: Occupational Training Center, 1957.

Inventory of the County Archives of Colorado, No. 6, Bent County (Las Animas). Denver: Historical Records Survey, 1938.

Lytle, Ruth Rebecca. *Historic Old Bent County.* Thesis, University of Denver, 1931.

Vickers, W B and O L Baskin & Co. *History of the Arkansas Valley, Colorado; Illustrated.* Chicago: O L Baskin Historical Publishers, 1881.

Warren, Hugh M. *The History of Bent County, Colorado.* Thesis, Colorado State College of Education, 1939.

Historical Assets Colorado

Boulder County

Introduction

Established: 1861   Population: 326,078

Formed from: Original

Adjacent Counties: Larimer, Weld, Broomfield, Jefferson, Gilpin, Grand

County Seat: Boulder

Other Communities: Lafayette, Longmont, Louisville, Erie, Jamestown, Lyons, Nederland, Superior, Ward, Allenspark, Altona, Bark Ranch, Coal Creek, Crisman, Eldora, Eldorato Springs, Glendale, Gold Hill, Hidden Lake, Leyner, Mountain Meadows, Niwot, Sugarloaf, Sunshine, Valmont, Wondervu, Caribou, Canfield, Gooding, Hygiene, Highland, Liggett, Morey, Pleasant View Ridge, Tabor

Website, https://www.bouldercounty.org

Area Codes: 303, 719

Zip Codes: 80025, 80026, 80027, 80301, 80302, 80303, 80304, 80305, 80306, 80307, 80308, 80309, 80310, 80314, 80455, 80466, 80471, 80501, 80502, 80510, 80516, 80533, 80516, 80533, 80540, 80544

Historical Assets Colorado

Boulder County Courthouse built circa 1867

Boulder County Courthouse built circa 1885

Boulder County Courthouse

Boulder County Justice Center

Courthouses & County Government

Boulder County
   https://www.bouldercounty.org
Boulder County Courts (Justice Center)(20th Judicial District), 1777 6th St, Boulder, CO 80302, 303-441-3750; http://www.courts.state.co.us/Courts/County/Index.cfm?County_ID=62
Boulder County Courthouse, 1324 Pearl St, Boulder, CO 80302; http://www.courts.state.co.us/Courts/County/Index.cfm?County_ID=62
Longmont Courthouse, 1035 Kimbark St, Longmont, CO 80501, 720-564-2522; http://www.courts.state.co.us/Courts/County/Index.cfm?County_ID=62
Assessor, 1325 Pearl St, Boulder, CO 80302, 303-441-3530; http://www.bouldercounty.org/dept/assessor/pages/default.aspx
Board of County Commissioners, 1325 Pearl St, Boulder, CO 80302, 303-441-3500, https://www.bouldercounty.org
Clerk & Recorder, 1750 33rd Street, Boulder, CO 80301, 303-413-7770; http://www.bouldercounty.org/dept/clerkrecorder/pages/default.aspx

Boulder County

Clerk & Recorder, 529 Coffman St, Longmont, CO 80501, (303) 413-7710; http://www.bouldercounty.org/dept/clerkrecorder/pages/default.aspx

Clerk & Recorder, 1376 Miners Dr, Lafayette, CO 80026; http://www.bouldercounty.org/dept/clerkrecorder/pages/default.aspx

Coroner, 5610 Flatiron Pkwy, Boulder, CO 80301, 303-441-3535; https://www.bouldercounty.org/departments/coroner/

Elections, 1750 33rd St, Ste 200, Boulder, CO 80301, 303-413-7740; https://www.bouldercounty.org/elections/

Public Health, 3450 Broadway, Boulder, CO 80304, 303-441-1100; http://www.bouldercounty.org/dept/publichealth/pages/default.aspx

Transportation, 2525 13th St, Boulder, CO 80304, 303-441-3900; https://www.bouldercounty.org/transportation/

Treasurer, 1325 Pearl St, 1st Fl, Boulder, CO 80306, 303-441-3520; http://www.bouldercounty.org/dept/Treasurer/pages/default.aspx

Treasurer, 529 Coffman St, Ste 120, Longmont, CO 80504; http://www.bouldercounty.org/dept/Treasurer/pages/default.aspx

Treasurer, 400 E Simpson, Ste 105, Lafayette, CO 80027; http://www.bouldercounty.org/dept/Treasurer/pages/default.aspx

County Records

Birth 1866	Marriage 1864	Divorce 1864
Death 1866	Land 1865	Probate 1862
Court 1862		

Early birth and death records were kept by the Department of Health

County & Municipal Records Held at the State Level

The Colorado State Archives

Physical Records	Longmont	**Records on Master Film**
Assessor	North Longmont	Assessor
Clerk & Recorder	Ward	Clerk & Recorder
Coroner		County Commissioners
County Commissioners	**Records on Film**	County Court
County Court	Clerk & Recorder	District Court
District Court	District Court	Combined Court
Probate Court	School Districts	Finance
Public Trustee	Treasurer	Land Use/Building
Sheriff	**Cities**	Police
Treasurer	Boulder	School Districts
WPA Historical Records	North Longmont	Sheriff
WPA Religious Institutions Survey	Ward	Treasurer
WPA Boulder		**Cities**
Cities		Boulder
Boulder		Lafayette
Eldora		Longmont
Jamestown		Louisville
Lafayette		North Longmont
		Ward

Historical Assets Colorado

The Denver Public Library
    American Queen & Klondyke Gold Mining Company Records, 1880-1904
    Big Five Mining Company Records, 1892-1921
    Chicago Colorado Colony Executive Council Minutes, 1871
    Colorado Bureau of Mines Records, 1897-1915
    Colorado Deeds, 1868-1911
    Colorado Theatre Program Collection, 1900-
    Crags Mountain Summer Resort Records, 1908
    Eagle Rock Tungsten Production Company Records, 1916
    Election Notice, 1871, Colorado Territorial Secretary
    Goodhue Farms Company Records, 1917
    Institute for African American Leadership Records, 1994-2010
    Humboldt Gold Mining & Milling Company Records, 1918-1919
    Pine Creek Mining District Association Records, 1895
    Poorman Silver Mines Records, 1891-1893
    Rough & Ready Irrigating Canal Records, 1885
    Sunset Gold Mining & Milling Company Records, 1904-1906
    Warpath Lode Mining Claim, 1880
    Washburn Mining Company Records, 1904-1920
    WPA Historical Records Survey
    WWI Draft Registration Cards (microfilm)

School Districts

School Districts, http://www.adcogov.org/local-school-districts
Boulder Valley School District RE-2, 6500 E Arapahoe Rd, Boulder, CO 80303, 303-447-1010; https://www.bvsd.org
Estes Park School District R-3, 1605 Brodie Ave, Estes Park, CO 80517, 970-586-2361; https://www.estesschools.org/
St Vrain Valley, School District, 395 S Pratt Pkwy, Longmont, CO 80501, 303-776-6200; https://www.svvsd.org/

Historic School Districts

1. Superior
2. Shamrock, Dry Creek
3. Boulder
4. Valmont
5. Davidson, Whitney
6. Burlington
7. Niwot, Modoc
8. Montgomery, Upper St Vrain
9. Pella, Hygiene
10. Baseline
11. Jamestown
12. Ward
13. Bader, Upper Left Hand
14. White Rock, Carle's Dist
15. Marshall, Furnace
16. Pleasant View, Carle's
17. Longmont
18. Middle Boulder, Nederland
19. Caribou
20. Batchelder
21. Hygiene, Goss
22. Altona, Left Hand Canyon
23. Armstrong, Lerey Bardo
24. Gold Hill, Goodwill
25. Bashor, Upper St Vrain South
26. Ryssby, Swede District
27. Wallstreet, Four Mile & Sugarloaf Cutoff
28. Sunshine
29. Louisville, Southeast Corner County
30. Pine Grove, Bear Canyon
31. Salina
32. Crisman
33. Silver Spruce, Orodelfan
34. Sugarloaf, Osburn
35. Chapman, Northeast Corner County

Boulder County

36. Eldorado Springs, Hawthorn, South Boulder
37. Culver, Therfeler [??] Creek
38. Magnolia
39. Rowena, Glendale
40. Springdale
41. Fairview, Ballarat
42. Beasley
43. Broomfield
44. Potato Hill
45. Pleasant View Ridge
46. Canfield
47. Lyons
48. Nelson
49. Bunce
50. Lee Hill
51. Sunset
52. Lafayette
53. Noland
54. Eggleston
55. Stony Lake
56. Eldora
57. Pine Cliffe
58. Pine Glade, Camp Frances
59. Allenspark
60. Hessie
61. Willow Glen
62. Gooding
63. Lake View
64. Sunnyside
65. Valley View, Valley Road
66. Monarch
67. Nederland

Fraternal Organizations

Granges
Valmont, No. 5, Boulder, Valmont, 12 Dec 1873
Washington, No. 8, Boulder, Longmont, 19 Dec 1873
Left Hand, No. 9, Boulder, Niwot/Modoc, 20 Dec 1873
Harmony, No. 14, Boulder, Valmont, 23 Dec 1873
St Vrain, No. 16, Boulder, Pella, 26 Dec 1873
Longmont, No. 27, Boulder, Longmont, 5 Jan 1874
South Boulder, No. 28, Boulder, Valmont, 6 Jan 1874
Lower St Vrain, No. 29, Boulder, St Vrain, 10 Jan 1874
Coal Creek, No. 30, Boulder, Boulder, 10 Jan 1874
Burlington, No. 31, Boulder, Longmont, 14 Jan 1874
Haystack, No. 36, Boulder, Haystack Mountain, 19 Jan 1874
Grand Island, No. 63, Boulder, Nederland, 27 June 1874
Dry Creek Valley, No. 90, Boulder, Broomfield, 24 Aug 1889
Pleasant View, No. 94, Boulder, Longmont, 24 Jan 1890
Altona, No. 127, Boulder, Hygiene, 24 Feb 1891
Rocky Mountain, No. 128, Boulder, Longmont, 12 Mar 1891
Longmont, No. 130, Boulder, Longmont, 28 Jan 1892
Boulder Valley, No. 131, Boulder, Lafayette, 13 Nov 1893
Hygiene, No. 134, Boulder, Hygiene, 26 Feb 1896
Crescent, No. 136, Boulder, Broomfield, 20 Oct 1898
Highland Lake, No. 140, Boulder, Longmont, 27 June 1899
Clarkston Valley, No. 157, Boulder, Louisville, 29 May 1907
Pleasant View, No. 164, Boulder, Davidson, 1 May 1908
St Vrain, No. 205, Boulder, Longmont, 14 Mar 1912
Liberty, No. 216, Boulder, Longmont, 30 Sept 1913
South Boulder, No. 225, Boulder, Boulder, 27 Mar 1914
Liberty Hall, No. 459, Boulder, Longmont, 14 June 1945
Rinn Valley, No. 466, Boulder, Longmont, 8 July 1946
County Line, No. 484, Weld/Boulder, Longmont/Erie?, 28 Aug 1958

Historical Assets Colorado

Masons
  Ancient Free & Accepted Masons
    Rocky Mountain, No. 3, Boulder, Gold Hill, 2 Aug 1861
    Columbia, No. 14, Boulder, Columbia City, 7 Oct 1867
    Boulder, No. 14, Boulder, Boulder, 27 Jan 2018
    Saint Vrain, No. 23, Boulder, Longmont, 24 Sept 1872
    Boulder, No. 45, Boulder, Boulder, 21 Sept 1881
    Eureka, No. 66, Boulder, Coal Creek, 21 Sept 1887
    Lafayette, No. 91, Boulder, Lafayette, 20 Sept 1892
    Mount Auduon, No. 107, Boulder, Ward, 20 Sept 1899
  Royal Arch Masons
    Boulder, No. 7, Boulder, Boulder
    Longmont, No. 8, Boulder, Longmont
  Knights Templar
    Mount Sinai Commandery, No. 7, Boulder, Boulder, 1882 Dec 10
    Longs Peak Commandery, No. 12, Boulder, Longmont, 1884 June 2
  Eastern Star
    Queen Esther, No. 5, Boulder, Boulder
    Columbine, No. 11, Boulder, Longmont
    Excelsior, No. 66, Boulder, Lafayette

Odd Fellows
    Ward, No. 22, Boulder, Ward
    Longmont, No. 29, Boulder, Longmont, 1877 Nov 5
    Bi-Metal, No. 44, Boulder, Gold Hill
    Jamestown, No. 79, Boulder, Jamestown
    Lafayette, No. 91, Boulder, Lafayette
    Louisville, No. 94, Boulder, Louisville
    St Vrain, No. 102, Boulder, Lyons
    Silver Queen, No. 112, Boulder, Boulder
    Hygiene, No. 124, Boulder, Hygiene
    Niwot, No. 154, Boulder, Niwot
  Rebekahs
    Boulder, No. 5, Boulder, Boulder
    Silver Spruce, No. 16, Boulder, Longmont
    Excelsior, No. 30, Boulder, Lyons
    Ivy, No. 51, Boulder, Boulder
    Welcome, No. 72, Boulder, Lafayette
    Flagstaff, No. 108, Boulder, Boulder
    St Vrain, No. 119, Boulder, Hygiene

Knights of Pythias
    Boulder, No. 12, Boulder, Boulder, Spring 1880
    Excelsior, No. 54, Boulder, Longmont
    Lignite, No. 64, Boulder, Lafayette
    Calanthe, No. 66, Boulder, Louisville

Boulder County

Columbia, No. 68, Boulder, Ward, 1891 Apr 22
Boulder, No. 76, Boulder, Boulder

Pythian Sisters
Silver State, No. 8, Boulder, Boulder
Lady Lignite, No. 10, Boulder, Lafayette
Rathbone, No. 54, Boulder, Louisville
Victory, No. 72, Boulder, Louisville

Benevolent Protective Order of Elks
Boulder, No. 566, Boulder, Boulder
Longmont, No. 1055, Boulder, Longmont
Tri-City, No. 2541, Boulder, Louisville

City & Town Halls

Boulder, 3170 Broadway, Boulder, CO 80304, 303-413-7260, https://bouldercolorado.gov

Lafayette, 1290 S PUblic Rd, Lafayette, CO 80026, 303-665-5588, https://cityoflafayette.com

Longmont, 350 Kimbark St, Longmont, CO 80501, 303-776-6050, https://www.longmontcolorado.gov

Louisville, 749 Main St, Louisville, CO 80027, 303-666-6565, https://www.louisvilleco.gov

Jamestown, P.O. Box 298, Jamestown, CO 80455, 303-449-1806

Lyons, 432 5th Ave, Lyons, CO 80540, 303-823-6622, http://www.townoflyons.com

Nederland, 45 W 1st St, Nederland, CO 80466, 303-258-3266, https://nederlandco.org/government/town-hall/

Superior, 124 E Coal Creek Dr, Superior, CO 80027, 303-499-3675, https://www.superiorcolorado.gov

Ward, https://www.ward-co.org

Eldorato Springs, https://www.eldoradosprings.com/our-community

Gold Hill, https://goldhilltown.com

Archives & Manuscript Collections

Boulder County Records Archive (digital); https://www.bouldercounty.org/records/public/

Carnegie Library for Local History, 1125 Pine St, Boulder, CO 80306-1326, (303) 441-3100, https://localhistory.boulderlibrary.org

City of Boulder Records Archive (digital); https://bouldercolorado.gov/central-records/document-archive

Colorado Chautauqua Association, Archive and History Room, 900 Baseline Rd, Boulder, CO 80302, (303) 442-3282, https://www.chautauqua.com/preservation/archives/

Longmont Museum and Cultural Center, 400 Quail Rd, Longmont, CO 80501, (303) 651-8374, https://www.longmontcolorado.gov/departments/departments-e-m/museum

Norlin Library, Archives & Special Collections, Univ of Colorado, 1720 Pleasant St, UCB 184, Boulder, CO 80309-0184, (303) 492-7521, https://www.colorado.edu/libraries/

Historical Assets Colorado

Historical & Genealogical Societies
Boulder Genealogical Society, c/o Carnegie Library, 1125 Pine St, P.O. Box 3246, Boulder, CO 80303-3246, (303) 441-3110, http://www.bouldergenealogy.org

Colorado Chautauqua Association, Archive and History Room, 900 Baseline Rd, Boulder, CO 80302, (303) 442-3282, https://www.chautauqua.com/preservation/archives/

Historic Boulder, 1200 Pearl St, Ste 70, Boulder, CO 80302, (303) 444-5192, http://www.historicboulder.org

Lafayette Historical Society, Miner's Museum, 108 E Simpson St, P.O. Box 186, Lafayette, CO 80026, (303) 665-7030, https://www.cityoflafayette.com/463/Miners-Museum

Longmont Genealogical Society, P.O. Box 6081, Longmont, CO 80501-2077, (303) 776-9931, http://longmontgenealogicalsociety.org

Louisville Historical Commission, Historical Museum, 1001 Main St, Louisville, CO 80027, (303) 665-9048, https://www.louisvilleco.gov/government/departments/home-museum

Lyons Historical Society, Lyons Redstone Museum, 340 High St, P.O. Box 9, Lyons, CO 80540, (303) 823-6692, http://lyonsredstonemuseum.com

Nederland Area Historical Society, Nederland Mining Museum & Gillaspie House, 200 N Bridge St, P.O. Box 1252, Nederland, CO 80466, (303) 258-0567, http://www.nederlandmuseums.org

Niwot Historical Society, Firehouse Museum, 195 2nd Ave, P.O. Box 354, Niwot, CO 80544, http://www.niwothistoricalsociety.org

Saint Vrain Historical Society, Old Mill Park, 237 Pratt St, P.O. Box 705, Longmont, CO 80502-0705, (303) 776-1870, http://www.stvrainhistoricalsociety.com

Local Libraries
Boulder Public Library, 1000 Canyon Blvd, P.O. Drawer H, Boulder, CO 80306, (303) 441-3100, http://www.boulder.lib.co.us

Carnegie Library for Local History, 1125 Pine St, Boulder, CO 80306-1326, (303) 441-3100, https://localhistory.boulderlibrary.org

Lafayette Public Library, 775 W Baseline Rd, Lafayette, CO 80026, (303) 665-5200, https://cityoflafayette.com/945/Library

Longmont Public Library, 350 Kimbark St, Longmont, CO 80501, (303) 651-8470, https://www.longmontcolorado.gov/departments/departments-e-m/library

Louisville Public Library, 951 Spruce St, Louisville, CO 80027, (303) 335-4849, https://www.louisvilleco.gov/government/departments/louisville-library

Lyons Regional Library, 451 4th Ave, P.O. Box 619, Lyons, CO 80540, (303) 823-5165, http://lyons.colibraries.org, https://nederland.colibraries.org

Nederland Community Library, 200 Hwy 72, PO Box 836, Nederland, CO 80466, (303) 258-1101,

Norlin Library & Special Collections, Univ of Colorado, 1720 Pleasant St, UCB 184, Boulder, CO 80309-0184, (303) 492-7521, https://www.colorado.edu/libraries/

Ward Public Library, 66 Columbia St, Ward, CO 80481, https://www.ward-co.org/category/ward-public-library/

Boulder County

Links
CO GenWeb
http://cogenweb.com/boulder/
Cyndi's List
https://www.cyndislist.com/us/co/counties/boulder/
FamilySearch Wiki
https://www.familysearch.org/wiki/en/Boulder_County,_Colorado_Genealogy
Linkpendium
http://www.linkpendium.com/boulder-co-genealogy/
RootsWeb Wiki
https://wiki.rootsweb.com/wiki/index.php/Boulder_County,_Colorado
Wikipedia
https://en.wikipedia.org/wiki/Boulder_County,_Colorado

Historic Hotels
1909 Hotel Boulderado, 2115 13th St, Boulder, CO 80302, 303-442-4344, https://www.boulderado.com

1898* Boulder Chautauqua Cottages (*the first cottage was built around 1900), 900 Baseline Rd, Boulder, CO 80302, 303-442-3282, https://www.chautauqua.com

Museums & Historic Sites
Agricultural Heritage Center, 8348 Ute Hwy, Longmont, CO 80503, (303) 776-8688, https://www.bouldercounty.org/open-space/education/museums/agricultural-heritage-center/

Callahan House & Garden, 312 Terry St, Longmont, CO 80501, (303) 776-5191, https://www.longmontcolorado.gov/departments/departments-a-d/community-services-department/callahan-house

CU Heritage Center Museum, Old Main, 3rd Fl, 1600 Pleasant St, 459 UCB, Boulder, CO 80309, (303) 492-6329, https://www.colorado.edu/alumni/heritagecenter

Dougherty Museum, 8306 Hwy 287, Longmont, CO 80504, (303) 776-2520, https://www.bouldercounty.org/open-space/education/museums/dougherty-museum/

Gold Hill Museum, 661 Pine St, P.O. Box 2015, Gold Hill, CO 80466, (303) 442-2249, http://www.goldhillmuseum.org

Historic Hover Home & Farmstead, 1303-1309 Hover St, Longmont, CO 80502, (303) 774-7810, http://www.stvrainhistoricalsociety.com

James F Bailey Assay Office Museum, 6352 Fourmile Canon Dr, Boulder, CO 80302, (303) 776-8848, https://www.bouldercounty.org/open-space/education/museums/assay-office/

Lafayette Historical Society, Miner's Museum, 108 E Simpson St, P.O. Box 186, Lafayette, CO 80026, (303) 665-7030, https://www.cityoflafayette.com/463/Miners-Museum

Longmont Museum and Cultural Center, 400 Quail Rd, Longmont, CO 80501, (303) 651-8374, https://www.longmontcolorado.gov/departments/departments-e-m/museum

Historical Assets Colorado

Louisville Historical Commission, Historical Museum, 1001 Main St, Louisville, CO 80027, (303) 665-9048, https://www.louisvilleco.gov/government/departments/home-museum

Lyons Historical Society, Lyons Redstone Museum, 340 High St, P.O. Box 9, Lyons, CO 80540, (303) 823-6692, http://lyonsredstonemuseum.com

Museum of Boulder, 2205 Broadway, Boulder, CO 80302-7224, (303) 449-3464, https://museumofboulder.org

Nederland Area Historical Society, Nederland Mining Museum & Gillaspie House, 200 N Bridge St, P.O. Box 1252, Nederland, CO 80466, (303) 258-0567, http://www.nederlandmuseums.org

Niwot Historical Society, Firehouse Museum, 195 2nd Ave, P.O. Box 354, Niwot, CO 80544, http://www.niwothistoricalsociety.org

Old St Stephen's 1881 Church, 470 Main St, Longmont, CO 80501, http://www.stvrainhistoricalsociety.com

Saint Vrain Historical Society, Old Mill Park, 237 Pratt St, P.O. Box 705, Longmont, CO 80502-0705, (303) 776-1870, http://www.stvrainhistoricalsociety.com

Special Events & Scenic Locations

The Boulder County Fair is held in July and August each year. Boulder County Fair, Boulder County Fairgrounds, 9595 Nelson Rd, Longmont, CO 80501, 720-864-6460, https://www.bouldercountyfair.org.

Boulder has multitudes of annual events and festivals. There is a good calendar of those events here, https://www.bouldercoloradousa.com/events/annual-events/

Arapaho National Forest
Roosevelt National Forest
Indian Peak Wilderness
James Peak Wilderness
Eldorado Canyon State Park
Continental Divide National Scenic Trail
Peak to Peak Scenic and Historic Byway
Colorado Chautauqua National Historic District

Ghost Towns & Other Sparsely Populated Places

Altona, Boulder Junction, Burns Junction, Camp Frances, Canon Mine, Caribou, Chapman, Coal Park, Columbia City, Crisman, Dixon's Mill, Eldora, Gold Hill Station, Hessie, Highland, Hygiene, Idaho Creek, Jamestown, Langford, Leyner, Magnolia, Marshall Junction, Noland, Northrup, Oredel [Oradel], Ryssby, Salina, Secor, Seven Hills, Springdale, Sunset, Sunshine, Tower Junction, Tungsten, Valmont, White Rock, Zangs Spur

Newspapers

Town & Country Shopper. (Boulder, Colo.) 1???-196?
The Black Diamond World. (Louisville, Boulder County, Colo.) 1???-19??
Louisville-Lafayette Advance. (Louisville, Colo.) 18??-1???

Boulder County

The Local Miner. (Boulder, Colo.) 18??-1???
The Daily Herald. (Boulder, Colo.) 18??-18??
Boulder County Herald. (Boulder, Colo.) 18??-1904
The Home Mirror. (Longmont, Colo.) 18??-1???
The Boulder News and Banner. (Boulder, Colo.) 18??-1???
Boulder Valley News. (Boulder City, Colo.) 1867-1???
The Boulder County News. (Boulder, Boulder County, Colo.) 1869-1878
The Boulder County Pioneer. (Boulder, Boulder County, Colo.) 1869-1869
The Caribou Post. (Caribou, Colo.) 1871-18??
The Colorado Press. (Longmont, Boulder County, Colo.) 1871-1872
Burlington Free Press. (Burlington, Colo.) 1871-1???
The Colorado Press. (Longmont, Boulder County, Colo.) 1871-1872
The Longmont Press. (Longmont, Boulder Co., Colo.) 1872-1888
Rocky Mountain Eagle. (Boulder, Colo.) 1873-1???
The Republican Extra. (Boulder, Colo.) 1875-1???
The Colorado Banner. (Boulder, Colo.) 1875-1883
Sunshine Courier. (Sunshine, Colo.) 1875-1878
Valley Home and Farm. (Longmont, Boulder County, Colo.) 1878-1879
The Boulder News and Courier. (Boulder, Colo.) 1878-18??
Longmont Ledger. (Longmont, Boulder Co., Colo.) 1878-1969
The Boulder County Courier. (Boulder, Colo.) 1878-1878
Real Estate Bulletin. (Longmont, Boulder County, Colo.) 1879-1???
Daily News. (Boulder, Colo.) 1880-1???
The Daily Colorado Banner. (Boulder, Colo.) 1880-1???
The Boulder Herald. (Boulder, Colo.) 1880-1???
The Boulder County Herald. (Boulder, Colo.) 1880-19??
The Boulder Sentinel. (Boulder, Colo.) 1884-1890
The Boulder News. (Boulder, Colo.) 1888-19??
The Longmont Times. (Longmont, Boulder County, Colo.) 1888-1???
The Progress. (Longmont, Colo.) 1888-1???
The Boulder Tribune. (Boulder, Colo.) 1889-1921
The Camera. (Boulder, Colo.) 1890-1891
Longs Peak Rustler. (Lyons, Colo.) 1890-1???
The Ward Miner. (Ward, Boulder Co., Colo.) 1891-1902
Daily Camera. (Boulder, Colo.) 1891-1928
Copper Rock Champion. (Copper Rock, Colo.) 1892-1???
The Lafayette Lignite. (Lafayette, Boulder County, Colo.) 1893-1???
The Daily Times. (Longmont, Colo.) 1893-1931
Lyons Topics. (Lyons, Colo.) 1894-1???
The Grange Exponent. (Boulder, Col.) 1896-1???
The Eldora Miner. (Eldora, Boulder County, Colo.) 1897-1???
Wall Street Gold Miner. (Wall Street Camp, Delphi P.O., Boulder County, Colo.) 1897-1???
The Colorado Representative. (Boulder, Colo.) 1897-1???
The Lafayette News. (Lafayette, Boulder County, Colo.) 1898-1906
The Longmont Call. (Longmont, Boulder County, Colo.) 1898-1931

Historical Assets Colorado

The Friday Social and Industrial Review. (Boulder, Colo.) 1899-1???
The Longmont Citizen-News successor to The Boulder County's Oldest Weekly News. (Longmont, Colo.) 19??-19??
The Longmont Citizen. (Longmont, Colo.) 19??-19??
The Wall Paper. (Boulder, Colo.) 19??-19??
Broomfield Star. (Broomfield, Colo.) 19??-1973
Broomfield Enterprise. (Broomfield, Colo.) 19??-1986
Longmont Times-Call. (Longmont, Colo.) 19??-1957
Louisville Times. (Louisville, Colo.) 19??-Current
The Lyons Recorder. (Lyons, Colo.) 1900-19??
The Eldora Record. (Eldora, Colo.) 19??-19??
The Boulder County Miner. (Wall Street, Boulder County, Colo.) 1902-1920
The Semi-Weekly Times. (Boulder, Colo.) 1903-1903
The Weekly Times. (Boulder, Colo.) 1903-1904
The Daily Herald. (Boulder, Colo.) 1904-1916
The Boulder County Times. (Boulder, Colo.) 1904-1907
The Lafayette Leader. (Lafayette, Colo.) 1905-1910
The News Free Press. (Lafayette, Boulder County, Colo.) 1906-1910
The Daily Ledger. (Longmont, Colo.) 1907-19??
The Lafayette Leader and News Free Press, Vol. 13. (Lafayette, Colo.) 1910-1917
Niwot Weekly News. (Niwot, Boulder County, Colo.) 1912-19??
The Boulder Morning News. ([Boulder, Colo.]) 1914-1916
The Boulder News-Herald. (Boulder, Colo.) 1916-1932
Lafayette Leader-News. (Lafayette, Colo.) 1917-1917
The Lafayette Leader. (Lafayette, Colo.) 1917-1954
The Progressive Citizen. (Boulder, Colo.) 1917-19??
The Colorado Granger. (Boulder, Colo.) 192?-Current
The Record. (Boulder, Colo.) 1920-19??
The Niwot Tribune. (Niwot, Boulder County, Colo.) 1921-1958
The Boulder County Miner and Farmer. (Boulder, Colo.) 1921-1947
The Rocky Mountain American. ([Boulder, Colo.]) 1925-1925
Boulder Daily Camera. (Boulder, Colo.) 1928-1973
The Hygiene Herald. (Lyons, Boulder Co., Colo.) 1931-1933
The Boulder Advertiser. (Boulder, Colo.) 1932-19??
The Boulder County Journal. (Boulder, Colo.) 1932-1933
The Journal. (Boulder, Colo.) 1933-19??
The Lyons News. (Lyons, Boulder Co., Colo.) 1946-19??
The Boulder County Journal. (Boulder, Colo.) 1947-19??
Boulder Reporter. ([Boulder, Colo.]) 1952-19??
Colorado Daily. (Boulder, Colo.) 1953-Current
The Boulder Valley Lens Leader. (Boulder County, Colo.) 1954-1954
The Lafayette Leader incorporating The Boulder Valley Lens Leader. (Lafayette, Colo.) 1954-1954
The Lafayette Leader. (Lafayette, Colo.) 1954-19??
Longmont Daily Times-Call. (Longmont, Colo.) 1957-1962
Town & Country Shopper Review. (Boulder, Colo.) 196?-1968

Boulder County

The Nederland Bugle. (Nederland, Boulder County, Colo.) 1960-19??
The Daily Times-Call. (Longmont, Colo.) 1962-1964
Longmont Daily Times-Call. (Longmont, Colo.) 1964-1981
Town & Country Review. (Boulder, Colo.) 1968-19??
The Longmont Commercial Ledger. (Longmont, Boulder County, Colo.) 1969-1969
Commercial Ledger. (Longmont, Boulder County, Colo.) 1969-1970
The New Lyons Recorder. (Longmont, Colo.) 1969-1981
The Longmont Scene. (Longmont, Colo.) 1970-1971
Boulder Express. (Boulder, Colo.) 1970-19??
Boulder. (Boulder, Colo.) 1970-1972
The Boulder County Commercial Ledger. (Longmont, Boulder County, Colo.) 1970-1971
Snake Ranch News. (Boulder, Colo.) 1971-1972
The Longmont Scene and The Boulder County Commercial Ledger. (Longmont, Colo.) 1971-1973
Mountain Press. (Nederland, Colo.) 1972-19??
Front Range People's Press. (Boulder, Colo.) 1972-197?
Mountain Messenger. (Nederland, Colo.) 1973-1???
The Longmont Scene. (Longmont, Colo.) 1973-19??
The Daily Camera. (Boulder, Colo.) 1973-Current
The Front Range Daily Star. (Broomfield, Colo.) 1973-1973
Nederland Dispatch. (Nederland, Colo.) 1974-19??
Lafayette Times. (Lafayette, Colo.) 1974-1975
Allenspark Wind. (Allenspark, Colo.) 1974-Current
Town & Country. (Boulder, Colo.) 1974-1975
Town & Country Review. (Boulder, Colo.) 1975-19??
Lafayette News. (Lafayette, Colo.) 1975-Current
The Some Times. (Boulder, Colo.) 1977-19??
The Mountain-Ear. (Nederland, Colo.) 1977-Current
The Handicapped Coloradan. (Denver, Colo.) 1978-Current
The New Tribune. ([Boulder, Colo.) 198?-1988
Daily Times-Call. (Longmont, Colo.) 1981-Current
Lyons Recorder. (Lyons, Colo.) 1981-1987
The Boulder Courant. (Boulder, Colo.) 1983-1986
The Niwot Recorder. (Niwot, Colo.) 1984-1984
The Recorder. (Niwot, Colo.) 1984-1986
Town & Country Chronicle. (Niwot, Co) 1986-198?
Broomfield Enterprise Sentinel. (Broomfield, Colo.) 1986-Current
The Boulder Courier. (Boulder, Colo.) 1987-1987
The Old Lyons Recorder. (Lyons, Colo.) 1987-Current
The Old Recorder. (Niwot, Colo.) 1988-1989
The County Recorder. (Lyons, Co) 1989-Current

Places on the National Register

Allens Park, Thunder Lake Trail—Bluebird Lake Trail, Roughly along N. St. Vrain Cr., W. of Wild Basin Ranger Stn.

Historical Assets Colorado

Allenspark, Bunce School, CO 7 S of Allenspark
Boulder, Arnett-Fullen House, 646 Pearl St.
Boulder, Boulder County Poor Farm, Address Restricted
Boulder, Boulder Creek Bridge, CO 119 at milepost 39.13
Boulder, Carnegie Library, 1125 Pine St.
Boulder, Chautauqua Auditorium, Chautauqua Park
Boulder, Colorado Chautauqua, 900 Baseline Rd., Chautauqua Park
Boulder, Columbia Cemetery, Along 9th St., bounded by Pleasant and College Aves.
Boulder, Downtown Boulder Historic District, CO 19
Boulder, First Baptist Church of Boulder, 1237 Pine St.
Boulder, Fox Mine Office, 1226 S. Cherryvale Rd.
Boulder, Fox Stone Barn, S. Cherryvale Rd., .5 mi. S of US 36
Boulder, Highland School, 885 Arapahoe Ave.
Boulder, Hotel Boulderado, 2115 13th St.
Boulder, McKenzie Well, Near Independence Rd. and CO 119
Boulder, Mount St. Gertrude Academy, 970 Aurora St.
Boulder, Norlin Quadrangle Historic District, University of Colorado campus
Boulder, Northern Colorado Power Company Substation, 1590 Broadway
Boulder, Squires-Tourtellot House, 1019 Spruce St.
Boulder, Swedish Evangelical Lutheran Church of Ryssby, N. 63rd St.
Boulder, US Post Office—Boulder Main, 1905 Fifteenth St.
Boulder, Walker Ranch Historic District, W of Boulder
Boulder, Walker Ranch Historic District (Boundary Increase), 7.5 mi. W of Boulder off Flagstaff Rd.
Boulder, Weiser, Martha, House, 4020 N. 75th St.
Boulder, Woodward-Baird House, 1733 Canyon Blvd.
Eldora, Denver, Northwestern and Pacific Railway Historic District, SW of Eldora
Eldora, Eldora Historic District, Roughly Eaton Pl., 6th, Pearl, and 4th Sts., Huron Ave., 6th St., Eldorado Ave., and 7th St., Klondyke Ave. & Tenth St.
Eldora, Gold Miner Hotel, 601 Klondyke Ave.
Eldora, Gold Miner Hotel (Boundary Increase), 601 Klondyke Ave.
Estes Park, Thunder Lake Patrol Cabin, Thunder Lake
Estes Park, Wild Basin House, Wild Basin
Estes Park, Wild Basin Ranger Station and House, Wild Basin
Gold Hill, Gold Hill Historic District, Roughly bounded by North St., Pine St., Boulder St., Gold Run St., and College St.
Gold Hill, Snowbound Mine, Co. Rd. 52
Hygiene, Church of the Brethren, 17th Ave.
Jamestown, Jamestown Mercantile Building, Main St.
Jamestown, Jamestown Town Hall, 118 Main St.
Jamestown, Jamestown Town Hall (Boundary Increase), 118 Main St.
Lafayette, Boulder Valley Grange No. 131, 3400 N. Ninety-fifth St.
Lafayette, Congregational Church, 300 E. Simpson St.
Lafayette, Kullgren House, 209 E. Cleveland St.
Lafayette, Lafayette House, 600 E. Simpson St.
Lafayette, Lewis House, 108 E. Simpson St.

Boulder County

Lafayette, Miller House, 409 E. Cleveland St.
Lafayette, Shannon Farm, 1341 N. 95th St.
Lafayette, Terrace, The, 207 E. Cleveland St.
Longmont, Callahan, T. M., House, 312 Terry St.
Longmont, Dickens Opera House, 300 Main St.
Longmont, East Side Historic District, Roughly bounded by Long's Peak Ave., Collyer St., Fourth Ave., and Emery St.
Longmont, Empson Cannery, 15 3rd Ave.
Longmont, Hoverhome and Hover Farmstead, 1303-1309 Hover Rd.
Longmont, Longmont Carnegie Library, 457 Fourth Ave.
Longmont, Longmont College, 546 Atwood St.
Longmont, Longmont Fire Department, 667 4th Ave.
Longmont, St. Stephen's Episcopal Church, 1881, 470 Main St.
Longmont, West Side Historic District, Roughly bounded by Fifth, Terry, Third, and Grant
Louisville, Denver Elevator—Grain Elevator, Tract 712 near CO 42
Louisville, Ginacci House, 1116 LaFarge St.
Louisville, Jacoe Store, 1001 Main St.
Louisville, Lackner's Tavern, 1006 Pine
Louisville, LaSalla House, 1124 Main St.
Louisville, National Fuel Company Store, 801 Main St.
Louisville, Petrelli—DelPizzo House, 1016 Main St.
Louisville, Rhoades House, 1024 Grant
Louisville, Robinson House, 301 Spruce
Louisville, Stolmes House, 616 Front St.
Louisville, Tego Brothers Drugstore—State National Bank of Louisville, 700 Main St.
Louisville, Thomas House, 700 Lincoln
Lyons, First Congregational Church of Lyons, High and 4th Sts.
Lyons, Longmont Power Plant, Old Apple Valley Rd.
Lyons, Lyons Railroad Depot, 400 block of Broadway
Lyons, Lyons Sandstone Buildings, U.S. 36 and CO 7
Lyons, North St. Vrain Creek Bridge, CO 7 at milepost 32.98
Meeker Park, Sandbeach Lake Trail, S. of Lookout Mt.
Nederland, Cardinal Mill, Address Restricted
Nederland, Rocky Mountain Mammoth Mine, 4879 Magnolia Dr
Rollinsville, Denver, Northwestern and Pacific Railway Historic District—Rollinsville & Middle Park Wagon Road (Boundary Increase), Rollins Pass
Salina, Little Church in the Pines, 414 Gold Run Rd.
Salina, Salina School, 536 Gold Run Rd.
Sunshine, Sunshine School, 355 Co. Rd. 83
Wall Street, Wall Street Assay Office (Boundary Increase), Area W and across Wall St. from Assay Office
Wallstreet, Wall Street Assay Office, 6352 Four Mile Canyon Dr.
Ward, Denver, Boulder and Western Railway Historic District, CO 72
Ward, Modoc Mill, N of Ward

Historical Assets Colorado

Ward, Ward Congregational Church, 41 Modoc
Ward, Ward School, 66 Columbia

USGS Historic Places

Boulder, Boulder County Hospital, 40.0372078, -105.2802681
Boulder, Highland Elementary School, 40.013319, -105.2847128
Boulder, Mount Saint Gertrude Academy, 40.003319, -105.280546
Boulder, Unitarian Church, 40.013319, -105.2838794
Erie, Leyners Hayfield Airport, 40.0460959, -105.1124841
Gold Hill, Gold Hill Post Office, 40.0630415, -105.4041612
Louisville, Bridge School, 39.98739, -105.19667
Lyons, Lefthand Fire Protection District Central Station, 40.1328652, -105.2862221
Lyons, Lefthand Fire Protection District Station 3, 40.1325707, -105.2888741
Nederland, Cardinal, 39.9697091, -105.547777
Nederland, Caribou, 39.9808202, -105.5786115
Nederland, Grand Island, 39.9708202, -105.6033346
Nederland, Hessie, 39.954987, -105.600001
Niwot, Arapahoe School, 40.0155408, -105.1785979
Niwot, Base Line School, 40.0005411, -105.2352667
Niwot, Pleasant View School, 40.0405411, -105.2444335
Raymond, Peaceful Valley Post Office, 40.1313744, -105.4977758
Tungsten, Tungsten, 39.9719312, -105.4761079
Unknown, Crags Post Office, 0, 0
Unknown, Pinecliffe Post Office, 0, 0

Grand Army of the Republic Posts

Nathaniel Lyon, No. 5, Boulder, Boulder, 1881
McPherson, No. 6, Boulder, Longmont, 1905

USGS Historic Military Places

None

Military Bases

None

Post Offices

Allenspark	1896 Aug 18	1905 Nov 30	
Allenspark 2	1906 May 5		80510
Altona	1879 Oct 2	1916 July 15	
Balarat	1879 Sept 12	1887 May 13*	
Belle Monte	1866 Jan 3	1866 Aug 31	
Big Elk	1915 June 3	1917 Sept 15	
Boulder	1859 Apr 22		80302
Broomfield	1884 Sept 26		80020
Bunce	1895 Oct 12	1901 May 31	

Boulder County

Burlington	1862 Nov 6	1873 Apr 14	
Canfield	1878 Mar 28	1906 June 15	
Cardinal	1905 July 13	1919 Oct 15*	
Caribou	1871 Jan 31	1917 Mar 31	
Coal Creek	1864 Apr 9	1873 Oct 29	
Coal Park	1890 May 5	1895 May 13	
Coalpark	1895 May 13	1896 Oct 5	
Copper Rock	1892 June 30	1915 Dec 15*	
Coraville	1887 Aug 19	1888 Nov 21	
Crags	1911 Mar 4	1913 Sept 13	
Crescent	1907 Feb 5	1922 Nov 15*	
Crescent	1959 Oct 16	[now in Golden]	
Crisman	1876 July 20	1918 May 31*	
Davidson	1873 Dec 4	1878 Oct 15*	
Delphi	1895 Oct 31	1898 Apr 18	
Downer	1904 Aug 9	1915 Apr 15	
Eagle Rock	1876 June 22	1877 June 20	
Eldora	1897 Feb 13	1977 Sept 8	
Eldorado Springs	1930 May 1		80025
Eversman	1899 Sept 7	1900 Aug 31	
Ferberite	1916 May 27	1918 Oct 15	
Frances	188 Oct 26	1907 Jan 15	
Glacier Lake	1906 Mar 3	1908 Aug 15	
Gold Dirt	1861 Aug 13	1867 Oct 11	
Gold Hill	1863 Jan 13	1894 June 4*	
Goldhill	1895 June 4	1952 May 31*	
Gorham	1899 Aug 31	1942 Jan 15*	
Gresham	1895 July 17	1912 Nov 30	
Gulch	1892 June 20	1893 Jan 7	
Hawthorne	1906 Sept 12	1930 May 1	
Hessie	1898 Mar 19	1902 June 30	
Hygiene	1883 June 25		80533
Ironsides	1898 Apr 22	1898 May 11	
Jamestown	1867 Jan 8	1930 July 15	
Jamestown 2	1934 June 19		80455
Lafayette	1889 Feb 4		80026
Lakewood	1912 Oct 1	1920 Dec 31	
Langford	1881 Aug 5	1899 Aug 31*	
Left Hand	1872 Apr 25	1879 Dec 26	
Longmont	1873 Apr 14		80501
Louisville	1878 May 21		80027
Lyons	1882 May 18		80540
Magnolia	1876 May 16	1920 Dec 31	
Marshall	1878 Aug 2	1893 Apr 10*	
Middle Boulder	1871 Sept 13	1874 Mar 2	
Modoc	1874 June 18	1879 Oct 31	

Historical Assets Colorado

Nederland	1874 Mar 2		80466
Ni Wot	1873 Apr 2	1895 May 2*	
Niwot	1895 May 2		80544
Noland	1890 July 16	1901 Aug 31*	
Orodelfan	1876 June 9	1881 Jan 3	
Osborn	1880 Sept 20	1885 Feb 4	
Peaceful Valley	1917 June 26	1935 June 29	
Pella	1871 Apr 5	1885 Nov 12	
Penn	1882 Mar 6	1882 July 18	
Pinecliffe	1909 Mar 8		80471
Primos	1907 May 17	1913 Feb 13	
Puzzler	1898 May 10	1903 Nov 14	
Rockville	1877 July 16	1878 May 7	
Rowena	1894 Mar 16	1918 July 31*	
Salina	1874 Nov 19	1925 Jan 1	
Shelton	1904 May 13	1904 Sept 23	
Springdale	1881 May 3	1911 July 5	
Sugar Loaf	1867 Sept 30	1944 Feb 29*	
Sunset	1883 Sept 25	1921 Nov 15*	
Sunshine	1875 Feb 26	1913 Aug 31	
Superior	1896 Dec 14	1955 Jan 31	
Tungsten	1916 July 10	1949 Nov 30	
Valmont	1865 Sept 15	1901 June 29	
Vesuvius	1908 Apr 15	1908 June 15	
Wallstreet	1898 Apr 18	1921 Sept 15	
Ward	1894 Sept 11		80481
Ward District	1863 Jan 13	1894 Sept 11	
Wheelman	1900 June 2	1902 July 31	
Whitney	1868 Apr 27	1871 July 3	

Topo Quads

Allenspark	401500N	400730N	1053000W	1053730W
Boulder	400730N	400000N	1051500W	1052230W
Eldorado Springs	400000N	395230N	1051500W	1052230W
Gold Hill	400730N	400000N	1052230W	1053000W
Hygiene	401500N	400730N	1050730W	1051500W
Lafayette	400000N	395230N	1050000W	1050730W
Longmont	401500N	400730N	1050000W	1050730W
Louisville	400000N	395230N	1050730W	1051500W
Lyons	401500N	400730N	1051500W	1052230W
Nederland	400000N	395230N	1053000W	1053730W
Niwot	400730N	400000N	1050730W	1051500W
Raymond	401500N	400730N	1052230W	1053000W
Tungsten	400000N	395230N	1052230W	1053000W
Ward	400730N	400000N	1053000W	1053730W

Boulder County

Suggested Reading

Aldrich, John K. *Ghosts of Boulder County: A Guide to the Ghost Towns and Mining Camps of Boulder County, Colorado*. Denver: Columbine Ink, 2008.

Boulder County, Colorado: its Mines of Gold, Silver, Copper and Coal. Boulder, CO: Boulder Board of Trade, 1882.

Courtney, Chellee. *Digging up Dirt: The Gold Hill Cemetery, Gold Hill, Colorado*. Niwot, CO: Iron Gate Publishing, 2019.

Dyni, Anne Quinby. *Back to the Basics: the Frontier Schools of Boulder County, Colorado*. Boulder, CO: Book Lode, 1991.

Fritz, Percy Stanley. *Mining Districts of Boulder County, Colorado*. NL: University of Colorado History Department, 1933.

History of Clear Creek and Boulder Valleys, Colorado. Chicago: O L Baskin & Co, 1880.

Lambrecht, Mona. *Boulder, 1859-1919*. Charleston, SC: Arcadia Pub, 2008.

Mining in Boulder County, Colorado: Silver Jubilee Edition. Boulder, CO: Boulder County Metal Mining Association, 1919.

Mohlenkamp, Steve and Silvia Pettem. *Portrait of Boulder*. Helena, MT: Farcountry Press, 2013.

Noel, Thomas J and Dan W Corson. *Boulder County: An Illustrated History*. Carlsbad, CA: Heritage Media Corp, 1999.

Pettem, Silvia. *Boulder: A Sense of Time and Place Revisited*. Charleston, SC: History Press, 2010.

Pettem, Silvia. *Boulder: Evolution of a City*. Boulder, CO: University Press of Colorado, 2006.

Schoolland, John B. *Boulder Then and Now: Picturesque Boulder and Gems of Boulder County*. Boulder, CO: Johnson Pub Co, 1982.

Historical Assets Colorado

Broomfield County

Introduction

Established: 2001   Population: 69,267
Formed from: Boulder, Jefferson, Weld, Adams
Adjacent Counties: Boulder, Jefferson, Weld, Adams
County Seat: Broomfield
  Other Communities: None
Website, https://www.broomfield.org
Area Codes: 303, 719
Zip Codes: 80020, 80023, 80038

Historical Assets Colorado

Broomfield Combined Courts Center

Courthouses & County Government

Broomfield County
   https://www.broomfield.org
Broomfield City Council, One Descombes Dr, Broomfield, CO 80020, 303-469-3301, https://www.broomfield.org/954/Council-Members
Broomfield County Courthouse (17th Judicial District), 17 Descombes Dr, Broomfield, CO 80020, 720-887-2100; http://www.courts.state.co.us/Courts/County/Index.cfm?County_ID=56
Broomfield, Assessor, One DesCombes Dr, Broomfield, CO 80020, 303-464-5819; http://www.broomfield.org/assessor/
Clerk & Recorder, One DesCombes Dr, Broomfield, CO 80020, 303-464-5819; http://www.broomfield.org/clerkandrecorder/
Elections, 1 Descombes Dr, Broomfield, CO 80020, 303-464-5857; https://www.broomfield.org/153/Elections
Public Health, 6 Garden Center, Broomfield, CO 80020, 720-887-2200; http://www.broomfield.org/hhs/Public_Health_Environment/index.shtml
Transportation (Engineering), 1 Descombes Dr, Broomfield, CO 80020, 303-438-6380; https://www.broomfield.org/1078/Transportation-Information
Treasurer, 1 DesCombes Dr, Broomfield, CO 80020, 303-464-5819; http://www.broomfield.org/Treasurer/

Broomfield County

County Records
Birth 2001
Death 2001
Court 2001
Marriage 2001
Land 2001
Divorce 2001
Probate 2001

County & Municipal Records Held at the State Level

The Colorado State Archives
Physical Records	Records on Film	Records on Master Film
None	None	None
Cities	**Cities**	**Cities**
Broomfield	Broomfield	Broomfield

The Denver Public Library
None

School Districts
School Districts, http://www.adcogov.org/local-school-districts

Boulder Valley School District RE-2, 6500 E Arapahoe Rd, Boulder, CO 80303, 303-447-1010; https://www.bvsd.org

Adams District 12 Five Star Schools, 1500 E 128th Ave, Thornton, CO 80241, 720-972-4000; https://www.adams12.org/

Weld County Reorganized School District RE-8, 200 S Fulton Ave, Fort Lupton, CO 80621, 303-857-3200; https://www.weld8.org/

Historic School Districts
None

Fraternal Organizations
Because Broomfield county was established in 2001, we have not discovered any fraternal orders that have formed in this county. Look for Broomfield residents to be members of fraternal orders in Boulder, Jefferson, Adams and Weld counties.

City Hall
Broomfield, 1 Descombes Dr, Broomfield, CO 80020, 303-438-6300, https://www.broomfield.org

Archives & Manuscript Collections
National Archives at Denver, 17101 Huron St, Broomfield, CO 80023, 303-604-4740, https://www.archives.gov/denver

Historical & Genealogical Societies
Anthem Ranch Genealogical Society, 16151 Lowell Blvd, Broomfield, CO 80023

Broomfield Genealogical Society, c/o Mamie Doud Eisenhower Public Library, 3 Community Park Rd, Broomfield, CO 80020, https://broomfieldgensoc.com

Historical Assets Colorado

Local Libraries
Mamie Doud Eisenhower Public Library, 3 Community Park Rd, Broomfield, CO 80020-3781, (720) 887-2300, https://broomfield.flatironslibrary.org

Links
CO GenWeb
http://cogenweb.com/broomfield/

Cyndi's List
https://www.cyndislist.com/us/co/counties/broomfield/

FamilySearch Wiki
https://www.familysearch.org/wiki/en/Broomfield_County,_Colorado_Genealogy

Linkpendium
http://www.linkpendium.com/broomfield-co-genealogy/

RootsWeb Wiki
https://wiki.rootsweb.com/wiki/index.php/Broomfield_County,_Colorado

Wikipedia
https://en.wikipedia.org/wiki/Broomfield_County,_Colorado

Historic Hotels
None

Museums & Historic Sites
None

Special Events & Scenic Locations
Broomfield Days is held in September each year in Midway Park, 1270 W Midway Blvd, Broomfield, CO 80020. For a full schedule of events, https://www.broomfield.org/361/Broomfield-Days

Broomfield keeps a calendar of annual events here, https://www.broomfield.org/2560/Events

Ghost Towns & Other Sparsely Populated Places
None

Newspapers
Broomfield Star. (Broomfield, Colo.) 19??-1973
Broomfield Enterprise. (Broomfield, Colo.) 19??-1986
The Front Range Daily Star. (Broomfield, Colo.) 1973-1973
Broomfield Enterprise Sentinel. (Broomfield, Colo.) 1986-Current

Places on the National Register
None

Broomfield County

USGS Historic Places
None

Grand Army of the Republic Posts
None

USGS Historic Military Places
None

Military Bases
None

Post Offices
Broomfield   1884 Sept 26   80020

Topo Quads
None

Suggested Reading
Pettem, Silvia. *Broomfield: Changes Through Time*. Longmont, CO: Book Lode, 2001.
Spitler, Laura and Louis Walther Spitler. *Gem of the Mountain Valley: A History of Broomfield*. NL: Broomfield Centennial-Bicentennial Commission, 1975.
Turner, Carol. *Legendary Locals of Broomfield, Colorado*. Charleston, SC: Arcadia Publishing, 2014.

Historical Assets Colorado

Chaffee County

Introduction

Established: 1861   Population: 17,809

Formed from: Original

Adjacent Counties: Lake, Park, Fremont, Saguache, Gunnison, Pitkin

County Seat: Salida

Other Communities: Buena Vista, Poncha Springs, Garfield, Johnson Village, Maysville, Smeltertown, Alpine, Americus, Belleview, Browns Canon, Centerville, Cleora, Futurity, Granity, Hamilton, Nathrop, Newett, Princeton, Riverside, Rockdale, St Elmo, Stonewall, Turret, Vicksburg, Winfield

Website, http://www.chaffeecounty.org

Area Codes: 719

Zip Codes: 81201, 81211, 81227, 81228, 81236, 81242

Historical Assets Colorado

Chaffee County Courthouse

Courthouses & County Government

Chaffee County
  http://www.chaffeecounty.org/
Chaffee County Courthouse (11th Judicial District), 142 Crestone, Salida, CO 81201, 719-539-2561; http://www.courts.state.co.us/Courts/County/Index.cfm?County_ID=28
Assessor, 104 Crestone Ave, Salida, CO 81201, 719-539-4016; http://www.chaffee-county.org/Assessor
Board of County Commissioners, 104 Crestone Ave, Salida, CO 81201, 719-539-2218, http://www.chaffeecounty.org/Commissioners
Clerk & Recorder, 104 Crestone Ave, Salida, CO 81201, 719-539-6913; http://www.chaffeecounty.org/Clerk-and-Recorder
Clerk & Recorder (Buena Vista), 112 Linderman Ave, Buena Vista, CO 81211, 719-395-8296; Clerk & Recorder (Salida), 104 Crestone Ave, Salida, CO 81201, 719-539-6913; https://www.chaffeecountyclerk.org/; http://www.chaffeecounty.org/Clerk-and-Recorder
Coroner, P.O. Box 613, Salida, CO 81201, 719-221-8733; http://www.chaffeecounty.org/Coroner
Public Health, 448 E 1st St, Ste 137, Salida, CO 81201, 719-539-4510; http://www.chaffee-hhs.org/chaffee-county-public-health/
Transportation (Road & Bridge) (Salida), 10360 County Rd 120, Salida, CO 81201, 719-539-4591; Transportation (Road & Bridge) (Buena Vista), 521 Gregg Dr, Buena Vista, CO 81211; http://www.chaffeecounty.org/Road-and-Bridge
Treasurer, 104 Crestone Ave, Salida, CO 81201, 719-539-6808; http://www.chaffee-county.org/Treasurer

Chaffee County

County Records
Birth Unk
Death Unk
Court 1880
Marriage 1890
Land 1890
Divorce 1880
Probate 1880

Clerk & Recorder has very few 19th Century birth or death records
CSA has naturalization records from 1881

County & Municipal Records Held at the State Level

The Colorado State Archives

Physical Records
Assessor
Clerk & Recorder
County Court
District Court
Justice Court
WPA Historical Records
WPA Religious Institutions
   Survey
WPA Salida
Cities
   Salida

Records on Film
1885 Census
District Court
School Districts
Cities
   Salida

Records on Master Film
Clerk & Recorder
County Court
District Court
Combined Courts
School Districts
Cities
   Cleora
   Salida

The Denver Public Library
Chaffee County, Colorado Mining Companies Records, 19098
Lucky Mine Records, 1880-1934
Mary Murphy Gold Mining Company Records, 1886, 1911-1939
Notary Ledger Book of Salida, CO, 1919-1922
Romley, Colorado Post Office Records, 1914-1924
Salida Gold Mining & Investment Company Records, 1898
WWI Draft Registration Cards (microfilm)

School Districts
School Districts, http://www.adcogov.org/local-school-districts
Buena Vista School Dist No R-31, 113 N Court St, Buena Vista, CO 81211, 719-395-7000; http://www.bvschools.org/
Salida School District R32, 310 E 9th St, Salida, CO 81201, 719-530-5469; http://www.salidaschools.com/

Historic School Districts
1. Granite
2. Centerville
3. Poncha
4. Maysville
5. Smelter, Adobe Park
6. Free Gold, Buena Vista
7. Salida
8. [1881]
9. Buena Vista
10. Garfield
11. Riverside
12. St Elmo, Alpine
13. Nathrop
14. Missouri Park, Pinion Grove, Masonic Park
15. [1882]
16. Riverside, Pine Creek
17. [1882]
18. Turret, Nelson
19. Mt Princeton, Hortense
20. Nathrop, Gas Creek

Historical Assets Colorado

21. Monarch
22. [1884]
23. [1884]
24. Sand Park
25. Clear Creek, Granite
26. Buena Vista, Mt Princeton
27. Bear Creek, Buena Vista, Berrian
28. Cleora
29. Valley View
30. Brown's Canon, Salida

Fraternal Organizations

Granges
Princeton, No. 121, Chaffee, Buena Vista, 5 Nov 1890
College Peaks, No. 414, Chaffee, Buena Vista, 24 May 1934
Poncha Springs, No. 417, Chaffee, Salida, 31 July 1935

Masons

Ancient Free & Accepted Masons
Mount Princeton, No. 49, Chaffee, Buena Vista, 20 Sept 1882
Salida, No. 57, Chaffee, Salida, 17 Sept 1884

Royal Arch Masons
Salida, No. 17, Chaffee, Salida

Knights Templar
Salida Commandery, No. 17, Chaffee, Salida, 1891 Mar 12

Eastern Star
Buena Vista, No. 18, Chaffee, Buena Vista
Topaz, No. 27, Chaffee, Salida

Odd Fellows
Buena Vista, No. 42, Chaffee, Buena Vista
Poncha Springs, No. 47, Chaffee, Poncha Springs, 1882 Apr 6
Salida, No. 54, Chaffee, Salida
Monarch, No. 55, Chaffee, Monarch
Granite, No. 117, Chaffee, Granite

Rebekahs
Miriam, No. 10, Chaffee, Salida

Knights of Pythias
Shavano, No. 16, Chaffee, Maysville, 1881 May
Iron Mountain, No. 19, Chaffee, Salida
Buena Vista, No. 88, Chaffee, Buena Vista, 1893 May 31

Pythian Sisters
None

Benevolent Protective Order of Elks
Salida, No. 808, Chaffee, Salida

City & Town Halls
Salida, 448 E 1st St, Salida, CO 81201, 719-539-4555, https://cityofsalida.com
Buena Vista, 210 E Main St, Buena Vista, CO 80211, 719-395-8643, http://www.buenavistaco.gov
Poncha Springs, 330 Burnett Ave, Poncha Springs, CO 81242, 719-59-6882, http://www.ponchaspringscolorado.us

Chaffee County

Archives & Manuscript Collections
Salida Archive (digital), http://salidaarchive.info/research/

Historical & Genealogical Societies
Buena Vista Heritage Association, Courthouse Museum, 506 E Main, P.O. Box 1414, Buena Vista, CO 81211, (719) 395-8458, http://www.buenavistaheritage.org

Clear Creek Canyon Historical Society of Chaffee County, P.O. Box 2181, Granite, CO 81228, (719) 486-2942, https://www.facebook.com/ClearCreekCanyonHistoricalSociety/

Salida Museum Association, Historical Museum, 406 1/2 Rainbow Blvd, Salida, CO 81201, (970) 539-7483, http://salidamuseum.org

Local Libraries
Salida Regional Library, 405 E Street, Salida, CO 81201, 719-539-4826, https://www.salidalibrary.org

Buena Vista Public Library, 131 Linderman Ave, P.O. Box 2019, Buena Vista, CO 81211-2019, (719) 395-8700, http://www.buenavistalibrary.org

Links
CO GenWeb
http://cogenweb.com/chaffee/

Cyndi's List
https://www.cyndislist.com/us/co/counties/chaffee/

FamilySearch Wiki
https://www.familysearch.org/wiki/en/Chaffee_County,_Colorado_Genealogy

Linkpendium
http://www.linkpendium.com/chaffee-co-genealogy/

RootsWeb Wiki
https://wiki.rootsweb.com/wiki/index.php/Chaffee_County,_Colorado

Wikipedia
https://en.wikipedia.org/wiki/Chaffee_County,_Colorado

Historic Hotels
None

Museums & Historic Sites
Buena Vista Depot Museum, Hwy 24 & Main St, Buena Vista, CO 81211, (719) 395-8458, https://www.buenavistaheritage.org/Depot—And-Caboose

Buena Vista Heritage Association, Courthouse Museum, 506 E Main, P.O. Box 1414, Buena Vista, CO 81211, (719) 395-8458, http://www.buenavistaheritage.org

Salida Museum Association, Historical Museum, 406 1/2 Rainbow Blvd, Salida, CO 81201, (970) 539-7483, http://salidamuseum.org

Turner Farm and Apple Orchard Museum, 829 W Main St, Buena Vista, CO 81211, (719) 395-8458, https://www.buenavistaheritage.org/Turner-Farm

Historical Assets Colorado

Special Events & Scenic Locations

The Chaffee County Fair is held at the fairgrounds each year. Chaffee County Fairgrounds, 10165 CO Rd 120, Salida, CO 81201, 719-539-6151, http://www.chaffee-county.org/fairgrounds

FourteenerNet keeps a good calendar of events for the region, http://www.fourteenernet.com/things-to-do/major-events

The Buena Vista Chamber of Commerce keeps a calendar of events, https://www.buenavistacolorado.org/events/

The City of Salida also keeps a calendar of local events, https://cityofsalida.com/events/

Browns Canyon National Monument
Buffalo Peaks Wilderness
Collegiate Peaks Wilderness
San Isabel National Forest
Arkansas Headwaters Recreation Area
American Discovery Trail
Colorado Trail
Continental Divide National Scenic Trail
Great Parks Bicycle Route
Western Express Bicycle Route

Ghost Towns & Other Sparsely Populated Places

Alpine, Alpine Tunnel, Americus, Arbourville, Arena, Babcock, Banker Mine, Beaver City, Belleview, Brown's Canon, Cascade, Cashe Creek, Centreville, Charcoal, Cleora, Clohseys Lake, Cottonwood Springs, Divide, Fisher, Garfield, Granite, Hamilton, Hancock, Hartsville, Harvard City, Haywood Springs, Hecla Junction, Higgins, Hortense, Interlaken, Iron City, Kraft, Lady Murphy, Mary Murphy, Maysville, McGee's, Mears Junction, Midway, Monarch (Camp Monarch, Chaffee City), Mount Princeton, Nathrop, Otto, Raspberry, Riverside, Rockdale, Romley (Murphy's Switch), Saint Elmo (Forest City), Schwanders, Shavano (Clifton), Shirley, Silverdale, Smeltertown, Stonewall, Swiss Boy, Tasmania, Tomichi, Turret, Venice, Vicksburg, Wild Horse, Winfield

Newspapers

The Chaffee County Democrat. (Buena Vista, Chaffee County, Colo.) 1???-19??
Colorado Republican. (Buena Vista, Colo.) 1???-19??
The Colorado Republic. (Buena Vista, Colo.) 1???-1???
The Granite Mining Journal. (Granite, Chaffee County, Colo.) 18??-19??
Chrysolite Mountain Bugle. (Grizzly Gulch, near Alpine, Chaffee County, Colo.) 1879-1???
St. Elmo Mountaineer. (St. Elmo, Colo.) 1880-????
Mountain Mail. (South Arkansas Colo.) 1880-1883
The Chaffee County Press. (Nathrop, Colo.) 1880-????
The South Arkansas Miner. (Maysville, Colo.) 1880-188?

Chaffee County

The Maysville Miner. (Maysville, Colo.) 188?-1???
The Poncha Herald. (Poncha Springs, Colo.) 188?-1???
The Chaffee County Times. (Buena Vista, Chaffee County, Colo.) 1880-1886
Mine, Stack, and Rail. (Buena Vista, Colo.) 188?-1???
Poncho Springs Herald. (Poncho Springs, Colo.) 1881-1???
Buena Vista Herald. (Buena Vista, Chaffee County, Colo.) 1881-1???
Chaffee County Democrat. (Maysville, Colo.) 1881-1???
Salida Daily Mountain Mail. (Salida, Colo.) 1882-1883
Salida Daily Sentinel. (Salida, Colo.) 1882-1???
The Wasp. (Buena Vista, Colo.) 1883-1???
The Buena Vista Wasp. (Buena Vista, Colo.) 1883-????
Salida Weekly Mail. (Salida, Colo.) 1883-1885
Salida Daily Mail. (Salida, Colo.) 1883-1885
Salida Daily News. (Salida, Colo.) 1883-1888
The Weekly Mail. (Salida, Colo.) 1883-1883
The Buena Vista Democrat. (Buena Vista, Colo.) 1883-1892
Salida Mail. (Salida, Colo.) 1885-1937
Salida Real Estate Guide. (Salida, Chaffee County, Colo.) 1885-1???
Salida News. (Salida, Colo.) 1888-1890
Salida Semi-Weekly News. (Salida, Colo.) 1890-1???
The Salida Sentinel. (Salida, Colo.) 1891-1???
The Colorado Democrat. (Buena Vista, Chaffee County, Colo.) 1892-1895
Chaffee County Record. (Salida, Colo.) 1893-1898
Granite Pay-Streak. (Granite, Chaffee County, Colo.) 1894-1???
The Chaffee County News. (Buena Vista, Chaffee County, Colo.) 1895-1???
The Chaffee County Republican. (Buena Vista, Chaffee County, Colo.) 1895-1897
The Whitehorn News. (Whitehorn, Chaffee County, Colo.) 1897-19??
The Chaffee County Republic. (Buena Vista, Chaffee County, Colo.) 1897-1???
The Granite Courier. (Granite, Chaffee County, Colo.) 1898-1???
The Salida Record. (Salida, Colo.) 1898-1926
Turret Gold Belt. (Turret, Colo.) 1899-19??
Chaffee County Republican. (Buena Vista, Colo.) 19??-1976
The Chronicle. (Salida, Colo.) 1904-19??
The Salida Semi-Weekly Record. (Salida, Colo.) 1926-1926
The Salida, Colorado, Record. (Salida, Colo.) 1926-1926
The Salida Record. (Salida, Colo.) 1927-1964
Mail Bulletin. (Salida, Colo.) 1933-1936
The Salida Daily Mail. (Salida, Colo.) 1936-1948
Salida Daily Mail-Record. (Salida, Colo.) 1948-1955
Moly Mountain News. (Climax, Colo.) 1949-19??
Mountain Mail. (Salida, Colo.) 1956-Current
Chaffee County Times. (Buena Vista, Colo.) 1976-Current

Places on the National Register

Buena Vista, Behrman Ranch, 31715 US 24 N.
Buena Vista, Bonney, J. M., House, 408 Princeton Ave.

Historical Assets Colorado

Buena Vista, Bridge over Arkansas River, U.S. Hwy 24
Buena Vista, Chaffee County Courthouse and Jail Buildings, 501 E. Main St
Buena Vista, Grace Episcopal Church, Main and Park Ave.
Buena Vista, Jacobs Building, 414 Main St.
Buena Vista, Vicksburg Mining Camp, 15 mi. NW of Buena Vista on SR 390
Buena Vista, Winfield Mining Camp, 15 mi. NW of Buena Vista
Granite, Littlejohn Mine Complex, SW of Granite
Maysville, Maysville School, S of US 50
Poncha Springs, Hutchinson Ranch, 2 mi. E of Poncha Springs on U.S. 50
Poncha Springs, Poncha Springs Schoolhouse, 330 Burnett St.
Romley, Morley Bridge, Chaffee Cty Rd. 297 at milepost 2.40
Salida, Alexander House, 846 F St.
Salida, Bode—Stewart House, 803 F St.
Salida, Brown's Canyon Bridge, Cty. Rd. 191 crossing the Arkansas R.
Salida, Chaffee County Poor Farm, 8495 County Rd. 160
Salida, Corbin, E.W., House, 303 E. 5th St.
Salida, F Street Bridge, F St.
Salida, Gray, Garret and Julia, Cottage, 125 E. 5th St.
Salida, Heister House, 102 Poncha Blvd.
Salida, Hutchinson Ranch (Boundary Increase), 8911 W. I-50
Salida, Jackson, F.A., House, 401 E. 1st St.
Salida, Manhattan Hotel, 225 F St.
Salida, Ohio-Colorado Smelting and Refining Company Smokestack, NE of Salida at jct. of SR 150 and 152
Salida, Salida Downtown Historic District, Roughly bounded by Arkansas River, RR Track, 3rd and D Sts.
Salida, Valley View School, 8465 Co. Rd. 140
St. Elmo, St. Elmo Historic District, Pitkin, Gunnison, 1st., Main and Poplar Sts.
Vicksburg, Crescent Moly Mine No. 100 and Mining Camp, Address Restricted

USGS Historic Places

Cumberland Pass, Old Alpine Tunnel, 38.6477734, -106.4066926
Garfield, Monarch, 38.5405525, -106.3141907
Garfield, Shavano, 38.6027747, -106.2903008
Mount Antero, Mount Princeton Hot Springs, 38.7330521, -106.1669631
Mount Ouray, Shirley, 38.4244426, -106.128352
Nathrop, Nathrop, 38.7472183, -106.0755712
Nathrop, Swan, 38.6799964, -106.0419591
Saint Elmo, Alpine, 38.7111077, -106.2769666
Saint Elmo, Hancock, 38.6402738, -106.3658582
Saint Elmo, Iron City, 38.7086072, -106.3380793
Saint Elmo, Romley, 38.6749959, -106.3700248
Saint Elmo, Saint Elmo, 38.7047182, -106.3480796
Saint Elmo, Stonewall, 38.6311072, -106.359747
Salida West, CMRS Airdrome Airport, 38.5413862, -106.1039059
Salida West, Salida Airport, 38.5191641, -106.0700158

Chaffee County

Unknown, Arbourville, 0, 0
Unknown, Babcock, 0, 0
Unknown, Bullion City, 0, 0
Unknown, Greens Gulch, 0, 0
Unknown, Hartsville, 0, 0
Unknown, Hartz, 0, 0
Unknown, Hortense, 0, 0
Unknown, Jennings, 0, 0

Grand Army of the Republic Posts

Torbert, No. 11, Chaffee, Poncha Springs
Joe Hutchinson, No. 18, Chaffee, Buena Vista
Phil Sheridan, No. 18, Chaffee, Buena Vista
Edwin M Stanton, No. 37, Chaffee, Salida, 1883

USGS Historic Military Places

None

Military Bases

None

Post Offices

Name	Established	Discontinued	ZIP
Alpine	1874 Oct 26	1904 June 30	
Antero	1895 Oct 5	1896 Apr 3	
Arbourville	1879 Sept 12	1881 Aug 15	
Arkansas	1880 June 16	1881 Mar 28	
Bath	1893 July 25	1904 July 28*	
Brown Canon	1904 Mar 9	1908 June 30	
Browns Canon	1888 May 8	1893 July 25	
Buena Vista	1879 Sept 18		81211
Calumet	1882 Jan 24	1885 Feb 9	
Carmel	1881 June 15	1882 Oct 26	
Centreville	1868 Apr 22	1930 Apr 30	
Chaffee	1879 June 6	1883 May 14	
Chalk Creek	1879 Aug 29	1880 Sept 8	
Cleora	1876 Dec 5	1882 Mar 7	
Cochem	1897 June 5	1899 May 8	
Columbus	1882 Apr 10	1884 Aug 11	
Conrow	1881 Aug 15	1882 Nov 9	
Cottonwood Springs	1879 July 28	1895 Nov 11*	
Divide	1874 June 24	1885 Aug 19	
Dolomite	1886 Oct 11	1890 Aug 27	
Dora	1906 Jan 10	1906 Nov 30	
Fisher	1889 Sept 12	1890 Aug 15	
Free Gold	1880 Apr 12	1881 Apr 6	
Garfield	1880 July 8	1911 Feb 28	

Historical Assets Colorado

Garfield 2	1911 Sept 9		
Granite	1868 Nov 30		
Hancock	1880 Sept 10	1904 Dec 31	
Helena	1866 Oct 16	1880 Mar 10	
Heywood	1884 June 20	1888 Feb 15	
Higgins	1890 Aug 27	1895 Apr 22*	
Hortense	1877 May 11	1907 Sept 14*	
Hummel	1882 Oct 3	1883 Oct 26	
Kraft	1882 Feb 14	1888 May 8	
Krain	1917 Mar 24	1919 June 14	
Mahonville	1876 Feb 28	1879 Sept 18	
Maysville	1879 July 28	1893 Dec 23	
Mears	1879 Sept 29	1888 Apr 25*	
Meily	1882 June 29	1885 June 16*	
Monarch	1883 May 14	1903 Nov 30	
Mount Princeton	1889 Sept 17	1899 June 19	
Mount Princeton Hot Springs	1926 Aug 21	1936 May 15	
Nathrop	1880 Sept 8		81236
Neva	1882 May 17	1882 Oct 6	
Newett	1895 Apr 22	1918 Aug 10*	
Poncha Springs	1924 Nov 22		81242
Poncho Springs	1877 Mar 13	1924 Nov 22*	
Riverside	1872 May 22	1905 June 19	
Romley	1886 Jan 15	1924 Oct 30*	
Saint Elmo	1880 June 23	1952 Oct 15	
Salida	1881 Mar 28		81201
Shavano	1880 Aug 4	1880 Nov 30	
Shavano 2	1930 Jan 4	1930 Sept 20	
Silverdale	1882 Jan 23	1882 May 25	
Skinner	1897 Feb 20	1899 Feb 1	
Sylvanite	1898 May 16	1898 July 28	
Turret	1898 Feb 28	1939 Oct 31*	
Vicksburgh	1881 May 3	1885 July 30	
Whitehorn	1897 July 22	1916 Nov 15	
Winfield	1881 July 5	1912 Sept 15	

Topo Quads

Buena Vista East	385230N	384500N	1060000W	1060730W
Buena Vista West	385230N	384500N	1060730W	1061500W
Maysville	383730N	383000N	1060730W	1061500W
Mount Antero	384500N	383730N	1060730W	1061500W
Nathrop	384500N	383730N	1060000W	1060730W
Poncha Pass	383000N	382230N	1060000W	1060730W
Saint Elmo	384500N	383730N	1061500W	1062230W
Salida East	383730N	383000N	1055230W	1060000W

Chaffee County

Salida West	383730N	383000N	1060000W	1060730W
Wellsville	383000N	382230N	1055230W	1060000W

Suggested Reading

Aldrich, John K. *Ghosts of Chaffee County: a Guide to the Ghost Towns and Mining Camps of Chaffee and Eastern Gunnison Counties, Colorado.* Lakewood, CO: Centennial Graphics, 2000.

Danielson, Kay Marnon. Chaffee County: the First 125 Years. Salida, CO: Greater Arkansas River Nature Association, 2004.

Danielson, Kay Marnon. *Salida, Colorado.* Chicago: Arcadia, 2002.

Dodge, Joseph V. *History of Old Lake County: Lake and Chaffee, Colorado Territory, Colorado State, 1800-1900.* Coal Creek, CO: Rocky Mountain Books, 1999.

Humbeutel, Lacy. *Nuggets from Chalk Creek.* Colorado Springs, CO: Century One Press, 1975.

Shaputis, June and Suzanne Kelly. *History of Chaffee County.* Buena Vista, CO: Buena Vista Heritage, 1982.

Swift, Kim Maurice. *Heart of the Rockies: A History of the Salida Area.* Colorado Springs, CO: Century One Press, 1980.

Vickers, W B and O L Baskin & Co. *History of the Arkansas Valley, Colorado; Illustrated.* Chicago: O L Baskin Historical Publishers, 1881.

Vinette, A. B*uena Vista and Tributary Mining Camps: A Sketch of the Mines of Cottonwood and La Plata Districts, Chaffee, County, Colorado.* Buena Vista, CO: Times Book and Job Rooms, 1882.

Historical Assets Colorado

Cheyenne County

Introduction

Established: 1889 Population: 1,836
Formed from: Bent, Elbert
Adjacent Counties: Kit Carson, Lincoln, Kiowa
County Seat: Cheyenne Wells
  Other Communities: Kit Carson, Arapahoe, Wild Horse
Website, http://www.co.cheyenne.co.us
Area Codes: 719
Zip Codes: 80802, 80810, 80825, 80862

Historical Assets Colorado

Cheyenne County Courthouse

Cheyenne County 19th Century Courthouse

Courthouses & County Government

Cheyenne County
http://www.co.cheyenne.co.us

Cheyenne County Courthouse (15th Judicial District), 51 S 1st St, Cheyenne Wells, CO 80810, 719-767-5649; http://www.courts.state.co.us/Courts/County/Index.cfm?County_ID=49

Assessor, 51 S 1st St, Cheyenne Wells, CO 80810, 719-767-5664; http://www.co.cheyenne.co.us/countydepartments/assessor.htm

Board of County Commissioners, 51 S 1st St E, Cheyenne Wells, CO 80810, 719-767-5872, http://www.co.cheyenne.co.us/electedofficials.htm

Clerk & Recorder, 51 S 1st St, Cheyenne Wells, CO 80810, 719-767-5685; http://www.co.cheyenne.co.us/countydepartments/clerkandrecorder.htm

Coroner, P.O. Box 297, Cheyenne Wells, CO 80810, 719-342-0187; http://www.co.cheyenne.co.us/countydepartments/countycoroner.htm

Public Health, 560 W 6 N, Cheyenne Wells, CO 80810, 719-767-5616; http://www.co.cheyenne.co.us/countydepartments/publichealth.htm

Transportation (Road & Bridge), 51 S 1st St, Cheyenne Wells, CO 80810, 719-767-5872; http://www.co.cheyenne.co.us/countydepartments/roadandbridge.htm

Treasurer, 51 S 1st St, Cheyenne Wells, CO 80810, 719-767-5657; http://www.co.cheyenne.co.us/countydepartments/Treasurer.htm

County Records

Birth 1910	Marriage 1906	Divorce 1920
Death 1911	Land 1906	Probate 1920
Court 1920		

Early birth and death records were kept by the Vital Records Office
CSA Birth 1893
CSA Death 1893
CSA Delayed Birth Certificates 1965

Cheyenne County

County & Municipal Records Held at the State Level

The Colorado State Archives

Physical Records	Records on Film	Records on Master Film
Assessor	Assessor	Assessor
Clerk & Recorder	Clerk & Recorder	Clerk & Recorder
Social Services		Treasurer
WPA Historical Records		
WPA Religious Institutions Survey		
WPA Cheyenne Wells		

The Denver Public Library
WWI Draft Registration Cards (microfilm)

School Districts

School Districts, http://www.adcogov.org/local-school-districts
Cheyenne County School District, 301 N 5th St W, Cheyenne Wells, CO 80810, 719-767-5866; https://www.cheyennesd.net/

Historic School Districts

1. Kit Carson
2. Cheyenne Wells
3. First View
4. Waterville
5. Arapahoe
6. Ardrey
7. Pfost
8. Wild Horse
9. Aroya
10. [1896]
11. [1901]
12. [1896]
13.
14. [1896]
15.
16.
17.
18.
19. [1896]

Fraternal Organizations

Granges
Kit Carson, No. 226, Cheyenne, Kit Carson, 4 Apr 1914

Masons

Ancient Free & Accepted Masons
Cheyenne Wells, No. 132, Cheyenne, Cheyenne Wells, 21 Sept 1909

Royal Arch Masons
None

Knights Templar
None

Eastern Star
Cheyenne Wells, No. 110, Cheyenne, Cheyenne Wells

Odd Fellows
Ivanhoe, No. 100, Cheyenne, Cheyenne Wells
Ivanhoe, No. 153, Cheyenne, Cheyenne Wells
Cheyenne Wells, No. 153, Cheyenne, Cheyenne Wells

Historical Assets Colorado

Rebekahs
Prairie Queen, No. 44, Cheyenne, Cheyenne Wells

Knights of Pythias
Sherman, No. 67, Cheyenne, Cheyenne Wells

Pythian Sisters
None

Benevolent Protective Order of Elks
None

City & Town Halls

Cheyenne Wells, 151 S 1st St W, Cheyenne Wells, CO 80810, 719-767-8985, http://townofcheyennewells.com/

Kit Carson, P.O. Box 376, Kit Carson, CO 80825, 719-962-3248, http://kitcarsoncolorado.com

Archives & Manuscript Collections

None

Historical & Genealogical Societies

Eastern Colorado Historical Society, Old Jail Museum, 85 W 2nd St, P.O. Box 771, Cheyenne Wells, CO 80810, (719) 767-5907, https://www.facebook.com/EasternColoradoHistoricalSociety/

Kit Carson Historical Society, Historical Museum, 202 W Hwy 287, P.O. Box 67, Kit Carson, CO 80825, (719) 962-3306, https://www.colorado.com/history-museums/kit-carson-museum

Local Libraries

Cheyenne Wells Public Library, 151 S 1st West St, PO Box 939, Cheyenne Wells, CO 80810-0939, 719-767-5138, https://eastcheyenne.biblionix.com/catalog/

Links

CO GenWeb
http://cogenweb.com/cheyenne/

Cyndi's List
https://www.cyndislist.com/us/co/counties/cheyenne/

FamilySearch Wiki
https://www.familysearch.org/wiki/en/Cheyenne_County,_Colorado_Genealogy

Linkpendium
http://www.linkpendium.com/cheyenne-co-genealogy/

RootsWeb Wiki
https://wiki.rootsweb.com/wiki/index.php/Cheyenne_County,_Colorado

Wikipedia
https://en.wikipedia.org/wiki/Cheyenne_County,_Colorado

Cheyenne County

Historic Hotels
None

Museums & Historic Sites
Eastern Colorado Historical Society, Old Jail Museum, 85 W 2nd St, P.O. Box 771, Cheyenne Wells, CO 80810, (719) 767-5907, https://www.facebook.com/Eastern-ColoradoHistoricalSociety/

Kit Carson Historical Society, Historical Museum, 202 W Hwy 287, P.O. Box 67, Kit Carson, CO 80825, (719) 962-3306, https://www.colorado.com/history-museums/kit-carson-museum

Mountain States Telephone & Telegraph Museum, 60 S 1st St, Cheyenne Wells, CO 80810, (719) 767-5865, https://www.colorado.com/museums/mountain-states-telephone-and-telegraph-museum

Special Events & Scenic Locations
Cheyenne County's Tumbleweed Fair & Rodeo takes place in July most years. Cheyenne County Fairgrounds, W 6th St W, Cheyenne Wells, CO 80810, https://cheyenne.extension.colostate.edu/cheyenne-county-fair-rodeo/

Old Military Trail (Fort Wallace, KS to Fort Lyon, CO)
Omaha Trail
Smoky Hill Trail
Texas-Montana Cattle Trail

Ghost Towns & Other Sparsely Populated Places
Arapahoe, Arena, Aroya, Ascalon, Chemung, First View, Kanorado, Kit Carson, Namouna, Sorrento, Wild Horse

Newspapers
Cheyenne Republican. (Cheyenne Wells, Cheyenne County, Colo.) 1???-1913
Cheyenne Wells Record. (Cheyenne Wells, Cheyenne County, Colo.) 1???-1969
Cheyenne Wells Gazette. (Cheyenne Wells, Bent County, Colo.) 1887-1???
Raisor's Pointer. (Cheyenne Wells, Colo.) 1888-1???
Weekly Herald. (Cheyenne Wells, Colo.) 1889-1???
Kit Carson Herald. (Kit Carson, Cheyenne County, Colo.) 19??-19??
The Wild Horse Times. (Wild Horse, Cheyenne County, Colo.) 19??-1919
Eastern Colorado Times. (Cheyenne Wells, Colo.) 1912-1913
The Cheyenne County News. (Cheyenne Wells, Cheyenne County, Colo.) 1913-19??
Cheyenne Record. (Cheyenne Wells, Cheyenne County, Colo.) 1913-19??
The Range Ledger And The Cheyenne Wells Record. (Cheyenne Wells, Colo.) 1969-Current

Historical Assets Colorado

Places on the National Register
Cheyenne Wells, Cheyenne County Courthouse, 51 S. 1st St.
Cheyenne Wells, Cheyenne County Jail, 85 W. Second St.
Dumont, Dumont School, 150 Co. Rd. 260

USGS Historic Places
None

Grand Army of the Republic Posts
None

USGS Historic Military Places
None

Military Bases
None

Post Offices

Arapahoe	1906 May 5		80802
Arena	1910 May 2	1923 Apr 30	
Aroya	1889 Sept 17	1965 Mar 26	
Chemung	1906 Dec 22	1910 Aug 15	
Cheyenne Wells 2	1895 Oct 2		80810
Firstview	1907 June 25	1961 Nov 24	
Kit Carson	1869 Dec 29	1881 May 17	
Kit Carson	1882 Feb 14		80825
Medill	1910 Dec 1	1920 May 15	
Mount Pearl	1911 July 27	1923 Jan 31	
Pilot	1899 Sept 11	1903 Sept 30*	
Sorrento	1907 July 29	1918 Feb 14	
Wild Horse	1877 Jan 5	1877 May 25	
Wild Horse 2	1904 Apr 13		80862

Topo Quads

Arapahoe	385230N	384500N	1020730W	1021500W
Arapahoe NW	390000N	385230N	1020730W	1021500W
Arsenic Lake	384500N	383730N	1025230W	1030000W
Arsenic Lake SW	383730N	383000N	1025230W	1030000W
Big Spring	390000N	385230N	1024500W	1025230W
Cheyenne Wells	385230N	384500N	1021500W	1022230W
Cheyenne Wells NE	390000N	385230N	1021500W	1022230W
Cheyenne Wells NW	390000N	385230N	1022230W	1023000W
Cheyenne Wells SW	385230N	384500N	1022230W	1023000W
Dunlap Ranch	383730N	383000N	1024500W	1025230W
East of Lewis Lake	384500N	383730N	1023730W	1024500W

Cheyenne County

Eureka Creek North	390000N	385230N	1023730W	1024500W
Eureka Creek South	385230N	384500N	1023730W	1024500W
Firstview	385230N	384500N	1023000W	1023730W
Galatea	383730N	383000N	1030000W	1030730W
Galatea NE	384500N	383730N	1030000W	1030730W
Kit Carson	385230N	384500N	1024500W	1025230W
Kit Carson NW	390000N	385230N	1025230W	1030000W
Lake Albert	383730N	383000N	1020730W	1021500W
Lake Albert NW	384500N	383730N	1020730W	1021500W
Landsman Hill	390000N	385230N	1023000W	1023730W
Lewis Lake	384500N	383730N	1024500W	1025230W
North of Brandon	383730N	383000N	1022230W	1023000W
North of Chivington	383730N	383000N	1023000W	1023730W
North of Sheridan Lake	383730N	383000N	1021500W	1022230W
Oswald Ranch	383730N	383000N	1023730W	1024500W
Sanders Ranch	390000N	385230N	1030000W	1030730W
Sorrento	385230N	384500N	1025230W	1030000W
South Ladder Creek	384500N	383730N	1022230W	1023000W
South of Cheyenne Wells	384500N	383730N	1021500W	1022230W
South of Firstview	384500N	383730N	1023000W	1023730W
Wild Horse	385230N	384500N	1030000W	1030730W

Suggested Reading

Blevins, Terry W. *Our Heritage: a Collection of Tales of East Central Colorado.* Stratton, CO: East Central Council of Local Governments, 1983.

Cheyenne County History. Cheyenne Wells, CO: Eastern Colorado Historical Society, 1979.

Homesteaders and Other Early Settlers, 1900-1930, Western Cheyenne County, Colorado. NL: Kit Carson Historical SOciety, 1985.

Sterns, Betty J. *The War Years and the Veterans of Cheyenne-Kowa County, Colorado.* Dallas: Curtis Media, 1995.

Historical Assets Colorado

Clear Creek County

Introduction

Established: 1861   Population: 9,088

Formed from: Original

Adjacent Counties: Jefferson, Gilpin, Park, Summit, Grand

County Seat: Georgetown

Other Communities: Idaho Springs, Empire, Silver Plume, Downieville, Lawson, Dumont, Floyd Hill, St Mary's, Upper Bear Creek

Website, https://www.clearcreekcounty.us

Area Codes: 303, 720

Zip Codes: 80436, 80438, 80444, 80452, 80476

Historical Assets Colorado

Clear Creek County Courthouse

Clear Creek County Courthouse built 1868

Courthouses & County Government

Clear Creek County
https://www.co.clear-creek.co.us
Clear Creek County Courthouse (5th Judicial District), 405 Argentine St, Georgetown, CO 80444, 303-679-4220; http://www.courts.state.co.us/Courts/County/Index.cfm?County_ID=8
Assessor, 405 Argentine St, Georgetown, CO 80444, 303-679-2322; http://www.co.clear-creek.co.us/index.aspx?nid=188
Board of County Commissioners, 405 Argentine St, Georgetown, CO 80444, 303-679-2312, https://www.clearcreekcounty.us
Clerk & Recorder, 405 Argentine St, Georgetown, CO 80444, 303-679-2339; http://www.co.clear-creek.co.us/index.aspx?nid=104
Coroner, P.O. Box 2037, Idaho Springs, CO 80452, 970-409-2720; https://www.co.clear-creek.co.us/index.aspx?nid=134
Public Health, 1531 Colorado Blvd, Idaho Springs, CO 80452, 303-670-7540; http://www.co.clear-creek.co.us/index.aspx?nid=637
Transportation (Road & Bridge), 3549 County Rd 312, Dumont, CO 80436, 303-679-2334; https://www.co.clear-creek.co.us/index.aspx?nid=128
Treasurer, 405 Argentine St, Georgetown, CO 80444, 303-679-2353; http://www.co.clear-creek.co.us/index.aspx?NID=193

County Records

Birth Unk	Marriage 1882	Divorce 1862
Death Unk	Land 1862	Probate 1862
Court 1862		

Clear Creek County

County & Municipal Records Held at the State Level

The Colorado State Archives

Physical Records
Clerk & Recorder
County Court
District Court
Justice Court
Treasurer
WPA Historical Records
WPA Religious Institutions
   Survey
WPA Georgetown
Cities
   Georgetown
   Idaho Springs
   Silver Plume

Records on Film
Clerk & Recorder
Cities
Georgetown
Silver Plume

Records on Master Film
Clerk & Recorder
County Court
District Court
Combined Courts
County Commissioners
School Districts
Sheriff
Cities
   Georgetown
   Idaho Springs
   Silver Plume

The Denver Public Library

Abstract Ledger, 1862-1864
Argo Mine Letter, 1886
Atlantic-Pacific Railway Tunnel Company Records, 1881-1896
Baker & Franklin Mines Records, 1866-1876
Big Five Mining Companies Records, 1892-1921
Board of Selectmen Records, 1868-1874
Board of Trustees Minutes, 1882-1883
Clear Creek County, Colorado Mining Companies Records, 1862-1940
Clear Creek County Records, 1861-1933
Clear Creek Placer & Mining Company Records, 1925-1929
Colorado Theatre Program Collection, 1900-
Commonwealth Power & Electric Company Records, 1907-1913
Consolidated Seaton Mountain Mining Company Letters, 1882
Fulton Gold Mining Company Records, 1865-1915
Georgetown & Breckenridge Wagon Road Company Records, 1867
Maumee Gold Mining Company Records, 1909-1910
Pay Rock Silver Mines Records, 1891-1900
Radium Hot Springs Records, 1924-1930
Republican Mountain Silver Mines Letters, 1896-1899
Silver Spring Mining Company Records, 1860-1866
Stevens Mining Company Letter Books, 1875-1884
Syndicated Rocky Mountain Water Users Records, 1935
Theatre Programmes Scrapbooks, 1896-1913
Whale Mining & Milling Company Correspondence, 1894
Yates House Records, 1879
WWI Draft Registration Cards (microfilm)

Historical Assets Colorado

School Districts
School Districts, http://www.adcogov.org/local-school-districts
Clear Creek School District RE-1, P.O. Box 3399, Idaho Springs, CO 80452, 303-567-3850; http://www.ccsdre1.org/

Historic School Districts

1. Empire
2. Beaver Brook
3. Georgetown
4. Dumont
5. Idaho Springs
6. Silver Plume
7. Silver Dale
8. Silver Creek
9. Lamartine
10. Lawson
11. Brookvale
12. Freeland
13.
14. Brownville
15. [1882]
16. [1885]
17. [1885]
18. [1885]
19. Alice

Fraternal Organizations

Granges
None

Masons

Ancient Free & Accepted Masons
Empire, No. 8, Clear Creek, Empire City, 6 Nov 1865
Washington, No. 12, Clear Creek, Georgetown, 7 Oct 1867
Georgetown, No. 12, Clear Creek, Georgetown, 13 Apr 1916
Idaho Springs, No. 26, Clear Creek, Idaho Springs, 21 Sept 1875
Georgetown, No. 48, Clear Creek, Georgetown, 20 Sept 1882

Royal Arch Masons
Georgetown, No. 4, Clear Creek, Georgetown
Idaho Springs, No. 30, Clear Creek, Idaho Springs

Knights Templar
Georgetown Commandery, No. 4, Clear Creek, Georgetown, 1880 Jan 24
Crusader Commandery, No. 29, Clear Creek, Idaho Springs, 1903 Nov 16

Eastern Star
Georgetown, No. 42, Clear Creek, Georgetown
Idaho Springs, No. 51, Clear Creek, Idaho Springs

Odd Fellows
Georgetown, No. 5, Clear Creek, Georgetown, 1868 Mar 27
Harmony, No. 18, Clear Creek, Georgetown
Silver Plume, No. 25, Clear Creek, Silver Plume
Wildey, No. 33, Clear Creek, Idaho Springs, 1879 Oct 30
Ridgely, No. 50, Clear Creek, Freeland
Empire, No. 119, Clear Creek, Empire

Rebekahs
None

Knights of Pythias
Columbian, No. 7, Clear Creek, Georgetown, 1876 Feb 23
Clear Creek, No. 9, Clear Creek, Silver Plume

Clear Creek County

Idaho, No. 13, Clear Creek, Idaho Springs
Georgetown, No. 17, Clear Creek, Georgetown

Pythian Sisters
May, No. 22, Clear Creek, Idaho Springs
Free Coinage, No. 24, Clear Creek, Silver Plume

Benevolent Protective Order of Elks
Idaho Springs, No. 607, Clear Creek, Idaho Springs

City & Town Halls

Georgetown, 404 6th St, Georgetown, CO 80444, 303-569-2555, http://www.townof-georgetown.us

Idaho Springs, 1711 Miner St, Idaho Springs, CO 80452, 303-567-4421, https://www.colorado.gov/idahosprings

Empire, 30 Park Ave, Empire, CO 80438, 303-569-2978, http://www.empirecolorado.us

Silver Plume, 710 Main St, Silver Plume, 80476, 303-569-2363, https://www.silver-plumeco.com

Archives & Manuscript Collections

Clear Creek County Archives, 405 Argentine St, P.O. Box 2000, Georgetown, CO 80444, (303) 670-7531, https://www.co.clear-creek.co.us/187/Archives-Records

Historical & Genealogical Societies

Alvarado Cemetery Association, P.O. Box 98, Idaho Springs, CO 80452

Historic Georgetown, Hamill House Museum, 305 Argentine, P.O. Box 667, Georgetown, CO 80444, (303) 569-2840, http://www.historicgeorgetown.org

Historical Society of Idaho Springs, 2060 Miner St, P.O. Box 1318, Idaho Springs, CO 80452, (303) 567-4382, http://www.historicidahosprings.com

Local Libraries

John Tomay Memorial Library-Georgetown Library, 605 6th St, P.O. Box 338, Georgetown, CO 80444-0338, (303) 569-2620, https://cccld.org

Idaho Springs Public Library, 219 14th Ave, P.O. Box 1509, Idaho Springs, CO 80452, (303) 567-2020, https://cccld.org

Links

CO GenWeb
http://stanwyck.com/CCGilpin/

Cyndi's List
https://www.cyndislist.com/us/co/counties/clear-creek/

FamilySearch Wiki
https://www.familysearch.org/wiki/en/Clear_Creek_County,_Colorado_Genealogy

Linkpendium
http://www.linkpendium.com/clear_creek-co-genealogy/

Historical Assets Colorado

RootsWeb Wiki
https://wiki.rootsweb.com/wiki/index.php/Clear_Creek_County,_Colorado

Wikipedia
https://en.wikipedia.org/wiki/Clear_Creek_County,_Colorado

Historic Hotels
None

Museums & Historic Sites
Argo Gold Mine & Mill Museum, 2350 Riverside Dr, P.O. Box 1990, Idaho Springs, CO 80452, (303) 567-2421, https://argomilltour.com

Bowman White House Museum, 901 Rose St, Georgetown, CO 80444, (303) 569-3489, https://www.historicgeorgetown.org

Clear Creek Historic Mining & Milling Museum, 23rd Ave & Riverside, P.O. Box 1498, Idaho Springs, CO 80452, (303) 567-2421, https://www.facebook.com/pages/Clear-Creek-Historic-Mining-And-Milling-Museum/474345336079887

George Rowe Museum at the Schoolhouse, 905 Main St, Silver Plume, CO 80476, (303) 569-2562, https://www.facebook.com/GeorgeRoweMuseum

Georgetown Energy Museum, 600 Griffith St, P.O. Box 398, Georgetown, CO 80444, (303) 204-9873, http://www.georgetownenergymuseum.org

Georgetown Loop Historic Mining & Railroad Museum, 646 Loop Dr, P.O. Box 249, Georgetown, CO 80444, (888) 456-6777, http://www.georgetownlooprr.com

Hotel de Paris Museum, 409 6th Ave, P.O. Box 746, Georgetown, CO 80444, (303) 569-2311, http://www.hoteldeparismuseum.org

Historic Georgetown, Hamill House Museum, 305 Argentine, P.O. Box 667, Georgetown, CO 80444, (303) 569-2840, http://www.historicgeorgetown.org

James Underhill Museum & Victorian Garden, 1416 Miner St, P.O. Box 1318, Idaho Springs, CO 80452, (303) 567-2020, http://historicidahosprings.com/museums/

Special Events & Scenic Locations
Idaho Springs hosts the annual Dynamite Days festival in September, https://clearcreekcounty.org/events/dynamite-days/2020-09-26/

Georgetown hosts an annual Christmas Market weekends throughout December, https://www.historicgeorgetown.org/christmas-events.html

Clear Creek County keeps a list of events here: https://clearcreekcounty.org/events/

Pike National Forest
Roosevelt National Forest
James Peak Wilderness
Mount Evans Wilderness
American Discovery Trail
Continental Divide National Scenic Trail
Grays Peak National Recreation Trail
Mount Evans National Recreation Trail
Guanella Pass Scenic Byway
Mount Evans Scenic Byway

Clear Creek County

Georgetown Loop Historic Mining and Railroad Park
Georgetown-Silver Plume National Historic District

Ghost Towns & Other Sparsely Populated Places

94 (Ninety-Four), Alice (Yorktown), Bakerville, Bonito, Brookvale, East Idaho Springs, Empire, Fall River, Floyd Hill, Freeland (Trail Creek Camp), Gilson Gulch, Graymount, Hall's, Kohinoor, Lamartine, Lawson, Lebanon, North Empire (Upper Empire), Red Elephant, Silver Creek (Daileyville, Chinn City), Silver Dale, Silver Plume, Spanish Bar, Waldorf, Yankee (Yankee Hill)

Newspapers

Daily Courier. (Georgetown, Colo.) 18??-18??
The Colorado Miner. (Georgetown, Colo.) 1867-1888
The Colorado Miner. (Georgetown, Colo.) 1869-1869
Daily Colorado Miner. (Georgetown [Colo.]) 1872-1874
The Idaho Springs Reporter. (Idaho Springs, Colo.) 1872-1872
The Centennial. (Georgetown, Colo.) 1876-1???
Georgetown Courier. (Georgetown, Colo.) 1877-1957
Idaho Springs Advance. (Idaho Springs, Clear Creek County, Colo.) 1880-1???
The Silver Plume Coloradoan. (Silver Plume, Colo.) 1881-1884
Silver Plume Mining News. (Silver Plume, Clear Creek County, Colo.) 1881-1???
Colorado Mining Gazette. (Idaho Springs, Colo.) 1882-1901
The Idaho Springs News. (Idaho Springs, Clear Creek County, Colo.) 1883-1905
The Silver Standard. (Silver Plume, Colo.) 1885-1907
Colorado Jack Rabbit. (Silver Plume, Colo.) 1885-1885
The Arbitrator. (Georgetown, Colo.) 1886-1???
The Georgetown Miner. (Georgetown, Colo.) 1890-1891
The Colorado Miner. (Georgetown, Colo.) 1891-1???
Clear Creek Reporter. (Idaho Springs, Clear Creek County, Colo.) 1892-1???
The Idaho Springs Iris. (Idaho Springs, Clear Creek County, Colo.) 1892-1892
The Georgetown Herald. (Georgetown, Colo.) 1899-1902
Idaho Springs Siftings. (Idaho Springs, Colo.) 1900-1905
Gold Rush Gazette. (Idaho Springs, Colo.) 19??-19??
The Idaho Springs Mining Gazette. (Idaho Springs, Colo.) 1901-19??
Empire True Fissure. (Empire, Colo.) 1901-19??
Clear Creek Topics. (Georgetown, Colo.) 1902-19??
Clear Creek Democrat. (Georgetown, Colo.) 1904-19??
The Idaho Springs Siftings-News. (Idaho Springs, Colo.) 1905-19??
Clear Creek Miner. (Idaho Springs, Colo.) 1910-19??
The Clear Creek Mining Journal. (Idaho Springs, Colo.) 1924-19??
The Clear Creek Mining Journal-Gazette. (Idaho Springs, Colo.) 1927-19??
The Clear Creek Mining Journal. (Idaho Springs, Colo.) 1933-1968
The Front Range Journal. (Idaho Springs And Central City, Colo.) 1968-198?
Georgetown Crucible. (Georgetown, Colo.) 1970-1970
The Clear Creek Courant. (Georgetown, Colo.) 1973-1982

Historical Assets Colorado

The Clear Creek Courant & Evergreen Today. (Idaho Springs, Colo.) 1982-1984
The Clear Creek Courant. (Idaho Springs, Colo.) 1984-Current

Places on the National Register
Dumont, Mill City House, 247 Co. Rd. 308
Empire, Mint Saloon, 13 E. Park Ave. (US 40)
Empire, Peck House, 83 Sunny Ave.
Evergreen, Evans, Anne, Mountain Home, Address Restricted
Georgetown, Alpine Hose Company No. 2, 507 5th St.
Georgetown, Georgetown Loop Railroad, Runs between Georgetown and Silver Plume
Georgetown, Grace Episcopal Church, Taos St., between 4th and 5th Sts.
Georgetown, Hamill House, Argentine and 3rd Sts.
Georgetown, Hotel de Paris, Alpine St.
Georgetown, McClellan House, 919 Taos St.
Georgetown, Ore Processing Mill and Dam, 1 mi. SW of Georgetown off I-70
Georgetown, Toll House, S side of Georgetown adjacent to I-70
Georgetown-Silver Plume, Georgetown-Silver Plume Historic District, I-70
Idaho Springs, Argo Tunnel and Mill, 2517 Riverside Dr.
Idaho Springs, Bryan Hose House, Jct. of Illinois and Virginia Sts.
Idaho Springs, Echo Lake Park, Along CO 103 and CO 5 SW of Idaho Springs
Idaho Springs, Evans-Elbert Ranch, Upper Bear Creek Rd.
Idaho Springs, Hose House No. 2, 600 Colorado Blvd.
Idaho Springs, Idaho Springs Downtown Commercial District, Roughly bounded by Center Alley, 14th Ave., Riverside Dr., and Idaho St.
Idaho Springs, Methodist Episcopal Church, 1414 Colorado Blvd.
Idaho Springs, Miner Street Bridge, Miner St.
Idaho Springs, Summit Lake Park, Mt. Evans Rd., SW of Idaho Springs
Silver Plume, Lebanon and Everett Mine Tunnels, NE of Silver Plume, adjacent to I-70 right-of-way
Silver Plume, Silver Plume Depot, Off I-70

USGS Historic Places
Central City, Yankee, 39.8263763, -105.6238902
Empire, Ninetyfour, 39.8274874, -105.6363907
Georgetown, Silverdale, 39.6916541, -105.6961153
Unknown, Waldorf Post Office, 0, 0

Grand Army of the Republic Posts
Thornburg No. 2, Clear Creek, Georgetown
E D Baker, No. 30, Clear Creek, Idaho Springs

USGS Historic Military Places
None

Clear Creek County

Military Bases
None

Post Offices

Alice	1898 Aug 20	1938 Dec 31*	
Belford	1884 Mar 7	1884 Aug 11	
Brookvale	1876 July 24	1942 Apr 30*	
Brownsville	1871 Apr 7	1875 Dec 1	
Dumont	1880 May 17		80436
East Argentine	1867 Aug 26	1867 Nov 15	
Elephant	1881 June 28	1881 Nov 7	
Empire	1886 May 7		80438
Empire City	1861 June 28	1886 May 7	
Floyd Hill	1912 Sept 9	1937 June 30	
Freeland	189 Jan 16	1908 Sept 15	
Georgetown	1866 June 19		80444
Graymont	1884 May 19	1884 Oct 16	
Hukill	1879 May 12	1880 May 10	
Idaho	1862 Mar 22	1876 Apr 7	
Idaho Springs	1876 Sept 18		80452
Lamartine	1889 Nov 27		
Lawson	1877 June 29	1966 Aug 31	
Lombard	1914 Dec 30	1919 July 15	
Marshallpark	1902 July 25	1903 Nov 14	
Mill City	1861 July 5	1879 May 26*	
Red Elephant	1878 Dec 19	1881 Apr 22	
Silver Plume	1875 Dec 1	1896 Jan	
Silverplume	1896 Jan		80476
Spanish Bar	1860 Dec 13	1886 July 9	
Waldorf	1906 Oct 5	1912 Feb 29	
Yankee	1893 Nov 2	1910 Feb 28	
Yates	1882 Sept 4	1883 Feb 8	

Topo Quads

Georgetown	394500N	393730N	1053730W	1054500W
Harris Park	393730N	393000N	1053000W	1053730W
Idaho Springs	394500N	393730N	1053000W	1053730W
Meridian Hill	393730N	393000N	1052230W	1053000W
Mount Evans	393730N	393000N	1053730W	1054500W
Willow Creek Ranch	400000N	395230N	1020000W	1020730W

Suggested Reading

Aldrich, John K. *Ghosts of Clear Creek County: a Guide to the Ghost Towns and Mining Camps of Clear Creek County, Colorado.* Lakewood, CO: Centennial Graphics, 1992.

Historical Assets Colorado

Annals of Clear Creek County, Colorado. NL: NP, 1911.

Cushman, Samuel. *The Mines of Clear Creek County, Colorado*. Denver: Times Steam Printing House, 1876.

Dugan, Ben M. *Mines of Clear Creek County*. Charleston, SC: Arcadia Publishing, 2013.

Gaffney, Hank. *Visiting Clear Creek County's Interesting Past*. Dumont, CO: H Gaffney, 1987.

History of Clear Creek and Boulder Valleys, Colorado. Chicago: O L Baskin & Co, 1880.

History of Clear Creek County: Tailings, Tracks & Tommyknockers. Denver: Historical Society of Idaho Springs, 2004.

Lewis, Allan C. *Colorado & Southern Railway: Clear Creek Narrow Gauge*. Charleston, SC: Arcadia Pub, 2004.

Pioneer History: *Clear Creek County, Colorado*. Lakewood, CO: Foothills Genealogical Society of Colorado, 1994.

Conejos County

Introduction
Established: 1861   Population: 8,256
Formed from: Original
Adjacent Counties: Rio Grande, Alamosa, Costilla, Archuleta
County Seat: Conejos
  Other Communities: Antonito, La Jara, Manassa, Romeo, Sanford, Capulin
Website, https://www.conejoscounty.org
Area Codes: 719
Zip Codes: 81120, 81124, 81129, 81140, 81141, 81148, 81151

Historical Assets Colorado

Conejos County Courthouse

Old Conejos County Courthouse in Antonito

Courthouses & County Government

Conejos County
https://www.conejoscounty.org
Conejos County Courthouse (12th Judicial District), 6683 County Rd 13, Conejos, CO 81129, 719-376-5465; http://www.courts.state.co.us/Courts/County/Index.cfm?County_ID=33
Assessor, 6683 County Rd 13, Conejos, CO 81129, 719-376-5585; http://www.conejoscounty.org/Webpages/assesshome.html
Board of County Commissioners, 6683 CO 13, Conejos, CO 81129, 719-376-5654, https://www.conejoscounty.org/departments/elected/commissioners
Clerk & Recorder, 6683 County Rd 13, Conejos, CO 81129, 719-376-5422; http://www.conejoscounty.org/Webpages/crhome.html
Coroner, P.O. Box 447, Manassa, CO 81141, 719-843-5815; https://www.conejoscounty.org/departments/elected/coroner
Public Health, 19023 State Hwy 285 S, La Jara, CO 81140, 719-274-4307; http://www.conejoscounty.org/Webpages/nursingservices.html
Schools; https://www.conejoscounty.org/departments/community/school
Transportation (Road & Bridge), 6683 County Rd 13, Conejos, CO 81129, 719-376-5772 x4; https://www.conejoscounty.org/departments/business/roadbridge
Treasurer, 6683 County Rd 13, Conejos, CO 81129, 719-376-5919; http://www.conejoscounty.org/Webpages/Treasurer.html

County Records

Birth 1877	Marriage 1940	Divorce 1889
Death 1918	Land 1900	Probate 1900
Court 1862		

CSA has Naturalization records from 1882

Conejos County

County & Municipal Records Held at the State Level

The Colorado State Archives

Physical Records
Clerk & Recorder
County Commissioners
County Court
District Court
Sheriff
WPA Historical Records
WPA Religious Institutions Survey

Records on Film
1885 Census
County Commissioners
County Court
District Court
School Districts

Records on Master Film
Clerk & Recorder
District Court
School Districts

The Denver Public Library
Colorado Deeds, 1868-1911
Petition from Public Officers and Other Loyal Citizens, 1864
WPA Historical Records Survey
WWI Draft Registration Cards (microfilm)

School Districts

School Districts, http://www.adcogov.org/local-school-districts
North Conejos School District RE1-J, 7889 US Hwy 285, La Jara, CO 81140, 719-274-5178; https://www.northconejos.com/
Sanford School District, 1 West St, Sanford, CO 81151, 719-274-5167; https://www.sanfordschools.org/

Historic School Districts

1. La Jara
2. Lobatos
3. San Antone
4. Las Mesitas
5. Morgan
6. Sanford
7. Conejos
8. Los Sauses
9. Fox Creek
10. Antonio
11. Los Cerritos
12. El Brazo
13. Capulin
14. Ortiz
15. Excelsior, Norton [Joint with Alamosa]
16. La Isla, Paine
17. Carmel [Joint with Alamosa]
18. Gomez
19. [1889]
20. [1889]
21. [1889]
22. San Antonio
23. [1890]
24. Star [Joint with Alamosa]
25. Espinoza
26. San Rafael
27. Mogote, Canyon
28. Romeo
29. Hot Creek
30. Manassa
31.
32. North Terrace
33.
34.
35. South Terrace
36. La Florida
37. Victoria

Fraternal Organizations

Granges
None

Historical Assets Colorado

Masons
Ancient Free & Accepted Masons
None
Royal Arch Masons
None
Knights Templar
None
Eastern Star
None
Odd Fellows
Antonito, No. 63, Conejos, Antonito
Rebekahs
None
Knights of Pythias
La Jara, No. 42, Conejos, La Jara, 1888 Oct 15
Pythian Sisters
Nomne
Benevolent Protective Order of Elks
None

City & Town Halls
Conejos (shared with Conejos County)
Antonito, 515 River St, Antonito, CO 81120, 719-376-2355
La Jara, 221 Broadway St, La Jara, CO 81140, 719-274-5363, https://www.colorado.gov/townoflajara
Manassa, 401 Main St, Manassa, CO 81141, 719-843-5207

Archives & Manuscript Collections
None

Historical & Genealogical Societies
None

Local Libraries
Conejos County Library, 17703 US Hwy 285, La Jara, CO 81140, (719) 274-5858, https://conejos.colibraries.org
Antonito Library, 201 Main St, Antonito, CO 81120

Links
CO GenWeb
http://cogenweb.com/conejos/
Cyndi's List
https://www.cyndislist.com/us/co/counties/conejos/

Conejos County

FamilySearch Wiki
https://www.familysearch.org/wiki/en/Conejos_County,_Colorado_Genealogy

Linkpendium
http://www.linkpendium.com/conejos-co-genealogy/

RootsWeb Wiki
https://wiki.rootsweb.com/wiki/index.php/Conejos_County,_Colorado

Wikipedia
https://en.wikipedia.org/wiki/Conejos_County,_Colorado

Historic Hotels

None

Museums & Historic Sites

Conejos County Museum, 5045 US Hwy 285, P.O. Box 829, Antonito, CO 81120, (719) 580-4070, https://www.museumtrail.org/conejos-county-museum.html

Jack Dempsey Museum, 412 Main St, P.O. Box 130, Manassa, CO 81141, (719) 843-5207, https://www.museumtrail.org/jack-dempsey-museum.html

Sanford Colorado History Museum, 778 Main St, Sanford, CO 81151, (719) 274-4382, https://www.museumtrail.org/sanford-museum.html

Special Events & Scenic Locations

I did not find information about a Conejos County Fair, although they do have a fairgrounds complex where events take place. Conejos County Arena Complex, 17705 US Hwy 285, La Jara, CO 81140, 719-274-0189

Old Spanish National Historic Trail
Pike's Stockade
Continental Divide National Scenic Trail
Los Caminos Antiguos Scenic and Historic Byway

Ghost Towns & Other Sparsely Populated Places

Catherin, Cockrell, Conejos, Cumbres, Henry, La Sauses, Los Cerritos, Los Sauches, Manassas Station, Ortiz, Osier, Platoro, San Rafael, Sanford, Stunner, Sublette, Sunflower

Newspapers

Alamosa Journal. (Alamosa, Colo.) 1884-1885
The Alamosa Independent-Journal. (Alamosa, Colo.) 1885-1914
The Sentinel. (Alamosa, Colo.) 1886-????
San Luis Valley Courier. (Alamosa, Colo.) 1889-1900
The Antonito Ledger. (Antonito, Conejos County, Colo.) 1892-1927
The Weekly Lance. (Alamosa, Colo.) 1895-1???
The La Jara Chronicle. (La Jara, Conejos County, Colo.) 1896-19??
La Voz Del Valle. (Antonito, Colo.) 1898-19?? | Languages: Spanish

Historical Assets Colorado

    La Aurora. (Antonito, Colo.) 19??-???? | Languages: Spanish
    The Alamosa Courier. (Alamosa, Conejos County, Colo.) 1901-1917
    The Alamosa Empire. (Alamosa, Colo.) 1909-19??
    The La Jara Enterprise. (La Jara, Conejos County, Colo.) 1910-1916
    The Platoro Miner. (Platoro, Colo.) 1913-19??
    The La Jara Gazette. (La Jara, Conejos County, Colo.) 1916-1917
    The Enterprise combined with The Gazette. (La Jara, Conejos County, Colo.) 1917-1917
    The La Jara Gazette and La Jara Enterprise. (La Jara, Conejos County, Colo.) 1917-1917
    La Jara Gazette combined with The Enterprise. (La Jara, Colo.) 1917-1926
    La Jara Gazette. (La Jara, Conejos County, Colo.) 1926-1981
    The Ledger-News. (Antonito, Conejos County, Colo.) 1927-1981
    The Valley Courier. (Alamosa, Colo.) 1955-Current
    Conejos County Citizen. (La Jara, Colo.) 1981-1985
    The Citizen. (La Jara, Colo.) 1985-1987
    The Conejos County Citizen. (La Jara, Conejos County, Colo.) 1987-Current

Places on the National Register
    Antonito, Costilla Crossing Bridge, Cty. Rd. over Rio Grande River
    Antonito, Denver & Rio Grande Railroad San Juan Extension (Boundary Increase), Railway corridor from Antonito, CO to Chama, NM via Cubres Pass
    Antonito, Engine No. 463, Off U.S. 285
    Antonito, Palace Hotel, 429 Main St.
    Antonito, S.P.M.D.T.U. Concilio Superior, 603 Main St.
    Antonito, Warshauer Mansion, 515 River St.
    La Jara, La Jara Depot, Broadway and Main Sts.
    Sanford, McIntire Ranch, Approx. 1.5 mi. N. of Co. Rd. V
    Sanford, Pike's Stockade, 4 mi. E of Sanford on CO 136

USGS Historic Places
    Cumbres, Cumbres Post Office, 37.0197328, -106.4478106
    La Jara, Lama Airfield, 37.2608424, -105.9291891
    Manassa, Lama Airport, 37.2472316, -105.9303002
    Platoro, Platoro Post Office, 37.3519502, -106.5328145

Grand Army of the Republic Posts
    None

USGS Historic Military Places
    None

Military Bases
    None

Conejos County

Post Offices

Antonito	1881 Jan 24		81120
Arboles	1882 Dec 13		81121
Broyles	1905 Sept 29	1908 Oct 31	
Capulin	1881 Aug 10	1922 July 14	
Capulin 2	1923 Sept 21		81120
Catherin	1888 Sept 25	1890 Oct 18	
Cenicero	1894 Apr 13	1902 Mar 14	
Cockrell	1879 Oct 15	1892 Dec 22	
Conejos	1862 Feb 25		81129
Cumbres	1889 Nov 25	1937 Feb 27*	
Del Norte	1883 Jan 28		81132
Del Rio	1942 Aug 13	1946 Jan 31	
Ephriam	1881 July 5	1888 June 2	
Espinoza	1905 Feb 4	1933 Sept 15	
Freedom	1901 May 14	1905 Apr 15	
Henry	1889 Nov 29	1896 Feb 21*	
Joya	1904 May 27	1904 May 28	
La Jara	1884 July 15		81140
La Sauses	1890 June 25	1895 Feb 28	
Lado	1884 Feb 24	1885 Mar 9	
Lajara	1875 Mar 5	1884 May 15	
Lasauses	1895 Feb 28	1920 July 31	
Lobatos	1902 Mar 14	1920 Dec 13*	
Los Cerritos	1889 June 3	1914 Apr 15	
Los Sauses	1882 July 21	1883 Feb 15	
Loyton	1884 Sept 10	1884 Oct 2	
Manassa	1879 Feb 3		81141
Mogote	1897 Aug 27	1920 Dec 31	
Morgan	1900 Aug 25	1901 May 14	
Navajoe	1878 Sept 17	1879 Nov 6	
Newcomb	1884 May 15	1886 May 13	
Ortiz	1890 May 23	1943 Jan 12*	
Osier	1882 May 15	1928 May 31*	
Pagosa Springs	1878 June 7		81147
Paisaje	1906 June 25	1920 Dec 31	
Piedra	1879 May 16	1927 June 30*	
Platoro	1888 Mar 12	1919 Apr 30	
Price	1880 Sept 27	1882 Aug 31	
Romeo	1901 July 24		81148
San Antonio	1880 Nov 26	1881 Jan 24	
San Rafael	1890 May 17	1895 Jan 24	
Sanford	1881 July 5		81151
Stunner	1886 Oct 2	1914 Jan 31*	
Sunflower	1889 June 3	1892 Jan 14	

Historical Assets Colorado

Terrace	1894 Dec 18	1900 Apr 14		
Vadner	1884 Sept 18	1885 July 31		

Topo Quads

Antonito	370730N	370000N	1060000W	1060730W
Centro	372230N	371500N	1060730W	1061500W
Fox Creek	370730N	370000N	1060730W	1061500W
Goshawk Dam	371500N	370730N	1060000W	1060730W
La Jara Canyon	371500N	370730N	1061500W	1062230W
Lobatos	370730N	370000N	1055230W	1060000W
Manassa	371500N	370730N	1055230W	1060000W
Manassa NE	371500N	370730N	1054500W	1055230W
Osier	370730N	370000N	1061500W	1062230W
Platoro	372230N	371500N	1063000W	1063730W
Red Mountain	372230N	371500N	1062230W	1063000W
Spectacle Lake	371500N	370730N	1062230W	1063000W
Terrace Reservoir	372230N	371500N	1061500W	1062230W
Vicente Canyon	371500N	370730N	1060730W	1061500W

Suggested Reading

Feitz, Leland. *Conejos County: a Quick History of Colorado's Land of Many Contrasts.* Colorado Springs, CO: Little London Press, 1998.

Inventory of the County Archives of Colorado, No. 11, Conejos County (Conejos). Denver: Historical Records Survey, 1938.

Mead, Frances Harvey. *Conejos County.* Colorado Springs, CO: Century One Press, 1984.

Memories of South Conejos (Memorias de Conejos del Sur). NL: NP, 1975.

Costilla County

Introduction

Established: 1861   Population: 3,524

Formed from: Original

Adjacent Counties: Huerfano, Las Animas, Conejos, Alamosa

County Seat: San Luis

  Other Communities: Blanca, Fort Garland, San Acacio, Chama, Garcia

Website, https://www.colorado.gov/costillacounty

Area Codes: 719

Zip Codes: 81123, 81126, 81133, 81138, 81152

Historical Assets Colorado

Costilla County Courthouse

Courthouses & County Government

Costilla County
   https://www.colorado.gov/pacific/costillacounty
Costilla County Courthouse (12th Judicial District), 304 Main St, San Luis, CO 81152, 719-672-3681; http://www.courts.state.co.us/Courts/County/Index.cfm?County_ID=34
Assessor, P.O. Box 344, San Luis, CO 81152, 719-672-3642; http://www.colorado.gov/cs/Satellite/CNTY-Costilla/CBON/1251594973867
Board of County Commissioners, 352 Main St, San Luis, CO 81152, 719-672-3372, https://www.colorado.gov/pacific/costillacounty/board-county-commissioners
Clerk & Recorder, 400 Gasper St, San Luis, CO 81152, 719-672-3301; http://www.colorado.gov/cs/Satellite/CNTY-Costilla/CBON/1251593793203
Coroner, San Pablo, CO 81153, 719-580-3426; https://www.colorado.gov/pacific/costillacounty/county-coroner-0
Public Health, P.O. Box 99, San Luis, CO 81152, 719-672-3332; http://www.colorado.gov/cs/Satellite/CNTY-Costilla/CBON/1251595053805
Transportation (Road & Bridge), 352 Main St, San Luis, CO 81152, 719-672-0217; https://www.colorado.gov/pacific/costillacounty/road-bridge
Treasurer, P.O. Box 348, San Luis, CO 81152, 719-937-7672; http://www.colorado.gov/cs/Satellite/CNTY-Costilla/CBON/1251595035177

County Records

Birth Unk
Death Unk
Court 1874

Marriage 1853
Land 1853

Divorce Unk
Probate 1874

Costilla County

County & Municipal Records Held at the State Level

The Colorado State Archives

Physical Records
Assessor
County Commissioners
County Court
District Court
Treasurer
WPA Historical Records
WPA Religious Institutions
  Survey

Records on Film
County Court
District Court
School Districts

Records on Master Film
District Court
Combined Courts
San Luis Valley Historical
  Society
School Districts
Cities
  San Luis

The Denver Public Library
Costilla County School Records, 1892-1893
San Luis Museum Cultural & Commercial Center Records, 1984-1985
WPA Historical Records Survey
WWI Draft Registration Cards (microfilm)

School Districts
School Districts, http://www.adcogov.org/local-school-districts
Sierra Grande School District R-30, 17523 Hwy 160, Blanca, CO 81123, 719-379-3259; http://www.sierragrandeschool.net/
Centennial School District No. R-1, 14644 Hwy 1159, San Luis, CO 81152, 719-672-3322; http://www.centennialschool.net/

Historic School Districts

1. San Luis
2. Garcia, La Costilla
3. [1878]
4. El Valle, San Pablo
5. Old San Acacio
6. Chama
7. San Francisco, La Valley
8. Jarosa, Rio Grande
9. San Acacio, Zapato
10. Blanca, Placer
11. Russell
12. Mesita
13. Fort Garland
14. Canyon
15. [1888]
16. [1889]
17. [1889]
18. [1889]
19. [1890]
20. [1889]
21. [1889]
22. Los Fuertes
23. [1891]
24. [1896]
25. [1900]

Fraternal Organizations

Granges
Jarosa, No. 373, Costilla, Jarosa, 30 May 1918

Masons

Ancient Free & Accepted Masons
San Acacio, No. 155, Costilla, San Acacio, 21 Sept 1921

Royal Arch Masons
None

Knights Templar
None

Historical Assets Colorado

Eastern Star
None
Odd Fellows
None
Rebekahs
None
Knights of Pythias
None
Pythian Sisters
None
Benevolent Protective Order of Elks
None

City & Town Halls

San Luis, 408 Main St, San Luis, CO 81152, 719-672-3321, http://www.townofsanluisco.org

Blanca, 601 Main St, Blanca, CO 81123, 719-379-3461, http://users.gojade.org/~blancaco/

Archives & Manuscript Collections

None

Historical & Genealogical Societies

Fort Garland Heritage Association, Old Fort Garland Museum, 29477 Hwy 159, P.O. Box 368, Fort Garland, CO 81133-0368, (719) 379-3512, http://www.coloradohistory.org

Local Libraries

Costilla County Library, 413 Gasper St, P.O. Box 351, San Luis, CO 81152-0351, (719) 672-3309, https://www.colorado.gov/pacific/costillacounty/public-library-system

Blanca Fort Garland Library, 17591 US 160, Blanca, CO 81123, (719) 379-3456, https://www.colorado.gov/pacific/costillacounty/public-library-system

Links

CO GenWeb
http://cogenweb.com/costilla/
Cyndi's List
https://www.cyndislist.com/us/co/counties/costilla/
FamilySearch Wiki
https://www.familysearch.org/wiki/en/Costilla_County,_Colorado_Genealogy
Linkpendium
http://www.linkpendium.com/costilla-co-genealogy/

Costilla County

RootsWeb Wiki
https://wiki.rootsweb.com/wiki/index.php/Costilla_County,_Colorado
Wikipedia
https://en.wikipedia.org/wiki/Costilla_County,_Colorado

Historic Hotels
None

Museums & Historic Sites
Fort Garland Heritage Association, Old Fort Garland Museum, 29477 Hwy 159, P.O. Box 368, Fort Garland, CO 81133-0368, (719) 379-3512, http://www.coloradohistory.org

Sangre de Cristo Heritage Center, 401 Church Pl, P.O. Box 9, San Luis, CO 81152, (719) 672-0999, https://www.museumtrail.org/sangre-de-cristo-heritage-center.html

Special Events & Scenic Locations
The town of San Luis hosts an annual Fiesta de Santiago y Santa Ana in July, http://www.townofsanluisco.org/santana.html

San Isabel National Forest
Fort Garland State History Museum
Los Caminos Antiguos Scenic and Historic Byway
Old Spanish National Historic Trail

Ghost Towns & Other Sparsely Populated Places
Baldy, Fort Garland, Garland, Garnett, Garrison, Hayes, Isle, McGinty, Montville, Mosca, Placer, Russell (Sangre de Cristo, Placer Isle), San Acacio, San Pedro, Stanley, Streator, Trinchera, Zapato

Newspapers
The Mosca Herald. (Mosca, Costilla County, Colo.) 18??-19??
The Colorado Independent. (Garland, Costilla County, Colo.) 1877-1???
Fort Garland Republican. (Fort Garland, Colo.) 1888-1???
The Valley Herald and El Heraldo Del Valle. (San Luis, Colo.) 19??-19?? | Languages: English, Spanish
The Mesita Herald. (Mesita, Costilla County, Colo.) 19??-19??
The San Luis Valley News. (Fort Garland, Colo.) 1907-1949
El Democrata Del Condado De Costilla. (San Luis, Colo.) 1923-1939 | Languages: English, Spanish
Costilla County Free Press. (San Luis, Colo.) 1948-Current | Languages: English, Spanish
The San Luis Valley News and The Valley Herald. (Blanca, Colo.) 1949-19??
The Valley Courier. (Alamosa, Colo.) 1955-Current

Historical Assets Colorado

The Citizen. (La Jara, Colo.) 1985-1987
The Conejos County Citizen. (La Jara, Conejos County, Colo.) 1987-Current

Places on the National Register
Blanca, San Luis Southern Railway Trestle, abandoned section of Costilla Cty Rd. 12
Charma, Iglesia de la Inmaculada Concepcion, 21529 Cty. Rd. P.6
Fort Garland, Fort Garland, On CO 159, 1 block S of U.S. 10
Los Fuertes, Capilla de San Isidro, 21801 Cty. Rd. KS
San Francisco, Iglesia de San Francisco de Assisi, 23531 Cty. Rd. J.2
San Luis, Plaza de San Luis de la Culebra, CO 159
San Luis, Rito Seco Creek Culvert, CO 142 at milepost 33.81
San Luis, Salazar, A.A., House, 603 Main St.
San Luis, San Luis Bridge, Off CO 159
San Pedro, Iglesia de San Pedro y San Pablo, 11423 Cty. Rd. 21
Viejo San Acacio, Capilla de Viejo San Acacio, 14152 Cty. Rd. 14.8

USGS Historic Places
Fort Garland, Skinkle Landing Strip, 37.3855649, -105.4847345
Fort Garland SW, Escheman Landing Strips, 37.3672323, -105.4416786
San Luis, San Luis Airport, 37.1916818, -105.4636233
San Luis, San Luis High School, 37.2080703, -105.4236236
Trinchera Ranch, Garland City, 37.4525087, -105.3422311

Grand Army of the Republic Posts
None

USGS Historic Military Places
None

Military Bases
None

Post Offices

Bernice	1901 Feb 26	1902 May 16	
Blanca	1894 Oct 5	15 Feb 1902*	
Blanca 2	1908 Oct 28		81123
Chama	1907 May 3		81126
Coryell	1887 Aug 29	1890 Jan 8	
Costilla	1862 Nov 13	[now in NM]	
Eastdale	1895 Apr 27	1909 July 15	
Fort Garland	1862 Feb 25		81133
Garcia	1916 Feb 6		
Garland	1877 July 24	1878 June 27	
Garnett	1888 Mar 3	1921 Sept 30	
Garrison	1891 Jan 26	1896 July 17	

Costilla County

Hirst	1899 June 19	1901 July 31	
Hooper	1896 July 17		81136
Jaroso	1911 Mar 10		81138
Lavalley	1903 Aug 14	1918 Aug 15	
Laveta Pass	1904 Jan 5	1911 Apr 13	
Manzanares	1901 Feb 19	1902 Mar 31	
Margaret	1899 May 22	1900 Mar 31	
Medano Springs	1874 Jan 29	1879 June 20*	
Mesita	1910 May 27		81142
Meyer	1885 Aug 25	1885 Dec 10	
Montville	1887 Feb 28	1900 Jan 31	
Mosca	1890 Dec 30		81146
Mosco	1880 May 24	1882 Feb 1	
Norman	1890 June 25	1890 Oct 16	
Orean	1881 June 22	1887 Feb 28	
Rio Grande	1874 Mar 13	1877 Apr 18	
Russell	1876 May 12	1956 July 31*	
San Acacio	1909 Nov 11		81150
San Luis	1862 Feb 25		81152
San Pablo	1893 Jan 7		81153
Stanley	1890 Jan 8	1891 Sept 2	
Streator	1888 Apr 23	1890 Dec 30	
Underhill	1872 Mar 28	1873 May 20	
Veta Pass	1911 Apr 13	1935 Apr 30	
Wayside	1875 Feb 15	1878 Sept 10	
Zapato	1879 Apr 30	1900 Sept 15*	

Topo Quads

Blanca SE	372230N	371500N	1053000W	1053730W
Fort Garland	373000N	372230N	1052230W	1053000W
Fort Garland SW	372230N	371500N	1052230W	1053000W
Garcia	370730N	370000N	1053000W	1053730W
Kiowa Hill	370730N	370000N	1054500W	1055230W
La Valley	370730N	370000N	1051500W	1052230W
Mesito Reservoir	371500N	370730N	1053730W	1054500W
Ojito Peak	372230N	371500N	1051500W	1052230W
Russell	373730N	373000N	1051500W	1052230W
San Acacio	371500N	370730N	1053000W	1053730W
San Luis	371500N	370730N	1052230W	1053000W
Sanchez Reservoir	370730N	370000N	1052230W	1053000W
Sky Valley Ranch	370730N	370000N	1053730W	1054500W
Taylor Ranch	371500N	370730N	1051500W	1052230W
Trinchera Ranch	373000N	372230N	1051500W	1052230W

Historical Assets Colorado

Suggested Reading

Gibson, C E. *Stories from Costilla County*. Denver: Civil Works Administration, 1934.

Inventory of the County Archives of Colorado, No. 12, Costilla County (San Luis). Denver: Historical Records Survey, 1938.

Petty, Hazel Bean. *The History of Costilla County as Revealed by its Cemeteries*. Dissertation, Adams State College, 1971.

Sewell, Clarinda Knight. *Clarinda's Story of San Luis Valley Roots*. Monte Vista, CO: C K Sewell, 1983.

Crowley County

Introduction
Established: 1911   Population: 5,823
Formed from: Bent, Otero
Adjacent Counties: Lincoln, El Paso, Otero, Kiowa, Pueblo
County Seat: Ordway
  Other Communities: Crowley, Olney Springs, Sugar City
Website, https://www.colorado.gov/crowleycounty
Area Codes: 719
Zip Codes: 81033, 81034, 81062, 81063, 81076

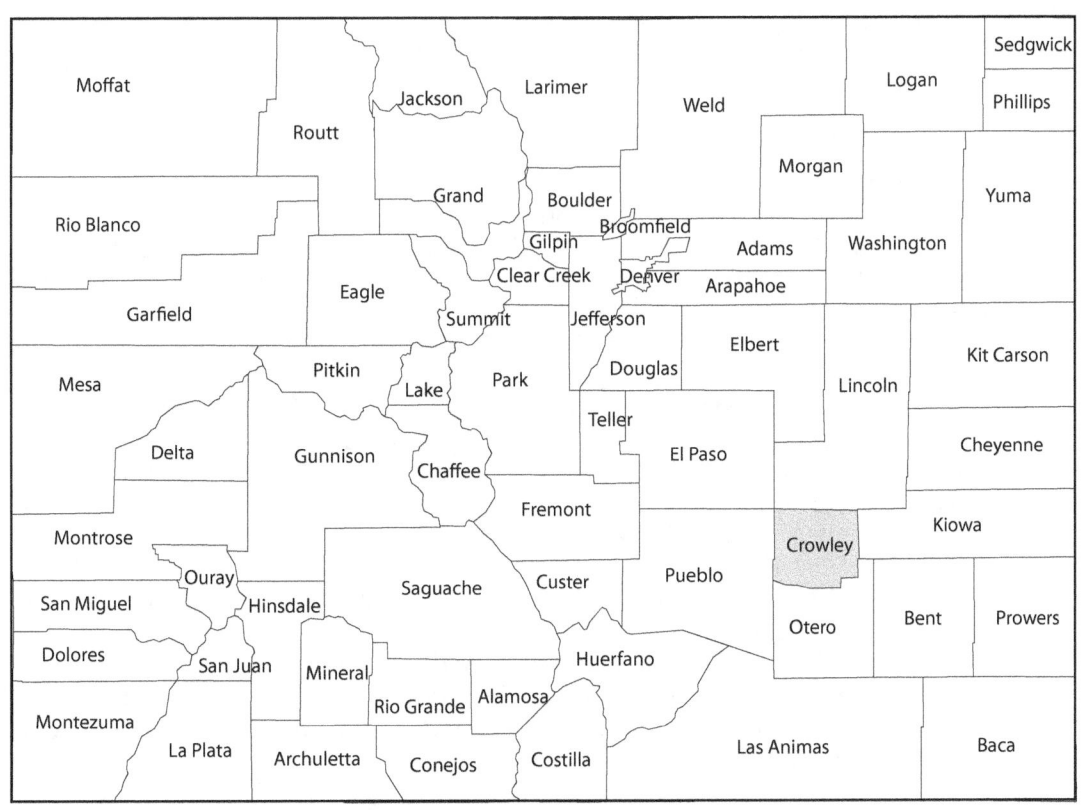

Historical Assets Colorado

Crowley County Courthouse

Courthouses & County Government

Crowley County
https://www.colorado.gov/crowleycounty
Crowley County Courthouse (16th Judicial District), 110 E 6th, Ordway, CO 81063, 719-267-4468; http://www.courts.state.co.us/Courts/County/Index.cfm?County_ID=53
Assessor, 631 Main St, Ordway, CO 81063, 719-267-5229; http://www.crowleycounty.net/assessor.htm
Board of County Commissioners, 603 Main St, Ordway, CO 81063, 719-267-5555, https://www.colorado.gov/pacific/crowleycounty/administration-0
Clerk & Recorder, 631 Main St, Ordway, CO 81063, 719-267-5225; http://www.crowleycounty.net/clerk.htm
Coroner, 603 Main St, Ste 2, Ordway, CO 81063, 719-267-5555 x3; https://www.colorado.gov/pacific/crowleycounty/coroner
Public Health, 603 Main St, Ordway, CO 81063, 719-267-5247; http://www.crowleycounty.net/health.htm
Transportation (Road & Bridge), 603 Main St, Ste 2, Ordway, CO 81063, 719-267-5555 x3; https://www.colorado.gov/pacific/crowleycounty/road-and-bridge
Treasurer, 631 Main St, Ordway, CO 81063, 719-267-5227; http://www.crowleycounty.net/Treasurer.htm

Crowley County

County Records
Birth 1909
Death Unk
Court 1874
Marriage 1864
Land 1864
Divorce Unk
Probate Unk

County & Municipal Records Held at the State Level

The Colorado State Archives

Physical Records
District Court
WPA Historical Records
WPA Religious Institutions Survey

Records on Film
Clerk & Recorder
District Court
School Districts

Records on Master Film
County Court
District Court
Combined Courts
School Districts

The Denver Public Library
WWI Draft Registration Cards (microfilm)

School Districts
School Districts, http://www.adcogov.org/local-school-districts
Crowley County School District RE-1J, 1001 Main St, Ordway, CO 81063, 719-267-3117; http://www.cck12.net/

Historic School Districts

1. Crowley
2. North Fowler
3. Manzanola
4.
5.
6.
7. Olney Springs
8.
9.
10.
11.
12. Ordway Public
13.
14.
15.
16. Numa
17. [1913]
18.
19.
20.
21. [1913]
22.
23.
24.
25. Sugar City
26. [1913]
27. Lolita
28.
29.
30. [1915]
31. Grand View, Pleasant Hill
32. Antelope Mesa, Bluff Springs

Fraternal Organizations

Granges
Numa, No. 213, Crowley, Ordway, 18 Jan 1913
King Center, No. 269, Crowley, Olney Springs, 14 Mar 1916
Sand Arroyo, No. 299, Crowley, Sugar City, 18 Aug 1916
Antelope Mesa, No. 325, Crowley, Olney Springs,
Pearl Spring Valley, No. 340, Crowley, Ordway/Sugarbeet, 30 Apr 1917

Masons

Ancient Free & Accepted Masons
Ordway, No. 135, Crowley, Ordway, 20 Sept 1910

Historical Assets Colorado

Royal Arch Masons
None

Knights Templar
None

Eastern Star
Meredith, No. 89, Crowley, Ordway

Odd Fellows
Samaritan, No. 133, Crowley, Sugar City
Ordway, No. 150, Crowley, Ordway

Rebekahs
Prairie Flower, No. 133, Crowley, Ordway

Knights of Pythias
None

Pythian Sisters
None

Benevolent Protective Order of Elks
None

City & Town Halls

Ordway, 232 Main St, Ordway, CO 81063, 719-267-3134, https://www.townofordway.com
Olney Springs, 401 Warner, Olney Springs, CO 81062, 719-267-5567, https://www.colorado.gov/pacific/crowleycounty/olney-springs
Sugar City, 205 Colorado St, Sugar City, CO 81076, 719-267-3729, https://www.colorado.gov/pacific/crowleycounty/sugar-city

Archives & Manuscript Collections

None

Historical & Genealogical Societies

None

Local Libraries

Community Library, 1007 Main St, Ordway, CO 81063, (719) 267-3823
Louis Goodrich Memorial Library, 503 Warner Ave, Olney Springs, CO 81062, (719) 267-3111

Links

CO GenWeb
http://cogenweb.com/crowley/

Cyndi's List
https://www.cyndislist.com/us/co/counties/crowley/

Crowley County

FamilySearch Wiki
https://www.familysearch.org/wiki/en/Crowley_County,_Colorado_Genealogy
Linkpendium
http://www.linkpendium.com/crowley-co-genealogy/
RootsWeb Wiki
https://wiki.rootsweb.com/wiki/index.php/Crowley_County,_Colorado
Wikipedia
https://en.wikipedia.org/wiki/Crowley_County,_Colorado

Historic Hotels
None

Museums & Historic Sites
Crowley County Heritage Center, 300 Main St, P.O. Box 24, Crowley, CO 81033, (719) 267-3384, http://www.crowleyheritagecenter.com

Special Events & Scenic Locations
Crowley County Days is held at the Foxley (Crowley County) Fairgrounds, County Ln 17, Ordway, CO 81063, 719-267-5555, https://www.facebook.com/pages/Crowley-County-Fair-Grounds/101962786618497

Crowley County keeps a list of annual festivals and events here, https://www.colorado.gov/pacific/crowleycounty/festivals

TransAmerica Trail Bicycle Route

Ghost Towns & Other Sparsely Populated Places
King Center, Pultney

Newspapers
The Ordway News. (Ordway, Otero County, Colo.) 1896-1???
The Crowley County Leader. (Ordway, Crowley County, Colo.) 19??-1927
The Saccharine Gazette. (Sugar City, Otero County, Colo.) 1900-1915
The Ordway New Era and Crowley County Leader. (Ordway, Crowley County, Colo.) 19??-19??
The Ordway New Era. (Ordway, Colo.) 1902-1927
The Sugar City Gazette. (Sugar City, Crowley County, Colo.) 1915-1924
The Gazette. (Sugar City, Crowley County, Colo.) 1924-1926
The Sugar City Gazette. (Sugar City, Crowley County, Colo.) 1926-1942
The Crowley County Gazette. (Sugar City, Crowley County, Colo.) 1941-1942

Places on the National Register
Crowley, Crowley School, 301 Main St.

Historical Assets Colorado

USGS Historic Places
Hardesty Reservoir, Fowler Golf Course, 38.0930617, -104.026905
Ordway, Orahood Airstrip, 38.2013943, -103.7657834
Ordway, Ordway Airport, 38.2102831, -103.7602275
Sugar City, Rocky Ford Auxiliary Army Air Field Number 1, 38.1341667, -103.6875
The Pinnacles, Sand Arroya Airport, 38.45278, -103.52994

Grand Army of the Republic Posts
Blackmar, No. 29, Crowley, Ordway

USGS Historic Military Places
Sugar City, Rocky Ford Auxiliary Army Air Field Number 1 , 38.1341667, -103.6875

Military Bases
None

Post Offices

Crowley	1914 Dec 18		81033
Hester	1905 June 16	1912 Nov 30	
Olney Springs	1909 Mar 24		81062
Ordway	1890 June 25		81063
Sugar City	1900 Mar 27		81076

Topo Quads

Antelope Mesa	382230N	381500N	1035230W	1040000W
Box Springs	383000N	382230N	1033730W	1034500W
Cheraw	380730N	380000N	1033000W	1033730W
Elder	380730N	380000N	1035230W	1040000W
Fowler	381500N	380730N	1040000W	1040730W
Grandview School	383000N	382230N	1040000W	1040730W
Grandview School SE	382230N	381500N	1040000W	1040730W
Lake Henry	382230N	381500N	1033730W	1034500W
Manzanola	380730N	380000N	1034500W	1035230W
Meredith Hill	381500N	380730N	1033000W	1033730W
Nero Hill	382230N	381500N	1034500W	1035230W
Olney Springs	381500N	380730N	1035230W	1040000W
Ordway	381500N	380730N	1034500W	1035230W
Sugar City	381500N	380730N	1033730W	1034500W
Windmill Lake	383000N	382230N	1034500W	1035230W

Suggested Reading
Crowley County Centennial, 1911-2011, Special Edition. Aurora, CO: NP: 2011.
The History of Crowley County, Colorado: A Collection of General History and Family Stories of Crowley County. Dallas: Taylor Pub Co, 1980.

Custer County

Introduction

Established: 1877   Population: 4,445

Formed from: Fremont

Adjacent Counties: Fremont, Pueblo, Huerfano, Saguache

County Seat: Westcliffe

Other Communities: Silver Cliff, Cold Spring, Fairview, Greenwood, McKenzie Junction, San Isabel, Tanglewood Acres, Wetmore, Colfax, Galena, Querida, Rosita, Ula

Website, http://www.custercountygov.com

Area Codes: 719

Zip Codes: 81252, 81253

Historical Assets Colorado

Custer County Courthouse

Courthouses & County Government

Custer County
   http://www.custercountygov.com
Custer County Courthouse (11th Judicial District), 205 S 6th St, Westcliffe, CO 81252, 719-783-2274; http://www.courts.state.co.us/Courts/County/Index.cfm?County_ID=29
Assessor, 205 S 6th St, Westcliffe, CO 81252, 719-783-2218; http://www.custercountygov.com/index.php?pg=assessor
Board of County Commissioners, 205 S 6th St, Westcliffe, CO 81252, 719-783-2552, http://www.custercountygov.com/index.php?pg=commissioners
Clerk & Recorder, P.O. Box 150, Westcliffe, CO 81252, 719-793-2441; http://www.custercountygov.com/index.php?pg=clerk
Coroner, P.O. Box 29, Westcliffe, CO 81252, 719-371-4686; http://www.custercountygov.com/index.php?pg=sheriff
Public Health, 704 Edwards St, Westcliffe, CO 81252, 719-783-3369; http://oem.custercountygov.com/ph.htm
Transportation (Road & Bridge), 213 N 4th St, Westcliffe, CO 81252, 719-783-2281; http://www.custercountygov.com/index.php?pg=roadbridge
Treasurer, 205 S 6th St, Westcliffe, CO 81252, 719-783-2341; http://www.custercountygov.com/index.php?pg=Transportation

County Records

Birth Unk
Death Unk
Court 1900
CSA Birth & Death 1941

Marriage 1876
Land 1876

Divorce 1900
Probate 1900

Custer County

County & Municipal Records Held at the State Level

The Colorado State Archives

Physical Records
Clerk & Recorder
County Court
District Court
WPA Historical Records
WPA Religious Institutions
 Survey
Cities
 Silver Cliff

Records on Film
1885 Census
Clerk & Recorder
County Court
Cities
 Silver Cliff

Records on Master Film
Clerk & Recorder
County Court
Combined Courts
Probate Court
School Districts
Cities
 Silver Cliff

The Denver Public Library
Custer County Register of Electors, 1879-1882
New Hope Baptist Church in Wetmore, 1871-1876, 1913-1926
WWI Draft Registration Cards (microfilm)

School Districts
School Districts, http://www.adcogov.org/local-school-districts
Custer County Schools, 709 Main St, Westcliffe, CO 81252, 719-783-2291; https://www.custercountyschools.org/

Historic School Districts

1. Rosita
2. Beck
3. Knuth
4. Colfax
5. Ula
6. Fairview
7. Greenleaf
8. Brush Creek
9. Wetmore
10. [1878]
11. [1878]
12. Querida
13. Silver Cliff
14. Froze Creek
15. Willows
16. canda
17. Dry Lake
18. Jenkins Park
19. Augusta
20. Silver Park
21. Antelope
22. [1884]
23. Ilse
24. West Cliffe
25. [1887]
26. Adobe
27.
28.
29.
30.
31.
32.
33.
34. [1886]
35.
36. [1898]

Fraternal Organizations

Granges
San Isabel, No. 400, Custer, Wetmore, 4 Mar 1926
Sangre de Christo, No. 402, Custer, Westcliffe, 1 June 1926

Masons

Ancient Free & Accepted Masons
Rosita, No. 36, Custer, Rosita, 17 Sept 1879
Silver Cliff, No. 38, Custer, Westcliffe, 22 Sept 1880

Royal Arch Masons
None

Historical Assets Colorado

Knights Templar
None

Eastern Star
Silver Cliff, No. 24, Custer, Silver Cliff
Sangre de Christo, No. 134, Custer, Westcliffe

Odd Fellows
Rosita, No. 21, Custer, Rosita
Silver Cliff, No. 34, Custer, Silver Cliff
Ilse, No. 66, Custer, Ilse, 1886 May 15

Rebekahs
None

Knights of Pythias
Silver Cliff, No. 14, Custer, Silver Cliff, 1880 Nov 6

Pythian Sisters
None

Benevolent Protective Order of Elks
None

City & Town Halls
Westcliffe, 1000 Main St, Westcliffe, CO 81252, 719-783-2282, https://www.colorado.gov/townofwestcliffe
Silver Cliff, 612 Main St, Silver Cliff, CO 81252, 719-783-2615, https://www.silvercliffco.com

Archives & Manuscript Collections
None

Historical & Genealogical Societies
Custer County Historical & Genealogical Society, P.O. Box 436, Westcliffe, CO 81252, (719) 783-2837, http://genealogytrails.com/colo/custer/
Custer County Historical Society, 59000 Hwy 69, Westcliffe, C, 81252, (719) 783-9448

Local Libraries
West Custer County Library District, 209 Main St, P.O. Box 689, Westcliffe, CO 81252-0689, (719) 783-9138, http://www.westcusterlibrary.org
Wetmore Community Library, 95 County Rd 393, PO Box 18, Wetmore, CO 81253-0018, (719) 784-6669, https://wetmore.colibraries.org

Links

CO GenWeb
http://cogenweb.com/custer/

Cyndi's List
https://www.cyndislist.com/us/co/counties/custer/

Custer County

FamilySearch Wiki
https://www.familysearch.org/wiki/en/Custer_County,_Colorado_Genealogy

Linkpendium
http://www.linkpendium.com/custer-co-genealogy/

RootsWeb Wiki
https://wiki.rootsweb.com/wiki/index.php/Custer_County,_Colorado

Wikipedia
https://en.wikipedia.org/wiki/Custer_County,_Colorado

Historic Hotels
None

Museums & Historic Sites
Silver Cliff Museum, 606 Main St, P.O. Box 835, Silver Cliff, CO 81252, (719) 783-2615, https://visitcustercounty.com/silver-cliff-museum/

Special Events & Scenic Locations
The Custer County Fairgrounds, 90 CO Rd 241, Westcliffe, CO 81252, https://www.facebook.com/events/westcliffe-colorado/custer-county-fair/937765103281683/

The Custer County Chamber of Commerce keeps a calendar of events here: https://visitcustercounty.com/our-events/

San Isabel National Forest
Sangre de Christo Wilderness
Frontier Pathways National Scenic and Historic Byway
TransAmerica Trail Bicycle Route
Western Express Bicycle Route

Ghost Towns & Other Sparsely Populated Places
Augusta, Bassick City (Querida), Blackburn, Colfax, Custer City, Fairview, Galena, Govetown, Greenwood, Ilse, Querida, Rosita (Brown's Spring), Ula, Wetmore

Newspapers
The Sierra Journal. (Rosita, Custer County, Colo.) 18??-1886
Silver Cliff Rustler. (Silver Cliff, Custer County, Colo.) 18??-1908
Wet Mountain Tribune. (Westcliffe, Colo.) 18??-Current
The Rosita Index. (Rosita, Colo.) 1875-18??
The Silver Cliff Miner. (Silver Cliff, Colo.) 1878-1???
The Silver Cliff Daily Prospect. (Silver Cliff, Colo.) 1879-1???
The Daily Miner. (Silver Cliff, Colo.) 1879-18??
The Silver Cliff Weekly Prospect. (Silver Cliff, Colo.) 1880-????
The Silver Cliff Weekly Herald. (Silver Cliff, Colo.) 1881-1882
The Daily Herald. (Silver Cliff, Colo.) 1882-1???
The Weekly Herald. (Silver Cliff, Colo.) 1882-1???

Historical Assets Colorado

Places on the National Register
Beulah, Mingus Homestead, Off CO 165 N of jct. with Ophir Cr. Rd., San Isabel NF
Westcliffe, Beckwith Ranch, 64159 CO 69
Westcliffe, Hope Lutheran Church, 310 S. 3rd St.
Westcliffe, Kennicott Cabin, 63161 CO 69
Westcliffe, National Hotel—Wolff Building, 201 Second St.
Westcliffe, Westcliff School, 304 4th St.
Westcliffe, Westcliffe Jail, 116 Second St.
Westcliffe, Willows School, Willows Ln. (Co. Rd. 141) between Muddy Ln. (Co. Rd. 155) and Schoolfield Rd. (Co. Rd. 328)
Wetmore, Wetmore Post Office, 682 Co. Rd. 395

USGS Historic Places
Beckwith Mountain, Cress Field, 38.1902768, -105.5638923
Beckwith Mountain, Ula, 38.15005, -105.50192

Grand Army of the Republic Posts
E V Sumner, No. 24, Custer, Silver Cliff, 1883
John M Oliver, No. 72, Custer, Westcliffe

USGS Historic Military Places
None

Military Bases
None

Post Offices

Augusta	1890 May 5	1902 Apr 15
Bassick	1917 May 19	1920 Dec 31
Blackburn	1881 Aug 1	1889 May 11
Blumenau	1870 May 2	1890 Oct 9*
Camargo	1881 Apr 19	1881 Nov 31
Cleveland	1885 Feb 5	1886 May 13
Clinton	1879 Aug 4	1881 Oct 13
Colfax	1870 May 2	1879 Jan 16
Dora	1879 July 11	1883 Oct 31
Fairview	1882 Oct 24	1913 Aug 15*
Focus	1921 May 5	1926 Oct 30
Forestdale	1914 Oct 17	1926 Apr 30
Gove	1883 Dec 6	1888 Oct 9
Greenwood	1872 Feb 16	1918 June 29
Ilse	1884 Aug 14	1929 Sept 30*
Keating	1914 Dec 18	1924 Nov 6
Millbrook	1893 Mar 2	1895 Nov 7
Neeley	1888 Feb 16	1888 Dec 12

Custer County

Querida	1880 Jan 12	1906 May 14*		
Rosita	1874 July 8	1966 Dec 2		
San Isabel	1936 June 18	1938 Dec 31		
Silver Cliff	1878 Oct 30		81249	
Silver Park	1879 July 28	1881 Feb 2		
Ula	1871 Dec 1	1891 May 4		
Westcliffe	1881 July 14	1882 Nov 21		
Westcliffe 2	1886 Jan 22		81252	
Wetmore	1881 Apr 19		81253	

Topo Quads

Aldrich Gulch	380730N	380000N	1052230W	1053000W
Bear Creek	380000N	375230N	1050730W	1051500W
Beckwith Mountain	381500N	380730N	1053000W	1053730W
Deer Peak	380730N	380000N	1050730W	1051500W
Devils Gulch	380000N	375230N	1051500W	1052230W
Hardscrabble Mtn	381500N	380730N	1050730W	1051500W
Mount Tyndall	381500N	380730N	1051500W	1052230W
Rosita	380730N	380000N	1051500W	1052230W
Westcliffe	381500N	380730N	1052230W	1053000W

Suggested Reading

Custer County Women's Club. *Reflections: Bicentennial-Centennial 1976, Custer County, Colorado*. Pueblo, CO: Pride City Printing, 1989.

Dodds, Joanne West and Edwin Lloyd Dodds. *Custer County at a Glance: Featuring Rosita, Silver Cliff and Westcliffe*. Pueblo, CO: Focal Plain, 2007.

Dodds, Joanne West. *Custer County: Mountains, Mines and Ranches*. Pueblo, CO: Paperworks, 1992.

History of Custer County, Colorado Stockgrowers. NL: Custer County Cattle Growers' Association, 1966.

Murray, Robert A and Dale R Andrus, Frederic J Athearn. *Las Animas, Huerfano and Custer: Three Colorado Counties on a Cultural Frontier: A History of the Raton Basin*. Denver: Colorado Bureau of Land Management, 1979.

Southern Colorado: Historical and Descriptive of Fremont and Custer Counties with their Principal Towns. Canon City, CO: Binckley & Hartwell, 1879.

Vickers, W B and O L Baskin & Co. *History of the Arkansas Valley, Colorado; Illustrated*. Chicago: O L Baskin Historical Publishers, 1881.

Historical Assets Colorado

Delta County

Introduction

Established: 1883 Population: 29,979

Formed from: Gunnison

Adjacent Counties: Gunnison, Montrose, Mesa

County Seat: Delta

Other Communities: Cedaredge, Crawford, Hotchkiss, Orchard City, Paonia, Austin, Cory, Eckert, Lazear

Website, https://www.deltacounty.com

Area Codes: 970

Zip Codes: 81410, 81413, 81414, 81415, 81416, 81418, 81419, 81420, 81428

Historical Assets Colorado

Delta County Courthouse

Delta County 19th Century Courthouse

Courthouses & County Government

Delta County
https://www.deltacounty.com

Delta County Courthouse (7th Judicial District), 501 Palmer St, Delta, CO 81416, 970-874-6280; http://www.courts.state.co.us/Courts/County/Index.cfm?County_ID=15

Assessor, 501 Palmer St, Delta, CO 81416, 970-874-2120; http://www.deltacounty.com/index.aspx?id=60

Board of County Commissioners, 501 Palmer St, Delta, CO 81416, 970-874-2111; https://www.deltacounty.com/36/Commissioners

Clerk & Recorder, 501 Palmer St, Delta, CO 81416, 970-874-2150; http://www.delta-county.com/index.aspx?id=59

Coroner, 682A 1725 Road, Delta, CO 81416, 970-874-5918; https://www.deltacounty.com/362/Coroner

Elections (Clerk & Recorder's office); https://www.deltacounty.com/325/Elections

Public Health, 560 Dodge St, Delta, CO 81416, 970-874-2030; http://www.deltacounty.com/index.aspx?nid=7

Transportation (Road & Bridge), 501 Palmer St, Ste 227, Delta, Co 81416, 970-874-2101; https://www.deltacounty.com/16/Road-and-Bridge

Treasurer, 501 Palmer St, Ste 202, Delta, CO 81416, 970-874-2135; http://www.deltacounty.com/index.aspx?nid=28

County Records

Birth 1897	Marriage 1883	Divorce 1883
Death 1883	Land 1883	Probate 1883
Court 1883		

Delta County

County & Municipal Records Held at the State Level

The Colorado State Archives

Physical Records
Clerk & Recorder
WPA Historical Records
WPA Religious Institutions Survey

Records on Film
1885 Census
Clerk & Recorder

Records on Master Film
Clerk & Recorder
County Court
District Court
Combined Courts
School Districts

The Denver Public Library
Honor Roll: Men from Delta County, 1917-1919
WWI Draft Registration Cards (microfilm)

School Districts

School Districts, http://www.adcogov.org/local-school-districts
Delta County School District 50J, 145 W 4th St, Delta, CO 81416, 970-874-4438; http://www.deltaschools.com/

Historic School Districts

1. Delta
2. Hotchkiss
3. Paonia
4. Columbine, Liberty
5. Lamborn Mesa
6. Coalby
7. Grand View, Dove
8. (united with 3)
9. Fairview
10. Read
11. Hurst
12. Rogers Mesa, Lazear
13. [1887]
14. Crawford
15. Cottonwood
16. [1891]
17. Roubideau, Knoll
18. Eckert
19. Stewart Mesa, Bone Mesa
20. Clear Fork
21. Midway
22. Cedaredge
23. Cory, Mound
24. Tongue Creek
25. Fruitland Mesa, Hotchkiss
26. Rogers Mesa
27.
28. Crawford
29.
30.
31.
32. Ariel, Fruitland Mesa
33. Bowie
34. East Redlands, West Redlands, Leroux Creek, Redlands Mesa
35.
36. Cedaredge, Sand Creek

Fraternal Organizations

Granges
Paonia, No. 83, Delta, Paonia, 7 Apr 1888
Surface Creek, No. 88, Delta, Delta, 4 Mar 1889
Garnet, No. 89, Delta, Delta, 6 Mar 1889
Hotchkiss, No. 107, Delta, Hotchkiss, 1 May 1890
Fairview, No. 108, Delta, Delta, 9 May 1890
Fruitland Mesa, No. 317, Delta, Crawford, 6 Jan 1917
Lambert, No. 439, Delta, Paonia, 21 Sept 1936
Stewart, No. 440, Delta, Paonia, 23 Sept 1936
Saddle Mountain, No. 473, Delta, Crawford, 27 Feb 1953
Redlands Mesa, No. 487, Delta, Hotchkiss, 13 Nov 1958
Hotchkiss, No. 488, Delta, Hotchkiss, 11 Dec 1958

Historical Assets Colorado

Masons
　Ancient Free & Accepted Masons
　　Delta, No. 62, Delta, Delta, 16 Sept 1885
　　Mount Lamorn, No. 102, Delta, Hotchkiss, 22 Sept 1897
　　Paonia, No. 121, Delta, Paonia, 18 Sept 1906
　　Eckert, No. 136, Delta, Eckert, 20 Sept 1910
　Royal Arch Masons
　　Delta, No. 38, Delta, Delta
　　Zion, No. 46, Delta, Paonia
　Knights Templar
　　Delta Commandery, No. 34, Delta, Delta, 1915 May 10
　Eastern Star
　　Garnet, No. 39, Delta, Delta
　　Paonia, No. 74, Delta, Paonia
　　Hotchkiss, No. 81, Delta, Hotchkiss
　　Spruce, No. 129, Delta, Cedaredge
Odd Fellows
　　Mount Lamborn, No. 101, Delta, Paonia
　　Crawford, No. 106, Delta, Crawford
　　North Fork, No. 110, Delta, Hotchkiss
　　Delta, No. 116, Delta, Delta
　　Paonia, No. 132, Delta, Paonia, 1900 Mar 24
　　Peach Belt, No. 149, Delta, Cedaredge
　　Eckert, No. 168, Delta, Eckert
　Rebekahs
　　May Queen, No. 23, Delta, Eckert
　　Katherine, No. 65, Delta, Delta
　　Paonia, No. 77, Delta, Paonia
　　Elberta, No. 106, Delta, Cedaredge
Knights of Pythias
　　Grand Mesa, No. 84, Delta, Delta
　　Hotchkiss, No. 119, Delta, Hotchkiss
　Pythian Sisters
　　Delta, No. 22, Delta, Delta
　　Columbine, No. 44, Delta, Delta
　　Paonia, No. 57, Delta, Paonia
　　Excelsior, No. 62, Delta, Hotchkiss
Benevolent Protective Order of Elks
　　Delta, No. 1235, Delta, Delta
　　Hotchkiss, No. 1807, Delta, Hotchkiss

Delta County

City & Town Halls

Delta, 360 Main St, Delta, CO 81416, 970-874-7566, https://cityofdelta.net

Cedaredge, 235 W Main St, Cedaredge, CO 81413, 970-856-3123, https://www.cedaredgecolorado.com

Crawford, 425 CO 92, Crawford, CO 81415, 970-921-4725, https://www.colorado.gov/crawford

Hotchkiss, 276 W Main St, Hotchkiss, CO 81419, 970-872-3663, http://www.townofhotchkiss.com

Orchard City, 9661 2100 Rd, Orchard City, CO 81410, 970-835-3337, https://www.orchardcityco.org

Paonia, 214 Grand Ave, Paonia, CO 81428, 90-527-4102, http://www.townofpaonia.com

Archives & Manuscript Collections

None

Historical & Genealogical Societies

Delta County Historical Society, Delta County Museum, 251 Meeker St, P.O. Box 681, Delta, CO 81416-1914, (970) 874-8721, https://www.colorado.com/history-museums/delta-county-museum

Hotchkiss-Crawford Historical Society, Historical Museum, 180 2nd St, P.O. Box 727, Hotchkiss, CO 81419, (970) 872-3780, https://www.facebook.com/Hotchkiss-CrawfordHistoricalMuseum/

Surface Creek Historical Society, Pioneer Town Museum, 315 SW 3rd Ave, P.O. Box 906, Cedaredge, CO 81413, (970) 856-7554, http://www.pioneertown.org

Local Libraries

Delta County Public Library, 211 W 6th St, Delta, CO 81416, (970) 874-9630, http://www.deltalibraries.org

Cedaredge Public, 180 SW 6th Ave, PO Box 548, Cedaredge, CO 81413-0548, (970) 399-7674, https://deltalibraries.org/

Crawford Community Library, 545 Hwy 92, PO Box 201, Crawford, CO 81415-0201, (970) 399-7783, https://deltalibraries.org

Hotchkiss Public Library, 149 E Main St, P.O. Box 540, Hotchkiss, CO 81419-0540, (970) 399-7781, https://deltalibraries.org

Paonia Public Library, 2 Third St, P.O. Box 969, Paonia, CO 81428-0969, (970) 399-7881, http://www.deltalibraries.org/

Links

CO GenWeb
http://cogenweb.com/delta/

Cyndi's List
https://www.cyndislist.com/us/co/counties/delta/

FamilySearch Wiki
https://www.familysearch.org/wiki/en/Delta_County,_Colorado_Genealogy

Historical Assets Colorado

Linkpendium
http://www.linkpendium.com/delta-co-genealogy/

RootsWeb Wiki
https://wiki.rootsweb.com/wiki/index.php/Delta_County,_Colorado

Wikipedia
https://en.wikipedia.org/wiki/Delta_County,_Colorado

Historic Hotels
None

Museums & Historic Sites
Delta County Historical Society, Delta County Museum, 251 Meeker St, P.O. Box 681, Delta, CO 81416-1914, (970) 874-8721, https://www.colorado.com/history-museums/delta-county-museum

Fort Uncompahgre Living History Museum, 360 Main St, Delta, CO 81416, (970) 874-7973, http://www.fortuncompahgre.org

Hotchkiss-Crawford Historical Society, Historical Museum, 180 2nd St, P.O. Box 727, Hotchkiss, CO 81419, (970) 872-3780, https://www.facebook.com/Hotchkiss-CrawfordHistoricalMuseum/

Surface Creek Historical Society, Pioneer Town Museum, 315 SW 3rd Ave, P.O. Box 906, Cedaredge, CO 81413, (970) 856-7554, http://www.pioneertown.org

Special Events & Scenic Locations
The Delta County Fair & Rodeo is held in August most years. Delta County Fairgrounds, 403 Fair Grounds (S 4th St), Hotchkiss, CO 81419, 970-234-3971, https://deltacountyfair.com.

Delta County keeps a calendar of festivals and events here: https://www.deltacountycolorado.com/play/ongoing-events/

Dominguez Canyon Wilderness
Dominguez-Escalante National Conservation Area
Grand Mesa National Forest
Gunnison Gorge National Conservation Area
Gunnison Gorge Wilderness
Crawford State Park
Sweiter Lake State Park
American Discovery Trail
Crag Crest National Recreation Trail
Old Spanish National Historic Trail
Grand Mesa Scenic and Historic Byway
West Elk Loop Scenic Byway

Ghost Towns & Other Sparsely Populated Places
Chipeta, Crawford, Dominguez, Duncan, Escalante, Hotchkiss, Roubideau

Delta County

Newspapers
Delta Chief. (Delta, Delta County, Colo.) 1883-1886
Delta County Advertiser. (Delta, Colo.) 1885-????
The Delta Independent. (Delta, Colo.) 1886-19??
The Delta County Laborer. (Delta City, Delta County, Colo.) 1890-1897
The Delta Laborer. (Delta, Delta County, Colo.) 1897-1902
The North Fork Times. (Hotchkiss, Colo.) 1897-19??
The Delta Press. (Delta, Colo.) 19??-19??
Davis' Auction Bulletin. (Delta, Colo.) 19??-19??
The Paonia Gazette. (Paonia, Delta County, Colo.) 19??-19??
Delta Evening Telegram. (Delta, Colo.) 19??-19??
The Delta County Laborer. (Delta, Delta County, Colo.) 1902-1908
Surface Creek Champion. (Cedaredge, Delta County, Colo.) 1904-1943
The Paonia Booster. (Paonia, Colo.) 1904-1912
The Newspaper. (Paonia, Colo.) 1904-1910
The Paonia Newspaper. (Paonia, Colo.) 1904-1904
The Hotchkiss Herald. (Hotchkiss, Colo.) 1905-1969
The Crawford Chronicle. (Crawford, Colo.) 1907-19??
Delta County Tribune and Delta County Laborer. (Delta, Colo.) 1908-1908
Delta County Tribune. (Delta, Colo.) 1908-19??
The Paonia Newspaper. (Paonia, Colo.) 1910-1911
Paonia's Market Day Herald. (Paonia, Colo.) 1910-19??
The Paonia Progressive and The Paonia Newspaper. (Paonia, Colo.) 1911-19??
The Austin Journal. (Austin, Delta County, Colo.) 1911-1914
The Paonian and The Paonia Booster. (Paonia, Colo.) 1912-1912
The Paonian. (Paonia, Colo.) 1912-1978
The West Slope. (Austin, Delta County, Colo.) 1914-1917
Delta Daily Independent. (Delta, Colo.) 1929-1939
The Boomerang. (Delta, Colo.) 1930-1930
The Free Press. (Delta, Colo.) 1930-19??
Delta County Daily Independent. (Delta, Colo.) 1939-1940
Delta County Independent. (Delta, Colo.) 1940-Current
Surface Creek News. (Cedaredge, Colo.) 1948-1956
The Sentry. (Cedaredge, Colo.) 1968-19??
The North Fork Herald-Chronicle. (Hotchkiss, Colo.) 1969-1978
The North Fork Times. (Paonia, Colo.) 1975-1990
The North Fork's Paonian Herald-Chronicle. (North Fork Valley, Delta County, Colo.) 1978-1979
The North Fork's Paonian-Herald. (Paonia, Colo.) 1979-1979
Paonia Paonian-Hotchkiss Herald. (Paonia, Colo.) 1979-1979
Paonian-Herald. (Paonia, Colo.) 1979-1982

Places on the National Register
Austin, Ferganchick Orchard Rock Art Site, Address Restricted
Cedaredge, Stolte House, 1812 CO 65
Cedaredge, Surface Creek Livestock Company Silos, 315 SW 3rd St.

Historical Assets Colorado

Delta, Delta County Bank Building, 301 and 305 Main St.
Delta, Egyptian Theater, 452 Main St.
Delta, First Methodist Episcopal Church of Delta, 199 E. Fifth St.
Delta, Garnethurst, 509 Leon St.
Delta, US Post Office and Federal Building—Delta Main, 360 Meeker St.
Eckert, First Presbyterian Church of Eckert, 13011 and 13025 CO 65
Hotchkiss, Hotchkiss Homestead, 422 Riverside Dr.
Hotchkiss, Hotchkiss Hotel, 101 Bridge St.
Hotchkiss, Hotchkiss Methodist Episcopal Church, 285 N. 2nd St.
Paonia, Curtis Hardware Store, 228 Grand Ave.
Paonia, Mathews House, 40647 Matthews Ln.
Paonia, Paonia First Christian Church, 235 Box Elder Ave.

USGS Historic Places

Grand Mesa, Grand Mesa Post Office, 39.0402581, -107.9497893
Hotchkiss, Hotchkiss-Crawford Historical Museum, 38.7980404, -107.7200587
Lazear, Hurst School, 38.8005396, -107.7817267
Orchard City, Hawkins Ranch Airport, 38.8413719, -107.8761744
Paonia, Community Care Hospital of America, 38.8647096, -107.5817238

Grand Army of the Republic Posts

George B McClellan, No. 76, Delta, Delta
North Fork, No. 86, Delta, Hotchkiss
Paonia, No. 111, Delta, Delta

USGS Historic Military Places

None

Military Bases

None

Post Offices

Alda	1913 May 2	1914 Dec 15	
Austin	1905 May 19		81410
Bowie	1907 Feb 5	1967 July 14	
Cedaredge	1894 Dec 5		81413
Chipeta	1895 June 14	1895 Sept 7	
Coalby	1906 Apr 11	1912 Aug 15	
Cory	1895 Mar 12		81414
Crawford	1883 Apr 14		81415
Delta	1882 Jan 5		81416
Dominguez	1907 Aug 17	1913 Oct 31	
Eckert	1891 Oct 27		81418
Grand Mesa	1927 June 23	1958 Aug 31	
Hotchkiss	1882 Oct 3		81419

Delta County

Lazear	1912 Jan 29		81420
Marion	1885 Feb 6	1886 Aug 27	
Paonia	1882 June 7		81428
Read	1898 Apr 22	1934 Jan 31	
Robideau	1909 Feb 27	1918 July 15	
Verne	1903 Oct 12	1903 Dec 30	
Welcome	1910 June 22	1912 Aug 31	

Topo Quads

Black Ridge	384500N	383730N	1074500W	1075230W
Cedaredge	390000N	385230N	1075230W	1080000W
Delta	384500N	383730N	1080000W	1080730W
Dry Creek	390000N	385230N	1074500W	1075230W
Electric Mountain	390730N	390000N	1073000W	1073730W
Good Point	384500N	383730N	1081500W	1082230W
Grand View Mesa	384500N	383730N	1073730W	1074500W
Gray Reservoir	390000N	385230N	1073730W	1074500W
Hotchkiss	385230N	384500N	1073730W	1074500W
Lazear	385230N	384500N	1074500W	1075230W
North Delta	385230N	384500N	1080000W	1080730W
Olathe NW	384500N	383730N	1075230W	1080000W
Orchard City	385230N	384500N	1075230W	1080000W
Roubideau	384500N	383730N	1080730W	1081500W

Suggested Reading

Doherty, Deborah V and Julie Wise. Delta, *Colorado: the First Hundred Years*. Delta, CO: D V Coherty, 1981.

Fay, Abbott. *Grand Mesa Country: Stories from Mesa and Delta Counties in Colorado*. Montrose, CO: Western Reflections Pub, 2005.

Rockwell, Wilson. *Delta County: the Formative Years*. NL: NP, 1975.

Wetzel, James K. *A Spirit Returns: Delta County, Colorado: A Pictoral History*. Virginia Beach, VA: Donning Co Publishers, 2003.

Historical Assets Colorado

Denver County

Introduction

Established: 1901   Population: 619,968

Formed from: Arapahoe

Adjacent Counties: Adams, Jefferson, Arapahoe

County Seat: Denver

  Other Communities: Glendale, Holly Hills

Website, https://www.denvergov.org

Area Codes: 303, 720

Zip Codes: 80201-80212, 80216-80220, 80222-80224, 80230, 80231, 80236-80239, 80243, 80244, 80246, 80248-80251, 80256, 80257, 80259, 80261-80266, 80271, 80273, 80274, 80281, 80290, 80291, 80293, 80294, 80299

Historical Assets Colorado

Denver City & County Courthouse and Civic Center

Courthouses & County Government

Denver County
https://www.denvergov.org/content/denvergov/en.html
Denver City Council, 1437 Bannock St, Denver, CO 80202, 720-337-2000, https://www.denvergov.org/content/denvergov/en/denver-city-council.html
Denver City & County Building (Civil Matters), 1437 Bannock St, Denver, CO 80202, 720-865-8301; http://www.denvergov.org
Denver County Courthouse (Criminal Matters)(2nd Judicial District), 520 W Colfax Ave, Denver, CO 80204, 720-865-8301; http://www.courts.state.co.us/Courts/County/Index.cfm?County_ID=3
Assessor, 201 W Colfax Ave, Denver, CO 80202, 720-913-1311; http://www.denvergov.org/Default.aspx?alias=www.denvergov.org/assessor
Clerk & Recorder, 201 W Colfax Ave, Denver, CO 80202, 720-865-8400; http://www.denvergov.org/Default.aspx?alias=www.denvergov.org/clerkandrecorder
Coroner (Medical Examiner), 500 Quivas St, Denver, CO 80204, 720-337-7600; https://www.denvergov.org/content/denvergov/en/environmental-health/our-divisions/office-of-the-medical-examiner.html
Elections, 200 W 14th Ave, Ste 100, Denver, CO 80204, 720-913, 8683; https://www.denvergov.org/content/denvergov/en/denver-elections-divison.html
Public Health, 4300 Cherry Creek Dr S, Denver, CO 80245, 303-692-2200; http://www.denvergov.org/Default.aspx?alias=www.denvergov.org/deh
Transportation Engineering, 201 W Colfax Ave, Dept 2, Denver, CO 80202; https://www.denvergov.org/content/denvergov/en/denver-development-services/help-me-find-/transportation-engineering.html
Treasurer, 201 W Colfax Ave, Dept 1009, Denver, CO 80202, 720-913-9300; http://www.denvergov.org/Default.aspx?alias=www.denvergov.org/treasury

Denver County

County Records

Birth 1906	Marriage 1897	Divorce 1901
Death Unk	Land 1901	Probate 1901
Court 1901		

CSA Birth 1872, Births Outside of Denver City Limits 1891
CSA Delayed Birth Certificates 1942
CSA Death 1888
CSA Infant Deaths 1930
CSA Burial Permits 1907
CSA County Physicians Records 1908
CSA Hospital Admission Register 1891
CSA Hospital Death Register 1887
CSA Undertakers Shippers Record 1916

County & Municipal Records Held at the State Level

The Colorado State Archives

Physical Records
Assessor
Building
Board of Aldermen
Board of Supervisors
City Clerk
City Council
Clerk & Recorder
Coroner
County Commissioners
County Court
District Court
Probate Court
Superior Court
Fire
Police
Mountain Parks
Public Trustee
Public Works
Sheriff
Surveyor
Treasurer
WPA Historical Records
WPA Religious Institutions Survey
Cities
  Denver
  Early Denver
  Argo
  Auraria
  Barnum
  Berkley
  Denver City
  Elyria
  Harman
  Globeville
  Highlands
  Montclair
  North Denver
  South Denver
  Valverde
  Westwood

Records on Film
Assessor
Clerk & Recorder
County Court
District Court
Probate Court
Superior Court
Treasurer
Cities
  Denver
  Early Denver
  Argo
  Auraria
  Barnum
  Berkley
  Denver City
  Elyria
  Harman
  Globeville
  Highlands
  Montclair
  North Denver
  South Denver
  Valverde
  Westwood

Records on Master Film
Assessor
Auditor
Board of Equalization
Cemetery District
City Clerk
City Council
Clerk & Recorder
County Court
District Court
Juvenile Court
Probate Court
Superior Court
Election Commission
Health & Hospitals
Mountain Parks
Museums
Planning
Police
Public Welfare
School District
Sheriff
Treasurer
Water
Cities
  Denver
  Early Denver
  Argo
  Auraria

Historical Assets Colorado

Barnum	Harman	North Denver
Berkley	Globeville	South Denver
Denver City	Highlands	Valverde
Elyria	Montclair	Westwood

The Denver Public Library
- 1885 Colorado Census
- Abstracts of Title, 1860-1969
- Alps Gold Mining Company Records, 1889-1907
- American Institue of Architects, Colorado Records, 1954
- Auditor's Office Records, 1922-1984
- Board of Adjustment for Zoning Records, 1925-1968
- Board of Park Commissioners Records, 1893-1916
- Board of Water Commissioners, Water Tap Papers, 1872-1987
- Building Permits 1889-1955
- City Council Records, 1859-2011
- Clayton College Records, 1851-1999
- Colorado Deeds, 1868-1911
- Colorado Genealogical Society Records, 1849-2017
- Colorado-Missouri Society Genealogical Records, 1938-1940
- Colorado State Council of Defense Records, 1918-1919
- Colorado State Engineers Office Records, 1907-1908
- Colorado Taxpayers Protective League Records, 1914-1917
- Community Planning & Development Records, 1955-2005
- Denver & Arapahoe County Real Estate Records, 1886-1974
- Denver American Indian Commission Records, 1987-2008
- Denver Building Department Records, 1893-1960
- Denver Charter Convention Records, 1903
- Denver Civil Service Commission Records, 1904-1952
- Denver Landmarks, 1987-1999
- Denver Model City Program Records, 1966-1976
- Denver Police Department Intelligence Bureau Files, 1950-2002
- Denver Public School Records, 1890-2018
- Denver Regional Council of Government Records, 1970-1991
- Denver Street Department Letters, 1894-1916
- Denver Tramway Corporation Records, 1888-1975
- Department of Finance, Treasury Division Records, 1864-1978
- Departmentt of Finance, Assessment Division Records, 1863-1985
- Department of Improvement and Parks Records, 1895-1959
- Department of Public Office Buildings Records, 1939-1987
- Department of Public Works Records, 1890-2003
- Department of Safety and Exise, Police Department Records, 1900-1982
- Development Engineering Services Records, 1893-1995
- Election Division Records, 1920-1991
- Hampton Heights Civil Association Records, 1974-2001
- Kansas-Burroughs Consolidated Mining Company Records, 1870-1906
- LaCrosse Gold Mining Company Records, 1877-1905

Denver County

Maumee Gold Mining Company Records, 1909-1910
Marriage License Applications, 1903-2003
Marriage Licenses & Certificates, 1952-1965
Marriage Records, 1859-1901
Montclair Lateral Irrigation Company Records, 1910-1911
Municipal Building Records, 1916-1933
New York-Central Gold Mining Company Records, 1896-1909
Office of Television Services Records, 1985-1991
Origin of the Adult Blind Home, 1933
Planning and Land Office Records, 1950-1959
Presbyterian-St Luke's Medical Center Records, 1890-2009
Probate Court Records, 1930-1989
Rocky Mountain Arsenal Records, 1952-1966
Treasurer's Certificates of Purchase, 1894-1939
WWI Draft Registration Cards (microfilm)

School Districts

School Districts, http://www.adcogov.org/local-school-districts
Denver Public Schools, 1860 Lincoln St, Denver, CO 80203, 720-423-3200; https://www.dpsk12.org/

Historic School Districts

Denver School District No. 1

Fraternal Organizations

Granges
Green Valley, No. 158, Denver, Valverde, 15 June 1907
Cherry Gardens, No. 165, Denver, Denver/Capitol Hill Station, 9 May 1908
Sable, No. 167, Denver, Montclair, 25 Aug 1908
Garden Home, No. 407, Denver, Denver, 12 Mar 1930
Liberty, No. 437, Denver, Denver, 26 June 1936
Alameda Community, No. 474, Denver, Denver, 12 Mar 1953
Mile High, No. 492, Denver, Denver, 10 Apr 1962

Masons

Ancient Free & Accepted Masons
Pythagoras, No. 41, Denver, Denver, 24 Jan 2016
Marquis de Lafayette, No. 41, Denver, Denver, 25 Jan 2019
Albert Pike, No. 117, Denver, Denver, 16 Sept 1903
Arapahoe, No. 130, Denver, Denver, 22 Sept 1908
Berkeley, No. 134, Denver, Denver, 20 Sept 1910
Liberty, No. 134, Denver, Denver, 26 Jan 2002
South Gate, No. 138, Denver, Denver, 20 Sept 1910
Inspiration, No. 143, Denver, Denver, 15 Sept 1914
Henry M Teller, No. 144, Denver, Denver, 15 Sept 1914
Columine, No. 147, Denver, Denver, 19 Sept 1916

Historical Assets Colorado

Park Hill, No. 148, Denver, Denver, 19 Sept 1916
Liberty, No. 150, Denver, Denver, 18 Sept 1918
Palestine, No. 151, Denver, Denver, 18 Sept 1918
Centennial, No. 151, Denver, Denver, 26 Jan 1996
Emulation, No. 154, Denver, Denver, 21 Sept 1921
East Denver, No. 160, Denver, Denver, 16 Sept 1925
George Washington, No. 161, Denver, Denver, 16 Sept 1925
Paul Revere, No. 162, Denver, Denver, 16 Sept 1925
Lawrence N Greenleaf, No. 169, Denver, Denver, 18 Sept 1928
Jacques DeMolay, No. 171, Denver, Denver, 14 Sept 1949
William W Cooper, No. 172, Denver, Denver, 14 Sept 1949
Joppa Daylight, No. 174, Denver, Denver, 23 Jan 1952
Malta, No. 178, Denver, Denver, 18 Mar 1953
Cherry Point, No. 179, Denver, Denver, 25 Jan 1982
Friendship, No. 185, Denver, Denver, 27 Jan 1960
Cherry Point, No. 186, Denver, Denver, 27 Jan 1960
Perfection, No. 193, Denver, Denver, 23 Jan 1968

Royal Arch Masons
Highlands, No. 39, Denver, Denver
South Denver, No. 42, Denver, Denver
Park Hill, No. 50, Denver, Denver

Knights Templar
Highlands Commandery, No. 30, Denver, Denver, 1907 Sept 7
Ascalon Commandery, No. 31, Denver, Denver, 1910 Apr 12
Coronal Commandery, No. 36, Denver, Denver, 1917 June 11

Eastern Star
Radiant, No. 12, Denver, Denver
Denver, No. 59, Denver, Denver
Electa, No. 60, Denver, Denver
Fern, No. 94, Denver, Denver
Temple, No. 96, Denver, Denver
Unity, No. 97, Denver, Denver
Oriental, No. 98, Denver, Denver
Daylight, No. 101, Denver, Denver
South Gate, No. 104, Denver, Denver
Inspiration, No. 107, Denver, Denver
Park Hill, No. 109, Denver, Denver
Golden Sheaf, No. 111, Denver, Denver
Golden Rule, No. 115, Denver, Denver
Capitol Hill, No. 119, Denver, Denver
East Denver, No. 123, Denver, Denver
Areme, No. 124, Denver, Denver
Washington Park, No. 126, Denver, Denver
Melody, No. 141, Denver, Denver
Fidelity, No. 144, Denver, Denver

Denver County

Prince Hall Masons
    Rocky Mountain Lodge No. 1, Arapahoe, Denver, 1876
    Mount Evans Lodge No. 7, Denver, Denver, 1960

Prince Hall Order of the Eastern Star
    Lone Star Chapter No. 1, Denver, Denver
    Evergreen Chapter No. 3, Denver, Denver
    Lone Star Chapter, No. 15, Denver, Denver
    Electa Chapter No. 16, Denver, Denver
    Evergreen Chapter, No. 36, Denver, Denver

Prince Hall Heroines of Jericho
    Josephine F Brown Court No. 1, Denver, Denver

Prince Hall Scottish Rite
    Mountain Plains Consistory No. 33, Denver, Denver

Prince Hall Order of the Golden Circle
    Mountain & Plains Assembly No. 49, Denver, Denver

Prince Hall Holy Royal Arch Masons
    D R Butler Chapter No. 1, Denver, Denver

Prince Hall Knights Templar
    Ira C Meadows Commandery No. 1, Denver, Denver

Odd Fellows
    Barnham, No. 3, Denver, Denver
    Queen City, No. 56, Denver, Denver
    Englewood, No. 57, Denver, Englewood
    Burnham, No. 57, Denver, Denver
    Norden, No. 61, Denver, Denver
    Washington, No. 72, Denver, Denver
    Enterprise, No. 85, Denver, Denver
    Buckingham, No. 93, Denver, Denver
    Fairmount, No. 96, Denver, Denver
    Capital, No. 96, Denver, Denver
    Silver State, No. 97, Denver, Denver
    Harman, No. 105, Denver, Denver
    Denver, No. 120, Denver, Denver

Rebekahs
    Star of the East, No. 48, Denver, Denver
    Justicia, No. 49, Denver, Denver
    Pleiades, No. 67, Denver, Denver
    Linnea, No. 110, Denver, Denver
    Daylight, No. 121, Denver, Denver
    Rainbow, No. 139, Denver, Denver

Knights of Pythias
    South Side, No. 127, Denver, Denver

Pythian Sisters
    Fern, No. 14, Denver, Denver
    Capitol, No. 51, Denver, Denver

Historical Assets Colorado

Benevolent Protective Order of Elks
None

City Hall
Denver (City & County Building), 1437 Bannock St, Denver, CO 80202, 720-337-2000, https://www.denvergov.org

Archives & Manuscript Collections
Anderson Academic Commons, Special Collections, University of Denver, 2150 E Evans Ave, Denver, CO 80208-2007, (303) 871-2905, https://library.du.edu/collections-archives/specialcollections/index.html

Archives of the Archdiocese of Denver, 1300 S Steele St, Denver, CO 80210, (303) 722-4687, https://www.archden.org/archives/

Archives of the Episcopal Diocese of Colorado, 1300 Washington, Denver, CO 80203, (303) 837-1173, https://episcopalcolorado.org

Auraria Library, Special & Digital Collections, 1100 Lawrence St, Denver, CO 80204-2095, (303) 556-2805, https://library.auraria.edu/about/special-collections

Bailey Library & Archives, Denver Museum of Nature & Science, 2001 Colorado Blvd, Denver, CO 80205, (303) 370-6089, https://www.dmns.org/science/archives/

Blair Caldwell African American Research Library, 2401 Welton St, Denver, CO 80205-3015, (720) 865-2401, https://www.denverlibrary.org/content/blair-caldwell-african-american-research-library

Colorado Division of State Archives and Public Records, 1313 Sherman St, Rm 120, Denver, CO 80203-3534, (303) 866-2055, https://www.colorado.gov/archives

Denver Public Library-Western History & Genealogy, 10 W 14th Ave Pkwy, Denver, CO 80204-2731, (720) 865-1821, https://www.denverlibrary.org

Ira J Taylor Library & Margaret E Scheve Archives, Iliff School of Theology, 2323 E Iliff Ave, Denver, CO 80210, (303) 765-3173, https://library.iliff.edu/archives/

Ira M Beck Memorial Collection of Rocky Mountain Jewish History, Sturm Hall, 2000 E Asbury Ave, Denver, CO 80208, (303) 871-3020, https://www.du.edu/ahss/cjs/rmjhs/archives/

Stephen H Hart Research Center, History Colorado, 1200 Broadway, Denver, CO 80203, (303) 866-2305, https://www.historycolorado.org/visit-our-stephen-h-hart-research-center

Historical & Genealogical Societies
Association of Professional Genealogists, Colorado Chapter, P.O. Box 40431, Denver, CO 80204, https://www.apgen.org/chapters/colorado/index.html

Black Genealogy Search Group of Colorado, P.O. Box 7276, Denver, CO 80207, (303) 445-2150, http://bgsgden.com

Colorado Council of Genealogical Societies, P.O. Box 40270, Denver, CO 80224-0379, (303) 688-9652, http://cocouncil.org

Colorado Genealogical Society, P.O. Box 9218, Denver, CO 80209-0218, (303) 571-1535, http://www.cogensoc.us

Colorado Genealogical Society, Computer Interest Group, P.O. Box 9218, Denver, CO 80209-0218, https://cigcolorado.org

Denver County

Colorado Society of Hispanic Genealogy, 2300 S Patton Ct, Denver, CO 80219-5212, http://www.hispanicgen.org

Colorado Welsh Society, P.O. Box 103192, Denver, CO 80250, (303) 427-7188, http://coloradowelshsociety.org

Historic Denver, 1420 Ogden St, Ste 202, Denver, CO 80218, (303) 534-5288, http://www.historicdenver.org

History Colorado, Colorado Heritage Center, 1200 Broadway, Denver, CO 80203, (303) 447-8679, http://www.historycolorado.org

Jewish Genealogical Society of Colorado, P.O. Box 460442, Denver, CO 80246, http://www.jgsco.org

National Railway Historical Society, Intermountain Chapter, 4303 Brighton Blvd, P.O. Box 16664, Denver, CO 80216, (303) 298-0377, http://www.cozx.com/nrhs/

Rocky Mountain Jewish Historical Society, Univ of Denver, Sturm Hall, 2000 E Asbury Ave, Rm 157, Denver, CO 80208-0001, (303) 871-3016, http://www.du.edu/cjs/rmjhs

Society of Rocky Mountain Archivists, Colorado State Archives, 1313 Sherman St, Denver, CO 80203, (307) 766-2553, https://www.srmarchivists.org

Tenth Circuit Historical Society, 1801 California St, Ste 4200, Denver, CO 80202, (303) 298-5701, http://www.10thcircuithistory.org

WISE Family History Society (Wales, Ireland, Scotland, England), P.O. Box 40658, Denver, CO 80204-0658, (303) 922-8856, http://www.wise-fhs.org

Local Libraries

Denver Public Library-Western History & Genealogy, 10 W 14th Ave Pkwy, Denver, CO 80204-2731, (720) 865-1821, https://www.denverlibrary.org

Colorado State Library, Colorado Virtual Library Collection, 201 E Colfax Ave, No 309, Denver, CO 80203-1799, (303) 866-6900, http://www.cde.state.co.us/cdelib; https://www.coloradovirtuallibrary.org

Saint John's Cathedral Library, 1350 Washington St, Denver, CO 80203, (303) 831-7115, http://www.sjcathedral.org/Library

Links

CO GenWeb
http://cogenweb.com/denver/

Cyndi's List
https://www.cyndislist.com/us/co/counties/denver/

FamilySearch Wiki
https://www.familysearch.org/wiki/en/Denver_County,_Colorado_Genealogy

Linkpendium
http://www.linkpendium.com/denver-co-genealogy/

RootsWeb Wiki
https://wiki.rootsweb.com/wiki/index.php/Denver_County,_Colorado

Wikipedia
https://en.wikipedia.org/wiki/Denver_County,_Colorado

Historical Assets Colorado

Historic Hotels

1891 Oxford Hotel, 1600 17th St, Denver, CO 80202, 303-628-4500, https://www.theoxfordhotel.com

1892 Brown Palace Hotel, 321 17th St, Denver, CO 0202, 303-297-3111, https://www.brownpalace.com

*1881 Crawford Hotel (located in the 1881 Union Station), 1701 Wynkoop St, Denver, CO 80202, 720-460-3700, https://www.thecrawfordhotel.com

Museums & Historic Sites

Barco Library & Cable Center Museum, 2000 Buchtel Blvd, Denver, CO 80210, (303) 871-4885, http://www.cablecenter.org

Black American West Museum and Heritage Center, 3091 California St, Denver, CO 80205, (303) 292-2566, https://bawmhc.org

Boettcher Mansion Museum, 400 E 8th Ave, Denver, CO 80203, (303) 866-5344, https://www.colorado.gov/governor-residence

Buckhorn Exchange Restaurant and Museum, 1000 Osage St, Denver, CO 80204, (303) 534-9505, http://www.buckhorn.com

Colorado Sports Hall of Fame, 1701 Mile High Stadium Cr #500, Denver, CO 80204, (720) 258-3888, http://www.coloradosports.com

Delaney Farm Museum, 170 S Chambers Rd, Aurora, CO 80205, (303) 739-6660, https://dug.org/about-delaney-community-farm

Denver Firefighters Museum, 1326 Tremont Pl, Denver, CO 80204, (303) 892-1436, http://www.denverfirefightersmuseum.org

Denver Museum of Nature & Science, 2001 Colorado Blvd, Denver, CO 80205, (303) 322-7009, https://www.dmns.org

Forney Museum of Transportation, 4303 Brighton Blvd, Denver, CO 80216, (303) 297-1113, http://www.forneymuseum.org

Four Mile Historic Park Museum, 715 S Forest St, Denver, CO 80246, (303) 399-1859, http://www.fourmilepark.org

Grant-Humphreys Mansion Museum, 770 Pennsylvania St, Denver, CO 80203, (303) 894-2506, https://www.historycolorado.org/grant-humphreys-mansion

Historic Fort Logan, 3742 W Princeton Cr, P.O. Box 36011, Denver, CO 80236, (303) 789-3568, http://www.friendsofhistoricfortlogan.org

History Colorado, Colorado Heritage Center, 1200 Broadway, Denver, CO 80203, (303) 447-8679, http://www.historycolorado.org

Mizel Museum, 400 S Kearney St, Denver, CO 80224, (303) 394-9993, http://www.mizelmuseum.org

Molly Brown House Museum, 1340 Pennsylvania St, Denver, CO 80203, (303) 832-4092, http://www.mollybrown.org

Molly Brown Summer House Museum, 7595 W Yale Ave, Denver, CO 80227, (303) 253-8349, http://www.mollybrownsummerhouse.com

Museo de las Americas, 861 Santa Fe Dr, Denver, CO 80204, (303) 571-4401, http://www.museo.org

Stiles African American Heritage Center, 2607 Glenarm Pl, Denver, CO 80205, (303) 294-0597, http://www.stilesheritagecenter.org

Denver County

United States Mint Museum, 320 W Colfax Ave, Denver, CO 80204, (303) 844-3332, https://www.usmint.gov/about/mint-tours-facilities/denver

Wings Over the Rockies Air & Space Museum, 7711 N Academy Blvd, Hanger 1, Denver, CO 80230, (303) 860-5360, http://www.wingsmuseum.org

Special Events & Scenic Locations

The Denver County Fair is held in July most years at the National Western Complex, 4655 Humboldt St, Denver, CO 80216, 303-297-1166, https://denvercountyfair.org

Denver is also famous for the National Western Stock Show & Rodeo that takes place in January each year at the National Western Complex, https://national-western.com

Visit Denver keeps a calendar of annual events and festivals here: https://www.denver.org/events/annual/

Ghost Towns & Other Sparsely Populated Places

Argo, Auraria, Barnum, Berkeley (North Denver), Colfax, Elyria, Globeville, Harman, Highlands, Montana City, Montclair, South Denver, Valverde, Westwood

(Most of these towns are now neighborhoods within the City of Denver)

Newspapers

The Denver Democrat and National Standard. (Denver, Colo.) 1???-1905
Johannes Steel Challenge. (Denver, Colo.) 1???-19??
South Denver Eye & Bulletin. (Denver, Colo.) 1???-19??
The Colorado Tourist and Hotel Reporter. (Denver and Colorado Springs [Colo.]) 1???-19??
The Denver Leader. (Denver, Colo.) 1???-1971
The Denver Citizen. (Denver, Colo.) 1???-19??
The Highland Chief. (Denver, Colo.) 18??-19??
The Daily Colorado Price Current and Livestock Journal. (Denver, Colo.) 18??-1897
Colorado Farm and Livestock Journal. (Denver, Colo.) 18??-1???
The Colorado Farmer. (Denver, Colo.) 18??-1???
The Colorado Evening Sun. (Denver, Colo.) 18??-1???
Rocky Mountain Illustrated Weekly. (Denver, Colo.) 18??-1897
The Denver Examiner. (Denver, Colo.) 18??-1916
The Elite. ([Denver, Colo.]) 18??-1885
Daily Fair Programme. (Denver, Colo.) 18??-1???
Denver Hotel Bulletin. (Denver, Colo.) 18??-19??
The Evening Star. (Denver, Colo.) 18??-1???
Rocky Mountain Cricket. (Denver, Colo.) 18??-1???
The Silver Age. (Denver, Colo.) 18??-1???
The State Mining Journal. (Denver, Colo.) 18??-1???
The Rocky Mountain Farmer and Miner. (Denver, Colo.) 18??-19??
Tri-Weekly Commonwealth & Republican. (Denver City, Colo. Territory [I.e. Denver, Colo.]) 18??-18??

Historical Assets Colorado

The Kansas City Times. (Denver, Colo.) 18??-18??
The Challenge. (Denver, Colo.) 18??-1???
The Rocky Mounty Celt and Globeville Chronicle. (Denver And Globeville, Colo.) 18??-1???
Arizona Copper Miner. (Denver, Colo.) 181?-18??
Rocky Mountain News. (Cherry Creek, Kan. Terr. [Denver, Colo.]) 1859-1864
Weekly Rocky Mountain News. (Denver, Colo.) 1859-19??
Cherry Creek Pioneer. (Denver City, Kan. [i.e. Denver, Colo.]) 1859-1859
The Denver Bulletin : and Supplement to The Rocky Mountain News. (Denver, Jefferson [Colo.]) 1860-1860
The Denver Weekly Bulletin : and Supplement to The Rocky Mountain News. (Denver, Jefferson [Colo.]) 1860-1860
Rocky Mountain Herald. (Denver, Colo.) 1860-1861
Denver Weekly Mountaineer. (Denver, Colo.) 1860-1861
Daily Denver Mountaineer. (Denver, Colo. Terr. [Colo.]) 1860-1861
The Daily Herald and Rocky Mountain Advertiser. (Denver, Colo.) 1860-1861
Daily Rocky Mountain News. (Denver, Jefferson [Colo.]) 1860-1879
The Daily Colorado Republican and Rocky Mountain Herald. (Denver City, Colorado Territory [Denver, Colo.]) 1861-1862
The Weekly Colorado Republican and Rocky Mountain Herald. (Denver City, Colorado Territory. [Denver, Colo.]) 1861-1862
The Weekly Commonwealth and Republican. (Denver City, Colo. Territory [Denver, Colo.]) 1862-1863
The Daily Commonwealth. (Denver City, Colorado Territory [Denver, Colo.]) 1863-1864
The Weekly Commonwealth. (Denver City, Colorado Territory [Denver, Colo.]) 1863-1864
The Weekly Rocky Mountain News. (Denver, Colo.) 1864-1865
The Weekly Denver Gazette. (Denver, Colo.) 1865-1???
The Daily Denver Gazette. (Denver, Colo.) 1865-1869
The Rocky Mountain News. (Denver, Colo.) 1865-1872
The Colorado Leader. (Denver, Colo.) 1867-18??
The Denver Daily. (Denver, Colo.) 1867-1867
The Daily Colorado Tribune. (Denver, Colo.) 1867-1871
The Weekly Colorado Tribune. (Denver, Colo.) 1867-1868
The Colorado Tribune. (Denver, Colo.) 1867-1867
The Rocky Mountain Herald. (Denver, Colo.) 1868-1976
The Colorado Tribune. (Denver, Colo.) 1869-18??
The Daily Gazette and Commercial Advertiser. (Denver, Colo.) 1869-1???
The Daily Denver Times. (Denver, Colo.) 1869-1870
Denver Daily Democrat. (Denver, Colo.) 187?-18??
The Colorado Weekly Republican. (Denver, Colo.) 187?-1???
Colorado Journal. (Denver, Colo.) 187?-1??? | Languages: German
Presbyterian Home Missions. (Denver, Colo.) 187?-1874
The Denver Press. (Denver, Colo.) 1871-1901
The Denver Tribune. (Denver, Colo.) 1871-1875

Denver County

The Denver Tribune. (Denver, Colo.) 1871-1884
Rocky Mountain Leader. (Denver, Colo.) 1872-1873
Daily Denver Times. (Denver, Colo.) 1872-1875
Weekly Rocky Mountain News. (Denver, Colo.) 1872-19??
The Denver Times. (Denver, Colo.) 1872-1926
Colorado Journal. (Denver, Colo.) 1872-1901 | Languages: German
Weekly Denver Times. (Denver, Colo.) 1873-1875
Colorado Agriculturalist and Stock Journal. (Denver, Colo.) 1873-1???
Denver Mirror. (Denver, Colo.) 1873-1879
Colorado Democrat. (Denver, Colo.) 1874-1???
The Weekly Colorado Democrat. (Denver, Colo.) 1874-????
Daily Colorado Transcript. (Denver, Colo.) 1875-1???
The Denver Weekly Times. (Denver, Colo.) 1875-1895
Denver Daily Times. (Denver, Colo.) 1875-1886
Denver Daily Tribune. (Denver, Colo.) 1875-1879
The Daily Democrat. (Denver, Colo.) 1876-18??
The Weekly Democrat. (Denver, Colo.) 1876-18??
Kansas and Colorado Illustrated Monthly Newspaper. (Kansas City, Mo. And Denver, Colo.) 1878-1???
Weekly Republican. (Denver, Colo.) 1878-1884
Colorado Rural Life. (Denver, Colo.) 1879-1880
The Denver Republican. (Denver, Colo.) 1879-1884
Denver Tribune. (Denver, Colo.) 1879-1884
Colorado Post. (Denver, Colo.) 1879-1??? | Languages: German
The Daily Hotel Reporter. (Denver, Colo.) 1879-1???
The Colorado Antelope. (Denver, Colo.) 1879-1879
Rocky Mountain News. (Denver, Colo.) 1879-1935
Denver Daily Republican. (Denver, Colo.) 1879-1???
Inter-Ocean. (Denver, Colo.) 1880-1???
The Great West. (Denver, Colo.) 1880-1882
Pomeroy's Democrat. (Denver, Colo.) 1880-1???
Montclair Mirror. (Denver, Colo.) 188?-19??
The Denver Detective. (Denver, Colo.) 188?-1???
Denver Argus. (Denver, Colo.) 188?-1???
The Western Churchman. (Denver, Colo.) 188?-1???
The Rocky Mountain Celt. (Denver, Colo.) 1881-1???
Sunday Morning Paragraph. (Denver, Colo.) 1881-188?
Our Opinion. (Denver, Colo.) 1881-18??
Evening Truth. (West Denver, Colo.) 1881-1882
The Truth. (West Denver, Colo.) 1881-1881
Denver Evening Press. (Denver, Colo.) 1881-1???
Die Sonntags-Post. (Denver, Colo.) 1881-1??? | Languages: German
Denver Journal Of Commerce. (Denver, Colo.) 1881-????
Queen Bee. (Denver, Colo.) 1882-1895
The Denver World. (Denver, Colo.) 1882-1???
Republican Journal. (Denver, Colo.) 1882-1???

Historical Assets Colorado

The Denver Mercury. (Denver, Colo.) 1882-1???
Denver Evening World. (Denver, Colo.) 1882-1???
Evening Telegram. (Denver, Colo.) 1882-1???
The Denver Star. (Denver, Colo.) 1882-18??
Denver Weekly World. (Denver, Colo.) 1882-1???
Colorado Posten. (Denver, Colo.) 1882-188? | Languages: Danish, Norwegian, Swedish
Colorado Courier. (Denver, Colo.) 1882-1888
The Labor Enquirer. (Denver, Colo.) 1882-1888
North Denver Villa Park Telephone. (Denver, Colo.) 1883-18??
Home Journal. (Denver, Colo.) 1883-18??
Nya Colorado Posten. (Denver, Colo.) 1883-???? | Languages: Danish, Norwegian, Swedish
Opinion. (Denver, Colo.) 1884-1???
The Vidette. (Denver, Colo.) 1884-1???
Denver Tribune-Republican. (Denver, Colo.) 1884-1886
Weekly Tribune-Republican. (Denver, Colo.) 1884-1886
Denver Herold. (Denver, Colo.) 1884-1??? | Languages: German
Colorado Catholic. (Denver, Colo.) 1884-1899
La Stella. [Volume] (Denver, Colo.) 1885-1??? | Languages: English, Italian
The Colorado Graphic. (Denver, Colo.) 1886-19??
The Evening Times. (Denver, Colo.) 1886-1887
Field and Farm. (Denver, Colo.) 1886-1920
Denver Evening Telegram. (Denver, Colo.) 1886-1887
The Denver Evening Times. (Denver, Colo.) 1887-1???
Home Journal. (North Denver and Highlands [Colo.]) 1887-1???
North Denver and Highlands Home Journal. (North Denver and Highlands, Colo.) 1887-1887
The Denver Exchange Journal. (Denver, Colo.) 1887-1888
The Road. (Denver, Colo.) 1887-1896
The Weekly Republican. (Denver, Colo.) 1887-1913
Rocky Mountain Sentinel. (Denver, Colo.) 1887-19??
The Denver Republican. (Denver, Colo.) 1887-1913
The Individualist. (Denver, Colo.) 1887-????
The Rocky Mountain Advocate. (Denver, Colo.) 1887-1888
Denver Vecko-Blad. (Denver, Col.) 1888-1889 | Languages: Swedish
Colorado Exchange Journal. (Denver, Colo.) 1888-1891
The Mountain Mirror. (Denver, Colo.) 1888-1???
The Western Standard. (Denver, Colo.) 1888-1???
The Arbitrator. (Denver, Colo.) 1889-1???
Denver Fidibus. (Denver, Colo.) 1889-189? | Languages: German
Svenska Korrespondenten. (Denver, Colo.) 1889-1901 | Languages: English, Swedish
The Mining Exchange Journal. (Denver, Colo.) 1889-1892
The Cow-Boy Roundup. (Denver, Colo.) 1889-1???
The Golden Perhaps. (Denver, Colo.) 1889-1???
The Statesman. (Denver, Colo.) 1889-1906

Denver County

The Bugle Call and The Plain Dealer. (Denver, Colo.) 189?-19??
Denver Fidibus-Herold. (Denver, Colo.) 189?-1901 | Languages: German
The Denver Dispatch. (Denver, Colo.) 1890-1???
The Illustrated Rocky Mountain Globe. (Denver, Colo.) 189?-1901
The Colorado Democrat. (Denver, Colo.) 189?-1???
La Patria. (Denver, Colo.) 189?-1??? | Languages: Italian
Denver Commercial Review. (Denver, Colo.) 1890-1???
Colorado State Capital. (Denver, Colo.) 1890-1???
Cheely's Democrat. (Denver, Colo.) 1890-1???
The African Advocate. (Denver, Colo.) 1890-1???
The Denver Financial News. (Denver, Colo.) 1890-1???
The Tomahawk. (Denver, Colo.) 1890-1???
The Rocky Mountain Forum. (Denver, Colo.) 189?-19??
The Denver Bee. (Denver, Colo.) 189?-1???
West Denver Review. (West Denver, Colo.) 189?-1???
The Colorado and Texas Exchange Journal. (Denver, Colo.) 1891-1???
The Colorado Sun. (Denver, Colo.) 1891-1???
The People. (Denver, Colo.) 1891-1???
Next. (Denver, Colo.) 1892-1???
The Western Irishman. (Denver, Colo.) 1892-1???
The Evening Post. (Denver, Colo.) 1892-1895
Il Roma. (Denver, Colo.) 1892-1920 | Languages: Italian
Progress. (Denver, Colo.) 1893-1???
The Daily Mining Record. (Denver, Colo.) 1893-1913
Industrial Advocate. (Denver, Colo.) 1893-1900
The Colorado Weekly Sun. (Denver, Colo.) 1893-1895
Rocky Mountain American. (Denver, Colo.) 1893-1???
The Daily State Mining Journal. (Denver, Colo.) 1893-1893
The Prohibition Globe. (Denver, Colo.) 1893-1???
The Democratic Record. (Denver, Colo.) 1893-1???
National Populist. (Denver, Colo.) 1893-1???
The Altrurian. (Denver [Colo.]) 1894-1901
Co-Operation. (University Park, Colo.) 1894-1???
The Bi-Metallist. (Denver, Colo.) 1894-1???
The Daily Populist. (Denver, Colo.) 1894-1???
The Special Post. (Denver, Colo.) 1895-1???
Our National Crisis. (Denver, Colo.) 1895-1???
The Denver Evening Post. (Denver, Colo.) 1895-1900
The Denver Weekly Times-Sun. (Denver, Colo.) 1895-1901
The Colorado Statesman. (Denver, Colo.) 1895-1961
The New Road. (Denver, Colo.) 1896-1898
The Grip Of Gold. (Denver, Colo.) 1896-1???
Las Dos Repúblicas. (Denver, Colo.) 1896-1??? | Languages: Spanish
The National Standard. (Denver, Colo.) 1897-19??
Daily Denver Stockman. (Denver, Colo.) 1897-1900
Illustrated Sentinel. (Denver, Colo.) 1897-1898

Historical Assets Colorado

The Daily Journal. (Denver, Colo.) 1897-Current
Illustrated Sentinel Weekly. (Denver, Colo.) 1898-1899
George's Weekly (The New Road). (Denver, Colo.) 1898-1898
George's Weekly (The Road). (Denver, Colo.) 1898-1900
Clay's Review. (Denver, Colo.) 1898-19??
The Denver Democrat. (Denver, Colo.) 1899-19??
Der Unterhaltungs-Bote. ([Denver, Colo.]) 1899-1899 | Languages: German
Illustrated Weekly. (Denver, Colo.) 1899-1908
South Side Citizen. (Denver, Colo.) 1899-1???
The Woman's Crier and Illustrated Free-Thinker. (Denver, Colo.) 1899-1???
The Intermountain Catholic. (Salt Lake City [Utah] ;) 1899-1920
Denver Weekly Post. (Denver, Colo.) 190?-1914
Denver Civic News. (Denver, Colo.) 19??-19??
The Mountain Plains Seniors' Gazette. (Denver, Colo.) 19??-????
The Liberty Press. (Denver, Colo.) 19??-19??
Public Ledger. (Denver, Colo.) 19??-19??
Denver Chronicle. (Denver, Colo.) 19??-19??
The Harpoon. (Denver, Colo.) 19??-19??
The Weekly Journal. (Denver, Colo.) 19??-19??
The Barnum News. (Denver, Colo.) 19??-19??
The Denver Catholic. (Denver, Colo.) 1900-1905
The Clarion : El Clarin. (Denver, Colo.) 19??-19??
Actionews. (Denver, Colo.) 19??-197?
United Labor Bulletin. (Denver, Colo.) 19??-1915
The Rocky Mountain Monthly. (Denver, Colo.) 19??-19??
Equality. (Denver, Colo.) 1900-19??
Rocky Mountain Mirror. (Denver, Colo.) 19??-19??
The Denver Citizen and "Business." (Denver, Colo.) 1900-1901
George's Weekly. (Denver, Colo.) 1900-1907
The Register. (Denver, Colo.) 19??-????
Eco. (Denver, Colo.) 19??-1973 | Languages: English, Spanish
Rokkī Nippon = Rocky Nippon. (Denver, Colo.) 19??-1943 | Languages: English, Japanese
Pabor's Pictorial : with which is incorporated The Rocky Mountain Globe, Denver Press, and Rocky Mountain World. (Denver, Colo.) 1901-1901
Daily Edition Denver Record-Stockman. (Denver, Colo.) 1901-19??
Denver Record-Stockman. (Denver, Colo.) 1901-1919
Svensk Amerikanska Western Svenska Korrespondenten. (Denver, Colo.) 1901-1913 | Languages: English, Swedish
Columbia. (Denver, Colo.) 1901-19?? | Languages: Swedish
The Rocky Mountain Miner. (Denver, Colo.) 1901-19??
The Denver Post. (Denver, Colo.) 1901-Current
Colorado Chronicle. (Denver, Colo.) 1901-1903
Colorado Herold. (Denver, Colo.) 1902-1918 | Languages: German
The Rocky Mountain Magazine. (Denver, Colo.) 1903-1906
The Jewish Outlook. (Denver, Colo.) 1903-1913

Denver County

The Clarion-Advocate. (Denver, Colo.) 1904-19??
The Forum. (Denver, Colo.) 1904-1905
The Denver Democrat. (Denver, Colo.) 1905-1955
Denver Catholic Register. (Denver, Colo.) 1905-1967
Il Risveglio = The Awakening. (Denver, Colo.) 1906-1952 | Languages: English, Italian
The Denver Express. (Denver, Colo.) 1906-1926
The Rocky Mountain Screech Owl. (Denver, Colo.) 1906-19??
Franklin's Paper The Statesman. (Denver, Colo.) 1906-1912
La Capitale. (Denver, Colo.) 1907-1926 | Languages: Italian
Illustrated Weekly The Inter-Mountain Farmer. (Denver, Colo.) 1908-19??
Thursday Edition Denver Record-Stockman. (Denver, Colo.) 1912-1914
Franklin's Paper The Denver Star. (Denver, Colo.) 1912-1913
Svensk-Amerikanska Western. (Denver, Colo.) 1913-1928 | Languages: English, Swedish
The Daily Mining and Financial Record. (Denver, Colo.) 1913-1922
The Colorado Worker. (Denver, Colo.) 1913-19??
The Denver Call. (Denver, Colo.) 1913-19??
The Denver Star. (Denver, Colo.) 1913-1963
The New Great Divide. (Denver, Colo.) 1914-1914
The Great Divide. (Denver, Colo.) 1914-19??
The Commercial. (Denver, Colo.) 1914-1919
Denver Labor Bulletin. (Denver, Colo.) 1915-19??
The Denver Jewish News. (Denver, Colo.) 1915-1925
The Clipper. (Denver, Colo.) 1916-19??
Colorado Herold Greeley Edition. (Denver, Colo.) 1917-1918 | Languages: German
The Western Oil World. (Denver, Colo.) 1917-19??
Weekly Colorado Herold. (Denver, Colo.) 1918-1927 | Languages: German
The Colorado Leader. (Denver, Colo.) 1918-19??
Kakushu Jiji = Colorado Times. (Denver, Colo.) 1918-1969 | Languages: English, Japanese
Denver Daily Record Stockman. (Denver, Colo.) 1919-1939
Tenshun, 21!. (Denver, Colo.) 1919-19??
The Denver Commercial. (Denver, Colo.) 1919-1926
The Bulletin. (Denver, Colo.) 192?-1943
La Frusta. (Denver, Colo) 1920-19?? | Languages: Italian
Protestant Herald. (Denver, Colo.) 192?-1926
The Colorado Republican. (Denver, Colo.) 1920-Current
Colorado Labor Advocate. (Denver, Colo.) 192?-Current | Languages: English, Spanish
The Weekly Comet. (Denver, Colo.) 192?-1923 | Languages: English, Yiddish
Hill's Monthly. (Denver, Colo.) 1921-19??
The Oil Shale Outlook. (Denver, Colo.) 1921-19??
The Inland Oil Index. (Casper, Wyo.) 1922-1941
The Mining and Financial Record. (Denver, Colo.) 1922-1924
Sunday Colorado Herold. (Denver, Colo.) 1922-1933 | Languages: German

Historical Assets Colorado

Denver Mirror. (Denver, Colo.) 1922-19??
Colorado. (Denver, Colo.) 1923-1971
Western Jewish World. (Denver, Colo.) 1923-19?? | Languages: English, Yiddish
Park Hill Bulletin. (Denver, Colo.) 1924-19??
Denver Mining & Financial Record. (Denver, Colo.) 1924-1928
Westerns Nyheter = The Western News. (Denver, Colo.) 1924-1928 | Languages: English, Swedish
Intermountain Jewish News. (Denver, Colo.) 1925-Current
The Register. (Denver) 1925-19??
The Denver Evening News. (Denver, Colo.) 1926-1928
Herald-Dispatch. (Denver, Colo.) 1926-19??
The Rocky Mountain Canary. (Denver, Colo.) 1926-19??
Denver Morning Post. (Denver, Colo.) 1927-1928
The Register. (Denver, Colo.) 1927-1967
Denver Mining Record. (Denver, Colo.) 1928-1939
The Barnum Booster. (Denver, Colo.) 1928-19??
Svensk-Amerikanska Western Och Westerns Nyheter = The Western News. (Denver, Colo.) 1928-1928 | Languages: English, Swedish
Westerns Nyheter Svensk-Amerikanska Western = The Western News. (Denver, Colo.) 1929-1931 | Languages: English, Swedish
The Register. (Denver, Colo.) 1930-1947
Westerns Nyheter = The Western News. (Denver, Colo.) 1931-1941 | Languages: English, Swedish
El Imparcial. (Denver, Colo.) 1932-19?? | Languages: Spanish
The Register. (Denver, Colo.) 1932-1938
Park Hill Topics. (Denver, Colo.) 1933-19??
Colorado Herold. (Denver, Colo.) 1933-1942 | Languages: German
The Register. ([Denver, Colo.]) 1934-1959
Sunday Colorado Herold. (Denver, Colo.) 1934-19?? | Languages: German
The Civic Sentinel. (Denver, Colo.) 1935-19??
Capitol Hill News. (Denver, Colo.) 1935-19??
The Trumpet = La Tromba. (Denver, Colo.) 1935-19?? | Languages: English, Italian
Denver Rocky Mountain News. (Denver, Colo.) 1935-1937
Rocky Mountain News. (Denver, Colo.) 1937-2009
Latin American News. (Denver, Colo.) 1938-19?? | Languages: English, Spanish
East Side Journal. (Denver, Colo.) 1938-19??
The Lake Shore Visitor-Register. (Denver, Colo.) 1938-1959
Denver Mining Record and Machinery Journal. (Denver, Colo.) 1939-1941
Denver Times. (Denver, Colo.) 1939-1947
Rocky Mountain Tourist News. (Denver, Colo.) 1939-19??
The Westwood News. (Denver, Colo.) 194?-19??
Green Light. (Denver, Colo.) 1940-19??
Denver Ordnance News and Shopping Guide. (Denver, Colo.) 1941-19??
The Mining Record. (Denver, Colo.) 1941-1964
Lowry Field. (Lowry Field, Denver, Colo.) 1941-1941
The Lowry Field Rev-Meter. (Denver, Colo.) 1941-1943

Denver County

The Western News. (Denver, Colo.) 1941-1979 | Languages: English, Swedish
The Union. (Denver, Colo.) 1942-1954 | Languages: English, Spanish
Bizerte Rattler. (Denver, Colo.) 1943-19??
Buckley Armorer. (Denver, Colo.) 1943-19??
The Bulletin Free Press. (Denver, Colo.) 1943-1966
The Rev-Meter. (Denver, Colo.) 1943-1945
The Denver Post. (Denver, Colo.) 1943-1945
The Buckley Air-Scoop. (Buckley Field, Colo.) 1943-19??
Rokkī Shimpō = Rocky Shimpo. (Denver, Colo.) 1943-1961 | Languages: English, Japanese
The Colorado Nail. (Denver, Colo.) 1944-1944
Pan-American News. (Denver, Colo.) 1945-19?? | Languages: English, Spanish
Rocky Mountain Sports. (Denver, Colo.) 1945-19??
The Lowry Field Rev-Meter. (Denver, Colo.) 1945-1945
Service Record. (Denver, Colo.) 1945-194?
Challenge. (Denver, Colo.) 1946-19?? | Languages: English, Spanish
The Denver Evening Whirl. (Denver, Colo.) 1946-19??
Antena : Spanish News. (Denver, Colo.) 1947-19?? | Languages: English, Spanish
American Commentator. (Denver, Colo.) 1947-19??
Pioneer Village News. (Pioneer Village, Denver, Colo.) 1948-19??
The Colorado Journal. (Denver, Colo.) 1948-19??
East Denver Journal. (East Denver, Colo.) 1949-????
Cervi's Rocky Mountain Journal. (Denver, Colo.) 1949-1974
L'unione combined with "Il Risveglio." (Pueblo, Colo.) 1949-1949 | Languages: Italian
Lowry Airmen. ([Denver, Colo.]) 1949-1954
The Denver Inquirer. (Denver, Colo.) 1952-1953
Il Risveglio L'unione. (Denver, Colo.) 1952-1955 | Languages: English, Italian
The Colorado Clarion. (Denver, Colo.) 1953-19?? | Languages: English, Spanish
The Mine-Mill Union. (Denver, Colo.) 1954-1967 | Languages: English, Spanish
Airmen. ([Denver, Colo.]) 1954-195?
The Colorado Democrat. (Denver, Colo.) 1955-1977
Il Risveglio = The Awakening. (Denver, Colo.) 1955-1956 | Languages: English, Italian
The Awakening. (Denver, Colo.) 1956-19??
The Register. (Denver, Colo.) 1956-1967
The Denver Dispatch. (Denver, Colo.) 1957-19??
The Overland News. (Denver, Colo.) 1957-1958
Lowry Airman. (Denver, Colo.) 1957-Current
El Sol. (Denver, Colo.) 1958-19?? | Languages: English, Spanish
The Catholic Register. ([Altoona, Pa., I.e. Denver, Colo.]) 1959-Current
Park Hill Actionews. (Denver, Colo.) 1960-196?
Park Hill Reporter. (Denver, Colo.) 1961-19??
The Denver Blade. (Denver, Colo.) 1961-19??
Rocky Mountain Jiho. (Denver, Colo.) 1962-Current
El Tiempo. (Denver, Colo.) 1962-1964 | Languages: English, Spanish
The Jeffco Tusker. (Denver, Colo.) 1963-19??

Historical Assets Colorado

The Mining And Natural Resources Record. ([Denver) 1964-1968
Side III. (Denver, Colo.) 1965-19??
Southland News. (Denver, Colo.) 1966-1970
Reform Call. (Denver, Colo.) 1967-19??
Denver News Week. (Denver, Colo.) 1967-19??
The Register. ([Denver, Colo.]) 1967-1972
Teleidoscopic Collage. (Denver, Colo.) 1967-1968
Solid Muldoon. (Denver, Colo.) 1967-1968
El Gallo. (Denver, Colo.) 1967-???? | Languages: English, Spanish
Metro West. (Denver, Colo.) 1968-19??
Neighborhood Journal. (Denver, Colo.) 1968-19??
The Mountain Free Press. (Denver, Colo.) 1968-19??
The Mining Record. (Denver) 1968-Current
The Colorado Graphic. (Denver, Colo.) 1969-19??
Chinook. (Denver, Co.) 1969-1972
The Denver Drum. (Denver, Colo.) 197?-19??
Hoa Binh. (Denver, Col.) 197?-19??
The Denver Weekly News. (Denver) 1971-Current
The Crime Paper. (Denver, Colo.) 1971-19??
News Letter. (Denver, Colo.) 1971-1980
The Colorado Leader. (Denver, Colo.) 1971-Current
The Drum. (Denver, Colo.) 1971-19??
The Straight Creek Journal. (Denver, Colo.) 1972-1980
Dispatch-Sentinel. (Denver, Colo.) 1972-1980
Big Mama Rag. (Denver, Colo.) 1972-1984
Journal-Sentinel. (Denver, Colo.) 1972-1977
El Eco Maya. (Denver, Colo.) 1973-1974 | Languages: English, Spanish
Ken-Caryl Ranch News. ([Littleton, Colo.]) 1974-19??
Rhinoceros. (Denver, Colo) 1974-197?
Southeast Denver Times. (Denver, Colo.) 1974-19??
Rocky Mountain Journal. ([Denver, Colo.]) 1974-1981
El Eco. (Denver, Colo.) 1974-197? | Languages: English, Spanish
A Journal of Occurances. (Denver, Colo.) 1975-19??
Life on Capitol Hill. (Denver, Colo.) 1975-Current
La Voz Hispana De Colorado. (Denver, Colo.) 1975-1987 | Languages: English, Spanish
The Colorado Statesman. (Denver, Colo.) 1977-2017
Westminster Journal Sentinel. (Denver, Colo.) 1977-1979
The Handicapped Coloradan. (Denver, Colo.) 1978-Current
The Wall Street Journal. [Volume] (Denver, Colo.) 1978-Current
The Stapleton Innerline. (Denver, Colo.) 1979-Current
Westminster Sentinel. (Denver, Colo.) 1979-1991
Denbŏ Sinbo = The Korean Denver News. (Aurora, Co.) 198?-Current | Languages: Korean
Greater Park Hill Newsletter. (Denver, Colo.) 1980-Current
The Urban Spectrum : Spreading The News About People Of Color. (Aurora, Colo.) 198?-Current

Denver County

Camp Crier. ([Denver, Colo.) 1983-????
City Edition. (Denver, Colo.) 1983-Current
Foothills Independent. (Denver, Colo.) 1985-????
Village Independent. (Denver, Colo.) 1985-1985
Denver Herald Dispatch. (Denver, Co) 1987-19??
The New Political Newspaper. (Denver, Colo.) 1988-1988
La Voz. (Denver, Co) 1988-2002 | Languages: English, Spanish
Rocky Mountain Oil Journal. (Denver, Co) 199?-Current
La Voz Nueva. (Denver, Co) 2002-2010 | Languages: English, Spanish
Denver Herald Dispatch & Sheridan Sun. (Denver, Co) 2002-Current
La Voz Bilingüe. (Denver, Co) 2010-Current

Places on the National Register

Denver, 19th Street Bridge, 19th St.
Denver, Alamo Placita Park, Roughly bounded by Speer Blvd., First Ave., and Clarkson St.
Denver, All Saints Episcopal Church, 2222 W. 32nd Ave.
Denver, Altamaha Apartments, 1490 Lafayette St.
Denver, Annunciation Church, 3601 Humboldt St.
Denver, Arcanum Apartments, 1904 Logan St.
Denver, Arno Apartments, 325 E. Eighteenth Ave.
Denver, Auraria 9th Street Historic District, 9th St. from Curtis to Champa St.
Denver, Austin Building, 2400—2418 E. Colfax and 1742 Josephine St.
Denver, Avoca Lodge, 2690 S. Wadsworth Blvd.
Denver, Bailey House, 1600 Ogden St.
Denver, Bancroft, Caroline, House, 1079—81 Downing St. and 1180 E. 11th
Denver, Bastien's Restaurant, 3503 E. Colfax Ave.
Denver, Bats Grocery Store, 4336 Clayton St.
Denver, Baur Confectionery Company, 1512-14 Curtis St.
Denver, Belcaro, 3400 Belcaro Dr.
Denver, Bennett—Field House, 740 Clarkson St
Denver, Berkeley Lake Park, Roughly bounded by N side of Berkeley Lake, Tennyson St., W. Forty-sixth Ave., and Sheridan Blvd.
Denver, Berkeley School, 5025—5055 Lowell Blvd.
Denver, Bluebird Theater, 3315—3317 E. Colfax Ave.
Denver, Bonfils Memorial Theater, 1475 Elizabeth St.
Denver, Boston Building, 828 17th St.
Denver, Bouvier-Lothrop House, 1600 Emerson St.
Denver, Bowman, William Norman, House—Yamecila, 325 King St.
Denver, Brinker Collegiate Institute, 1725—1727 Tremont Pl.
Denver, Brown Palace Hotel, 17th St. and Tremont Pl.
Denver, Brown, J. S., Mercantile Building, 1634 18th St.
Denver, Brown, Molly, House, 1340 Pennsylvania St.
Denver, Brueger Brothers Building and Annex, 1732-1740 Champa St.
Denver, Bryant—Webster Elementary School, 3635 Quivas St.
Denver, Buchtel Bungalow, 2100 S. Columbine St.

Historical Assets Colorado

Denver, Building at 1389 Stuart Street, 1389 Stuart St.
Denver, Building at 1390 Stuart Street, 1390 Stuart St.
Denver, Building at 1435 Stuart Street, 1435 Stuart St.
Denver, Building at 1444 Stuart Street, 1444 Stuart St.
Denver, Building at 1471 Stuart Street, 1471 Stuart St.
Denver, Burlington Hotel, 2205 Larimer St.
Denver, Butters, Alfred, House, 1129 Pennsylvania
Denver, Byers-Evans House, 1310 Bannock St.
Denver, Campbell, Richard Crawford, House, 909 York St.
Denver, Capitol Life Insurance Building, 1600 Sherman St.
Denver, Carter-Rice Building, 1623-1631 Blake St.
Denver, Cathedral of the Immaculate Conception, NE corner of Colfax Ave. and Logan St.
Denver, Central Presbyterian Church, 1660 Sherman St.
Denver, Chamber of Commerce Building, 1726 Champa St.
Denver, Chamberlin Observatory, 2930 E. Warren Ave.
Denver, Chapel No. 1, Reeves St. on Lowry AFB
Denver, Chappell, Delos Allen, House, 1555 Race St.
Denver, Chateau, The, 900 Sherman St.
Denver, Cheesman Park, Roughly bounded by E. Thirteenth Ave., High St., E. Eigth Ave., and Franklin St.
Denver, Cheesman Park Duplex, 1372 S. Pennsylvania St.
Denver, Cheesman Park Esplanade, Roughly bounded by Eighth Ave., High St., Seventh Ave. Pkwy., and Williams St.
Denver, Christ Methodist Episcopal Church, 2201 Ogden St.
Denver, City Park, Roughly bounded by E. Twenty-third Ave., Colorado Blvd., E. Seventeenth Ave., and York St.
Denver, City Park Esplanade, City Park Esplanade from E. Colfax Ave. to E. Seventeenth Ave.
Denver, City Park Golf, Roughly bounded by E. Twenty-sixth Ave., Colorado Blvd., E. Twenty-third Ave., and York St.
Denver, Civic Center Historic District, Roughly bounded by W. Colfax, E. Colfax, Grant, E. 14th, Broadway, E. 13th, W. 13th, Bannock, W. 14th, and Delaware
Denver, Clayton, George W., Trust and College, 3801 Martin Luther King Blvd.
Denver, Clements Rowhouse, 2201—2217 Glenarm Pl.
Denver, Clermont Street Parkway, Clermont St. Pkwy. from E. Third Ave. to E. Sixth Ave.
Denver, Cole Neighborhood Historic District, 3200—3300 Vine and Race Sts.
Denver, Colorado Governor's Mansion, 400 E. 8th Ave.
Denver, Colorado National Bank Building, 918 17th St.
Denver, Colorado State Capitol Annex Building and Boiler Plant, 1341 Sherman St.
Denver, Cornwall Apartments, 1317 Ogden St., 912 E. 13th Ave.
Denver, Country Club Historic District, Roughly bounded by 1st and 4th Aves., Race and Downing Sts.
Denver, Country Club Historic District (Boundary Increase), Between Downing & University, E. 4th Ave. and N of Alameda Ave.

Denver County

Denver, Cranmer House, 200 Cherry St.
Denver, Cranmer Park, Roughly bounded by E. Third Ave., Cherry St., E. First Ave., and Bellaire St.
Denver, Crawford Hill Mansion, 969 Sherman St.
Denver, Creswell Mansion, 1244 Grant St.
Denver, Crocker, F. W., and Company Steam Cracker Factory, 1862 Blake St.
Denver, Croke-Patterson-Campbell Mansion, 428—430 E. 11th Ave.
Denver, Curry-Chucovich House, 1439 Court Pl.
Denver, Curtis-Champa Streets District, Roughly bounded by Arapahoe, 30th, California, and 24th Sts.
Denver, Curtis-Champa Streets Historic District (Boundary Increase), Roughly 30th, Stout, Downing and Arapahoe Sts.
Denver, Daniels and Fisher Tower, 1101 16th St.
Denver, Denver Athletic Club, 1325 Glenarm Pl.
Denver, Denver City Cable Railway Building, 1801 Lawrence St.
Denver, Denver City Railway Company Building, 1635 17th St., 1734-1736 Wynkoop St.
Denver, Denver Civic Center, Roughly Grant to Cherokee Streets and 14th to Colfax Avenues
Denver, Denver Civic Center Classroom Building, 1445 Cleveland Pl.
Denver, Denver Dry Goods Company Building, 16th and California Sts.
Denver, Denver Medical Depot, 3800 York St.
Denver, Denver Mint, W. Colfax Ave. and Delaware St.
Denver, Denver Municipal Auditorium, 1323 Champa St.
Denver, Denver Orphans' Home, 1501 Albion St.
Denver, Denver Public Library, 1357 Broadway
Denver, Denver Tramway Powerhouse, 1416 Platte St.
Denver, Dickinson Branch Library, 1545 Hooker St.
Denver, Doud, John and Elvira, House, 750 Lafayette St.
Denver, Downing Street Parkway, Downing St. Pkwy. from E. Bayaud Ave. to E. Third Ave.
Denver, Downtown Denver Central YMCA and Annex, 25 E. Sixteenth Ave.
Denver, Dow-Rosenzweig House, 1129 E. 17th Ave.
Denver, Doyle—Benton House, 1301 Lafayette St.
Denver, Dunning-Benedict House, 1200 Pennsylvania St.
Denver, Dunwoody, William J., House, 2637 W. 26th Ave.
Denver, East Fourth Avenue Parkway, E. Fourth Ave. Pkwy. from Gilpin St. to Williams St.
Denver, East High School, 1545 Detroit St.
Denver, East Seventeenth Avenue Parkway, E. Seventeenth Ave. Pkwy. from Colorado Blvd. to Monaco St. Pkwy.
Denver, East Seventh Avenue Parkway, E. Seventh Ave. Pkwy. from Williams St. to Colorado Blvd.
Denver, East Sixth Avenue Parkway, E. Sixth Ave. Pkwy. from Colorado Blvd. to Quebec St.
Denver, Elitch Theatre, W. 38th Ave. and Tennyson St.

Historical Assets Colorado

Denver, Elsner, John, House, 2810 Arapahoe St.
Denver, Emerson School, 1420 Ogden St.
Denver, Emmanuel Shearith Israel Chapel, 1201 10th St.
Denver, Enterprise Hill Historic District, Bounded by 21st and 22nd Aves., Tremont and Glenarm Pls.
Denver, Eppich Apartments, 1266 Emerson St.
Denver, Equitable Building, 730 17th St.
Denver, Evans Memorial Chapel, University of Denver campus
Denver, Evans School, 1115 Acoma St.
Denver, Field, Eugene, House, 715 S. Franklin St.
Denver, Fire Station No. 1, 1326 Tremont Pl.
Denver, First Baptist Church of Denver, 230 E. 14th Av.—1373 Grant St.
Denver, First Congregational Church, 980 Clarkson St.
Denver, First National Bank Building, 818 17th St.
Denver, Fisher, William G., House, 1600 Logan St.
Denver, Fitzroy Place, 2160 S. Cook St.
Denver, Fleming-Hanington House, 1133 Pennsylvania
Denver, Flower, John S., House, 1618 Ogden St.
Denver, Flower-Vaile House, 1610 Emerson St.
Denver, Ford, Barney L., Building, 1514 Blake St.
Denver, Ford, Justina, House, 3091 California St.
Denver, Forest Street Parkway, Forest St. Pkwy. from Seventeenth Ave. to Montview Blvd.
Denver, Foster, A. C., Building, 912 16th St.
Denver, Foster, Ernest LeNeve, House, 2105 Lafayette St.
Denver, Four-Mile House, 715 S. Forest St.
Denver, Fourth Church of Christ, Scientist, 3101 W. 31st Ave.
Denver, Gates, Russell and Elinor, Mansion, 1365-1375 Josephine
Denver, Gebhard Mansion, 2253 Downing St.
Denver, General Electric Building, 1441 18th St.
Denver, Glenarm Place Historic Residential District, 2417-2462 Glenarm Pl.
Denver, Grafton, The, 1001-1020 E. 17th Ave.
Denver, Grant-Humphreys Mansion, 770 Pennsylvania St.
Denver, Grimm, S. A., Block, 2031—2033 Curtis St.
Denver, Guerrieri-Decunto House, 1650 Pennsylvania St.
Denver, Hamburger, George, Block, 2199 Arapahoe
Denver, Hanigan—Canino Terrace, 1421—1435 W. Thirty-fifth Ave.
Denver, Haskell House, 1651 Emerson St.
Denver, Helene Apartment Building, 1052 Pearl St.
Denver, Hendrie and Bolthoff Warehouse Building, 1743 Wazee
Denver, Highland Park, Roughly bounded by Highland Park Pl., Federal Blvd., and Fairview Pl.
Denver, Highland Park Historic District, Bounded by Zuni St., Dunkeld Pl., Clay St., and 32nd Ave.
Denver, Highlands Masonic Lodge, 3220 Federal Blvd.
Denver, House at 1750 Gilpin Street, 1750 Gilpin St.

Denver County

Denver, Hover, W.A., and Company Building, 1390 Lawrence St.
Denver, Humboldt Street Historic District, Humboldt St. between E. 10th and E. 12th Sts.
Denver, Hungarian Freedom Park, Roughly bounded by Speer Blvd., First Ave., and Clarkson St.
Denver, Ideal Building, 821 17th St.
Denver, Iliff Hall, 2201 S. University Blvd.
Denver, Inspiration Point, Roughly bounded by W. Fiftieth Ave., Sheridan Blvd., W. Forty-ninth Ave., and Fenton St.
Denver, Joshel, Lloyd M., House, 220 S. Dahlia St.
Denver, Joslin Dry Goods Company Building, 934 16th St.
Denver, Keating, Jeffery and Mary, House, 1207 Pennsylvania St.
Denver, Kerr House, 1900 E. 7th Ave. Pkwy
Denver, Kistler Stationery Company Building, 1636 Champa St.
Denver, Kistler-Rodriguez House, 700 E. 9th Ave.
Denver, Kittredge Building, 511 16th St.
Denver, Kohn House, 770 High St.
Denver, Kopper's Hotel and Saloon, 1215-1219 20th St.
Denver, Lang, William, Townhouse, 1626 Washington St.
Denver, Larimer Square, 1400 block of Larimer St.
Denver, Larimer Square Historic District (Boundary Increase), 1404 Larimer St.
Denver, Leeman Auto Company Building, 550 Broadway
Denver, LeFevre, Owen E., House, 1311 York St.
Denver, Lewis, A. T., and Son Department Store, 800—816 Sixteenth St.
Denver, Lewis, A. T., New Building, 1531 Stout St.
Denver, Littleton Creamery—Beatrice Foods Cold Storage Warehouse, 1801 Wynkoop St.
Denver, Loretto Heights Academy, 3001 S. Federal Blvd.
Denver, Lowry Field Brick Barracks, 200 N. Rampart Way
Denver, Macedonia Baptist Church, 3240 Adams St.
Denver, Masonic Temple Building, 1614 Welton St.
Denver, McClintock Building, 1550-58 Califorinia St./622-40 16th St.
Denver, McCourt, Peter, House, 1471 High St.
Denver, McPhee and McGinnity Building, 2301 Blake St.
Denver, McPhee and McGinnity Paint Factory, 2519 Walnut St.
Denver, Midland Savings Building, 444 17th St.
Denver, Midwest Steel and Iron Works Company Complex, 25 Larimer St.
Denver, Moffat Station, 2105 15th St.
Denver, Monaco Street Parkway, Monaco St. Pkwy. from E. First Ave. to Montview Blvd.
Denver, Montclair Park, Roughly bounded by E. Twelfth Ave., Onieda St., and Richthofen Pkwy.
Denver, Montgomery Court, 215 E. Eleventh Ave.
Denver, Montview Boulevard, Montview Blvd. from Colorado Blvd. to Monaco St. Pkwy.
Denver, Montview Boulevard Presbyterian Church, 1980 Dahlia St.

Historical Assets Colorado

Denver, Moore, Dora, Elementary School, E. 9th Ave. and Corona St.
Denver, Mosque of the El Jebel Shrine, 1770 Sherman St.
Denver, Motor Coach Division Building—Denver Tramway Company, 3500 Gilpin St.
Denver, Neef, Frederick W., House, 2143 Grove St.
Denver, Neusteter Building, 720 Sixteenth St.
Denver, New Terrace, 900—914 E. Twentieth Ave.
Denver, Niblock—Yacovetta Terrace, 1301—1319 W. Thirty-fifth Ave.
Denver, Nordlund House, 330 Birch St.
Denver, Norman Apartments, 99 S. Downing St.
Denver, Ogden Theatre, 935 E. Colfax Ave.
Denver, Old Highland Business District, 15th and Boulder Sts.
Denver, Oriental Theater, 4329-39 W. 44th Ave.
Denver, Orlando Flats, 2330 Washington St.
Denver, Overland Cotton Mill, 1314 W. Evans Ave.
Denver, Oxford Hotel, 1612 17th St.
Denver, Pacific Express Stable, 2363 Blake St.
Denver, Palmer, Judge Peter L. House, 1250 Ogden St.
Denver, Palmer—Ferril House, 2123 Downing St.
Denver, Paramount Theater, 519 16th St.
Denver, Park Hill, Bounded by Colorado Blvd., E. 26th Ave., Dahlia St., and E. Montview Blvd.
Denver, Pearce-McAllister Cottage, 1880 Gaylord St.
Denver, Peters Paper Company Warehouse, 1625—1631 Wazee St.
Denver, Photography and Armament School Buildings, Lowry Air Force Base, 125 and 130 Rampart Way and 7600 East First Place
Denver, Pierce-Haley House, 857 Grant St.
Denver, Potter Highlands Historic District, Roughy bounded by W. Thirty-eighth, Zuni, and W. Thirty-second Sts., and Federal Blvd.
Denver, Pride of the Rockies Flour Mill, 2100 20th St.
Denver, Public Service Building, 910 15th St.
Denver, Railway Exchange Addition and Railway Exchange New Building, 1715 Champa St. and 909 17th St.
Denver, Ray Apartments Buildings, 1550 and 1560 Ogden St.
Denver, Raymond, Wilbur S., House, 1572 Race St.
Denver, Richthofen Castle, 7020 E. 12th Ave.
Denver, Richthofen Monument, Richthofen Pkwy. at Oneida St.
Denver, Richthofen Place Parkway, Richthofen Pl. Pkwy. from Monaco St. Pkwy. to Oneida St.
Denver, Robinson House, 3435 Albion St.
Denver, Rocky Mountain Bank Note Company Building, 1080 Delaware St.
Denver, Rocky Mountain Hotel, 2301 7th St.
Denver, Rocky Mountain Lake Park, Roughly bounded by I-70, Federal Blvd., W. Forty-sixth Ave., and Lowell Blvd.
Denver, Romeo Block, 2944 Zuni St.
Denver, Root, Amos H., Building, 1501—1529 Platte St.

Denver County

Denver, Rossonian Hotel, 2650 Welton St.
Denver, Roth, Henry, House, 5, 7, and 9 S. Fox St.
Denver, Saint Philomena Catholic Parish School, 940 Fillmore St.
Denver, Saint Thomas Theological Seminary, 1300 S. Steele
Denver, San Rafael Historic District, Roughly bounded by E. Twenty-sixth Ave., Downing St., E. Twentieth Ave., and Washington St.
Denver, Schleier, George, Mansion, 1665 Grant St.
Denver, Schlessinger House, 1544 Race St.
Denver, Schmidt, George, House, 2345 7th St.
Denver, Sheedy Mansion, 1115-1121 Grant St.
Denver, Sherman Street Historic District, Approx. 1000 to 1099 Sherman St.
Denver, Sixth Avenue Community Church, 3250 E Sixth Ave
Denver, Smith House, 1801 York St.
Denver, Smith, Milo A., House, 1360 Birch St.
Denver, Smith, Pierce T., House, 1751 Gilpin St.
Denver, Smith's Irrigation Ditch, Washington Park
Denver, South Marion Street Parkway, S. Marion St. Pkwy. from E. Virginia Ave. to E. Bayaud Ave. at Downing St.
Denver, South Platte River Bridges, I-25 at milepost 210.53
Denver, South Side—Baker Historic District, Roughly bounded by W. Fifth Ave., Broadway, W. Alameda Ave., and W. Fox St.
Denver, Speer Boulevard, Speer Blvd. from W. Colfax Ave. to Downing St.
Denver, Spratlen-Anderson Wholesale Grocery Company—Davis Brothers Warehouse, 1450 Wynkoop St.
Denver, St. Andrews Episcopal Church, 2015 Glenarm Pl.
Denver, St. Dominic's Church, 3005 W. 29th Ave.
Denver, St. Elizabeth's Church, 1062 11th St.
Denver, St. Elizabeth's Retreat Chapel, 2825 W. 32nd Ave.
Denver, St. Ignatius Loyola Church, Jct. of E. 23rd Ave. and York St.
Denver, St. John's Cathedral, 14th and Washington Sts.
Denver, St. Joseph's Polish Roman Catholic Church, 517 E. 46th Ave
Denver, St. Joseph's Roman Catholic Church of Denver, 600 Galapago
Denver, St. Mark's Parish Church, 1160 Lincoln St.
Denver, St. Patrick Mission Church, 3325 Pecos St.
Denver, St. Paul's English Evangelical Lutheran Church, 1600 Grant St.
Denver, Stanley Arms, 1321-1333 E. Tenth Ave.
Denver, Stanley School—Montclair School, 1301 Quebec St.
Denver, Stearns House, 1030 Logan St.
Denver, Stonemen's Row Historic District, South side 28th Ave. between Umatilla and Vallejo Sts.
Denver, Sugar Building, 1530 16th St.
Denver, Sunken Gardens, Roughly bounded by Speer Blvd., W. Eighth Ave., Delaware, and Elati Sts.
Denver, Swallow Hill Historic District, Roughly Bounded by Clarkson St., E. Seventeenth Ave., Downing St., E Colfax Ave.
Denver, Tallmadge and Boyer Block, 2926-2942 Zuni St.

Historical Assets Colorado

Denver, Tears-McFarlane House, 1200 Williams St.
Denver, Telephone Building, 931 14th St.
Denver, Temple Emanuel, 24 Curtis St.
Denver, Temple Emanuel, 51 Grape St.
Denver, Temple Emanuel, 1595 Pearl St.
Denver, Thomas, H. H., House, 2104 Glenarm Pl.
Denver, Tilden School for Teaching Health, Jct. of W. Fairview Pl. and Grove St.
Denver, Tivoli Brewery Company, 1320—1348 10th St.
Denver, Tramway Building, 1100 14th St.
Denver, Treat Hall, E. 18th Ave. and Pontiac St.
Denver, Trinity United Methodist Church, E. 18th Ave. and Broadway
Denver, U.S. Customhouse, 721 19th St.
Denver, U.S. Post Office and Federal Building, 18th and Stout Sts.
Denver, Union Station, 17th St. at Wynkoop
Denver, Union Warehouse, 1514 17th St.
Denver, University Boulevard, University Blvd. from E. Iowa Ave. to E. Alameda Ave.
Denver, US National Bank, 817 17th St.
Denver, Vine Street Houses, 1415, 1429, 1435, 1441, 1453 Vine St.
Denver, Walters, Manuella C., Duplex, 1728 & 1732 Gilpin St.
Denver, Washington Park, Roughly bounded by E. Virginia Ave., S. Franklin St., E. Louisiana Ave., and S. Downing St.
Denver, Weckbaugh House, 1701 E. Cedar Ave.
Denver, West Forty-sixth Avenue Parkway, W. Forty-sixth Ave. Pkwy. from Stuart St. to Grove St.
Denver, West Side Court Building, 924 W. Colfax Ave.
Denver, Westside Neighborhood, 1311—1466 Lipan St., 1305—1370 Kalamath St., 931—1126 W. 14th Ave., 1312—1438 Maraposa St., & 1008-1118 W. 13th Ave.
Denver, Williams Street Parkway, Williams St. Pkwy. from E. Fourth Ave. to E. Eighth Ave.
Denver, Wood-Morris-Bonfils House, 707 Washington St.
Denver, Zall House, 5401 East Sixth Avenue Parkway
Denver, Zang, Adolph J., House, 1532 Emerson St.
Denver, Zang, Adolph, Mansion, 709 Clarkson St.
Denver, Zeitz Buckhorn Exchange, 1000 Osage St.

USGS Historic Places

Arvada, Alcott School, 39.7735978, -105.0444274
Arvada, Ashland School, 39.7585979, -105.0174821
Arvada, Bethany Christian Church, 39.7663889, -105.0530556
Arvada, Boulevard School, 39.7513758, -105.0258158
Arvada, Faith United Methodist Church, 39.7622222, -105.0525
Arvada, Highland Park Historical District, 39.7608333, -105.0180556
Arvada, Offielo Nursing Home, 39.7638756, -105.0297048
Arvada, Queen of Heaven M C Memorial School, 39.7849865, -105.0260935
Arvada, Remington Elementary School, 39.78224, -105.00685

Denver County

Arvada, Saint Claras Orphanage, 39.7566535, -105.0369273
Arvada, Saint Dominics School, 39.7588757, -105.0260936
Arvada, Saint Mary Magalene School, 39.7577647, -105.052761
Arvada, Saint Patricks School, 39.7647089, -105.0063707
Arvada, Smedley Elementary School, 39.77498, -105.00968
Arvada, Tilden School For Teaching Health, 39.7616667, -105.0266667
Commerce City, Cure d'Ars School, 39.7624869, -104.93109
Commerce City, Denver Medical Depot, 39.7708333, -104.9597222
Commerce City, Elyria Branch Library, 39.7822222, -104.9641667
Commerce City, Elyria School, 39.7824866, -104.9647023
Commerce City, Glenarm Place Historic Residential District, 39.7516667, -104.98
Commerce City, Holy Rosary School, 39.7810976, -104.9797029
Commerce City, Manual High School, 39.7563757, -104.9666469
Commerce City, Sacred Heart School, 39.7599868, -104.981092
Commerce City, Stapleton International Airport, 39.7741536, -104.8796989
Commerce City, Word Up Christian Center, 39.7502778, -104.975
Englewood, Alameda School, 39.7116538, -104.9902593
Englewood, Bethesda PsycHealth Hospital, 39.6713764, -104.9349796
Englewood, Boettcher School, 39.7458202, -104.9727584
Englewood, Booth Memorial Hospital, 39.7319316, -104.9191452
Englewood, Byers Alternative High School, 39.7135982, -104.9797034
Englewood, Byers Elementary School, 39.7119444, -104.9902778
Englewood, Cathedral High School, 39.7458202, -104.9819254
Englewood, Christ Triumphant Lutheran Church, 39.7163889, -104.9919444
Englewood, Colorado Psychiatric Hospital, 39.7306396, -104.939671
Englewood, Convent of the Good Shepherd, 39.6922096, -104.9413686
Englewood, Denver County Criminal Court, 39.739257, -104.9911474
Englewood, Denver International School, 39.7465485, -104.9295077
Englewood, Ellsworth Elementary School, 39.7158205, -104.9441463
Englewood, Elmwood School, 39.7280426, -104.9960928
Englewood, Emerson School, 39.7388758, -104.9749807
Englewood, Evans School, 39.7341536, -104.989148
Englewood, Fire Station Number 18, 39.7497222, -104.9411111
Englewood, Gove Middle School, 39.73783, -104.93982
Englewood, Grace School, 39.7308205, -104.9274789
Englewood, Lafayette Historic District, 39.7488889, -104.9708333
Englewood, Lowry Air Force Base, 39.7230556, -104.8919444
Englewood, Merchant Station Denver Post Office, 39.745, -104.9916667
Englewood, Montclair Annex School, 39.7374872, -104.9038667
Englewood, Museum of Western Art, 39.7447222, -104.9883333
Englewood, Park Avenue Hospital, 39.7410981, -104.969425
Englewood, Philips Elementary School, 39.7480427, -104.9119226
Englewood, Pitts Elementary School, 39.6524877, -104.9266462
Englewood, Public School 1 Charter School, 39.73352, -104.99252
Englewood, Rocky Mountain Hebrew Academy, 39.71086, -104.93093
Englewood, Rosedale Elementary School, 39.6744318, -104.9844261

Historical Assets Colorado

Englewood, Saint John School, 39.7260982, -104.956369
Englewood, Saint Joseph High School, 39.7263759, -104.9955372
Englewood, Saint Luke Hospital, 39.7466536, -104.9802587
Englewood, Sherman Elementary School, 39.7197093, -104.9835924
Englewood, Spears Hospital, 39.7313761, -104.920812
Englewood, Stevens Elementary School, 39.7344314, -104.9569245
Englewood, Swallow Hill Historic District, 39.7416667, -104.9755556
Englewood, Temple Emanuel, 39.7416667, -104.9802778
Englewood, Thatcher School, 39.6847095, -104.9835927
Englewood, Twilight Golf Club, 39.6974874, -104.9069228
Englewood, University Hills Lutheran School, 39.65947, -104.92967
Englewood, University of Colorado Health Services Center, 39.7305427, -104.939146
Englewood, Washington Park School, 39.6960984, -104.9644251
Fort Logan, Belmont School, 39.7030428, -105.0452612
Fort Logan, Beth Israel Hospital, 39.7436111, -105.035
Fort Logan, Denver Lutheran High School, 39.6955428, -105.0283163
Fort Logan, Denver Public Schools Night High School, 39.6762, -105.02732
Fort Logan, Emmanuel Sherith Israel Chapel, 39.7441667, -105.0038889
Fort Logan, Fort Logan, 39.6427778, -105.0377778
Fort Logan, Islamic Center of Ahl-Al-Beit, 39.7133333, -105.0352778
Fort Logan, McNichols Sports Arena, 39.7427778, -105.0227778
Fort Logan, Mile High Stadium, 39.7466536, -105.0224824
Fort Logan, Perry School, 39.7177649, -105.0397054
Fort Logan, Rishel Middle School, 39.70864, -105.01141
Fort Logan, Saint Anthony of Padua School, 39.702765, -105.0369276
Fort Logan, Saint Cajetan School, 39.743598, -105.0060931
Fort Logan, Saint Cajetan's Catholic Church, 39.7427778, -105.0052778
Fort Logan, Saint Elizabeth School, 39.742209, -105.0016485
Fort Logan, Saint Elizabeth's Catholic Church, 39.7427778, -105.0022222
Fort Logan, Westwood Elementary School, 39.7008333, -105.0355556
Unknown, Overland Park Post Office, 0, 0

Grand Army of the Republic Posts
Byron L Carr, No. 14, Denver, Denver, 1903

USGS Historic Military Places
Commerce City, Denver Medical Depot, 39.7708333, -104.9597222
Englewood, Lowry Air Force Base, 39.7230556, -104.8919444
Fort Logan, Fort Logan, 39.6427778, -105.0377778

Military Bases
None

Post Offices
Alcott	1896 May 18	1904 June 30
Argo	1881 Apr 11	1911 Sept 15

Denver County

Denver	1866 Feb 13		80202
Denver Mills	1892 Jan 20	1918 Sept 30*	
Elyria	1895 Feb 15	1904 Jan 15	
Harman	1887 Aug 16	1904 Jan 16	
Loretto	1896 Sept 28	1966 Mar 11	
Montclair	1888 July 3	1912 Mar 31	
Overland	1892 Apr 12	1920 Feb 14	
Stockyards	1898 Apr 16	1904 Jan 15	
Valverde	1889 Oct 14	1908 Feb 29	

Topo Quads

Fort Logan	394500N	393730N	1050000W	1050730W
Highlands Ranch	393730N	393000N	1045230W	1050000W
Littleton	393730N	393000N	1050000W	1050730W

Suggested Reading

Arps, Louisa Ward. *Denver in Slices*. Denver: Sage Books, 1959.

Goodstein, Phil H. *The Denver History Index*. Denver: New Social Publications, 2013.

King, Clyde L. *History of the Government of Denver*. Denver: The Fisher Book Company, 1911.

Smiley, Jerome C. *History of Denver*. Denver: Times-Sun Pub Co, 1901.

Tonge, Thomas. *Denver by Pen and Picture*. Denver: Denver Dry Goods Co, 1898.

Vickers, W B. *History of the City of Denver, Arapahoe County*, Colorado. Chicago: O L Baskin & Co, 1880.

Wharton, Junius E. *History of the City of Denver from its Earliest Settlement to the Present Time*. Denver: Byers & Dailey, 1866.

Historical Assets Colorado

Dolores County

Introduction
Established: 1881   Population: 2,064
Formed from: Ouray
Adjacent Counties:
County Seat: Dove Creek
  Other Communities: Rico, Cahone
Website, http://www.dolorescounty.org
Area Codes: 970
Zip Codes: 81320, 81324, 81332

Historical Assets Colorado

Dolores County Courthouse   Dolores County 19th Century Courthouse

Courthouses & County Government

Dolores County
    http://www.dolorescounty.org/
Dolores County Courthouse (22nd Judicial District), 409 N Main St, Dove Creek, CO 81324, 970-677-2258; http://www.courts.state.co.us/Courts/County/Index.cfm?County_ID=65
Assessor, P.O. Box 478, Dove Creek, CO 81324, 970-677-2385; http://www.dolorescounty.org/government/dolores_county_assessor.html
Board of County Commissioners, 409 N Main St, Dove Creek, CO 81324, 970-677-2383, http://www.dolorescounty.org/departments-and-contacts/#commissioners?option=commissioners
Clerk & Recorder, 409 N Main St, Dove Creek, CO 81324, 970-677-2381; http://www.dolorescounty.org/government/dolores_county_clerk_and_recorder.html
Coroner, 409 N Main St, Dove Creek, CO 81324, 970-677-2383; http://www.dolorescounty.org/county-services/#the-coroner?option=the-coroner
Public Health, 497 W 4th St, Dove Creek, CO 81324, 970-677-2387; http://www.dolorescounty.org/services/county_public_health_services.html
Transportation (Road & Bridge), 8477 Road 7.7, Dove Creek CO 81324, 970-677-2328; http://www.dolorescounty.org/departments-and-contacts/
Treasurer, 409 N Main St, Dove Creek, CO 81324, 970-677-2386; http://www.dolorescounty.org/government/dolores_county_Transportation Treasurer_and_public_trustee.html

County Records

Birth 1887   Marriage 1887   Divorce 1881
Death 1887   Land 1887   Probate 1881
Court 1881
CSA has Naturalization records from 1881

Dolores County

County & Municipal Records Held at the State Level
The Colorado State Archives

Physical Records
Coroner
County Court
District Court
Combined Courts
WPA Historical Records
WPA Religious Institutions
   Survey
WPA Rico
Cities
Rico

Records on Film
1885 Census

Records on Master Film
Clerk & Recorder
County Court
School Districts

The Denver Public Library
WWI Draft Registration Cards (microfilm)

School Districts
School Districts, http://www.adcogov.org/local-school-districts
Dolores County School District RE-2J, 425 N Main St, Dove Creek, CO 81324, 970-677-2522; https://www.dc2j.org

Historic School Districts
1. Rico
2. Lower Lavender, Middle Lavender
3. Dunton
4. Dove Creek
5. Independence
6. Peel, Egnar
7. Coal Bed
8. Oak Grove
9. Cahone
10. Little Grove
11. Upper Lavender

Fraternal Organizations
Granges
Dove Creek, No. 446, Dolores, Dove Creek, 25 Feb 1939
Masons
Ancient Free & Accepted Masons
Rico, No. 79, Dolores, Rico, 16 Sept 1890
Charles L Young, No. 177, Dolores, Dove Creek, 23 Jan 1952
Royal Arch Masons
None
Knights Templar
None
Eastern Star
Rico, No. 31, Dolores, Rico
Vesper, No. 146, Dolores, Dove Creek
Odd Fellows
Silver Crescent, No. 40, Dolores, Rico

Historical Assets Colorado

Rebekahs
None

Knights of Pythias
Silver Glance, No. 82, Dolores, Rico

Pythian Sisters
None

Benevolent Protective Order of Elks
None

City & Town Halls

Dove Creek, 505 W 4th St, Dove Creek, CO 81324, 970-677-2255, https://www.colorado.gov/dovecreek

Rico, 2 Commercial St, Rico, CO 81332, 970-967-2865, https://www.colorado.gov/pacific/ricocolorado

Archives & Manuscript Collections

None

Historical & Genealogical Societies

Dolores County Historical Society, 409 Main St, P.O. Box 453, Dove Creek, CO 81324, (970) 677-2283, http://cogenweb.com/dolores/dgsociety.html

Rico Historical Society, Historical Museum, 15 S Glasgow Ave, Rico, CO 81332, https://www.facebook.com/ricohistory/

Local Libraries

Dolores County Library, 525 Main St, PO Box 578, Dove Creek, CO 81324-0578, (970) 677-2389, https://www.facebook.com/DCPublicLibrary/

Rico Public Library, 2 N Short St, PO Box 69, Rico, CO 81332-0069, (970) 967-2103, https://rico.colibraries.org

Links

CO GenWeb
http://cogenweb.com/dolores/

Cyndi's List
https://www.cyndislist.com/us/co/counties/dolores/

FamilySearch Wiki
https://www.familysearch.org/wiki/en/Dolores_County,_Colorado_Genealogy

Linkpendium
http://www.linkpendium.com/dolores-co-genealogy/

RootsWeb Wiki
https://wiki.rootsweb.com/wiki/index.php/Dolores_County,_Colorado

Wikipedia
https://en.wikipedia.org/wiki/Dolores_County,_Colorado

Dolores County

Historic Hotels
None

Museums & Historic Sites
Rico Historical Society, Historical Museum, 15 S Glasgow Ave, Rico, CO 81332, https://www.facebook.com/ricohistory/

Special Events & Scenic Locations
The Dolores County Fair is held in August most years at the Dolores County Fairgrounds, 6798 Cty Rd 3.7, Dove Creek, CO 86038, 970-677-2283, http://www.dolorescounty.org/fairgrounds/

Dolores County keeps a calendar of annual events on Eventbrite: https://www.eventbrite.com/d/co—dolores/festivals/

Calico National Recreation Trail
Canyons of the Ancient National Monument
Lizard Head Wilderness
Old Spanish National Historic Trail
San Juan National Forest
Great Parks Bicycle Route
Western Express Bicycle Route
San Juan Skyway National Scenic Byway

Ghost Towns & Other Sparsely Populated Places
Dunton, Lavender, Lizard Head, Montelores, Rico

Newspapers
The Rico News. (Rico, Dolores County, Colo.) 18??-1???
Dolores News. (Rico, Ouray Co., Colo.) 1879-1886
The Rico Clipper. (Rico, Colo.) 1882-1???
Rico Record. (Rico, Colo.) 1883-1886
Rico News-Record. (Rico, Colo.) 1886-????
The Rico Democrat. (Rico, Dolores County, Colo.) 1891-1891
The Rico Weekly Sun. (Rico, Dolores County, Colo.) 1891-1891
The Rico Sun. (Rico, Dolores County, Colo.) 1891-18??
The Rico News-Sun. (Rico, Dolores County, Colo.) 1896-1901
The Rico Item. (Rico, Dolores County, Colo.) 19??-1932
The Rico News. (Rico, Dolores County, Colo.) 1901-19??
The Rico-Dove Creek News. (Rico, Dolores County, Colo.) 1933-19??
The Dove Creek Press. (Dove Creek, Colo.) 1940-1952
The Dove Creek Press and San Juan Record. (Dove Creek, Colo.) 1952-1953
The Dove Creek Press. (Dove Creek, Colo.) 1953-1977
Dove Creek Dolores County Press. (Dove Creek, Colo.) 1977-1979
Dove Creek Press. (Dove Creek, Dolores County, Colo.) 1980-Current

Historical Assets Colorado

Places on the National Register
Cahone, Ansel Hall Ruin, Address Restricted
Dolores, Beaver Creek Massacre Site, Address Restricted
Rico, Dey Building, 3 N. Glasgow
Rico, Kauffman, William, House, Silver St.
Rico, Rico City Hall, NE corner of Commercial and Mantz Sts.

USGS Historic Places
Dolores Peak, Dunton Post Office, 37.7727718, -108.0939632
Narraguinnep Mountain, Fort Narraguinnep Historical Site, 37.7302683, -108.5762058
Rico, Burns, 37.7241616, -108.0253497
Unknown, Disappointment Post Office, 0, 0

Grand Army of the Republic Posts
Hazen, No. 63, Dolores, Rico

USGS Historic Military Places
None

Military Bases
None

Post Offices

Alkali	1916 May 6	rescinded	
Beaty	1902 Aug 20	1903 Jan 2	
Cahone	1916 May 21	1884 June 9	
Cahone 2	1920 June 12		81320
Disappointment	1919 Apr 19	1920 June 30	
Dove Creek	1915 Jan 16		81324
Dunton	1892 Aug 9	1954 Nov 30*	
Egnar	1917 May 28		81325
Hermitage	1904 Oct 17	1907 June 29	
Jual	1918 Jan 28	1918 Sept 14	
Lavender	1888 Aug 10	1915 Feb 27*	
Lizard Head	1892 July 23	1895 Oct 31	
Molding	1919 Sept 16	1924 Feb 29	
Northdale	1918 May 23	1946 Aug 31*	
Rico	1879 Aug 25		81332
Squaw Point	1920 Nov 3	1926 May 15	
Willow Gulch	1921 Mar 28	1927 Dec 31	

Topo Quads

Cahone	374500N	373730N	1084500W	1085230W
Champagne Spring	374500N	373730N	1085230W	1090000W

Dolores County

Clyde Lake	374500N	373730N	1080730W	1081500W
Doe Canyon	374500N	373730N	1083730W	1084500W
Dove Creek	375230N	374500N	1085230W	1090000W
Glade Mountain	375230N	374500N	1083000W	1083730W
Groundhog Reservoir	375230N	374500N	1081500W	1082230W
Narraguinnep Mtn	374500N	373730N	1083000W	1083730W
Nipple Mountain	374500N	373730N	1081500W	1082230W
Northdale	375230N	374500N	1090000W	1090730W
Rico	374500N	373730N	1080000W	1080730W
Ruin Canyon	373730N	373000N	1085230W	1090000W
Secret Canyon	375230N	374500N	1084500W	1085230W
South Mountain	375230N	374500N	1082230W	1083000W
The Glade	375230N	374500N	1083730W	1084500W
Willow Spring	374500N	373730N	1082230W	1083000W

Suggested Reading

Fleming J and Inez Towne. *Rico: A Brief History*. NL: NP, 1987.

Historical Assets Colorado

Douglas County

Introduction

Established: 1861   Population: 285,465

Formed from: Original

Adjacent Counties: Jefferson, Arapahoe, Elbert, El Paso, Teller

County Seat: Castle Rock

Other Communities: Castle Pines, Lone Tree, Sedalia, Larkspur, Parker, Roxborough, Dakan, Deckers, Greenland, Meridian, Franktown, Highlands Ranch, Louviers, Perry Park, Roxborough Park

Website, https://www.douglas.co.us

Area Codes: 303, 720

Zip Codes: 80104, 80108, 80109, 80116, 80118, 80124, 80125, 80126, 80129, 80130, 80131, 80134, 80135, 80138, 80163

Historical Assets Colorado

Douglas County early Courthouse

Douglas County 19th Century Courthouse

Douglas County Courthouse

Courthouses & County Government

Douglas County
https://www.douglas.co.us/

Douglas County Courthouse (18th Judicial District), 4000 Justice Way, Castle Rock, CO 80109; http://www.courts.state.co.us/Courts/County/Index.cfm?County_ID=58

Assessor, 301 Wilcox St, Castle Rock, CO 80104, 303-660-7450; http://www.douglas.co.us/assessor/

Douglas County

Board of County Commissioners, 1100 3rd St, Castle Rock, CO 80104, 303-660-7401, https://www.douglas.co.us/government/commissioners/

Clerk & Recorder, 301 Wilcox St, Castle Rock, CO 80104, 303-660-7446; http://www.douglas.co.us/clerk/

Coroner, 4000 Justice Wy, Castle Rock, CO 80109, 303-814-7150; https://www.douglas.co.us/coroner/

Elections, 125 Stephanie Pl, Castle Rock, CO 80109, 303-660-7444; https://www.douglas.co.us/elections/

Public Health, 6162 S Willow Dr, Ste 100, Greenwood Village, CO 80111, 303-220-9200; http://www.tchd.org/

Transportation, 100 3rd St, Castle Rock, CO 80104, 303-660-7400; https://www.douglas.co.us/transportation/

Treasurer, 100 3rd St, Ste 120, Castle Rock, CO 80104, 303-660-7455; http://www.douglas.co.us/Treasurer/

County Records

Birth Unk	Marriage 1864	Divorce Unk
Death Unk	Land 1864	Probate Unk
Court Unk		
CSA Delayed Birth Certificates 1941		

County & Municipal Records Held at the State Level

The Colorado State Archives

Physical Records	**Records on Film**	**Records on Master Film**
Assessor	1885 Census	Assessor
Clerk & Recorder	Assessor	Attorney
Coroner	Clerk & Recorder	Building
County Commissioners	County Court	Clerk & Recorder
County Court	District Court	County Court
District Court	Combined Courts	District Court
Justice Court	Justice Court	Combined Courts
Public Trustee	School Districts	County Commissioners
Surveyor		District Attorney
Treasurer		Finance
WPA Historical Records		Motor Vehicles
WPA Religious Institutions Survey		Planning
		Public Trustee
		School Districts
		Treasurer

The Denver Public Library

District Court Depositions, 1933
WWI Draft Registration Cards (microfilm)

Historical Assets Colorado

School Districts
School Districts, http://www.adcogov.org/local-school-districts
Douglas County School District RE-1, 620 Wilcox St, Castle Rock, CO 80104, 303-387-0100; https://www.dcsdk12.org/

Historic School Districts
1. Sedalia
2. Franktown
3. Spring Valley
4. Gann
5. Jarre Creek
6. Glen Grove
7. Indian Park
8. Fonder
9. Welte
10. [1878]
11. [1878]
12. Lower Lake Gulch
13. Upper Lake GUlch
14. Goldale
15. Larkspur, Stone Canon
16. Plum Creek
17. Lone Tree
18. [1878]
19. [1888]
20. Cherry
21. Sylvia
22. East Cherry
23. Greenland
24. Irving
25. [1883]
Jt26. Columbine
27. West Creek, Elton, Pine Grove
28. Happy Canyon
29. [1890]
Jt30. Hill Top
31. Round Top
32. Oaklands
Jt33. Cedar Grove
34. Roxborough Park
35. Flintwood
36. Louviers
37. Parker
38. Castle Rock
39. Baldridge

Fraternal Organizations

Granges
Fonder, No. 32, Douglas, Franktown/Fonderville, 14 Jan 1874
Pleasant Valley, No. 33, Douglas, Bear Canyon/Sedalia, 15 Jan 1874
Sedalia, No. 40, Douglas, Sedalia, 22 Jan 1874
Larkspur, No. 44, Douglas, Larkspur, 23 Jan 1874
Greenland, No. 52, Douglas, Greenland, 17 Feb 1874
Castle Rock, No. 62, Douglas, Castle Rock, 17 June 1874
Rich Valley, No. 64, Douglas, Greenland/Larkspur, 27 July 1874
Sunflower, No. 162, Douglas, Sedalia, 13 Dec 1907
Pikes Peak, No 163, Douglas, Franktown, 14 Mar 1908
Great Divide, No. 166, Douglas, Case, 10 June 1908
Golden Rod, No. 192, Douglas, Castle Rock, 15 Dec 1910
Pine Ridge, No. 199, Douglas, Parker/Bayfield, 28 Apr 1911

Masons

Ancient Free & Accepted Masons
Douglas, No. 153, Douglas, Castle Rock, 8 Oct 1919

Royal Arch Masons
None

Knights Templar
None

Eastern Star
Martha, No. 135, Douglas, Castle Rock

Douglas County

Odd Fellows
Castle Rock, No. 139, Douglas, Castle Rock
Sedalia, No. 142, Douglas, Sedalia

Rebekahs
Jasmine, No. 83, Douglas, Sedalia

Knights of Pythias
None

Pythian Sisters
None

Benevolent Protective Order of Elks
Douglas County, No. 2873, Douglas, Castle Rock

City & Town Halls
Castle Rock, 100 Wilcox St, Castle Rock, CO 80104, 303-660-1015, http://www.crgov.com
Castle Pines, 360 Village Square Ln, Castle Pines, CO 80108, 303-705-0200, https://www.castlepinesco.gov
Lone Tree, 9220 Kimmer Dr, Lone Tree, CO 80124, 303-708-1818, https://cityoflonetree.com
Larkspur, 9524 S Spruce Mountain Rd, Larkspur, CO 80118, 303-681-2324, https://www.townoflarkspur.org
Parker, 20120 Main St, Parker, CO 80138, 303-841-0353, https://www.parkeronline.org
Highlands Ranch, 62 Plaza Dr, Highlands Ranch, CO 80129, 303-791-0430, https://highlandsranch.org
Perry Park, P.O. Box 183, Larkspur, CO 80118, http://perrypark.org

Archives & Manuscript Collections
Douglas County Library & History Research Center, 100 S Wilcox St, Castle Rock, CO 80104, (303) 688-7730, http://douglascountyhistory.org

Historical & Genealogical Societies
Castle Rock Genealogical Society, P.O. Box 1881, Castle Rock, CO 80104, http://crcgs.com
Castle Rock Historical Society, Denver & Rio Grande RR Station Museum, 420 Elbert St, Castle Rock, CO 80104, (303) 814-3164, http://castlerockmuseum.org
Colorado Historic Cemetery Association, P.O. Box 924, Castle Rock, CO 80104, https://www.coloradohistoriccemeteries.org
Deer Trail Pioneer Historical Society, Deer Trail Pioneer Museum, 2nd Ave & Fir St, P.O. Box 176, Deer Trail, CO 80105, (303) 769-4542, https://www.colorado.gov/pacific/townofdeertrail/deer-trail-pioneer-historical-museum
Highlands Ranch Genealogical Society, c/o Highlands Ranch Library, 9292 Ridgeline Blvd, Highlands Ranch, CO 80129, http://hrgenealogy.wordpress.com/
Historic Douglas County, P.O. Box 2032, Castle Rock, CO 80104, http://www.historicdouglascounty.org

Historical Assets Colorado

Larkspur Historical Society, 5254 Grimes Ln, Larkspur, CO 80118, (303) 681-3537, http://www.larkspurhistoricalsociety.com

Parker Area Historical Society, Schoolhouse Museum, 19650 E Mainstreet, P.O. Box 604, Parker, CO 80134, http://www.parkerhistory.org

Parker Genealogical Society, P.O. Box 2672, Parker, CO 80134, https://sites.rootsweb.com/~copgs/index.html

Saint Andrew Society of Colorado, 344 Southpark Rd, Highlands Ranch, CO 80126-2232, (720) 675-7268, http://coloradoscots.com

Local Libraries

Douglas County Library & History Research Center, 100 S Wilcox St, Castle Rock, CO 80104, (303) 688-7730, http://douglascountyhistory.org

Douglas County Libraries-Lone Tree Branch, 10055 Library Wy, Lone Tree, CO 80124, (303) 791-7323, https://www.dcl.org/lone-tree/

Douglas County Libraries-Parker Branch, 20105 Mainstreet, Parker, CO 80138, (303) 791-7323, https://www.dcl.org/parker/

Links

CO GenWeb
http://cogenweb.com/douglas/

Cyndi's List
https://www.cyndislist.com/us/co/counties/douglas/

FamilySearch Wiki
https://www.familysearch.org/wiki/en/Douglas_County,_Colorado_Genealogy

Linkpendium
http://www.linkpendium.com/douglas-co-genealogy/

RootsWeb Wiki
https://wiki.rootsweb.com/wiki/index.php/Douglas_County,_Colorado

Wikipedia
https://en.wikipedia.org/wiki/Douglas_County,_Colorado

Historic Hotels

None

Museums & Historic Sites

Castle Rock Historical Society, Denver & Rio Grande RR Station Museum, 420 Elbert St, Castle Rock, CO 80104, (303) 814-3164, http://castlerockmuseum.org

Deer Trail Pioneer Historical Society, Deer Trail Pioneer Museum, 2nd Ave & Fir St, P.O. Box 176, Deer Trail, CO 80105, (303) 769-4542, https://www.colorado.gov/pacific/townofdeertrail/deer-trail-pioneer-historical-museum

Parker Area Historical Society, Schoolhouse Museum, 19650 E Mainstreet, P.O. Box 604, Parker, CO 80134, http://www.parkerhistory.org

Douglas County

Special Events & Scenic Locations

The Douglas County Fair & Rodeo is held in July and August most years at the Douglas County Fairgrounds, 500 Fairgrounds Rd, Castle Rock, CO 80104, 720-733-6900, https://www.douglascountyfairandrodeo.com.

Historic Douglas County has a calendar of events here: https://www.historicdouglascounty.org/sponsorships.

The Castle Rock Chamber of Commerce keeps a list of events here: https://castlerock.org/signature-events/.

The Douglas County Fairgrounds & Events Center's calendar is here: https://eventscenter.douglas.co.us.

American Discovery Trail
Colorado Trail
Devils Head National Recreation Trail
Highline Canal National Recreation Trail
Platte River Greenway National Recreation Trail
Ridgeline Open Space Trail

Ghost Towns & Other Sparsely Populated Places

Acequia, Bear Canon, Dakan, Deansbury, Douglass City, Glade, Greenland, Hill Top, Larkspur, Lehigh Coal Mine, Nighthawk, Plateau, Rock Ridge, Struby, Toluca, Tomah, Wohlhurst

Newspapers

The Parker News. (Parker, Douglas County, Colo.) 1???-19??
The Great West. (Omaha [Neb.] ;) 18??-1???
The News Letter. (Castle Rock, Colo.) 1872-1???
Douglas County News. (Frankstown, Colo.) 1873-1879
Castle Rock Independent. (Castle Rock, Colo.) 1879-1881
The Castle Rock Journal. (Castle Rock, Colo.) 1880-1908
Douglas County News. (Castle Rock, Colo.) 1890-1???
The Press. (Parker, (Douglas County), Colo.) 19??-1978
The Record-Journal of Douglas County. (Castle Rock, Douglas County, Colo.) 1908-1923
The Inland Oil Index. (Casper, Wyo.) 1922-1941
The Record-Journal. (Castle Rock, Colo.) 1923-19??
Douglas County News. (Castle Rock, Colo.) 1949-1979
Palmer Lake-Monument News. (Palmer Lake, Colo.) 1965-1972
Town & Country Squire. (Castle Rock, Colo.) 1973-1973
The Castle Rock Town & Country Squire. (Castle Rock, Colo.) 1973-19??
Castle Rock's Douglas County Town & Country Squire. (Castle Rock, Colo.) 1973-1975
Palmer Lake-Monument-Woodmoor News. (Castle Rock, Colo.) 1973-1975
Douglas County Town & Country Squire. (Castle Rock, Colo.) 1975-19??
Tri-Lakes Tribune. (Castle Rock, Colo.) 1975-1977

Historical Assets Colorado

The Wednesday Press. (Parker (Douglas County) Colo.) 1978-1979
Parker News-Press. (Parker, Colo.) 1979-1983
Douglas County News-Press. (Castle Rock, Colo.) 1979-1983
Colorado Legal Squire. (Castle Rock, Colo.) 1980-1985
Douglas County Daily News-Press. (Castle Rock, Colo.) 1983-1987
Parker Daily News-Press. (Parker, Colo.) 1983-1987
The Parker Trail. (Parker, Colo.) 1984-Current
Impact Along The Front Range. (Castle Rock, Colo.) 1985-19??
Daily News-Press. (Castle Rock, Co) 1987-1992
Daily News-Press. (Parker, Colo.) 1987-Current
Douglas County News-Press. (Castle Rock, Co) 1992-Current

Places on the National Register

Castle Rock, Castle Rock Depot, 420 Elbert St.
Castle Rock, Castle Rock Elementry School, 3rd and Cantril Sts.
Castle Rock, First National Bank of Douglas County, 300 Wilcox St.
Castle Rock, Hammar, Benjamin, House, 203 Cantril St.
Castle Rock, Keystone Hotel, 219 and 223 4th St.
Denver, Bear Canon Agricultural District, S of Denver on both sides of CO 105 from CO 67 S to Jarre Creek
Franktown, Cherry Creek Bridge, CO 83 at milepost 46.30
Franktown, Evans Homestead Rural Historic Landscape, Address Restricted
Franktown, Franktown Cave, Address Restricted
Franktown, Pike's Peak Grange No. 163, 3093 CO 83
Larkspur, American Federation of Human Rights Headquarters, 9070 S. Douglas Blvd.
Larkspur, Sinclaire, Reginald, House, 6154 Perry Park Rd.
Larkspur, Spring Valley School, E of Larkspur at Spring Valley and Lorraine Rds.
Littleton, Lamb Spring, Address Restricted
Louviers, Louviers Village, Louviers Blvd.,Hillcrest Dr.,Triangle Dr., Main St.,Valley View St, 1st, 2nd, 3rd and 4th Sts.
Louviers, Louviers Village Club, Jct. of Louviers Blvd. and First St.
Palmer Lake, Glen Grove School, N of Palmer Lake off Perry Park Rd.
Palmer Lake, Quick, Ben, Ranch and Fort, 6695 W. Plum Creek Rd.
Parker, Ruth Memorial Methodist Episcopal Church, 19670 E. Mainstreet
Sedalia, Cherokee Ranch, N of Co. Rd. 85 and S of Daniels Park Rd.
Sedalia, Church of St. Philip-in-the-Field and Bear Canon Cemetery, 5 mi. S of Sedalia on CO 105
Sedalia, Daniels Park, Along Douglas Co. Rd. 67 NE of Sedalia
Sedalia, Devils Head Lookout, South Platte District, Pike National Forest
Sedalia, Indian Park School, 10 mi. (16 km) W of Sedalia on CO 67
Sedalia, Kinner, John, House, 6694 Perry Park Rd.
Sedalia, Santa Fe Railway Water Tank, US 85 W of jct. with CO 67
Waterton, Roxborough State Park Archaeological District, Address Restricted

Douglas County

USGS Historic Places
Dawson Butte, Glen Grove School, 39.2605464, -104.9510941
Dawson Butte, Oakland School, 39.3702676, -104.9555381
Deckers, Deckers Post Office, 39.2547125, -105.2269382
Highlands Ranch, Carriage Club Census Designated Place, 39.5282155, -104.8952756
Highlands Ranch, Heritage Hills Census Designated Place, 39.5438825, -104.876874
Kassler, South Metro Fire Rescue Station 41, 39.4777485, -105.006874
Littleton, Bowen Farms Number 1 Airport, 39.5497104, -105.0341509
Littleton, South Metro Fire Rescue Station 42, 39.5069755, -105.0730095
Russellville Gulch, Kostroski Airport, 39.3655459, -104.6777529
Sedalia, Denver-Douglas Landing Strip, 39.4141562, -104.8774795
Sedalia, Littleton-Sedalia Landing Area, 39.4680444, -104.9910945
Westcreek, Westcreek Lake, 39.1616577, -105.1655461

Grand Army of the Republic Posts
J G Blunt, No. 65, Douglas, Castle Rock

USGS Historic Military Places
None

Military Bases
None

Post Offices

Acequia	1874 Jan 30	1900 July 14*	
Bear Canyon	1863 Apr 7	1879 Aug 4*	
Bennet Springs	1862 Dec 20	1865 Sept 12	
Bethesda	1902 Mar 28	1909 Sept 15	
Bijou Basin	1869 Apr 8	1907 Mar 30*	
Case	1897 Aug 7	1913 June 24	
Castle Rock	1871 Apr 5	1874 May 18	
Castle Rock 2	1874 May 18		80104
Cherry	1900 Apr 7	1920 Aug 31	
Cheyenne Wells	1869 Feb 10	1870 Apr 11	
Colfax	1862 July 14	1863 Oct 21	
Daffodil	1896 Apr 11	1908 Feb 19	
Dakan	1896 Dec 30	1898 Aug 2	
Deane	1879 Dec 19	1884 Oct 16	
Deansbury	1890 June 23	1892 Feb 3	
Deckers	1908 Feb 19	1933 Nov 15	
Douglas	1874 May 18	1886 Dec 12	
Franktown	1862 Sept 8		80116
Frosts Ranch	1871 Feb 8	1872 Feb 12	
Glen Grove	1869 Nov 29	1877 July 24	
Golddale	1882 June 29	1885 Feb 12	

Historical Assets Colorado

Gomers Mills	1870 June 13	1882 June 27*	
Hill Top	1890 Feb 17	1896	
Hilltop	1896	1943 Dec 31	
Hugo	1871 Dec 1		80821
Huntsville	1860 Mar 24	1871 Dec 13*	
Irving	1913 June 24	1920 Apr 15	
Keystone	1869 Apr 8	1872 Oct 28	
Keystone Ranch	1863 Apr 7	1865 June 16	
Kiowa	1868 Feb 14		80117
Larkspur	1871 Dec 13	1892 July 27	
Larkspur 2	1892 Aug 26		80118
Louviers	1907 June 25		80131
New Memphis	1872 Jan 8	1874 May 18	
Parker	1870 Dec 8		80134
Pemberton	1896 Jan 23	1902 Apr 14	
Perry	1890 June 21	1895 Mar 23	
Perry Park	1892 Mar 11	1906 Jan 31	
Pine Grove	1873 Dec 8	1882 Mar 17*	
Platte Canon	1877 Oct 11	1879 Dec 19	
Rock Butte	1869 Sept 20	1874 Oct 22*	
Rock Ridge	1872 Feb 13	1892 Mar 22	
Running Creek	1868 Apr 14	1883 Mar 12*	
Russellville	1862 May 22	1862 Sept 8	
Sedalia	1872 Apr 8		80135
Spring Valley	1865 Mar 27	1885 July 31	
Strongia Springs	1911 Sept 27	1932 Jan 15	
Strontia	1903 Oct 3	1903 Dec 1	
Tyler	1895 Nov 27	1897 July 30	
Virginia	1869 Sept 29	1871 Feb 8	
Westcreek	1902 Apr 14	1968 Nov 6*	

Topo Quads

Castle Rock North	393000N	392230N	1044500W	1045230W
Castle Rock South	392230N	391500N	1044500W	1045230W
Dakan Mountain	391500N	390730N	1050000W	1050730W
Dawson Butte	392230N	391500N	1045230W	1050000W
Devils Head	392230N	391500N	1050000W	1050730W
Greenland	391500N	390730N	1044500W	1045230W
Larkspur	391500N	390730N	1045230W	1050000W
Parker	393730N	393000N	1044500W	1045230W
Sedalia	393000N	392230N	1045230W	1050000W

Suggested Reading

Appleby, Susan Consola. *Fading Past: the Story of Douglas County, Colorado*. Palmer Lake, CO: Fitter Press, 2001.

Boyd, Shaun K. *Douglas County*. Charleston, SC: Arcadia Publishing, 2017.

Douglas County

Castle Rock Writers. *Chronicles of Douglas County, Colorado*. Charleston, SC: The History Press, 2014.

Meyer, Betty. *A Survey of Douglas County History*. NL: NP. 19__.

Moore, Anne. *A History of Douglas County, 1820 to 1910*. Thesis, University of Denver, 1970.

Smith, Edwin W. *Historical Sketch of that Portion of Douglas County, Colorado known as West Plum Creek, 1869-1900*. NL: State Historical Society of Colorado, 1950.

Historical Assets Colorado

Eagle County

Introduction

Established: 1883   Population: 52,197

Formed from: Summit

Adjacent Counties: Grand, Summit, Lake, Pitkin, Garfield, Routt

County Seat: Eagle

Other Communities: Avon, Basalt, Gypsum, Minturn, Red Cliff, Vail, Dotsero, Edwards, El Jebel, Fulford, McCoy, Wolcott, Bond, Eagle-Vail, Sweetwater, Gilman

Website, https://www.eaglecounty.us

Area Codes: 970

Zip Codes: 80423, 80426, 80463, 81620, 81621, 81631, 81632, 81637, 81645, 81649, 81655, 81657, 81658

Historical Assets Colorado

Eagle County Courthouse

Eagle County 19th Century Courthouse

Courthouses & County Government

Eagle County
https://www.eaglecounty.us

Eagle County Courthouse (Justice Center)(5th Judicial District), 885 Chambers Ave, Eagle, CO 81631, 970-328-6373; http://www.courts.state.co.us/Courts/County/Index.cfm?County_ID=9

Eagle County Courthouse (El Jebel), 20 Eagle County Dr, Ste B, Carbondale, CO 81623, 970-704-2740; http://www.courts.state.co.us/Courts/County/Index.cfm?County_ID=9

Assessor, 500 Broadway, Eagle, CO 81631, 970-328-8640; http://www.eaglecounty.us/Assessor/

Board of County Commissioners, 500 Broadway, Eagle, CO 81631, 970-328-8605, https://www.eaglecounty.us/Commissioners/

Clerk & Recorder, 500 Broadway, Eagle, CO 81631, 970-328-8723; http://www.eagle-county.us/Clerk/

Coroner, P.O. Box 5200, Eagle, CO 81631, 970-328-8864; https://www.eaglecounty.us/Coroner/

Public Health, 551 Broadway, Eagle, CO 81631, 970-328-8840; http://www.eagle-county.us/publichealth/

Transportation (Road & Bridge), P.O. Box 250, Eagle, CO 81631, 970-328-3540; https://www.eaglecounty.us/Road/

Treasurer, 500 Broadway, Ste 106, Eagle, CO 81631, 970-328-8860; http://www.eaglecounty.us/Treasurer/

County Records

Birth 1894	Marriage 1883	Divorce 1883
Death 1897	Land 1883	Probate 1883
Court 1883		

Eagle County

County & Municipal Records Held at the State Level

The Colorado State Archives

Physical Records
Clerk & Recorder
County Court
District Court
WPA Historical Records
WPA Religious Institutions
 Survey
WPA Eagle
Cities
 Red Cliff

Records on Film
1885 Census
District Court

Records on Master Film
Clerk & Recorder
County Court
District Court
Combined Courts
School Districts
Treasurer
Cities
 Avon
 Red Cliff

The Denver Public Library
None

School Districts

School Districts, http://www.adcogov.org/local-school-districts
Eagle County School District RE 50, 948 Chambers Ave, Eagle, CO 81631, 970-328-6321; https://www.eagleschools.net/

Historic School Districts

1. Red Cliff
2. Pando, Mitchell
3. Upper and Lower Sheep Horn
4. Eagle
5. Upper Gypsum
6. Gilman
7. El Jebel, Luby, Roaring Fork
8. Burns
9. Avon
10. Lower Brush, Brush Creek
11. Minturn
12. [1890]
13. Edwards
14. Wolcott
15. Sloss, Peachblow
16. Gypsum
17. Upper Brush, Fulford
18. McCoy
19. Ruedi

J1. Basalt [Joint with Pitkin]
J2. Sweetwater [Joint with Garfield]
J3. Emma [Joint with Pitkin]
J4. McCoy [Joint with Routt]
J5. [1890]
J6. Cattle Creek [Joint with Garfield]

J13. [1904]
J14. [1904]

Fraternal Organizations

Granges
Eagle, No. 114, Eagle, Gypsum, 24 Oct 1890
Empire, No. 115, Eagle, Castle/Gypsum, 27 Oct 1890
Castle, No. 116, Eagle, Castle/Gypsum, 28 Oct 1890
Avon, No. 117, Eagle, Edwards, 30 Oct 1890

Masons
Ancient Free & Accepted Masons
Eagle, No. 43, Eagle, Red Cliff, 21 Sept 1881
Castle, No. 122, Eagle, Eagle, 18 Sept 1906

Historical Assets Colorado

Royal Arch Masons
None

Knights Templar
None

Eastern Star
Eagle, No. 86, Eagle, Eagle
Battle Mountain, No. 120, Eagle, Minturn

Odd Fellows
Silver Wave, No. 45, Eagle, Red Cliff
Gilman, No. 95, Eagle, Gilman
Crown, No. 146, Eagle, Gypsum

Rebekahs
Free Silver, No. 47, Eagle, Basalt
Crater, No. 105, Eagle, Gypsum

Knights of Pythias
Battle Mountain, No. 18, Eagle, Red Cliff, 1882 Jan 9
Eagle, No. 83, Eagle, Basalt
Fisher's Peak, No. 92, Eagle, Eagle

Pythian Sisters
None

Benevolent Protective Order of Elks
None

City & Town Halls

Eagle, 1050 Chambers Ave, Eagle, CO 81631, 970-328-6427, https://www.townofeagle.org
Avon, 100 Mikaela Wy, Avon, CO, 970-748-4000, https://www.avon.org
Basalt, 101 Midland Ave, Basalt, CO 81621, 970-927-4701, https://www.basalt.net
Gypsum, 50 Lundgren Blvd, Gypsum, CO 81637, 970-524-7514, https://townofgypsum.com
Minturn, 302 Pine St, Minturn, CO 81645, 970-827-4104, https://www.minturn.org
Red Cliff, 400 Pine St, Red Cliff, CO 81649, 970-827-5303, https://www.colorado.gov/townofredcliff
Vail, 75 S Frontage Rd, Vail, CO 81657, 970-479-2100, https://www.vailgov.com
Edwards, https://edwards-colorado.com
Eagle-Vail, https://www.eaglevail.org

Archives & Manuscript Collections

Eagle Valley Library District & Local History Archive, 600 Broadway, P.O. Box 240, Eagle, CO 81631-0240, (970) 328-8800, http://www.evld.org

Historical & Genealogical Societies

Eagle County Historical Society, P.O. Box 192, Eagle, CO 81631, (970) 845-7741, http://eaglecountyhistoricalsociety.com

Eagle County

Local Libraries
Eagle Valley Library District & Local History Archive, 600 Broadway, P.O. Box 240, Eagle, CO 81631-0240, (970) 328-8800, http://www.evld.org

Avon Branch Library, 200 Benchmark Rd, PO Box 977, Avon, CO 81620-0977, (970) 949-6797, https://www.evld.org

Basalt Regional Library District, 14 Midland Ave, Basalt, CO 81621, (970) 927-4311, https://www.basaltlibrary.org

Gypsum Public Library, 48 Lundgren Blvd, PO Box 979, Gypsum, CO 81637-0979, 970-524-5080, https://www.evld.org/about/hours-and-locations/gypsum-public-library

Vail Public Library, 292 W Meadow Dr, Vail, CO 81620, (970) 479-2184, http://www.vaillibrary.com

Links
CO GenWeb
http://cogenweb.com/eagle/

Cyndi's List
https://www.cyndislist.com/us/co/counties/eagle/

FamilySearch Wiki
https://www.familysearch.org/wiki/en/Eagle_County,_Colorado_Genealogy

Linkpendium
http://www.linkpendium.com/eagle-co-genealogy/

RootsWeb Wiki
https://wiki.rootsweb.com/wiki/index.php/Eagle_County,_Colorado

Wikipedia
https://en.wikipedia.org/wiki/Eagle_County,_Colorado

Historic Hotels
None

Museums & Historic Sites
Colorado Snow Sports Museum Hall of Fame, 231 S Frontage Rd E, Vail Village, P.O. Box 1976, Vail, CO 81657, (970) 476-1876, https://www.snowsportsmuseum.org

Special Events & Scenic Locations
The Eagle County Fair & Rodeo is held in July most years at the Eagle County Fairgrounds, 426 Fairgrounds Rd, Eagle, CO 81631, 970-328-3646, https://www.eaglecounty.us/fairrodeo/

Eagle Outside has a calendar of events here: https://eagleoutside.com/event/event-calendar/

The Eagle County Chamber of Commerce has a calendar of festival and events here: https://eaglechamber.co/eagle-events/

Historical Assets Colorado

White River National Forest
Eagles Nest Wilderness
Flat Tops Wilderness
Holy Cross Wilderness
Sylvan Lake State Park
Colorado Trail
Continental Divide National Scenic Trail
Two Elk National Recreation Trail
Vail Pass National Recreation Trail
Colorado River Headwaters National Scenic Byway
Top of the Rockies National Scenic Byway

Ghost Towns & Other Sparsely Populated Places

Allenton, Aspen Junction, Belden, Camp Hale, Castles, Cooper, Frying Pan, Fulford (Nolan's Creek Camp, Camp Fulford), Gilman, Gold Park, Gypsum, Holy Cross City, Hopkins, McCoy, Meredith, Mill Pond, Mitchell, Ogle, Pando, Peachblow, Red Cliff, Rio Aquilla, Rock Creek, Ruedi, Sherman, Sherwood, Sloane, Tennessee Pass, Thomasville, Wolcott

Newspapers

Eagle County Times. (Red Cliff, Colo.) 18??-1???
Eagle County Examiner. (Eagle, Eagle County, Colo.) 18??-1???
Eagle River Shaft. (Red Cliff, Summit County, Colo.) 18??-1???
The Times. (Red Cliff, Colo.) 1886-1???
The Pusher. (Aspen Junction, Eagle County, Colo.) 1891-1???
The Fulford Signal. (Fulford, Eagle County, Colo.) 1893-1???
The Eagle County Blade. (Red Cliff, Colo.) 1894-19??
The Basalt Journal. (Basalt, Eagle County, Colo.) 1897-19??
The Eagle County News. (Red Cliff, Colo.) 19??-1922
The Vail Villager and Eagle County Review. (Vail, Colo.) 19??-1979
The Eagle Valley Enterprise. (Eagle, Eagle County, Colo.) 1901-1916
Western Slope Enterprise The Eagle Valley Enterprise. (Eagle, Colo.) 1916-1917
Western Slope Enterprise. (Eagle, Colo.) 1917-1918
Eagle Valley Enterprise and Western Slope Enterprise. (Eagle, Colo.) 1918-1919
Eagle Valley Enterprise. (Eagle, Colo.) 1919-Current
The Holy Cross Trail. (Red Cliff, Colo.) 1922-1941
The Camp Hale Ski-Zette. (Camp Hale, Colo.) 1942-19??
The Vail Trail. (Vail, Colo.) 1965-Current
News. (Vail, Colo.) 1979-1981
News and Eagle County Review. (Vail, Colo.) 1981-19??
The Avon-Beaver Creek Times. (Avon, Colo.) 1982-1991
The ABC Times. (Avon, Co) 1991-Current

Places on the National Register

Basalt, Archeological Site 5EA484, Address Restricted
Dotsero, Dotsero Bridge, I-70 Service Rd. at milepost 133.51

Eagle County

Eagle, Eagle River Bridge, US 6 at milepost 150.24
Eagle, Upper Brush Creek School, Between Coulter Meadow & W. Brush Cr. Rds.
Gypsum, First Evangelical Lutheran Church, 400 2nd St.
Leadville, Camp Hale Site, Address Restricted
McCoy, Waterwheel, SE of McCoy at Colorado River
Minturn, Notch Mountain Shelter, Notch Mtn. Summit, White River NF
Minturn, Tigiwon Community House, FSR 707, Holy Cross Dist., White River NF
Radium, Yarmony Archeological Site, Address Restricted
Red Cliff, Red Cliff Bridge, U.S. 24
State Bridge, State Bridge, Off CO 131
Thomasville, Woods Lake Resort, 11 mi. N of Thomasville at Woods Lake

USGS Historic Places

Eagle, Eagle County Historical Museum, 39.6577635, -106.8286507
Minturn, Astor City, 39.5499861, -106.408918
Minturn, Tigiwon Post Office, 39.5233194, -106.420307
Mount of the Holy Cross, Holy Cross City, 39.4149868, -106.4780853
Ruedi Reservoir, Ruedi, 39.3663742, -106.7980938
Sheephorn Mountain, Abbet Place, 39.9216527, -106.4219755
State Bridge, Orestod, 39.8680426, -106.6842033
Unknown, Troutville Post Office, 0, 0

Grand Army of the Republic Posts

Battle Mountain, No. 55, Eagle, Red Cliff

USGS Historic Military Places

None

Military Bases

None

Post Offices

Aspen Junction	1890 Feb 13	1895 June 19	
Avon	1900 Nov 26		81620
Basalt	1895 June 9		81621
Blaine	1884 July 7	1939 Sept 15	
Bond			80423
Burns	1895 May 14		80426
Castle	1885 Feb 18	1891 Sept 3	
Cleveland	1883 Mar 21	1884 Aug 14	
Cooper	1886 July 31	1890 Feb 6	
Copper Spur	1929 Oct 1	1955 Feb 28	
Copperton	1917 Mar 17	1917 Aug 11	
Coppertown	1922 Dec 8	1929 Oct 1	
Derby	1888 Aug 16	1889 Sept 16	

253

Historical Assets Colorado

Dotsero	1883 June 29	1948 Feb 29*	
Eagle	1891 Sept 3		81631
Edwards	1883 July 10		81632
Emma	1883 Nov 23	1949 May 31*	
Fulford	1892 Feb 5	1910 May 15	
Gilman	1886 Nov 3	1986 Apr 22	
Gold Park	1881 Mar 31	1883 Oct 5	
Gypsum	1883 June 14		81637
Holy Cross	1882 Jan 23	1905 Aug 7*	
McCoy	1891 May 23		80463
Minturn	1889 Sept 17		81345
Mitchell	1883 Apr 2	1909 Mar 31	
Pando	1891 Dec 26	1942 May 31*	
Peach Blow	1890 Nov 24	1909 Aug 21	
Red Cliff	1880 Feb 4	1895 Feb 7	
Red Cliff 2	1979 Apr 2		81649
Redcliff	1895 Feb 7	1979 Apr 1	
Riland	1913 Sept 24	1946 Nov 26	
Robinson	1881 Feb 17	1911 Feb 28*	
Roudebush	1880 Dec 15	1883 Apr 2	
Ruedi	1889 Aug 6	1941 Nov 15	
Seven Castles	1913 Dec 11	1918 Aug 10	
Sheephorn	1895 Jan 17	1951 Dec 31	
Sherman	1890 June 30	1892 July 5	
Sloss	1909 Aug 21	1931 July 31	
Squaw Creek	1884 July 14	1888 Jan 14	
State Bridge	1909 Nov 8	1915 Apr 15	
Taylor	1882 Sept 28	1886 July 31	
Tennessee Pass	1890 Feb 6	1893 July 27	
Tigiwon	1929 June 5	1942 Sept 30	
Troutville	1909 Dec 6	1954 Dec 31	
Vail	1963 Oct 1		81657
Wolcott	1889 Sept 12		81655
Yarmony	1908 Feb 3	1908 May 11	

Topo Quads

Burns South	395230N	394500N	1065230W	1070000W
Castle Peak	395230N	394500N	1064500W	1065230W
Climax	392230N	391500N	1060730W	1061500W
Copper Mountain	393000N	392230N	1060730W	1061500W
Crooked Creek Pass	393000N	392230N	1063730W	1064500W
Eagle	394500N	393730N	1064500W	1065230W
Edwards	394500N	393730N	1063000W	1063730W
Fulford	393730N	393000N	1063730W	1064500W
Grouse Mountain	393730N	393000N	1063000W	1063730W
Gypsum	394500N	393730N	1065230W	1070000W

Eagle County

Homestake Reservoir	392230N	391500N	1062230W	1063000W
Lava Creek	395230N	394500N	1063000W	1063730W
Leadville North	392230N	391500N	1061500W	1062230W
Meredith	392230N	391500N	1063730W	1064500W
Minturn	393730N	393000N	1062230W	1063000W
Mount Jackson	393000N	392230N	1063000W	1063730W
Mount of the Holy Cross	393000N	392230N	1062230W	1063000W
Mount Powell	395230N	394500N	1061500W	1062230W
Nast	392230N	391500N	1063000W	1063730W
Pando	393000N	392230N	1061500W	1062230W
Piney Peak	395230N	394500N	1062230W	1063000W
Red Cliff	393730N	393000N	1061500W	1062230W
Red Creek	393000N	392230N	1064500W	1065230W
Ruedi Reservoir	392230N	391500N	1064500W	1065230W
State Bridge	395230N	394500N	1063730W	1064500W
Suicide Mountain	393730N	393000N	1065230W	1070000W
The Seven Hermits	393730N	393000N	1064500W	1065230W
Toner Reservoir	393000N	392230N	1065230W	1070000W
Vail East	394500N	393730N	1061500W	1062230W
Vail Pass	393730N	393000N	1060730W	1061500W
Vail West	394500N	393730N	1062230W	1063000W
Willow Lakes	394500N	393730N	1060730W	1061500W
Wolcott	394500N	393730N	1063730W	1064500W
Woody Creek	392230N	391500N	1065230W	1070000W

Suggested Reading

100 Years of History: a Gypsum, Colorado Walking Tour. Eagle, CO: Eagle County Historical Society, 2011.

Aldrich, John K. *Ghosts of Eagle and Grand Counties: Stories from the Ghost Towns and Mining Camps of Eagle, Grand, Jackson, Larimer and Routt Counties, Colorado.* Denver: Columbine Ink, 2009.

Braun, Sharon and Perie Uva Whipple Noble. *History of Eagle, Brush Creek, Fulford, Eagle, County, Colorado.* NL: NP, 1970.

Heicher, Kathy. *The Bridges of Eagle County: a Story of Pioneers, Politics, and Progress.* Denver: Colorado Bridge Enterprise, 2015.

Heicher, Kathy. *Eagle County Characters.* Charleston, SC: The History Press, 2013.

McCabe, William. *A Descriptive History of Eagle County, Colorado: Relating to Mining, Agriculture, Stock and Scenery.* Red Cliff, CO: NP, 1899.

Strasinger, Bruce. *A History of Mining in Eagle County, Colorado.* NL: Bruce Stasinger, 2003.

Historical Assets Colorado

El Paso County

Introduction

Established: 1861 Population: 699,232

Formed from: Original

Adjacent Counties: Douglas, Elbert, Lincoln, Crowley, Pueblo, Fremont, Teller

County Seat: Colorado Springs

Other Communities: Fountain, Manitou Springs, Calhan, Green Mountain Falls, Monument, Palmer Lake, Ramah, Black Forest, Cascade-Chipita Park, Cimarron Hills, Ellicott, Gleneagle, Peyton, Rock Creek Park, Security-Widefield, Stratmoor, Woodmoor, Alta Vista, Crystola, Eastonville, Falcon, La Foret, Rush, Tructon, Yoder

Website, https://www.elpasoco.com

Area Codes: 719

Zip Codes: 80106, 80132, 80133, 80808, 80809, 80817, 80819, 80829, 80831, 80832, 80833, 80840, 80841, 80864, 80901, 80902, 80903, 80904, 80905, 80906, 80907, 80908, 80909, 80910, 80911, 80912, 80913, 80914, 80915, 80916, 80917, 80918, 80919, 80920, 80921, 8092, 80924, 80925, 80926, 80927, 80928, 80929, 80930, 80931, 80932, 80933, 80934, 80935, 80936, 80937, 80938, 80939, 80941, 80942, 80946, 80947, 80949, 80950, 80951, 80960, 80962, 80970, 80977, 80995, 80997

Historical Assets Colorado

El Paso County Justice Center

El Paso County early Courthouse

Courthouses & County Government

El Paso County
https://www.elpasoco.com/

El Paso County Courthouse (Records Center) (4th Judicial District), 270 S Tejon, Colorado Springs, CO 80901, 719-452-5000; http://www.courts.state.co.us/Courts/County/Index.cfm?County_ID=6

Assessor, 1675 W Garden of the Gods, Colorado Springs, CO 80907, 719-520-6600; http://asr.elpasoco.com/Pages/default.aspx

Board of County Commissioners, 2880 International Cr, Colorado Springs, CO 80910, 719-520-6485, https://bocc.elpasoco.com/

Clerk & Recorder, 1675 W Garden of the Gods, Colorado Springs, CO 80907, 719-520-6202; http://car.elpasoco.com/Pages/default.aspx

Coroner, 2741 E Las Vegas St, Colorado Springs, CO 80906, 719-390-2450; https://coroner.elpasoco.com/

Public Health, 1675 Garden of the Gods Rd, Ste 2044, Colorado Springs, CO 80907, 719-578-3199; http://www.elpasocountyhealth.org/

Transportation (Road & Bridge); https://publicworks.elpasoco.com/road-bridge/

Treasurer, 1675 Garden of the Gods Rd, Ste 2100, Colorado Springs, CO 80907, 719-520-7900; http://trs.elpasoco.com/Pages/default.aspx

County Records

Birth 1890	Marriage 1861	Divorce 1903
Death 1893	Land 1861	Probate 1876
Court 1876		

El Paso County

County & Municipal Records Held at the State Level

The Colorado State Archives

Physical Records
Assessor
Clerk & Recorder
Coroner
County Commissioners
County Court
District Court
Justice Court
Sheriff
Treasurer
WPA Historical Records
WPA Religious Institutions Survey
WPA Fountain, Manitou Springs
Cities
Bachelor/Wasson
Colorado City
Colorado Springs
Ellicott/Yoder
Monument
Mound City
Palmer Lake

Records on Film
1885 Census
Clerk & Recorder
District Court
Treasurer
Cities
Colorado City
Colorado Springs
Falcon
Florissant
Fountain
Fremont
Goldfield
Green Mountain Falls
Monument
Mound City
Palmer Lake
South Altman

Records on Master Film
Assessor
Clerk & Recorder
County Court
District Court
Combined Courts
District Attorney
Planning
Public Trustee
School Districts
Sheriff
Social Services
Treasurer
Cities
Colorado Springs
Monument
Palmer Lake

The Denver Public Library
Air Force Academy Site Selection Board Records, 1949
Banning-Lewis Ranch Records, 1915-2001
El Paso County Mining Companies Records, 1901
Historical Society of the Pikes Peak Region Records, 1951-1961
Tax Assessment Notebook, 1989
WWI Draft Registration Cards (microfilm)

School Districts

School Districts, http://www.adcogov.org/local-school-districts
Academy School District No. 20, 1110 Chapel Hills Dr, Colorado Springs, CO 80920, 719-234-1200; https://www.asd20.org
Calhan School District RJ-1, 800 Bulldog Dr, Calhan, CO 80808, 719-347-2766; https://www.calhanschool.org/
Cheyenne Mountain School District No. 12, 1775 LaClede St, Colorado Springs, CO 80905, 719-475-6100; https://www.cmsd.k12.co.us/
Colorado Springs School District 11, 1115 N El Paso St, Colorado Springs, CO 80903, 719-520-2000; https://www.d11.org/
Edison School District No. 54 JT, 14550 Edison Rd, Yoder, CO 80864, 719-478-2125; https://www.edison54jt.org/
Falcon School District 49, 10850 E Woodmen Rd, Peyton, CO 80831, 719-495-1100; https://www.d49.org/

Historical Assets Colorado

Fountain-Fort Carson School District 8, 10665 Jimmy Camp Rd, Fountain, CO 80817, 719-382-1300; https://www.ffc8.org/

Hanover School District No. 28, 7930 Indian Village Heights, Fountain, CO 80817, 719-382-1260 x 412; http://www.hanoverhornets.org/

Lewis-Palmer Consolidated School District No. 38, 146 N Jefferson St, Monument, CO 80132, 719-488-4700; https://www.lewispalmer.org/

Manitou Springs School District 14, 405 El Monte Pl, Manitou Springs, CO 80829, 719-685-2024; https://www.mssd14.org/

Miami-Yoder School District 60 JT, 420 S Ruth Rd, Rush, CO 80833, 719-478-2186; https://miamiyoder.com/

Peyton School District 23 JT, 18320 Main St, Peyton, CO 80831, 719-749-2330; http://www.peyton.k12.co.us/

Widefield School District 3, 1820 Main St, Colorado Springs, CO 80911, 719-391-3000; https://www.wsd3.org/

Historic School Districts

1. Calhan
2. Harrison
3. Drennan, Tructon, Widefield, Security
4. [1878]
5. Lewis
6. [1878]
7. Sun View
8. Fountain
9. Wigwam
10. [1878]
11. Colorado Springs
12. Cheyenne Mountain
13. [1878]
14. Manitou Springs
15. Bijou Basin [Joint with Elbert]
16. Calhan
17. Amo, Surber, Falcon
18. Table Rock
19. Monument
20. Woodmen, Academy
21. Eastonville
22. Ellicott
23. Peyton
24. [1889]
25. Monument
26. Columbine [Joint with Douglas]
27. Elton, Pine Grove
28. Squirrel Creek, Hanover
29. Miami, Yoder
30. Eastonville
31. Crystola [Joint with Teller]
32. Table Rock
33. Palmer Lake
34. Granger
35. Glen Eyrie
36. [1888]
37. Peyton, Falcon
38. Lewis, Palmer, Black Forrest, Forest View
39. Lytle [Joint with Fremont]
40. Peyton
41. Corona
42. Bald Mountain, Green Mountain Falls
43. Cascade
44. Ellicott
45. Alta Vista
46. Ramah
47. Columbine
48. Excelsior, Fairplay
49. Falcon
50. Calhan, Peyton
51. [1891]
52. Peyton
53. Washington
54. Edison
55. Peyton
56. [1892]
57. [1895]
58. Shadeland
59. Big Sandy
60. Jt Miami/Yoder
61. Calhan

Jt100. Big Sandy

Fraternal Organizations

Granges
Fountain, No. 22, El Paso, Fountain, 10 Jan 1874
El Paso, No. 23, El Paso, El Paso, 12 Jan 1874
Monument, No. 24, El Paso, Monument, 13 Jan 1874
Alma, No. 38, El Paso, Southwater, 17 Jan 1874
Wheatland, No. 48, El Paso, Colorado Springs, 7 Mar 1874

El Paso County

Divide, No. 53, El Paso, Spring Valley/Monument, 18 Feb 1874
Huerfano, No. 55, El Paso, Butte Valley, 20 Mar 1874
Cheyenne, No. 65, El Paso, Colorado Springs, 8 Aug 1874
Comanche, No. 207, El Paso, Hargisville, 4 May 1912
Fountain Valley, No. 253, El Paso, Fountain, 11 June 1915
Chico Basin, No. 261, El Paso, Hanover, 7 Jan 1916
Blue Bell, No. 265, El Paso, Squirrel Creek, 26 Feb 1916
Drennan, No. 278, El Paso, Colorado Springs, 26 Apr 1916
Signal Rock, No. 284, El Paso, Yoder, 13 May 1916
Ellicott, No. 298, El Paso, Ellicott, 10 July 1916
Trinton, No. 302, El Paso, Yoder, 30 Sept 1916
Mountain View, No. 411, El Paso, Ellicott, 26 Feb 1932
Higbee, No. 427, El Paso, Higbee, 15 Jan 1936
Richards, No. 428, El Paso, Richards, 26 Feb 1936
Washington, No. 462, El Paso, Calhan, 2 Apr 1946
Edison, No. 465, El Paso, Yoder, 7 June 1946
Mount Herman, No. 470, El Paso, Monument, 5 May 1948
Pine Ridge, No. 471, El Paso, Calhan, 4 Feb 1949
El Paso, No. 480, El Paso, Colorado Springs, 28 June 1957,

Masons

  Ancient Free & Accepted Masons

    El Paso, No. 13, El Paso, Colorado Springs, 7 Oct 1867
    Manitou, No. 68, El Paso, Manitou Springs, 21 Sept 1887
    Colorado Springs, No. 76, El Paso, Colorado Springs,
    Colorado City, No. 76, El Paso, Colorado City, 18 Sept 1889
    Tejon, No. 104, El Paso, Colorado Springs, 21 Sept 1898
    Ramah, No. 165, El Paso, Ramah, 22 Sept 1926
    Fountain Valley, No. 191, El Paso, Fountain, 28 Jan 1964
    Centurion Daylight, No. 195, EL Paso, Monument, 22 Jan 1979
    Enlightenment, No. 198, El Paso, Colorado Springs, 26 Jan 2008

  Royal Arch Masons

    Colorado Springs, No. 6, El Paso, Colorado Springs

  Knights Templar

    Pikes Peak Commandery, No. 6, El Paso, Colorado Springs, 1881 Apr 18

  Eastern Star

    Glen Eyrie, No. 8, El Paso, Colorado Springs
    Ruxton, No. 10, El Paso, Manitou
    Ramona, No. 11, El Paso, Colorado Springs
    Ramona, No. 12, El Paso, Manitou
    Centennial, No. 58, El Paso, Colorado Springs
    Faith, No. 140, El Paso, Ramah

  Prince Hall Masons

    Pikes Peak Lodge No. 5, El Paso, Colorado Springs, 1878
    Mountain Post Military Lodge No. 26, El Paso, Fort Carson, 1978

Historical Assets Colorado

Prince Hall Order of the Eastern Star
    Magnolia Chapter No. 14, El Paso, Colorado Springs
    Elizabeth Chapter, No. 14, El Paso, Colorado Springs
    Carroll Chapter, No. 61, El Paso, Colorado Springs

Prince Hall Heroines of Jericho
    Dorothy L Harrison Court No. 2, El Paso, Colorado Springs

Prince Hall Scottish Rite
    Pikes Peak Consistory No. 81, El Paso, Colorado Springs

Prince Hall Order of the Golden Circle
    Pikes Peak Assenbly No. 52, El Paso, Colorado Springs

Prince Hall Holy Royal Arch Masons
    Randall A Baker Chapter No. 2, El Paso, Colorado Springs

Prince Hall Knights Templar
    Prince of Peace Commandery No. 2, El Paso, Colorado Springs

Odd Fellows
    Manitou, No. 15, El Paso, Colorado Springs, 1872 Oct 19
    Manitou, No. 18, El Paso, Colorado Springs, 1872 Oct 19
    Pikes Peak, No. 38, El Paso, Colorado Springs
    Manitou, No. 71, El Paso, Manitou Springs
    Colorado City, No. 77, El Paso, Colorado Springs
    Coronado, No. 83, El Paso, Roswell
    Calhan, No. 115, El Paso, Calhan
    Monument, No. 115, El Paso, Monument, 1906 Feb 22
    Colorado Springs, No. 140, El Paso, Colorado Springs
    Rogers, No. 175, El Paso, Fountain
    Ramah, No. 178, El Paso, Ramah

Rebekahs
    Naomi, No. 1, El Paso, Colorado City
    Monte Rosa, No. 4, El Paso, Colorado Springs
    Naomi, No. 15, El Paso, Colorado Springs
    Fountain, No. 59, El Paso, Fountain
    Colorado City, No. 89, El Paso, Colorado Springs
    Sunshine, No. 92, El Paso, Colorado Springs

Knights of Pythias
    Myrtle, No. 34, El Paso, Colorado Springs
    El Paso, No. 47, El Paso, Colorado City
    Koerner, No. 50, El Paso, Colorado Springs, 1889 Mar 18
    Garden of the Gods, No. 53, El Paso, Roswell, 1889 Oct 10
    Manitou, No. 57, El Paso, Manitou Springs
    Sunrise, No. 97, El Paso, Eastonville
    Majestic, No. 104, El Paso, Falcon, 1896 Aug 20
    Syracuse, No. 111, El Paso, Colorado Springs
    Sublime, No. 123, El Paso, Colorado Springs

El Paso County

Pythian Sisters
Hermione, No. 1, El Paso, Colorado Springs
Fidelity, No. 2, El Paso, Manitou
Crystal, No. 5, El Paso, Colorado City
Logan, No. 36, El Paso, Falcon
Sunshine, No. 50, El Paso, Eastonville
Sublime, No. 53, El Paso, Colorado Springs

Benevolent Protective Order of Elks
Colorado Springs, No. 309, El Paso, Colorado Springs

City & Town Halls

Colorado Springs, 107 N Nevada Ave, Colorado Springs, CO 80903, 719, 385-5986, https://coloradosprings.gov

Fountain, 116 S Main St, Fountain, CO 80817, 719-322-2000, https://www.fountain-colorado.org

Manitou Springs, 606 Manitou Ave, Manitou Springs, CO 80829, 719-685-5481, https://www.manitouspringsgov.com

Calhan, 556 Colorado Ave, Calhan, CO 80808, 719-347-2586, https://www.calhan.co

Green Mountain Falls, 10615 Green Mountain Falls Rd, Green Mountain Falls, CO 80819, 719-684-9414, https://www.colorado.gov/greenmountainfalls

Monument, 645 Beacon Lite Rd, Monument, CO 80132, 719-481-2954, https://www.townofmonument.org

Palmer Lake, 42 Valley Crescent St, Palmer Lake, CO 80133, 719-481-2953, https://www.townofpalmerlake.com

Ramah, 113 S Commercial St, Ramah, CO 80832, 719-541-2163, https://ramah.colorado.gov

Archives & Manuscript Collections

Catholic Diocese of Colorado Springs Archives, 228 N Cascade Ave, Colorado Springs, CO 80903, (719) 636-2345, https://www.diocs.org/departments/office-of-the-chancellor/archives

Charles Leaming Tutt Library & Special Collections, Colorado College, 14 E Cache la Poudre St, Colorado Springs, CO 80903, (719) 389-6668, http://www.coloradocollege.edu/library/specialcollections/special.html

Colorado Springs Pioneer Museum & Archives, Starsmore Center for Local History, 215 S Tejon St, Colorado Springs, CO 80903, (719) 385-5650, http://www.cspm.org

Grand Lodge A.F. & A.M. of Colorado, 1130 Panorama Dr, Colorado Springs, CO 80904, (719) 471-9587, http://www.coloradofreemasons.org

McDermott Library & Clark Special Collections Branch, United States Air Force Academy, 2354 Fairchild Dr, Suite 3A10, USAF Academy, CO 80840-6214, (719) 333-4749, https://usafa.libguides.com/spc

Historical & Genealogical Societies

American Nimismatic Association, Money Museum, 818 N Cascade Ave, Colorado Springs, CO 80903, (719) 632-2646, http://www.money.org

Historical Assets Colorado

Manitou Springs Historical Society, Miramont Castle, 9 Capitol Hill Ave, Manitou Springs, CO 80829, (719) 685-1011, http://www.miramontcastle.org

Masonic Grand Lodge of Colorado, 1130 Panorama Dr, Colorado Springs, CO 80904, (719) 471-9587, http://www.coloradofreemasons.org

National Railway Historical Society, Colorado Midland Chapter, P.O. Box 824, Colorado Springs, CO 80901, (719) 533-1311, https://nrhs.com/chapters/colorado/colorado-midland

National Society of the Colonial Dames of America in the State of Colorado, McAllister House Museum, 423 N Cascade Ave, Colorado Springs, CO 80903, (970) 635-7925, http://mcallisterhouse.org

Negro Historical Association of Colorado Springs (NHACS), c/o Colorado Springs Pioneers Museum, 215 S Tejon St, Colorado Springs, CO 80903, (719) 385-5990, http://www.cspm.org/finding-aidsinventories/negro-historical-association-of-colorado-springs/

Old Colorado City Historical Society, Historical Museum, 1 S 24th St, Colorado Springs, CO 80904-3319, (719) 636-1225, https://occhs.org

Palmer Lake Historical Society, Lucretia Vaile Museum, 66 Lower Glenway, P.O. Box 662, Palmer Lake, CO 80133, (719) 559-0837, http://www.palmerdividehistory.org

Pikes Peak Genealogical Society, P.O. Box 1262, Colorado Springs, CO 80901, (719) 630-8407 FAX, http://www.ppgs.org

Local Libraries

Pikes Peak Library District-Penrose, Genealogical Collection, 20 N Cascade, P.O. Box 1579, Colorado Springs, CO 80902, (719) 531-6333 x2252, http://library.ppld.org/SpecialCollections/

Albert B Simpson Historical Library, Christian & Missionary Alliance, 8595 Explorer Dr, P.O. Box 35000, Colorado Springs, CO 80935-3500, (719) 599-5999, http://www.cmalliance.org

Calhan Library, 600 Bank St, Calhan, CO 80808, (719) 531-6333, https://ppld.org/calhan-library

Fountain Library, 230 S Main St, Fountain, CO 80817, (719) 531-6333, https://ppld.org/fountain-library

Grant Library, Fort Carson, 1637 Flint St, Fort Carson, CO 80913-4105, (719) 526-2350, https://carson.armymwr.com/programs/grant-library

Kraemer Family Library, University of Colorado at Colorado Springs, 1420 Austin Bluffs Pkwy, P.O. Box 7150, Colorado Springs, CO 80933-7150, (719) -262-3295, https://www.uccs.edu/library/

Manitou Springs Public Library, 701 Manitou Ave, Manitou Springs, CO 80829-1887, (719) 685-5206, http://ppld.org/manitou-springs-library

Monument Library, 1706 Lake Woodmoor Dr, PO Box 1688, Monument, CO 80132-1688, (719) 531-6333, https://ppld.org/monument-library

Palmer Lake Library, 66 Lower Glenway St, Palmer Lake, CO 80133, (719) 531-6333, https://ppld.org/palmer-lake-library

Pikes Peak Library District-East Library, 5550 N Union Blvd, Colorado Springs, CO 80901, (719) 531-6333, https://ppld.org/east-library

El Paso County

Security Public Library, 715 Aspen Dr, Security, CO 80911, (719) 391-3195, https://www.securitypubliclibrary.org

Trimble Library, Nazarene Bible College, 1111 Academy Park Loop, Colorado Springs, CO 80910-3717, (719) 596-5110, https://www.nbc.edu/library/

Links

CO GenWeb
http://cogenweb.com/elpaso/

Cyndi's List
https://www.cyndislist.com/us/co/counties/el-paso/

FamilySearch Wiki
https://www.familysearch.org/wiki/en/El_Paso_County,_Colorado_Genealogy

Linkpendium
http://www.linkpendium.com/el_paso-co-genealogy/

RootsWeb Wiki
https://wiki.rootsweb.com/wiki/index.php/El_Paso_County,_Colorado

Wikipedia
https://en.wikipedia.org/wiki/El_Paso_County,_Colorado

Historic Hotels

1874 The Cliff House at Pikes Peak, 306 Canon Ave, Manitou Springs, CO 80829, 719-785-1000, https://www.thecliffhouse.com

1918 The Broadmoor, 1 Lake Ave, Colorado Springs, CO 80906, 800-755-5011, https://www.broadmoor.com

Museums & Historic Sites

4th Infantry Division Museum-Mountain Post Historical Center, Bldg 6012 B Nelson Blvd, Fort Carson, CO 80913, (719) 524-0915, http://mountainposthistoricalcenter.org

American Nimismatic Association, Money Museum, 818 N Cascade Ave, Colorado Springs, CO 80903, (719) 632-2646, http://www.money.org

Colorado Springs Pioneer Museum & Archives, Starsmore Center for Local History, 215 S Tejon St, Colorado Springs, CO 80903, (719) 385-5650, http://www.cspm.org

Ghost Town Museum, 400 S 21st St, Colorado Springs, CO 80904, (719) 634-0696, http://www.ghosttownmuseum.com

Manitou Cliff Dwellings Museum, 10 Cliff Rd, P.O. Box 272, Manitou Springs, CO 80829, (719) 685-5242, http://www.cliffdwellingsmuseum.com

Manitou Springs Heritage Center, 517 Manitou Ave, Manitou Springs, CO 80829, (719) 685-1454, http://www.manitouspringsheritagecenter.org

Manitou Springs Historical Society, Miramont Castle, 9 Capitol Hill Ave, Manitou Springs, CO 80829, (719) 685-1011, http://www.miramontcastle.org

National Museum of World War II Aviation, 765 Aviation Wy, Colorado Springs, CO 80916, (719) 637-7559, https://www.worldwariiaviation.org

Historical Assets Colorado

National Society of the Colonial Dames of America in the State of Colorado, McAllister House Museum, 423 N Cascade Ave, Colorado Springs, CO 80903, (970) 635-7925, http://mcallisterhouse.org

Old Colorado City Historical Society, Historical Museum, 1 S 24th St, Colorado Springs, CO 80904-3319, (719) 636-1225, https://occhs.org

Palmer Lake Historical Society, Lucretia Vaile Museum, 66 Lower Glenway, P.O. Box 662, Palmer Lake, CO 80133, (719) 559-0837, http://www.palmerdividehistory.org

Penrose Heritage Museum, 11 Lake Cr, Colorado Springs, CO 80906, (719) 577-7065, https://www.elpomar.org/About-Us/museum-and-legacy-properties/penrose-heritage-museum-1/

Peterson Air & Space Museum, 21st Space Wing/MU, 150 E Ent Ave, Peterson AFB, CO 80914, (719) 556-4915, http://www.petemuseum.org

Pikes Peak Auto Hill Climb Museum, Penrose Heritage Museum, 11 Lake Cr, Colorado Springs, CO 80906, (719) 685-5996, http://ppihc.org/2020-pikes-peak-hill-climb-museum-hall-of-fame-nominations-are-now-open/

Pikes Peak Historic Street Railway Museum, 2333 Steel Dr, Colorado Springs, CO 80907, (719) 475-9508, http://www.coloradospringstrolleys.com

Pikes Peak Radio & Electronics Museum, 6735 Earl Dr, Colorado Springs, CO 80918, (719) 550-5810, http://www.pikespeakradiomuseum.com

Pro Rodeo Hall of Fame Museum, 101 Pro Rodeo Dr, Colorado Springs, CO 80919, (719) 528-4761, http://www.prorodeo.com; http://www.prorodeohalloffame.com

Rock Ledge Ranch Historic Site Museum, 3105 Gateway Rd, Colorado Springs, CO 80904, (719) 578-6777, http://www.rockledgeranch.com

Rocky Mountain Motorcycle Museum, 5867 N Nevada Ave, Colorado Springs, CO 80918, (719) 487-8005, http://www.themotorcyclemuseum.com/

Turin Shroud Center of Colorado, 8755 Scarborough Dr, P.O. Box 25326, Colorado Springs, CO 80918, (719) 599-5755, http://www.shroudofturin.com

United States Space Foundation Headquarters & Discovery Center, 4425 Arrowswest Dr, Colorado Springs, CO 80907, (719) 576-8000, http://www.spacefoundation.org

US Air Force Academy Visitor Center, 2346 Academy, USAF Academy, CO 80840, (719) 333-2025, https://www.usafa.edu

Western Museum of Mining & Industry, 225 Northgate Blvd, Colorado Springs, CO 80921, (719) 488-0880, http://www.wmmi.org

Will Rogers Shrine of the Sun, 4250 Cheyenne Mountain Zoo Rd, Colorado Springs, CO 80906, (719) 633-9925, https://www.cmzoo.org/visit/will-rogers-shrine-of-the-sun/

World Figure Skating Museum, 20 1st St, Colorado Springs, CO 80906, (719) 635-5200, http://www.worldskatingmuseum.org

Special Events & Scenic Locations

The El Paso County Fair is held most years during July, at the El Paso County Fair & Events Complex, 366 10th St, Calhan, CO 80808, 719=520-7880, https://www.elpasocountyfair.com.

El Paso County

Visit Colorado Springs has a calendar of annual events here: https://www.visitcos.com/events-calendar/annual/
El Paso County keeps a calendar of events here: https://www.elpasoco.com/category/events/
Pike National Forest
Cheyenne Mountain State Park
Pikes Peak National Historic Landmark
USAFA Cadet Area National Historic District
American Discovery Trail
Barr National Recreation Trail
Bear Creek Canon State Park
Bear Creek Regional Park and Nature Center
Calhan Paint Mines
Fountain Creek Nature Center
Manitou Springs Incline Trail
New Santa Fe Trail
Pike Peak Greenway
White House Ranch National Recreation Trail

Ghost Towns & Other Sparsely Populated Places

Alnwick, Beaumont, Bellevue, Bierstadt, Big Sandy, Bijou Basin, Borst, Butte's, Cable Junction, Colorado City, Culver Siding, Dyersville, Edgerton, El Paso, Elsmere, Florrisant, Franceville, Franceville Junction, Garden of the Gods, Gwillimville, Half Way House, Hulbert, Husted, Ivywild, Jimmy's Camp, Kelker, Kenmuir, Little Buttes, Lytle, Manitou Iron Springs, Manitou Junction, McConnellsville, McFerran, Minnehaha, Morland, Mountain View, Old Zounds, Patterson, Peyton, Pike View, Pring, Ramah, Rock Creek Park, Roswell, Saddle Horse, Summit, Summit Park, Sunview, Table Rock, Tip Top, Ute Park, Widefield, Wigwam, Williamsville

Newspapers

The Fountain Herald. (Fountain, Colo.) 1???-19??
The Daily Transcript and Mining News. (Colorado Springs, Colo.) 1???-1911
The Queen Bee. (Colorado Springs, Colo.) 1???-1???
The Colorado Tourist and Hotel Reporter. (Denver and Colorado Springs [Colo.]) 1???-19??
The Weekly Miner. (Cripple Creek, Colo.) 18??-1???
Strawberries and Cream. (Colorado Springs [Colo.]) 18??-1???
The Mining Investor. (Colorado. Springs., Colo.) 18??-19??
Falcon Herald. (Falcon, El Paso Co., Colo.) 18??-1???
The Colorado City Journal. (Colorado City, Colo. Territory [Colo.]) 1861-1???
The Colorado Weekly Mountaineer. (Colorado Springs, Colo.) 187?-1882
Colorado Free Press and El Paso County Advertiser. (Colorado Springs, Colo.) 187?-187?
Out West. (Colorado Springs, C.T.) 1872-1872
The Republic. (Colorado Springs, Colo.) 1873-????
Colorado Mountaineer. (Colorado Springs [Colo.) 1873-187?

Historical Assets Colorado

The Colorado Springs Gazette and El Paso County News. (Colorado Springs [Colo.]) 1873-1878
Deaf Mute Index. (Colorado Springs, Colo.) 1874-????
The Monument Mentor. (Monument, Colo.) 1878-1???
Saturday Night. (Colorado Springs [Colo.]) 1878-1???
The New West. (Colorado Springs, Colo.) 1878-1???
The Daily Gazette. (Colorado Springs, Colo.) 1878-1887
The Weekly Gazette. (Colorado Springs, Colo.) 1878-19??
El Paso County Republic. (Colorado Springs, Colo.) 188?-1891
Colorado Springs Republic. (Colorado Springs, Colo.) 188?-1891
The Magnet. (Colorado Springs, Colo.) 1880-1???
Weekly Republic. (Colorado Springs, Colo.) 1881-1882
Daily Republic. (Colorado Springs, Colo.) 1881-1???
Weekly Republic and Colorado Mountaineer. (Colorado Springs, Colo.) 1882-1883
The Manitou Item. (Manitou, Colo.) 1882-1???
Weekly Republic. (Colorado Springs, Colo.) 1883-1883
Colorado State Republic. (Colorado Springs, Colo.) 1883-18??
Daily Times. (Colorado Springs, Colo.) 1884-1???
The Manitou Springs Journal. (Manitou Springs, Colo.) 1885-19??
The Weekly Times. (Colorado Springs, Colo.) 1885-????
The Hour. (Colorado Springs, Colo.) 1885-1???
El Paso County Register. (Monument, El Paso County, Colo.) 1885-1???
Colorado Springs Gazette. (Colorado Springs, Colo.) 1887-1946
Pike's Peak Herald. (Colorado Springs, Colo.) 1887-1893
The Saturday Mail. (Colorado Springs, Colo.) 1888-1???
Mountain Falls Echo. (Colorado Springs, Colo.) 1888-1889
Falcon News. (Falcon ;) 1888-1???
The Green Mountain Falls Echo. (Colorado Springs, Colo.) 1889-1???
The Colorado City Iris. (Colorado City, El Paso County, Colo.) 1889-1891
Pike's Peak Daily News. (Manitou, Colo.) 189?-19??
The West Creek Times. (West Creek, El Paso County, Colo.) 189?-1???
The Tiger. (Colorado Springs, Colo.) 189?-19??
The Edgewood Sun. (Colorado Springs, Colo.) 189?-189?
Republic and Telegraph. (Colorado Springs, Colo.) 1891-1893
Pike's Peak News. (Manitou Springs, Colo.) 1891-189?
The Iris. (Colorado City, El Paso County, Colo.) 1891-1905
The Cripple Creek Prospector. (Fremont, El Paso County, Colo.) 1891-1???
The Sun. (Colorado Springs, Colo.) 1891-1???
The Morning Times. (Cripple Creek, El Paso County, Colo.) 1891-1900
The Weekly Journal. (Cripple Creek, Colo.) 1893-1???
The Plaindealer. (Colorado Springs, Colo.) 1893-1???
Cripple Creek Sunday Herald. (Cripple Creek, Colo.) 1893-1???
The Evening Telegraph. (Colorado Springs, Colo.) 1893-1901
The Weekly Telegraph. (Colorado Springs, Colo.) 1893-19??
The Cripple Creek Morning Times. (Cripple Creek, Colo.) 1894-????
The Morning Journal. (Cripple Creek, Colo.) 1894-1895

El Paso County

El Paso County Democrat. (Colorado Springs, Colo.) 1894-1922
Co-Operation. (Colorado Springs, Colo.) 1894-1???
The Gillett Forum. (Gillett, El Paso County, Colo.) 1895-1???
The Cripple Creek Mail. (Cripple Creek, Colo.) 1895-1898
The Cripple Creek Times. (Cripple Creek, El Paso County, Colo.) 1896-1896
The Weekly Cripple Creek Times. (Cripple Creek, El Paso County, Colo.) 1896-1901
The Western Enterprise. (Colorado Springs, Colo.) 1896-1912
Cripple Creek Citizen. (Cripple Creek, Colo.) 1897-1???
The Colorado City Argus. (Colorado City, Colo.) 1899-19??
The Pikes Peak Journal. (Manitou Springs, Colo.) 19??-200?
Westside Story. (Colorado Springs [Colo.]) 19??-19??
The Colorado Springs Times. (Colorado Springs [Colo.]) 19??-1974
The Security Advertiser and The Fountain Valley News. (Fountain, Colo.) 19??-19??
The WCTU Messenger. (Colorado Springs, Colo.) 19??-19??
El Paso County Advertiser & News. (Fountain, Colo.) 19??-Current
Advertiser-News. (Fountain, Colo.) 19??-19??
The Pink Iconoclast. (Colorado Springs, Colo.) 190?-19??
The Calhan News. (Calhan, El Paso County, Colo.) 1901-1924
The Labor News. (Colorado Springs, Colo.) 1901-19??
Colorado Telegraph. (Colorado Springs, Colo.) 1901-1901
The Evening Mail. (Colorado Springs, Colo.) 1901-1901
The Evening Telegraph and Evening Mail. (Colorado Springs, Colo.) 1901-1901
The Evening Telegraph. (Colorado Springs, Colo.) 1902-1904
Colorado Springs Telegraph. (Colorado Springs, Colo.) 1904-1905
The Colorado City Iris. (Colorado City, Colo.) 1905-1914
Public Opinion. (Colorado Springs, Colo.) 1905-19??
The Colorado Springs Evening Telegraph. (Colorado Springs, Colo.) 1905-1910
The Daily Iris. (Colorado City, Colo.) 1908-1908
The Daily Anti-Saloon Advocate. (Colorado City, Colo.) 1909-19??
The Evening Herald. (Colorado Springs, Colo.) 1909-1910
The Herald-Telegraph. (Colorado Springs, Colo.) 1910-1911
The Daily Transcript Court House Reporter. (Colorado Springs, Colo.) 1911-1911
The Daily Transcript. (Colorado Springs, Colo.) 1911-19??
The Cheyenne News and The Ivywild Times. (Ivy Wild, Colo.) 1912-19??
The Evening Telegraph. (Colorado Springs, Colo.) 1912-1920
The Colorado City Independent and The Colorado City Iris. (Colorado City, Colo.) 1914-1915
The Colorado City Independent. (Colorado City, Colo.) 1915-1916
The Daily Independent. (Colorado City [Colo.]) 1916-19??
The Independent. (Colorado City, Colo.) 1916-19??
Colorado Springs Independent. (Colorado Springs, Colo.) 1917-19??
Pikes Peak Oil News. (Colorado Springs, Colo.) 1920-19??
Colorado Springs Evening Telegraph. (Colorado Springs, Colo.) 1920-1921
Colorado Springs Evening and Sunday Telegraph. (Colorado Springs, Colo.) 1921-1923
Ute Pass Weekly News. (Colorado Springs, Colo.) 1922-19??

Historical Assets Colorado

Colorado Springs Farm News and El Paso County Democrat. (Colorado Springs, Colo.) 1923-1924
Colorado Springs Evening Telegraph. (Colorado Springs, Colo.) 1923-1946
The Calhan News and The Ramah Record. (Calhan, El Paso County, Colo.) 1924-1947
Colorado Springs Farm News. (Colorado Springs, Colo.) 1925-1936
Colorado Springs Observer. (Colorado Springs, Colo.) 1926-19??
Commonsense Weekly. (Colorado Springs, Colo.) 1931-19??
The Voice of Colorado. (Colorado Springs, Colo.) 1936-19??
Colorado Springs News. (Colorado Springs, Colo.) 1937-1955
Colorado Springs Advertiser. (Colorado Springs, Colo.) 1938-1949
Camp Carson Mountaineer. (Colorado Springs, Colo.) 1942-1954
Wingspread. (Colorado Springs, Colo.) 1942-19??
Die Pw Woche. ([Camp Carson, Colo.) 1943-1945 | Languages: German
Lager-Rundschau. (Pow-Camp Carson, Colo.) 1945-194? | Languages: German
Colorado Springs Gazette-Telegraph. (Colorado Springs, Colo.) 1946-1997
The Calhan News. (Calhan, El Paso County, Colo.) 1947-1949
Colorado Springs Free Press. (Colorado Springs, Colo.) 1947-1949
The Colorado Voice. (Colorado Springs, Colo.) 1948-19??
The Morning Free Press. (Colorado Springs, Colo.) 1949-1951
Free Press. (Colorado Springs, Colo.) 1949-1949
The Colorado Springs Morning Free Press. (Colorado Springs, Colo.) 1949-1949
Aerospace Observer. (Colorado Springs, Colo.) 195?-19??
The Fountain Valley News. (Security Village, Colo.) 195?-19??
The Free Press. (Colorado Springs, Colo.) 1951-1970
The Mountaineer. (Colorado Springs, Colo.) 1954-197?
The Skyline Observer. (Ent AFB [Colorado Springs, Colo.]) 1955-196?
Colorado Farm News. (Colorado Springs, Colo.) 1955-1955
Week End. (Colorado Springs, Colo.) 1955-19??
The Columbine Herald. (Palmer Lake, Colo.) 1956-19??
Sam's People & Politics. (Colorado Springs, Colo.) 1958-19??
Sam's People & Politics of The Pikes Peak Region. (Colorado Springs, Colo.) 1958-1958
Black Forest News and Divide Courier. (Black Forest, Colo.) 1960-19??
Black Forest News. (Black Forest, Colo.) 1960-1960
The Northeast Mail. (Colorado Springs, Colo.) 196?-1973
El Paso County Courier. (Colorado Springs, Colo.) 1965-19??
Palmer Lake-Monument News. (Palmer Lake, Colo.) 1965-1972
Colorado Springs Sentinel. ([Colorado Springs, Colo.]) 1969-19??
Fort Carson Mountaineer. (Colorado Springs, Colo.) 197?-1976
The Black Forest News & East Colorado Springs Crier. (Black Forest, Colo.) 197?-1981
Westsider. (Colorado Springs, Colo) 1970-19??
Fountain-Widefield-Security Weekly Times. (Fountain Valley [Colo.) 197?-1973
Colorado Springs Sun. (Colorado Springs, Colo.) 1970-1986
The Crime Paper. (Denver, Colo.) 1971-19??

El Paso County

Ivy Wild-Cheyenne Mountain Weekly Times. (Colorado Springs [Colo.]) 1971-1972
Westside Town and Country Weekly Times. ([Colorado Springs, Colo.]) 1971-1973
The New Day. (Manitou Springs, Colo.) 1971-19??
Colorado Springs Sun Centennial/Progress 1872/1972. ([Colorado Springs, Colo.]) 1972-19??
Fountain Valley Weekly Times. (Fountain Valley [Colo.]) 1972-19??
Ivy Wild-Cheyenne Mountain-Pikes Peak Park Weekly Times. (Colorado Springs [Colo.) 1972-1973
Ivy Wild-Cheyenne Mountain-Pikes Peak Park Times. (Colorado Springs [Colo.) 1973-19??
The Times West Edition. (Colorado Springs, Colo.) 1973-19??
Westside Times. (Colorado Springs, Colo.) 1973-1973
The Times Northeast Edition. (Colorado Springs [Colo.]) 1973-1973
The Times South Edition. (Colorado Springs [Colo.]) 1973-1973
The Times Fountain Valley. (Fountain Valley [Colo.]) 1973-19??
Fountain, Widefield, Security Times. (Fountain Valley [Colo.]) 1973-1973
Northeast Mail Times. (Colorado Springs [Colo.]) 1973-1973
Palmer Lake-Monument-Woodmoor News. (Castle Rock, Colo.) 1973-1975
The Times Weekly Journal. (Colorado Springs, Colo.) 1974-1974
The Weekly Times Journal. (Colorado Springs, Colo.) 1974-19??
Triangle Echo. (Green Mountain Falls, Colo.) 1975-1976
Tri-Lakes Tribune. (Castle Rock, Colo.) 1975-1977
Mountain Echo. (Green Mountain Falls [Colo.]) 1976-19??
Mountaineer. (Colorado Springs, Colo.) 1976-19??
The Tribune. ([Monument, Colo.]) 1977-Current
The Wellspring. (Colorado Springs, Colo.) 1978-198?
The Calhan News and Ramah Record. (Simla, Colo.) 1979-1979
The Calhan News. (Simla, Colo.) 1979-1985
Northern Light. (Colorado Springs, Colo.) 198?-19??
The Cheyenne Edition. (Colorado Springs, Colo.) 1981-19??
The Black Forest News. (Black Forest, Colo.) 1981-19??
The Weekly Northern Light. (Colorado Springs, Colo.) 1982-19??
Colorado Springs Minority Press. (Colorado Springs, Colo.) 1982-19??
Springs Business. ([Colorado Springs, Colo.]) 1983-1984
El Paso Advertiser And News. (Fountain, Colo.) 1984-19??
The Catholic Herald : The Newspaper for the Diocese of Colorado Springs. (Colorado Springs, Colo.) 1984-Current
Sand Creek Edition. (Colorado Springs, Colo.) 1986-1987
Hispania News. (Colorado Springs, Colo.) 1993-Current | Languages: English, Spanish
The Gazette. (Colorado Springs, Colo.) 1997-Current

Places on the National Register
Black Forest, Evans, J.G., Barn, Hodgen Rd.
Calhan, Calhan Paint Mines Archeological District, Approx. 0.5 mi. SE of jct. S. Calhan Rd. and Paint Mine Rd.

Historical Assets Colorado

Calhan, Calhan Rock Island Railroad Depot, 252 ft. W of Denver St. on Rock Island RR right-of-way
Cascade, Eastholme, 4445 Haggerman AVe.
Colorado Springs, Alamo Hotel, 128 S. Tejon St.
Colorado Springs, Atchison, Topeka and Santa Fe Passenger Depot, 555 E. Pikes Peak Ave.
Colorado Springs, Bemis Hall, 920 N. Cascade Ave.
Colorado Springs, Bemis, Judson Moss, House, 506 N. Cascade Ave.
Colorado Springs, Black Forest School, 6770 Shoup Rd.
Colorado Springs, Boulder Crescent Place Historic District, 9 and 11 W. Boulder St. and 312, 318, and 320 N. Cascade
Colorado Springs, Burgess House, 730 N. Nevada Ave.
Colorado Springs, Carlton House, Pine Valley, US Air Force Academy
Colorado Springs, Chadbourn Spanish Gospel Mission, 402 S. Conejos St.
Colorado Springs, Chambers Ranch, 3202 Chambers Way
Colorado Springs, City Hall of Colorado City, 2902 W. Colorado Ave.
Colorado Springs, Claremont, 21 Broadmoor Ave.
Colorado Springs, Colorado Springs Airport, Jct. of Ent Ave. and Peterson Blvd. (Peterson Air Force Base)
Colorado Springs, Colorado Springs and Cripple Creek District Railway—Corley Mountain Highway, Gold Camp Rd. and Forest Rd. 370
Colorado Springs, Colorado Springs City Auditorium, 231 E. Kiowa St.
Colorado Springs, Colorado Springs City Hall, 107 N. Nevada Ave.
Colorado Springs, Colorado Springs Day Nursery, 104 E. Rio Grande St.
Colorado Springs, Colorado Springs Fine Arts Center, 30 W. Dale St.
Colorado Springs, Colorado Springs Public Library—Carnegie Bldg, 21 W. Kiowa St.
Colorado Springs, Cossitt, Frederick H., Memorial Hall, 906 N. Cascade Ave.
Colorado Springs, Cottonwood Creek Bridge, On Vincent Dr. over Cottonwood Creek.
Colorado Springs, Cutler Hall, 912 N. Cascade Ave.
Colorado Springs, DeGraff Building, 116-118 N. Tejon
Colorado Springs, Dodge—Hamlin House, 1148 N. Cascade Ave., 1122 Wood Ave.
Colorado Springs, Drennan School, 20500 Drennan Rd.
Colorado Springs, Edgeplain, 1106 N. Nevada Ave.
Colorado Springs, El Paso County Courthouse, 215 S. Tejon St.
Colorado Springs, El Pomar Estate, 1661 Mesa Ave.
Colorado Springs, Emmanuel Presbyterian Church, 419 Mesa Rd.
Colorado Springs, Evergreen Cemetery, 1005 S. Hancock Ave.
Colorado Springs, First Congregational Church, 20 E. St. Vrain St.
Colorado Springs, Fort Collins Municipal Railway No. 22, 2333 Steel Dr.
Colorado Springs, Giddings Building, 101 N. Tejon St.
Colorado Springs, Glen Eyrie, 3280 N. 30th St.
Colorado Springs, Grace and St. Stephen's Episcopal Church, 631 N. Tejon St.
Colorado Springs, Gwynne—Love House, 730 N. Cascade Ave.
Colorado Springs, Hagerman Mansion, 610 N. Cascade Ave.
Colorado Springs, Lennox House, 1001 N. Nevada Ave.
Colorado Springs, Lindley—Johnson—Vanderhoof House, 1130 N. Cascade Ave.
Colorado Springs, Maytag Aircraft Building, 701 S. Cascade Ave.

El Paso County

Colorado Springs, McAllister House, 423 N. Cascade Ave.
Colorado Springs, McGregor Hall, 930 N. Cascade Ave.
Colorado Springs, Midland Terminal Railroad Roundhouse, 600 S. 21st St.
Colorado Springs, Montgomery Hall, Colorado College, 1030 N. Cascade Ave.
Colorado Springs, Monument Valley Park, Approx. bounded by Monroe, Culebra, Westview, Bijou Sts, BN&SF, and W edge of main N/S trail, N. of Del Norte
Colorado Springs, Navajo Hogan, 2817 N. Nevada Ave.
Colorado Springs, North Cheyenne Canon Park, 2120 N. Cheyenne Canon Rd.
Colorado Springs, North End Historic District, Roughly bounded by Monument Valley Wood, Nevada Ave., Madison and Unitah Sts.
Colorado Springs, North Weber Street-Wahsatch Avenue Historic Residential District, N. Weber St. between Boulder and Del Norte St., and N. Wahsatch Ave. between St. Vrain and Columbia St.
Colorado Springs, Old Colorado City Historic Commercial District, N side of Colorado Ave. from 24th St., W to 2611 Colorado Ave., also includes 115 S. 26 St. and 2418 W. Pikes Peak Ave.
Colorado Springs, Palmer Hall, 116 E. San Rafael
Colorado Springs, Pauline Chapel, 2 Park Ave.
Colorado Springs, People's Methodist Episcopal Church, 527 E. St. Vrain St.
Colorado Springs, Pikes Peak, 15 mi. W of Colorado Springs in Pike National Forest
Colorado Springs, Pioneer Cabin, 11 mi. N of Colorado Springs off I-25 on grounds of U.S. Air Force Academy
Colorado Springs, Plaza Hotel, 830 N. Tejon St.
Colorado Springs, Ponderosa Lodge, 6145 Shoup Rd.
Colorado Springs, Rice, Ida M., House, 1196 N. Cascade Ave.
Colorado Springs, Rio Grande Engine No. 168, 9 S. Sierra Madre
Colorado Springs, Second Midland School, 815 S. 25th St.
Colorado Springs, Shove Memorial Chapel, 1010 N. Tejon St.
Colorado Springs, Shrine of the Sun, 4250 Cheyenne Mountain Zoo Rd.
Colorado Springs, St. Mary's Catholic Church, 26 W. Kiowa St.
Colorado Springs, Stockbridge House, 2801 W. Colorado Ave.
Colorado Springs, Taylor Memorial Chapel, 6145 Shoup Rd.
Colorado Springs, Ticknor Hall, 926 Cascade Ave.
Colorado Springs, US Post Office and Federal Courthouse—Colorado Springs Main, 210 Pikes Peak Ave.
Colorado Springs, Van Briggle Pottery Company, 1125 Glen Ave./231 W. Uintah St.
Colorado Springs, Wolfe, John, House, 905 W. Cheyenne Rd.
Colorado Springs, Y.W.C.A., 130 E. Kiowa St.
Falcom, Black Squirrel Creek Bridge, US 24 at milepost 327.33
Fountain, Old Livery Stable, 217 W. Missouri
Mainitou Springs, US Post Office—Manitou Springs Main, 307 Canon Ave.
Manitou Springs, Barker House, 819 Manitou
Manitou Springs, Briarhurst, 404 Manitou Ave.
Manitou Springs, Bridge over Fountain Creek, Rt. 24
Manitou Springs, Cliff House, 306 Canon Ave.
Manitou Springs, Crystal Valley Cemetery, Plainview Ave.

Historical Assets Colorado

Manitou Springs, First Congregational Church, 101 Pawnee Ave.
Manitou Springs, Keithley Log Cabin Development District, Roughly bounded by Santa Fe Pl., Crystal Rd., and Spur Rd.
Manitou Springs, Manitou Bathhouse, 934 Manitou Ave.
Manitou Springs, Manitou Springs Bridges (2), Park Ave. and Cannon Ave. over Fountain Creek
Manitou Springs, Manitou Springs Historic District, Roughly bounded by El Paso Blvd., Ruxton Ave., US 24, and Iron Mt. Ave.
Manitou Springs, Miramont, 9 Capitol Hill
Manitou Springs, Wheeler Bank, 717—719 Manitou Ave.
Monument, Lewis, Inez Johnson, School, 146 Jefferson St.
Ramah, First Presbyterian Church of Ramah, 113 S. Commercial St.
U.S. Air Force Academy, United States Air Force Academy, Cadet Area, Roughly between Cadet Drive and Faculty Drive
Widefield, Little Fountain Creek Bridge, CO 115 at milepost 36.84

USGS Historic Places

Cascade, Cascade Post Office, 38.8966566, -104.9722013
Cascade, Crags Siding, 38.8799901, -104.9494224
Cherry Valley School, Pine Grove School, 39.129714, -104.7344203
Colorado Springs, South Junior High School, 38.8241594, -104.8213632
Corral Bluffs, Bledsoe Ranch, 38.8355512, -104.5194128
Ellicott, Drennan School, 38.7519411, -104.4494105
Elsmere, Peterson Army Air Field, 38.8127778, -104.71
Elsmere, Peterson Field, 38.8230505, -104.7155283
Elsmere, Rocky Mountain Airport, 38.7830509, -104.7341391
Falcon, Dustrude Ranch, 38.8897166, -104.6052486
Fountain, Pikes Peak Airport, 38.7336072, -104.701916
Haegler Ranch, Eisco Airport, 38.9163825, -104.4383001
Manitou Springs, Cheyenne Mountain School Cabin, 38.7647118, -104.903862
Manitou Springs, Old Mountain View, 38.833877, -104.9913655
Mount Pittsburg, Pinehurst Ranch, 38.5816621, -104.9422009
Peyton, Combs Ranch Airport, 39.1191571, -104.4646898
Pikeview, Elkhorn Ranch, 38.9644368, -104.857201
Pikeview, Pine Valley Airport, 38.9744372, -104.8177557
Pikeview, Pine Valley Ranch, 38.9694369, -104.8583123
Rush NW, Peakview Airport, 38.9201978, -104.1518176
Timber Mountain, Avery Ranch, 38.5261098, -104.8235887
Timber Mountain, Earley Ranch, 38.5341651, -104.8266441
Unknown, Green Post Office, 0, 0
Unknown, Halfway Post Office, 0, 0
Woodland Park, Green Mountain Falls Post Office, 38.9349905, -105.0169263

Grand Army of the Republic Posts

Palmer, No. 19, El Paso, Colorado Springs
Colorado Springs, No. 22, El Paso, Colorado Springs, 1882

El Paso County

Pike's Peak, No. 40, El Paso, Manitou
J E Stevens, No. 52, El Paso, Minneapolis
Cpt C F Coleman, No. 57, El Paso, Monument

USGS Historic Military Places

Corral Bluffs, Schriever Air Force Base, 38.8024275, -104.5161575
Elsmere, Peterson Air Force Base, 38.8235726, -104.69501
Elsmere, Peterson Army Air Field, 38.8127778, -104.71
Palmer Lake, United States Air Force Academy Cadet Area, 39.008635, -104.890288
Pikeview, United States Air Force Academy, 38.9984961, -104.8540895
Timber Mountain, Fort Carson, 38.5555596, -104.842556

Military Bases

Air Force Academy
2346 Academy Drive, Air Force Academy, CO 80840, 719-333-2025
Home of the Cadet Wing, 10th Air Base Wing, 306th Flying Training Group+

Cheyenne Mountain Air Force Base
101 Norad Rd, Colorado Springs, CO 80906, 719-474-1110
Former home of NORAD, North American Aerospace Defence Command, now headquartered at Peterson Air Force Base

Fort Carson Army Base
6001 Wetzel Ave, Fort Carson, CO 80913, 719-526-5811
Home to 71st Ordnance Group, 10th Combat Support Hospital, 4th Infantry Division, 4th Engineer Batallion, 10th Special Forces Group, 43rd Sustainment Brigade, 13th Air Support Operations Squadron (US Air Force), 759th Military Police Batallion.

Peterson Air Force Base
Platte Ave & N Powers Blvd, Colorado Springs, CO 80915, 719-556-7321
Home of the 21st Air Wing, 821st Air Base Group, 721st Mission Support Group

Schriever Air Force Base
1560 Enoch Rd, Schriever AFB, CO 80930, 719-567-1110
Home to the 50th Space Wing, 21st Medical Group, 310th Space Wing

Post Offices

Albano	1904 Oct 27	1912 Nov 30
Alnwick	1887 Aug 11	1893 Oct 26
Altman	1894 Jan 18	1895 Feb 20
Amo	1899 Apr 14	1916 July 31*
Anaconda	1893 Dec 7	1917 Nov 15*
Arequa	1894 July 9	rescinded
Bardeen	1917 Mar 7	1924 May 31
Barry	1892 Mar 1	1893 Dec 7
Bassetts Mills	1869 June 15	1872 Sept 13*

Historical Assets Colorado

Big Sandy	1876 Dec 13	1888 Nov 24*	
Bijou Basin	1869 Apr 8	1907 Mar 30*	
Black Forest	1960 Apr 16		
Boaz	1895 Mar 7	1898 Oct 31	
Burt	1910 Mar 24	1916 Aug 15	
Buttes	1895 Jan 24	1922 Apr 15	
Calhan	1888 Nov 24		80808
Cascade	1887 Aug 16		80809
Chipita Park	1935 Mar 9	1881	
Colorado City	1860 Mar 24	1917 June 30	
Colorado Springs	1871 Dec 1		80901
Cragmor	1927 Feb 5	1935 Dec 31	
Cripple Creek	1892 June 20		80813
Crows Roost	1913 Nov 4	1916 July 31	
Curtis	1901 Oct 15	1915 Mar 15	
Divide	1889 July 26		80814
Dragoo	1915 Apr 19	1916 Aug 15	
Drennan	1922	1951 Oct 5	
Easton	1872 May 6	1883 Sept 28*	
Eastonville	1883 Sept 28	1932 May 11	
Edgerton	1870 June 16	1902 Aug 28*	
Edlowe	1896 Jun 9	1899 June 16	
El Paso	1862 Oct 21	1893 July 11	
Elkton	1895 Apr 2	1926 Nov 15	
Ellicott	1895 Apr 29	1916 July 31	
Elsmere	1889 Nov 18	1890 Feb 4	
Falcon	1888 Oct 10	1942 Sept 14	
Florissant	1872 Nov 20		80816
Fountain	1864 Aug 8		80817
Fountain Valley School		1957 May 18	1980 June 28
Franceville	1881 Nov 2	1894 May 14	
Franceville Junction	1892 Mar 12	1899 Nov 15	
Fremont	1891 July 29	1892 June 20*	
Gillett	1894 Aug 29	1913 Mar 15*	
Gleneath	1910 Oct 22	1916 July 31	
Glenn	1896 Sept 23	1903 Dec 5*	
Goldfield	1895 May 5	1932 June 3	
Goldrock	1896 Apr 14	1896 Aug 31	
Granger	1883 Jan 12	1888 Dec 13	
Green	1894 Sept 28	1901 June 25	
Green Mountain Falls	1888 Aug 28	1894 Sept 28	
Green Mountain Falls 2		1901 June 25	80819
Gwillimsville	1878 Apr 18	1890 Sept 25	
Halfway	1903 Aug 21	1917 May 31	
Hanover	1913 June 10	1921 Apr 30	
Hibbard	1920	1922	

El Paso County

Highpark	1896 June 2	1917 May 31*	
Holtwold	1889 Jan 16	1917 Feb 28*	
Horace	1896 June 5	1899 Mar 8	
Husted	1878 Oct 1	1920 Oct 15*	
Ivywild	1891 Sept 14	1895 July 31	
Jimmy Camp	1878 May 17	1879 Feb 14	
Kelker	1912 Apr 30	1914 Aug 31	
Lawrence	1892 Feb 3	1898 Apr 22	
Love	1894 Dec 29	1902 July 15	
Lowland	1908 Aug 13	1909 Jan 15	
Lytle	1885 Aug 12	1920 Mar 5	
Macon	1895 Feb 20	1899 May 12	
Majors	1911 May 22	1912 Nov 30	
Manitou	1872 Oct 31	1936 Jan 1*	
Manitou Park	1888 Mar 19	1890 Feb 20	
Manitou Park 2	1890 June 30	1892 Feb 17	
Manitou Springs	1886 Feb 27	1892 May 20	
Manitou Springs 2	1936 Jan 1		80829
McFerran	1889 Jan 19	1896 July 30	
Midland	1892 June 27	1899 Aug 31*	
Monument	1869 Apr 8		80132
Morland	1891 Dec 9	1892 Feb 4	
Mosby	1910 Mar 24	1913 Nov 30	
Mound	1893 Mar 3	1882 Feb 1	
Myers	1891 Aug 11	1894 May 10	
Newfield	1896 July 30	1898 May 28	
North Pole	1956 Aug 1		
O Z	1877 Jan 29	1889 Aug 8	
Pacific	1880 Mar 10		
Palmer	1887 Mar 22	1912 June 17*	
Palmer Lake	1887 Apr 26	1894 Sept 11	
Palmer Lake 2	1912 June 17		80133
Peyton	1889 Feb 14		80831
Pikeview	1902 Aug 28	1957 July 31	
Ramah	1889 Aug 8		
Rosa	1895 Jan 11	1895 May 7	
Roswell	1889 Feb 1	1908 Apr 30	
Rush	1908 Feb 15		80833
Saint Peters	1905 Nov 14	1907 Dec 31	
Seward	1896 Aug 6	1899 Oct 12	
Signal	1896 May 1	1898 May 23	
Southwater	1872 Jan 4	1878 Oct 1	
Squirrel Creek	1911 Jan 24	1916 July 31	
Sublime	1903 May 28	1909 Aug 31	
Suffolk	1879 Feb 5	1885 Sept 11	
Summit Park	1873 Sept 1	1892 July 15*	

Historical Assets Colorado

Sun View	1877 Oct 15	1896 May 27*	
Surber	1895 June 11	1916 July 31	
Table Rock	1873 Dec 15	1893 Nov 11	
Tacony	1915 Mar 25	1942 July 31	
Torrington	1896 Sept 14	1903 Nov 14	
Turkey Creek	1877 July 16	1881 Oct 25	
United States Air Force Academy		1958 June 28	80840
Victor	1894 June 7		80860
Waverly	1897 May 1		
Wayne	1909 Jan 15	1912 Nov 30	
Weissport	1875 July 21	1887 Mar 22*	
Wheatland	1869 Aug 19	1873 Oct 26	
Wigwam	1882 June 26	1922 May 31*	
Woodland Park	1873 Sept 1		80863
Woodmen	1912 Jan 20	1949 Jan 31	
Yoder	1904 Apr 21		80864

Topo Quads

Big Springs Ranch	385230N	384500N	1041500W	1042230W
Black Forest	390730N	390000N	1043730W	1044500W
Buttes	383730N	383000N	1043730W	1044500W
Calhan	390730N	390000N	1041500W	1042230W
Cascade	390000N	385230N	1045230W	1050000W
Cheyenne Mountain	384500N	383730N	1044500W	1045230W
Colorado Springs	385230N	384500N	1044500W	1045230W
Corral Bluffs	385230N	384500N	1043000W	1043730W
Eastonville	390730N	390000N	1043000W	1043730W
Edison School	383730N	383000N	1040730W	1041500W
Ellicott	385230N	384500N	1042230W	1043000W
Elsmere	385230N	384500N	1043730W	1044500W
Falcon	390000N	385230N	1043000W	1043730W
Falcon NW	390000N	385230N	1043730W	1044500W
Fountain	384500N	383730N	1043730W	1044500W
Fountain NE	384500N	383730N	1043000W	1043730W
Fountain SE	383730N	383000N	1043000W	1043730W
Haegler Ranch	390000N	385230N	1042230W	1043000W
Hanover	383730N	383000N	1042230W	1043000W
Hanover NE	384500N	383730N	1041500W	1042230W
Hanover NW	384500N	383730N	1042230W	1043000W
Hanover SE	383730N	383000N	1041500W	1042230W
Holcolm Hills	390000N	385230N	1041500W	1042230W
Manitou Springs	385230N	384500N	1045230W	1050000W
Monument	390730N	390000N	1044500W	1045230W
Mount Big Chief	384500N	383730N	1045230W	1050000W
Mount Deception	390730N	390000N	1050000W	1050730W
Mount Pittsburg	383730N	383000N	1045230W	1050000W

El Paso County

Northgate	410000N	405230N	1061500W	1062230W
Palmer Lake	390730N	390000N	1045230W	1050000W
Peyton	390730N	390000N	1042230W	1043000W
Pikes Peak	385230N	384500N	1050000W	1050730W
Pikeview	390000N	385230N	1044500W	1045230W
Ramah South	390730N	390000N	1040730W	1041500W
Rush NW	390000N	385230N	1040730W	1041500W
Timber Mountain	383730N	383000N	1044500W	1045230W
Truckton	384500N	383730N	1040730W	1041500W
Woodland Park	390000N	385230N	1050000W	1050730W
Yoder	385230N	384500N	1040730W	1041500W

Suggested Reading

Breckenridge, Juania L and John P Breckenridge. *El Paso County Heritage*. Dallas: Curtis Media, 1985.

Foster, Dora. *Colorado Yesterdays*. Colorado Springs, CO: NP, 1961.

Gandy, Willard Eugene. *The History of the Town of Monument, El Paso County, Colorado*. Thesis Western State College of Colorado, 1951.

Peyton, Colorado, 1860-1968. Peyton, CO: Peyton High School, 1968.

Schweda, James T. *History of the Ewl Paso County Sheriff's Office, Colorado Springs, Colorado, 1861-1976*. NL: NP, 1977.

Vickers, W B and O L Baskin & Co. *History of the Arkansas Valley, Colorado; Illustrated*. Chicago: O L Baskin Historical Publishers, 1881.

Historical Assets Colorado

Elbert County

Introduction

Established: 1874   Population: 23,086

Formed from: Douglas, Greenwood

Adjacent Counties: Arapahoe, Lincoln, El Paso, Douglas

County Seat: Kiowa

Other Communities: Elizabeth, Simla, Elbert, Ponderosa Park, Agate, Fondis, Matheson

Website, https://www.elbertcounty-co.gov

Area Codes: 719

Zip Codes: 80101, 80107, 80117, 80830, 80835

Historical Assets Colorado

Elbert County Courthouse

Elbert County 19th Century Courthouse

Courthouses & County Government

Elbert County
https://www.elbertcounty-co.gov
Elbert County Courthouse (18th Judicial District), 751 Ute St, Kiowa, CO 80117, 303-621-2131; http://www.courts.state.co.us/Courts/County/Index.cfm?County_ID=59
Assessor, P.O. Box 26, Kiowa, CO 80117, 303-621-3101; http://www.elbertcounty-co.gov/dept_assessor.php
Board of County Commissioners, 215 Comanche St, Kiowa, CO 80117, 710-639-5850, https://www.elbertcounty-co.gov/commissioners.php
Clerk & Recorder, 210 Comanche St, Kiowa, CO 80117, 303-621-3128; http://www.elbertcounty-co.gov/dept_clerk.php
Coroner, 303-646-5599; https://www.elbertcounty-co.gov/elected_offices/coroner.php#.VRssXuESPEY
Elections, 440 Comanche St, Kiowa, CO 80117, 303-621-3127; https://www.elbert-county-co.gov/elections.php
Public Health, 75 Ute Ave, Kiowa, CO 80117, 720-621-3144; http://www.elbertcountyhealth.com/
Transportation (Road & Bridge), 218 Cheyenne St, Kiowa, CO 80117, 303-621-3157; https://www.elbertcounty-co.gov/road_and_bridge.php
Treasurer, 215 Comanche St, Kiowa, CO 80117, 303-621-3120; https://www.elbert-county-co.gov/treasurer.php

Elbert County

County Records

Birth Unk
Death 1893
Court 1876
CSA Birth 1880
CSA Death 1893
CSA Burial Permits 1908
CSA Disinterment Permits [nd]

Marriage 1861
Land 1861

Divorce Unk
Probate 1876

County & Municipal Records Held at the State Level

The Colorado State Archives

Physical Records
Assessor
Clerk & Recorder
Coroner
County Commissioners
County Registrar
County Court
District Court
Combined Courts
Justice Court
Public Trustee
Surveyor
Treasurercal Records
WPA Religious Institutions Survey
WPA Elizabeth, Kiowa
Cities
  Elizabeth
  Kiowa

Records on Film
Clerk & Recorder
County Court
District Court
School Districts
Cities
  Elizabeth

Records on Master Film
Clerk & Recorder
County Commissioners
County Court
District Court
Combined Courts
Public Trustee
School Districts
Treasurer
Cities
  Elizabeth

The Denver Public Library
WWI Draft Registration Cards (microfilm)

School Districts

School Districts, http://www.adcogov.org/local-school-districts

Agate School District 300, 41032 2nd, Agate, CO 80101, 719-764-2741; https://www.agateschools.net/

Big Sandy School District 100J, 10891 CR 125, Simla, CO 80835, 719-541-2291; https://bigsandy100j.com/

Calhan School District RJ-1, 800 Bulldog Dr, Calhan, CO 80808, 719-347-2766; https://www.calhanschool.org/

Elbert School District 200, 24489 Main St, Elbert, CO 80106, 303-648-3030; http://www.elbertschool.org/

Elizabeth School District, 634 S Elbert St, Elizabeth, CO 80107, 303-646-1836; https://www.elizabethschooldistrict.org/

Historical Assets Colorado

Kiowa School District C-2, 525 Comanche St, Kiowa, CO 80117, 303-621-2220; https://www.kiowaschool.org/
Limon School District RE-4J, 912 Badger Wy, Limon, CO 80828, 719-775-2350; http://limonbadgers.com/
Peyton School District 23 JT, 18320 Main St, Peyton, CO 80831, 719-749-2330; http://www.peyton.k12.co.us/

Historic School Districts

1. Elizabeth
2. Kiowa
3. East Lincoln
4. Sidney
5. Keysar
6. Kutch
7. Lundy
8. Lost
9. Osborn
10. James
11. Elbert
12. Kuln's Crossing
13. Schley
14. Locust Grove
15. Bijou Basin
16. High Point, Progressive
17. Pleasant Plains, Union Dale
18. Horseshoe
19. Wedemeyer
20. Union Valley
21. Waynee
22. [1888]
23. [1888]
24. Pines
25. Rattlesnake Hill
26. Hopewell
27. [1888]
28. Siam
29. South Bijou Valley, South Bijou Basin
30. Hill Top
31. Kanya
32. Glazier
33. Cedar Grove
34. Holt
35. Maul
36. Springdale
37. [1900]
38. Cirbo]
39. Willow Grove
40. Snell
41. River Bend
42. West Lincoln
43. Simla
44. Norton
45. Mountain View
46. Matheson
47. Bijou Valley
48. Twin Meadows
49.
50. Agate

UH1. Elizabeth Union
UH2. Simla Union
UH3. Agate Union
Jt1. Lincoln [Joint with Lincoln]

Fraternal Organizations

Granges

Kiowa, No. 59, Elbert, Middle Kiowa, 14 Apr 1874
Running Creek, No. 60, Elbert, Running Creek, 14 Apr 1874
Excelsior, No. 66, Elbert, Middle Kiowa, 29 Oct 1874
Bijou Basin, No. 67, Elbert, Bijou Basin, 30 Oct 1874
Bijou, No. 147, Elbert, Fondis, 5 Dec 1903
Banner, No. 210, Elbert, Kiowa, 20 Apr 1912
Harmony, No. 211, Elbert, Elizabeth, 27 Aug 1912
Kiowa, No. 223, Elbert, Kiowa, 21 Feb 1914
Elbert, No. 248, Elbert, Elbert, 17 Apr 1915
Bijou, No. 276, Elbert, Kiowa, 21 Apr 1916
Norton, No. 280, Elbert, Ramah, 6 May 1916
Cedar, No. 327, Elbert, Agate, 17 Mar 1917
Cheyenne, No. 338, Elbert, Keysor, 12 Apr 1917
Lincoln, No. 343, Elbert, Matheson, 4 May 1917
Keysor, No. 348, Elbert, Matheson, 2 June 1917
Pleasant Plains, No. 351, Elbert, Limon, 25 May 1917

Elbert County

Masons
    Ancient Free & Accepted Masons
        Kiowa, No. 116, Elbert, Kiowa, 16 Sept 1903
    Royal Arch Masons
        None
    Knights Templar
        None
    Eastern Star
        Kiowa, No. 116, Elbert, Kiowa
Odd Fellows
    Kiowa, No. 24, Elbert, Kiowa
    Simla, No. 24, Elbert, Simla
    Elbert, No. 86, Elbert, Elbert
    Fowler, No. 108, Elbert, Elizabeth
    Rebekahs
        Simla, No. 88, Elbert, Simla
        Pine Ridge, No. 100, Elbert, Elizabeth
Knights of Pythias
    None
    Pythian Sisters
        None
Benevolent Protective Order of Elks
    None

City & Town Halls
Kiowa, 404 Comanche St, Kiowa, CO 80117, 303-621-2366, https://www.townofkiowa.com
Elizabeth, 151 S Banner St, Elizabeth, CO 80107, 303-646-4166, https://www.townofelizabeth.org
Simla, 323 Pueblo Ave, Simla, CO 80835, 719-541-2468, https://townofsimla.com
Elbert, https://www.townofelbert.com

Archives & Manuscript Collections
None

Historical & Genealogical Societies
Elbert County Historical Society, Historical Museum, 515 Comanche St, P.O. Box 43, Kiowa, CO 80117, (303) 621-2229, http://www.elbertcountymuseum.org

Local Libraries
Pines & Plains Libraries - Kiowa, 331 Comanche, P.O. Box 538, Kiowa, CO 80117, (303) 621-2111, https://pplibraries.org
Elizabeth Library of Pines & Plains, 651 Beverly St, Elizabeth, CO 80107, (303) 646-3416, https://pplibraries.org

Historical Assets Colorado

Simla Library of Pines & Plains, 504 Washington Ave, Simla, CO 80535, (719) 541-2573, https://pplibraries.org

Links

CO GenWeb
http://cogenweb.com/elbert/

Cyndi's List
https://www.cyndislist.com/us/co/counties/elbert/

FamilySearch Wiki
https://www.familysearch.org/wiki/en/Elbert_County,_Colorado_Genealogy

Linkpendium
http://www.linkpendium.com/elbert-co-genealogy/

RootsWeb Wiki
https://wiki.rootsweb.com/wiki/index.php/Elbert_County,_Colorado

Wikipedia
https://en.wikipedia.org/wiki/Elbert_County,_Colorado

Historic Hotels

None

Museums & Historic Sites

Bailey Saddleland Museum, 20140 Cty Rd 125, Simla, CO 80835, (719) 541-2736, https://www.baileysaddleshopandmuseum.com

Elbert County Historical Society, Historical Museum, 515 Comanche St, P.O. Box 43, Kiowa, CO 80117, (303) 621-2229, http://www.elbertcountymuseum.org

Rambler Ranch Museum, 36370 Forest Tr, Elizabeth, CO 80107, (720) 833-8129, https://www.ramblerranch.com

Special Events & Scenic Locations

The Elbert County Fair takes place in July and August most years, at the Elbert County Fairgrounds, 95 Ute Ave, iowa, CO 80117, 303-621-3162, http://www.elbertcountyfair.com.

There is a list of Elbert County Festivals on Eventbrite here: https://www.eventbrite.com/d/co—elbert/festivals/

And a calendar of "Things to Do" in Elbert County here: https://www.eventbrite.com/d/co—elbert/events/

Ghost Towns & Other Sparsely Populated Places

Agate, Bland, Cameron, Cedar Point, Clemmons, Eastonville, Fondis, Godfrey, Gomers Mills, Holtwold, Hoyt, Kuhn's Crossing, Lowland, Mattison, Orsburn, Resolis, River Bend, Rosalias, Sidney

Elbert County

Newspapers
Elbert County News-Tribune. (Elizabeth, Colo.) 1???-19??
The Divide Review and Elbert County Democrat. (Kiowa, Colo.) 1???-1920
County Seat News-Tribune. (Kiowa, Colo.) 1???-19??
The Elbert County Tribune. (Elbert, Elbert County, Colo.) 18??-1920
The Eastonville Herald. (Eastonville, El Paso County, Colo.) 18??-1???
Elbert County Banner. (Elizabeth, Elbert County, Colo.) 1887-19??
The Western Recorder. (Elbert, Elbert County, Colo.) 1897-1898
The Elizabeth Eye. (Elizabeth, Colo.) 1899-1???
The Simla Herald. (Simla, Colo.) 1915-1916
The Simla Sun. (Simla, Elbert County, Colo.) 1916-1949
Elbert County Tribune and Elbert County Banner. (Elizabeth, Colo.) 1920-1921
The Divide Review. (Kiowa, Colo.) 1920-1941
Elbert County Tribune. (Elizabeth, Colo.) 1921-19??
Elbert County News. (Elbert, Colo.) 1922-19??
The Divide Review with which is combined The Elizabeth News-Tribune. (Kiowa, Elbert County, Colo.) 1941-1946
The Divide Review. (Kiowa, Elbert County, Colo.) 1946-1960
Pike View Farmer. (Simla, Colo.) 1949-1966
The Rainbelt Echo. (Elizabeth, Elbert County, Colo.) 1950-1960
Elbert County News. (Kiowa, Colo.) 1960-Current
Ranchland Farm News. (Simla, Colo.) 1966-1982
The Elbert County Country Squire. (Elizabeth, Colo.) 1973-198?
The Calhan News and Ramah Record. (Simla, Colo.) 1979-1979
The Calhan News. (Simla, Colo.) 1979-1985

Places on the National Register
Elbert, St. Mark United Presbyterian Church, 225 Main St.

USGS Historic Places
Elbert, Flying Lazy D Ranch Airport, 39.1622907, -104.5344376
Elizabeth, Dead Stick Ranch Airport, 39.3399878, -104.520246
Kiowa, Kiowa Division, 39.345265, -104.4541331
Unknown, Elbert Division, 0, 0

Grand Army of the Republic Posts
Elbert County, No. 103, Elbert, Elizabeth
Byron L Carr, No. 107, Elbert, Fondis

USGS Historic Military Places
None

Military Bases
None

Historical Assets Colorado

Post Offices

Agate	1882 Apr 24		80101
Arriba	1889 Feb 4		80804
Arroya	1877 Jan 16	1881 Jan 17	
Avendale	1889 Feb 5	1890 Sept 12	
Beloit	1888 Mar 27	1893 Sept 29	
Benko	1915 Sept 18	1917 Mar 31	
Bethune	1889 Jan 19	1905 May 15	
Beuck	1918 Mar 23	1918 May 1	
Bland	1883 May 25	1921 Feb 15	
Bovina	1899 Jan 8	1955 Nov 30	
Bowser	1888 June 9	1888 Oct 12	
Buick	1916 Sept 19	1925 Aug 15*	
Burlington	1887 Apr 29		80807
Carlisle	1887 July 21	1890 June 9	
Chenoweth	1897 Jan 16	1900 Sept 29	
Claremont	1888 Sept 11	1906 Mar 24	
Claud	1882 Oct 30	1888 Apr 3	
Clemmons	1882 Oct 23	1898 Oct 31	
Clermont	1881 Mar 25	1883 July 23	
Elbert	1875 Mar 12	1880 July 27	
Elbert 2	1882 June 27		80106
Elizabeth	1882 Apr 24		80107
Flagler	1888 Oct 12		80815
Fondis	1895 Nov 25	1954 July 15	
Gebhard	1881 Apr 8	1882 Apr 24	
Godfrey	1908 Jan 29	1908 Apr 11	
Goff	1888 Apr 23	1910 June 15	
Gomers Mills	1870 June 13	1882 June 27*	
Graceland	1908 Apr 20	1911 Sept 30	
Hargisville	1908 May 20	1915 Nov 15	
Holtwold	1889 Jan 16	1917 Feb 28*	
Hoyt	1888 Mar 27	1888 Nov 10	
Hugo	1871 Dec 1		80821
Kanza	1907 July 19	1917 Apr 14	
Keysor	1906 May 24	1938 Feb 28	
Kiowa	1868 Feb 14		80117
Kuhns Crossing	1879 Apr 10	1920 Jan 31	
Kutch	1899 July 17	1971 Jan 31*	
Laketon	1884 Oct 9	1886 Mar 27	
Landsman	1883 Mar 27	1918 May 31	
Matheson	1915 Feb 17		80830
Mattison	1889 Feb 13	1915 Feb 17	
Melville	1889 Jan 24	1890 Jan 21	
Norton	1899 June 29	1915 June 15	
Oranola	1888 July 7	1889 Feb 19	

Elbert County

Orsburn	1885 Mar 2	1896 Jan 28		
Resolis	1890 July 26	1914 Jan 15		
River Bend	1875 Jan 4	1939 Jan 31		
Running Creek	1868 Apr 14	1883 Mar 12*		
Schley	1899 June 27	1913 Oct 15		
Seibert	1888 Oct 17		80834	
Simla	1909 Aug 12		80835	
Tuttle	1883 Mar 27	1918 July 31		
Vona	1889 Jan 19	1905 Oct 14		
Wolfcreek	1910 Mar 15	1919 Mar 15		
Yoman	1904 Feb 11	1904 May 12		

Topo Quads

Agate	393000N	392230N	1035230W	1040000W
Alta Vista	390730N	390000N	1040000W	1040730W
Barking Dog Spg	393000N	392230N	1034500W	1035230W
Beuck Draw	392230N	391500N	1035230W	1040000W
Big Gulch	392230N	391500N	1041500W	1042230W
Bijou	393000N	392230N	1040730W	1041500W
Bijou Basin	391500N	390730N	1042230W	1043000W
Bijou SW	392230N	391500N	1040730W	1041500W
Cabin Gulch	393000N	392230N	1043000W	1043730W
Cattle Gulch	393000N	392230N	1040000W	1040730W
Cherry Valley Sch	391500N	390730N	1043730W	1044500W
Elbert	391500N	390730N	1043000W	1043730W
Elizabeth	392230N	391500N	1043000W	1043730W
Fondis	391500N	390730N	1041500W	1042230W
Holtwold Store	390000N	385230N	1040000W	1040730W
Kiowa	392230N	391500N	1042230W	1043000W
Kiowa NE	393000N	392230N	1041500W	1042230W
Kiowa NW	393000N	392230N	1042230W	1043000W
Kuhns Crossing	392230N	391500N	1040000W	1040730W
Kutch	390000N	385230N	1034500W	1035230W
Kutch NW	390000N	385230N	1035230W	1040000W
Kutch SE	385230N	384500N	1034500W	1035230W
Kutch SW	385230N	384500N	1035230W	1040000W
Lake	391500N	390730N	1033730W	1034500W
Limon	392230N	391500N	1033730W	1034500W
Long Creek	390730N	390000N	1033730W	1034500W
Matheson	391500N	390730N	1035230W	1040000W
Matheson NE	391500N	390730N	1034500W	1035230W
Matheson SE	390730N	390000N	1034500W	1035230W
Matheson SW	390730N	390000N	1035230W	1040000W
Ponderosa Park	393000N	392230N	1043730W	1044500W
Punkin Center	385230N	384500N	1033730W	1034500W
Punkin Center NW	390000N	385230N	1033730W	1034500W

Historical Assets Colorado

Ramah North	391500N	390730N	1040730W	1041500W
River Bend	392230N	391500N	1034500W	1035230W
Rush	385230N	384500N	1040000W	1040730W
Russellville Gulch	392230N	391500N	1043730W	1044500W
Simla	391500N	390730N	1040000W	1040730W
T Draw	393000N	392230N	1033730W	1034500W

Suggested Reading

Blevins, Terry W. *Our Heritage: a Collection of Tales of East Central Colorado*. Stratton, CO: East Central Council of Local Governments, 1983.

Corbett, Ethel Rae. *Western Pioneer Days: Biographies and Genealogies of Early Settlers, with History of Elbert County, Colorado*. Denver: Corbett, 1974.

Gabehart, Margee. *History of Elbert County, Colorado*. Dallas: Curtis Media Corp, 1989.

History of Elbert County. Simla, CO: Simla High School, 1959.

Richards, Clarice E. *A Tenderfoot Bride: Tales from an Old Ranch*. Lincoln, NE: University of Nebraska Press, 1988.

Thompson, *Brad and LaRiea Thompson. Through the Years: a Look at Some History: Elbert, Colorado*. NL: NP, 2006.

Fremont County

Introduction

Established: 1861   Population: 46,824

Formed from: Original

Adjacent Counties: Teller, El Paso, Custer, Saguache, Chaffee, Park

County Seat: Canon City

Other Communities: Florence, Brookside, Coal Creek, Portland, Rockvale, Williamsburg, Coaldale, Cotopaxi, Howard, Lincoln Park, Penrose, Hillside, Parkdale, Swissvale, Texas Creek, Wellsville, Chandler, Siloam, Whitehorn

Website, https://www.fremontco.com

Area Codes: 719

Zip Codes: 81212, 81215, 81221, 81222, 81223, 81226, 81232, 81240, 81244, 81290

Historical Assets Colorado

Fremont County Courthouse

Fremont County 19th Century Courthouse

Courthouses & County Government

Fremont County
https://www.fremontco.com/

Fremont County Courthouse (11th Judicial District), 136 Justice Center Rd, Canon City, CO 81212, 719-269-0100; http://www.courts.state.co.us/Courts/County/Index.cfm?County_ID=30

Assessor, 615 Macon St, Canon City, CO 81212, 719-276-7310; http://www.fremontco.com/assessor/index.shtml

Board of County Commissioners, 615 Macon Ave, Canon City, CO 81212, 719-276-7300, https://www.fremontco.com/commissioners/board-county-commissioners

Clerk & Recorder, 615 Macon St, Canon City, CO 81212, 719-276-7330; http://www.fremontco.com/clerkandrecorder/

Coroner, 615 Macon Ave, Rm LL7, Canon City, CO 81212, 719-276-7358; https://www.fremontco.com/coroner/coroner

Public Health, 172 Justice Center Rd, Canon City, CO 81212, 719-275-1626; http://www.fremontco.com/nursingservices/index.shtml

Treasurer, 615 Macon Ave, Rm 104, Canon City, CO 81212, 719-276-7380; http://www.fremontco.com/Treasurer/index.shtml

County Records

Birth Unk	Marriage 1861	Divorce 1900
Death Unk	Land 1861	Probate 1900
Court 1900		
CSA Birth 1941		

Fremont County

County & Municipal Records Held at the State Level

The Colorado State Archives

Physical Records
1885 Census
Clerk & Recorder
County Commissioners
County Court
District Court
Sheriff
Treasurer
WPA Historical Records
WPA Religious Institutions Survey
Cities
Canon City

Records on Film
1885 Census
Clerk & Recorder
County Commissioners
District Court
Treasurer
Cities
Canon City

Records on Master Film
1885 Census
Clerk & Recorder
County Court
District Court
Combined Courts
School Districts
Treasurer
Cities
Canon City

The Denver Public Library

Fremont & Pueblo County Mining Companies Records, 1894
WPA Historical Records Survey
WWI Draft Registration Cards (microfilm)

School Districts

School Districts, http://www.adcogov.org/local-school-districts
Canon City School District RE-1, 101 N 14th St, Canon City, CO 81212, 719-276-5700; https://www.canoncityschools.org/
Cotopaxi School District Fremont RE-3, 345 County Rd 12, Cotopaxi, CO 81223, 719-942-4131; http://www.cotopaxire3.org/
Fremont School District RE-2, 403 W 5th St, Florence, CO 81226, 719-784-4856; http://www.re-2.org/

Historic School Districts

1. Canon City
2. Florence
3. Portland
4. Fruitmere, Fourmile
5. Garden Park
6. Upper Beaver
7. Mt View
8. [1878]
9. Foster
10. [1878]
11. Concrete
12. Tucker
13. Stout Creek
14. Brookside, Brewster
15. Coal Creek
16. Parkdale, 12 Mile
17. Coaldale, Yellow Pine
18. [1881]
19. Oak Creek
20. Tallahasse, Cottonwood
21. Rockvale
22. Tribble
23. [1883]
24. Wilmont
25. Skagway
26. Hillsdale, Code Park, Hillside
27. Fourmile
28. Wellsville
29. [1891]
30. [1891]
31. Cramer
32. Chandler
33. Brush Hollow, Fairview
34. [1891]
35. [1901]
36. [1902]
37. Calcite, Howard
38. Kenwood
Jt39. Lytle
40.
41. Cotopaxi
42.
43.
44.
45.
46.
47.
48. Webster Park, Wilson Creek
49. Guffy, Foster

Historical Assets Colorado

50. Penrose
51. West Fremont
52.
53.
54.
55. [1891]
56. [1891]

Fraternal Organizations

Granges
Florence, No. 49, Fremont, Florence, 9 Mar 1874
Colfax, No. 70, Fremont, Colfax/Canon City, 30 Oct 1875
New Hope, No. 72, Fremont, Greenwood/Canon City, 1 May 1876
Royal Gorge, No. 382, Fremont, Canon City, 14 Jan 1919
Beaver Park, No. 396, Fremont, Penrose, 4 Feb 1926
Coaldale-Cotopaxi, No. 397, Fremont, Coaldale, 6 Feb 1926
Pleasant Valley, No 398, Fremont, Howard, 11 Feb 1926
Hillside, No. 399, Fremont, Hillside, 2 Mar 1926

Masons
Ancient Free & Accepted Masons
Mount Moriah, No. 15, Fremont, Canon City, 6 Oct 1868
Fremont, No. 97, Fremont, Florence, 19 Sept 1894

Royal Arch Masons
Canon City, No. 14, Fremont, Canon City
Florence, No. 35, Fremont, Florence

Knights Templar
Canon City Commandery, No. 9, Fremont, Canon City, 1883 Nov 12

Eastern Star
Canon City, No. 21, Fremont, Canon City
Florence, No. 25, Fremont, Florence
Coal Creek, No. 88, Fremont, Coal Creek

Odd Fellows
Unity, No. 3, Fremont, Canon City, 1972 Dec 1
Canon City, No. 7, Fremont, Canon City, 1868 Nov 10
Coal Creek, No. 32, Fremont, Coal Creek
Golden Star, No. 53, Fremont, Cotopaxi, 1883 July 4
Rockvale, No. 62, Fremont, Rockvale
Fremont, No. 98, Fremont, Florence

Rebekahs
Salome, No. 7, Fremont, Florence
Harmony, No. 96, Fremont, Canon City

Knights of Pythias
Hercules, No. 21, Fremont, Coal Creek
Petroleum, No. 36, Fremont, Florence
Coeur de Leon, No. 48, Fremont, Canon City
Empire, No. 77, Fremont, Rockvale, 1892 Jan 8

Pythian Sisters
Western Star, No. 7, Fremont, Rockvale/Coal Creek
Columbian, No. 13, Fremont, Florence

Fremont County

Benevolent Protective Order of Elks
Canon City, No. 610, Fremont, Canon City
Florence, No. 611, Fremont, Florence

City & Town Halls
Canon City, 128 Main St, Canon City, CO 81212, 719-269-9011, https://www.canoncity.org
Florence, 600 W 3rd St, Florence, CO 81226, 719-784-4848, https://www.colorado.gov/florencecolorado
Brookside, 1720 Brookside Ave, Canon City, CO 81212, 719-276-3436, https://www.colorado.gov/pacific/townofbrookside/town-brookside-colorado
Coal Creek, 615 Main St, Coal Creek, CO 81221, 719-784-6150, https://www.colorado.gov/coalcreekco
Rockvale, 156 Rockafellow St, Rockvale, CO 81244, 719-784-4125, https://www.colorado.gov/pacific/townofrockvale/rockvale
Williamsburg, 1 John St, Florence, CO 81226, 719-784-4511, http://williamsburgcolorado.com

Archives & Manuscript Collections
IOOF Grand Lodge of Colorado, 1545 Phelps Ave, Canon City, CO 81212, (719) 275-1606, https://ioofcolorado.org

Historical & Genealogical Societies
Canon City Heritage Association, Royal Gorge Regional Museum and History Center, 612 Royal Gorge Blvd, P.O. Box 1460, Canon City, CO 81212-3751, (719) 269-9018, https://museum.canoncity.org
Florence Historical Society, Price Pioneer Museum, 100 E Front St, P.O. Box 87, Florence, CO 81226, (719) 784-1904, https://www.florencepioneermuseum.org
Fremont County Historical Society, Prospect Heights Jail Museum, 1321 S 4th St, P.O. Box 965, Canon City, CO 81212, https://fremontheritage.com/fc-historical-society/

Local Libraries
Canon City Public Library & Fremont County Local History Center, 516 Macon St, Canon City, CO 81212-3380, (719) 269-9020, http://ccpl.lib.co.us
John C Fremont Public Library, 130 Church Ave, Florence, CO 81226, (719) 784-4649, https://www.jcfld.org
Penrose Community Library, 35 7th Ave, Penrose, CO 81240, (719) 372-6017, https://penrose.colibraries.org

Links
CO GenWeb
http://cogenweb.com/fremont/
Cyndi's List
https://www.cyndislist.com/us/co/counties/fremont/

Historical Assets Colorado

FamilySearch Wiki
https://www.familysearch.org/wiki/en/Fremont_County,_Colorado_Genealogy

Linkpendium
http://www.linkpendium.com/fremont-co-genealogy/

RootsWeb Wiki
https://wiki.rootsweb.com/wiki/index.php/Fremont_County,_Colorado

Wikipedia
https://en.wikipedia.org/wiki/Fremont_County,_Colorado

Historic Hotels

None

Museums & Historic Sites

Colorado Territorial Prison Museum, 201 N 1st St, Canon City, CO 81212, (719) 269-3015, http://www.prisonmuseum.org

Canon City Heritage Association, Royal Gorge Regional Museum and History Center, 612 Royal Gorge Blvd, P.O. Box 1460, Canon City, CO 81212-3751, (719) 269-9018, https://museum.canoncity.org

Florence Historical Society, Price Pioneer Museum, 100 E Front St, P.O. Box 87, Florence, CO 81226, (719) 784-1904, https://www.florencepioneermuseum.org

Fremont County Historical Society, Prospect Heights Jail Museum, 1321 S 4th St, P.O. Box 965, Canon City, CO 81212, https://fremontheritage.com/fc-historical-society/

Royal Gorge Dinosaur Experience, 44895 W Hwy 50, Canon City, CO 81212, (719) 275-2726, https://dinoxp.com

Special Events & Scenic Locations

The Fremont County Fair is held most years in July and August at the Royal Gorge Rodeo Grounds, 1595 S 9th St, Canon City, CO 81212, https://www.royalgorgerodeo.org.

The Canon City Chamber of Commerce has a calendar of events here: http://www.canoncity.com/events

Fremont County keeps a calendar of events here: http://www.fremontcolorado.com/Events.aspx

Pike National Forest
San Isabel National Forest
Sangre de Christo Wilderness
Arkansas Headwaters Recreation Area
Gold Belt Tour National Scenic and Historic Byway
American Discovery Trail
Trans America Trail Bicycle Route
Western Express Bicycle Route

Fremont County

Ghost Towns & Other Sparsely Populated Places

Adelaide, Adobe, Beaver Creek, Bridge Three, Brookside, Burnito, Chandler, Clelland, Cliff Junction, Coaldale, Cotopaxi, Currant Creek, Echo, Fairy Glen, George, Glendale, Hanging Bridge, Hillside, Howard, Macon, Marsh, Oak Creek, Oak Creek Junction, Parkdale, Reno, Soda Springs, Spike Buck, Swissvale, Texas Creek, Toll Gate, Vallie, Wellsville, Williamsburg, Woodruff, Yorkville

Newspapers

The Canon City Record Fremont County Leader. (Canon City, Colo.) 1???-1925
Canon City Reporter. (Canon City, Colo.) 18??-1???
Canon Times. (Canon City, J.t. [Colo.]) 1860-1861
Cañon City Times. (Cañon City, Colo.) 1861-18??
Cañon City Times. (Cañon City, Colo.) 1872-1877
Canon City Free Press. (Canon City, Colo.) 1874-1???
Cañon City Avalanche. (Cañon City, Colo.) 1875-1877
The Fremont County Record. (Canon City, Colo.) 1877-18??
The Mining Gazette. (Canon, Colo.) 1880-1???
The Daily Express. (Canon City, Colo.) 1882-1???
The Weekly Express. (Canon City, Colo.) 1882-????
Coal Creek Enterprise. (Coal Creek, Colo.) 1882-1???
Cañon City Record. (Cañon City, Colo.) 1883-192?
Canon City Mercury. (Canon City, Colo.) 1884-????
The Advance. (Canon City, Colo.) 1884-????
The Gate City. (Canon City, Colo.) 1885-1???
Florence Oil Refiner. (Florence, Fremont County, Colo.) 1887-1892
Canon City Clipper. (Canon City, Fremont County, Colo.) 1888-1905
Florence Refiner. (Florence, Colo.) 189?-1901
The Oil Refiner. (Florence, Fremont County, Colo.) 1892-189?
The Coal Miners' Journal. (Rockvale, Colo.) 1893-1???
Florence News. (Florence, Colo.) 1893-1???
The Florence Chronicle. (Florence, Colo.) 1895-1895
The Daily Chronicle. (Florence, Colo.) 1895-1???
The Weekly Chronicle. (Florence, Colo.) 1895-1???
The Florence Daily Herald. (Florence, Colo.) 1896-1???
The Whitehorn News. (Whitehorn, Chaffee County, Colo.) 1897-19??
Canon City Times. (Canon City, Colo.) 1898-1911
The Florence Daily Tribune. (Florence, Colo.) 1898-1903
The Florence Citizen. (Florence, Colo.) 1898-1914
The Canon City Daily Record. (Canon City, Colo.) 1898-1906
Florence Daily Citizen. (Florence, Colo.) 1899-19??
Penrose Press. (Penrose, Fremont County, Colo.) 19??-19??
The Fremont County Sun. (Canon City, Colo.) 19??-1983
The Daily American. (Canon City, Colo.) 19??-19??
The Fremont Trader. (Canon City, Colo.) 19??-19??
Ex Parte. (Florence, Colo.) 1901-1901

Historical Assets Colorado

Ex Parte and Florence Refiner. (Florence, Colo.) 1901-1903
The Daily Tribune. (Florence, Colo.) 1903-19??
Ex Parte. (Florence, Colo.) 1903-1912
The Daily Record. (Canon City, Colo.) 1906-1926
The Daily Citizen. (Florence, Colo.) 1909-1913
The Canon City Record with which is consolidated The Canon City Cannon. (Canon City, Colo.) 1911-192?
The Fremont County Leader and Canon City Times. (Canon City, Fremont County, Colo.) 1911-1912
Paradox. (Rockvale, Fremont County, Colo.) 1911-1925
The Fremont County Leader. (Canon City, Fremont County, Colo.) 1912-19??
The Fremont Democrat Ex Parte. (Florence, Colo.) 1912-1912
The Fremont Democrat. (Florence, Colo.) 1913-19??
Florence Daily Citizen. (Florence, Colo.) 1913-1939
The Citizen-Democrat. (Florence, Colo.) 1914-19??
The Fremont County Daily News. (Canon, City, Colo.) 1924-19??
The Canon City Record. (Canon City, Colo.) 1925-1969
The Florence Paradox. (Florence, Fremont County, Colo.) 1925-19??
Canon City Daily Record. (Canon City, Colo.) 1926-1989
The Florence Daily News. (Florence, Fremont County, Colo.) 1927-19??
The Citizen. (Florence, Colo.) 1937-1943
The Citizen with which is consolidated The Penrose Press. (Florence, Fremont County, Colo.) 1943-1948
The Florence Citizen with which is incorporated The Penrose Press. (Florence, Fremont County, Colo.) 1948-1957
The Sun. (Canon City, Colo.) 1951-19??
The Florence Citizen. (Florence, Colo.) 1957-1988
The Valley Voice. (Howard, Colo.) 1980-1984
The Fremont County Sun and County Newspaper/Trader. (Canon City, Colo.) 1983-Current
The Fremont Observer. (Canon City, Colo.) 1987-Current
The Citizen. (Florence, Colo.) 1988-1990
Daily Record. (Canon City, Colo.) 1989-Current
Canon City Shopper. (Canon City, Colo.) 1989-19??
The Florence Citizen. (Florence, Colo.) 1990-Current

Places on the National Register

Canon City, Atwater, Samuel H., House, 821 Macon Ave.
Canon City, Canon City Downtown Historic District, Roughly Main St. from 3rd to 9th Sts. and Macon Ave.
Canon City, Canon City Downtown Historic District (Boundary Increase), 602 Macon Ave.
Canon City, Canon City Municipal Building, 612 Royal Gorge Blvd.
Canon City, Canon City State Armory, 110 Main St.
Canon City, Christ Episcopal Church, 802 Harrison Ave.
Canon City, Colorado Women's Prison, 201 N. 1st St.

Fremont County

Canon City, Deputy Warden's House, 105 Main
Canon City, First Presbyterian Church, Macon and 7th Sts.
Canon City, Greenwood Cemetery, 1251 S. 1st St.
Canon City, Holy Cross Abbey, US 50
Canon City, McClure House, 323-331 Main St.
Canon City, Mount Saint Scholastica Academy, East Building, 615 Pike Ave.
Canon City, Oil Spring, Address Restricted
Canon City, Robison Mansion, 12 Riverside Dr.
Canon City, Royal Gorge Bridge and Incline Railway, NW of Canon City
Canon City, South Canon High School, 1020 Park Ave.
Canon City, US Post Office and Federal Building—Canon City Main, Fifth St. and Macon Ave.
Florence, Bridge No. 10/Adelaide Bridge, Fremont Cty. Rd.
Florence, Main Street Bridge, CO 115 at milepost 8.90
Florence, Rio Grande Railroad Viaduct, CO 120 at milepost 0.17
Florence, US Post Office—Florence Main, 121 N. Pikes Peak St.
Portland, Portland Bridge, SR 120
Swissvale, Rouch Gulch Bridge, US 50 at milepost 230.12

USGS Historic Places

Rockvale, Chandler, 38.373055, -105.2005456
Royal Gorge, Buckskin Joe Post Office, 38.4763859, -105.3269362

Grand Army of the Republic Posts

Greenwood, No. 10, Fremont, Canon City, 1881
Ethan Allen, No. 56, Fremont, Coal Creek
John C Fremont, No. 83, Arapahoe, Littleton
Gen A J Smith, No. 102, Fremont, Florence

USGS Historic Military Places

Rockvale, Chandler, 38.373055, -105.2005456
Royal Gorge, Buckskin Joe Post Office, 38.4763859, -105.3269362

Military Bases

Rockvale, Chandler, 38.373055, -105.2005456
Royal Gorge, Buckskin Joe Post Office, 38.4763859, -105.3269362

Post Offices

Adelaide	1878 Sept 27	1901 Nov 15*
Anita	1892 June 30	1894 May 10
Barehills	1896 Apr 28	1901 June 29
Beaver	1902 Apg 11	1910 Apr 30
Beaver Creek	1862 Oct 3	1902 Apr 11*
Boaz	1895 Mar 7	1898 Oct 31
Brewster	1899 Oct 9	1916 Sept 30*

Historical Assets Colorado

Brookside	1888 May 21	1909 Mar 15	
Buckskin Joe	1961 June 1	1966 Mar 31	
Calcite	1904 June 29	1930 Apr 30	
Canon City	1860 Dec 13		81212
Canyon City	1904 July 30	1905 Dec 15	
Chandler	1890 Aug 4	1942 Oct 31	
Clonmell	1898 July 18	1901 Feb 7	
Coal Creek	1873 Nov 4	1894 May 31	
Coal Creek 2	1964 July 1		81221
Coalcreek	1894 May 31	1964 July 1	
Coaldale	1891 Feb 16		81222
Colfax	1870 May 2	1879 Jan 16	
Concrete	1908 May 28	1921 May 31	
Copperfield	1907 June 18	1910 Dec 31	
Cotopaxi	1880 May 25		81223
Cramer	1901 Feb 7	1904 June 30	
Currant	1894 Oct 2	1901 Feb 28	
Currant Creek	1870 Aug 29	1894 Oct 2	
Cyanide	1895 Oct 23	1907 May 31	
Driscoll	1896 May 2	1896 May 27	
Eldred	1892 Sept 9	1907 Dec 15	
Fairy	1881 May 18	1881 Sept 28	
Fidler	1881 June 17	1882 Oct 26	
Florence	1873 May 8		81226
Ford	1881 Jan 4	1885 Sept 10	
Galena	1877 Feb 16	1885 Nov 4*	
Glendale	1877 Dec 28	1909 May 8	
Grape	1883 June 4	1887 Jan 13	
Hatton	1882 June 12	1887 Aug 10	
Hayden Creek	1878 May 4	1880 Feb 10	
Heathton	1906 Dec 28	1908 May 15	
Hendricks	1887 Jan 31	1891 Feb 16	
Hickman	1866 Dec 10	1869 Sept 20*	
Hillsdale	1880 Feb 18	1880 Aug 2	
Hillside	1884 Jan 24		
Howard	1877 Mar 19		81233
Juniper	1881 Jan 10	1881 Oct 17	
Kalbaugh	1898 Nov 2	1900 Feb 15	
Kenwood	1926 Apg 16	1929 Dec 31	
Littell	1911 Dec 7	1915 Jan 15	
Manoa	1900 May 14	1907 Dec 31	
Marigold	1895 Oct 31	1902 June 30	
Micanite	1904 Sept 30	1925 Sept 30	
Palmer	1880 Feb 10	1887 Jan 31	
Parkdale	1880 Aug 16	1970 July 31*	
Penrose	1877 Dec 28		81240

Fremont County

Pleasant Valley	1877 Mar 19	1882 July 26	
Portland	1900 Mar 20	1952 Aug 31	
Pyrolite	1915 Apr 20	1926 Apr 16	
Radiant	1904 Dec 20	1915 Apr 20	
Rockdale	1882 Mar 17	1882 Apr 12	
Rockvale	1882 Apr 12		81244
Rosita	1874 July 8	1966 Dec 2	
Royal Gorge	1949 July 21		
Sunol	1892 Sept 8	1894 Oct 18	
Texas	1882 May 12	1884 Jan 21	
Texas Creek	1872 Aug 27	1882 Mar 31	
Texas Creek 2	1885 Sept 10		81250
Titusville	1881 Oct 12	1883 Aug 13	
Toof	1881 Apr 21	1883 Jan 8	
Ula	1871 Dec 1	1891 May 4	
Wellsville	1880 Dec 13	1896 Aug 13	
Whitehorn	1897 July 22	1916 Nov 15	
Wilbur	1894 Sept 11	1913 July 15	
Williamsburgh	1882 Jan 10	1916 Oct 31	
Wulstenville	1871 July 21	1871 Dec 4	
Yorkville	1875 Nov 4		

Topo Quads

Arkansas Mountain	383000N	382230N	1053730W	1054500W
Bushnell Peak	382230N	381500N	1055230W	1060000W
Canon City	383000N	382230N	1050730W	1051500W
Coaldale	382230N	381500N	1054500W	1055230W
Cooper Mountain	383730N	383000N	1050730W	1051500W
Cotopaxi	382230N	381500N	1053730W	1054500W
Curley Peak	382230N	381500N	1051500W	1052230W
Echo	383000N	382230N	1053000W	1053730W
Florence	383000N	382230N	1050000W	1050730W
Florence SE	382230N	381500N	1050000W	1050730W
Gribble Mountain	383730N	383000N	1052230W	1053000W
Hall Gulch	383730N	383000N	1053000W	1053730W
Hillside	382230N	381500N	1053000W	1053730W
Hobson	382230N	381500N	1045230W	1050000W
Howard	383000N	382230N	1054500W	1055230W
Iron Mountain	382230N	381500N	1052230W	1053000W
Jack Hall Mountain	383730N	383000N	1054500W	1055230W
McIntyre Hills	383000N	382230N	1052230W	1053000W
Phantom Canyon	383730N	383000N	1050000W	1050730W
Pierce Gulch	383000N	382230N	1045230W	1050000W
Rice Mountain	383730N	383000N	1051500W	1052230W
Rockvale	382230N	381500N	1050730W	1051500W
Royal Gorge	383000N	382230N	1051500W	1052230W
Waugh Mountain	383730N	383000N	1053730W	1054500W

Historical Assets Colorado

Suggested Reading

Ahart, Barbara Joan Allen. *Pioneers of Fremont County, Colorado*. Canon City, CO: B Ahart, 2003.

Campbell, Rosemae Wells. *From Trappers to Tourists: Fremont County, Colorado, 1830-1950*. Colorado Springs, CO: Century One Press, 1972.

Cresto, Antoinette. *King Coal: Coal Mining in Fremont County*. Florence, CO: Florence Citizen, 1980.

Hurley, Paul. *Fremont County Ranchers and Cowboys*. Canon City, CO: Master Printers, 1972.

Inventory of the County Archives of Colorado, No. 22, Fremont County (Canon City). Denver: Historical Records Survey, 1938.

McGinn, Elinor M. *If Walls Could Speak: Vignettes of Some pre-1900 Buildings Actively Serving Fremont County*. Canon City, CO. Fremont-Custer Historical Society, 1984.

Southern Colorado: Historical and Descriptive of Fremont and Custer Counties with their Principal Towns. Canon City, CO: Binckley & Hartwell, 1879.

Vickers, W B and O L Baskin & Co. *History of the Arkansas Valley, Colorado; Illustrated*. Chicago: O L Baskin Historical Publishers, 1881.

Wulsten, Carl. *The Silver Region of the Sierra Mojada (Wet Mountains) and Rosita, Fremont County, Colorado*. Denver: Tribune Steam Printing House, 1876.

Garfield County

Introduction

Established: 1883   Population: 58,095

Formed from: Summit

Adjacent Counties: Rio Blanco, Routt, Eagle, Pitkin, Mesa

County Seat: Glenwood Springs

  Other Communities: Rifle, Carbondale, New Castle, Silt, Parachute, Battlement Mesa, Catherine, Cattle Creek, Chacra, Mulford, No Name

Website, https://www.garfield-county.com

Area Codes: 970

Zip Codes: 81601, 81602, 81623, 81635, 81636, 81647, 81650, 81652

Historical Assets Colorado

Garfield County Courthouse

Courthouses & County Government

Garfield County
https://www.garfield-county.com
Garfield County Courthouse (9th Judicial District), 109 8th St, Glenwood Springs, CO 81601, 970-945-5075; http://www.courts.state.co.us/Courts/County/Index.cfm?County_ID=24
Garfield County Courthouse (Rifle), 200 E 18th St, Rifle, CO 81650, 970-625-5100; http://www.courts.state.co.us/Courts/County/Index.cfm?County_ID=24
Assessor, 109 8th St, Glenwood Springs, CO 81601, 970-945-9134; http://www.garfield-county.com/assessor/index.aspx
Board of County Commissioners, 108 8th St, Glenwood Springs, CO 81601, 970-945-5004, https://www.garfield-county.com/
Clerk & Recorder, 144 E 3rd St, Rifle, CO 81650, 970-625-0882; http://www.garfield-county.com/clerk-recorder/index.aspx
Clerk & Recorder, 109 8th St, Glenwood Springs, CO 81601, 970-384-3700; http://www.garfield-county.com/clerk-recorder/index.aspx
Coroner, 1806 Medicine Bow Ct, Silt, CO 81652, 970-665-6335; https://www.garfield-county.com/coroner/index.aspx
Public Health, 195 W 14th St, Rifle, CO 81650, 970-625-5200; http://www.garfield-county.com/public-health/index.aspx
Transportation (Road & Bridge), 7300 Hwy 82, Glenwood Springs, 81601, 970-945-1223; https://www.garfield-county.com/road-bridge/index.aspx
Transportation (Road & Bridge), 0298 County Rd 333A, Rifle, CO 81650, 970-625-8601; https://www.garfield-county.com/road-bridge/index.aspx
Treasurer, 109 8th St, Ste 204, Glenwood Springs, CO 81601, 970-945-6382; http://www.garfield-county.com/Treasurer/index.aspx
Treasurer, 144 E 3rd St, Rifle, CO 81650, 970-625-0926; http://www.garfield-county.com/Treasurer/index.aspx

Garfield County

County Records
Birth 1883
Death 1883
Court 1892
Marriage 1883
Land 1883
Divorce 1906
Probate 1892

County & Municipal Records Held at the State Level
The Colorado State Archives

Physical Records
Clerk & Recorder
County Court
District Court
Justice Court
WPA Historical Records
WPA Religious Institutions Survey
WPA Glenwood Springs
Cities
Newcastle

Records on Film
Clerk & Recorder

Records on Master Film
Assessor
Building
County Court
District Court
Combined Courts
School Districts
Sheriff
Treasurer
Cities
Glenwood Springs

The Denver Public Library
Garfield County History Scrapbook, 1936
WPA Historical Records Survey
WWI Draft Registration Cards (microfilm)

School Districts
School Districts, http://www.adcogov.org/local-school-districts
De Beque School District 49JT, 730 Minter Ave, De Beque, CO 81630, 970-283-5596; https://www.dbschools.org/
Garfield School District RE-2, 839 Whiteriver Ave, Rifle, CO 81650, 970-665-7600; https://www.garfieldre2.org/
Garfield School District 16, 460 Stone Quarry Rd, Parachute, CO 81635, 970-285-5701; http://www.garfield16.org/
Roaring Fork School District RE-1, 400 Sopris Ave, Carbondale, CO 81623, 970-384-6000; http://www.rfsd.k12.co.us/
Eagle County School District RE 50, 948 Chambers Ave, Eagle, CO 81631, 970-328-6321; https://www.eagleschools.net/

Historic School Districts
1. Glenwood Springs
Jt2. Sweetwater
3. [1886]
4. Peach Valley
5. Corn Creek, Stone Canon
6. Upper Cattle Creek, Spring Valley
7. Upper Parachute
8. Catherine
9. [1885]
10. New Castle
11. Book Cliff
12. Carbondale
13. Antlers
14. [1896]
15. Lower Cattle Creek
16. Grand Valley
17. [1889]
18. Wallace Creek
19. Garfield Creek
20. Austin
Jt21. Rio Blanco
22. Larson
23. Fairview

Historical Assets Colorado

24. Sunlight
25. Cardiff
26. Crystal Springs
27. Mamon Creek
28. Cache Creek
29. Lower Highmore
30. [1892]
31. Beaver Creek
32. Canon Creek
33. [1892]
34. Kimball Creek
35. [1904]
36. [1904]
37. Elk Park
38. Holmes Mesa
39. [1920]
40. Grand View
41. Hunter Mesa
42. Dry Hollow
43. Morrisania
44. Four Mlie
45. [1923]
46.
47. Carr Creek
48. Missouri Heights
49.
50.
51.
52.
53.
54.
55. [1892]
56. [1892]

C1. Silt
C2. Rifle

Fraternal Organizations

Granges
Excelsior, No. 100, Garfield, Parachute/Rifle, 29 Mar 1890
Rifle, No. 104, Garfield, Rifle, 14 Apr 1890
Beaver, No. 112, Garfield, Parachute/Rifle, 6 Oct 1890
Union, No. 113, Garfield, Carbondale, 21 Oct 1890
New Castle, No. 124, Garfield, New Castle, 3 Feb 1891
Eureka, No. 125, Garfield, Carbondale, 4 Feb 1891
Mt Sopris, No. 126, Garfield, Carbondale, 5 Feb 1891
Peach Valley, No. 387, Garfield, New Castle, 4 Oct 1919
Elk Creek, No. 415, Garfield, New Castle, 23 Nov 1934
Divide Creek, No. 481, Garfield, Silt, 14 Sept 1957,

Masons

Ancient Free & Accepted Masons
Glenwood, No. 65, Garfield, Glenwood Springs, 21 Sept 1887
Carbondale, No. 82, Garfield, Carbondale, 16 Sept 1890
Rifle, No. 129, Garfield, Rifle, 22 Sept 1908

Royal Arch Masons
Glenwood, No. 22, Garfield, Glenwood Springs
Rifle, No. 48, Garfield, Rifle

Knights Templar
Glenwood Springs Commandery, No. 20, Garfield, Glenwood Spgs, 1891 Aug 31

Eastern Star
Crystal, No. 57, Garfield, Carbondale
Erica, No. 69, Garfield, Glenwood Springs
Jewel, No. 77, Garfield, Rifle

Odd Fellows
Book Cliff, No. 45, Garfield, Rifle
Glenwood, No. 68, Garfield, Glenwood Springs
Mount Sopris, No. 75, Garfield, Carbondale
Grand River, No. 107, Garfield, New Castle
Silt, No. 170, Garfield, Silt

Garfield County

Rebekahs
Elizabeth-Forget-Me-Not, No. 46, Garfield, Rifle
Yampah, No. 73, Garfield, Glenwood Springs
Seven Stars, No. 91, Garfield, Carbondale
New Castle, No. 114, Garfield, New Castle

Knights of Pythias
New Castle, No. 79, Garfield, New Castle
Garfield, No. 86, Garfield, Glenwood Springs, 1893 Jan 9

Pythian Sisters
New Castle, No. 30, Garfield, New Castle

Benevolent Protective Order of Elks
Rifle, No. 2195, Garfield, Rifle
Glenwood Springs, No. 2286, Garfield, Glenwood Springs

City & Town Halls

Glenwood Springs, 101 8th St, Glenwood Springs, CO 81601, 870-384-6400, http://www.ci.glenwood-springs.co.us
Rifle, 202 Railroad Ave, Rifle, CO 81650, 970-665-6400, https://www.rifleco.org
Carbondale, 511 Colorado Ave, Carbondale, CO 81623, 970-963-2733, https://www.carbondalegov.org
New Castle, 450 W Main St, New Castle, CO 81647, 970-984-2311, https://www.newcastlecolorado.org
Silt, 231 N 7th St, Silt, CO 81652-970-876-2353, https://www.townofsilt.org
Parachute, 222 Grand Valley Wy, Parachute, CO 81635, 970-285-7630, https://www.colorado.gov/parachutecolorado
Battlement Mesa, 1117 River Bluff Rd, Parachute, CO 81635, 970-285-7000, http://bmmetrodistrict.com

Archives & Manuscript Collections

None

Historical & Genealogical Societies

Carbondale Historical Society, Thompson House Museum, 301 Lewies Ln, Carbondale, CO 81623, (970) 414-1078, https://www.carbondalehistory.org
Frontier Historical Society, Historical Museum, 1001 Colorado Ave, Glenwood Springs, CO 81601-3319, (970) 945-4448, http://www.glenwoodhistory.com
Marble Historical Society, Historical Museum, 412 W Main St, Marble, CO 81623, (970) 963-9815, http://marblehistory.org
New Castle Historical Society, Historical Museum, 116 N 4th St, P.O. Box 883, New Castle, CO 81647, (970) 984-2311, https://www.newcastlecolorado.org/community/page/history-highland-cemetery-and-museum
Silt Historical Society, Historical Museum, 707 Orchard, P.O. Box 401, Silt, CO 81652, (970) 876-5801, https://silthistorical.org

Historical Assets Colorado

Local Libraries
Carbondale Branch Library, 320 Sopris Ave, Carbondale, CO 81623, (970) 963-2889, https://www.gcpld.org

Garfield County Public Library System-Parachute Branch, 244 Grand Valley Way, Parachute, CO 81635-9608, (970) 285-9870, https://www.gcpld.org

Glenwood Springs Branch Library, 815 Cooper Ave, Glenwood Springs, CO 81601, (970) 945-5958, https://www.gcpld.org

New Castle Branch Library, 402 W Main, P.O. Box 320, New Castle, CO 81647-0320, (970) 984-2347, http://www.gcpld.org

Rifle Branch Library, 207 East Ave, Rifle, CO 81650, (970) 625-3471, https://www.gcpld.org

Silt Branch Library, 680 Home Ave, Silt, CO 81652, (970) 876-5500, https://www.gcpld.org

Links
CO GenWeb
http://cogenweb.com/garfield/

Cyndi's List
https://www.cyndislist.com/us/co/counties/garfield/

FamilySearch Wiki
https://www.familysearch.org/wiki/en/Garfield_County,_Colorado_Genealogy

Linkpendium
http://www.linkpendium.com/garfield-co-genealogy/

RootsWeb Wiki
https://wiki.rootsweb.com/wiki/index.php/Garfield_County,_Colorado

Wikipedia
https://en.wikipedia.org/wiki/Garfield_County,_Colorado

Historic Hotels
1893 Hotel Colorado, 526 Pine St, Glenwood Springs, CO 81601, 970-945-6511, https://www.hotelcolorado.com

1915 Hotel Denver, 402 7th St, Glenwood Springs, CO 81601, 970-945-6565, https://thehoteldenver.com

Museums & Historic Sites
Carbondale Historical Society, Thompson House Museum, 301 Lewies Ln, Carbondale, CO 81623, (970) 414-1078, https://www.carbondalehistory.org

Frontier Historical Society, Historical Museum, 1001 Colorado Ave, Glenwood Springs, CO 81601-3319, (970) 945-4448, http://www.glenwoodhistory.com

Marble Historical Society, Historical Museum, 412 W Main St, Marble, CO 81623, (970) 963-9815, http://marblehistory.org

New Castle Historical Society, Historical Museum, 116 N 4th St, P.O. Box 883, New Castle, CO 81647, (970) 984-2311, https://www.newcastlecolorado.org/community/page/history-highland-cemetery-and-museum

Garfield County

Rifle Heritage Center, 337 East Ave, Rifle, CO 81650, (970) 625-4862, https://www.rifleheritagecenter.com

Silt Historical Society, Historical Museum, 707 Orchard, P.O. Box 401, Silt, CO 81652, (970) 876-5801, https://silthistorical.org

Vintage Ski World Museum, 1676 CO Rd 100, Carbondale, CO 81623, (970) 963-9025, http://www.vintageskiworld.com

Special Events & Scenic Locations

The Garfield County Fair & Rodeo is held in July and August most years, at the Garfield County Fairground, 1001 Railroad Ave, Rifle, CO 81650, 970-625-2514, https://www.garfieldcountyfair.com.

There is a calendar of Garfield County events on Eventbrite here: https://www.eventbrite.com/d/co—garfield/events/

There is a calendar of events in or near Rifle here: https://www.colorado.com/co/rifle/festivals-events

Flat Tops Wilderness
Grand Mesa National Forest
Harvey Gap State Park
Rifle Falls State Park
Rifle Gat State Park
Routt National Forest
White River National Forest
Dinosaur Diamond Prehistoric Highway National Scenic Byway
Flat Tops Trail Scenic Byway
West Elk Loop Scenic Byway

Ghost Towns & Other Sparsely Populated Places

Allen, Antlers, Austin, Balzac, Cardiff, Chacra, Coal Mine, Coalridge, Coryell, Ferguson, Glenwood, Highmore, Leon, Marion, Morris, No Name, Rockford, Sands, Satank, Shoshone, Siloam Springs, Silt, South Canon, Sunshine, Una, West Glenwood, Wheeler

Newspapers

The Grand Valley News. (Grand Valley, Garfield County, Colo.) 1???-19??
New Castle Nonpareil. (New Castle, Colo.) 18??-1905
The Glenwood Echo and Advocate. (Glenwood Springs, Colo.) 188?-????
The New Empire. (Glenwood Springs, Colo.) 188?-1889
The Ute Chief. (Glenwood Springs, Colo.) 1885-1???
The Meeker Herald. (Meeker, Colo.) 1885-Current
The Glenwood Echo. (Glenwood Springs, Garfield County, Colo.) 1885-1891
Glenwood Springs Advocate. (Glenwood Springs, Colo.) 1886-1886
Glenwood Daily News. (Glenwood Springs, Colo.) 1887-1889
Glenwood Springs Republican. (Glenwood Springs, Colo.) 1887-1892
The Avalanche. (Carbondale, Garfield County, Colo.) 1888-1891

Historical Assets Colorado

Glenwood Springs Ute Chief. (Glenwood Springs, Colo.) 1888-1889
Rio Blanco News. (Meeker, Colo.) 1889-1892
Glenwood Springs Ute Chief-News. (Glenwood Springs, Colo.) 1889-1???
The Daily New Empire. (Glenwood Springs, Colo.) 1889-1???
The People's Herald. (Glenwood Springs, Colo.) 189?-1???
The Rifle Reveille. (Rifle, Garfield County, Colo.) 1890-1916
The Pool. (Glenwood Springs, Colo.) 1890-1???
The Avalanche and Glenwood Echo. (Glenwood Springs, Colo.) 1891-1891
The Avalanche Echo. (Glenwood Springs, Colo.) 1891-1???
The Avalanche in it Daily. (Glenwood Springs, Colo.) 1891-1892
The Republican. (Glenwood Springs, Colo.) 1892-1892
The Avalanche. (Glenwood Springs, Colo.) 1892-1900
The Weekly Ledger. (Glenwood Springs, Colo.) 1892-1893
The New Castle News. (New Castle, Colo.) 1893-1???
The Ledger. (Glenwood Springs, Colo.) 1893-1896
The People's Herald and Glenwood Springs Republican. (Glenwood Springs, Colo.) 1893-189?
The Parachute Index. (Parachute, Garfield County, Colo.) 1895-1???
The Weekly Ledger. (Glenwood Springs, Colo.) 1896-1896
The Glenwood Post and The Weekly Ledger. (Glenwood Springs, Colo.) 1897-1897
The Glenwood Post. (Glenwood Springs, Colo.) 1897-Current
The Glenwood Daily Post. (Glenwood Springs, Colo.) 1897-1???
The Carbondale Item. (Carbondale, Garfield County, Colo.) 1898-19??
Glenwood Springs Morning Reminder. (Glenwood Springs, Colo.) 19??-1967
Garfield County Leader. (Silt, Garfield County, Colo.) 19??-19??
The Glenwood High Country Gazette. (Glenwood Springs, Colo.) 19??-19??
The Daily Avalanche. (Glenwood Springs, Colo.) 1900-19??
The Morning Reminder. (Glenwood Springs, Colo.) 19??-19??
The Daily Advance. (Glenwood Springs, Colo.) 1903-19??
The Rifle Telegram. (Rifle, Colo.) 1903-1916
The Garfield County Democrat and The New Castle Nonpareil. (New Castle, Garfield County, Colo.) 1905-19??
The Garfield County News. (Silt, Garfield County, Colo.) 1911-19??
Silt Searchlight. (Silt, Garfield County, Colo.) 1913-19??
The Telegram-Reveille. (Rifle, Colo.) 1916-1920
The Rifle Telegram. (Rifle, Colo.) 1920-Current
The Crystal River Empire. (Carbondale, Garfield County, Colo.) 1923-19??
The Daily Post-Reminder. (Glenwood Springs, Colo.) 193?-1936
The Glenwood Daily Post. (Glenwood Springs, Colo.) 1936-19??
Western Colorado Farm and Ranch Reporter. (Rifle, Colo.) 1950-19??
Glenwood Springs Sage. (Glenwood Springs, Colo.) 1959-1967
The Glenwood Springs Reminder Record. (Glenwood Springs, Colo.) 1964-19??
Sage Reminder. (Glenwood Springs, Colo.) 1967-1976
Glenwood Gazette. (Glenwood Springs, Colo.) 1968-19??
The Gazette Shopper. (Glenwood Springs, Colo.) 1968-19??
The Roaring Fork Valley Journal. (Carbondale, Colo.) 1975-1975

Garfield County

The Roaring Fork Review & Valley Journal. (Carbondale, Colo.) 1975-1977
The Free! Weekly Newspaper. (Glenwood Springs, Colo.) 1976-1977
The Weekly Newspaper. ([Glenwood Springs, Colo.]) 1976-1976
The Rocky Mountain Observer. ([Glenwood Springs, Colo.]) 1976-1977
The Roaring Fork Valley Journal. (Carbondale, Colo.) 1977-1987
The Weekly Newspaper & The Rocky Mountain Observer. (Glenwood Springs, Colo.) 1977-1981
The Weekly Newspaper. (Glenwood Springs, Colo.) 1981-1985
The Free Weekly Newspaper. (Glenwood Springs, Colo.) 1985-1987
Valley West Dispatch. (Parachute, Colo.) 1987-????
The Valley Journal. (Carbondale, Colo.) 1987-Current
The Free Weekly. (Glenwood Springs, Colo.) 1987-19??

Places on the National Register
Battlement Mesa, Battlement Mesa Schoolhouse, 7201 300 Rd.
Carbondale, Holland—Thompson Property, 1605 CO 133
Carbondale, Missouri Heights School, Cty Rd. 102, 0.5 mi. E of jct. with Cty Rd. 100
Carbondale, Satank Bridge, Cty. Rd. 106
Glenwood Springs, Canyon (Canon) Creek School, District No. 32, 0566 Cty Rd. 137
Glenwood Springs, Cardiff Coke Ovens, Co. Rt. 116, approximately 1.5 mi. S. of Glenwood
Glenwood Springs, Citizens National Bank Building, 801 Grand Ave.
Glenwood Springs, Earnest Ranch, 6471 Co. Rd. 117
Glenwood Springs, Glenwood Springs Hydroelectric Plant, 601 6th St.
Glenwood Springs, Hotel Colorado, 526 Pine St.
Glenwood Springs, South Canon Bridge, Cty. Rd. 134
Glenwood Springs, Starr Manor, 901 Palmer Ave.
Glenwood Springs, Sumers Lodge, 1200 Mountain Dr.
Glenwood Springs, Taylor, Edward T., House, 903 Bennett Ave.
Parachute, Wasson—McKay Place, 259 Cardinal Way
Rifle, Havemeyer-Willcox Canal Pumphouse and Forebay, W of Rifle
Rifle, Rifle Bridge, Off SR 6/24 over Colorado River
Rifle, US Post Office—Rifle Main, Railroad Ave. and Fourth St.
Silt, Nunns, John Herbert, House, 311 N. 7th St.

USGS Historic Places
Carbonate, Carbonate, 39.7430376, -107.3467219
Glenwood Springs, Frontier Historical Society Museum, 39.5435931, -107.3264428
Unknown, Atchee Post Office, 0, 0
Unknown, Trappers Lake Post Office, 0, 0

Grand Army of the Republic Posts
W S Hancock, No. 66, Garfield, Glenwood Springs
Mount Sopris, No. 68, Garfield, Carbondale
Gen Shields, No. 78, Garfield, New Castle
Myron W Reed, No. 108, Garfield, Rifle

Historical Assets Colorado

USGS Historic Military Places
None

Military Bases
None

Post Offices

Name	Established	Discontinued	ZIP
Antlers	1891 July 1	1954 Apr 30*	
Atchee	1905 Sept 26	1940 Apr 30*	
Austin	1890 July 21	1896 Jun 6	
Axial	1893 Mar 6	1958 Apr 30*	
Balzac	1891 May 23	1903 Mar 13	
Barlow	1883 June 25	1884 Mar 28	
Carbonate	1881 Apr 13	1886 Nov 15	
Carbondale	1887 Jan 6	1887 Feb 14	
Carbondale 2	1887 May 14		81623
Cardiff	1889 Aug 1	1918 July 31	
Catherine	1892 Oct 18	1902 Feb 15	
Chapman	1884 May 19	1888 Apr 23	
Coalridge	1889 Aug 6	1893 Oct 26*	
Dailey	1900 Sept 6	1903 Dec 14	
Early Spring	1883 Apr 20	1883 July 20	
El Jebel	1973 May 1		
Emma	1883 Nov 23	1949 May 31*	
Farwell	1888 Apr 25	1888 Sept 18	
Ferguson	1883 APR 16	1891 July 1	
Glenwood Springs	1884 Mar 28		81601
Grand Valley	1904 Aug 19	1980 July 4	
Gresham	1883 June 20	1884 Dec 1	
Hecla	1891 Apr 29	1895 June 11	
Highmore	1889 Mar 21	1931 Oct 15	
Marion	1889 Aug 6	1912 Jan 31*	
Meeker	1871 Sept 29		81641
Morris	1902 Jan 15	1903 Apr 15	
Newcastle	1888 Apr 23		81647
Parachute	1885 July 27	1904 Aug 19	
Parachute 2	1980 July 4		81635
Rangely	1885 Sept 10		81648
Rangley	1884 Aug 26	1885 Sept 10	
Raven	1898 Aug 11	1939 Apr 29	
Rifle	1884 Apr 23		81650
Riland	1913 Sept 24	1946 Nov 26	
Satank	1882 June 27	1904 July 14	
Shoshone	1907 Sept 3	1910 June 30	
Silt	1898 Oct 27		81652
South Canon	1905 Aug 21	1916 Sept 30	

Garfield County

Sunlight	1897 Oct 19	1912 Sept 2*		
Trappers Lake	1927 May 26	1934 Oct 31		
Vulcan	1892 Oct 6	1893 Oct 23		
Waterman	1888 May 21			
White River	1888 Aug 15	1908 Mar 15		

Topo Quads

Adams Lake	394500N	393730N	1072230W	1073000W
Anvil Points	393730N	393000N	1075230W	1080000W
Badger Wash	392230N	391500N	1085230W	1090000W
Basalt	392230N	391500N	1070000W	1070730W
Baxter Pass	393730N	393000N	1085230W	1090000W
Broken Rib Creek	394500N	393730N	1070730W	1071500W
Calf Canyon	393730N	393000N	1083730W	1084500W
Carbonate	394500N	393730N	1071500W	1072230W
Carbondale	393000N	392230N	1070730W	1071500W
Carbonera	393000N	392230N	1085230W	1090000W
Cattle Creek	393000N	392230N	1071500W	1072230W
Center Mountain	393000N	392230N	1072230W	1073000W
Circle Dot Gulch	393730N	393000N	1080730W	1081500W
Corcoran Peak	392230N	391500N	1083000W	1083730W
Cottonwood Pass	393730N	393000N	1070000W	1070730W
De Beque	392230N	391500N	1080730W	1081500W
Deep Creek Point	394500N	393730N	1073000W	1073730W
Deep Lake	395230N	394500N	1071500W	1072230W
Desert Gulch	393730N	393000N	1082230W	1083000W
Dotsero	394500N	393730N	1070000W	1070730W
Douglas Pass	393730N	393000N	1084500W	1085230W
Flatiron Mountain	392230N	391500N	1073000W	1073730W
Forked Gulch	393730N	393000N	1080000W	1080730W
Garvey Canyon	393000N	392230N	1083730W	1084500W
Gibson Gulch	393000N	392230N	1073000W	1073730W
Glenwood Springs	393730N	393000N	1071500W	1072230W
Hawxhurst Creek	392230N	391500N	1075230W	1080000W
Henderson Ridge	393730N	393000N	1083000W	1083730W
Highline Lake	392230N	391500N	1084500W	1085230W
Hightower Mountain	392230N	391500N	1073730W	1074500W
Horse Mountain	394500N	393730N	1074500W	1075230W
Housetop Mountain	392230N	391500N	1080000W	1080730W
Howard Canyon	393000N	392230N	1084500W	1085230W
Hunter Mesa	393000N	392230N	1073730W	1074500W
Leon	393000N	392230N	1070000W	1070730W
Long Point	393000N	392230N	1081500W	1082230W
Middle Dry Fork	393000N	392230N	1083000W	1083730W
Mount Blaine	393730N	393000N	1081500W	1082230W
Mount Sopris	392230N	391500N	1070730W	1071500W

Historical Assets Colorado

New Castle	393730N	393000N	1073000W	1073730W
North Mamm Peak	393000N	392230N	1074500W	1075230W
Parachute	393000N	392230N	1080000W	1080730W
Quaker Mesa	392230N	391500N	1072230W	1073000W
Red Pinnacle	393000N	392230N	1080730W	1081500W
Rifle	393730N	393000N	1074500W	1075230W
Rifle Falls	394500N	393730N	1073730W	1074500W
Ruby Lee Reservoir	392230N	391500N	1083730W	1084500W
Rulison	393000N	392230N	1075230W	1080000W
Shoshone	393730N	393000N	1070730W	1071500W
Silt	393730N	393000N	1073730W	1074500W
South Mamm Peak	392230N	391500N	1074500W	1075230W
Stony Ridge	392230N	391500N	1071500W	1072230W
Storm King Mtn	393730N	393000N	1072230W	1073000W
Sugarloaf Mountain	395230N	394500N	1070000W	1070730W
Sweetwater Lake	395230N	394500N	1070730W	1071500W
The Saddle	393000N	392230N	1082230W	1083000W
Trappers Lake	400000N	395230N	1070730W	1071500W
Wagon Track Ridge	392230N	391500N	1081500W	1082230W
Winter Flats	392230N	391500N	1082230W	1083000W

Suggested Reading

Arthur, Kathleen. *The Arthur Ranch on East Divide Creek: Memories of Western Colorado in the 1960s and 70s.* San Bernardino, CA: NP, 2013.

Boulton, Alice. Silt, *Colorado Homesteads, 1880-1940: Settling an Isolated Valley.* Silt, CO: Silt Historical Park, 2006.

Boulton, Margaret Irene Trust and Owen Boulton. *Reflections of Dry Hollow Ranch Memories.* Silt, CO: Silt Historical Society, 1966.

Inventory of the County Archives of Colorado, No. 23, Garfield County (Glenwood Springs). Denver: Historical Records Survey, 1941.

Loshbaugh, Harrette and Charles Loshbaugh. *Recollections of Life in Rifle, 1920-1995.* Rifle, CO: Silt Historical Society, 1996.

Murray, Erlene Durrant. *Lest We Forget: a Short History of Early Grand Valley, Colorado, Originally Called Parachute, Colorado.* Parachute, CO: mPress ink, 2003.

Rifle Shots: a Story of Rifle Colorado (Garfield County). Rifle, CO: Rifle Reading Club, 1973.

Shrull, Dale and Paul S Kimball. *The Legend of the Burning Mountain: an Early History of New Castle.* Glenwood Springs, CO: Stoney Mountain Pub, 2000.

Urquhart, Lena M. *Roll Call: the Violent and Lawless.* Denver: Golden Bell Press, 1967.

Witt, Anita McCune. *They Came from Missouri: the History of Missouri Heights, Colorado.* Glenwood Springs, CO, Gran Farnum, 1998.

Gilpin County

Introduction
Established: 1861   Population: 5,828
Formed from: Original
Adjacent Counties: Boulder, Jefferson, Clear Creek, Grand
County Seat: Central City
   Other Communities: Black Hawk, Coal Creek, Rollinsville, Russell Gulch
Website, http://www.gilpincounty.org
Area Codes: 720
Zip Codes: 80422, 80427, 80474

Historical Assets Colorado

Gilpin County Courthouse

Courthouses & County Government

Gilpin County
   http://www.gilpincounty.org
Gilpin County Courthouse (1st Judicial District), 2960 Dory Hill Rd, Black Hawk, CO 80422, 303-582-5522; http://www.courts.state.co.us/Courts/County/Index.cfm?County_ID=1
Assessor, 203 Eureka St, Central City, CO 80427, 303-582-5451; http://www.co.gilpin.co.us/Assessor/default.htm
Board of County Commissioners, 200 Eureka St, Central City, CO 80427, http://www.gilpincounty.org/board_of_county_commissioners
Clerk & Recorder, 203 Eureka St, Central City, CO 80427, 303-582-5321; http://www.co.gilpin.co.us/clerkrecorder/index.html
Coroner, P.O. Box 333, Central City, CO 80428, 303-515-4333; http://www.gilpin-county.org/departments/county_coroner
Public Health, 101 Norton Dr, Black Hawk, CO 80422, 303-582-5803; http://www.co.gilpin.co.us/Public%20Health/homedefault.htm
Treasurer, 203 Eureka St, Central City, CO 80427, 303-582-5222; http://www.co.gilpin.co.us/Treasurer/default.htm

County Records

Birth Unk	Marriage 1860	Divorce Unk
Death Unk	Land 1860	Probate Unk
Court Unk		
CSA Death 1941		
CSA Burial 1942		

Gilpin County

County & Municipal Records Held at the State Level

The Colorado State Archives

Physical Records
Assessor
Clerk & Recorder
County Commissioners
County Court
District Court
Justice Court
WPA Historical Records
WPA Religious Institutions
　Survey
WPA Central City
Cities
　Black Hawk
　Central City

Records on Film
1885 Census
Clerk & Recorder
County Court
District Court
Mining Districts
School Districts
Cities
　Black Hawk
　Central City

Records on Master Film
Clerk & Recorder
County Court
District Court
Justice/Justice of the Peace
　Court
Probate Court
Mining District Records
School Districts
Cities
　Black Hawk
　Central City

The Denver Public Library
Alps Gold Mining Company Records, 1889-1907
Bates-Hunter Mining Company Records, 1869-1893
Bates Mining Company Account Book, 1864-1866
Big Five Mining Companies Records, 1892-1921
Bobtail Gold Mining Company Records, 1864-1876
California Gold Mining Company Records, 1889-1892
Central City Board of Alderman Minutes 1864-1867
Chain O'Mines Records, 1928-1934
Chris Paul Grocery Book, 1903-1906
Colorado Bureau of Mines Records, 1897-1915
Colorado Deeds, 1868-1911
Colorado Gold Mining Company Records, 1861-1864
Conlee Burroughs Mine Company Records, 1890-1903
Corydon Leasing Company Records, 1912
East Boston Mining Company Records, 1901-1905
Eight Associates Records, 1864-1865
German Insurance Company Records, 1886-1894
Gilpin County Mining Companies Records, 1859-1945
Gilpin County Opera House Association Stock Certificates, 1882-1914
Gilpin County Receipt Collection, 1879-1880
Gilpin County Voting Records, 1895-1903
Gilpin Tramway Company Records, 1889
Hubert Mining Company Records, 1895
Jefferson Mine Pool Account Book, 1894
Kansas-Burroughs COnsolidated Mining Company Records, 1870-1906
Kansas Mine Records, 1879-1880
LaCrosse Gold Mining Company Records, 1877-1905
Leavenworth Gold Mining Company Records, 1864-1866
London Deep Mines Company Records, 1932-1937

Historical Assets Colorado

Maumee Gold Mining Company Records, 1909-1910
Millers Joint Stock Mining Company Record Book, 1858-1869
National Gold Mining & Milling Company Minute Book, 1899-1901
Nevadaville Records, 1873-1896, 1907
New York-Central Gold Mining Company Records, 1896-1909
Pewabic Gold Mining Company Records, 1866-1870
Pine Creek Mining District Association Records, 1895
Quartz Hill Mining & Tunneling Company Records, 1875-1899
Ridgewood Mining Company Records, 1932-1933
Rio Claro Milling & Mines Company Records, 1908-1915
Rollins Gold & Silver Mining Company Records, 1880-1887
Rocky Mountain National Bank Records, 1866-1941
Savage Leasing Company Account Book, 1911-1929
Transatlantic Fire Insurance Company Records, 1890-1906
Twolon Mining Company Records, 1903-1905
Western Mill Company Day Book & Journal, 1861-1864
Whale Mining & Milling Company Correspondence, 1894
Whipple Gold Mining Company Account Book, 1878-1880
WWI Draft Registration Cards (microfilm)

School Districts

School Districts, http://www.adcogov.org/local-school-districts
Boulder Valley School District RE-2, 6500 E Arapahoe Rd, Boulder, CO 80303, 303-447-1010; https://www.bvsd.org
Gilpin County School District RE-1, 10595 Hwy 119, Black Hawk, CO 80422; http://gilpin.k12.co.us/

Historic School Districts

1. Central City
2. Bald Mountain, Nevadaville
3. Black Hawk
4. Lake Gulch, Rollinsville
5. Russell Gulch
6. Hughesville
7. Rollinsville
8. Mountain House
9. Bay State
10. Thorne Lake
11. Apex
12. Quartz Valley
13. East Portal, Tolland

Jt 67. Nederland

Fraternal Organizations

Granges
Gilpin, No. 368, Gilpin, Blackhawk, 6 Apr 1918

Masons

Ancient Free & Accepted Masons
Nevada, No. 4, Gilpin, Nevadaville, 10 Dec 1861
Central, No. 6, Gilpin, Central City, 6 Oct 1868
Chivington, No. 6, Gilpin, Central City, 10 Dec 1861
Black Hawk, No. 11, Gilpin, Black Hawk, 1 Oct 1866

Gilpin County

Royal Arch Masons
Central City, No. 1, Gilpin, Central City

Knights Templar
Central City Commandery, No. 2, Gilpin, Central City, 1866 Nov 8

Eastern Star
Golden Queen, No. 17, Gilpin, Central City

Odd Fellows
Rocky Mountain, No. 2, Gilpin, Central City, 1865 June 13
Colorado, No. 3, Gilpin, Black Hawk, 1866 May 16
Nevada, No. 6, Gilpin, Bald Mountain, 1868 Sept 23
Rising Star, No. 20, Gilpin, Central City, 1875
Russell Gulch, No. 41, Gilpin, Russell Gulch
Scandia, No. 60, Gilpin, Black Hawk

Rebekahs
None

Knights of Pythias
Black Hawk, No. 4, Gilpin, Black Hawk
Gilpin, No. 5, Gilpin, Central City
Richmond, No. 37, Gilpin, Bald Mountain

Pythian Sisters
Calanthe, No. 34, Gilpin, Central City
Black Hawk, No. 41, Gilpin, Black Hawk

Benevolent Protective Order of Elks
Central City, No. 557, Gilpin, Central City

City & Town Halls

Central City, 116 Lawrence St, Central City, CO 80427, https://www.colorado.gov/centralcity
Black Hawk, 201 Selak St, Black Hawk, CO 80422, 303-582-5221, https://www.cityofblackhawk.org

Archives & Manuscript Collections

None

Historical & Genealogical Societies

Central City Opera House Association, Historical Museum, 124 Eureka St, P.O. Box 218, Central City, CO 80427, (303) 623-7167, http://centralcityopera.org
Gilpin County Historical Society, Gilpin County Museum, 228 E First High St, P.O. Box 247, Central City, CO 80427-0247, (303) 582-5283, http://www.gilpinhistory.org

Local Libraries

Gilpin County Public Library, 15131 CO 119, Black Hawk, CO 80422, (303) 582-5777, https://www.gilpinlibrary.org

Historical Assets Colorado

Links
CO GenWeb
http://stanwyck.com/CCGilpin/
Cyndi's List
https://www.cyndislist.com/us/co/counties/gilpin/
FamilySearch Wiki
https://www.familysearch.org/wiki/en/Gilpin_County,_Colorado_Genealogy
Linkpendium
http://www.linkpendium.com/gilpin-co-genealogy/
RootsWeb Wiki
https://wiki.rootsweb.com/wiki/index.php/Gilpin_County,_Colorado
Wikipedia
https://en.wikipedia.org/wiki/Gilpin_County,_Colorado

Historic Hotels
None

Museums & Historic Sites
Central City Opera House Association, Historical Museum, 124 Eureka St, P.O. Box 218, Central City, CO 80427, (303) 623-7167, http://centralcityopera.org

Coeur d'Alene Mine Shaft House Museum, Academy Hill, Central City, CO 80427, https://www.gilpinhistory.org/coeur-d-alene-mine

Gilpin County Historical Society, Gilpin County Museum, 228 E First High St, P.O. Box 247, Central City, CO 80427-0247, (303) 582-5283, http://www.gilpinhistory.org

Lace House Museum, 161 Main St, Black Hawk, CO 80422, (303) 582-5382

Thomas House Museum, 209 Eureka St, Central City, CO 80427, https://www.gilpinhistory.org/thomas-house

Washington Hall Museum, 117 Eureka St, Central City, CO 80427, https://www.gilpinhistory.org/washington-hall

Special Events & Scenic Locations
The Gilpin County Fair is held in July most years at the Gilpin County Fairgrounds, 230 Norton Dr, Black Hawk, CO 80422, 303-582-9106, https://gilpincountyfair.com

Gilpin County keeps a calendar of events here: http://www.gilpincounty.org/eventscalendar

Arapaho National Forest
James Peak Wilderness
Roosevelt National Forest
Golden Gate Canyon State Park
Continental Divide National Scenic Trail

Gilpin County

Peak to Peak Scenic and Historic Byway
Central City-Black Hawk Historic District

Ghost Towns & Other Sparsely Populated Places

American City, Apex, Bald Mountain, Baltimore, Cottonwood, East Portal, Missouri City, Mountain City, Nevadaville (Bald Mountain, Nevada City), Nugget, Rollinsville, Russell Gulch, Smith Hill, Tiptop, Tolland (Mammoth), Wide Awake

Newspapers

The Colorado Herald. (Central [City], Colo.) 18??-1???
The Post. (Black Hawk, Colo.) 18??-1???
The Weekly Mining Journal. (Black Hawk, Colo.) 18??-1866
Rocky Mountain Gold Reporter and Mountain City Herald. (Mountain City, Jefferson [Central City, Colo.]) 1859-1859
Colorado Mining Life. (Central City, Colo.) 1862-18??
Tri-Weekly Mining Life. (Central City, Colo.) 1862-18??
The Tri-Weekly Miner's Gazette. (Central City, Colo.) 1862-1863
Tri-Weekly Miner's Register. (Central City, Colo.) 1862-1863
The Colorado Miner. (Black Hawk, C.t. [Colo.]) 1863-1???
The Daily Colorado Miner. (Black Hawk [Colo.]) 1863-1???
The Weekly Miners' Register. (Central City, Colo. Terr. [Colo.]) 1863-1868
The Daily Mining Journal. (Black Hawk, Colo.) 1863-1866
The Daily Miners' Register. (Central City, Colo.) 1863-1868
The Weekly Colorado Mining Journal. (Black Hawk, Colo.) 1864-1???
The Weekly Colorado Times. ([Black Hawk] Colorado) 1866-1868
The Daily Colorado Times. (Black Hawk, Colo.) 1866-1868
The Weekly Colorado Herald. (Central City, Colo.) 1868-1875
The Daily Colorado Herald. (Central City, Colo.) 1868-18??
Weekly Central City Register. (Central City, Colo.) 1868-1875
Daily Central City Register. (Central City, Colo.) 1868-1877
Daily Black Hawk Journal. (Black Hawk, Colo.) 1872-1873
The Coach. (Central City, Colo.) 1872-1873
Central City Weekly Register. (Central City, Colo.) 1875-1878
The Post. (Central City, Colo.) 1876-1???
Daily Register. (Central City, Colo.) 1877-1878
Daily Town Talk. (Central City, Colo.) 1877-18??
Daily Central Register. (Central City, Colo.) 1878-1878
The Evening Call. (Central City, Colo.) 1878-1878
Weekly Central City Register. (Central City, Colo.) 1878-1878
The Daily Register-Call. (Central City, Colo.) 1878-1890
Weekly Register-Call. (Central City, Colo.) 1878-Current
Weekly Ledger. (Central City, Colo.) 1883-????
Black Hawk Times. (Black Hawk, Colo.) 1886-1887
Gilpin County Observer. (Central City, Colo.) 1887-1897
Black Hawk Advertiser. (Black Hawk, Colo.) 1888-1???
The Pine Creek Gold Belt. (Pine Creek, Colo.) 1896-1???

Historical Assets Colorado

Gilpin County Republican. (Central City, Colo.) 1896-1???
The Pine Cone. (Apex, Colo.) 1897-1???
The Star. (Black Hawk, Colo.) 1897-1897
The Black Hawk Star. (Black Hawk, Colo.) 1897-1???
Gilpin Observer. (Central City, Colo.) 1897-1921
Black Hawk Independent. (Black Hawk, Colo.) 1898-1???
The Gilpin Miner. (Central City, Colo.) 1898-1???
The Herald. (Tolland, Colo.) 19??-19??
Gilpin County Miner. (Central City, Colo.) 193?-19??
The Central City Tommy-Knawker. (Central City, Gilpin County, Colo.) 1953-1968
The Front Range Journal. (Idaho Springs And Central City, Colo.) 1968-198?
The Little Kingdom Come. (Central City, Colo.) 1970-Current

Places on the National Register
Central City, Central City Opera House, Eureka St.
Central City, Central City—Black Hawk Historic District, On SR 119
Central City, Teller House, Eureka St.
Pinecliffe, Winks Panorama, SW of Pinecliffe
Pinecliffe, Winks Panorama (Boundary Increase), 213 Winks Way
Russell Gulch, Russell Gulch I.O.O.F. Hall No. 47—Wagner and Askew, 81 Russell Gulch Rd.

USGS Historic Places
Gilpin, Central City, American City, 39.8724873, -105.5872225
Gilpin, Central City, Apex, 39.8655851, -105.5702458
Gilpin, Central City, Wideawake, 39.8499875, -105.5216644
Gilpin, Nederland, Baltimore, 39.9033205, -105.5744444
Gilpin, Nederland, Perigo, 39.8791541, -105.5308315
Gilpin, Nederland, Phoenix, 39.9285982, -105.5355541
Gilpin, Nederland, Tolland Post Office, 39.9049872, -105.5891671

Grand Army of the Republic Posts
Ellsworth, No. 20, Gilpin, Central City

USGS Historic Military Places
None

Military Bases
None

Post Offices

Apex	1894 Nov 12	1932 Apr 30
Bald Mountain	1869 Dec 16	1921 Oct 15
Baltimore	1896 Aug 28	1904 Oct 26
Black Hawk	1871 Feb 8	1895 Jan 30

Gilpin County

Black Hawk 2	1950 July 1		80422
Black Hawk Point	1862 Dec 6	1871 Feb 8	
Blackhawk	895 Jan 30	1950 July 1	
Central City	1869 Oct 8		80427
Colorado Sierra	1966 Aug 16	1980 May 1*	
East Portal	1923 Oct 12	1962 Jan 24*	
Gilpin	1897 Apr 7	1917 Sept 29	
Gold Dirt	1861 Aug 13	1867 Oct 11	
Missouri City	1860 Mar 24	1863 Jan 3	
Mountain City	1860 Jan 17	1869 Oct 8	
Nevada	1861 Jan 12	1869 Dec 16	
Nugget	1895 Nov 21	1901 Mar 15	
Pactoulus	1911 Mar 9	1912 Oct 15	
Perigo	1895 Mar 2	1905 Mar 15*	
Rollinsville	1871 Jan 31		80474
Russell Gulch	1879 Setp 29	1943 May 31	
South Boulder	1865 Dec 14	1869 Nov 22	
Tiptop	1890 Apr 18	1890 Dec 24	
Tolland	1904 Oct 26	1944 June 30	

Topo Quads

Black Hawk	395230N	394500N	1052230W	1053000W
Central City	395230N	394500N	1053000W	1053730W
Squaw Pass	394500N	393730N	1052230W	1053000W

Suggested Reading

Abbott, Dan and Dell A McCoy. *The Gilpin Railroad Era: Black Hawk, Central City, Nevadaville, Russell Gulch*. Denver: Sundance Books, 2009.

Brown, Robert L. *Central City and Gilpin County: Then and Now*. Caldwell, ID: Caxton Printers, 1994.

Cushman, Samuel and J P Waterman. *Central City, Black Hawk and Nevadaville: From the Earliest Settlement until Statehood: 1859-1876*. Aurora, CO: NP, 1991.

Cushman, Samuel. *The Gold Mines of Gilpin County, Colorado*. Central City, CO: Register Steam Printing House, 1876.

Granruth, Alan. *Bald Mountain Cemetery, Gilpin County, Colorado: History, Records and Inscriptions*. Lakewood, CO: Foothills Genealogical Society of Colorado, 1996.

Granruth, Alan et al. *The Little Kingdom of Gilpin: Gilpin County, Colorado*. NL: Gilpin Historical Society, 2000.

Leslie, Darlene, Kelle Rankin-Sunter, Deborah Wightman and William D MacKenzie. *Central City: the Richest Square Mile on Earth: and the History of Gilpin County*. NL: TB Pub, 1990.

The Little Kingdom of Gilpin: Smallest County in the State. Central City, CO: Register-Call Print, 1940.

Historical Assets Colorado

Grand County

Introduction

Established: 1874   Population: 14,843

Formed from: Summit

Adjacent Counties: Larimer, Gilpin, Boulder, Clear Creek, Summit, Eagle, Jackson, Routt

County Seat: Hot Sulphus Springs

Other Communities: Fraser, Granby, Grand Lake, Kremmling, Winter Park, Parshall, Tabernash, Radium

Website: https://co.grand.co.us

Area Codes: 970

Zip Codes: 80442, 80446, 80447, 80451, 80459, 80468, 80478, 80482

Historical Assets Colorado

Grand County Courthouse

Courthouses & County Government
Grand County
https://www.co.grand.co.us
Grand County Courthouse (14th Judicial District), 307 Moffat Ave, Hot Sulphur Springs, CO 80451, 970-725-3357; http://www.courts.state.co.us/Courts/County/Index.cfm?County_ID=45
Assessor, 308 Byers Ave, Hot Sulphur Springs, CO 80451, 970-725-3060; http://co.grand.co.us/Assessor/Assessor.html
Board of County Commissioners, 308 Byers Ave, Hot Sulphur Springs, CO 80451, 970-725-3100, https://www.co.grand.co.us/203/Board-of-County-Commissioners
Clerk & Recorder, 308 Byers Ave, Hot Sulphur Springs, CO 80451, 970-725-3347; http://co.grand.co.us/Clerk/clerkand.htm
Coroner, 1003 Eagle Ave, P.O. Box 828, Kremmling, CO 80459, 970-724-0083; https://www.co.grand.co.us/124/Coroner
Elections, 308 Byers Ave, P.O. Box 120, Hot Sulphur Springs, CO 80451, 970-725-3065; https://www.co.grand.co.us/147/Elections
Public Health, 150 Moffat Ave, Hot Sulphur Springs, CO 80451, 970-725-3288; http://co.grand.co.us/publichealth.html
Transportation (Road & Bridge), P.O. Box 9, 467 E Topaz Ave, Granby, CO 80446, 970-887-2123; https://www.co.grand.co.us/244/Road-Bridge
Treasurer, 308 Byers Ave, Hot Sulphur Springs, CO 80451, 970-725-3061; http://co.grand.co.us/Treasurer/Treasurer.html

County Records
Birth 1907	Marriage 1874	Divorce 1880
Death Unk	Land 1874	Probate 1880
Court 1880		

Grand County

County & Municipal Records Held at the State Level

The Colorado State Archives

Physical Records
Clerk & Recorder
County Court
District Court
Surveyor
WPA Historical Records
WPA Religious Institutions
    Survey
Cities
    Granby
    Hot Sulphur Springs
    Kremmling

Records on Film
Clerk & Recorder
Cities
    Hot Sulphur Springs
    Kremmling

Records on Master Film
Clerk & Recorder
County Court
District Court
Combined Courts
Probate Court
School Districts
Sheriff
Treasurer
Cities
    Hot Sulphur Springs
    Winter Park

The Denver Public Library

Big Lake Land & Irrigation Company Records, 1908-1914
Colorado Arlberg Club Records, 1921-2005
Grand County Mining Records, 1883
WWI Draft Registration Cards (microfilm)

School Districts

School Districts, http://www.adcogov.org/local-school-districts
East Grand School District No. 2, 299 CR 611, P.O. Box 125, Granby, CO 80446, 970-887-2581; http://www.egsd.org/
West Grand School District, No. 1, 715 Kinsey Ave, P.O. Box 515, Kremmling, CO 80459, 970-724-3217; https://www.wgsd.us/

Historic School Districts

1. Hot Sulphur Springs
2. Fraser
3. Grand Lake
4. [1883]
5. Kremmling
6. Colorow
7. Upper Williams Fork, Willow View
8. Blacktail, Radium
9. [1885]
Jt10. Hill Crest
11.
12. Muddy Valley
13. Willow Creek
14. Grandby
15. Sleepy Hollow, Knight
16. Tabernash
17. Lower Williams Fork, Columbine
18. [1920]
19. Troublesome
20. Parshall
21. Mountain View, Union High

Fraternal Organizations

Granges

Williams Park, No. 254, Grand, Scholl, 19 June 1915
Granby, No. 255, Grand, Granby, 26 June 1915

Masons

Ancient Free & Accepted Masons

High Country, No. 163, Grand, Kremmling, 27 Apr 2001

Historical Assets Colorado

    Mount Wolford, No. 163, Grand, Kremmling, 16 Sept 1925
    High Country, No. 181, Grand, Granby, 28 Jan 1959

Royal Arch Masons
None

Knights Templar
None

Eastern Star
Starlight, No. 127, Grand, Kremmling

Odd Fellows
Elk Mountain, No. 50, Grand, Kremmling
Grand Valley, No. 156, Grand, Grand Valley

Rebekahs
Delila, No. 71, Grand, Grand Valley
Dora, No. 111, Grand, Kremmling

Knights of Pythias
None

Pythian Sisters
None

Benevolent Protective Order of Elks
None

City & Town Halls

Hot Sulphur Springs, 513 Aspen St, Hot Sulphur Springs, CO 80451, 970-725-3933, http://www.hotsulphurspringsco.com
Fraser, 153 Fraser Ave, Fraser, CO 80442, 970-726-5491, https://frasercolorado.com
Granby, Zero W Jasper Ave, Granby, CO 80446, 970-887-2501, https://www.townofgranby.com
Grand Lake, 1026 Park Ave, Grand Lake, CO 80447, 970-627-3435, http://www.townofgrandlake.com
Kremmling, 200 Eagle Ave, Kremmling, CO 80459, 970-724-3249, http://www.townofkremmling.org
Winter Park, 50 Vaxquez Rd, Winter Park, CO 80482, 970-726-8081, https://wpgov.com

Archives & Manuscript Collections

Grand County Archive Center (digital); https://www.co.grand.co.us/Archive.aspx

Historical & Genealogical Societies

Grand County Historical Association, Grand County Museum & Pioneer Village, 110 E Byers Ave, P.O. Box 165, Hot Sulphur Springs, CO 80451, (970) 725-3939, http://www.grandcountymuseum.com
Grand Lake Area Historical Society, 610 Center Dr, P.O. Box 656, Grand Lake, CO 80447, (970) 627-9277, http://grandlakehistory.org

Grand County

Local Libraries

Hot Sulphur Springs Library, 105 Moffat, PO Box 336, Hot Sulphur Springs, CO 80451-0336, (970) 725-3942, https://www.gcld.org

Fraser Valley Library, 421 Norgren Rd, PO Box 160, Fraser, CO 80442-0421, (970) 726-5689, https://www.gcld.org

Granby Library, 55 Zero St, Granby, CO 80446, (970) 887-2149, http://www.gcld.org

Juniper Library, 316 Garfield St, P.O. Box 506, Grand Lake, CO 80447, (970) 627-8353, https://www.gcld.org/juniper-library

Kremmling Library, 300 S 8th St, PO Box 1240, Kremmling, CO 80459-1240, (970) 724-9228, https://www.gcld.org

Links

CO GenWeb
http://cogenweb.com/grand/

Cyndi's List
https://www.cyndislist.com/us/co/counties/grand/

FamilySearch Wiki
https://www.familysearch.org/wiki/en/Grand_County,_Colorado_Genealogy

Linkpendium
http://www.linkpendium.com/grand-co-genealogy/

RootsWeb Wiki
https://wiki.rootsweb.com/wiki/index.php/Grand_County,_Colorado

Wikipedia
https://en.wikipedia.org/wiki/Grand_County,_Colorado

Historic Hotels

None

Museums & Historic Sites

Cottage Camp Museum, 775 Lake Ave, Grand Lake, CO 80447, http://grandlakehistory.org/museums/cottage-camp/

Cozens Ranch Museum, 77849 US Hwy 40, Fraser, CO 80442, (970) 726-5488, https://grandcountyhistory.org/museums/cozens-ranch-museum/

Emily Warner Field Aviation Museum, 1023 County Rd 610, Granby, CO 80446, (970) 531-1100, https://grandcountyhistory.org/museums/emily-warner-field-aviation-museum/

Grand County Historical Association, Grand County Museum & Pioneer Village, 110 E Byers Ave, P.O. Box 165, Hot Sulphur Springs, CO 80451, (970) 725-3939, http://www.grandcountymuseum.com

Heritage Park Museum, 114 N 4th St, P.O. Box 204, Kremmling, CO 80459, (970) 724-9390, https://grandcountyhistory.org/museums/heritage-park-museum/

Kaufman House Museum, 407 Pitkin Ave, Grand Lake, CO 80447, (970) 627-9644, http://grandlakehistory.org/museums/kauffman-house-museum/

Historical Assets Colorado

Special Events & Scenic Locations

The Grand County-Middle Park Fair & Rodeo is held in July and August most years at the Grand County Fairgrounds, 210 11th St, Kremmling, CO 80459, https://www.middleparkfairandrodeo.com

Visit Grand County has a calendar of events here: https://www.visitgrandcounty.com/calendar

Arapahoe National Forest
Arapaho National Recreation Area
Byers Peak Wilderness
Continental Divide National Scenic Trail
Indian Peaks Wilderness
Never Summer Wilderness
Ptarmigan Peak Wilderness
Routt National Forest
Sarvis Creek Wilderness
Vasquez Peak Wilderness
Great Parks Bicycle Route
TransAmerica Trail Bicycle Route
Colorado River Headwaters National Scenic Byway
Trail Ridge Road-Beaver Meadow National Scenic Byway

Ghost Towns & Other Sparsely Populated Places

Arrow, Colorow, Corona, Coulter, Crescent, Fraser, Grand Lake, Kremmling, Lulu City, Parshall, Selak, Troublesome

Newspapers

The North Park Miner. (Teller, Colo.) 1881-188?
The Middle Park Times. (Hot Sulphur Springs, Colo.) 1881-1922
The Grand County Times. (Teller, Colo.) 1881-1???
Grand County Messenger. (Hot Sulphur Springs, Colo.) 1887-1???
The Kremmling News. (Kremmling, Grand County, Colo.) 19??-1922
Granby Sky-Hi News. (Granby, Colo.) 19??-1989
The Grand County News. (Kremmling, Grand County, Colo.) 1903-19??
The Grand County Advocate. (Sulpher Springs, Grand County, Colo.) 1905-19??
The Grand County Citizen. (Fraser, Colo.) 1911-19??
The Fraser Times. (Fraser, Grand County, Colo.) 1914-19??
The Kremmling Register. ([Hot Sulpher Springs, Colo.]) 192?-193?
Middle Park Times and Kremmling News. (Hot Sulfer [Sulphur] Springs, Grand County, Colo.) 1922-1932
The Kremmling Register. (Kremmling, Grand County, Colo.) 1925-19??
The Kremmling Record. (Kremmling, Grand County, Colo.) 1926-1932
Middle Park Times and Kremmling Register. (Hot Sulphur Springs, Colo.) 193?-1936
The Middle Park Times and Kremmling Record. (Hot Sulphur Springs, Grand County, Colo.) 1936-1975

Grand County

Grand Lake Pioneer. (Grand Lake, Colo.) 1940-19??
Sky-Hi News. (Granby, Colo.) 1945-19??
Middle Park Times. (Kremmling, Colo.) 1975-Current
Winter Park Manifest. (Winter Park, Colo.) 1977-1981
Manifest. (Winter Park, Colo.) 1981-1984
Winter Park Manifest. (Winter Park, Colo.) 1984-Current
Sky-Hi News. (Granby, Colo.) 1989-Current

Places on the National Register

Estes Park, East Inlet Trail, Rocky Mountain National Park
Estes Park, Milner Pass Road Camp Mess Hall and House, Milner Pass Rd.
Estes Park, Timber Creek Campground Comfort Station No. 245, Timber Creek Campground
Estes Park, Timber Creek Campground Comfort Station No. 246, Timber Creek Campground
Estes Park, Timber Creek Campground Comfort Station No. 247, Timber Creek Campground
Estes Park, Timber Creek Road Camp Barn, Approx. 200 yards S of Columbine Lake Rd., 450 yards W of Kawuneeche Visitor Center
Estes Park vicinity, Timberline Cabin, Fall River Rd.
Fraser, Cozens Ranch House, CO 40 1 1/2 mi. S of Fraser
Grand Lake, Dutchtown, Ditch Rd.
Grand Lake, Grand Lake Lodge, 15500 US 34
Grand Lake, Grand River Ditch, N of Grand Lake
Grand Lake, Greenwood Lodge, 161 CR 451
Grand Lake, Holzwarth Historic District, N of Grand Lake on Trail Ridge Rd.
Grand Lake, Kauffman House, NW corner of Pitkin and Lake Ave.
Grand Lake, Little Buckaroo Ranch Barn, 20631 Trail Ridge Rd., Rocky Mountain National Park
Grand Lake, Lulu City Site, N of Grand Lake on Trail Ridge Rd.
Grand Lake, Shadow Mountain Lookout, SE of Grand Lake in Rocky Mountain National Park
Grand Lake, Shadow Mountain Trail, E. side of Shadow Mt. Lake
Grand Lake, Tonahutu Creek Trail, Roughly along Tonahutu Cr. to Flattop Mt.
Kremmling, Barger Gulch Locality B, Address Restricted
Kremmling, Yust, E. C., Homestead, S of Kremmling off CO 9
Rand, Kenjockety, Address Restricted

USGS Historic Places

East Portal, Corona, 39.9344314, -105.6852818
Fall River Pass, Lulu City, 40.4455391, -105.8480671
Fraser, Winter Park Highlands Airport, 39.9969309, -105.8650115
Granby, Elkdale Post Office, 40.040264, -105.8811236
Granby, Granby Sports Park Airport, 40.0485971, -105.9389038
Unknown, Heeney Post Office, 0, 0
Unknown, Monarch Post Office, 0, 0

Historical Assets Colorado

Grand Army of the Republic Posts
None

USGS Historic Military Places
None

Military Bases
None

Post Offices

Arrow	1905 Mar 21	1915 Mar 15	
Blainvale	1882 June 20	1884 Sept 18*	
Bowen	1883 May 25	1901 Sept 30	
Bowenton	1881 Aug 10	1884 Aug 21	
Canadian	1881 Mar 6	1891 July 3	
Clarkson	1892 July 28	1898 Dec 8	
Colorow	1882 May 24	1903 May 20	
Cornwall	1879 Oct 31	1882 Nov 20	
Coulter	1884 Aug 14	1905 Oct 14	
Del Norte	1883 Jan 28		81132
Elkdale	1920 June 17	1925 Sept 30	
Elwood	1882 Sept 18	1899 Aug 16*	
Fairfax	1884 Jan 14	1885 July 9	
Fraser	1876 July 26		80442
Gaskill	1880 Oct 22	1886 Nov 11	
Granby	1905 Oct 26		80446
Grand Lake	1879 Jan 10	1895 Jan 30	
Grand Lake 2	1938 Apr 1		80447
Grandlake	1895 Jan 30	1938 Apr 1	
Granger	1902 Oct 14	1903 Jan 12	
Haworth	1885 Aug 26	1898 Mar 17	
Hayden	1875 Nov 15	1881 Aug 1*	
Hebron	1884 July 11	1922 Feb 15	
Henry	1884 Apr 16	1886 Feb 18	
Hermitage	1878 May 17	1884 Jan 10*	
Hideaway Park	1949 Aug 4	1980 Oct 1	
Homelake	1919 Feb 11	1965 Dec 3	
Hot Sulphur Springs	1874 Sept 10	1894 June 26	
Hot Sulphur Springs 2	1912 Feb 15		80451
Jasper	1882 Nov 20	1927 Feb 15*	
Kinsey	1891 Oct 24	1895 June 19	
Kremmling	1885 Feb 12	1891 Oct 24	
Kremmling 2	1895 June 19		80459
Lariat	1881 Aug 5	1884 Apr 16	
Leal	1904 Sept 17	1930 Apr 30	

Grand County

Lehman	1903 Mar 31	1911 Oct 4	
Liberty	1887 Oct 11	1898 Apr 30	
Loyton	1884 Sept 10	1884 Oct 2	
Lulu	1880 July 26	1883 Nov 26	
Martin	1898 Aug 24	1934 Nov 30	
Monarch	1907 Feb 12	1922 Feb 15*	
Monte Vista	1886 Feb 18		81144
Nichols	1903 Dec 22	1904 Apr 2	
Norma	1896 Dec 16	1899 Dec 15	
Parma	1886 Mar 20	1910 June 15*	
Parshall	1906 Nov 17		80468
Pearmont	1907 Apr 8	1918 July 31	
Piedra	1875 Jan 27	1878 Mar 24	
Radium	1906 Feb 9	1974	
Rand	1883 Sept 3	1886 Nov 13	
Rand 2	1887 June 2		80473
Red Mountain	188 Apr 8	1878 Sept 5	
Scholl	1901 Nov 27	1930 Jan 31	
Selak	1883 July 11	1893 Sept 29	
South Fork	1876 Feb 10	1909 Sept 9	
South Fork 2	1910 Nov 9		81154
Spicer	1884 Apr 29	1954 June 30	
Stillwater	1911 Oct 4	1930 Oct 30	
Sulphur Springs	1894 June 26	1912 Feb 15	
Summit	1876 Feb 10	1880 Nov 17*	
Summitville	1880 Nov 17	1947 Nov 25*	
Tabernash	1905 Sept 30		80478
Teller	1880 July 19	1886 Dec 16	
Troublesome	1878 Mar 15	1935 May 15*	
Twelve Mile	1879 June 19	1880 Aug 5	
Val Moritz	1973 Apr 1	1975 Mar 21	
Wagon Wheel Gap	1875 Aug 27	1957 Sept 30*	
Walden	1881 Feb 28		80470
Wason	1891 Dec 26	1904 Apr 30	
West Portal	1923 Oct 12	1939 Dec 1	
Winter Park	1939 Dec 1		80482

Topo Quads

Battle Mountain	400000N	395230N	1060730W	1061500W
Berthoud Pass	395230N	394500N	1054500W	1055230W
Bottle Pass	400000N	395230N	1055230W	1060000W
Byers Peak	395230N	394500N	1055230W	1060000W
Cabin Creek	401500N	400730N	1060000W	1060730W
Corral Peaks	401500N	400730N	1060730W	1061500W
Dillon	394500N	393730N	1060000W	1060730W
East Portal	400000N	395230N	1053730W	1054500W

Historical Assets Colorado

Empire	395230N	394500N	1053730W	1054500W
Fraser	400000N	395230N	1054500W	1055230W
Gore Pass	400730N	400000N	1063000W	1063730W
Granby	400730N	400000N	1055230W	1060000W
Gunsight Pass	401500N	400730N	1061500W	1062230W
Hinman Reservoir	401500N	400730N	1062230W	1063000W
Hot Sulphur Springs	400730N	400000N	1060000W	1060730W
Isolation Peak	401500N	400730N	1053730W	1054500W
Junction Butte	400730N	400000N	1061500W	1062230W
King Creek	400000N	395230N	1061500W	1062230W
Kremmling	400730N	400000N	1062230W	1063000W
Loveland Pass	394500N	393730N	1055230W	1060000W
Monarch Lake	400730N	400000N	1053730W	1054500W
Parshall	400730N	400000N	1060730W	1061500W
Radium	400000N	395230N	1063000W	1063730W
Shadow Mountain	401500N	400730N	1054500W	1055230W
Sheephorn Mtn	400000N	395230N	1062230W	1063000W
Squaw Creek	395230N	394500N	1060730W	1061500W
Strawberry Lake	400730N	400000N	1054500W	1055230W
Sylvan Reservoir	400000N	395230N	1060000W	1060730W
Trail Mountain	401500N	400730N	1055230W	1060000W
Tyler Mountain	401500N	400730N	1063000W	1063730W
Ute Peak	395230N	394500N	1060000W	1060730W

Suggested Reading

Aldrich, John K. *Ghosts of Eagle and Grand Counties: Stories from the Ghost Towns and Mining Camps of Eagle, Grand, Jackson, Larimer and Routt Counties, Colorado.* Denver: Columbine Ink, 2009.

Black, Robert C III. *Island in the Rockies: the Pioneer Era of Grand County, Colorado.* Granby, CO: Grand County Pioneer Society, 1969.

Hamilton, Penny Rafferty and Patricia Shapiro. *A to Z: Your Grand County History Alphabet.* Hot Sulphur Springs, CO: Grand County Historical Association, 2017.

Hamilton, Penny Rafferty. *Granby, Then and Now: A Quick History.* Granby, CO: Greater Granby Chamber of Commerce, 2005.

Gunnison County

Introduction

Established: 1877   Population: 15,24

Formed from: Lake

Adjacent Counties: Pitkin, Chaffee, Saguache, Hinsdale, Ouray, Delta, Montrose, Mesa

County Seat: Gunnison

Other Communities: Crested Butte, Marble, Mount Crested Butte, Pitkin, Almont, Doyleville, Ohio City, Parlin, Powderhorn, Sapinero, Somerset, Tincup, Pittsburg, Baldwin

Website, https://www.gunnisoncounty.org

Area Codes: 970

Zip Codes: 81210, 81224, 81225, 81230, 81231, 81237, 81239, 81241, 81243, 81434

Historical Assets Colorado

Gunnison County Courthouse

Gunnison County Historic Courthouse

Courthouses & County Government

Gunnison County
https://www.gunnisoncounty.org

Gunnison County Courthouse (7th Judicial District), 200 E Virginia St, Gunnison, CO 81230, 970-641-3500; http://www.courts.state.co.us/Courts/County/Index.cfm?County_ID=16

Assessor, 221 N Wisconsin, Gunnison, CO 81230, 970-641-1085; http://www.gunnisoncounty.org/assessor.html

Board of County Commissioners, 200 E Virginia Ave, Gunnison, CO 81230, 970-641-0248, https://www.gunnisoncounty.org/127/County-Commissioners

Clerk & Recorder, 221 N Wisconsin, Gunnison, CO 81230, 970-641-1516; http://www.gunnisoncounty.org/clerk_recorder.html

Gunnison County

Coroner, 106 S Taylor St #2, Gunnison, CO 81230, 970-641-9213; https://www.gunnisoncounty.org/142/Coroners-Office

Public Health, 225 N Pine St, Ste E, Gunnison, CO 81230, 970-641-0209; http://www.gunnisoncounty.org/health_human_services.html

Treasurer, 221 N Wisconsin, Gunnison, CO 81230, 970-641-2231; http://www.gunnisoncounty.org/Treasurer.html

County Records

Birth 1880	Marriage 1877	Divorce 1877
Death 1880	Land 1877	Probate 1877
Court 1877		
CSA Birth 1941		

County & Municipal Records Held at the State Level

The Colorado State Archives

Physical Records	Records on Film	Records on Master Film
Clerk & Recorder	1885 Census	Clerk & Recorder
County Court	Clerk & Recorder	County Court
District Court	District Court	District Courts
Sheriff	Sheriff	Combined Courts
Treasurer	**Cities**	School Districts
WPA Historical Records	Gunnison	Sheriff
WPA Religious Institutions Survey	Mount Crested Butte	**Cities**
Cities		Crested Butte
Gunnison		Gunnison
Marble		Mount Crested Butte
Mount Crested Butte		

The Denver Public Library

Bank of Irwin Records, 1880
Crested Butte Town Council Records, 1894-1921
Gunnison County Mining Companies Records, 1883, 1931
Gunnison County Pioneer Days, 1935-1946
Tincup Colorado Records, 1881-1953
WWI Draft Registration Cards (microfilm)

School Districts

School Districts, http://www.adcogov.org/local-school-districts

Gunnison Watershed School District, No. RE-1J, 800 N Boulevard St, Gunnison, CO 81230, 970-641-7770; https://www.gunnisonschools.net/

Delta County School District 50J, 145 W 4th St, Delta, CO 81416, 970-874-4438; http://www.deltaschools.com/

Montrose County School District RE-1J, 930 Colorado Ave, Ste B, MOntrose, CO 81401, 970-249-7726; http://www.mcsd.org/

Historical Assets Colorado

Historic School Districts

1. Gunnison
2. Parlin
3. Doyleville
4. Marble
5. Pitkin
6. Tin Cup
7. Floresta, Irwin
8. Crested Butte
9. White Pine
10. Fairview
11. Castleton
12. Goose Creek, Lake Fork
13. Ohio City
14. Powderhorn
15. Spencer
16. Glacier
17. Iola
18. Jack's Cabin
19. Vulcan
20. Sapinero
21. Cunningham
22. Paragon
23. Baldwin
24. Anthracite
25. Cebolla
26. Hillside
27. Vader
28. Lake Fork, Riverside, Gateview
29. Rimrock
30. Somerset

Fraternal Organizations

Granges
Minaret, No. 109, Gunnison, Minaret, 20 May 1890
Tumichi, No. 110, Gunnison, Doyleville, 28 May 1890
Tabeguache, No. 485, Gunnison, Gunnison, 22 Sept 1958

Masons

Ancient Free & Accepted Masons
Gunnison, No. 39, Gunnison, Gunnison, 21 Sept 1881
Gunnison Valley, No. 39, Gunnison, Gunnison, 25 Jan 1993
Pitkin, No. 40, Gunnison, Pitkin, 21 Sept 1881
Tin Cup, No. 52, Gunnison, Tin Cup, 18 Sept 1883
Crested Butte, No. 58, Gunnison, Crested Butte, 17 Sept 1884
Marble, No. 137, Gunnison, Marble, 20 Sept 1910

Royal Arch Masons
Gunnison, No. 16, Gunnison, Gunnison

Knights Templar
Gunnison Commandery, No. 8, Gunnison, Gunnison, 1883 May 28

Eastern Star
Waunita, No. 37, Gunnison, Gunnison

Odd Fellows
Gunnison, No. 39, Gunnison, Gunnison
Pitkin, No. 43, Gunnison, Pitkin
Elk Mountain, No. 52, Gunnison, Crested Butte, 1883 June 7

Rebekahs
Vashti, No. 43, Gunnison, Gunnison
Pine Tree, No. 116, Gunnison, Crested Butte

Knights of Pythias
Snowy Range, No. 43, Gunnison, Crested Butte
Gunnison, No. 112, Gunnison, Gunnison, 1900 Oct 22

Pythian Sisters
Silver State, No. 29, Gunnison, Crested Butte

Gunnison County

Benevolent Protective Order of Elks
Gunnison, No. 1623, Gunnison, Gunnison

City & Town Halls
Gunnison, 201 W Virginia Ave, Gunnison, CO 81230, 970-641-8000, http://www.cityofgunnison-co.gov
Crested Butte, 507 Maroon Ave, Crested Butte, CO 81224, 970-349-5338, https://www.crestedbutte-co.gov
Marble, 407 Main St, Marble, CO 81623, https://www.townofmarble.com
Mount Crested Butte, 911 Gothic Rd, Mount Crested Butte, CO 81225, 970-349-6632, https://mtcrestedbuttecolorado.us
Pitkin, http://www.pitkincolorado.com
Ohio City, https://www.gunnisoncounty.org/628/Ohio-City
Tincup, http://www.tincupco.com

Archives & Manuscript Collections
Gunnison County Archive (digital); https://www.gunnisoncounty.org/Archive.aspx
Leslie J Savage Library Archives & Special Collections, Western State College, 600 N Adams St, Gunnison, CO 81231, (970) 943-2153, http://www.western.edu/academics/leslie-j-savage-library

Historical & Genealogical Societies
Gunnison County Historic Preservation Commission, 200 E Virginia Ave, Gunnison, CO 81230, (970) 641-5347, https://www.gunnisoncounty.org/193/Historic-Preservation-Commission
Gunnison County Pioneer and Historical Society, Pioneer Museum, 803 E Tomichi Ave, P.O. Box 418, Gunnison, CO 81230, (970) 641-4350, http://www.gunnisonpioneermuseum.com

Local Libraries
Gunnison County Public Library, 307 N Wisconsin St, Gunnison, CO 81230-2627, (970) 641-3845, https://www.gunnisoncountylibraries.org
Crested Butte Library, 507 Maroon St, PO Box 489, Crested Butte, CO 81224-0489, (970) 349-6535, https://www.gunnisoncountylibraries.org/crested-butte-library/

Links
CO GenWeb
http://cogenweb.com/gunnison/
Cyndi's List
https://www.cyndislist.com/us/co/counties/gunnison/
FamilySearch Wiki
https://www.familysearch.org/wiki/en/Gunnison_County,_Colorado_Genealogy
Linkpendium
http://www.linkpendium.com/gunnison-co-genealogy/

Historical Assets Colorado

RootsWeb Wiki
https://wiki.rootsweb.com/wiki/index.php/Gunnison_County,_Colorado
Wikipedia
https://en.wikipedia.org/wiki/Gunnison_County,_Colorado

Historic Hotels
None

Museums & Historic Sites
Crested Butte Mountain Heritage Museum, 331 Elk Ave, P.O. Box 2480, Crested Butte, CO 81224, (970) 349-1880, http://www.crestedbuttemuseum.com

Gunnison County Pioneer and Historical Society, Pioneer Museum, 803 E Tomichi Ave, P.O. Box 418, Gunnison, CO 81230, (970) 641-4350, http://www.gunnison-pioneermuseum.com

Marin Museum of Bicycling and Mountain Bike Hall of Fame Museum, 122 Teocalli Rd, P.O. Box 845, Crested Butte, CO 81224, (970) 349-6482, https://mmbhof.org

Special Events & Scenic Locations
The Gunnison County Cattlemen's Days is held in July most years at the Fred Field Western Heritage Center and Fairgrounds, 275 S Spruce, Gunnison, CO 81230, https://www.cattlemensdays.com

The Gunnison Valley Calendar of events is here: https://gunnisonvalleycalendar.com.

Gunnison County keeps a calendar of events here: https://www.colorado.com/co/gunnison/festivals-events

Paonia State Park
Curecanti National Recreation Area
Gunnison National Forest
White River National Forest
Collegiate Peaks WIlderness
Fossil Ridge Wilderness
Maroon Bells-Snowmass Wilderness
Powderhorn Wilderness
Raggeds Wilderness
West Elk Wilderness
American Discovery Trail
Colorado Trail
Continental Divide National Scenic Trail
Old Spanish National Historic Trail
Great Parks Bicycle Route
Western Express Bicycle Route
West Elk Loop Scenic Byway
Silver Thread Scenic Byway

Gunnison County

Ghost Towns & Other Sparsely Populated Places

Abbeyville, Aberdeen, Aberdeen Junction, Allen, Almont, Alpine Station, Anthracite, Atlantic, Baldwin, Bonita, Bowerman, Bowman, Castleton, Cebolla, Cosden, Crooks, Crookton, Crystal, Currecanti, Dorchester, Doyleville, Elkton, Floresta (Ruby, Ruby-Anthracite), Forest Hill, Gate View, Glaciers, Gothic, Grabiola, Gunnison Smelter, Hierro, Hillerton, Hinkles, Iola (under Blue Mesa Reservoir), Irwin, Jack's Cabin, Jackson, Kebler, Kezar, Lake Junction, Marble, Marion, Midway, Minaret, Mound, Mount Carbon, North Star (Lakes Camp), Ohio City (Eagle City, Gold Creek), Oversteg, Parlin, Pie Plant, Pitkin, Pittsburgh, Powderhorn, Prospect, Quartz, Red Mountain, Sapinero, Schofield (Scofield), Sherrod, Teachout, Tincup, Trimble Stage Stop, Valley Spur, Vidals Spur, Vulcan, Waunita Hot Springs, White Pine, Woodstock, Youman

Newspapers

Weekly News-Democrat. (Gunnison, Colo.) 18??-1???

The Marble City Times and Clarence Chronicle. (Marble, Gunnison County, Colo.) 18??-1894

The Marble Times (formerly The Crystal River Current). (Marble, Gunnison County, Colo.) 18??-1???

The Occident. (Hillerton, Gunnison County, Colo.) 1879-1???

The Tin Cup Miner. (Tin Cup, Colo.) 188?-????

Elk Mountain Bonanza. (Gothic, Colo.) 1880-1881

The Gunnison Democrat. (Gunnison, Colo.) 1880-1881

The Gunnison News. (Gunnison, Colo.) 1880-1881

The Gunnison Review. (West Gunnison, Colo.) 1880-1882

The Pitkin Independent. (Pitkin, Colo.) 1880-1???

The Elk Mountain Pilot. (Irwin, (Ruby Camp), Gunnison County, Colo.) 1880-19??

Gunnison Daily Democrat. (Gunnison, Colo.) 1880-18??

White Pine Journal. (White Pine, Colo.) 1881-1???

Gothic Miner. (Gothic, Colo.) 1881-1881

The Free Press. (Gunnison, Colo.) 1881-1882

The Gunnison News and Democrat. (Gunnison, Colo.) 1881-1881

The Gunnison Daily News Democrat. (Gunnison, Colo.) 1881-1882

Gunnison Daily Review. (Gunnison, Colo.) 1881-1882

Crested Butte Republican. (Crested Butte, Colo.) 1881-1883

The Pitkin Mining News. (Pitkin, Colo.) 1881-18??

The Garfield Banner. (Tin Cup, Gunnison County, Colo.) 1881-1882

The Tin Cup Record. (Virginia City, Colo.) 1881-18??

Gunnison Advertiser. (Gunnison, Colo.) 1881-1???

The Messenger. (Montrose, Colo.) 1882-1882

Montrose Messenger. (Montrose, Colo.) 1882-1???

Silver Record. (Gothic, Colo.) 1882-1???

Grand Junction News. (Grand Junction, Gunnison Co., Colo.) 1882-1914

Daily News-Democrat. (Gunnison, Colo.) 1882-1???

Gunnison Daily Review-Press. (Gunnison, Colo.) 1882-1883

Historical Assets Colorado

Gunnison Review-Press. (Gunnison, Colo.) 1882-1891
Tin Cup Banner. (Tin Cup, Gunnison County, Colo.) 1882-1???
Gunnison Review-Press. (Gunnison, Colo.) 1883-1891
Crested Butte Gazette. (Crested Butte, Colo.) 1883-1884
The Sun. (Gunnison, Colo.) 1883-1884
The Tri-Weekly Sun. (Gunnison, Colo.) 1883-????
The Herald. (Tomichi, Colo.) 1883-18??
White Pine Cone. (White Pine, Colo.) 1883-18??
The Daily Gazette. (Crested Butte, Colo.) 1884-1???
The Gunnison Republican. (Gunnison, Colo.) 1884-1885
New Democrat and Tin Cup Mining District Advocate. (Tin Cup, Colo.) 1885-????
The Gunnison Weekly Republican. (Gunnison, Colo.) 1885-????
Crystal River Current. (Crystal, Colo.) 1886-18??
The Pitkin Miner. (Pitkin, Gunnison County, Colo.) 1890-1929
The Gunnison Tribune. (Gunnison, Colo.) 1891-1904
The Gunnison News. (Gunnison, Colo.) 1891-1901
The Silver Lance. (Crystal, Colo.) 1892-1899
The Pitkin Bulletin. (Pitkin, Gunnison County, Colo.) 1893-1???
The Pick and Drill. (Dubois, Gunnison County, Colo.) 1893-1???
Dubois Chronicle. (Dubois, Colo.) 1894-1???
The People's Champion. (Gunnison, Gunnison County, Colo.) 1894-1901
Marble City Times. (Marble, Colo.) 1894-19??
The Daily People's Champion. (Gunnison, Colo.) 1898-1???
The Marble Times and Crystal Silver Lance. (Marble, Colo.) 1899-19??
The Weekly Citizen. (Crested Butte, Colo.) 1899-19??
The Vulcan Times. (Vulcan, Colo.) 1900-19??
Crested Butte Citizen. (Crested Butte, Colo.) 190?-19??
Mt. Crested Butte Mountain Sun. (Crested Butte, Colo.) 19??-1990
The Gunnison News and People's Champion. (Gunnison, Colo.) 1901-1902
The Gunnison Republican. (Gunnison, Colo.) 1901-1929
Gunnison News-Champion. (Gunnison, Colo.) 1902-1904
The Bowerman Herald. (Bowerman, Colo.) 1903-19??
Gunnison News-Champion and Tribune. (Gunnison, Colo.) 1904-1905
Gunnison News-Champion. (Gunnison, Colo.) 1905-1932
The Marston Wizard. (Almont, Colo.) 1906-19??
The Marble Age. (Marble, Colo.) 1909-19??
The Marble Booster. (Marble, Gunnison County, Colo.) 1911-19??
The Gunnison Empire. (Gunnison, Colo.) 1917-19??
The Marble Column. (Marble, Gunnison County, Colo.) 1923-19??
The Gunnison Republican and Pitkin Miner. (Gunnison, Colo.) 1929-1932
Gunnison News-Champion and The Gunnison Republican. (Gunnison, Colo.) 1932-1946
The Echo. (Gunnison, Colo.) 1932-1935
The Gunnison Courier. (Gunnison, Colo.) 1935-1947
The Gunnison Courier. (Gunnison, Colo.) 1946-1947
The Courier. (Gunnison, Colo.) 1947-1965

Gunnison County

Gunnison News-Champion. (Gunnison, Colo.) 1947-1975
The Gunnison County Globe. (Gunnison, Colo.) 1957-1975
Chronicle. (Crested Butte, Colo.) 1962-1985
Crested Butte Chronicle. (Crested Butte, Colo.) 1962-1978
Western State Prospector. (Gunnison, Colo.) 1963-1963
The Gunnison Courier. (Gunnison, Colo.) 1965-1975
Crested Butte Pilot. (Crested Butte, Colo.) 1972-1985
Crystal River Current. (Marble, Colo.) 1973-????
The Gunnison Country Times. (Gunnison, Colo.) 1975-Current
Chronicle. (Crested Butte, Colo.) 1978-1985
Gunnison County Community Herald. (Gunnison, Colo.) 1982-Current
Chronicle and Pilot. (Crested Butte, Colo.) 1985-1985
Crested Butte Chronicle & Pilot. (Crested Butte, Colo.) 1985-200?
Mountain Sun. (Crested Butte, Colo.) 1990-Current
The Crested Butte News : The Official Newspaper of Crested Butte and Mt. Crested Butte. (Crested Butte, Colo.) 2001-Current

Places on the National Register

Crested Butte, Crested Butte Denver and Rio Grande Railroad Depot, 716 Elk Ave.
Crested Butte, Town of Crested Butte, Roughly bounded by Maroon Ave., Eighth St., White Rock Ave., and First St.
Crested Butte, Town of Crested Butte (Boundary Increase and Boundary Decrease), Roughly bounded by Gothic Ave., 6th St., White Rock Ave., and First St.
Crystal, Crystal Mill, Cty. Rd. 3, 7 mi. SE of Marble
Gunnison, Chance Gulch Site, Address Restricted
Gunnison, Curecanti Archeological District, Address Restricted
Gunnison, Edgerton House, 514 W. Gunnison Ave.
Gunnison, Fisher-Zugelder House and Smith Cottage, 601 N. Wisconsin St.
Gunnison, Gunnison River Bridge I, US 50 Service Rd. at milepost 155.41
Gunnison, Gunnison River Bridge II, US-50 Service Rd. at milepost 155.59
Gunnison, Vienna Bakery—Johnson Restaurant, 122-124 N. Main St.
Gunnison, Webster Building, 229 N. Main St.
Marble, Haxby House, 101 W. Silver
Marble, Marble City State Bank Building, 105 W. Main St.
Marble, Marble High School, 412 Main St.
Marble, Marble Mill Site, Park and W. 3rd Sts.
Marble, Marble Town Hall, 407 Main St.
Marble, Parry, William D., House, 115 Main St.
Marble, St. Paul's Church, 123 State St.
Pitkin, Alpine Tunnel Historic District, Along the Denver, South Park and Pacific RR tracks from Quartz to Hancock
Sapinero, Rimrock School, Cty. Rd. 24

USGS Historic Places

Big Mesa, Iola, 38.4749917, -107.0972716
Crested Butte, Crested Butte High School, 38.8708257, -106.9825451

Historical Assets Colorado

Crested Butte, Saint Patricks Catholic Church, 38.870548, -106.9892121
Crested Butte, Town of Crested Butte Marshalls Office-Stone Jail, 38.8691591, -106.9875453
Doyleville, Doyleville School, 38.4366604, -106.6064217
Gothic, Gothic Post Office, 38.959158, -106.9897676
Gunnison, Aberdeen, 38.545825, -106.925321
Marble, State of Colorado Standard School, 39.0719328, -107.1936601
Mount Axtell, Floresta Post Office, 38.8419375, -107.1228269
Pitkin, Campbelltown, 38.6122163, -106.5653083
Powderhorn, Midway, 38.343882, -107.0539375
Powderhorn, Vulcan, 38.3455484, -107.0014356
Unknown, Almont Post Office, 0, 0
Unknown, Cebolla Post Office, 0, 0
Unknown, Cosden, 0, 0
Unknown, Dorchester Post Office, 0, 0
Unknown, Lodge Post Office, 0, 0
Unknown, North Star, 0, 0
Unknown, Sherrod Post Office, 0, 0
Unknown, Tomichi, 0, 0
Unknown, Waunita Hot Springs Post Office, 0, 0

Grand Army of the Republic Posts

Dick Yates, No. 14, Gunnison, Pitkin
Gunnison, No. 17, Gunnison, Gunnison
Tomichi, No. 29, Gunnison, White Pine, 1883
Elk Mountain, No. ?, Gunnison, Irwin

USGS Historic Military Places

None

Military Bases

None

Post Offices

Abbeyville	1882 Nov 20	1884 Dec 3	
Aberdeen	1890 Feb 15	1891 June 16	
Allen	1881 Aug 1	1892 Mar 11	
Almont	1882 Mar 6	1913 July 21*	
Almont 2			81210
Anthracite	1884 Nov 14	1896 Dec 30	
Argenta	1880 July 2	1880 Aug 23	
Ashcroft	1880 Aug 12	1912 Nov 30*	
Aspen	1880 June 7		81611
Baldwin	1883 Sept 17	1902 Mar 31	
Baldwin2	1909 June 26	1948 Sept 30	
Bardine	1903 Mar 11	1908 Oct 15	

Gunnison County

Barnum	1876 Mar 20	1881 June 7	
Bittner	1905 Sept 7	rescinded	
Bowerman	1903 Oct 28	1910 May 27	
Bowman	1880 June 7	1882 Apr 28	
Cameville	1882 Nov 7	1890 Aug 20	
Camp Center	1925 Feb 12	1930 Jan 15	
Castleton	1882 Dec 8	1894 Oct 11	
Cebolla	1894 Mar 20	1935 Sept 14	
Chance	1894 Nov 24	1901 Dec 14	
Chaney	1892 Aug 25	1894 May 10	
Chipeta	1881 Oct 21	1882 Sept 15	
Chloride	1881 Aug 5	1882 Jan 3	
Clarence	1892 Feb 4	1892 Mar 2	
Cloud	1881 May 18	1881 Nov 3	
Cosden	1883 Aug 28	1885 Feb 4	
Cox	1903 Apr 25	1905 Feb 15	
Crested Butte	1879 May 26		81224
Crookstown	1904 May 25	1906 Feb 28	
Crooksville	1878 June 3	1885 Dec 15	
Crystal	1882 July 28	1909 Oct 31	
Curran	1880 Aug 8	1880 Sept 10	
Dayton	1897 Jan 26	1911 Oct 31	
Delta	1882 Jan 5		81416
Dorchester	1900 Aug 21	1912 July 31	
Doyleville	1881 Oct 24	1969 Apr 4*	
Drake	1881 Sept 13	1882 Oct 5	
Drew	1884 Feb 7	1886 Mar 29	
Dubois	1894 Jan 9	1910 Feb 28	
Elgin	1882 Oct 11	1885 Sept 10	
Elko	1881 Aug 15	1884 Sept 24	
Elkton	1881 July 14	1882 Nov 15	
Emma	1881 Sept 27	1882 Nov 10	
Floresta	1897 Jan 16	1919 Nov 15	
Gateview	1892 Mar 11	1895 Nov 7	
Gilman	1882 Sept 4	1883 Feb 5	
Glacier	1914 Apr 20	1915 Nov 30	
Gothic	1879 Aug 5	1914 Jan 31*	
Grand Junction	1882 May 26		81524
Gunnison	1876 Oct 2		81230
Haverly	1880 Aug 30	1880 Nov 22	
Hawxhurst	1882 Aug 25	1892 Mar 3	
Hillerton	1879 May 26	1882 Nov 20	
Homeville	1879 June 26	1904 May 14*	
Hotchkiss	1882 Oct 3		81419
Iowa	1896 June 24	1963 Aug 16	
Irwin	1879 Sept 12	1900 June 5*	

345

Historical Assets Colorado

Jacks Cabin	1909 Jan 25	1918 Mar 30	
Jackson		1893 Feb 20	
Kannah	1882 June 29	1882 Sept 11	
Kezar	1882 May 17	1896 June 24	
Lawrence	1883 Feb 5	1884 Feb 11	
Lodge	1911 Apr 13	1920 Feb 14	
Los Pinos	1877 Feb 23	1881 Jan 13	
Marble	1890 Mar 19	1942 Oct 31*	
Minaret	1890 Feb 25	1896 Nov 14	
Montrose	1882 Feb 14		81401
Mount Carbon	1884 Aug 26	1909 June 26	
Mount Crested Butte	1981 Dec		
Naturita	1882 Sept 15		81422
North Star	1889 Oct 11	1894 May 18	
Northstar	1900 Oct 16	1903 Apr 30	
Ohio	1880 June 15		
Orson	1882 Oct 3	1894 June 20*	
Oversteg	1882 Aug 1	1905 Mar 15	
Paonia	1882 June 7		81428
Paradox	1882 Jan 9		81429
Parlin	1879 Oct 24		81239
Pieplant	1904 Aug 24	1906 May 14	
Pitkin	1879 Sept 12		81241
Pittsburgh	1881 July 22	1896 Dec 30	
Powderhorn	1880 Jan 12	1881 Apr 22	
Powderhorn 2	1881 May 18		81243
Prospect	1886 Nov 9	1890 Dec 24	
Providence	1898 May 17	1900 Mar 31	
Quartz	1882 Aug 7	1886 Mar 29	
Quartzville	1879 June 9	1879 Sept 1	
Ragged Mountain	1919 Apr 11	1956 Mar 31	
Red Mountain	1880 Dec 13	1881 Nov 7	
Roaring Fork	1880 Apr 13	1880 July 29	
Ruby	1879 Oct 31	1895 Apr 27*	
Sage	1880 Nov 22	1882 Sept 18	
Sapinero	1882 Nov 23	1988 Nov 24	
Schofield	1880 Sept 20	1886 Nov 19	
Sherrod	1904 July 18	1906 Apr 30	
Sidney	1881 Jan 4	1887 Mar 20	
Sillsville	1903 Nov 7	1910 June 15*	
Snowmass	1882 July 21	1883 Aug 13	
Somerset	1903 Mar 19		81434
Spencer	1894 Sept 10	1907 Sept 14*	
Spring	1881 Apr 19	1881 Oct 31	
Standish	1885 Sept 10	1886 Oct 25	
Stevens	1881 June 9	1882 Mar 21	

Gunnison County

Suttle	1882 Aug 25	1883 Apr 12
Tin Cup	1879 July 22	1895 May 7
Tincup	1895 May 7	1918 Jan 31
Tolifaro	1896 Feb 20	1898 Apr 16
Tomichi	1880 Aug 23	1899 Nov 30*
Tucker	1896 Dec 28	1897 Nov 10
Tumichi	1879 Oct 24	1880 Aug 23
Turner	1881 Apr 19	1881 Oct 14
Uncompaghre	1880 Oct 14	1906 Nov 30
Ute	1882 Feb 3	1882 May 26
Virginia	1879 July 22	1880 Feb 28
Vulcan	1895 Aug 2	1912 Aug 15
Waunita	1885 Sept 10	1908 Apr 15*
Waunita Hot Springs	1910 May 27	1942 Oct 31
White Pine	1880 Aug 12	1894 Apr 14
Whitepine	1894 Apr 14	1954 Apr 30*
Woodstock	1881 Aug 5	1884 Aug 12*

Topo Quads

Almont	384500N	383730N	1064500W	1065230W
Alpine Plateau	381500N	380730N	1071500W	1072230W
Anthracite Range	385230N	384500N	1070730W	1071500W
Big Mesa	383000N	382230N	1070000W	1070730W
Big Soap Park	384500N	383730N	1071500W	1072230W
Bowie	390000N	385230N	1073000W	1073730W
Buckhorn Lakes	382230N	381500N	1073730W	1074500W
Bull Mountain	390730N	390000N	1072230W	1073000W
Carpenter Ridge	383000N	382230N	1070730W	1071500W
Cathedral Peak	383730N	383000N	1073000W	1073730W
Cement Mountain	385230N	384500N	1064500W	1065230W
Courthouse Mtn	381500N	380730N	1073000W	1073730W
Crawford	384500N	383730N	1073000W	1073730W
Crested Butte	385230N	384500N	1065230W	1070000W
Crystal Creek	384500N	383730N	1063730W	1064500W
Cumberland Pass	384500N	383730N	1062230W	1063000W
Curecanti Needle	383000N	382230N	1072230W	1073000W
Doyleville	383000N	382230N	1063000W	1063730W
Fairview Peak	384500N	383730N	1063000W	1063730W
Flat Top	384500N	383730N	1065230W	1070000W
Garfield	383730N	383000N	1061500W	1062230W
Gateview	382230N	381500N	1070730W	1071500W
Gunnison	383730N	383000N	1065230W	1070000W
Houston Gulch	383000N	382230N	1063730W	1064500W
Iris	383000N	382230N	1064500W	1065230W
Iris NW	383000N	382230N	1065230W	1070000W
Italian Creek	390000N	385230N	1063730W	1064500W

Historical Assets Colorado

Little Soap Park	383730N	383000N	1071500W	1072230W
Lost Lake	382230N	381500N	1072230W	1073000W
Marcellina Mtn	390000N	385230N	1070730W	1071500W
Matchless Mountain	385230N	384500N	1063730W	1064500W
McIntosh Mountain	383730N	383000N	1070000W	1070730W
Minnesota Pass	385230N	384500N	1072230W	1073000W
Mount Axtell	385230N	384500N	1070000W	1070730W
Mount Guero	384500N	383730N	1072230W	1073000W
Mount Harvard	390000N	385230N	1061500W	1062230W
Mount Ouray	383000N	382230N	1060730W	1061500W
Mount Yale	385230N	384500N	1061500W	1062230W
Oh-be-joyful	390000N	385230N	1070000W	1070730W
Pahlone Peak	383000N	382230N	1061500W	1062230W
Paonia	385230N	384500N	1073000W	1073730W
Paonia Reservoir	390000N	385230N	1071500W	1072230W
Parlin	383730N	383000N	1063730W	1064500W
Pitkin	383730N	383000N	1063000W	1063730W
Poison Draw	382230N	381500N	1071500W	1072230W
Powderhorn	382230N	381500N	1070000W	1070730W
Powderhorn Lakes	381500N	380730N	1070730W	1071500W
Rudolph Hill	381500N	380730N	1070000W	1070730W
Sapinero	383000N	382230N	1071500W	1072230W
Sargents	383000N	382230N	1062230W	1063000W
Sheep Mountain	381500N	380730N	1072230W	1073000W
Signal Peak	383730N	383000N	1064500W	1065230W
Somerset	390000N	385230N	1072230W	1073000W
Spring Hill Creek	382230N	381500N	1065230W	1070000W
Squirrel Creek	384500N	383730N	1070000W	1070730W
Taylor Park Reservoir	385230N	384500N	1063000W	1063730W
Tincup	385230N	384500N	1062230W	1063000W
Washboard Rock	382230N	381500N	1073000W	1073730W
West Beckwith Mtn	385230N	384500N	1071500W	1072230W
West Elk Peak	384500N	383730N	1070730W	1071500W
West Elk Peak SW	383730N	383000N	1070730W	1071500W
Whitepine	383730N	383000N	1062230W	1063000W
Winfield	390000N	385230N	1062230W	1063000W
X Lazy F Ranch	383730N	383000N	1072230W	1073000W

Suggested Reading

Aldrich, John K. *Ghosts of Chaffee County: a Guide to the Ghost Towns and Mining Camps of Chaffee and eastern Gunnison Counties, Colorado.* Lakewood, CO: Centennial Graphics, 2000.

Carnahan, John W. *History of Ohio City, Colorado, 1880-1920.* Gunnison, CO: N:, 1969.

Gunnison County

Chappell, Gordon S, Cornelius W Hauck and Richard W Richardson. *Narrow Gauge Transcontinental Through Gunnison County: Black Canyon Revisited*. NL: Colorado Railroad Museum, 1971.

Dahm, John. *History of Quarts, Colorado*. Gunnison, CO: NP, 1970.

Eldorado of Colorado. Chicago: H S Reed & Company, 1884.

Gunnison County Stockgrowers Since 1894: Tops in Cattle. Denver: Colorado Cattlemen's Association, 1967.

Perry, Eleanor. *Taylor Park, Colorado's Shangri-la: a History of Taylor Park, Gunnison County, Colorado*. Buena Vista, CO: Eleanor Harrington, 1989.

Rockwell, Noraetta Piatt. *The Early History of Gunnison County, Colorado Schools*. Thesis Western State College of Colorado, 1953.

Wallace, Betty. *Epitaph for an Editor: a Century of Journalism in Hinsdale and Gunnison Counties, 1875-1975*. Gunnison, CO: B&B Printers, 1987.

Historical Assets Colorado

Hinsdale County

Introduction

Established: 1874   Population: 843

Formed from: Conejos

Adjacent Counties: Gunnison, Saguache, Mineral, Archuleta, La Plata, San Juan, Ouray

County Seat: Lake City

Other Communities: Cathedral, Piedra, Bear Town, Burrows Park, Capitol City, Carson, Henson, Old Carson

Website, https://www.colorado.gov/hinsdalecounty

Area Codes: 970

Zip Codes: 81235

Historical Assets Colorado

Hinsdale County's 1877 Courthouse

Courthouses & County Government

Hinsdale County
   https://www.colorado.gov/hinsdalecounty
Hinsdale County Courthouse (7th Judicial District), 317 Henson St, Lake City, CO 81235, 970-944-2227; http://www.courts.state.co.us/Courts/County/Index.cfm?County_ID=17
Assessor, 317 Henson St, Lake City, CO 81235, 970-944-2224; http://www.hinsdalecountycolorado.us/assessor.html
Board of County Commissioners, 311 Jenson St, Lake City, CO 81235, 970-944-2225, https://www.colorado.gov/pacific/hinsdalecounty/county-commissioners-3
Clerk & Recorder, 317 Henson St, Lake City, CO 81235, 970-944-2228; http://www.hinsdalecountycolorado.us/clerk.html
Coroner, P.O. Box 277, Lake City, CO 81235, 970-944-2806; https://www.colorado.gov/pacific/hinsdalecounty/hinsdale-county-coroner
Public Health, 304 3rd St, Lake City, CO 81235, 970-944-0321; http://www.hinsdalepublichealth.com/
Transportation (Road & Bridge), 1775 N Hwy 149, Lake City, CO 81235, 970-944-2400; https://www.colorado.gov/pacific/hinsdalecounty/road-bridge-department
Treasurer, P.O. Box 336, Lake City, CO 81235, 970-944-2223; https://www.colorado.gov/pacific/hinsdalecounty/treasurer-2

County Records

Birth 1900	Marriage 1880	Divorce 1874
Death Unk	Land 1874	Probate 1874
Court 1874		

Hinsdale County

County & Municipal Records Held at the State Level

The Colorado State Archives

Physical Records
Clerk & Recorder
County Commissioners
County Court
Justice Court
Treasurer
WPA Historical Records
WPA Religious Institutions
  Survey
Cities
  Lake City

Records on Film
Clerk & Recorder
County Commissioners
County Court
District Court

Records on Master Film
Clerk & Recorder
Coroner
County Commissioners
County Court
District Court
Justice of the Peace Court
People vs Alferd Packer
School Districts
Sheriff

The Denver Public Library

Crooke's Mining & Smelting Company Records, 1883
Hinsdale County Mining Companies Records, 1891-1921
WPA Historical Records Survey
WWI Draft Registration Cards (microfilm)

School Districts

School Districts, http://www.adcogov.org/local-school-districts
Hinsdale County School District RE-1, 614 N Silver St, Lake City, CO 81235, 970-944-2314; http://www.lakecityschool.org/district.html
Archuleta School District 50JT, 309 Lewis St, Pagosa Springs, CO 81147, 970-264-2794; https://www.mypagosaschools.com/

Historic School Districts

1. Lake City
2. Capitol City
3. Creede
4. Henson
5. Cathedral, Powderhorn
6. Lakeshore
7. Upper Piedra, Debs, Pagosa Springs
8. Hermit, Creede

Fraternal Organizations

Granges
None

Masons

Ancient Free & Accepted Masons
Crystal Lake, No. 34, Hinsdale, Lake City, 18 Sept 1878

Royal Arch Masons
Lake City, No. 9, Hinsdale, Lake City

Knights Templar
None

Eastern Star
Lake City, No. 36, Hinsdale, Lake City

Historical Assets Colorado

Odd Fellows
Silver Star, No. 27, Hinsdale, Lake City

Rebekahs
Deborah, No. 18, Hinsdale, Lake City

Knights of Pythias
None

Pythian Sisters
None

Benevolent Protective Order of Elks
None

City & Town Halls

Lake City, P.O. Box 544, Lake City, CO 81235, 970-944-2333, http://www.townoflakecity.co

Archives & Manuscript Collections

None

Historical & Genealogical Societies

Hinsdale County Historical Society, Lake City (Hinsdale County) Museum, 130 N Silver St, P.O. Box 353, Lake City, CO 81235, (970) 944-2050, http://www.lakecitymuseum.com

Local Libraries

Lake City Public Library, 206 Silver St, PO Box 607, Lake City, CO 81235-0607, (970) 944-2615, http://www.lakecitypubliclibrary.com

Links

CO GenWeb
http://cogenweb.com/hinsdale/

Cyndi's List
https://www.cyndislist.com/us/co/counties/hinsdale/

FamilySearch Wiki
https://www.familysearch.org/wiki/en/Hinsdale_County,_Colorado_Genealogy

Linkpendium
http://www.linkpendium.com/hinsdale-co-genealogy/

RootsWeb Wiki
https://wiki.rootsweb.com/wiki/index.php/Hinsdale_County,_Colorado

Wikipedia
https://en.wikipedia.org/wiki/Hinsdale_County,_Colorado

Historic Hotels

None

Hinsdale County

Museums & Historic Sites
Golconda Boarding House Museum, Cty Rd 21, Lake City, CO 81235
Hard Tack Mine Museum, Cty Rd 20, Lake City, CO 81235, (970) 944-2506
Hinsdale County Historical Society, Lake City (Hinsdale County) Museum, 130 N Silver St, P.O. Box 353, Lake City, CO 81235, (970) 944-2050, http://www.lake-citymuseum.com

Special Events & Scenic Locations
The Colorfest Arts & Crafts Fair is held in October most years at the Moseley Arts Center, 800 N Gunnison Ave, Lake City, CO 81235, 970-944-2527, https://www.facebook.com/LakeCityCO/posts/the-21st-colorfest-arts-crafts-fair-is-coming-up-this-saturday-10-am-to-4-pm-at-/101390580014852/
Lake City keeps a calendar of summer events here: https://www.lakecity.com/mountain-town-activities/seasons/61-summer-in-lake-city
And its featured events here: https://www.lakecity.com/36-featured-events

Gunnison National Forest
Rio Grande National Forest
San Juan National Forest
Uncompahgre National Forest
La Garita Wilderness
Powderhorn Wilderness
Uncompahgre Wilderness
Weminuche Wilderness
Colorado Trail
Continental Divide National Scenic Trail
West Lost Trail Creek National Recreation Trail
Alpine Loop National Scenic Back Country Byway
Silver Thread Scenic Byway

Ghost Towns & Other Sparsely Populated Places
Antelope Park, Antelope Springs, Beartown, Burrows Park, Capital/Capitol City (Galena City), Carson, Cathedral, Galena City, Henson, Lakeshore, Old Carson, Rose's Cabin, San Juan, Sherman, Sterling, Sunnyside, Tellurium, White Cross

Newspapers
Silver World. (Lake City, Hinsdale County, Colo.) 1875-1888
San Juan Crescent. (Lake City, Colo.) 1877-1878
Lake City Mining Register. (Lake City, Colo.) 1880-1885
Hinsdale Phonograph. (Lake City, Colo.) 1888-189?
Lake City Sentinel. (Lake City, Hinsdale County, Colo.) 1888-1???
The Phonograph. (Lake City, Colo.) 1891-1894
The Lake City Times. (Lake City, Hinsdale County, Colo.) 1891-1917
The Wason Miner. (Wason And Creede, Colo.) 1891-1???
The Teller Topics. (Bachelor, Teller P.O., Hinsdale County, Colo.) 1892-1???

Historical Assets Colorado

The Creede News. (Creede, Saguache County, Colo.) 1892-1???
The Creede Amethyst. (Amethyst And Creede, Colo.) 1892-1892
Creede Daily Herald. (Amethyst, Colo.) 1892-1???
The Daily Creede Candle. (Creede, Amethyst Postoffice, Colo.) 1892-1???
The Creede Candle. (Creede, Colo.) 1892-1930
The Creede Chronicle. (Creede, Colo.) 1892-1895
The Lake City Phonograph. (Lake City, Colo.) 1894-1???
The Daily Phonograph. (Lake City, Colo.) 1894-1???
Silver World and The Lake City Times. (Lake City, Colo.) 1917-1938
Lake City Tribune. (Lake City, Hinsdale County, Colo.) 1946-1948
Lake City Pioneer. (Lake City, Colo.) 1976-1979
Silver World. (Lake City, Colo.) 1978-1988
Lake City Silver World. (Lake City, Hinsdale County, Colo.) 1988-Current

Places on the National Register
Creede, Lost Trail Station, 81125 Forest Service Rd. 520
Lake City, Argentum Mining Camp, Address Restricted
Lake City, Capitol City Charcoal Kilns, Address Restricted
Lake City, Empire Chief Mine and Mill, Address Restricted
Lake City, Golconda Mine, Address Restricted
Lake City, Lake City Historic District, Roughly bounded by Bluff, Eighth, Lake, and First Streets
Lake City, Little Rome, Address Restricted
Lake City, Rose Lime Kiln, Co. Rd. 20 SW of Lake City
Lake City, Tellurium—White Cross Mining Camp, Address Restricted
Lake City, Tobasco Mine and Mill, S. of San Juan Co. Rd. 5 and Hinsdale Co. Rd. 34
Pagosa Springs, Debs School, 2783 McManus Rd.

USGS Historic Places
Finger Mesa, Carson, 37.8691646, -107.3622785
Lake City, Swanson Airport, 38.0772186, -107.2914447
Redcloud Peak, Whitecross Post Office, 37.9438854, -107.477836
Uncompahgre Peak, Capitol City, 38.0072181, -107.4667248
Unknown, Bachelor Cabins, 0, 0
Unknown, Childs Park Post Office, 0, 0

Grand Army of the Republic Posts
John A Rawlins, No. 28, Hinsdale, Lake City

USGS Historic Military Places
None

Military Bases
None

Hinsdale County

Post Offices

Antelope Springs	1876 May 5	1903 May 30	
Belford	1879 Dec 10	1881 Nov 21	
Burrows Park	1876 Sept 26	1882 Sept 28	
Capitol City	1877 May 18	1920 Oct 30	
Carson	1889 Sept 16	1903 Oct 15	
Cathedral	1898 July 18	1921 Sept 30	
Childs Park	1912 May 9	1919 Feb 28	
Debs	1915 Sept 10	1925 Jan 31	
Henson	1883 May 17	1913 Nov 30*	
Hermit	1904 July 6	1920 Sept 15	
Jennison	1875 Jan 15	1879 Apr 25*	
Lake City	1875 June 18		81235
Lakeshore	1896 Oct 19	1904 May 14*	
Lost Trail	1878 Jan 28	1894 May 10*	
Roses Cabin	1878 June 27	1887 Sept 19	
San Juan	1874 June 24	1923 Mar 8*	
Spar	1892 Aug 16	1895 Aug 23	
Sunnyside	1886 Apr 7	1891 Jan 3	
Teller	1892 Apr 29	1912 Mar 15	
Tellurium	1875 Aug 24	1880 Oct 4	
Timber Hill	1879 Apr 25	1881 Jan 3	
White Cross	1882 Sept 28	1912 May 15	

Topo Quads

Bear Mountain	373000N	372230N	1071500W	1072230W
Cannibal Plateau	380730N	380000N	1070730W	1071500W
Cimarrona Peak	373730N	373000N	1070730W	1071500W
Emerald Lake	373730N	373000N	1072230W	1073000W
Finger Mesa	375230N	374500N	1071500W	1072230W
Granite Lake	373730N	373000N	1071500W	1072230W
Granite Peak	373000N	372230N	1072230W	1073000W
Hermit Lakes	375230N	374500N	1070730W	1071500W
Howardsville	375230N	374500N	1073000W	1073730W
Lake City	380730N	380000N	1071500W	1072230W
Lake San Cristobal	380000N	375230N	1071500W	1072230W
Little Squaw Creek	374500N	373730N	1070730W	1071500W
Oakbrush Ridge	373000N	372230N	1070730W	1071500W
Palomino Mountain	373730N	373000N	1070000W	1070730W
Pole Creek Mtn	375230N	374500N	1072230W	1073000W
Redcloud Peak	380000N	375230N	1072230W	1073000W
Rio Grande Pyramid	374500N	373730N	1072230W	1073000W
Slumgullion Pass	380000N	375230N	1070730W	1071500W
Uncompahgre Peak	380730N	380000N	1072230W	1073000W
Weminuche Pass	374500N	373730N	1071500W	1072230W
Workman Creek	374500N	373730N	1070000W	1070730W

Historical Assets Colorado

Suggested Reading

Hinsdale County Historical Society. *A San Juan Tapestry: Hinsdale County Lake City, Colorado—Photographs—Memoirs*. Lake City, CO: Western Reflections Publishing Company, 2012.

Houston, Grant E and Barbara Baker. *An Official Guide to Historic Homes, Lake City, Colorado*. NL: Colorado Initiatives Program, 1889.

Inventory of the County Archives of Colorado, No. 27, Hinsdale County (Lake City). Denver: Historical Records Survey, 1939.

Smith, P David. *The Story of Lake City Colorado and its Surrounding Areas: Including the Tale of Alferd Packer—the Colorado Cannibal*. Lake City, CO: Western Reflections Publishing Company, 2016.

Wallace, Betty. *Epitaph for an Editor: a Century of Journalism in Hinsdale and Gunnison Counties, 1875-1975*. Gunnison, CO: B&B Printers, 1987.

Wright, Carolyn. *A History of Hinsdale County, Colorado*. NL: Carolyn Wright, 1960.

Huerfano County

Introduction

Established: 1861   Population: 6,711

Formed from: Original

Adjacent Counties: Pueblo, Las Animas, Costilla, Alamosa, Custer, Saguache

County Seat: Walsenburg

  Other Communities: Farisita, La Veta, Badito, Cuchara, Gardner, Navajo Ranch, Red Wing, Calumet, Alamo

Website, http://www.huerfano.us

Area Codes: 719

Zip Codes: 81040, 81055, 81089

Historical Assets Colorado

Huerfano County Courthouse

Courthouses & County Government

Huerfano County
  http://www.huerfano.us
Huerfano County Courthouse (3rd Judicial District), 401 Main St, Walsenburg, CO 81089, 719-738-1040; http://www.courts.state.co.us/Courts/County/Index.cfm?County_ID=4
Assessor, 401 Main St, Walsenburg, CO 81089, 719-738-1191; http://www.huerfano.us/Assessor_s_Office.php
Board of County Commissioners, 401 Main St, Walsenburg, CO 81089, 719-738-2370, http://www.huerfano.us/Commissioners_Corner.php
Clerk & Recorder, 401 Main St, Walsenburg, CO 81089, 719-738-2380; http://www.huerfano.us/Clerk_s_Office.php
Coroner, 401 Main St, Ste 201, Walsenburg, CO 81089, 719-738-2425; http://www.huerfano.us/coroner.php
Public Health, 412 Benedicta Ave, Trinidad, CO 81082, 719-846-2213; http://www.la-h-health.org/
Transportation (Road & Bridge), 401 Main St, Ste 105, Walsenburg, CO 81089, 719-738-3000 x 105; http://www.huerfano.us/Road_and_Bridge.php
Treasurer, 401 Main St, Ste 206, Walsenburg, CO 81089, 719-738-1280; http://www.huerfano.us/Treasurer_s_Office.php

County Records

Birth Unk   Marriage 1870   Divorce 1872
Death Unk   Land 1874   Probate 1872
Court 1872

Huerfano County

County & Municipal Records Held at the State Level

The Colorado State Archives

Physical Records
Assessor
Clerk & Recorder
County Commissioners
County Court
District Court
Treasurer
WPA Historical Records
WPA Religious Institutions Survey

Records on Film
1885 Census
Assessor
County Court
District Court
Combined Courts

Records on Master Film
Assessor
Clerk & Recorder
County Commissioners
County Court
District Court
Combined Courts
School Districts

The Denver Public Library
Huerfano County Township Records, 1880-1890
WWI Draft Registration Cards (microfilm)

School Districts
School Districts, http://www.adcogov.org/local-school-districts
Huerfano School District RE-1, 201 E 5th St, Walsenburg, CO 81089, 719-738-1520; http://www.lakecityschool.org/district.html
La Veta School District RE-2, 126 E Garland St, La Veta, CO 81055, 719-742-3662; https://lvk12.org/

Historic School Districts

1. St Mary's
2. Butte Valley
3. La Veta, Lower Badito
4. Walsenburg
5. Chama
6. Sharpsdale
7. [1878]
8. Farsita, Talpa
9. La Veta
10. Sand Arroyo
11. Gardner
12. Cucharas
13. [1881]
14. Sunrise Valley
15. Huajatolla
16. Ritter
17. Gordon, Rocky Mountain
18. Maes Creek
19. Walsen Cameron
20. Malachite
21. Cuchara Camps
22. Ideal
23. Maes, Birmingham
24. Bradford
25. Fairview
26. Apache
27. Rouse-Lester
28. Santa Clara
29. Bear Creek
30. Pictou-Toltec
31. Ravenwood
32. Oakview
33. Pryor
34. Yellowstone
35. Maitland
36. Pacheco
37. Pass Creek
38. Delcarbon
39. [1920]
40. Tioga
41. Laguna
42. Cucharas, Sandy
43. Rutledge
44. [1940]
45. Redwing
46. Buena Vista
47. Black Hills
48. Silver Mountain
49. Badito
50. Alamo
51. Ojo
52. Rahn
53. Turkey Ridge
54. North Veta
55. Sunnyside

Historical Assets Colorado

Fraternal Organizations

Granges
Spanish Peaks, No. 56, Huerfano, Spanish Peaks/Walsenburg, 10 Apr 1874
Walsenburg, No. 57, Huerfano, Walsenburg, 15 Apr 1874
Spanish Peaks, No. 447, Huerfano, La Veta, 29 June 1939
Mount Blanca, No. 448, Huerfano, Gardner, 4 Aug 1939

Masons

Ancient Free & Accepted Masons
Huerfano, No. 27, Huerfano, Walsenburg, 21 Sept 1875
La Veta, No. 59, Huerfano, La Veta, 17 Sept 1884

Royal Arch Masons
Walsenburg, No. 27, Huerfano, Walsenburg

Knights Templar
None

Eastern Star
Naomi, No. 14, Huerfano, Walsenburg
Mariposa, No. 63, Huerfano, La Veta

Prince Hall Masons
Spanish Peak Lodge, No. 17, Huerfano, Walsenburg

Odd Fellows
Unity, No. 70, Huerfano, Walsenburg
La Veta, No. 141, Huerfano, La Veta

Rebekahs
Blanco, No. 112, Huerfano, La Veta

Knights of Pythias
Diamond, No. 49, Huerfano, Walsenburg

Pythian Sisters
None

Benevolent Protective Order of Elks
None

City & Town Halls
Walsenburg, 525 S Albert Ave, Walsenburg, CO 81089, 719-738-1048, https://www.colorado.gov/walsenburg
La Veta, 111 Moore Ave, La Veta, CO 81055, 719-742-3631, http://www.townoflaveta-co.gov

Archives & Manuscript Collections
None

Historical & Genealogical Societies
Huerfano County Historical Society, Fort Francisco Museum, 306 S Main St, P.O. Box 428, La Veta, CO 81055, (719) 742-5501, https://www.franciscofort.org

Huerfano County

Huerfano County Historical Society, Walsenburg Mining Museum, 112 W 5th St, P.O. Box 134, Walsenburg, CO 81089, (719) 738-1992, http://www.huerfanohistory.org/mining-museum.html

Local Libraries

Spanish Peaks Library District, 415 Walsen Ave, Walsenburg, CO 81089, (719) 738-2774, http://www.spld.org

La Veta Public Library, 310 S Main St, P.O. Box 28, La Veta, CO 81055, (719) 742-3572, http://lvpl.org

Links

CO GenWeb
http://cogenweb.com/huerfano/

Cyndi's List
https://www.cyndislist.com/us/co/counties/huerfano/

FamilySearch Wiki
https://www.familysearch.org/wiki/en/Huerfano_County,_Colorado_Genealogy

Linkpendium
http://www.linkpendium.com/huerfano-co-genealogy/

RootsWeb Wiki
https://wiki.rootsweb.com/wiki/index.php/Huerfano_County,_Colorado

Wikipedia
https://en.wikipedia.org/wiki/Huerfano_County,_Colorado

Historic Hotels

1907 La Plaza Inn, 118 W 6th St, Walsenburg, CO 81089, 719-738-5700, http://www.laplazainnwalsenburg.com

Museums & Historic Sites

Francisco Fort Museum, 306 S Main St, P.O. Box 428, La Veta, CO 81055, (719) 742-5501, https://www.franciscofort.org

Huerfano County Historical Society, Fort Francisco Museum, 306 S Main St, P.O. Box 428, La Veta, CO 81055, (719) 742-5501, https://www.franciscofort.org

Huerfano County Historical Society, Walsenburg Mining Museum, 112 W 5th St, P.O. Box 134, Walsenburg, CO 81089, (719) 738-1992, http://www.huerfanohistory.org/mining-museum.html

Huerfano Heritage Center, 114 W 6th St, Walsenburg, CO 81089, (719) 738-2346, http://www.huerfanohistory.org/tirey-history-center.html

Special Events & Scenic Locations

The Huerfano County Fair is held in August most years at the Huerfano County Fairgrounds, 401-499 Moore Ave, La Veta, CO 81055, https://www.spanishpeakscountry.com/event/huerfano-county-fair/

Historical Assets Colorado

The Huerfano County 4-H Fair is held in July most years at the La Veta Fairgrounds, 501 Moore Ave, La Veta, CO 41055, https://www.facebook.com/pages/category/Sports—-Recreation/Huerfano-County-4-H-Fair-862164167171101/

The local newspaper, the Huerfano World Journal (publishing since 1884), has a calendar of upcoming events here: https://huerfanoworldjournal.com/category/upcoming-events/

Greenhorn Mountain Wilderness
Lathrop State Park
San Isabel National Forest
Sangre de Christo Wilderness
Spanish Peaks Wilderness
Highway of Legends Scenic Byway

Ghost Towns & Other Sparsely Populated Places

Apache, Autobees, Badito, Birmingham, Bradford, Butte Valley, Calumet, Conchito Junction, Cucharas, Gardner, Huerfano, Malachite, Mule Shoe, Ojo, Pictou, Pryor, Rouse, Rouse's Junction, Saint Mary's, Santa Clara, Santa Clara Junction, Scissors, Sharpsdale, Silver Lake, Talpa, Tioga, Tuna, Uptop (Old La Veta Pass), Ute, Veta Pass, Wahotoya

Newspapers

The Clarion. (Walsenburg, Colo.) 1???-19?? | Languages: English, Spanish
The Walsenburg Yucca. (Walsenburg, Colo.) 18??-19??
Huerfano Independent. (Walsenberg, Colo.) 1875-1??? | Languages: English, Spanish
The Huerfano Herald. (La Veta, Colo.) 1880-1883
The Huerfano Cactus. (Walsenburg, Colo.) 1883-18??
The Walsenburg Cactus. (Walsenburg, Colo.) 1885-1897
The Walsenburg World. (Walsenburg, Colo.) 1889-1933
The Huerfano Informer. (La Veta, Colo.) 1892-1???
Rouse Enterprise. (Walsenburg, Colo.) 1893-189?
The Advertiser. (La Veta, Colo.) 1895-1938
El Independiente. (Walsenburg, Colo.) 1896-1??? | Languages: Spanish
The Cuchara Valley Voice. (La Veta, Colo.) 19??-1986
The Independent. (Walsenburg, Huerfano County, Colo.) 1909-1915
The Independent y El Imparcial. (Walsenburg, Huerfano County, Colo.) 1915-1923
The Independent. (Walsenburg, Colo.) 1924-1933
The World-Independent. (Walsenburg, Colo.) 1933-1958
The La Veta Advertiser. (La Veta, Colo.) 1938-19??
Huerfano County News. (Walsenburg, Colo.) 1951-1951
Huerfano World. (Walsenburg, Colo.) 1958-2010

Places on the National Register

Farisita, Montoya Ranch, Address Resricted
La Veta, La Veta Pass Narrow Gauge Railroad Depot, Off U.S. 160

Huerfano County

La Veta, Lamme Hospital, 314 S. Main St.
La Veta, Veta Pass, 3652, 3665, 3688 Cty. Rd. 443
Le Veta, Francisco Plaza, 312 S. Main St.
Walsenburg, Huerfano County Courthouse and Jail, 400 Main St.
Walsenburg, Huerfano County High School, 415 Walsen Ave.
Walsenburg, Maitland Arroyo Bridge, CO 69 at Milepost 3.0

USGS Historic Places

Cuchara, Cuchara Camps Post Office, 37.3791796, -105.100281
Walsenburg North, Full Gospel Church, 37.6266667, -104.7830556
Walsenburg North, Huerfano County High School, 37.6308333, -104.7866667
Walsenburg South, Seventh Avenue Public School, 37.6197222, -104.7888889

Grand Army of the Republic Posts

Wadsworth, No. 32, Huerfano, La Veta
J B Hawkes, No. 61, Huerfano, Walsenburg

USGS Historic Military Places

None

Military Bases

None

Post Offices

Alamo	1923 Feb 21	1938 Oct 1
Apache	1878 May 31	1882 Nov 10
Apache 2	1894 Sept 10	1925 Aug 31*
Badito	1865 Sept 12	1910 Nov 15
Bents Fort	1863 June 4	1873 Dec 2
Birmingham	1883 May 25	1894 Sept 19
Bradford	1889 No 27	1895 Aug 21
Butte Valley	1869 July 6	1878 Aug 26*
Butte Valley 2	1938 Oct 1	1949 Sept 6
Cacharas	1879 Dec 8	1872 Sept 20
Camp Shumway	1911 Apr 13	1924 July 1
Capps	1894 Sept 26	1901 Aug 15
Carson	1868 Sept 23	1870 Dec 7*
Clover	1912 Dec 12	1922 Aug 31
Consolidated	1905 Sept 1	1905 Oct 26
Cuchara	1957 June 15	1959 June 30
Cuchara Camps	1916 Jan 20	1957 June 15
Cucharas	1872 Sept 20	1921 Jan 15*
Delcarbon	1915 Nov 20	1953 Dec 31
Dickson	1879 Jan 30	1885 Jan 7
Farisita	1923 Apr 2	1990 Apr 7

Historical Assets Colorado

Farr	1907 Dec 3	1946 Mar 26	
Fort Lyon	1862 Aug 2	1889 Dec 26	
Fort Wise	1860 Sept 5	1862 Aug 2	
Gardner	1871 Dec 15		81040
Gordon	1924 July 1	1937 Dec 15	
Grays Ranch	1863 Sept 1	1866 Feb 6	
Greenhorn	1866 Dec 10	1911 Dec 15*	
Hermosilla	1867 Mar 21	1872 Jan 15	
Hezron	1902 Jan 20	1912 Feb 14	
Houck	1883 Feb 13	1883 May 31	
Huerfano	1862 Feb 25	1879 Jan 20	
Huerfano Canon	1878 Apr 5	1890 Oct 16*	
Huerfano Canyon	1871 Apr 13	1871 Dec 15*	
Ideal	1910 Feb 24	1929 Nov 7	
La Veta	1876 Aug 17		81055
Larimer	1907 July 19	1914 Jan 21	
Lascar	1916 Jan 27	1949 Jan 20	
Lester	1910 Mar 5	1929 May 31	
Little Orphan	1865 May 1	1865 Sept 123	
Maitland	1898 Jan 31	1935 Apr 15	
Malachite	1880 Nov 22	1915 Apr 15	
Mayne	1905 July 27	1907 Dec 31	
McGuire	1905 Nov 4	1911 Apr 13	
McMillan	1900 Sept 7	1904 Sept 15	
Mooney	1896 Mar 26	1896 Apr 15	
Muriel	1903 Aug 18	1906 Jan 31*	
Mustang	1914 Jan 21	1940 Jan 31	
Niggerhead	1913 Sept 2		
North Veta	1920 Jan 13	1934 June 30*	
Nunda	1883 May 7	1888 Oct 24	
Oakview	1907 Dec 3	1930 May 31	
Ojo	1880 June 14	1928 Aug 15*	
Pauley	1920 Jan 6	1929 June 29	
Pictou	1889 Sept 12	1931 Oct 31	
Point of Rocks	1864 May 12	1865 May 16	
Pryor	1898 Feb 26	1996 Sept 14	
Quebec	1880 July 13	1884 Feb 18	
Rattlesnake Buttes	1918 Apr 15	1938 Oct 31	
Ravenwood	1910 Mar 4	1939 Mar 31	
Redwing	1914 May 22		
Rockland	1914 Dec 19	1915 May 20	
Round Oak	1908 Mar 16	1910 July 30	
Rouse	1889 Jan 24	1929 Nov 30	
Saint Marys	1867 Aug 7	1907 Dec 31*	
Santa Clara	1873 dec 17	1894 July 18*	
Scissors	1884 Feb 18	1894 Sept 26	

Huerfano County

Seguro	1895 Jan 4	1901 Setp 14		
Sharpsdale	1883 Nov 23	1934 June 15*		
Solar	1915 May 20	1926 Nov 10		
Spanish Peak	1871 June 15	1876 Aug 17		
Spanish Peaks	1920 Apr 21	1920 Oct 30		
Strong	1905 Mar 31	1929 May 31		
Tabeguache	1869 Feb 22	1869 Sept 20		
Talpa	1890 Oct 15	1912 Dec 31		
Tioga	1907 Nov 21	1954 Mar 15		
Toltec	1911 Apr 13	1953 Dec 31		
Tourist	1887 Oct 20	1887 Nov 29		
Trinidad	1862 June 17	1864 Sept 19		
Trinidad 2	1866 Feb 6		81082	
Ute	1888 Aug 12	1900 Apr 27		
Veta Pass	1889 June 15	1890 Oct 16		
Walsen	1902 Mar 29	1932 Oct 31		
Walsenburg	1892 Dec 22		81089	
Walsenburgh	1870 Dec 14	1892 Dec 22*		
Warrantsville	1876 July 10	1877 Sept 13		
Yellowstone Creek	1915 Aug 5	1916 Apr 15		

Topo Quads

Aguilar	373000N	372230N	1043730W	1044500W
Badito Cone	375230N	374500N	1050000W	1050730W
Black Hills	374500N	373730N	1045230W	1050000W
Blanca Peak	373730N	373000N	1052230W	1053000W
Creager Reservoir	375230N	374500N	1051500W	1052230W
Cuchara	373000N	372230N	1050000W	1050730W
Cucharas Pass	372230N	371500N	1050000W	1050730W
Cucharas Reservoir	374500N	373730N	1043000W	1043730W
Farisita	374500N	373730N	1050000W	1050730W
Gardner	375230N	374500N	1050730W	1051500W
Hayden Butte	375230N	374500N	1045230W	1050000W
Herlick Canyon	372230N	371500N	1045230W	1050000W
Huerfano Butte	375230N	374500N	1044500W	1045230W
La Veta	373730N	373000N	1050000W	1050730W
La Veta Pass	373730N	373000N	1050730W	1051500W
Lascar	375230N	374500N	1043730W	1044500W
Little Sheep Mtn	374500N	373730N	1050730W	1051500W
Maria Reservoir	374500N	373730N	1043730W	1044500W
McCarty Park	373000N	372230N	1050730W	1051500W
Mosca Pass	374500N	373730N	1052230W	1053000W
Pryor SE	373730N	373000N	1043000W	1043730W
Red Wing	374500N	373730N	1051500W	1052230W
Ritter Arroyo	373730N	373000N	1045230W	1050000W
Santa Clara	373000N	372230N	1044500W	1045230W

Historical Assets Colorado

South Rattlesnake Butte	374500N	373730N	1042230W	1043000W
Spanish Peaks	373000N	372230N	1045230W	1050000W
Trinchera Peak	372230N	371500N	1050730W	1051500W
Twin Peaks	373730N	373000N	1053000W	1053730W
Walsenburg North	374500N	373730N	1044500W	1045230W
Walsenburg South	373730N	373000N	1044500W	1045230W

Suggested Reading

Christofferson, Nancy. *Coal was King: Huerfano County's Mining History*. La Veta, CO: NP, 2000.

Clyne, Rick J. *Coal People: Life in Southern Colorado's Company Towns, 1890-1930*. Denver: History Colorado, 1999.

Faris-Avery, Kay Beth. *Along the Huerfano River*. Charleston, SC: Arcadia Publishing, 2016.

Murray, Robert A and Dale R Andrus, Frederic J Athearn. *Las Animas, Huerfano and Custer: Three Colorado Counties on a Cultural Frontier: A History of the Raton Basin*. Denver: Colorado Bureau of Land Management, 1979.

Owens, Robert Percy. *Huerfano Valley as I Knew it*. NL: NP, 1975.

Nardine, Henry. *In the Shadows of the Spanish Peaks: a History of Huerfano County, Colorado*. Walsenburg, CO: H Nardine, 1988.

Ree, Dorothy Rose. *Walsenburg, Crossroads Town: A History*. Walsenburg, CO, Independent Nocturn Publishing, 2006.

Jackson County

Introduction

Established: 1909   Population: 1,394

Formed from: Grand, Larimer

Adjacent Counties: Larimer, Grand, Routt

County Seat: Walden

Other Communities: Coalmont, Cowdrey, Gould, Rand, Brownlee, Hebron, Old Homestead, Owl, Pearl, Spicer, Teller City, Zirkel

Website, http://jacksoncountycogov.com

Area Codes: 970

Zip Codes: 80430, 80434, 80473, 80480

Historical Assets Colorado

Jackson County Courthouse

Courthouses & County Government

Jackson County
http://jacksoncountycogov.com

Jackson County Courthouse (8th Judicial District), 396 Lefever St, Walden, CO 80480, 970-723-4363; http://www.courts.state.co.us/Courts/County/Index.cfm?County_ID=21

Assessor, 396 Lafever St, Walden, CO 80480, 970-723-4751; https://jacksoncountycogov.com/jackson-county-assessor/

Board of County Commissioners, P.O. Box 1019, Walden, CO 80480, 970-999-2143, https://jacksoncountycogov.com/elected-officials/

Clerk & Recorder, 395 Lafever St, Walden, CO 80480, 303-723-4334; https://jacksoncountycogov.com/agendas-minutes/clerk-recorder/

Coroner, P.O. Box 293, Walden, CO 80480, 970-723-4242; http://jacksoncountycogov.com/coroner/

Public Health, 312 5th St, Walden, CO 80480, 970-723-8572; http://jacksoncountycogov.com/public-health/

Transportation, 188 Grant St, Walden, CO 80480, 970-723-4481; http://jacksoncountycogov.com/road-bridge/

Treasurer, P.O. Box 458, Walden, CO 80480, 970-723-4220; https://jacksoncountycogov.com/treasurer/

County Records

Birth 1909	Marriage 1909	Divorce 1909
Death 1909	Land 1909	Probate 1909
Court 1909		

Jackson County

County & Municipal Records Held at the State Level

The Colorado State Archives

Physical Records	Records on Film	Records on Master Film
District Court	District Court	Clerk & Recorder
WPA Historical Records	School Districts	County Court
WPA Religious Institutions Survey		District Court
WPA Walden		School Districts
		Treasurer

The Denver Public Library
WWI Draft Registration Cards (microfilm)

School Districts
School Districts, http://www.adcogov.org/local-school-districts
North Park School District R-1, 910 4th St, Walden, CO 80480, 970-723-3300; https://sites.google.com/northpark.k12.co.us/home/our-district

Historic School Districts

1. Walden
2. Coalmont
3. Cowdrey
4. Spicer
5. Rand
6. Haworth

Fraternal Organizations

Granges
None

Masons

Ancient Free & Accepted Masons
None

Royal Arch Masons
None

Knights Templar
None

Eastern Star
None

Odd Fellows
North Park, No. 118, Jackson, Walden

Rebekahs
Walden, No. 42, Jackson, Walden

Knights of Pythias
None

Pythian Sisters
None

Benevolent Protective Order of Elks
None

Historical Assets Colorado

City & Town Halls
Walden, 513 Harrison St, Walden, CO 80480, 970-723-4344, https://www.colorado.gov/townofwalden

Archives & Manuscript Collections
None

Historical & Genealogical Societies
North Park Pioneer Association, Historical Museum, 367 Logan St, P.O. Box 678, Walden, CO 80480, (970) 723-3282, http://www.nppioneermuseum.com

Local Libraries
Jackson County Public Library, 412 4th St, P.O. Box 398, Walden, CO 80480-0398, (970) 723-4602, http://jacksoncountycogov.com/library/

Links
CO GenWeb
http://cogenweb.com/jackson/

Cyndi's List
https://www.cyndislist.com/us/co/counties/jackson/

FamilySearch Wiki
https://www.familysearch.org/wiki/en/Jackson_County,_Colorado_Genealogy

Linkpendium
http://www.linkpendium.com/jackson-co-genealogy/

RootsWeb Wiki
https://wiki.rootsweb.com/wiki/index.php/Jackson_County,_Colorado

Wikipedia
https://en.wikipedia.org/wiki/Jackson_County,_Colorado

Historic Hotels
None

Museums & Historic Sites
North Park Pioneer Association, Historical Museum, 367 Logan St, P.O. Box 678, Walden, CO 80480, (970) 723-3282, http://www.nppioneermuseum.com

Special Events & Scenic Locations
The Jackson County-North Park Fair is held in September most years at the Jackson County Fairgrounds, 686 JCR 42, Walden, CO 80480.

Visit North Park Colorado posts notices of events here: https://www.facebook.com/VisitNorthParkCO

Jackson County

Colorado State Forest
State Forest State Park
Arapaho Nartional Wildlife Refuge
Routt National Forest
Mount Zirkel Wilderness
Never Summer Wilderness
Platte River Wilderness
Continental Divide National Scenic Trail
Great Parks Bicycle Route
TransAmerica Trail Bicycle Route
Cache la Poudre-North Park Scenic and Historic Byway

Ghost Towns & Other Sparsely Populated Places

Coalmont, Gould, King's Canyon, Park City, Pearl, Teller City

Newspapers

Kansas and Colorado Illustrated Monthly Newspaper. (Kansas City, Mo. And Denver, Colo.) 1878-1???
The North Park Miner. (Teller, Colo.) 1881-188?
North Park Union. (Walden, Larimer County, Colo.) 1896-19??
The North Park News. (Walden, Colo.) 1899-1???
Pearl Mining News. (Pearl, Colo.) 1901-19??
Pearl Mining Times. (Pearl, Colo.) 1902-19??
The New Era. (Walden, Colo.) 1906-19??
Jackson County Star. (Walden, Colo.) 191?-Current
Jackson County Times. (Walden, Colo.) 1911-19??

Places on the National Register

Cowdry, Hog Park Guard Station, Routt National Forest
Gould, Lake Agnes Cabin, 2.5 mi. from CO 14, near Cameron Pass

USGS Historic Places

Pearl, Pearl Post Office, 40.9852484, -106.5469787
Unknown, Lindland Post Office, 0, 0

Grand Army of the Republic Posts

None

USGS Historic Military Places

None

Military Bases

None

Historical Assets Colorado

Post Offices

Butler	1890 June 16	1911 Nov 30	
Chedsey	1917 May 12	1918 June 15	
Coalmont	1912 Mar 11	1893 Dec 21	
Cowdrey	1915 Apr 5		80434
Dryer	1916 Aug 31	1917 Oct 31	
Gould	1937 June 1	1973 Mar 14	
Hebron	1884 July 11	1922 Feb 15	
Higho	1889 June 14	1930 Aug 15	
Kings Canyon	1928 June 13	1936 Aug 31	
Larand	1914 Oct 8	1916 Aug 15	
Lindland	1922 Sept 18	1937 Apr 30	
Northgate	1912 Jan 16	1918 Feb 15	
Owl	1899 Dec 26	1918 Oct 31	
Paulus	1920 Dec 16	1933 Oct 31	
Pearl	1889 Jan 19	1919 Aug 30	
Peneold	1937 Feb 2	1937 June 1	
Rand	1883 Sept 3	1886 Nov 13	
Rand 2	1887 June 2		80473
Spicer	1884 Apr 29	1954 June 30	
Walden	1881 Feb 28		80470
Zirkel	1899 May 5	1911 Dec 30	

Topo Quads

Boettcher Lake	405230N	404500N	1063000W	1063730W
Bowen Mountain	402230N	401500N	1055230W	1060000W
Buffalo Peak	403000N	402230N	1061500W	1062230W
Chambers Lake	403730N	403000N	1054500W	1055230W
Clark Peak	403730N	403000N	1055230W	1060000W
Coalmont	403730N	403000N	1062230W	1063000W
Cowdrey	405230N	404500N	1061500W	1062230W
Delaney Butte	404500N	403730N	1062230W	1063000W
Eagle Hill	405230N	404500N	1060730W	1061500W
Fall River Pass	403000N	402230N	1054500W	1055230W
Gould	403730N	403000N	1060000W	1060730W
Gould NW	404500N	403730N	1060730W	1061500W
Hyannis Peak	402230N	401500N	1061500W	1062230W
Independence Mtn	410000N	405230N	1062230W	1063000W
Jack Creek Ranch	403000N	402230N	1060000W	1060730W
Johnny Moore Mtn	404500N	403730N	1060000W	1060730W
Kings Canyon	410000N	405230N	1060730W	1061500W
Lake Agnes	402230N	401500N	1063000W	1063730W
Lake John	405230N	404500N	1062230W	1063000W
MacFarlane Reservoir	403730N	403000N	1061500W	1062230W
Mount Richthofen	403000N	402230N	1055230W	1060000W

Jackson County

Owl Ridge	403730N	403000N	1060730W	1061500W
Parkview Mountain	402230N	401500N	1060730W	1061500W
Pearl	410000N	405230N	1063000W	1063730W
Pitchpine Mountain	404500N	403730N	1063000W	1063730W
Rabbit Ears Peak	403000N	402230N	1063000W	1063730W
Radial Mountain	402230N	401500N	1060000W	1060730W
Rand	403000N	402230N	1060730W	1061500W
Rawah Lakes	404500N	403730N	1055230W	1060000W
Shipman Mountain	405230N	404500N	1060000W	1060730W
Spicer Peak	403000N	402230N	1062230W	1063000W
Teal Lake	403730N	403000N	1063000W	1063730W
Walden	404500N	403730N	1061500W	1062230W
Whiteley Peak	402230N	401500N	1062230W	1063000W

Suggested Reading

Aldrich, John K. *Ghosts of Eagle and Grand Counties: Stories from the Ghost Towns and Mining Camps of Eagle, Grand, Jackson, Larimer and Routt Counties, Colorado*. Denver: Columbine Ink, 2009.

Bailey, Adah B. *History of Jackson County, Colorado*. Walden, CO: Jackson County Star, 1946.

Jackson County, Colorado. Walden, CO: Jackson County Library, 1967.

Kimball, Bev and Ken Kimball. *A History of Big Creek Valley and Pearl, Colorado*. NL: The Authors, 1988.

Historical Assets Colorado

Jefferson County

Introduction

Established: 1861 Population: 534,543

Formed from: Original

Adjacent Counties: Boulder, Broomfield, Adams, Denver, Arapahoe, Douglas, Teller, Park, Clear Creek, Gilpin

County Seat: Golden

Other Communities: Arvada, Edgewater, Lakewood, Littleton, Westminster, Wheat Ridge, Bow Mar, Lakeside, Morrison, Mountain View, Applewood, Aspen Park, Coal Creek, Columbine, Dakota Ridge, East Pleasant View, Evergreen, Fairmount, Genesee, Idledale, Indian Hills, Ken Caryl, Kittredge, West Pleasant View, Buffalo Creek, Conifer, Foxton, Pine, Pine Junction

Website, https://www.jeffco.us

Area Codes: 303, 720

Zip Codes: 80001, 80002, 80003, 80004, 80005, 80006, 80007, 80021, 80033, 8004, 80123, 80127, 80128, 80162, 80214, 80215, 80225, 80226, 80227, 80228, 80232, 80235, 80401, 80402, 80403, 80419, 80425, 80433, 80437, 80439, 80453, 80454, 80457, 80465, 80470

Historical Assets Colorado

Jefferson County Courthouse

Courthouses & County Government

Jefferson County
https://www.jeffco.us

Jefferson County Courthouse (1st Judicial District), 100 Jefferson County Pkwy, Golden, CO 80401, 303-271-6145; http://www.courts.state.co.us/Courts/County/Index.cfm?County_ID=2

Assessor, 100 Jefferson County Pkwy, Golden, CO 80419, 303-271-8600; https://www.co.jefferson.co.us/assessor/index.htm

Board of County Commissioners, 100 Jefferson County Pkwy, Golden, CO 81419, 303-271-8525, https://www.jeffco.us/663/Board-of-County-Commissioners

Clerk & Recorder, 100 Jefferson County Pkwy, Golden, CO 80419, 303-271-8186; https://www.co.jefferson.co.us/cr/index.htm

Coroner, 800 Jefferson County Pkwy, Golden, CO 80419, 303-271-6480; https://www.jeffco.us/665/Coroner

Elections, 3500 Illinois S:t, Ste 1100, Golden, CO 80401, 303-271-8111; https://www.jeffco.us/396/Elections

Public Health, 1801 19th St, Golden, CO 80401, 303-271-5700; http://jeffco.us/health/index.htm

Treasurer, 100 Jefferson County Pkwy, Golden, CO 80419, 303-271-8330; http://jeffco.us/Treasurer/index.htm

County Records

Birth 1907	Marriage 1868	Divorce 1863
Death 1868	Land 1867	Probate 1863
Court 1863		

Jefferson County

County & Municipal Records Held at the State Level

The Colorado State Archives

Physical Records
Clerk & Recorder
County Commissioners
County Court
District Court
Justice Court
Public Trustee
Treasurer
WPA Historical Records
WPA Religious Institutions
  Survey
Cities
  Golden
  Wheatridge

Records on Film
1885 Census
Clerk & Recorder
County Court
District Court
Cities
  Golden
  Wheatridge

Records on Master Film
Building
Clerk & Recorder
County Commissioners
County Court
District Court
Combined Courts
School Districts
Treasurer
Cities
  Arvada
  Golden
  Lakewood
  Wheatridge

The Denver Public Library

Blue Mountain Land & Homeowners Association Records, 1877-1994
Colorado Deeds, 1868-1911
Colorado Federation of Republican Women Records, 1938-2017
Colorado Ostrich Farm Company Records, 1907
Colorado Theatre Program Collection, 1900-
Genessee Ranch Ledger, 1870-1872
Golden Ditch & Flume Company Records, 1884-1886
History of Golden Notebooks, 1873-1914
Jefferson County Genealogy Records, 1800-1970
Jefferson County Mining Companies Records, 1896
PLAN Jeffco Records, 1871-1984
Rilliet Park Association Records, 1923-1999
Sylvania of the Rockies Summer Camp Records, 1864
WPA History of Golden, Jefferson County Colorado
WWI Draft Registration Cards (microfilm)

School Districts

School Districts, http://www.adcogov.org/local-school-districts
Jefferson County School District, R-1, 1829 Denver West Dr #27, Golden, CO 80401, 303-982-6500; https://www.jeffcopublicschools.org/

Historic School Districts

1. Golden
2. Arvada
3. Lottrodge
4. [1878]
5. [1878]
6. Fremont
7. Leyden
8. Wheatridge
9. Conifer
10. Grey Hill-Mt Douglas
11. [1878]
12. Ralston
13. Rpcl;amd
14. Maple Grove
15. Dun Creek
16. [1878]
17. Medlun
18. Pine
19. Pleasant Park
20. Fairmount
21. Edgewater

Historical Assets Colorado

22. Mt Morrison
23. Lothrop
24. South Platte
25. Lorraine-Mandalay
26. Hodgson
27. Columbine
28. [1878]
29. Belcher Hill
30. [1881]
31. Soda Creek
32. Fruitdale
33. Plainview
34. Kassler
35. Elk Creek
36. Lamb
37. [1889]
38. Parmalee Gulch
39. Semper
40. Buffalo Creek
41. Bancroft
42. Idledale
43. Wagner
44. Prospect Valley
45. [1897]
46. Sampton
47. Lakewood
48. Daniels
49. Denver View
50. Washington Heights
51. Mountain

C1. Bear Creek Valley
C2. Evergreen

Fraternal Organizations

Granges
Ralston, No. 2, Jefferson, Golden, 18 Aug 1873
Clear Creek Valley, No. 4, Jefferson, Arvada, 9 Dec 1873
Rocky Mountain, No. 10, Jefferson, Morrison/Gilman/Montana, 15 Dec 1873
Enterprise, No. 25, Jefferson, Arvada/Ralston, 16 Jan 1874
Bear Creek, No. 50, Jefferson, Cresswell/Morrison, 11 Mar 1874
Centennial, No. 73, Jefferson, Golden, 1 June 1876
Loch Lomond, No. 76, Jefferson, Golden, 19 July 1887
Crepwell, No. 82, Jefferson, Crepwell/Golden, 24 Mar 1888
Elk, No. 120, Jefferson, Pine, 12 Nov 1890
Maple Grove, No. 154, Jefferson, Edgewater, 27 Feb 1907
Wheat Ridge, No. 155, Jefferson, Wheat Ridge, 29 Mar 1907
Wild Rose, No. 160, Jefferson, Morrison, 16 Nov 1907
Bear Creek Valley, No. 161, Jefferson, Morrison, 30 Nov 1907
Lakewood, No. 172, Jefferson, Edgewater, 18 June 1909
Midway, No. 173, Jefferson, Mt Morrison, 28 June 1909
Fremont, No. 181, Jefferson, Golden, 30 Sept 1909
Elk Creek, No. 189, Jefferson, Pine, 25 June 1910
Genesee, No. 219, Jefferson, Golden, 11 Nov 1913
Evergreen, No. 227, Jefferson, Evergreen, 27 Apr 1914
Guy Hill, No. 237, Jefferson, Golden, 10 Mar 1915
Green Mountain, No. 409, Jefferson, Golden, 30 Sept 1931
Longs Peak, No. 450, Jefferson, Golden, 25 July 1940
Golden Gate, No. 451, Jefferson, Golden, 25 July 1940

Masons

Ancient Free & Accepted Masons
Golden City, No. 1, Jefferson, Golden, 2 Aug 1861
Arvada, No. 130, Jefferson, Arvada, 25 Jan 1996
Arvada, No. 141, Jefferson, Arvada, 17 Sept 1912
Edgewater, No. 159, Jefferson, Edgewater, 17 Sept 1924
Lakewood, No. 170, Jefferson, Lakewood, 17 Sept 1946
Wheat Ridge, No. 187, Jefferson, Wheat Ridge, 27 Jan 1960

Royal Arch Masons
Golden, No. 5, Jefferson, Golden

Jefferson County

Knights Templar
None

Eastern Star
Golden, No. 29, Jefferson, Golden
Mount Zion, No. 133, Jefferson, Golden
Friendship, No. 137, Jefferson, Arvada
Lakewood, No. 139, Jefferson, Lakewood
Evening Star, No. 142, Jefferson, Edgewater
Loyalty, No. 145, Jefferson, Westminster
Echo, No. 147, Jefferson, Evergreen

Odd Fellows
Golden, No. 13, Jefferson, Golden
Edgewater, No. 25, Jefferson, Edgewater
Morrison, No. 82, Jefferson, Morrison
Arvada, No. 145, Jefferson, Arvada
Pine, No. 157, Jefferson, Pine

Rebekahs
Golden, No. 8, Jefferson, Golden
Edgewater, No. 9, Jefferson, Edgewater
Arvada, No. 57, Jefferson, Arvada

Knights of Pythias
Golden, No. 10, Jefferson, Golden
Platte Valley, No. 122, Jefferson, Littleton

Pythian Sisters
None

Benevolent Protective Order of Elks
Lakewood, No. 1777, Jefferson, Lakewood
Westminster, No. 2227, Jefferson, Westminster
Arvada, No. 2278, Jefferson, Arvada
Evergreen, No. 2363, Jefferson, Evergreen
Golden, No. 2740, Jefferson, Golden

City & Town Halls

Golden, 911 10th St, Golden, CO 80401, 303-384-8000, https://www.cityofgolden.net

Arvada, 8101 Ralston Rd, Arvada, CO 80002, 720-898-7500, https://arvada.org

Edgewater, 1800 Harlan St, Edgewater, CO 80214, 303-235-8300, https://www.edgewaterco.com

Lakewood, 480 S Allison Pkwy, Lakewood, CO 80226, 303-987-7000, https://www.lakewood.org/Home

Littleton, 2255 W Berry Ave, Littleton, CO 80120, 303-795-3700, https://www.littletongov.org

Westminster, 4800 W 92nd Ave, Westminster, CO 80031, 303-658-2400, https://www.cityofwestminster.us

Historical Assets Colorado

Wheat Ridge, 7500 W 29th Ave, Wheat Ridge, CO 80033, 303-234-5900, https://www.ci.wheatridge.co.us

Bow Mar, 5395 Lakeshore Dr, Bow Mar, CO 80123, 303-794-6065, https://www.colorado.gov/townofbowmar

Morrison, 321 Hwy 8, Morrison, CO 80465, 303-697-8749, https://town.morrison.co.us

Mountain View, 4176 Benton St, Mountain View, CO 80212, 303-421-7282, http://www.townofmountainviewcolorado.org

Ken Caryl, 7676 S Continental Divide Rd, Littleton, CO 80127, 303-979-1876, https://ken-carylranch.org

Indian Hills, https://indianhillscolorado.com

Archives & Manuscript Collections

Arthur Lakes Library & Special Collections, Colorado School of Mines, 1500 Illinois St, Golden, CO 80401, (303) 273-3000, https://libguides.mines.edu/specialcollections/home

Arvada Historical Society, Marcetta Luz Historical Library & Archives, 6901 Wadsworth Blvd, Arvada, CO 80003, (303) 431-1261, http://www.arvadahistory.org/archives.html

Jefferson County Archives, 3500 Illinois St, Ste 2350, Golden, CO 80401, (303) 271-8448, https://www.jeffco.us/757/Archives

US Geological Survey Photographic Library, Denver Federal Ctr, Bldg 41 Rm 45, Denver, CO 80225-0046, (303) 236-1010, https://library.usgs.gov/photo/index.html#/

Historical & Genealogical Societies

American Historical Society of Germans from Russia, Denver Metro Chapter, 6733 Reed St, Arvada, CO 80033-4055, (303) 933-3180, https://www.ahsgr.org/page/DenverMetro

Arvada Historical Society, Marcetta Luz Historical Library & Archives, 6901 Wadsworth Blvd, Arvada, CO 80003, (303) 431-1261, http://www.arvadahistory.org/archives.html

Arvada Historical Society, McIlvoy House Museum, 7307 Grandview Ave, P.O. Box 419, Arvada, CO 80001, (303) 431-1261, http://arvadahistory.org

Conifer Historical Society, Little White Schoolhouse Museum, 26951 Barkley Rd, P.O. Box 295, Conifer, CO 80433, (303) 396-5975, https://www.coniferhistoricalsociety.org

Edgewater Historical Commission, 2401 Sheridan Blvd, Edgewater, CO 80214, (303) 238-7803, https://www.edgewaterco.com

Evergreen Mountain Area Historical Society, Hiwan Homestead Museum, 4208 S Timbervale Dr, P.O. Box 703, Evergreen, CO 80439, (303) 670-0784, http://jchscolorado.org

Foothills Genealogical Society, P.O. Box 150382, Lakewood, CO 80215-0382, (303) 642-7262, http://www.foothillsgenealogy.org

Friends of Dinosaur Ridge, 16831 W Alameda Pkwy, Morrison, CO 80465, (303) 697-3466, https://dinoridge.org

Jefferson County

Germanic Genealogical Society, P.O. Box 746255, Arvada, CO 80006, (720) 865-1821, https://germanicgensocco.wordpress.com

Golden Landmarks Association, 805 14th St, P.O. Box 1136, Golden, CO 80402, (303) 279-1236, http://goldenlandmarks.com

Grand Lodge of Colorado, Sons of Italy, P.O. Box 1231, Arvada, CO 80001, (303) 385-7025, http://www.osiacolorado.org

Jefferson County Historical Commission, 100 Jefferson County Pkwy, Ste 3550, Golden, CO 80419, (303) 271-8700, https://www.jeffco.us/3383/Historical-Commission

Ken-Caryl Ranch Historical Society, Ranch House, 7676 S Continental Divide Rd, Littleton, CO 80127, (303) 979-1876, https://ken-carylranch.org/events/historical-society/

Lakewood Historical Society, P.O. Box 260951, Lakewood, CO 80226, https://lakewoodhistoricalsociety.org

Morrison Historical Society, P.O. Box 208, Morrison, CO 80465, (303) 697-8526, http://morrisonhistory.wordpress.com/

Mountain Genealogists, P.O. Box 1004, Evergreen, CO 80439, http://www.mountaingenealogists.org

Palatines to America, Colorado Chapter, 7079 S Marshall St, Littleton, CO 80123-4607, (303) 827-4700, http://www.copalam.us

Swedish Genealogical Society of Colorado, P.O. Box 746255, Arvada, CO 80006, http://swedgensoc.org

Westminster Historical Society, Bowles House Museum, 3924 W 72nd Ave, Arvada, CO 80002, (303) 430-7929, https://www.westminstercohistory.com

Wheat Ridge Historical Society, Historical Museum, 4610 Robb St, P.O. Box 1833, Wheat Ridge, CO 80034-1833, (303) 467-0023, http://www.wheatridgehistoricalsociety.org

Local Libraries

Jefferson County Public Library-Golden Branch, 1019 10th St, Golden, CO 80401, (303) 235-5275, http://jeffcolibrary.org

Jefferson County Public Library-Arvada Library, 7525 W 57th Ave, Arvada, CO 80002, (303) 235-5275, https://jeffcolibrary.org

Jefferson County Public Library-Columbine, 7706 W Bowles Ave, Littleton, CO 80123, (303) 932-2690, https://jeffcolibrary.org

Jefferson County Public Library-Conifer Public, 10441 Hwy 73, Conifer, CO 80433, (303) 982-5310, https://jeffcolibrary.org

Jefferson County Public Library-Edgewater Branch, 1800 N Harlan St, Edgewater, CO 80214, (303) 235-5275, https://jeffcolibrary.org

Jefferson County Public Library-Evergreen Branch, 5000 State Hwy 73, Evergreen, CO 80439, (303) 674-0780, https://jeffcolibrary.org

Jefferson County Public Library-Lakewood, 10200 W 20th Ave, Lakewood, CO 80215, (303) 235-5275, http://jeffcolibrary.org

Jefferson County Public Library-Standley Lake, 8485 Kipling St, Arvada, CO 80005, (303) 456-0806, https://jeffcolibrary.org/locations/SL/

Jefferson County Public Library-Wheat Ridge Library, 5475 W 32nd Ave, Wheat Ridge, CO 80212, (303) 235-5275, https://jeffcolibrary.org

Historical Assets Colorado

Links

CO GenWeb
http://cogenweb.com/jefferson/

Cyndi's List
https://www.cyndislist.com/us/co/counties/jefferson/

FamilySearch Wiki
https://www.familysearch.org/wiki/en/Jefferson_County,_Colorado_Genealogy

Linkpendium
http://www.linkpendium.com/jefferson-co-genealogy/

RootsWeb Wiki
https://wiki.rootsweb.com/wiki/index.php/Jefferson_County,_Colorado

Wikipedia
https://en.wikipedia.org/wiki/Jefferson_County,_Colorado

Historic Hotels

None

Museums & Historic Sites

Arvada Center for the Arts and Humanities Museum, 6901 Wadsworth Blvd, Arvada, CO 80003, (303) 431-3080, http://www.arvadacenter.org

Arvada Flour Mill Museum, 7307 Grandview Blvd, Arvada, CO 80002, (303) 431-1261, http://www.arvadahistory.org

Arvada Historical Society, McIlvoy House Museum, 7307 Grandview Ave, P.O. Box 419, Arvada, CO 80001, (303) 431-1261, http://arvadahistory.org

Astor House Museum, 822 12th St, Golden, CO 80401, (303) 278-3557, http://www.astorhousemuseum.org

Bradford Washburn-American Mountaineering Museum, 710 10th St, Golden, CO 80401, (303) 996-2755, https://www.cmc.org/About/AmericanMountaineeringMuseum.aspx

Buffalo Bill Memorial Museum & Grave, 987 1/2 Lookout Mountain Rd, Golden, CO 80401, (303) 526-0744, http://www.buffalobill.org

Colorado Railroad Historical Foundation, Robert W Richardson Railroad Library, 17155 W 44th Ave, P.O. Box 10, Golden, CO 80402-0010, (303) 279-4591, http://coloradorailroadmuseum.org/library/

Colorado Railroad Museum, 17155 W 44th Ave, P.O. Box 10, Golden, CO 80403, (800) 365-6263, https://coloradorailroadmuseum.pastperfectonline.com

Conifer Historical Society, Little White Schoolhouse Museum, 26951 Barkley Rd, P.O. Box 295, Conifer, CO 80433, (303) 396-5975, https://www.coniferhistoricalsociety.org

Cussler Museum, 14959 W 69th Ave, Arvada, CO 80007, (303) 420-2795, http://www.cusslermuseum.com

Denver Museum of Miniatures, Dolls and Toys, 830 Kipling St, Lakewood, CO 80215, (303) 322-1053, http://www.dmmdt.org

Jefferson County

Evergreen Mountain Area Historical Society, Hiwan Homestead Museum, 4208 S Timbervale Dr, P.O. Box 703, Evergreen, CO 80439, (303) 670-0784, http://jchscolorado.org

Geology Museum, Colorado School of Mines, 1310 Maple St, Golden, CO 80401, (303) 274-3815, https://www.mines.edu/geology-museum/

Golden History Museum & Park, 1020 11th St, Golden, CO 80401, (303) 278-3557, https://www.goldenhistory.org/visit/history-park/

Heritage Lakewood Belmar Park, 801 S Yarrow St, Lakewood, CO 80226, (303) 987-7850, https://www.lakewood.org/Government/Departments/Community-Resources/Arts-and-Culture/Heritage-Lakewood

Humphrey Memorial Park & Museum, 620 S Soda Creek Rd, P.O. Box 2122, Evergreen, CO 80437, (303) 674-5429, http://www.hmpm.org

Rocky Mountain Quilt Museum, 200 Violet St #140, Golden, CO 80401, (303) 277-0377, http://www.rnqm.org

Westminster Historical Society, Bowles House Museum, 3924 W 72nd Ave, Arvada, CO 80002, (303) 430-7929, https://www.westminstercohistory.com

Special Events & Scenic Locations

The Jefferson County Fair & Festival is held in August most years, at the Jefferson County Fairgrounds, 15200 W 6th Ave, Golden, CO 80401, 303-271-6600, https://www.jeffco.us/fairgrounds

Jefferson County keeps a calendar of events here: https://www.jeffco.us/Calendar.aspx

Hiwan Homestead Museum
Lookout Mountain Nature Center
Ranson-Edwards Homestead Ranch
Chatfield State Park
Golden Gate Canyon State Park
Staunton State Park
Pike National Forest
Roosevelt National Forest
Lost Creek Wilderness
Rocky Flats National Wildlife Refuge
Two Ponds National Wildlife Refuge
South Platte Trail
American Discovery Trail
Apex National Recreation Trail
Big Dry Creek National Recreation Trail
Colorado Trail
Platte River Greenway National Recreation Trail
Two Ponds National Recreation Trail
Lariat Loop Scenic and Historic Byway

Historical Assets Colorado

Ghost Towns & Other Sparsely Populated Places

Arapahoe, Archer's, Beaver Brook, Big Hill, Buffalo Creek, Buffalo Tank, Chimney Gulch, Church's, Clay Spur, Cliff, Coal Tank, Creswell, Crossons, Crystal Lake, Dawson's, Deansbury, Dome Rock, Elk Creek, Fairmount, Forks Creek, Gaylor's Spur, Gillespie, Gilman, Glencoe, Granite Spur, Guy Gulch, Harris, Hutchinson, Lakeside, Lamb, Lee Siding, Lidderdale, Mayfield, Mill Gulch, Mount Carbon, Mount Falcon, Mount Vernon, Park Siding, Pine, Pine Grove, Platte Canon, Ralston, Riverside, Rock Spur, Semper, South Platte, Stevens Gulch, Stone Spur, Symes, Tinball, Tindale, Urmston, Vermillion, Wheatland

Newspapers

The Arvada Sun. (Arvada, Colo.) 1???-19??
The Morrison Bud. (Morrison, Colo.) 18??-1900
The Western Mountaineer. (Golden City, Jefferson [Colo.]) 1859-1860
Colorado Democrat. (Golden City, Colo.) 1863-1???
The Colorado Transcript. (Golden City, Colo.) 1866-1969
The Golden Globe. (Golden, Jefferson County, Colo.) 187?-19??
Golden Weekly Globe. (Golden, Colo.) 1873-187?
The Colorado Central. (Golden, Colo.) 1878-1???
Rocky Mountain Reveille. (Critchell, Colo.) 1899-1900
Jefferson County Graphic. (Morrison, Colo.) 1900-1908
The Arvada Jefferson Sentinel. (Lakewood, Co) 19??-19??
The Golden Outlook. (Golden, Colo.) 19??-19??
The Wheat Ridge Suburbanite. (Wheat Ridge, Colo.) 19??-19??
South Jefferson Times. (Littleton, Colo.) 19??-1991
The Arvada Enterprise. (Arvada, Colo.) 1908-1970
The Edgewater Record. (Edgewater, Colo.) 1911-19??
Mt. Morrison Independent. (Mt. Morrison, Colo.) 1912-1912
Wheat Ridge News. (Wheat Ridge, Colo.) 1913-19??
Morrison Monitor. (Mount Morrison, Jefferson County, Colo.) 1914-19??
The Jefferson County Republican and The Arvada Sun. (Golden, Colo.) 1919-1923
Jefferson County Republican. (Golden, Colo.) 1923-1949
Edgewater Tribune. (Edgewater, Colo.) 1923-19??
The Arvada Sun. (Arvada, Colo.) 1923-1923
The East Jefferson Sentinel. (Edgewater, Colo.) 1932-1948
The Register. (Denver, Colo. ;) 1936-1958
Arvada Paramount Weekly. (Arvada, Colo.) 1939-19??
The St. Cloud Register. (Denver, Colo.) 194?-1955
Denver Ordnance Bulletin. (Denver Ordnance Plant [Lakewood, Colo.]) 1941-1944
The Mountaineer. (Evergreen, Colo.) 1946-1948
The Jefferson Record. (Lakewood, Colo.) 1946-19??
Fillius Park Mountaineer. (Fillius Park, Evergreen, Colo.) 1948-1949
Edgewater Tribune. (Edgewater, Colo.) 1948-19??
The Mountain Parks Bulletin. (Evergreen, Colo.) 1949-19??
Jefferson Sentinel. (Lakewood, Colo.) 1949-1969

Jefferson County

The Mountain News. (Evergreen, Colo.) 1950-19??
Smoke Signals. (Indian Hills [Colo.) 1955-1958
Wheatridge Advocate. (Wheatridge, Colo.) 1957-19??
Canyon Courier. ([Indian Hills, Colo.]) 1958-Current
The Duluth Register. (Denver, Colo. ;) 1958-1970
Kernels of Political Thots 'N Observations. (Golden, Colo.) 1962-1962
Kernels. (Golden, Colo.) 1962-19??
The Southwest Sentry. ([Lakewood, Colo.]) 1965-19??
The Jefferson County Times. (Lakewood, Colo.) 1966-????
The Arvada Citizen. (Arvada, Colo.) 1966-1970
Golden Daily Transcript. (Golden City, Colo.) 1969-1976
The Jefferson City Sentinel. (Jefferson City [Lakewood], Colo.) 1969-1969
Lakewood Sentinel. (Lakewood, Colo.) 1969-1986
Wheat Ridge Sentinel. (Wheat Ridge, Colo.) 1969-1991
The Arvada Citizen Sentinel. (Arvada, Colo.) 1970-1970
The Arvada Citizen Sentinel and The Arvada Enterprise. (Arvada, Colo.) 1970-1973
The Arvada Citizen-Sentinel. ([Arvada, Colo.) 1974-1979
The Mountain Independent. (Jefferson And Park Counties, Colo.) 1975-19??
The Daily Transcript. (Golden, Colo.) 1976-1979
High Timber Times. (Conifer, Colo.) 1977-Current
The Colorado Transcript. (Golden, Colo.) 1979-1983
Arvada Sentinel. (Arvada, Colo.) 1979-19??
Jefferson County Transcript. (Golden, Co) 198?-2002
Wheat Ridge Transcript. (Golden, Co) 198?-Current
The Golden Transcript. (Golden, Colo.) 1983-Current
Foothills Independent. (Denver, Colo.) 1985-????
Village Independent. (Denver, Colo.) 1985-1985
Lakewood Independent. (Denver, Colo.) 1985-????
Arvada Independent. (Denver, Colo.) 1985-1985
Lakewood Jefferson Sentinel. ([Lakewood, Colo.]) 1986-1990
Lakewood Sentinel. ([Lakewood, Colo.]) 1990-199?
The Lakewood Jefferson Sentinel. (Lakewood, Co) 199?-199?
The Aurora Villager. (Englewood, Colo.) 1990-Current
Olde Towner : Arvada's Community Newspaper. (Arvada, Co) 199?-1999
The Wheat Ridge Jefferson Sentinel. (Arvada, Co) 1991-Current

Places on the National Register

Arvada, Arvada Downtown, Roughly bounded by Ralston Rd., Teller Rd., Grandview Ave. and Yukon St.
Arvada, Arvada Flour Mill, 5580 Wadsworth Blvd.
Arvada, Churches Ranch, 17999 W. 60th Ave.
Arvada, Reno Park Addition Historic District, Roughly bounded by Allison St., Ralston Rd., Yukon St., and Reno Dr.
Arvada, Russell-Graves House, 5605 Yukon St.
Arvada, Stocke—Walter Addition Historic District, Roughly along Saulsbury St., Ralston Rd., Grandview Ave., and Reed St.

Historical Assets Colorado

Buffalo Creek, Blue Jay Inn, Hwy. 126
Buffalo Creek, Green Mercantile Store, NW of Buffalo Creek
Buffalo Creek, Green Mountain Ranch, S of Buffalo Creek on Hwy. 126
Buffalo Creek, La Hacienda, On SR off U.S. 285
Conifer, Conifer Junction Schoolhouse, 26951 Barkley Rd.
Conifer, Midway House, 9345 U.S. 285
Denver, Tower of Memories, 8500 W. Twenty-ninth Ave.
Evergreen, Bergen Park, CO 74 S of I-40
Evergreen, Brook Forest Inn, 8136 S. Brook Forest Rd.
Evergreen, Corwina Park, O'Fallon Park, Pence Park, Roughly, area SE of jct. of Kittredge and Myers Gulch Rds.
Evergreen, Dedisse Park, 29614 Upper Bear Creek Rd.
Evergreen, Evergreen Conference District, CO 74
Evergreen, Everhardt Ranch, SE of Evergreen
Evergreen, Fillius Park, CO 74 NW of Evergreen
Evergreen, Hiwan Homestead, Meadow Dr.
Evergreen, Humphrey House, 620 S. Soda Creek Rd.
Golden, Ammunition Igloo, 15001 Denver W. Pkwy.
Golden, Astor House Hotel, 822 12th St.
Golden, Barnes—Peery House, 622 Water St.
Golden, Calvary Episcopal Church, 1300 Arapahoe St.
Golden, Camp George West Historic District, 15000 S. Golden Rd.
Golden, Colorado Amphitheater, 15001 Denver W. Pkwy.
Golden, Colorado National Guard Armory, 1301 Arapahoe St.
Golden, Colorow Point Park, 900 Colorow Rd.
Golden, Coors, Herman, House, 1817 Arapahoe St.
Golden, Deaton Sculptured House, 24501 Ski Hill Dr.
Golden, Denver and Rio Grande Western Railroad Caboose No. 0578, 17155 W. 44th Ave.
Golden, First Presbyterian Church of Golden—Unger House, 809 15th St.
Golden, Genesee Park, 26771 Genesee Ln.
Golden, Golden Cemetery, 755 Ulysses St.
Golden, Golden High School, 710 10th St.
Golden, Lariat Trail Scenic Mountain Drive, Lookout Mountain Rd. S of US 6 to Golden Reservoir
Golden, Lookout Mountain Park, 987 1/2 Lookout Mountain Rd.
Golden, Lorraine Lodge, SW of Golden
Golden, Loveland Building and Coors Building, 1122 and 1120 Washington Ave.
Golden, Magic Mountain Site, Address Restricted
Golden, Mount Vernon House, About 1 mi. S of Golden city limits at jct. of I-70, CO 26 and Mount Vernon Canyon Rd.
Golden, Quaintance Block, 805 13th St.
Golden, Queen of Heaven Orphanage Summer Camp, 20189 Cabrini Blvd.
Golden, Rio Grande Southern Railroad Engine No. 20, 17155 W. 44th Ave.
Golden, Rio Grande Southern Railroad, Motor No. 2, 17155 W. 44th Ave.
Golden, Rio Grande Southern Railroad, Motor No. 6, 17155 W. 44th Ave.

Jefferson County

Golden, Rio Grande Southern Railroad, Motor No. 7, 17155 W. 44th Ave.
Golden, Rockland Community Church and Cemetery, 24225 Rockland Rd.
Golden, Rocky Flats Plant, Approximately 2 mi. SE of jct. of CO 93 and CO 198
Golden, Rooney Ranch, S of Golden, jct. of Rooney Rd. and Alameda Pkwy.
Golden, Thiede Ranch, 22258 Shingle Creek Rd.
Golden, Twelfth Street Historic Residential District, Roughly bounded by 11th, 13th, Elm, and Arapahoe Sts.
Idledale, Little Park, Miller Ln. (CO 74) SW of Idledale
Idledale, Starbuck Park, CO 74 through Bear Creek Canyon, S of Idledale
Lakewood, Building 710, Defense Civil Preparedness Agency, Region 6 Operations Center, Denver Federal Center
Lakewood, Davies' Chuck Wagon Diner, 9495 W. Colfax Ave.
Lakewood, Denver and Intermountain Railroad Interurban No. 25, W. 6th Ave. & Kipling St.
Lakewood, Hill Section, Golden Hill Cemetery, 12000 W. Colfax Ave.
Lakewood, Jewish Consuptives' Relief Society, 6401 W. Colfax Ave.
Lakewood, Office of Civil Defense Emergency Operations Center, Denver Federal Center
Lakewood, Peterson House, 797 S. Wadsworth Blvd.
Lakewood, Schnell Farm, 3113 S. Wadsworth Blvd.
Lakewood, South Ranch, Address Restricted
Lakewood, Stone House, S of Lakewood off of S. Wadsworth Blvd.
Littleton, Bradford House II, N of Killdeer Ln.
Littleton, Hildebrande Ranch, 7 mi. SW of Littleton off Deer Creek Canyon Rd.
Morrison, Bear Creek Canyon Scenic Mountain Drive, CO 74 section between Morrison and Idledale
Morrison, Bradford House III Archeological Site, Address Restricted
Morrison, Bradford, Robert Boyles, Property, Address Restricted
Morrison, Craig, Katherine, Park, Along US 40/I-70 NW of Morrison
Morrison, District No. 17 School—Medlen School, Address Restricted
Morrison, Fort, The, 19192 CO 8
Morrison, LoDaisKa Site, Address Restricted
Morrison, Morrison Historic District, CO 8
Morrison, Morrison Schoolhouse, 226 Spring St.
Morrison, Red Rocks Park District, 16351 Co. Rd. 93
Pine, Staunton Ranch Rural Historic Landscape, 11559 Upper Ranch Dr.
Pine and South Platte, North Fork Historic District, Both sides of South Platte River from Pine to South Platte, in Red Pike National Forest
Pine and South Platte, North Fork Historic District (Boundary Increase), Longview, Foxton, Argyle and Pine Grove Expansions
Wheat Ridge, Baugh, James H., House, 11361 W. 44th Ave.
Wheat Ridge, Crown Hill Burial Park, 7777 W. 29th Ave.
Wheat Ridge, Fruitdale Grade School, 10801 W. 44th Ave.
Wheat Ridge, Pioneer Sod House, 4610 Robb St.
Wheat Ridge, Richards Mansion, 5349 W. 27th Ave.

Historical Assets Colorado

USGS Historic Places

Arvada, Allendale Cottage School Number 2, 39.8105422, -105.120263
Arvada, Alta Vista Cottage School, 39.8099865, -105.0930399
Arvada, Applewood Knolls Cottage School, 39.7585982, -105.1235966
Arvada, Arvada Seventh Day Adventist Christian School, 39.8125, -105.0755556
Arvada, Columbia Heights School, 39.7627646, -105.0574834
Arvada, East Arvada Junior High School, 39.8024865, -105.0777616
Arvada, Fitzmorris Cottage School, 39.8102644, -105.1113738
Arvada, Fruitdale School, 39.778598, -105.1191519
Arvada, Hoskinson Cottage School, 39.8105421, -105.099429
Arvada, Our Lady of the Rosary Academy, 39.77398, -105.05929
Arvada, Russell Cottage School, 39.7910978, -105.1044292
Arvada, Russell Elementary School, 39.79036, -105.08554
Arvada, Sands House Sanatarium, 39.7555425, -105.0555389
Arvada, Secrest Cottage School Number 1, 39.8197086, -105.077206
Arvada, Secrest Cottage School Number 2, 39.8163753, -105.0674834
Arvada, Swanson Cottage School Number 1, 39.8174863, -105.0577609
Arvada, Zerger Elementary School, 39.86188, -105.09737
Bailey, Cliffdale Post Office, 39.4086003, -105.3763853
Conifer, Flying J Ranch Airport, 39.5424884, -105.317771
Conifer, Meyer Ranch Airport, 39.5502685, -105.2807239
Fort Logan, Alameda Junior High School, 39.7124872, -105.0619283
Fort Logan, American Medical Center Cancer Research Center, 39.7435981, -105.0674838
Fort Logan, Axford Cottage School, 39.7222093, -105.0619283
Fort Logan, Bancroft School, 39.6969317, -105.0630396
Fort Logan, Belmont Junior High School, 39.7416537, -105.0563724
Fort Logan, Cleveland Heights Cottage School, 39.7158205, -105.0616505
Fort Logan, Lakewood's Historical Belmar Village, 39.7043041, -105.0844349
Fort Logan, Lasley Cottage School Number 3, 39.6949873, -105.071651
Fort Logan, Metropolitan Youth Education Center, 39.7480426, -105.0577613
Indian Hills, Indian Hills Post Office, 39.6166546, -105.2372124
Littleton, Columbine Airpark, 39.5894324, -105.1094308
Morrison, Cottage School Number 1, 39.700543, -105.136653
Morrison, Daniels School, 39.7388761, -105.1280413
Morrison, Denver University Research Institute, 39.7241541, -105.1594313
Morrison, Devinny Cottage School, 39.6916542, -105.1333196
Morrison, Glennon Heights Cottage School Number 2, 39.6969318, -105.1258194
Morrison, Mother Cabrini Orphanage, 39.7033209, -105.2258224
Platte Canyon, Dome Rock Post Office, 39.4216557, -105.1974907
Platte Canyon, Longview Post Office, 39.417489, -105.1938795
Unknown, Cloudcrest Post Office, 0, 0
Willow Lakes, Glennon Heights Cottage School Number 1, 39.7097083, -106.1275216

Jefferson County

Grand Army of the Republic Posts
Theodore H Dodd, No. 3, Jefferson, Golden
Maj Anderson, No. 88, Jefferson, Arvada

USGS Historic Military Places
Arvada, Rocky Flats Plant, 39.8915236, -105.2144915

Military Bases
None

Post Offices

Name	Opened	Closed	ZIP
Archers	1888 Sept 10	1893 July 25	
Arvada	1871 Feb 16		80001
Beaver Brook	1875 Apr 19	1892 May 31*	
Belleville	1881 Mar 7	1881 July 27	
Brightside	1900 Nov 13	1902 Nov 29*	
Brook Forest	1921 Oct 11	1949 Feb 15	
Buffalo Creek	1878 Aug 16		
Cheesman	1900 Mar 5	1904 Oct 31	
Cliff	1889 Jan 24	1923 Apr 5*	
Cliffdale	1923 Apr 5	1933 June 15	
Cloudcrest	1915 Apr 15	1918 Oct 15	
Conifer	1865 Apr 27	1929 Feb 28	
Conifer 2	1960 Oct 1		80433
Copperdale	1882 Mar 22	1883 Jan 30	
Creswell	1870 Oct 7	1908 Feb 15	
Critchell	1899 June 19	1945 Apr 30	
Crosson	1879 Aug 14	1885 Aug 25	
Crossons	1920 June 2	1931 Dec 31	
Crystal Lake	1892 June 28	1894 Nov 2	
Daffodil	1896 Apr 11	1908 Feb 19	
Daniels	1948 Apr 8	1954 July 1	
Dawson	1890 June 9	1894 June 30	
Deercreek	1896 Apr 24	1899 Dec 15	
Dome Rock	1880 July 12	1911 Apr 4	
East Tincup	1960 June 1	1963 Sept 1	
Edgewater	1892 Mar 1	1937 July 15	
El Rancho	1956 July 1		
Elk Creek	1864 Mar 23	1865 Apr 18	
Evergreen	1876 July 17		80439
Forks Creek	1878 Apr 5	1895 June 4	
Forkscreek	1895 June 4	1927 June 10	
Foxton	1909 Jan 21		80441
Gillespie	1890 May 24	1894 June 20	
Gilman	1874 Dec 17	1876 Aug 8	

Historical Assets Colorado

Golden	1876 June 27		80401
Golden City	1860 Apr 6	1876 June 27	
Golden Gate	1860 Sept 6	1863 Aug 19	
Grotto	1881 Mar 7	1882 Mar 21	
Herndon	1884 Feb 25	1884 Aug 1	
Hutchinson	1865 Apr 27	1894 Nov 16*	
Idledale	1930 Sept 1		80453
Indian Hills	1925 June 2		80454
Jefferson	1872 Mar 25	1873 Dec 12	
Jefferson 2			80456
Joylan	1918 Jan 28	1920 July 7	
Junction	1861 Aug 28	1863 Oct 22	
Kittredge	1923 Apr 2		80457
Lakeview	1892 Dec 3	1894 Feb 3	
Lakewood	1892 Apr 21	1942 Mar 31*	
Lamb	1890 June 11	1908 Feb 15	
Longview	1911 Apr 4	1937 Sept 15	
Magic Mountain	1960 July 16	1962 June 1	
Medlen	1896 Aug 15	1901 May 31	
Michigan House	1863 Feb 28	1863 May 5	
Morrison	1872 Dec 12	1908 June 8	
Morrison 2	1950 Aug 1		80465
Mount Morrison	1908 June 8	1950 Aug 1	
Mount Vernon	1860 May 9	1885 July 9*	
Mountain Park	1966 Aug 16	1978 Sept 23	
Olio	1872 Feb 16	1872 Aug 26	
Park Siding	1890 Dec 27	1896 May 21	
Phillipsburg	1896 July 2	1896 Oct 22	
Pine	1882 Mar 28	1961 July 22*	
Pine 2	1961 July 22		80470
Plainview	1909 Aug 26	1952 Apr 30*	
Platte Canon	1881 Mar 11	1893 May 21	
Ralston	1887 Apr 4	1887 Oct 27	
Ralstons	1863 Mar 16	1870 Jan 21*	
Resort	1880 Jan 15	1886 May 11*	
Ridge	1912 July 3	1954 June 30	
Sanatorium	1923 Mar 9	1928 Sept 1	
Semper	1882 Dec 28	1900 Aug 31	
South Platte	1899 Jan 31	1937 Sept 15	
Spivak	1928 Sept 1	1967 June 30	
Starbuck	1920 July 7	1930 Sept 1	
Symes	1887 Feb 9	1899 Jan 31	
Tindale	1891 Nov 2	1893 Feb 6	
Turkey Creek	1874 Dec 16	1875 Aug 24	
Urmston	1891 Mar 25	1900 Aug 15	
Vermilion	1881 Jan 3	1881 June 7	

Jefferson County

Wheat Ridge	1913 July 7		80033
Willowville	1879 Jan 8	1879 July 10	

Topo Quads

Bailey	393000N	392230N	1052230W	1053000W
Cheesman Lake	391500N	390730N	1051500W	1052230W
Conifer	393730N	393000N	1051500W	1052230W
Deckers	392230N	391500N	1050730W	1051500W
Evergreen	394500N	393730N	1051500W	1052230W
Golden	395230N	394500N	1050730W	1051500W
Green Mountain	392230N	391500N	1051500W	1052230W
Indian Hills	393730N	393000N	1050730W	1051500W
Kassler	393000N	392230N	1050000W	1050730W
McCurdy Mountain	391500N	390730N	1052230W	1053000W
Morrison	394500N	393730N	1050730W	1051500W
Pine	393000N	392230N	1051500W	1052230W
Platte Canyon	393000N	392230N	1050730W	1051500W
Ralston Buttes	395230N	394500N	1051500W	1052230W
Westcreek	391500N	390730N	1050730W	1051500W
Windy Peak	392230N	391500N	1052230W	1053000W

Suggested Reading

Bentley, Margaret V. *The Upper Side of the Pie Crust: an Early History of Southwestern Jefferson County, Conifer, Pine, Buffalo Creek, Colorado*. Evergreen, CO: Jefferson County Historical Society, 1996.

Dark, Ethel. *History of Jefferson County, Colorado*. Thesis, Colorado State College of Education, 1939.

From Scratch: a History of Jefferson County, Colorado. Golden, CO: Jefferson County Historical Commission, 1985.

Jefferson County Sheriff's Office: 1859-2009. Evansville, IN: M T Publishing, 2010.

Lomond, Carole and Stephen Knapp. *Jefferson County, Colorado: a Unique and Eventful History*. Golden, CO: Views Pub Co, 2009.

Ramstetter, Charles and Mary Ramstetter. *John Gregory Country: a Place Names and History of Ralston Buttes Quadrangle, Jefferson County, Colorado*. Golden, CO: C Lazy Three Press, 2013.

Robbins, Sara E. *Jefferson County, Colorado: the Colorful Past of a Great Community*. Lakewood, CO: Jefferson County Bank, 1062.

Ryan, Edna Sirois. *Narrative History of Buffalo Creek and Buffalo Park, Jefferson County, Colorado*. Denver: Claridge Printing Company, 1960.

Turner, Carol. *Notorious Jefferson County: Frontier Murder and Mayhem*. Charleston, SC: History Press, 2010.

Historical Assets Colorado

Kiowa County

Introduction

Established: 1889   Population: 1,398

Formed from: Cheyenne, Bent

Adjacent Counties: Cheyenne, Bent, Prowers, Otero, Crowley, Lincoln

County Seat: Eads

Other Communities: Haswell, Sheridan Lake, Brandon, Towner, Arlington, Chivington

Website, https://www.colorado.gov/kiowacounty/

Area Codes: 719

Zip Codes: 81021, 81036, 80145, 81071

Historical Assets Colorado

Kiowa County Courthouse

Kiowa County Courthouse 1903

Courthouses & County Government

Kiowa County
http://www.kiowacounty-colorado.com

Kiowa County Courthouse (15th Judicial District), 1305 Goff St, Eads, CO 81036, 719-438-5558; http://www.courts.state.co.us/Courts/County/Index.cfm?County_ID=50

Assessor, P.O. Box 295, Eads, CO 81036, 719-438-5521; http://www.kiowacounty-colorado.com/Kiowa_county_assessor.htm

Board of County Commissioners, 1305 N Goff St, Eads, CO 81036, 719-438-5810, https://www.colorado.gov/pacific/kiowacounty/commissioners-0

Clerk & Recorder, P.O. Box 37, Eads, CO 81036, 719-438-5421; http://www.kiowa-county-colorado.com/kiowa_county_clerk_&_recorder.htm

Coroner & Medical Examiner, P.O. Box 432, Eads, CO 81036, 719-438-2225; Public Health, 1206 Luther, Eads, CO 81036, 719-438-5782; http://www.kiowacounty-colo.com/publichealth.htm

County Records

Birth Unk	Marriage 1889	Divorce 1889
Death Unk	Land 1908	Probate 1889
Court 1889		

County & Municipal Records Held at the State Level

The Colorado State Archives

Physical Records	Records on Film	Records on Master Film
Clerk & Recorder	None	District Court
WPA Historical Records		School Districts
WPA Religious Institutions Survey		
WPA Eads		

Kiowa County

The Denver Public Library
WWI Draft Registration Cards (microfilm)

School Districts

School Districts, http://www.adcogov.org/local-school-districts
Kiowa County School District RE-1, 210 W 10th, Eads, CO 81036, 719-438-2218
Kiowa County School District RE-2, 13997 CR 71, Sheridan Lake, CO 81071, 719-729-3331

Historic School Districts

1. Eads
2. [1891]
3. Sheridan Lake, Stamiard Draw
4. Arlington
5. Fine Flat, Chivington
6. Galatea, Black Lake, Grand View, Prairie Center
7. Rush Creek
8. Chivington
9. Brandon, Shroud's Lake
10. Stuart, New Hope, Wolfe
11. Water Valley, Summit Ridge, Rush Creek, Brandon
12. Diston, Towner
13. Chivington, Sheridan Lake
14. Meadow Lee
15. Galatea
16. Towner
17. Pleasant Hill, Pleasant View, South Towner
18. Towner
19. [1890]
20. Prairie Queen
21. Hillcrest
22. [1890]
23. [1890]
24. Towner
25. Haswell
26. Inman, Prairie Valley
27. Sweetwater, Mustang Valley
28.
29.
30.
31.
32.
33.
34.
35.
36.
37.
38. [1903]

Fraternal Organizations

Granges
Kiowa, No. 206, Kiowa, Eads, 23 Mar 1912
Brandon, No. 230, Kiowa, Brancon, 25 Sept 1914
Chivington, No. 231, Kiowa, Chivington, 26 Sept 1914
Arlington, No. 250, Kiowa, Arlington, 15 May 1915
Tri-County, No. 264, Kiowa, Haswall, 19 Jan 1916
Valley, No. 274, Kiowa, Arlington, 1 July 1916
Kaswell, No. 282, Kiowa, Kaswell, 10 May 1916
Sheridan Lake, No. 293, Kiowa, Sheridan Lake, 17 June 1916
Prairie Rise, No. 315, Kiowa, Holly, 30 Dec 1916

Masons

Ancient Free & Accepted Masons
Unity, No. 142, Kiowa, Eads, 17 Sept 1912

Royal Arch Masons
None

Knights Templar
None

Historical Assets Colorado

>   **Eastern Star**
>   Bright Star, No. 106, Kiowa, Eads
>
>   **Odd Fellows**
>   Eads, No. 79, Kiowa, Eads, 1888 Aug 30
>   Prairie, No. 173, Kiowa, Sheridan Lake
>   Eads, No. 177, Kiowa, Eads
>
>   **Rebekahs**
>   Kiowa, No. 85, Kiowa, Eads
>
>   **Knights of Pythias**
>   None
>
>   **Pythian Sisters**
>   None
>
>   **Benevolent Protective Order of Elks**
>   None

City & Town Halls

>   **Eads**, 110 W 13th St, Eads, CO 81036, 719-438-5590, http://www.kcedfonline.org/eads.htm

Archives & Manuscript Collections

>   None

Historical & Genealogical Societies

>   None

Local Libraries

>   **Kiowa County Public Library**, 1305 N Goff St, PO Box 790, Eads, CO 81036-0790, (719) 438-5581, https://eads.colibraries.org

Links

>   **CO GenWeb**
>   http://cogenweb.com/kiowa/
>
>   **Cyndi's List**
>   https://www.cyndislist.com/us/co/counties/kiowa/
>
>   **FamilySearch Wiki**
>   https://www.familysearch.org/wiki/en/Kiowa_County,_Colorado_Genealogy
>
>   **Linkpendium**
>   http://www.linkpendium.com/kiowa-co-genealogy/
>
>   **RootsWeb Wiki**
>   https://wiki.rootsweb.com/wiki/index.php/Kiowa_County,_Colorado
>
>   **Wikipedia**
>   https://en.wikipedia.org/wiki/Kiowa_County,_Colorado

Kiowa County

Historic Hotels
None

Museums & Historic Sites
Kiowa County Museum, 1313 Maine St, Eads, CO 81036, (719) 438-2250
Sand Creek Massacre National Historic Site, 55411 Cty Rd W, Eads, CO 80136, (719) 438-5916, https://www.nps.gov/sand/index.htm

Special Events & Scenic Locations
The Kiowa County Fair & Rodeo is held at the Kiowa County Fair Grounds, 15103 Hwy 287, Eads, CO 81036, 719-438-5321, https://www.kiowacounty-colorado.com/kiowa_county_fairgrounds.htm
The local newspaper, The Kiowa County Press, keeps a calendar of upcoming events here: https://kiowacountypress.net/content/upcoming-events

Sand Creek Massacre National Historic Site
TransAmerica Trail Bicycle Route

Ghost Towns & Other Sparsely Populated Places
Arlington, Brandon, Chivington, Diston, Fergus, Galatea, Haskell, Haswell, Kilburn, Sheridan Lake, Stewart, Stuart, Towner, Water Valley, Whitney

Newspapers
Arlington Blizzard. (Arlington, Kiowa County, Colo.) 18??-1???
The Chivington Chief. (Chivington, Colo.) 18??-1???
The Water Valley Clarion. (Water Valley, Bent County, Colo.) 1887-1???
Kiowa County Press and The Brandon News. (Eads, Kiowa County, Colo.) 1887-1923
The Stuart Chronicle. (Stuart, Kiowa Co., Colo.) 1888-1889
The Brandon Bell. (Brandon, Colo.) 19??-19??
The Haswell Herald. (Haswell, Kiowa County, Colo.) 19??-19??
Colorado Farm and Ranch. (Sheridan Lake, Colo.) 1906-1917
The Westland. (Brandon, Colo.) 1916-1921
The Brandon News. (Brandon, Colo.) 1921-1923
Kiowa County Press and The Brandon News. (Eads, Kiowa County, Colo.) 1923-1968
Kiowa County Press. (Eads, Kiowa County, Colo.) 1968-Current

Places on the National Register
Eads, American Legion Hall, CO 287, N of Eads
Eads, Crow—Hightower House, 909 Maine St.
Eads, Eads Community Church, 110 E. 11th St.
Eads, Eads School Gymnasium, W. 10th & Slater Sts.
Eads, Sand Creek Massacre Site, Near jct. of Cty Rd. 54 and Cty Rd. W
Haswell, Hotel Holly—Haswell Hotel, 200 4th St.

Historical Assets Colorado

USGS Historic Places
Stuart, Budde Landing Strip, 38.4958493, -102.1432382

Grand Army of the Republic Posts
None

USGS Historic Military Places
None

Military Bases
None

Post Offices

Arlington	1887 Aug 16	2011 Oct 15	
Brandon	1888 May 19	1893 May 3	
Brandon	1908 May 28	1963 Feb 28	
Chivington	1887 Oct 24	1991 Jan 1	
Diston	1908 June 29	1908 Aug 15	
Eads	1887 Nov 18		81036
Fergus	1888 June 7	1890 Sept 2	
Galatea	1887 Dec 22	1948 July 31	
Haswell	1903 Mar 31		81045
Kilburn	1890 July 17	1891 Oct 2	
Queen Beach	1908 Nov 9	1911 Sept 30	
Segreganset	1914 July 4	1917 July 31	
Sheridan Lake	1887 Sept 20		81071
Stewart	1888 Apr 23	1899 Apr 25	
Stuart	1911 Mar 18	1912 Nov 20	
Sweetwater	1908 May 28	1918 Aug 15	
Towner	1888 Feb 20	1992 May 9	
Water Valley	1887 Sept 9	1894 Sept 12	

Topo Quads

Alkali Lake	383000N	382230N	1023730W	1024500W
Arlington	382230N	381500N	1031500W	1032230W
Arlington NE	383000N	382230N	1031500W	1032230W
Brandon	383000N	382230N	1022230W	1023000W
Chivington	383000N	382230N	1023000W	1023730W
Chivington SE	382230N	381500N	1023000W	1023730W
Eads	383000N	382230N	1024500W	1025230W
Haswell	383000N	382230N	1030730W	1031500W
Haswell NE	383000N	382230N	1030000W	1030730W
Haswell SE	382230N	381500N	1030000W	1030730W
Hawkins	383000N	382230N	1025230W	1030000W
Houston Lakes	382230N	381500N	1032230W	1033000W

Kiowa County

Lake Devore	382230N	381500N	1020730W	1021500W
Long Lake	382230N	381500N	1030730W	1031500W
Neenoshe Reservoir	382230N	381500N	1023730W	1024500W
Rose Ranch	382230N	381500N	1025230W	1030000W
Sheridan Lake	383000N	382230N	1021500W	1022230W
Sheridan Lake SE	382230N	381500N	1021500W	1022230W
Sheridan Lake SW	382230N	381500N	1022230W	1023000W
Stuart	383000N	382230N	1020730W	1021500W
Swede Lake	382230N	381500N	1024500W	1025230W
The Pinnacles	383000N	382230N	1033000W	1033730W
Todd Point	382230N	381500N	1033000W	1033730W
Towner	383000N	382230N	1020000W	1020730W
Towner SE	382230N	381500N	1020000W	1020730W
Trimble Lake	383000N	382230N	1032230W	1033000W

Suggested Reading

Eads High School Local History Project. *Kiowa County*. Charleston, SC: Arcadia Pub, 2010.

Harner, Ariana and Clark Secrest. *Children of the Storm: the True Story of the Pleasant Hill School Bus Tragedy*. Golden, CO: Fulcrum Publishing, 2001.

Jacobs, Ruthanna. *Kiowa County, Colorado, Centennial History, 1989*. Dallas: Curtis Media Corporation, 1989.

Teal, Roleta D and Betty Lee Jacobs. *Kiowa County*. Boulder, CO: Kiwoa County Bicentennial Committee, 1976.

Women on the Plains: *Pioneer Women, Kiowa County's Album*. Eads, CO: Kiowa County Public Library, 1983.

Historical Assets Colorado

Kit Carson County

Introduction

Established: 1889   Population: 8,270

Formed from: Elbert

Adjacent Counties: Yuma, Cheyenne, Lincoln, Washington

County Seat: Burlington

   Other Communities: Bethune, Flagler, Seibert, Stratton, Vona

Website, https://www.colorado.gov/kitcarsoncounty

Area Codes: 719, 970

Zip Codes: 80805, 80807, 80815, 80834, 80836, 80861

Historical Assets Colorado

Kit Carson County Courthouse

Courthouses & County Government

Kit Carson County
https://colorado.gov/kitcarsoncounty

Kit Carson County Courthouse (13th Judicial District), 251 16th St, Burlington, CO 80807, 719-346-5524; http://www.courts.state.co.us/Courts/County/Index.cfm?County_ID=38

Assessor, 251 16th St, Burlington, CO 80807, 719-346-8946; http://kitcarsoncounty.org/Assessor.html

Board of County Commissioners, 251 16th St, Burlington, CO 80807, 719-340-2308, https://kitcarsoncounty.colorado.gov/node/10299

Clerk & Recorder, 251 16th St, Burlington, CO 80807, 719-346-8638; http://kitcarsoncounty.org/Clerk___Recorder.html

Coroner, 1576 Lowell Ave, Ste B, Burlington, CO 80807, 719-346-9515; https://www.colorado.gov/pacific/kitcarsoncounty/coroner-5

Elections, 251 16th St, Ste 203, Burlington, CO 80807, 719-346-8638; https://colorado.gov/pacific/kitcarsoncounty/elections-26

Public Health, 252 S 14th St, Burlington, CO 80807, 719-346-7158; http://kitcarsoncounty.org/Health_and_Human_Service.html

Transportation (Road & Bridge), 815 15th St, Burlington, CO 80807, 719-346-8146; 324 Nebraska Ave, Stratton, CO 719-348-5282; 920 Ouray Ave, Flagler, CO 80815, 719-765-4665; https://colorado.gov/pacific/kitcarsoncounty/road-and-bridge-2

Treasurer, 251 16th St, Ste 203, Burlington, CO 80807, 719-346-8434; http://kitcarsoncounty.org/Treasurer.html

County Records

Birth Unk	Marriage 1908	Divorce 1910
Death Unk	Land 1908	Probate 1910
Court 1910		

Kit Carson County

County & Municipal Records Held at the State Level

The Colorado State Archives

Physical Records
County Court
District Court
WPA Historical Records
WPA Religious Institutions Survey
WPA Eads
Cities
  Burlington

Records on Film
Clerk & Recorder
District Court
Cities
  Burlington

Records on Master Film
Assessor
County Court
District Court
Historical & Genealogical Society Newspapers
School Districts
Treasurer
Cities
  Burlington

The Denver Public Library
WWI Draft Registration Cards (microfilm)

School Districts

School Districts, http://www.adcogov.org/local-school-districts

Arriba-Flagler School District C-20, 421 Julian Ave, Flagler, CO 80815, 719-765-4684; https://www.colorado.gov/af20

Bethune School District R-5, P.O. Box 127, Bethune, CO 80805, 719-346-7513; http://www.bethuneschool.com/

Burlington School District RE-6J, 2600 Rose Ave, Burlington, CO 80807, 719-346-8737; https://www.burlingtonk12.org/

Hi-Plains School District R-23, 350 Patriot Dr, Seibert CO 80834, 970-664-2636; http://www.hp-patriots.com/

Liberty School District J-4, 9332 Hwy 36, Joes, CO 80822, 970-358-4288; http://www.libertyschoolj4.com/

Stratton School District R-4, 219 Illinois Ave, Stratton, CO 80836, 719-348-5369; http://www.strattonschools.org/

Historic School Districts

1. Bethune
2. Emerson
3. Columbine, Prairie View
4. Carmichael
5. Peconic
6. Brammeier
7. Pious Point
8. Fair Haven
9. Seaman
10. Midway
11. Green Valley
12. Boger
13. Pond Creek
14. Grand View, White Plains, Mount Pleasant
15. Rose
16. Brownwood
17. Beaver Valley
18. Liberty
19. Second Central
20. East Fairview, West Fairview, Fair View
21. Pleasant View
22. Prairie View, Yale
23. Murphy
24. Prairie View, Blue View
25. Lone Star
26. Prairie View
27. Wilsonville
28. Union
29. Perkins, First Central
30. [1889]
31. Broadsword
32. Clearview
33. Plain View
34. Jewell
35. Flagler
36. Spring Rock, Nut Brook, Grand View
37. Seibert
38. Happy Hollow
39. Tuttle
40. Mount Pleasant, Pleasant Valley
41. Solid Center
42. Keehter
43. [1920]
44. Plainview
45. Prairie Star

Historical Assets Colorado

46. Progress
47. Rock Vale, Pleasant Meadow, Lucky Poll, Spring Creek
48. Ritzius
49. Idlewild
50. Norton
51. Hook
52. Bethel
53. Hell Creek
54. Ash View
55. Shield, Shiloh
56. Smelker
57. Stratton
58. Blakeman
59. Rock Cliff
60. Green Knoll
61. Vona
62. Busy Valley
63. [1920]
64. Plain View
65. Midway
66. Tip Top
67. West Point
68. Pleasant Valley
69. Vander Kool
70. Victory Heights
71. North Flatt
72. Prairie View
73. Prairie Gem
74. Pleasant Valley, Peaceful Valley
75. Sunny Slope, Sunny Side
76. Knapp

C1. Burlington
C2. Smoky Hill

Jt63. Clark
Jt79. Cement
Jt82. Kirk
Jt86. Cook
Jt87. Mount Pleasant
Jt92. Boden
Jt93. Newton

Fraternal Organizations

Granges
Grand Union, No. 183, Kit Carson, Tuttle, 26 Jan 1910
Golden Rule, No. 281, Kit Carson, Burlington, 6 May 1916
Fairview, No. 297, Kit Carson, Burlington, 8 July 1916
Mizpah, No. 305, Kit Carson, Burlington, 13 Nov 1916
Prairie View, No. 341, Kit Carson, Cole, 7 May 1917
Jewell, No. 344, Kit Carson, Burlington, 8 May 1917
Hermes, No. 346, Kit Carson, Hermes, xx May 1917
Bethel, No. 363, Kit Carson, Stratton, 23 Feb 1918
First Central, No. 383, Kit Carson, Stratton, 29 May 1919
Progress, No. 391, Kit Carson, Seibert, 27 Dec 1919
Mile Stone, No. 418, Kit Carson, Burlington, 6 Aug 1935

Masons

Ancient Free & Accepted Masons
Burlington, No. 77, Kit Carson, Burlington, 18 Sept 1889
Kit Carson, No. 127, Kit Carson, Flagler, 17 Sept 1907

Royal Arch Masons
None

Knights Templar
None

Eastern Star
Aurora, No. 73, Kit Carson, Burlington
Flagler, No. 113, Kit Carson, Flagler

Odd Fellows
Siebert, No. 37, Kit Carson, Siebert
Siebert, No. 52, Kit Carson, Siebert
Burlington, No. 84, Kit Carson, Burlington, 1889 Aug 22
Flagler, No. 135, Kit Carson, Flagler
Burlington, No. 152, Kit Carson, Burlington

Kit Carson County

Rebekahs
Comet, No. 123, Kit Carson, Burlington
Lotus, No. 128, Kit Carson, Seibert
Crystal, No. 130, Kit Carson, Flagler

Knights of Pythias
Lone Star, No. 51, Kit Carson, Burlington

Pythian Sisters
Star of Hope, No. 68, Kit Carson, Stratton
Northern Lights, No. 70, Kit Carson, Burlington

Benevolent Protective Order of Elks
None

City & Town Halls

Burlington, 415 15th St Burlington, CO 80807, 719-346-8652, https://www.burlingtoncolo.com

Flagler, 311 Main Ave, Flagler, CO 80815, 719-765-4571, http://flaglercolorado.com

Seibert, 201 Colorado Ave, Seibert, CO 80834, 970-664-2323

Stratton, 127 Colorado Ave, Stratton, CO 80836, 719-348-5612, https://www.colorado.gov/stratton

Archives & Manuscript Collections

None

Historical & Genealogical Societies

Flagler Historical Society, P.O. Box 263, Flagler, CO 80815, https://www.facebook.com/flaglerhistoricalsociety/

Local Libraries

Burlington Public Library, 321 14th St, Burlington, CO 80807-1607, (719) 346-8109, http://www.burlingtoncolo.com/160/Library

Flagler Community Library, 311 Main Ave, P.O. Box 367, Flagler, CO 80815-0367, (719) 765-4310, http://flaglercounty.org/departments/library/index.php

Stratton Public Library, 331 New York Ave, PO Box 267, Stratton, CO 80836-0267, (719) 348-5922, https://stratton.colibraries.org

Links

CO GenWeb
http://cogenweb.com/kitcarson/

Cyndi's List
https://www.cyndislist.com/us/co/counties/kit-carson/

FamilySearch Wiki
https://www.familysearch.org/wiki/en/Kit_Carson_County,_Colorado_Genealogy

Linkpendium
http://www.linkpendium.com/adams-co-genealogy/

Historical Assets Colorado

RootsWeb Wiki
https://wiki.rootsweb.com/wiki/index.php/Kit_Carson_County,_Colorado

Wikipedia
https://en.wikipedia.org/wiki/Kit_Carson_County,_Colorado

Historic Hotels
None

Museums & Historic Sites
Colorado Welcome Center Museum, 48265 Interstate 70, P.O. Box 157, Burlington, CO 80807, (719) 346-5554, https://www.colorado.com/colorado-official-state-welcome-center/colorado-welcome-center-burlington

Flagler Hospital Museum & Hal Borland Room, 311 Main Ave, Flagler, CO 80815, (719) 765-4571, https://www.colorado.com/historic-places-districts/flagler-hospital-museum-hal-borland-room

Kit Carson County Carousel & Museum, 815 15th St, Burlington, CO 80807, https://www.kitcarsoncountycarousel.com

Old Town Museum, 420 S 14th St, Burlington, CO 80807, (970) 346-7382, https://www.oldtownburlington.com

Second Central School Museum, 404 4th St, Flagler, CO 80815, (719) 765-4481, https://www.colorado.com/historic-places-districts/second-central-school-museum

Special Events & Scenic Locations
The Kit Carson County Fair & Rodeo takes place in July most years, at the Kit Carson Fairgrounds, 815 15th St, Burlington, CO 80807, 719-346-0111, https://kitcarsoncounty.colorado.gov/node/10286

The Kit Carson County Carousel keeps a blog that includes local events here: https://www.kitcarsoncountycarousel.com/blog

Philadelphia Toboggan Company Carousel #6 National Historic Landmark
Smoky Hill Trail

Ghost Towns & Other Sparsely Populated Places
Ashland, Avendale, Beloit, Carlisle, Chapin, Claremont, Flagler, Goff, Landsman, Seibert, Siding, Siebert, Tuttle, Vona, Wallet, Yale

Newspapers
The Prairie Settler. (Seibert, Colo.) 1???-19??
The Seibert Free Press. (Seibert, Kit Carson Co., Colo.) 18??-1???
The Weekly Register. (Flagler, Kit Carson Co., Colo.) 18??-1???
Burlington Blade. (Burlington, Kit Carson County, Colo.) 188?-1???
Rain-Belt Farmer. (North Smoky [Burlington], Colo.) 1890-1890
Burlington Republican. (Burlington, Colo.) 1890-1913
Kit Carson County Banner. (Burlington, Colo.) 1892-1896

Kit Carson County

The Burlington Call. (Burlington, Colo.) 19??-1944
The Seibert Settler. (Seibert, Colo.) 19??-19??
Kit Carson County Record. (Burlington, Colo.) 1901-19??
The Stratton Press. (Stratton, Colo.) 1908-19??
The Vona Enterprise. (Vona, Kit Carson County, Colo.) 1908-19??
The Stratton Democrat. (Stratton, Colo.) 1909-19??
The Flagler News. (Flagler, Kit Carson County, Colo.) 1913-Current
The Burlington Record. (Burlington, Colo.) 1931-Current
Stratton Spotlight. ([Stratton, Co) 198?-Current

Places on the National Register
Burlington, Burlington Gymnasium, 450 11th St.
Burlington, Burlington State Armory, 191 14th St.
Burlington, Elitch Gardens Carousel, Kit Carson County Fairgrounds
Burlington, Hudson, Sim, Motor Company, 1332 Senter Ave.
Burlington, Winegar Building, 494—498 Fourteenth St.
Flagler, Flagler Hospital, 311 Main Ave., P.O. Box 126
Vona, Spring Creek Bridge, US 24 at milepost 430.32

USGS Historic Places
Burlington, Burlington Municipal Airport, 39.3116667, -102.2841667
Kanorado NW, Silkman Farms Incorporated Airport, 39.4544393, -102.2132449
Tuttle, Tuttle, 39.4973848, -102.5108957

Grand Army of the Republic Posts
Gen Wolcott, No. 64, Kit Carson, Burlington

USGS Historic Military Places
None

Military Bases
None

Post Offices

Ashland	1890 Jan 14	1909 May 15	
Avendale	1889 Feb 5	1890 Sept 12	
Baltzer	1907 June 4	1907 Dec 14	
Beaverton	1910 Oct 17	1915 Nov 30	
Beloit	1888 Mar 27	1893 Sept 29	
Berry	1911 Apr 13	1912 Apr 15	
Bethune	1906 Sept 17		80807
Bonny	1915 June 3	1924 Feb 29	
Burlington	1887 Apr 29		80807
Carey	1910 Dec 12	1916 Dec 30	
Carlisle	1887 July 21	1890 June 9	

Historical Assets Colorado

Chapin	1890 Feb 15	1894 Nov 10	
Claremont	1888 Sept 11	1906 Mar 24	
Cole	1907 Mar 7	1919 May 31	
Dodgeville	1907 Sept 14	1907 Dec 14	
Elphis	1916 Dec 8	1923 Dec 31	
Farley	1908 Mar 31	1908 Oct 15	
Flagler	1888 Oct 12		80815
Goff	1888 Apr 23	1910 June 15	
Hanover	1908 July 7	1908 Oct 29	
Kukkuk	1907 Apr 24	1908 Apr 15	
Landsman	1883 Mar 27	1918 May 31	
Loco	1903 Mar 11	1922 May 31	
Morris	1907 Mar 18	1914 Mar 15	
Oriska	1910 Dec 22	1917 Dec 31	
Seibert	1888 Oct 17		80834
Stratton	1888 Sept 11		80836
Tuttle	1883 Mar 27	1918 July 31	
Valley	1898 June 2	1901 Aug 15	
Vansville	1907 Sept 14	1907 Nov 20	
Vona	1889 Jan 19	1905 Oct 14	
Vona	1907 Jan 21		80861
Wallet	1890 Apr 8	1907 May 15	
Yale	1891 Sept 10	1905 Nov 30	

Topo Quads

Alpine Ranch	390730N	390000N	1023000W	1023730W
Alpine Ranch NE	391500N	390730N	1023000W	1023730W
Alpine Ranch NW	391500N	390730N	1023730W	1024500W
Alpine Ranch SW	390730N	390000N	1023730W	1024500W
Bellyache Creek	390730N	390000N	1030000W	1030730W
Bethune	392230N	391500N	1022230W	1023000W
Big Spring Creek	390730N	390000N	1025230W	1030000W
Bledsoe Ranch	390730N	390000N	1030730W	1031500W
Burlington	392230N	391500N	1021500W	1022230W
Burlington NE	393000N	392230N	1021500W	1022230W
East of Rock Creek	390730N	390000N	1021500W	1022230W
East of Sevenmile Ranch	391500N	390730N	1030730W	1031500W
Flagler	392230N	391500N	1030000W	1030730W
Flagler NE	393000N	392230N	1030000W	1030730W
Flagler NW	393000N	392230N	1030730W	1031500W
Flagler Reservoir	392230N	391500N	1025230W	1030000W
Flagler SW	392230N	391500N	1030730W	1031500W
Kanorado NE	393000N	392230N	1020000W	1020730W
Kanorado NW	393000N	392230N	1020730W	1021500W

Kit Carson County

Mount Sunflower NW	391500N	390730N	1020730W	1021500W
Mount Sunflower SW	390730N	390000N	1020730W	1021500W
North of Big Spring	390730N	390000N	1024500W	1025230W
Peconic	392230N	391500N	1020730W	1021500W
Rock Creek	390730N	390000N	1022230W	1023000W
Seibert	392230N	391500N	1024500W	1025230W
Seibert NE	393000N	392230N	1024500W	1025230W
Seibert NW	393000N	392230N	1025230W	1030000W
Settlement	393000N	392230N	1022230W	1023000W
South of Bethune	391500N	390730N	1022230W	1023000W
South of Burlington	391500N	390730N	1021500W	1022230W
South of Flagler	391500N	390730N	1030000W	1030730W
South of Flagler Reservoir	391500N	390730N	1025230W	1030000W
South of Seibert	391500N	390730N	1024500W	1025230W
Stratton	392230N	391500N	1023000W	1023730W
Stratton NW	393000N	392230N	1023730W	1024500W
Tuttle	393000N	392230N	1023000W	1023730W
Vona	392230N	391500N	1023730W	1024500W

Suggested Reading

Bader, Roy and Alvis Bader. *History and Stories of the Kit Carson County Cattlemen and Women*. Burlington, CO: Kit Carson County Cattlemen's Association, 1963.

Blevins, Terry W. *Our Heritage: a Collection of Tales of East Central Colorado*. Stratton, CO: East Central Council of Local Governments, 1983.

Kit Carson County History Book Committee. *History of Kit Carson County, Colorado*. Dallas: Curtis Media Company, 1988.

Historical Assets Colorado

La Plata County

Introduction

Established: 1874   Population: 51,334

Formed from: Conejos, Lake

Adjacent Counties: San Juan, Hinsdale, Archuleta, Montezuma, Dolores

County Seat: Durango

Other Communities: Bayfield, Ignacio, Southern Ute, Allison, Bondad, Breen, Falfa, Gem Village, Hermosa, Hesperus, Kline, Marvel, Mayday, Oxford, Red Mesa, Tiffany, Gresill Mines, La Plata, Parrott City

Website, http://www.co.laplata.co.us

Area Codes: 970

Zip Codes: 81122, 81137, 81301, 81302, 81303, 81326, 81329

Historical Assets Colorado

La Plata County Courthouse

La Plata County 19th Century Courthouse

Courthouses & County Government
La Plata County
   http://www.co.laplata.co.us
La Plata County Courthouse (6th Judicial District), 1060 E 2nd Ave, Durango, CO 81301, 970-247-2304; http://www.courts.state.co.us/Courts/County/Index.cfm?County_ID=13
Assessor, 1060 E 2nd Ave, Durango, CO 81301, 970-382-6221; http://www.co.laplata.co.us/departments_officials/assessor
Board of County Commissioners, 1101 E 2nd Ave, Durango, CO 81301, 970-382-6219, http://www.co.laplata.co.us/government/board_of_county_commissioners
Clerk & Recorder, 98 Everett St, Durango, CO 81303, 970-382-6281; http://www.co.laplata.co.us/departments_and_elected_officials/clerk_recorder
Coroner, 1101 E 2nd Ave, Durango, CO 81301, 970-382-6397; http://www.co.laplata.co.us/government/elected_officials/coroner_s_office
Elections, 98 Everett St, Ste C, Durango, CO 81301, 970-382-6296; http://www.co.laplata.co.us/government/departments/elections
Public Health, 281 Sawyer Dr, Durango, CO 81302, 970-247-5702; http://sjbhd.org/
Transportation (Road & Bridge), 1365 S Camino del Rio, Durango, CO 81303, 970-382-6413; http://www.co.laplata.co.us/government/departments/road_and_bridge
Treasurer, 1060 Main Ave, Ste 103, Durango, CO 81301, 970-382-6352; http://co.laplata.co.us/departments_officials/Treasurer

County Records
Birth Unk   Marriage 1878   Divorce 1900
Death Unk   Land 1876   Probate 1900
Court 1900

La Plata County

County & Municipal Records Held at the State Level

The Colorado State Archives

Physical Records
County Court
District Court
Social Services (CCC, WPA)
WPA Historical Records
WPA Religious Institutions
 Survey
Cities
 Durango

Records on Film
County Court
District Court
Cities
 Durango

Records on Master Film
Clerk & Recorder
County Court
District Court
Finance
Public Trustee
School Districts
Sheriff
Treasurer
Cities
 Durango

The Denver Public Library
Montezuma & La Plata County Mining Companies Records, 1907
WWI Draft Registration Cards (microfilm)

School Districts
School Districts, http://www.adcogov.org/local-school-districts
Bayfield School District 10 JT-R, 24 Clover Dr, Bayfield, CO 81122, 970-884-2496; https://www.bayfield.k12.co.us/
Durango School District 9-R, 201 E 12th St, Durango, CO 81301, 970-247-5411; https://www.durangoschools.org/
Ignacio School District 11-JT, 455 Becker St, Ignacio, CO 81137, 970-563-0500; http://www.ignacioschools.org/

Historic School Districts

1. Animas City
2. Lightner Creek
3. Rockwood
4. Bayfield
5. Pinon Grove
6. Rockvale
7. Thompson Park
8. Columbus
9. Durango
10. Lowell
11. Trimble
12. Hermosa
13. Cascade
14. Sortais
15. Pargin
16. La Posta
17. Orr
18. Redmesa
19. Mayday
20. Hesperus
21. Ignacio
22. Florida
23. Oxford
24. Regnier
25. Allison
26. Cottonwood
27. Moss
28. Tiffany
29. Elco
30. Sunnyside
31. Center
32. Pleasant View
33. Long Lane
34. Marvel
35. Cherry Creek
36. Kline
37. Benn Spring
38. Independent

Fraternal Organizations

Granges
Animas Valley, No. 194, La Plata, Durango, 1 Apr 1911
Oxford, No. 196, La Plata, Oxford/Durango, 28 Apr 1911
Pine River, No. 197, La Plata, Bayfield, 29 Apr 1911

Historical Assets Colorado

Ignacio, No 198, La Plata, Ignacio, 6 May 1911
Florida, No. 306, La Plata, Griffith, 22 Nov 1916
Rimbons Valley, No. 307, La Plata, Ignacio, 1916
Mount Allison, No. 308, La Plata, Allison, 8 Dec 1916
Killkare, No. 309, La Plata, Oxford, 9 Dec 1916
Kline, No. 310, La Plata, Brien, 14 Dec 1916
Eureka, No. 311, La Plata, Durango, 4 Dec 1916
Morrison, No. 312, La Plata, Ignacio, 16 Dec 1916
Red Mesa, No. 313, La Plata, Red Mesa, 1 Jan 1917
Breen, No. 318, La Plata, Kline, 14 Jan 1917
Big Stick, No. 319, La Plata, Breen, 20 Jan 1917
Piedra, No. 461, La Plata, Bayfield, 2 Oct 1945
Marvel, No. 479, La Plata, Marvel, 1 Apr 1951
Oxford, No. 482, La Plata, Ignacio, 30 Dec 1957

Masons
Ancient Free & Accepted Masons
Durango, No. 46, La Plata, Durango, 1 Nov 1881
Durango/San Juan, No. 46, La Plata, Durango, 24 Jan 2015

Royal Arch Masons
San Juan, No. 15, La Plata, Durango

Knights Templar
Ivanhoe Commandery, No. 11, La Plata, Durango, 1884 Mar 4

Eastern Star
Electa, No. 8, La Plata, Durango
La Plata, No. 83, La Plata, Durango

Odd Fellows
Durango, No. 48, La Plata, Durango
Ignacio, No. 182, La Plata, Ignacio

Rebekahs
Sarah, No. 20, La Plata, Durango

Knights of Pythias
Montezuma, No. 22, La Plata, Durango

Pythian Sisters
None

Benevolent Protective Order of Elks
Durango, No. 507, La Plata, Durango

City & Town Halls
Durango, 949 E 2nd Ave, Durango, CO 81301, 970-375-5000, https://durangogov.org

Bayfield, 1199 Bayfield Pkwy, Bayfield, CO 81122, 970-884-9544, https://www.colorado.gov/townofbayfield

Ignacio, 540 Goddard Ave, Ignacio, CO 81137, 970-563-9494, https://www.colorado.gov/ignacio

La Plata County

Archives & Manuscript Collections
Animas Museum & Research Library, 3065 W 2nd Ave, P.O. Box 3384, Durango, CO 81302, (970) 259-2402, http://www.animasmuseum.org

John F Reed Library - Center for Southwest Studies, Fort Lewis College, 1000 Rim Dr, Durango, CO 81301-3999, (970) 247-7551, https://swcenter.fortlewis.edu

Historical & Genealogical Societies
La Plata County Historical Society, Animas School Museum, 3065 W 2nd Ave, P.O. Box 3384, Durango, CO 81302, (970) 259-2402, http://www.animasmuseum.org

Pine River Valley Heritage Society, Historical Museum, 11 W Mill St, Bayfield, CO 81122, (970) 884-7636, http://pineriverheritage.org

Southwest Colorado Genealogical Society, P.O. Box 371, Durango, CO 81302, http://www.swcogen.org

Local Libraries
Durango Public Library & Botanic Gardens, 1900 E 3rd Ave, Durango, CO 81301, (970) 375-3380, http://www.durangopubliclibrary.org

Pine River Public Library, 395 Bayfield Center Dr, P.O. Box 227, Bayfield, CO 81122-0227, (970) 884-2222, http://prlibrary.org

Links

CO GenWeb
http://cogenweb.com/laplata/

Cyndi's List
https://www.cyndislist.com/us/co/counties/la-plata/

FamilySearch Wiki
https://www.familysearch.org/wiki/en/La_Plata_County,_Colorado_Genealogy

Linkpendium
http://www.linkpendium.com/la_plata-co-genealogy/

RootsWeb Wiki
https://wiki.rootsweb.com/wiki/index.php/La_Plata_County,_Colorado

Wikipedia
https://en.wikipedia.org/wiki/La_Plata_County,_Colorado

Historic Hotels
1887 The Strater Hotel, 699 Main Ave, Durango, CO 81301, 970-375-7260, https://strater.com

1892 Rochester Hotel, 726 E 2nd Ave, Durango, CO 81301, 970-385-1920, https://www.rochesterhotel.com

1898 General Palmer Hotel, 567 Main Ave, Durango, CO 81301, 970-247-4747, http://generalpalmerhotel.com

Historical Assets Colorado

Museums & Historic Sites
Animas Museum & Research Library, 3065 W 2nd Ave, P.O. Box 3384, Durango, CO 81302, (970) 259-2402, http://www.animasmuseum.org

Durango & Silver Narrow Gauge Railroad Museum, 479 Main St, Durango, CO 81301, (970) 247-2733, https://www.durangotrain.com

La Plata County Historical Society, Animas School Museum, 3065 W 2nd Ave, P.O. Box 3384, Durango, CO 81302, (970) 259-2402, http://www.animasmuseum.org

Pine River Valley Heritage Society, Historical Museum, 11 W Mill St, Bayfield, CO 81122, (970) 884-7636, http://pineriverheritage.org

Southern Ute Cultural Center, 503 Ouray Dr, Ignacio, CO 81137, (970) 563-9583, https://www.southernutemuseum.org

Special Events & Scenic Locations
The La Plata County Fair is held in August most years, at the La Plata County Fairgrounds, 2500 Main Ave, Durango, CO 81301, 970-382-6463, http://co.laplata.co.us/government/departments/fairgrounds

Visit Durango has a calendar of events here: https://www.durango.org/events/

Historic Downtown Durango has a calendar of events here: https://www.downtown-durango.org/annual-events

What's Happening Durango has a calendar of events here: https://www.whatshappeningdurango.com/

San Juan National Forest
Weminuche Wilderness
Durango-Silverton Narrow-Gauge Railroad National Historic District
Colorado Trail
Old Spanish National Historic Trail
Great Parks Bicycle Route
San Juan Skyway National Scenic Byway

Ghost Towns & Other Sparsely Populated Places
Animas City, Bay City, Bocea, Dix, Florida, Greysill Mines, Hermosa, Hesperus, Home Ranch, Ignacio, La Boca, La Plata City, La Plata Junction, Los Pinos, Mayday, Needleton, Parrot City, Pine River, Porter, Rockwood, Trimble, Vallejo, Viceto

Newspapers
The Durango Democrat. (Durango, La Plata County, Colo.) 1???-1903
The Southwest. (Durango, Colo.) 1879-1884
The Durango Record. (Durango, Colo.) 1880-1882
Durango Herald. (Durango, Colo.) 1881-1886
The Daily South-West. (Durango, Colo.) 1881-1883
Durango Herald. (Durango, Colo.) 1881-1892
The Idea. (Durango, Colo.) 1884-1886
Durango Morning Herald. (Durango, Colo.) 1886-1892
The Daily Idea. (Durango, Colo.) 1887-1888

La Plata County

The Solid Muldoon. (Durango, Colo.) 1892-1895
Durango Herald. (Durango, Colo.) 1892-1895
The Solid Muldoon. [Microfilm Reel] (Durango, Colo.) 1892-1???
The Great Southwest. (Durango, Colo.) 1892-1893
The Daily Southwest. (Durango, Colo.) 1893-1895
The Durango Wage Earner. (Durango, Colo.) 1894-1905
The Durango Herald. (Durango, Colo.) 1895-1898
The Durango Herald And Daily Southwest. (Durango, Colo) 1895-1897
The Outlook. (Fort Lewis, Colo.) 1895-1???
Durango Evening Herald. (Durango, Colo.) 1897-1928
The Morning Democrat. (Durango, La Plata County, Colo.) 1897-1899
The Durango Democrat. (Durango, Colo.) 1899-1928
Durango Semi-Weekly Herald. (Durango, Colo.) 1899-1907
The Durango Telegraph. (Durango, Colo.) 1902-19??
Durango Weekly Democrat. (Durango, Colo.) 1903-19??
The Durango Weekly Banner and The Durango Wage Earner. (Durango, Colo.) 1906-1907
The Durango Wage Earner. (Durango, Colo.) 1907-19??
Semi-Weekly Herald. (Durango, Colo.) 1907-1917
The Bayfield Blade. (Bayfield, La Plata County, Colo.) 1909-1925
The Great Southwest. (Durango, Colo.) 1909-19??
Weekly Ignacio Chieftain. (Ignacio, La Plata County, Colo.) 1910-1917
The Farmer's Voice. (Durango, Colo.) 1910-19??
The Ignacio Chieftain. (Ignacio, La Plata County, Colo.) 1917-1925
The Ignacio Chieftain and The Bayfield Blade. (Ignacio, La Plata County, Colo.) 1925-1932
The Durango Klansman. (Durango, Colo.) 1925-192?
Durango Herald-Democrat. (Durango, Colo.) 1928-1952
The Durango News. (Durango, Colo.) 1930-1952
The Pine River Valley Chieftain and Bayfield Blade. (Ignacio, La Plata County, Colo.) 1932-1933
The Ignacio Chieftain. (Ignacio, La Plata County, Colo.) 1933-1934
The Ignacio Chieftain and Bayfield Blade. (Ignacio, La Plata County, Colo.) 1934-1965
Durango Herald-News. (Durango, Colo.) 1952-1960
The Basin Star. (Durango, Colo.) 1959-1962
The Southern Ute Drum. (Ignacio, Colo.) 1960-Current
The Durango Herald. (Durango, Colo.) 1960-Current
Chieftain. (Ignacio, La Plata County, Colo.) 1965-1972
The Chieftain and Bayfield Blade. (Ignacio, Colo.) 1972-1972
The Four Corners Chieftain and The Bayfield Blade. (Ignacio, Colo.) 1972-1972
The Four Corners Chieftain. (Ignacio, Colo.) 1972-1973
The Mountain Eagle incorporating The Four Corners Chieftain. (Durango, Colo.) 1973-1974
The Mountain Eagle. (Durango, Colo.) 1974-19??
Today. (Durango, Colo.) 1975-198?

Historical Assets Colorado

San Juan Journal. ([Durango, Colo.]) 1979-198?
Western Colorado Report. ([Durango, Colo.]) 1982-1983
Durango Weekly. (Durango, Colo.) 1992-1993
The Four Corners Weekly. (Durango, Colo.) 1993-Current
Four Corners Free Press. (Cortez, Co) 2003-Current

Places on the National Register

Bayfield, Spring Creek Archeological District, Address Restricted
Durango, Colorado Ute Power Plant, 14th St. and Animas River
Durango, Denver & Rio Grande Western RR Locomotive No. 315, 479 Main Ave.
Durango, Durango High School, 201 E. 12th St.
Durango, Durango Rock Shelters Archeology Site, Address Restricted
Durango, Durango-Silverton Narrow-Gauge Railroad, Right-of-way between Durango and Silverton
Durango, East Third Avenue Historic Residential District, E. 3rd. Ave. between 5th, and 15th Sts.
Durango, Main Avenue Historic District, Main Ave.
Durango, Newman Block, 801—813 Main Ave.
Durango, Ochsner Hospital, 805 Fifth Ave.
Durango, Rochester Hotel, 726 E. Second Ave.
Durango, Smiley Junior High School, 1309 E 3rd Ave.
Durango, Ute Mountain Ute Mancos Canyon Historic District, Address Restricted

USGS Historic Places

Columbine Pass, Logtown, 37.5516669, -107.5914484
Granite Peak, Tuckerville, 37.4925013, -107.485334
Loma Linda, Griffth, 37.2144476, -107.7961751
Unknown, Needleton Post Office, 0, 0
Vallecito Reservoir, Vallecito Post Office, 37.3752801, -107.5839466

Grand Army of the Republic Posts

Sedgwick, No. 12, La Plata, Durango

USGS Historic Military Places

None

Military Bases

None

Post Offices

Allison	1904 Aug 22	1954 Nov 30	
Animas	1886 July 10	1900 Sept 29	
Animas City	1877 May 24	1885 Aug 19	
Animas Forks	1875 Feb 8	1915 Nov 30*	
Bayfield	1899 Feb 25		81122

La Plata County

Breen	1901 July 19	1954 Nov 30	
Cascade	1880 June 14	1882 July 24*	
Castelar	1905 May 9	1912 June 30	
Columbus	1894 Nov 15	1903 Apr 30*	
Content	1901 Sept 21	1913 Oct 13	
Cortez	1887 June 21		81321
Dix	1890 Apr 8	1907 Dec 14*	
Dolores	1878 Apr 5		81323
Durango	1880 Nov 19		81301
Elco	1905 July 28	1914 May 31	
Emery	1892 Feb 5	1897 Nov 11	
Eureka	1875 Aug 9	1942 Apr 30	
Falfa	1924 Nov 19	1954 Nov 30	
Florida	1877 Aug 8	1881 Mar 31	
Fort Lewis	1880 Oct 5	1891 Oct 10	
Griffith	1909 Dec 2	1924 Nov 19	
Grommet	1904 May 3	1908 Jan 13	
Hermosa	1876 July 27	1900 Sept 29*	
Hesperus	1880 Oct 5		81326
Hewit	1882 July 14	1885 July 9*	
Howardsville	1874 June 24	1939 Oct 31*	
Ignacio	1882 Jan 31		81137
Kline	1904 Apr 22	1953 Mar 31	
La Boca	1909 Feb 23	1937 Sept 12	
La Plata	1882 July 24	1885 Dec 23	
Laboca	1895 Mar 2	1896 Mar 16	
Laplata	1894 Apr 21	1934 July 23*	
Lone Dome	1883 Oct 25	1894 Dec 6	
Los Pinos	1889 Jan 18	1899 Feb 25	
Mancos	1877 Feb 19		
Marvel	1904 Apr 22		81329
Mayday	1913 Sept 4	1914 Dec 31	
McQuiety	1894 Mar 16	1895 Aug 7	
Meserole	1882 Sept 12	1884 July 28	
Mineral Point	1875 Oct 29	1897 Jan 28*	
Morgan	1887 Oct 24	1891 May 4	
Murnane	1882 Nov 10	1886 July 8	
Needleton	1882 May 26	1910 Jan 31*	
Ouray	1875 Oct 28	1876 Mar 20	
Ouray 2	1876 May 9		81427
Oxford	1908 Jan 13	1954 Nov 30	
Pargin	1901 July 24	1903 Jan 15	
Parrott	1876 May 5	1898 Oct 31*	
Perin	1902 Apr 4	1903 Mar 24	
Perins	1907 Apr 10	1926 Aug 14	
Pine River	1878 July 15	1894 Apr 14	

Historical Assets Colorado

Pineriver	1894 Apr 14	1895 Sept 12	
Porter	1891 Oct 7	1908 Sept 15	
Red Mesa	197 Apr 24	1954 Nov 30	
Rockwood	1878 July 8	1917 Apr 14*	
Silverton	1875 Feb 1		81433
Tacoma	1906 Setp 25	1954 Nov 30	
Tiffany	1907 Dec 3	1954 Nov 30	
Toltec	1887 Jan 26	1887 Nov 21	
Uncapaghre	1875 Dec 20	1876 Mar 20	
Uncompaghre	1876 Mar 20	1877 Feb 23	
Vallecito	1901 Nov 15	1942 Mar 15*	
Viceto	1890 May 19	1891 Oct 15	
Walls	1896 Apr 25	1906 Aug 13	
Young	1882 Nov 7	1883 Mar 19	

Topo Quads

Allison	370730N	370000N	1072230W	1073000W
Baldy Mountain	372230N	371500N	1072230W	1073000W
Basin Mountain	371500N	370730N	1075230W	1080000W
Bayfield	371500N	370730N	1073000W	1073730W
Columbine Pass	373730N	373000N	1073000W	1073730W
Durango East	372230N	371500N	1074500W	1075230W
Durango West	372230N	371500N	1075230W	1080000W
Electra Lake	373730N	373000N	1074500W	1075230W
Elk Creek	373730N	373000N	1075230W	1080000W
Gem Village	371500N	370730N	1073730W	1074500W
Greasewood Canyon	370730N	370000N	1082230W	1083000W
Hermosa	373000N	372230N	1074500W	1075230W
Hesperus	372230N	371500N	1080000W	1080730W
Ignacio	370730N	370000N	1073730W	1074500W
Kline	371500N	370730N	1080000W	1080730W
La Plata	373000N	372230N	1080000W	1080730W
Lemon Reservoir	373000N	372230N	1073730W	1074500W
Loma Linda	371500N	370730N	1074500W	1075230W
Ludwig Mountain	372230N	371500N	1073000W	1073730W
Monument Hill	373000N	372230N	1075230W	1080000W
Mormon Reservoir	371500N	370730N	1080730W	1081500W
Mountain View Crest	373730N	373000N	1073730W	1074500W
Orphan Butte	373730N	373000N	1080000W	1080730W
Pargin Mountain	371500N	370730N	1072230W	1073000W
Red Horse Gulch	370730N	370000N	1081500W	1082230W
Redmesa	370730N	370000N	1080730W	1081500W
Rules Hill	372230N	371500N	1073730W	1074500W
Thompson Park	372230N	371500N	1080730W	1081500W

La Plata County

Trail Canyon	371500N	370730N	1081500W	1082230W
Vallecito Reservoir	373000N	372230N	1073000W	1073730W

Suggested Reading

A History of Southwestern La Plata County in Colorado. NL: Fort Lewis Mesa Reunion History Committee, 1991.

Cuthane, Albert Edward. *History of the Settlement of La Plata County, Colorado.* Thesis, University of Colorado, 1934.

Pioneers of Southwest La Plata County, Colorado. Fort Lewis Mesa Reunion History Committee, 1994.

Turner, Carol. *Notorious San Juans: Wicked Tales from Ouray, San Juan and La Plata Counties.* Charleston, SC: History Press, 2011.

Weber, Joseph C. *History of La Plata County, Colorado.* Thesis, Colorado State College of Education, 1939.

Wildfang, Frederic B. *La Plata: Tri-Cultural Traditions in the Upper San Juan Basin.* Chicago: Arcadia Pub, 2002.

Historical Assets Colorado

Lake County

Introduction

Established: 1861   Population: 7,310

Formed from: Original

Adjacent Counties: Eagle, Summit, Park, Chaffee, Pitkin

County Seat: Leadville

  Other Communities: Leadville North, Twin Lakes, Climax, Oro City

Website, http://www.lakecountyco.com

Area Codes: 719

Zip Codes: 80429, 80461, 81251

Historical Assets Colorado

Lake County Courthouse

Lake County 19th Century Courthouse

Courthouses & County Government
Lake County
   http://www.lakecountyco.com
Lake County Courthouse (5th Judicial District), 505 Harrison Ave, Leadville, CO 80461, 719-486-0535; http://www.courts.state.co.us/Courts/County/Index.cfm?County_ID=10
Assessor, 505 Harrison Ave, Leadville, CO 80461, 719-486-4110; http://www.lakecountyco.com/assessor/
Board of County Commissioners, 505 Harrison Ave, Leadville, CO 80461, 719-486-4102, http://www.lakecountyco.com/commissioner/
Clerk & Recorder, 505 Harrison Ave, Leadville, CO 80461, 719-486-1410; http://www.lakecountyco.com/clerkandrecorder/
Coroner, 719-486-1441; http://www.lakecountyco.com/coroner/
Elections, 719-486-4134
Public Health, 112 W 5th St, Leadville, CO 80461, 719-486-2413; http://www.lakecountyco.com/health/
Transportation (Road & Bridge); http://www.lakecountyco.com/roadandbridge/
Treasurer, P.O. Box 276, Leadville, CO 80461, 719-486-4117; http://www.lakecountyco.com/Treasurer/

County Records
Birth Unk   Marriage 1869   Divorce Unk
Death Unk   Land 1876   Probate 1879
Court 1879
County Clerk has some burial records from 1885
CSA Death 1886

Lake County

County & Municipal Records Held at the State Level

The Colorado State Archives

Physical Records
Clerk & Recorder
County Court
District Court
Justice Court
Treasurer
WPA Historical Records
WPA Religious Institutions Survey
Cities
Leadville

Records on Film
1885 Census
Clerk & Recorder
Treasurer

Records on Master Film
Clerk & Recorder
District Court
Combined Courts
School Districts
Cities
Leadville

The Denver Public Library
Gray's Peak, Snake River & Leadville Railroad Company Certificate, 1878-1883
Lake County Colorado Mining Companies Records, 1925, 1931
Leadville Assembly Records, 1952-1971
Leadville Church Programs Collection 1884-1899
London Deep Mines Company Records, 1932-1937
Oro City Assay Ledger, 1873-1878
WWI Draft Registration Cards (microfilm)

School Districts
School Districts, http://www.adcogov.org/local-school-districts
Lake County School District R-1, 328 W 5th St, Leadville, CO 80461, 719-486-6800; http://www.lakecountyschools.net/

Historic School Districts

1. [1878]
2. Leadville
3. Malta
4. Twin Lakes
5. Adelaide, Ibex
6. [1881]
7. [1881]
8. Soda Springs
9. Hayden
10. Crystal Lake
11. Malta
12. Tennessee Park
13. Stumptown, Climax
14. Climax
15. Soda Springs, Malta

Fraternal Organizations

Granges
None

Masons

Ancient Free & Accepted Masons
Ionic, No. 35, Lake, Leadville, 25 Oct 1878
Leadville, No. 35, Lake, Leadville, 15 Sept 1931
Corinthian, No. 35, Lake, Leadville, 25 Jan 1966
Leadville, No. 51, Lake, Leadville, 20 Sept 1882

Royal Arch Masons
Leadville, No. 10, Lake, Leadville

Historical Assets Colorado

Knights Templar
Mount of the Holy Cross Commandery, No. 5, Lake, Leadville, 1880 May 1

Eastern Star
Colorado, No. 2, Lake, Leadville

Odd Fellows
Oro, No. 16, Lake, Leadville
Chloride, No. 31, Lake, Leadville
Carbonate, No. 35, Lake, Leadville

Rebekahs
Cloud City, No. 38, Lake, Leadville

Knights of Pythias
Leadville, No. 11, Lake, Leadville, 1879 July 14
Progress, No. 20, Lake, Leadville
Banner, No. 29, Lake, Leadville, 1885 Nov 2

Pythian Sisters
Sunrise, No. 49, Lake, Gulch

Benevolent Protective Order of Elks
Leadville, No. 2363, Lake, Leadville

City & Town Halls

Leadville, 800 Harrison Ave, Leadville, CO 80461, 719-486-0349, https://www.colorado.gov/leadville

Archives & Manuscript Collections

Lake County Public Library Digital Collection; https://lakecountypubliclibrary.org/localhistory/digitalcollections

Historical & Genealogical Societies

Leadville Historical Association, House with the Eye Museum, 127 W 4th St, P.O. Box 911, Leadville, CO 80461, (719) 427-0895, https://leadville.com/the-house-with-the-eye-museum/

Local Libraries

Colorado Mountain History Collection, **Lake County Public Library**, 1115 Harrison Ave, Leadville, CO 80461-3398, (719) 486-0569, https://lakecountypubliclibrary.org/localhistory

Links

CO GenWeb
http://cogenweb.com/lake/

Cyndi's List
https://www.cyndislist.com/us/co/counties/lake/

FamilySearch Wiki

Lake County

https://www.familysearch.org/wiki/en/Lake_County,_Colorado_Genealogy

Linkpendium
http://www.linkpendium.com/lake-co-genealogy/

RootsWeb Wiki
https://wiki.rootsweb.com/wiki/index.php/Lake_County,_Colorado

Wikipedia
https://en.wikipedia.org/wiki/Lake_County,_Colorado

Historic Hotels

1886 Delaware Hotel, 700 Harrison Ave, Leadville, CO 80461, 800-748-2004, https://delawarehotel.com

Museums & Historic Sites

Healy House-Dexter Cabin Museum, 912 Harrison Ave, Leadville, CO 80461, (719) 486-0487, https://www.historycolorado.org/healy-house-museum-dexter-cabin

Leadville Historical Association, House with the Eye Museum, 127 W 4th St, P.O. Box 911, Leadville, CO 80461, (719) 427-0895, https://leadville.com/the-house-with-the-eye-museum/

Matchless Mine Museum, 414 W 7th St, P.O. Box 532, Leadville, CO 80461, (719) 486-0371, https://mininghalloffame.org/page/hours-and-location-matchless-mine

National Mining Hall of Fame Museum, 120 W 9th St, P.O. Box 981, Leadville, CO 80461, (719) 486-1229, http://www.mininghalloffame.org

Tabor Historic Home Museum, 116 E 5th St, Leadville, CO 80461, (719) 293-2391, https://www.facebook.com/pages/Tabor-Home-Museum/115978901757827

Tabor Opera House Museum, 308 Harrison Ave, P.O. Box 1004, Leadville, CO 80461, (719) 486-8409, http://www.taboroperahouse.net

Temple Israel Synagogue and Museum, 201 W 4th St, Leadville, CO 80461, (303) 709-7050, http://www.jewishleadville.org

Special Events & Scenic Locations

The Leadville Boom Days are held in August most years, http://www.leadvilleboomdays.org.

Leadville-Twin Lakes has a calendar of events here: https://www.leadvilletwinlakes.com/things-to-do/category/events/

Leadville maintains a calendar of events here: https://www.colorado.com/co/leadville/festivals-events

Leadville National Historic District
Arkansas Headwaters Recreation Area
San Isabel National Forest
Buffalo Peaks Wilderness
Collegiate Peaks Wilderness
Holy Cross Wilderness
Mount Massive Wilderness

Historical Assets Colorado

Leadville National Fish Hatchery
American Discovery Trail
Colorado Trail
Continental Divide National Scenic Trail
Mineral Belt National Recreation Trail
Top of the Rockies National Scenic Byway

Ghost Towns & Other Sparsely Populated Places

Adelaide City, Alexander, Alicante, Arkansas Junction, Birdseye, Brumley (Bromley, Bromley Station), Busk, Climax, Crane Park, Crystal Lake, Eilers, English Gulch, Everette (Halfway House, Seiden's House), Finntown, Fremont Pass, French Gulch, Interlaken, Keeldar, Leadville Junction, Lord's Ranch, Malta (Swill Town), Oro City (Agassiz, Kelly's Diggings, Poverty Flats, Boughtown, Shaptown, California Gulch), Pine Creek, Saint Kevin, Snowden, Soda Springs, Stringtown, Stumptown, Tabor City, Three Mile Tank, Twin Lakes

Newspapers

The Evening Chronicle. (Leadville, Colo.) 1???-1913
Pacific Echo. (Pendleton, Or.) 1???-1???
Carbonate Chronicle. (Leadville, Colo.) 18??-1987
The Weekly Herald. (Leadville, Colo.) 18??-1???
Leadville Pay-Streak. (Leadville, Colo.) 18??-1???
The News Reporter. (Leadville, Colo.) 18??-1902
The Lake County Reveille. (Leadville, Colo.) 187?-1???
The Daily Reveille. (Leadville, Colo.) 1878-1880
The Daily Eclipse. (Leadville, Colo.) 1878-1880
The Daily Chronicle. (Leadville, Colo.) 1879-1886
Carbonate Weekly Chronicle. (Leadville, Lake County, Colo.) 1879-18??
Leadville Weekly Herald. (Leadville, Colo.) 1879-1885
Leadville Daily Herald. (Leadville, Colo.) 1879-1884
The Democrat. (Leadville, Colo.) 1880-1???
Leadville Weekly Democrat. (Leadville, Colo.) 1880-1???
Leadville Deutsche Zeitung. (Leadville, Colo.) 1880-18?? | Languages: German
Leadville Democrat. (Leadville, Colo.) 1880-1885
The Leadville Herald. (Leadville, Colo.) 1884-1885
Leadville Herald Democrat. (Leadville, Colo.) 1885-1889
Leadville Daily Journal. (Leadville, Colo.) 1886-????
The Leadville Dispatch. (Leadville, Colo.) 1886-????
Leadville Evening Chronicle. (Leadville, Colo.) 1886-1???
The Herald Democrat. (Leadville, Colo.) 1889-1990
The Star. (Leadville, Colo.) 1892-1???
The Free Lance. (Leadville, Colo.) 1895-1???
Twin Lakes Miner. (Twin Lakes, Colo.) 1902-1911
The Evening News-Dispatch and The News-Reporter. (Leadville, Colo.) 1902-1903
The Evening News-Dispatch. (Leadville, Colo.) 1903-19??
The Leadville Press. (Leadville, Colo.) 1909-19??

Lake County

Lake County Miner. (Twin Lakes, Colo.) 1911-19??
Leadville Leader. (Leadville, Colo.) 1959-19??
The Twin Lakes Enterprise. (Twin Lakes, Colo.) 1967-19??
Generic News. ([Leadville, Colo.]) 1985-1985
Leadville Times. ([Leadville, Colo.]) 1985-19??
Leadville Herald Democrat. (Leadville, Colo.) 1990-Current

Places on the National Register

Leadville, Derry Mining Site Camp, W of US 24
Leadville, Dexter Cabin, 912 Harrison Ave.
Leadville, Hayden Ranch Headquarters, W. of US 24
Leadville, Healy House, 912 Harrison Ave.
Leadville, Leadville Historic District, Town of Leadville
Leadville, Leadville National Fish Hatchery, W of Leadville
Leadville, Matchless Mine, E 7th Rd
Twin Lakes, Interlaken Resort District, E of Twin Lakes off CO 82
Twin Lakes, Twin Lakes District, Both sides of CO 82

USGS Historic Places

Climax, Climax, 39.3688772, -106.1836335
Independence Pass, Brumley, 39.0894353, -106.5428076
Leadville North, Leadville Army Air Field, 39.2833333, -106.3333333
Leadville South, Adelaide, 39.247212, -106.2580785
Leadville South, Oro, 39.2352679, -106.2522449
Unknown, Longs Peak Post Office, 0, 0

Grand Army of the Republic Posts

James A Garfield, No. 9, Lake, Leadville, 1881

USGS Historic Military Places

Leadville North, Leadville Army Air Field, 39.2833333, -106.3333333

Military Bases

None

Post Offices

Adelaide	1878 Sept 27	1901 Nov 15*
Alexander	1879 Aug 1	1879 Oct 2
Alicante	1881 June 15	1887 Apr 22
Alpine	1874 Oct 26	1904 June 30
Arkansas Junction	1890 May 2	1918 Aug 10
Bond	1886 July 16	1888 Oct 25
Busk	1890 Dec 15	1894 Mar 2
Cash Creek	1862 Aug 2	1871 Feb 27
Centreville	1868 Apr 22	1930 Apr 30

Historical Assets Colorado

Cleora	1876 Dec 5	1882 Mar 7	
Climax	1887 Apr 22	1898 Apr 12	
Climax	1917 Dec 5		
Dayton	1866 Oct 16	1868 Nov 30	
Divide	1874 June 24	1885 Aug 19	
Everett	1881 Mar 31	1887 Dec 15	
Granite	1868 Nov 30		
Gunnison	1876 Oct 2		81230
Helena	1866 Oct 16	1880 Mar 10	
Hope	1885 Nov 3	1890 Nov 24	
Hortense	1877 May 11	1907 Sept 14*	
Howland	1879 Aug 8	1882 Sept 19	
Ibex	1896 Mar 7	1905 Apr 15*	
Interlaken	1887 Apr 29	1894 Apr 21*	
Ironhill	1883 June 18	1883 Oct 30	
Leadville	1877 July 16		80461
Mahonville	1876 Feb 28	1879 Sept 18	
Malta	1875 Oct 26	1955 July 31*	
Oro City	1861 Feb 16	1895 Sept 19	
Poncho Springs	1877 Mar 13	1924 Nov 22*	
Riverside	1872 May 22	1905 June 19	
Saint Kevin	1886 Jan 15	1890 Dec 24	
Snowden	1890 Nov 24	1883 Aug 31	
Soda Springs	1879 Aug 25	1902 Oct 31	
South Arkansas	1868 Apr 22	1877 Mar 13	
Tabor	1879 Apr 14	1881 Jan 27	
Tacoma	1883 Sept 20	1886 Mar 12*	
Tennessee Pass	1912 July 14	1959 Nov 30	
Twin Lakes	1879 Dec 19		
Wortman	1900 Sept 25	1919 Jan 15*	

Topo Quads

Granite	390730N	390000N	1061500W	1062230W
Independence Pass	390730N	390000N	1063000W	1063730W
Leadville South	391500N	390730N	1061500W	1062230W
Mount Champion	391500N	390730N	1063000W	1063730W
Mount Elbert	390730N	390000N	1062230W	1063000W
Mount Massive	391500N	390730N	1062230W	1063000W

Suggested Reading

Aldrich, John K. *Ghosts of Lake County: a Guide to the Ghost Towns and Mining Camps of Lake County and Eastern Pitkin County, Colorado*. Lakewood, CO: Centennial Graphics, 1997.

Blairm, Edward and E Richard Churchill. *Everybody Came to Leadville*. Fort Collins, CO: First Light Pub, 1997.

Lake County

Coquoz, Rene L. *The History of Medicine in Leadville and Lake County, Colorado.* Leadville, CO: NP, 1967.

History of Old Lake County: Lake and Chaffee: Colorado Territory, Colorado State. Coal Creek, CO: Rocky Mountain Books, 1999.

Goldberg, Larry Zelig. *Lake County Historical Inventory: Leadville, the History of a City Determined to Survive.* Boulder, CO: Western Interstate Commission for Higher Education, 1975.

Griswold, Don L and Jean Harvey Griswold. *History of Leadville and Lake County, Colorado: from Mountain Solitude to Metropolis.* Denver: University Press of Colorado, 1996.

Moriarty, Elizabeth. *The History of Lake County, Colorado.* Thesis, Colorado State Teachers College, 1930.

Voynick, Stephen M. *Leadville, a Miner's Epic.* Missoula, MT: Montana Press Pub Co, 1992.

Williamson, Ruby G. *The Lake County War: Upper Arkansas Valley, 1874-1881.* Gunnison, CO: B&B Printers, 1976.

Historical Assets Colorado

Larimer County

Introduction

Established: 1861   Population: 299,630

Formed from: Original

Adjacent Counties: Weld, Boulder, Grand, Jackson

County Seat: Fort Collins

> Other Communities: Loveland, Berthoud, Estes Park, Johnstown, Timnath, Wellington, Windsor, LaPorte, Red Feather Lakes, Bellvue, Buckeye, Campion, Cherokee Park, Drake, Glendevey, Glen Haven, Livermore, Kinikinik, Masonville, Pinewood Springs, Pingree Park, Poudre Park, Rustic, Teds Place, Waverly, Manhattan, Old Roach, Virginia Dale

Website, https://www.larimer.org

Area Codes: 970

Zip Codes: 80511, 80512, 80513, 80515, 80517, 80521, 80522, 80523, 80524, 80525, 80526, 80527, 80528, 80532, 80535, 80536, 80539, 80541, 80545, 80549, 80553

Historical Assets Colorado

Larimer County Courthouse

Early Larimer Courthouses circa 1865, 1868 and 1885

Courthouses & County Government

Larimer County
https://www.larimer.org

Larimer County Courthouse (Justice Center) (8th Judicial District), 201 La Porte Ave, Fort Collins, CO 80521, 970-498-6100; http://www.courts.state.co.us/Courts/County/Index.cfm?County_ID=22

Larimer County Courthouse (Loveland), 810 E 10th St, Loveland, CO 80537, 970-679-4420; http://www.courts.state.co.us/Courts/County/Index.cfm?County_ID=22

Assessor, 200 W Oak St, Fort Collins, CO 80521, 970-498-7050; http://www.larimer.org/assessor/

Board of County Commissioners, 200 W Oak St, Fort Collins, CO 80521, 970-498-7001, https://www.larimer.org/bocc

Clerk & Recorder, 200 W Oak St, Fort Collins, CO 80521, 970-498-7860; http://www.larimer.org/clerk/

Coroner, 1600 Prospect Park Way, Ste 101, Fort Collins, CO 80525, 970-498-6161; https://www.larimer.org/coroner

Larimer County

Elections, 200 W Oak St, 5th Fl, Fort Collins, CO 80521, 970-498-7820; https://www.larimer.org/clerk/elections

Public Health, 1525 Blue Spruce Dr, Fort Collins, CO 80524, 970-498-6700; http://www.larimer.org/health/

Transportation (Road & Bridge), 2643 Midpoint, Ste C, Fort Collins, CO 80525, 970-498-5650; https://www.larimer.org/roads

Treasurer, 200 W Oak St, 2nd Fl, Fort Collins, CO 80521, 970-498-7020; http://www.larimer.org/Treasurer/

County Records

Birth 1902
Death 1902
Court 1862
CSA Birth 1905
CSA Death 1908
CSA Delayed Birth Certificates 1942

Marriage 1862
Land 1862

Divorce 1862
Probate 1862

County & Municipal Records Held at the State Level

The Colorado State Archives

Physical Records
Assessor
Clerk & Recorder
County Commissioners
County Court
District Court
Justice Court
Probate Court
WPA Historical Records
WPA Religious Institutions Survey
WPA Loveland
Cities
  Fort Collins
  Loveland
  Wellington

Records on Film
Clerk & Recorder
District Court
Cities
  Fort Collins

Records on Master Film
Assessor
Clerk & Recorder
Coroner
County Commissioners
County Court
District Court
Justice of the Peace Court
District Attorney
Planning
Public Works
School Districts
Sheriff
Treasurer
Cities
  Estes Park
  Fort Collins

The Denver Public Library

Board of County Commissioners Report, 1889
History of the Jackson Ditch, 1890
Larimer County School District No. 56 Records, 1894-1920
WPA Historical Records Survey
WWI Draft Registration Cards (microfilm)

School Districts

School Districts, http://www.adcogov.org/local-school-districts

Historical Assets Colorado

Estes Park School District R-3, 1605 Brodie Ave, Estes Park, CO 80517, 970-586-2361; https://www.estesschools.org/
Poudre School District R-1, 2407 LaPorte Ave, Fort Collins, CO 80521, 970-482-7420; https://www.psdschools.org/
Thompson School District R2-J, 800 S Taft Ave, Loveland, CO 80537, 970-613-5000; https://www.thompsonschools.org/
St Vrain Valley School District, 395 S Pratt Pkwy, Longmont, CO 80501, 303-776-6200; https://www.svvsd.org/

Historic School Districts

1. Namaqua
2. St Louis, Loveland
3. Mountain View, Hillsborough, Kelim
4. LaPorte
5. Fort Collins
6. Sherwood, Riverside
7. Pleasant Valley
8. Weldon
9. Livermore, Ingleside, Owl Canyon
10. Mountain View, District No. 10
11. Michaud
12. Virginia Dale
13. Berthoud
14. Stratton Park, Poudre Park, Rist Canyon
15. Boxelder, Lower Boxelder
16. Pleasant View
17. Harmony
18. Stove Prairie, Buckhorn
19. Pinewood
20. Lonetree
21. Fairview, Timnath
22. Old Berthoud
23. Red Rock
24. Proctor
25. Tepfer, Cherokee Creek, Sloan, St Cloud, Cherokee Park
26. Plummer
27. Highland, Stout
28. Log Cabin, Adams
29. Jeffers
30. Estes Park
31. Fossil Creek
32. Mount Hope
33. Upper Boxelder
34. Wellington
35. District No. 35
36. Sunset
37. Culver, Pinedale [Jount with Boulder]
38. Twin Mounds [Joint with Weld]
39. Trilby
40. Soldier Canyon, Lamb
41. Rocky Ridge
42. Gleneyre, Roach
43. [1886]
44. [1888]
45. [1886]
46. [1886]
47. [1886]
48. North Park
49. Waverly
50. Bellvue
51. Masonville
52. Westerdoll
53. ELkhorn, Eggers
54. Summit
55. Buckeye
56. Westlake, Red Feather Lakes, Goldsborough
57. Lakeview [Joint with Weld]
58. Dry Creek
59. Moessner
60. Cache la Poudre, Old La Porte
61. Silver Dell, Meadow Hollow
62. Timnath Consolidated
63. Big Thompson Consolidated
64. Cache La Poudre Consolidated, Laporte Consolidated
65. Pingree Park, Eggers

Fraternal Organizations

Granges
Big Thompson, No. 6, Larimer, Big Thompson/St Louis, 13 Dec 1873
Collins, No. 7, Larimer, Fort Collins, 15 Dec 1873
Flora, No. 42, Larimer, Ft Collins, 23 Jan 1874
Berthoud, No. 81, Larimer, Berthoud, 20 Mar 1888
Virginia Dale, No. 122, Larimer, Virginia Dale, 27 Dec 1890
Agricultural College, No. 129, Larimer, Fort Collins, 14 Dec 1891
Union, No. 145, Larimer, Ft Collins, 12 Mar 1901
Poudre Valley, No. 146, Larimer, Timnath, 27 Feb 1902

Larimer County

Empire, No. 148, Larimer, Ft Collins, 24 Mar 1904
Eureka, No. 149, Larimer, Ft Collins, 6 Jan 1905
Mountain View, No. 150, Larimer, Laporte, 18 Feb 1905
College, No. 168, Larimer, Ft Collins, 16 Oct 1908
Buckhorn, No. 182, Larimer, Masonville/Loveland, 5 Jan 1910
Lower Box Elder, No. 186, Larimer, Fort Collins, 23 Feb 1910
Virginia Dale, No. 221, Larimer, Virginia Dale, 1 Nov 1913
Little Thompson, No. 454, Larimer, Berthoud, 4 May 1943
Cache la Poudre, No. 456, Larimer, Bellvue, 8 July 1944
Namaqua, No. 463, Larimer, Loveland, 15 Apr 1946

Masons

  Ancient Free & Accepted Masons

    Collins, No. 19, Larimar, Fort Collins, 28 Sept 1870
    Loveland, No. 53, Larimer, Loveland, 18 Sept 1883
    Berthoud, No. 83, Larimer, Berthoud, 16 Sept 1890
    Johnstown, No. 140, Larimer, Johnstown, 17 Sept 1912
    Estes Park, No. 183, Larimer, Estes Park, 28 Jan 1959
    Fidelity, No. 192, Larimer, Fort Collins, 29 Jan 1965
    Longs Peak, No. 197, Larimer, Loveland, 25 Jan 2003

  Royal Arch Masons

    Cache La Poudre, No. 11, Larimer, Fort Collins
    Loveland, No. 44, Larimer, Loveland

  Knights Templar

    DeMolay Commandery, No. 13, Larimer, Fort Collins, 1884 Oct 1
    Loveland Commandery, No. 38, Larimer, Loveland,

  Eastern Star

    Orient, No. 23, Larimer, Loveland
    Collins, No. 26, Larimer, Fort Collins
    Laurel, No. 44, Larimer, Berthoud

Odd Fellows

  Fort Collins, No. 19, Larimer, Fort Collins
  Timnath, No. 28, Larimer, Tinmath
  Loveland, No. 36, Larimer, Loveland
  Wellington, No. 95, Larimer, Wellington
  Berthoud, No. 99, Larimer, Berthoud
  Estes Park, No. 163, Larimer, Estes Park

  Rebekahs

    Delta, No. 25, Larimer, Fort Collins
    Grace, No. 58, Larimer, Loveland
    Bethel, No. 63, Larimer, Berthoud
    Longview, No. 103, Larimer, Wellington

Knights of Pythias

  Jerome, No. 73, Larimer, Spring Gulch
  Columbine, No. 99, Larimer, Berthoud

Historical Assets Colorado

Larimer, No. 101, Larimer, Fort Collins
Harmony, No. 102, Larimer, Loveland
  Pythian Sisters
Loveland, No. 30, Larimer, Loveland
  Benevolent Protective Order of Elks
Fort Collins, No. 804, Larimer, Fort Collins
Loveland, No. 1051, Larimer, Loveland

City & Town Halls

Fort Collins, 300 Laporte Ave, Fort Collins, CO 80521, 970-221-6878, https://www.fcgov.com

Loveland, 500 E 3rd St, Loveland, CO 80537, 970-962-2000, http://www.cityofloveland.org

Berthoud, 807 Mountain Ave, Berthoud, CO 80513, 970-532-2643, https://www.berthoud.org

Estes Park, 170 MacGregor Ave, Estes Park, CO 80517, 970-586-5331, https://www.colorado.gov/townofestespark

Johnstown, 450 S Parish Ave, Johnstown, CO 80534, 970-587-4664, https://www.townofjohnstown.com

Timnath, 4750 Signal Tree Dr, Timnath, Co 80547, 970-224-3211, https://timnath.org

Wellington, 3735 Cleveland Ave, Wellington, CO 80549, 970-568-3381, https://www.townofwellington.com

Windsor, 301 Walnut St, Windsor, CO 80550, 970-674-2400, https://www.windsorgov.com

Archives & Manuscript Collections

Baker Schneider Archives Vestig, 3740 Cleveland Ave, Wellington, CO 80549, (970) 490-2137

Fort Collins Museum of Discovery Local History Archive, 408 Mason Ct, Fort Collins, CO 80524, (970) 221-6738, http://www.fcmod.org

Sidney Heitman Germans from Russia Collection, Colorado State Univ, Morgan Library, 1201 Center Ave Mall, Fort Collins, CO 80523-1019, (970) 491-1844, https://mountainscholar.org/handle/10217/100072

William E Morgan Library, Colorado State Univ, Special Collections & Archives, 1201 Center Ave Mall, Fort Collins, CO 80523-1019, (970) 491-3977, https://lib.colostate.edu/find/archives-special-collections/

Historical & Genealogical Societies

Berthoud Historical Society, Little Thompson Valley Pioneer Museum, 228 Mountain Ave, P.O. Box 225, Berthoud, CO 80513, (970) 532-2147, http://www.berthoudhistoricalsociety.org

Estes Park Area Historical Society, Historical Museum, 200 4th St, P.O. Box 1691, Estes Park, CO 80517-6339, (970) 586-6256, https://www.colorado.gov/townofestespark/museum

Larimer County

Estes Park Genealogical Society, c/o Estes Park Public Library, 335 E Elkhorn Ave, Estes Park, CO 80517, (970) 586-8116, https://estesvalleylibrary.org/lifetoolkits/estes-park-genealogical-society/

Fort Collins Historical Society, 1413 Emigh St, Fort Collins, CO 80524, (970) 221-6738, https://fortcollinshistoricalsociety.org

Historic Larimer County, P.O. Box 1909, Fort Collins, CO 80522, http://historiclarimercounty.org

Larimer County Genealogical Society, P.O. Box 270737, Fort Collins, CO 80527, (970) 223-5874, http://www.lcgsco.org

Larimer County Pioneer Association, P.O. Box 1732, Fort Collins, CO 80522-1732, (970) 482-8590,

Poudre Landmarks Foundation, 108 N Meldrum St, Fort Collins, CO 80524, (970) 221-0533, http://www.poudrelandmarks.org

Local Libraries

Fort Collins Public Library, 201 Peterson St, Fort Collins, CO 80524-2990, (970) 221-6740, http://www.poudrelibraries.org

Berthoud Community Library, 236 Welch Ave, Berthoud, CO 80513-2259, (970) 532-2757, https://berthoud.colibraries.org

Loveland Public Library, 300 N Adams Ave, Loveland, CO 80537-5754, (970) 962-2665, https://lovelandpubliclibrary.org

Wellington Public Library, 3800 Wilson Ave, P.O. Box 416, Wellington, CO 80549-0416, (970) 568-3040, https://wellington.colibraries.org

Links

CO GenWeb
http://cogenweb.com/larimer/

Cyndi's List
https://www.cyndislist.com/us/co/counties/larimer/

FamilySearch Wiki
https://www.familysearch.org/wiki/en/Larimer_County,_Colorado_Genealogy

Linkpendium
http://www.linkpendium.com/larimer-co-genealogy/

RootsWeb Wiki
https://wiki.rootsweb.com/wiki/index.php/Larimer_County,_Colorado

Wikipedia
https://en.wikipedia.org/wiki/Larimer_County,_Colorado

Historic Hotels

1909 Stanley Hotel, 333 E Wonderview Ave, Estes Park, CO 80517, 970-577-4000, https://www.stanleyhotel.com

1923 Armstrong Hotel, 259 S College Ave, Fort Collins, CO 80524, 970-484-3883, https://thearmstronghotel.com

Historical Assets Colorado

Museums & Historic Sites

1879 Avery House Museum, 328 W Mountain Ave, Fort Collins, CO 80524, (970) 221-0533, https://poudrelandmarks.org/avery-house

Baldpate Inn Museum, 4900 S St Vrain, Estes Park, CO 80517, (970) 586-6151, http://www.baldpateinn.com

Bee Family Centennial Farm Museum, 4320 E Cty Rd 58, Fort Collins, CO 80524, (970) 482-9168, http://www.beefamilyfarm.com

Berthoud Historical Society, Little Thompson Valley Pioneer Museum, 228 Mountain Ave, P.O. Box 225, Berthoud, CO 80513, (970) 532-2147, http://www.berthoudhistoricalsociety.org

Colorado Computer Museum, 1241 W 8th St, Loveland, CO 80537, (970) 669-1258, http://www.trailedge.org

Enos Mills Cabin Museum, 6760 Hwy 7, Estes Park, CO 80517, (970) 586-4706, http://www.enosmills.com

Estes Park Area Historical Society, Historical Museum, 200 4th St, P.O. Box 1691, Estes Park, CO 80517-6339, (970) 586-6256, https://www.colorado.gov/townofestespark/museum

Estes Valley Library, Bond Park, 335 E Elkhorn Ave, P.O. Box 1687, Estes Park, CO 80517-1687, (970) 586-8116, https://estesvalleylibrary.org

Fall River Hydro Interpretive Center, 1746 Fish Hatchery Rd, Estes Park, CO 80517, (970) 577-7683, https://www.facebook.com/pages/Fall-River-Hydro-Interpretive-Center/136366289745327

Fort Collins Museum of Discovery Local History Archive, 408 Mason Ct, Fort Collins, CO 80524, (970) 221-6738, http://www.fcmod.org

Heard Museum, 315 W Creek Rd, Glen Haven, CO 80532, (970) 586-4849

Loveland Museum, 503 N Lincoln Ave, Loveland, CO 80537, (970) 962-2410, http://www.lovelandmuseumgallery.org

Lula W Dorsey Museum, YMCA of the Rockies, 90 Program Wy, P.O. Box 20500, Estes Park, CO 80511, (888) 613-9622, https://ymcarockies.org/activities/dorsey-museum/

MacGregor Ranch Museum, 180 MacGregor Ln, P.O. Box 4675, Estes Park, CO 80517, (970) 586-3749, http://www.macgregorranch.org

McCarty-Fickelm Home Museum, 645 7th St, Berthoud, CO 80513, (970) 453-9767, https://www.berthoudhistoricalsociety.org/mccarty-fickel-home-museum/

Stanley Hotel Museum, 333 Wonderview Ave, Estes Park, CO 80517, (970) 577-1903, http://www.stanleysteamcarmuseum.com/index.php/stanley-hotel

Stanley Museum of Estes Park, 517 Big Thompson Ave, P.O. Box 788, Estes Park, CO 80517, (970) 577-1903, https://www.allestespark.com/history_museums/stanley_museum.php

Timberlane Farm Museum, 2306 E 1st St, Loveland, CO 80537, (970) 663-7348, http://www.timberlandfarmmuseum.org

Webster House Museum, 301 E Olive St, Fort Collins, CO 80524, https://sites.google.com/site/fchistoricalsociety/

Larimer County

Special Events & Scenic Locations

The Larimer County Fair & Rodeo is held in July and August most years, at The Ranch Event Complex, 5280 Arena Cr, Loveland, CO 80538, 970-619-4009, http://www.treventscomplex.com/events/larimer-county-fair

Larimer County has a calendar of events here: https://www.larimer.org/events

Visit Fort Collins has a calendar of events here: https://www.visitftcollins.com/events/annual-events-calendar/

Cache la Poudre Wilderness
Comanche Peak Wilderness
Neota Wilderness
Rawah Wilderness
Rocky Mountain National Park
Roosevelt National Forest
Boyd Lake State Park
Lory State Park
Lindenmeier Prehistoric Site
Continental Divide National Scenic Trail
Greyrock Mountain National Recreation Trail
Mount McConnel National Recreation Trail
Round Mountain National Recreation Trail
Great Parks Bicycle Route
Poudre River Bicycle Trail
Spring Creek Bicycle Trail
Mason Bicycle Trail
Fossil Creek Bicycle Trail
Cathy Fromme Prairie Natural Area Bicycle Trail
Power Bicycle Trail
Loveland Recreation Bicycle Trail
Cache la Poudre-North Park Scenic and Historic Byway
Peak to Peak Scenic and Historic Byway
Trail Ridge Road-Beaver Meadow National Scenic Byway

Ghost Towns & Other Sparsely Populated Places

Adams, Alford, Alvord, Arkins, Bellevue, Bellevue Junction, Box Elder, Bristol, Butler, Canadian, Cliffs Spur, Dixon, Haworth, Hebron, Higho, Home, Homestead Meadows, Leschers, Lord's Spur, Malaby's, Manhattan, Miner, Moraine, Pearl, Pinewood, Pinkhampton, Poudre City, Pullen, Rand, Richan, Saint Cloud, Spicer, Stout (under Horsetooth Reservoir), Valdal, Valentine Spur, Virginia Dale, Walden, Wilde's Spur, Winona

Newspapers

The Argus. (Fort Collins, Colo.) 1???-19??
The Fort Collins Argus. (Fort Collins, Colo.) 1???-19??
The Larimer County Democrat. (Fort Collins, Colo.) 1???-1920

Historical Assets Colorado

The Fort Collins Prospectus. (Fort Collins, Larimer County, Colo.) 18??-1???
The Berthoud Blade. (Berthoud, Colo.) 18??-1893
Larimer County Express. (Fort Collins, Colo.) 1873-1880
Fort Collins Standard. (Fort Collins, Colo.) 1874-1876
The Fort Collins Courier. (Fort Collins, Colo.) 1878-1898
The Loveland Reporter. (Loveland, Colo.) 1880-1922
The Express. (Ft. Collins, Larimer County, Colo.) 1880-1882
The Daily Express. (Fort Collins, Colo.) 1881-1???
Daily Evening Courier. (Fort Collins, Colo.) 1882-1???
The News. (Loveland, Colo.) 1882-1???
The Weekly Express. (Fort Collins, Larimer County, Colo.) 1882-1883
The Express. (Fort Collins, Larimer County, Colo.) 1883-1885
The Larimer Bee. (Fort Collins, Colo.) 1885-1???
The Fort Collins Express. (Fort Collins, Larimer County, Colo.) 1885-1916
The Berthoud Beacon. (Berthoud, Colo.) 1886-????
The Manhattan, Prospector. (Manhattan, Colo.) 1887-1???
The City Druggist. (Fort Collins, Colo.) 1888-1???
The Leader. (Loveland, Larimer County, Colo.) 1892-1893
The Berthoud Bulletin. (Berthoud, Larimer County, Colo.) 1893-1980
The Loveland Register. (Loveland, Colo.) 1894-19??
North Park Union. (Walden, Larimer County, Colo.) 1896-19??
The Weekly Courier. (Fort Collins, Colo.) 1898-19??
The North Park News. (Walden, Colo.) 1899-1???
Larimer County Coloradoan. (Fort Collins, Colo.) 19??-19??
The Long View Successor to Larimer County Sun. (Fort Collins, Colo.) 19??-19??
The Big Thompson Valley News. (Loveland, Colo.) 19??-19??
Larimer County Guardian. (Fort Collins, Colo.) 19??-19??
Larimer County Illustrated News. (Fort Collins, Colo.) 19??-19??
The Fort Collins Courier. (Fort Collins, Colo.) 19??-1923
Fort Collins Times. (Fort Collins, Colo.) 19??-1959
Northern Colorado Star. (Fort Collins, Colo.) 19??-1969
Fort Collins Leader. (Fort Collins, Colo.) 19??-19??
The Wellington News. (Wellington, Colo.) 19??-????
The Evening Courier. (Fort Collins, Colo.) 1902-19??
The Wellington A Weekly Bulletin. (Wellington, Colo.) 1905-1909
The Loveland Herald. (Loveland, Colo.) 1906-19??
The Loveland Daily Register. (Loveland, Colo.) 1906-19??
Fort Collins Morning Express. (Fort Collins, Colo.) 1907-19??
The Beacon. (Fort Collins, Colo.) 1907-19??
The Loveland Daily Herald. (Loveland, Colo.) 1908-1922
The Mountaineer. (Estes Park, Colo.) 1908-19??
The Wellington Sun. (Wellington, Colo.) 1909-1945
The Fort Collins Review. (Fort Collins, Colo.) 1909-1916
The Wellington. (Wellington, Colo.) 1909-1909
The Courier Farmer. (Fort Collins, Colo.) 1911-1916
The Estes Park Trail. (Estes Park, Colo.) 1912-1914

Larimer County

The Fort Collins Express and The Fort Collins Review. (Fort Collins, Colo.) 1916-1916
The Fort Collins Express-Review. (Fort Collins, Colo.) 1916-1918
The Fort Collins Express. (Fort Collins, Colo.) 1916-1923
The Fort Collins Express. (Fort Collins, Larimer County, Colo.) 1918-1920
Estes Park Trail Talk. (Estes Park, Colo.) 1920-1920
The Larimer County Independent. (Fort Collins, Colo.) 1920-1930
Estes Park Trail. (Estes Park, Colo.) 1921-1971
The Loveland Reporter-Herald. (Loveland, Colo.) 1922-1962
The Fort Collins Express-Courier. (Fort Collins, Larmier County, Colo.) 1923-1945
The Herald. (Fort Collins, Colo.) 1925-19??
Fort Collins Mountain and Plains Weekly (and Larimer County Independent). (Fort Collins [Colo.]) 1930-19??
Mountain and Plains Weekly (and Larimer County Independent). (Fort Collins [Colo.]) 1930-1930
Mountain and Plains Farmer and The Larimer County Independent. (Fort Collins [Colo.]) 1930-1930
Fort Collins Coloradoan Continuing Fort Collins Express-Courier. (Fort Collins, Colo.) 1945-1966
Larimer County Sun Successor to The Wellington Sun. (Wellington, Colo.) 1945-1946
Fort Collins Coloradan. (Fort Collins, Colo.) 1945-1980
Larimer County Sun. (Wellington, Colo.) 1946-1948
Loveland Round-Up. (Loveland, Colo.) 1948-1959
The Long View. (Fort Collins, Colo.) 1948-1949
The Fort Collins News-Leader successor to The Long View. (Fort Collins, Colo.) 1949-19??
The Loveland News. (Loveland, Colo.) 1959-1959
The Larimer County Times-News. (Loveland, Colo.) 1960-19??
Larimer County Times (continuing The Fort Collins Times). (Fort Collins, Colo.) 1960-1960
Loveland Daily Reporter-Herald. (Loveland, Larimer County, Colo.) 1962-Current
Morning Star. (Fort Collins And Loveland, Colo.) 1964-19??
Loveland Star. (Loveland, Colo.) 1965-19??
Wellington Hi-Lites. (Wellington, Colo.) 1966-1973
The Mountain Gazette. (Estes Park, Colo.) 1968-1971
The Estes Park Trail-Gazette. (Estes Park, Colo.) 1971-Current
The Trail-Gazette. (Estes Park, Colo.) 1971-1971
Triangle Review. (Fort Collins, Colo.) 1973-1981
Wellington Hi-Lites, Inc. (Wekkington, Colo.) 1973-1983
The Coloradoan. (Fort Collins, Colo.) 1980-1984
The Berthoud Recorder. (Berthoud, Colo.) 198?-1987
Fort Collins Triangle Review. (Fort Collins, Colo.) 1981-1981
Fort Collins Review. (Fort Collins, Colo.) 1981-199?
The Review. (Fort Collins, Colo.) 1981-1981
Fort Collins Coloradoan. (Fort Collins, Colo.) 1984-Current
The Old Berthoud Recorder. (Berthoud, Colo.) 1987-2008

Historical Assets Colorado

Gândacul de Colorado. (Estes Park (Colo.)) 2001-Current | Languages: English, Romanian

Berthoud Weekly Surveyor. (Berthoud, Colo.) 2004-Current

Places on the National Register

Allenspark, East Longs Peak Trail—Longs Peak Trail—Keyhole Route—Shelf Trail, W of CO 7

Bellvue, Arrowhead Lodge, 34500 Poudre Canyon Hwy., Roosevelt NF

Bellvue, Bingham Homestead Rural Historic Landscape, 4916 Bingham Hill Rd. (County Rd 50E)

Bellvue, Flowers, Jacob and Elizabeth, House, 5200 W. Cty Rd. 52E

Bellvue, Pleasant Valley School, 4032 N. Co. Rd. 25E

Berthoud, Bimson Blacksmith Shop, 224 Mountain St.

Bethoud, Swanson, Gustav and Annie, Farm, 1932 N. CO 287

Estes Park, Baldpate Inn, 4900 S. CO 7

Estes Park, Bear Lake Comfort Station, Bear Lake

Estes Park, Clatworthy Place, 225 Cyteworth Rd.

Estes Park, Crags Lodge, 300 Riverside Dr.

Estes Park, Edgemont, 1861 Mary's Lake Rd.

Estes Park, Elkhorn Lodge, 530 W. Elkhorn Ave.

Estes Park, Fall River Entrance Historic District, Fall River Entrance

Estes Park, Fall River Pass Ranger Station, Fall River Pass

Estes Park, Fall River Pump House and Catchment Basin, near the top of Fall River Rd., Rocky Mountain National Park

Estes Park, Fall River Road, Fall River Rd.

Estes Park, Fern Lake Patrol Cabin, Fern Lake

Estes Park, Fern Lake Trail, Rocky Mountain National Park

Estes Park, Flattop Mountain Trail, Rocky Mountain Park

Estes Park, Gem Lake Trail, N. of Devils Gulch Rd. to Gem Lake

Estes Park, Glacier Basin Campground Ranger Station, Glacier Basin

Estes Park, Hewes—Kirkwood Inn, 465 Long Peak Rd.

Estes Park, Homestead Meadows Discontiguous District, Address Restricted

Estes Park, Lake Haiyaha Trail, Roughly along Bear, Nymph & Dream Lakes, then up Chaos Canyon

Estes Park, Leiffer House, S of Estes Park off CO 7

Estes Park, Lost Lake Trail, Roughly along N. Fork Big Thompson R.

Estes Park, MacGregor Ranch, 180 MacGregor Ave.

Estes Park, McGraw Ranch, McGraw Ranch Rd.

Estes Park, Mills, Enos, Homestead Cabin, S of Estes Park off CO 7

Estes Park, Moraine Lodge, W of Estes Park off U.S. 36 on Bear Lake Rd.

Estes Park, Moraine Park Museum and Amphitheater, Rocky Mtn National Park

Estes Park, Mountainside Lodge, 2515 Tunnel Rd.

Estes Park, Park Theatre, 130 Moraine Ave.

Estes Park, Rocky Mountain National Park Administration Building, CO Hwy 36

Estes Park, Rocky Mountain National Park Utility Area Historic District, Beaver Meadows Entrance Rd.

Larimer County

Estes Park, Snogo Snow Plow, Rocky Mountain National Park
Estes Park, Stanley Hotel, 333 Wonder View Ave.
Estes Park, Stanley Hotel District, 333 Wonder View Ave.
Estes Park, Stanley Hotel District (Stanley Power Plant Boundary Increase), Fish Hatchery Rd. at Fall R.
Estes Park, Trail Ridge Road, Rocky Mountain National Park
Estes Park, Twin Sisters Lookout, On Twin Sisters Peaks, Rocky Mountain National Park (ROMO)
Estes Park, Vaille, Agnes, Shelter, NW of Longs Peak along E. Longs Peak Trail, Rocky Mountain National Park (ROMO)
Estes Park, White, William Allen, Cabins, W of Estes Park of Moraine Park Visitor Center in Rocky Mountain National Park
Estes Park, Willard, Beatrice, Alpine Tundra Research Plots, US 34 at Rock Cut and Forest Canyon
Estes Park, Willow Park Patrol Cabin, Fall River Rd.
Estes Park, Willow Park Stable, Fall River Pass
Estes Park, Wind Ridge, 1397 Clara Dr.
Estes Park, Ypsilon Lake Trail, Along ridge between Ciquita Cr. & Roaring R.
Fort Collins, Ammons Hall, Colorado State University campus
Fort Collins, Anderson, Peter, House, 300 S. Howes St.
Fort Collins, Armstrong Hotel, 249-261 S. College Ave.
Fort Collins, Avery House, 328 W. Mountain Ave.
Fort Collins, Baker House, 304—304 1/2 E. Mulberry St.
Fort Collins, Bee Farm, 4320 E. Cty Rd. 58
Fort Collins, Botanical and Horticultural Laboratory, Colorado State University campus
Fort Collins, Bouton, Jay H., House, 113 N. Sherwood St.
Fort Collins, Fort Collins Armory, 314 E. Mountain Ave.
Fort Collins, Fort Collins Municipal Railway Birney Safety Streetcar No. 21, 1801 W. Mountain Ave.
Fort Collins, Fort Collins Post Office, 201 S. College Ave.
Fort Collins, Fuller, Montezuma, House, 226 W. Magnolia St.
Fort Collins, Great Western Sugar Company Effluent Flume and Bridge, Cache la Poudre R., 1/2 mi. W. of Timberline Rd.
Fort Collins, Harmony Mill, 131 Lincoln Ave.
Fort Collins, Kissock Block Building, 115-121 E. Mountain Ave.
Fort Collins, Laurel School Historic District, Off U.S. 287
Fort Collins, Lindenmeier Site, Address Restricted
Fort Collins, Maxwell, R. G., House, 2340 W. Mulberry St.
Fort Collins, McHugh-Andrews House, 202 Remington St.
Fort Collins, Mosman House, 324 E. Oak St.
Fort Collins, Old Town Fort Collins, Roughly bounded by College Ave., Mountain, Pine, Willow, and Walnut Sts.
Fort Collins, Opera House Block/Central Block Building, 117-131 N. College Ave.
Fort Collins, Plummer School, 2524 E. Vine Dr.
Fort Collins, Preston Farm, 4605 S. Ziegler Rd.

Historical Assets Colorado

Fort Collins, Robertson, T. H., House, 420 W. Mountain Ave.
Fort Collins, Spruce Hall, Colorado State University campus
Fort Collins, Waycott, Ernest, House, 1501 W. Mountain Ave.
Grand Lake, North Inlet Trail, Roughly along N. Inlet & Hallett Cr. to Flattop Mt.
Laporte, Greeley, Salt Lake and Pacific Railroad—Stout Branch, Approx. 1/2 mi. S. of jct. US 287 & Co.Rd. 28
LaPorte, Provost Homestead—Herring Farm Rural Historic Landscape, 2405 N Overland Trail
Livermore, Livermore Hotel and General Store, Address Restricted
Livermore, Soloman Batterson Ranch (Rural Historic Landscape), 603 Mount Moriah Rd
Loveland, Benson, A.S., House, 463 W. 5th St.
Loveland, Big Thompson River Bridge III, US 34 at milepost 85.15
Loveland, Big Thompson River Bridge IV, US 34 at milepost 86.04
Loveland, Borland, Maude Stanfield Harter, House, 610 N. Jefferson Ave.
Loveland, Chasteen's Grove, W of Loveland off U.S. 34
Loveland, Colorado and Southern Railway Depot, 405 Railroad Ave.
Loveland, Downtown Loveland Historic District, Roughly bounded by Railroad & Jefferson Aves., alleys between 3rd & 4th Sts. & 4th & 5th Sts.
Loveland, First United Presbyterian Church, 400 E. 4th St.
Loveland, Loveland State Amory, 201 S. Lincoln Ave.
Loveland, McCreery, William H., House, 746 N. Washington Ave.
Loveland, Milner—Schwarz House, 710 S. Railroad Ave.
Loveland, Peep O Day Park, 5445 Wild Ln.
Loveland, Rialto Theater, 228—230 E. Fourth Ave.
Loveland, Shaffer, Henry K. and Mary E., House, 1302 N. Grant Ave.
Virginia Dale, Virginia Dale Stage Station, Off US 287
Wellington, Buckeye School, off West County Rd 80
Wellington, First National Bank Building, 3728 Cleveland Ave.
Windsor, Kaplan—Hoover Site, Address Restricted

USGS Historic Places

Big Narrows, Eggers Post Office, 40.6908146, -105.4874929
Fort Collins, Fort Collins Downtown Airport, 40.5877602, -105.0410881
Fort Collins, Fossil Creek School, 40.5230382, -105.0774789
Fort Collins, Harmony School, 40.5233158, -105.0383109
Fort Collins, Holy Family School, 40.5910935, -105.0858119
Fort Collins, Plummer School, 40.5960935, -105.0299764
Glen Haven, Glen Haven Post Office, 40.4538722, -105.4491614
Loveland, Memorial Hospital, 40.3972057, -105.0902585
Old Roach, Tie Hack Dam, 40.8991428, -106.1097386
Red Feather Lakes, Red Feather Lakes Post Office, 40.802481, -105.5916629
Round Butte, Rawhide Strip, 40.9080395, -105.0841418
Rustic, Manhattan, 40.7322027, -105.5999976
Unknown, Association Camp Post Office, 0, 0
Unknown, Cherokee Park Post Office, 0, 0

Larimer County

Grand Army of the Republic Posts
George H Thomas, No. 7, Larimer, Fort Collins, 1881
A E Burnside, No. 15, Larimer, Loveland

USGS Historic Military Places
None

Military Bases
None

Post Offices

Adams	1885 Sept 10	1897 Jan 19	
Alford	1882 June 28	1909 Feb 15	
Arkins	1887 Feb 26	1906 Mar 31	
Association Camp	1916 May 29		
Bellvue	1884 June 24		80512
Berthoud	1878 Apr 4		80513
Big Thompson	1862 Nov 12	1878 Jan 10	
Bighorn	1898 Mar 3	1900 Feb 15	
Boiler	1914 Sept 3	1915 Sept 15	
Box Elder	1876 June 2	1877 Dec 26	
Box Elder 2	1884 Apr 29	1894 Oct 30	
Boxelder	1894 Oct 30	1924 Nov 19*	
Bristol	1877 Dec 26	1890 Dec 2	
Buckhorn	1878 Aug 2	1888 Aug 18	
Bulger	1909 Oct 4	1912 July 31	
Bush	1882 Oct 11	1885 Sept 10	
Butler	1890 June 16	1911 Nov 30	
Canadian	1881 Mar 6	1891 July 3	
Chambers	1880 Sept 21	1886 Aug 17	
Chambers Lake	1926 Sept 21		
Cherokee Park	1913 Feb 14	1933 May 31*	
Cowdrey	1901 Dec 21	1907 Jan 15	
Crescent	1880 Apr 7	1880 Nov 22	
Drake			80515
Eggers	1926 Apr 23	1944 Apr 30	
Elkhorn	1879 June 5	1917 Oct 31*	
Estes Park	1876 June 2		80517
Forks	1898 Apr 5	1905 June 15*	
Fort Collins	1865 June 27	1865 Oct 19	
Fort Collins 2	1866 May 12		80521
Glen Haven	1917 May 28	1924 July 31*	
Glen Haven 2	1926 May 18		80532
Glendevey	1902 May 19	1975 Jan 31	
Gleneyre	1895 June 16	1912 Apr 30	

Historical Assets Colorado

Haworth	1905 June 17	1906 May 31	
Hebron	1884 July 11	1922 Feb 15	
Higho	1889 June 14	1930 Aug 15	
Home	1882 Feb 7	1946 Mar 31	
Kelim	1915 Mar 2	1925 Oct 31*	
Kilburn	1895 June 4	1898 Nov 2	
La Porte	1862 July 15	1894 Dec 21*	
Laporte	1894 Dec 21		80535
Little Thompson	1875 Apr 5	1878 Apr 4	
Livermore	1871 Dec 1		80536
Logcabin	1903 June 24	1942 May 31	
Longs Peak	1909 July 23	1936 June 30	
Loveland	1872 Apr 4	1873 Jan 24	
Loveland 2	1878 Jan 10		80538
Manhattan	1887 Mar 19	1900 Dec 31	
Mason	1880 July 8	1880 Oct 5	
Masonville	1896 Sept 1		80541
Michigan	1880 July 26	1882 Feb 23	
Miner	1888 Mar 10	1894 Sept 5	
Moraine	1880 Mar 22	1902 Jan 27	
Moraine Park	1902 Jan 27	1921 Feb 15	
Mountearl	1896 Oct 28	1899 July 27	
Namaqua	1868 Jan 28	1879 Jan 3	
Otis	1881 Feb 15	1881 May 16	
Owl	1899 Dec 26	1918 Oct 31	
Pearl	1889 Jan 19	1919 Aug 30	
Petra	1882 May 17	1882 Sept 4	
Pinewood	1879 Feb 6	1921 June 30	
Pinkhampton	1879 Oct 24	1904 Sept 15	
Pullen	1888 May 15	1894 July 12	
Rand	1883 Sept 3	1886 Nov 13	
Rand 2	1887 June 2		80473
Red Feather Lakes	1924 July 2	1925 Jan 31	
Red Feather Lakes 2	1926 Aug 4		80545
Roach	1929 Dec 28	1941 Dec 31	
Ruction	1889 Aug 1	1889 Sept 16	
Saint Cloud	1884 May 9	1913 Feb 14	
Spicer	1884 Apr 29	1954 June 30	
Stout	1882 Sept 4	1908 July 31	
Teller	1880 July 19	1886 Dec 16	
Timnath	1884 July 10		80547
Trail Ridge	1937 July 9	1953 Dec 31	
Tyner	1879 Oct 24	1881 July 20	
Valdai	1889 June 14	1892 May 11	
Virginia Dale	1868 Jan 9	1868 Sept 28	
Virginia Dale 2	1871 Sept 14	1967 Jan 27	

Larimer County

Walden	1881 Feb 28		80470	
Waverly	1906 Feb 23	1912 May 15		
Wellington	1903 Aug 25		80549	
Westlake	1895 Apr 25	1898 July 22		
Wheatland	1875 Sept 24	1881 Feb 10		
Wilds	1926 Feb 11	1934 Jan 31		
Winona	1889 Feb 2	1893 May 18		
Zirkel	1899 May 5	1911 Dec 30		

Topo Quads

Big Narrows	404500N	403730N	1052230W	1053000W
Boston Peak	404500N	403730N	1054500W	1055230W
Buckeye	405230N	404500N	1050000W	1050730W
Buckhorn Mtn	403730N	403000N	1051500W	1052230W
Carter Lake Reservoir	402230N	401500N	1050730W	1051500W
Cherokee Park	410000N	405230N	1052230W	1053000W
Comanche Peak	403730N	403000N	1053730W	1054500W
Crystal Mountain	403730N	403000N	1052230W	1053000W
Drake	403000N	402230N	1051500W	1052230W
Eaton Reservoir	410000N	405230N	1053730W	1054500W
Estes Park	403000N	402230N	1053000W	1053730W
Fort Collins	403730N	403000N	1050000W	1050730W
Glen Haven	403000N	402230N	1052230W	1053000W
Glendevey	405230N	404500N	1055230W	1060000W
Grand Lake	402230N	401500N	1054500W	1055230W
Haystack Gulch	405230N	404500N	1052230W	1053000W
Horsetooth Reservoir	403730N	403000N	1050730W	1051500W
Kinikinik	404500N	403730N	1053730W	1054500W
Laporte	404500N	403730N	1050730W	1051500W
Livermore	405230N	404500N	1050730W	1051500W
Livermore Mtn	405230N	404500N	1051500W	1052230W
Longs Peak	402230N	401500N	1053000W	1053730W
Loveland	403000N	402230N	1050000W	1050730W
Masonville	403000N	402230N	1050730W	1051500W
McHenrys Peak	402230N	401500N	1053730W	1054500W
Old Roach	410000N	405230N	1060000W	1060730W
Panorama Peak	402230N	401500N	1052230W	1053000W
Pinewood Lake	402230N	401500N	1051500W	1052230W
Pingree Park	403730N	403000N	1053000W	1053730W
Poudre Park	404500N	403730N	1051500W	1052230W
Red Feather Lakes	405230N	404500N	1053000W	1053730W
Rustic	404500N	403730N	1053000W	1053730W
South Bald Mtn	405230N	404500N	1053730W	1054500W
Trail Ridge	403000N	402230N	1053730W	1054500W

Historical Assets Colorado

Virginia Dale	410000N	405230N	1051500W	1052230W
Wellington	404500N	403730N	1050000W	1050730W

Suggested Reading

Ahlbrandt, Arlene Briggs. *Memories of War Years: Memories of the Veterans of Fort Collins and Larimer County, Colorado*. Dallas: Curtis Media Corp, 1993.

Aldrich, John K. *Ghosts of Eagle and Grand Counties: Stories from the Ghost Towns and Mining Camps of Eagle, Grand, Jackson, Larimer and Routt Counties, Colorado*. Denver: Columbine Ink, 2009.

Dunn, Shirley P and Chloe J Bundy. *History of Fort Collins, Larimer, Colorado, 1864-1964: with Biographies, 1801-1964*. NL: NP, 1966.

Inventory of the County Archives of Colorado, No. 35, Larimer County (Fort Collins). Denver: Historical Records Survey, 1941.

Kniebes, Duane V and Susan Kniebes. *Cemeteries and Remote Burials in Larimer County, Colorado, Volume I: The Poudre and North, Including the Laramie River Valley and Livermore*. Niwot, CO: Iron Gate Publishing, 2018.

Kniebes, Duane V and Susan Kniebes. *Cemeteries and Remote Burials in Larimer County, Colorado, Volume II: South of the Poudre, Including Fort Collins, Loveland, and Berthoud*. Niwot, CO: Iron Gate Publishing, 2018.

Kniebes, Duane V and Susan Kniebes. *Cemeteries and Remote Burials in Larimer County, Colorado, Volume III: Estes Park Area and Rocky Mountain National Park, Including Park Property in Grand County*. Niwot, CO: Iron Gate Publishing, 2018.

Morris, Andrew J. *History of Larimer County, Colorado*. Dallas: Curtis Media, 1985.

Parrish, Shirley Rietveld. *The Epid of Larimer County*. Fort Collins, CO: Win-Art, 1959.

Watrous, Ansel. *History of Larimer County, Colorado*. Fort Collins, CO: Courtier Printing & Publishing Co, 1911.

Las Animas County

Introduction

Established: 1866   Population: 15,507

Formed from: Huerfano

Adjacent Counties: Otero, Pueblo, Bent, Baca, Costilla, Huerfano

County Seat: Trinidad

Other Communities: Aguilar, Branson, Cokedale, Kim, Starkville, El Moro, Hoehne, Jansen, Lynn, Segundo, Stonwall Gap, Valdez, Weston, Bonvcarbo, Delhi, Earl, Model, Thatcher, Trinchera, Tyrone, Villegreen, Brodhead, Delagua, Ludlow, Madrid, Morley, Sopris

Website, https://www.lasanimascounty.net

Area Codes: 719

Zip Codes: 81020, 81024, 81027, 81046, 81049, 81059, 81081, 81082, 81091

Historical Assets Colorado

Las Animas County Courthouse

Courthouses & County Government

Las Animas County
https://lasanimascounty.net

Las Animas County Courthouse (3rd Judicial District), 200 E 1st St, Trinidad, CO 81082, 719-846-3316; http://www.courts.state.co.us/Courts/County/Index.cfm?County_ID=5

Assessor, 200 E 1st St, Trinidad, CO 81082, 719-846-2295; http://lasanimascounty.org/index.php/departments/assessor.html

Board of County Commissioners, 200 E 1st St, Trinidad, CO 81082, 719-845-2593; https://www.lasanimascounty.net/departments/elected-officials/commissioners

Clerk & Recorder, 1st & Maple, Trinidad, CO 81082, 719-846-3314; http://lasanimascounty.org/index.php/departments/clerk-a-recorder

Coroner, 2309 E Main St, Trinidad, CO 81082, 719-845-9716; https://lasanimascounty.net/departments/elected-officials/coroner

Public Health, 412 Benedicta Ave, Trinidad, CO 81082, 719-846-2213; http://www.la-h-health.org/

Transportation (Road & Bridge), 2000 N Linden Ave, Trinidad, CO 81082, 719-846-2931; https://lasanimascounty.net/departments/business-offices/road-bridge

Treasurer, 200 E 1st St, Rm 204, Trinidad, CO 81082, 719-846-2981; http://www.lasanimascounty.net/index.php/departments/Treasurerpublic-trustee.html

County Records

Birth 1900	Marriage 1887	Divorce 1881
Death 1900	Land 1883	Probate 1881
Court 1881		

Las Animas County

County & Municipal Records Held at the State Level

The Colorado State Archives

Physical Records
Clerk & Recorder
County Court
District Court
Treasurer
WPA Historical Records
WPA Religious Institutions Survey
WPA Trinidad
Cities
Trinidad

Records on Film
1885 Census
Clerk & Recorder
County Court
District Court
School Districts

Records on Master Film
Clerk & Recorder
County Court
District Court
Combined Courts
School Districts

The Denver Public Library
WWI Draft Registration Cards (microfilm)

School Districts

School Districts, http://www.adcogov.org/local-school-districts

Aguilar Reorganized School District RE-6, 420 N Balsam, Aguilar, CO 81020, 719-941-4188; https://www.aguilarschools.com/

Branson Reorganized School District RE-82, 101 Saddle Rock Dr, Branson, CO 81027, 719-946-5531; https://www.bransonschoolonline.com/

Hoehne Reorganized School District 3, P.O. Box 91, Hoehne, CO 81046, 719-846-4457; http://www.hoehnesd.org/

Kim Reorganized School District 88, 425 State St, Kim, CO 81049, 719-643-5295; http://www.kimk12.org/

Primero Reorganized School District 2, 20200 Hwy 12, Weston, CO 81091, 719-868-2715; http://www.primeroschool.org/

Trinidad School District 1, 612 Park St, Trinidad, CO 81082, 719-846-3324; http://tsd1.org/

Historic School Districts

1. Trinidad
2. Coke Ovens, Cordova, Primero
3. Middle Fork, Vigil, Hoghne
4. Tijeras, Madrid
5. Garcia Plaza, North Garcia Plaza
6. Middle Apishapa, San Antonio, Aguilar
7. Vigil, Carpio Frequez, Jansen
8. Pulaski
9. Alfalfa, Ortiz
10. Trinchera Plaza, Wateyvale, Trinoa, Puza
11. Stonewall
12. Sareillo, Noverto Cordova Plaza
13. El Moro
14. Los Varos Plaza, Riley Canon
15. Abeyton, Trujillo Creek
16. La Junta, Weston
17. Barela
18. Stamford, Bon Carbo, Cokedale
19. Bent Canon, Earl and Perry
20. Trijoles, San Miguel
21. Engleville
22. Sunflower, Trujillo
23. Martinez Plaza, Upper Apishapa
24. Benito Cordova, Rivera
25. Alberson's, Jaryosa
26. Apishapa, Abyeta
27. Powell, Hicks
28. Riley Canon, Forbes Junction
29. Upper South Fork, Torres
30. Starkville, Central Starkville
31. Upper Spanish Peaks, Barela Mesa

Historical Assets Colorado

32. Lower Spanish Peaks, Morley
33. Floyd
34. Lower SOuth Fork, Cordova, San Isidro
35. Minneapolis, Alfalfa
36. Adams, Stonington, Barela, El Frisco
37. Correso Springs, Aspen Grove
38. Burro Canyon, Bon Carbo
39. Vilas, El Poso
40. Correso, Barnes, Greenville, Ludlow, Mountain View
41. Waterville, Bear Canyon, Vallaroso, Berwin
42. Boston, Lincoln, Sopris
43. Indianapolis, Hoehne
44. Troy, Wet Canyon
45. Plymouth, Augusta
46. Chicosa
47. Trinchera
48. Chicose, Cobert Canyon
49. Pinon Canyon, Pinon Ridge
50. El Moro, Coke Ovens
51. Victor Mines, Longfellow, Hastings, Delaqua
52. Lower Burro Canyon
53. North Starkville
54. Vega Ranch
55. Rapson, Rugby
56. South Starkville
57. Gulnare
58. El Ojito
59. Grey Creek
60. Zamora
61. Primero
62. Horn
63. St Thomas
64. Longs Canyon
65. Wilder
66. Pine Grove
67. Suffield
68. Beaman, Tercio
69. Broadhead
70. Round Prairie, Pinion, Red Rock
71. Sunny Side, Deora
72. Thatcher
73. Dalerose
74. Molino Canyon
75. Archuleta
76. Model
77. Apishipa
78. Crane
79. Abyeta
80. Pine View, Plainview
81. McArthur
82. Branson
83. Newcomb
84. Pleasant Valley
85. Cedar Vale, Cedar Valley
86. [1920]
87. Delhi
88. Kim
89. Prairie Star
90. Robbs
91. Ville Green
92. Nola
93. [1920]
94. Glendale
95. Plum Valley
96. Tobe
97. Riverside
98. Pine Log
99. Edenview
100. Rancho Viejo
101. Patches
102. [1920]
103. Cedar Hill South
104. Butte West, South Butte
105. Mount Pleasant
106. Mayland
107. Seven-D
108. [1920]
109. Center
110. [1920]
111. Roosevelt
112. [1920]
113. North Plains
114. White
115.
116. Lanford
117. Bunker HIll
118. Two Flues
119. Cotton Wood
120.
121. Green
122. Fallas Springs
123. Goodwill
124. Escondido
125. Longridge
126. Johnny Valley
127. Andrix
128. Shadel
129. Garcia Plaza, South Garcia Plaza
130. Sasanomos, Giggie

Fraternal Organizations

Granges
Horse Creek, No. 91, Las Animas, Las Animas, 12 Jan 1890
Bent, No. 95, Las Animas, Las Animas, 8 Feb 1890

Masons

Ancient Free & Accepted Masons
Las Animas, No. 28, Las Animas, Trinidad, 21 Sept 1875
Trinidad, No. 89, Las Animas, Trinidad, 20 Sept 1892

Royal Arch Masons
Trinidad, No. 23, Las Animas, Trinidad

Las Animas County

Knights Templar
Oriental Commandery, No. 18, Las Animas, Trinidad, 1891 Apr 23

Eastern Star
Trinidad, No. 1, Las Animas, Trinidad

Prince Hall Masons
Simpson Rest Lodge, No. 10, Las Animas, Trinidad

Prince Hall Order of the Eastern Star
Golden Star Chapter, No. 53, Las Animas, Trinidad
Magnolia Chapter, No. 56, Las Animas, Trinidad

Odd Fellows
Trinidad, No. 17, Las Animas, Trinidad
El Moro, No. 106, Las Animas, El Moro, 1893 Apr 21
Starkville, No. 127, Las Animas, Starkville

Rebekahs
None

Knights of Pythias
Rocky Mountain, No. 3, Las Animas, Trinidad
El Moro, No. 26, Las Animas, El Moro, 1884 Feb 4
Mineral, No. 91, Las Animas, Starkville
Peerless, No. 103, Las Animas, Aguilar
Spanish Peaks, No. 113, Las Animas, Hastings, 1901 Apr 11

Pythian Sisters
Columbine, No. 6, Las Animas, Trinidad
Equality, No. 6, Las Animas, Trinidad
Purity, No. 26, Las Animas, Engleville/Trinidad
Charity, No. 27, Las Animas, Starkville
Spanish Peaks, No. 28, Las Animas, Aguilar
McKinley, No. 45, Las Animas, Hastings
Columbine, No. 73, Las Animas, Aguilar

Benevolent Protective Order of Elks
Trinidad, No. 181, Las Animas, Trinidad

City & Town Halls

Trinidad, 135 N Animas St, Trinidad, CO 81082, 719-846-9843, https://www.trinidad.co.gov
Aguilar, 101 W Main St, Aguilar, Co 81020, 719-941-4360, http://www.aguilarco.us
Branson, https://www.bransoncolorado.com
Cokedale, 1 Elm St, Trinidad, CO 81082, 719-846-7428, https://www.colorado.gov/pacific/cokedale/contact-1

Archives & Manuscript Collections

None

Historical Assets Colorado

Historical & Genealogical Societies
Trinidad Historical Society, Bloom House Museum, 300 E Main St, P.O. Box 176, Trinidad, CO 81082, (719) 846-7217, http://www.trinidadco.com

Local Libraries
Carnegie Public Library, 202 N Animas St, Trinidad, CO 81082, (719) 846-6841, http://carnegiepubliclibrary.org

Aguilar Public Library, 146 W Main St, P.O. Box 578, Aguilar, CO 81020-0578, (719) 941-4426, http://www.aguilarco.us/aguilar-public-library/

Samuel Freudenthal Memorial Library, Trinidad State Junior College, 600 Prospect St, Trinidad, CO 81082, (719) 846-5593, http://www.trinidadstate.edu/library-ts/

Links
CO GenWeb
http://cogenweb.com/adams/

Cyndi's List
https://www.cyndislist.com/us/co/counties/las-animas/

FamilySearch Wiki
https://www.familysearch.org/wiki/en/Las_Animas_County,_Colorado_Genealogy

Linkpendium
http://www.linkpendium.com/las_animas-co-genealogy/

RootsWeb Wiki
https://wiki.rootsweb.com/wiki/index.php/Las_Animas_County,_Colorado

Wikipedia
https://en.wikipedia.org/wiki/Las_Animas_County,_Colorado

Historic Hotels
None

Museums & Historic Sites
Baca House, Trinidad History Museum, 312 E Main St, P.O. Box 377, Trinidad, CO 81082, (719) 846-7217, https://www.historycolorado.org/trinidad-history-museum

Colorado Welcome Center Museum, 309 Nevada Ave, Trinidad, CO 81082, (719) 846-9512, https://www.colorado.gov/pacific/trinidadwelcomecenter/contact-us-88

Santa Fe Trail Museum, 312 E Main St, Trinidad, CO 81082, (719) 846-7217, https://www.historycolorado.org/exhibit/santa-fe-trail-museum

Trinidad Historical Society, Bloom House Museum, 300 E Main St, P.O. Box 176, Trinidad, CO 81082, (719) 846-7217, http://www.trinidadco.com

Special Events & Scenic Locations
The Las Animas County Fair is held at the Las Animas County Fairgrounds, 2200 N Linden, Trinidad, Co 81082, 719-580-9182, https://www.facebook.com/LasAnimasCountyFair/

Las Animas County

The Trinidad Roundup Association's Chili/Salsa Festival is held in September most years at the Farmers Market in Cimino Park, http://trinidadroundup.homestead.com.

Visit Trinidad has a calendar of events here: https://visittrinidadcolorado.com/events/

Comanche National Grassland
Lake Dorothey State Wildlife Area
James M John State Wildlife Area
San Isabel National Forest
Spanish Peaks Wilderness
Trinidad Lake State Park
Mesa de Maya Historic Trail
Raton Pass National Historic Landmark
Santa Fe National Historic Trail
Trinidad State History Museum
Highway of Legends Scenic Byway
Santa Fe Trail National Scenic Byway

Ghost Towns & Other Sparsely Populated Places

Adair, Apishapa, Barela, Barnes, Bent Canyon, Berwind, Beshoar, Boaz, Branson, Brodhead, Butte City, Chappell, Chicosa Junction, Coke Oven, Delhi, Deuel, Downing, Earl, El Moro, Engle, Engleville Junction, Fair Grounds, Florbes, Forbes Junction, Forbes Mine, Guinare, Hastings, Hoehne, Jaroso, Kim, Long's Junction, Ludlow, Lynn, Madrid, Martinsen, Maxwell, Menger, Menger, Morley, Powell, Silvia, Sopris, Stamford, Starkville, Stonewall, Stonewall Gap, Tabaco, Thatcher, Thompson's, Trinchera, Troy, Tyrone, Valdez, Watervale, Weston, Wests, Whitford, Wootton

Newspapers

The Chronicle-News Weekly. (Trinidad, Colo.) 1???-19??
The Dry-Land Record. (Kim, Las Animas County, Colo.) 1???-1921
Trinidad Daily Times. (Trinidad, Las Animas, Colo.) 18??-1???
Peoples Monitor. (Trinidad, Colo.) 18??-1899
Anunciador de Trinidad. [Volume] (Trinidad, Colo.) 18??-1??? | Languages: English, Spanish
Daily News. (Trinidad, Colo.) 18??-????
The El Moro Dispatch. (El Moro, Las Animas Co., Colo.) 18??-1???
The Trinidad Enterprise. (Trinidad, Colo. Terr. [Colo.]) 1870-1875
Colorado Chronicle. (Trinidad, Colo.) 1873-1875
Trinidad Enterprise and Chronicle. (Trinidad, Colo.) 1875-1875
The Trinidadian. (Trinidad, Colo.) 1875-1???
The Enterprise and Chronicle. (Trinidad, Colo.) 1875-18??
The Colorado Pioneer. [Volume] (Trinidad, Colo.) 1875-1878
El Explorador. (Trinidad, Colo.) 1876-1877 | Languages: Spanish
The Chronicle-News. (Trinidad, Colo.) 1877-Current

Historical Assets Colorado

Trinidad Weekly News. (Trinidad, Colo.) 1878-18??
The Trinidad Enterprise. (Trinidad, Colo.) 1878-1880
The Trinidad Daily News. (Trinidad, Colo.) 1879-1889
The Colorado-New Mexico Cattlemen's Advertiser. (Trinidad, Colo.) 188?-1885
The Trinidad Republican. (Trinidad, Colo.) 1880-1???
The Weekly Advertiser. (Trinidad, Colo.) 188?-1901
Trinidad Weekly Times. (Trinidad, Las Animas County, Colo.) 1881-1??? | Languages: English, Spanish
Trinidad Times. (Trinidad, Las Animas Co., Colo.) 1881-1881
Trinidad Weekly Advertiser : El Anunciador de Trinidad. (Trinidad, Colo.) 1882-1??? | Languages: English, Spanish
Monday Morning Reporter. (Trinidad, Colo.) 1882-1???
Trinidad Daily Republican. (Trinidad, Colo.) 1882-1???
Trinidad Democrat. (Trinidad, Colo.) 1882-1???
Trinidad Democrat Daily Edition. (Trinidad, Colo.) 1882-1882
El Anciano. (Trinidad, Colo.) 1882-1??? | Languages: Spanish
The Trinidad Review. (Trinidad, Colo.) 1883-18??
The Daily Reporter. (Trinidad, Colo.) 1883-1???
Trinidad Daily Advertiser. (Trinidad, Colo.) 1883-1886
Cattlemen's Advertiser. (Trinidad, Colo.) 1885-1???
The Daily Advertiser. (Trinidad, Colo.) 1886-1898
Red Cross Banner. (Trinidad, Colo.) 1886-1???
The Citizen. (Trinidad, Colo.) 1887-1888
The Western World. (Boston, Las Animas County, Colo.) 1887-1???
Trinidad Weekly Citizen. (Trinidad, Las Animas County, Colo.) 1887-1???
The Troy Settler. (Troy, Las Animas County, Colo.) 1887-1???
The Boston Banner. (Boston, Las Animas County, Colo.) 1887-1???
The Daily Citizen. (Trinidad, Colo.) 1888-1888
Trinidad Daily Citizen. (Trinidad, Colo.) 1888-1890
Daily News. (Trinidad, Colo.) 1889-1898
Trinidad Chronicle. (Trinidad, Colo.) 1889-1???
The Tri-Weekly Lyre. (Trinidad, Colo.) 1889-1???
The Evening Chronicle. (Trinidad, Colo.) 1890-1???
El Progreso. (Trinidad, Colo.) 1891-19?? | Languages: Spanish
El Moro Monitor. (El Moro, Colo.) 1892-1???
The Morning Chronicle. (Trinidad, Colo.) 1896-1???
Daily Sentinel. (Trinidad, Colo.) 1897-1898
The Chronicle-News. (Trinidad, Colo.) 1898-Current
Daily Advertiser-Sentinel. (Trinidad, Colo.) 1898-1901
Forsyth's Chips. (Trinidad, Colo.) 1899-19??
The Weekly Monitor. (Trinidad, Colo.) 1899-1900
Las Animas County News. (Branson, Colo.) 19??-19??
The Twice-a-Week Monitor. (Trinidad, Colo.) 1900-1900
The Trinidad Monitor. (Trinidad, Colo.) 1900-1912
The Daily Advertiser. (Trinidad, Colo.) 1901-1906

Las Animas County

Corriere di Trinidad - The Trinidad Courier. (Trinidad, Colo.) 1902-1943 | Languages: English, Italian
El Anunciador. (Trinidad, Colo.) 1904-19?? | Languages: English, Spanish
The Trinidad Advertiser. (Trinidad, Colo.) 1906-1912
Trinidad Free Press. (Trinidad, Colo.) 191?-19??
The Aguilar Press. (Aguilar, Colo.) 1910-1934
Weekly Free Press. (Trinidad, Colo.) 1911-1915
The Advertiser-Monitor. (Trinidad, Colo.) 1912-19??
The Daily Free Press. (Trinidad, Colo.) 1913-191?
The Evening Picketwire. (Trinidad, Colo.) 1915-19??
The Free Press. (Trinidad, Colo.) 1915-19??
The National Issue. (Branson, Colo.) 1920-19??
General News. (Delhi, Colo.) 1920-1922
The Branson Leader. (Branson, Colo.) 1921-1???
The Kim-Country Record. (Kim, Las Animas County, Colo.) 1922-1970
General News and Timpas Times. (Dehli, Colo.) 1922-19??
The Trinidad Post. (Trinidad, Colo.) 1923-19??
The Evening Herald. (Trinidad, Colo.) 1928-19??
The Aquilar News. (Aquilar, Colo.) 1932-????
The Morning Shopper. (Trinidad, Colo.) 1932-1933
The Morning Light. (Trinidad, Colo.) 1933-19??
Las Animas County News. (Trinidad, Colo.) 1934-19??
News Pictorial. (Trinidad, Colo.) 1936-19??
Trinidad Herald. (Trinidad, Colo.) 1969-19??

Places on the National Register
Aguilar, Foster House Stage Station and Hotel Site, Address Restricted
Branson, 7-D School, Co. Rd. 171 N. of Co. Rd. 50.6
Branson, Pleasant Valley School, Co. Rd. 143 just S. of US Hwy 160
Cokedale, Cokedale Historic District, Roughly bounded by Church, Maple, Pine, Elm, and Spruce Sts.
Delhi, Santa Fe Trail Mountain Route Trail Segment—Delhi Vicinity I
Delhi, Santa Fe Trail Mountain Route Trail Segment—Delhi Vicinity II
Delhi, Santa Fe Trail Mountain Route Trail Segment—Delhi Vicinity III
Earl, Earl School, Address Restricted
Kim, Kim Schools, 425 State St.
Kim, Varros, Margarito, Homestead, Address Restricted
Kim, White School, Jct. of Co. Rd. 191 and Co. Rd. 30
La Junta, Rourke Ranch Historic District, Comanche National Grassland
Ludlow, Ludlow Tent Colony Site, Del Aqua Canyon Rd.
Madrid, Bridge over Burro Canon, CO 12
Trinchera, Trinchera Cave Archeological District, Address Restricted
Trinidad, Aultman House, 711 Colorado Ave.
Trinidad, Baca House and Outbuilding, 300 block of Main St.
Trinidad, Bloom, Frank G., House, 300 block of Main St.
Trinidad, Carnegie Public Library, 202 N. Animas St.

Historical Assets Colorado

Trinidad, Corazon de Trinidad, Roughly bounded by Purgatoire River on N and W, Walnut St. on E, and 3rd, W. 1st and Animas Sts. on S
Trinidad, East Street School, 206 East St.
Trinidad, Emerick, Charles, House, 1211 Nevada Ave.
Trinidad, First Baptist Church, 809 San Pedro St.
Trinidad, First Christian Church, 200 S. Walnut St.
Trinidad, First Methodist Episcopal Church, 216 Broom St.
Trinidad, Jaffa Opera House, 100—116 W. Main St.
Trinidad, Latuda, Frank, House, 431 W. Colorado Ave.
Trinidad, McCormick House, 1919 Pinon St.
Trinidad, Nichols House, 212 E. 2nd St.
Trinidad, US Post Office—Trinidad Main, 301 E. Main St.
Trinidad, Zion's German Lutheran Church, 510 Pine St.
Villegreen, Torres Cave Archeological Site, Address Restricted
Weston, Monument Lake Park Building and Hatchery Complex, 4789 CO 12

USGS Historic Places

Delagua, Delagua, 37.340016, -104.6630423
Doss Canyon North, Big Canyon Tyron Airport, 37.3930722, -103.8738478
Ludlow, Forbes, 37.2600168, -104.5647076
Ludlow, Forbes Junction, 37.2822387, -104.5388731
Madrid, Madrid, 37.127613, -104.641342
Madrid, Primero, 37.14252, -104.7416575
Trinidad West, Centennial Public School, 37.1741667, -104.5108333
Trinidad West, Lincoln School, 37.1325199, -104.5683206
Trinidad West, Park Street Public School, 37.1713889, -104.515
Trinidad West, Piedmont, 37.1377975, -104.5519313
Trinidad West, Rice Junior High School, 37.1680556, -104.5038889
Trinidad West, Saint Thomas, 37.1344642, -104.5574869
Trinidad West, Saint Thomas Public School, 37.1377778, -104.5636111
Trinidad West, Saint Thomas Roman Catholic Church, 37.1377778, -104.5627778
Trinidad West, Santa Fe Public School, 37.1797222, -104.5075
Trinidad West, Sopris, 37.134742, -104.5644316
Trinidad West, Sopris Plaza, 37.1405753, -104.5755428
Trinidad West, Viola, 37.1333533, -104.6005435
Unknown, Bowen, 0, 0

Grand Army of the Republic Posts

Trinidad No. 25, Las Animas, Trinidad, 1881
E R S Canby, No. 26, Las Animas, Trinidad, bef 1888
Jacob Abernathy, No. 29, Las Animas, Trinidad, bef 1888

USGS Historic Military Places

Rock Crossing, Pinon Canyon Maneuver Site, 37.4924676, -103.8761115

Las Animas County

Military Bases
None

Post Offices

Abeyta	1914 Dec 19	rescinded	
Abeyton	1884 Mar 7	1890 Aug 20	
Aguilar	1890 Dec 16		81020
Alcreek	1916 July 28	1935 Feb 28	
Alfalfa	1881 Apr 19	1923 Dec 15*	
Andrix	1920 Feb 16	1952 Dec 2	
Apishapa	1867 Aug 26	1911 Sept 27*	
Atlanda	1887 Dec 13	1899 Aug 31	
Atwell	1915 Jan 29	1920 Aug 31	
Augusta	1911 Sept 27	1928 May 15	
Aylmer	1899 Dec 14	1906 Sept 18*	
Badito	1865 Sept 12	1910 Nov 15	
Barela	1874 July 28	1931 Sept 30*	
Beacon	1910 Aug 11	1913 Nov 15	
Bent Canyon	1872 Mar 28	1902 June 30	
Bents Fort	1863 June 4	1873 Dec 2	
Berwind	1892 Mar 10	1931 May 30	
Beshoar	1901 Jan 25	1903 June 30	
Boncarbo	1917 Nov 15		81024
Boston	1887 Apr 14	1893 June 16	
Bowen	1906 Sept 18	1929 Jan 15	
Branson	1918 July 30		81027
Brazil	1895 May 14	1912 May 31*	
Brodhead	1902 Aug 14	1939 Apr 29*	
Brookfield	1887 Aug 30	1902 July 15	
Buster	1916 July 28	1927 July 30	
Carriso	1887 June 2	1895 July 11*	
Carriso Springs	1888 Aug 27	1890 May 17	
Carsonhart	1917 Nov 15		
Cedarhurst	1903 Aug 27	1913 Mar 31	
Chapel	1894 Dec 6	1895 Jan 3	
Chicosa	1890 May 19	1910 Aug 15*	
Clanda	1920 Feb 11	1926 Dec 31	
Clyde	1889 Feb 18	1920 June 15*	
Cokedale	1906 Dec 26		81032
Coloflats	1915 Aug 19	1918 July 30	
Cordova	1881 May 19	1889 Sept 9	
Corinth	1887 Mar 18	1887 Aug 12	
Cuatro	1903 Dec 21	1907 Aug 6	
Dalerose	1916 June 21	1943 Feb 28	
Davis	1878 Aug 6	1879 Apr 23	
Dean	1900 Apr 4	1913 June 15	

Historical Assets Colorado

Decatur	1888 July 25	1891 Aug 8	
Delagua	1903 Apr 30	1954 May 31	
Delhi	1908 Mar 16	1975 May 30*	
Dicks	1926 June 29	1935 Sept 30	
Dodsonville	1873 Dec 10	1876 Apr 17	
Downing	1886 Nov 3	1896 Sept 14	
Druce	1916 Aug 31	1922 May 2	
Duncan	1901 July 8	1916 Aug 17	
Earl	1895 July 31	1923 Dec 15*	
Edenview	1919 Feb 20	1920 Aug 31	
Edwest	1916 Nov 14	1919 Ded 26	
El Moro	1876 Apr 17	1896 Jan*	
Elmoro	Jan 1896	1933 Sept 15*	
Engle	1882 Mar 31	1913 Apr 15*	
Engleburg	1918 June 6	1923 Oct 31	
Flues	1915 Aug 26	1933 July 15	
Forbes	1889 Feb 13	1929 Jan 15*	
Forbes Junction	1906 Oct 25	1910 July 30	
Fort Lyon	1862 Aug 2	1889 Dec 26	
Fouret	1919 Sept 14		
Gillette	1888 July 25	1888 Oct 30	
Glenham	1873 May 19	1874 July 28	
Gotera	1916 Aug 17	1922 Jan 23	
Graycreek	1895 Jan 3	1921 Aug 31	
Green Canon	1909 Feb 4	1910 Aug 11	
Grinnell	1878 Dec 18	1883 July 10	
Gulnare	1890 Dec 16		81042
Hastings	1889 Sept 12	1939 Feb 15	
Hicks	1895 Apr 4	1918 Feb 15	
Higgins	1911 Dec 26	1914 June 15	
Hoehne	1886 Nov 2		81046
Hoopup	1919 Feb 26	1937 Dec 15*	
Humbar	1887 Aug 6	1887 Oct 27	
Indianapolis	1887 Aug 11	1889 May 16	
Irwin Canyon	1920 Mar 9	1924 Sept 30	
Jansen	1902 June 23	1974 May 24*	
Jaroso	1890 Dec 16	1894 Nov 16*	
Kant	1921 July 20	1925 Aug 15	
Katcina	1907 Apr 10	1907 Sept 12	
Kazan	1920 Feb 10	1931 May 9	
Kilroy	1917 Nov 15	1917 Nov 15	
Kim	1917 Jan 30		81049
Laub	1916 Dec 15	1923 Apr 30	
Link	1910 Jan 11	1912 Feb 29	
Linwood	1876 Apr 17	1886 Nov 11	
Lone Oak	1922 Jan 23	1928 Jan 14	

Las Animas County

Ludlow	1896 Feb 8	1954 May 31	
Madrid	1882 Oct 3	1917 Nov 30*	
Majestic	1900 Aug 21	1914 Dec 31	
Maldonado	1901 May 27	1905 Jan 14	
Martinsen	1889 June 3	1891 May 20	
Maxey	1889 Jan 19	1920 July 31*	
Menger	1891 July 15	1901 Nov 15	
Mesaview	1921 Oct 11	1922 Sept 30	
Minneapolis	1887 Aug 12	1899 Nov 15	
Model	1912 Oct 26		81059
Moore	1904 July 11	1904 Nov 17	
Morley	1882 Jan 11	1956 Aug 24*	
Ninaview	1915 Sept 20	1965 July 30	
Officer	1917 Feb 24	1938 June 30	
Onine	1918 June 6	1921 June 30	
Patches	1917 June 26	1928 July 14	
Patt	1919 Mar 11	1944 Feb 29	
Plum Valley	1917 Jan 9	1935 Aug 15	
Powell	1883 June 4	1896 June 8	
Primero	1901 Dec 11	1933 Apr 29	
Progress	1888 Sept 26	1895 Nov 19	
Pulaski	1874 Jan 27	1886 Nov 2	
Rapson	1911 Apr 4	1934 Oct 15*	
Raton	1878 Jan 31	1881 Apr 19	
Roby	1911 Nov 6	1912 Oct 26	
Rugby	1900 Mar 16	1947 Jan 31	
San Antonia	1875 July 21	1876 Aug 7	
San Jose	1873 Oct 6	1878 Dec 18	
San Pedro	1879 Jan 31	1879 May 23	
Segundo	1901 July 17		81070
Smith Canyon	1892 June 30	1893 Oct 23*	
Sopris	1888 July 25	1969 Jan 2	
Springfield	1887 June 2		81073
Springvale	1874 July 21	1875 Nov 9	
Stage Canyon	1919 Feb 11	1920 Nov 30	
Stamford	1883 May 2	1920 Apr 15*	
Starkville	1879 May 23		
Stevenson	1888 Feb 15	1888 Oct 30	
Stockville	1873 May 19	1875 June 1	
Stonewall	1878 Aug 6	1918 Jan 31	
Stonington	1888 Jan 20		81075
Strange	1881 Mar 21	1883 Oct 5	
Tabasco	1901 Sept 26	1925 Mar 14	
Tercio	1902 July 5	1949 Sept 30	
Thatcher	1883 Nov 9	1973 July 20*	
Tobe	1910 Dec 17	1960 Jan 31	

Historical Assets Colorado

Tollerburg	1909 Mar 18	1931 May 30	
Torres	1894 Sept 25	1918 Jan 31	
Trinchera	1889 Feb 14		80181
Trinidad 2	1866 Feb 6		81082
Troy	1887 Oct 27	1942 June 30	
Tyrone	1929 Aug 1	1968 Dec 6	
Valdez	1910 Apr 20	1961 Sept 15	
Vallorso	1918 Sept 14	1954 May 31	
Varros	1902 Sept 21	1903 Feb 14	
Vega Ranch	1916 Sept 21	1924 June 14	
Vigil	1894 Nov 5	1912 Dec 31	
Vilas	1887 June 20		81087
Villegreen	1917 Apr 21	1985 Nov 11	
Watervale	1888 July 6	1921 Mar 31*	
Wenger	1891 June 15	1891 July 15	
Weston	1889 Sept 9		81091
Wootton	1908 Dec 4	1922 Jan 14	
Wormington	1919 Apr 19	1934 Sept 29	
Yachita	1916 Oct 6	1918 July 31	
Yeiser	1904 Apr 16	1929 July 31	
Yetta	1916 Aug 5	1929 Aug 1	

Topo Quads

Abeyta	370730N	370000N	1040730W	1041500W
Andrix	372230N	371500N	1030730W	1031500W
Barela	370730N	370000N	1041500W	1042230W
Bates Lake	373730N	373000N	1040730W	1041500W
Beaty Canyon	373730N	373000N	1033000W	1033730W
Box Ranch	371500N	370730N	1034500W	1035230W
Branson	370730N	370000N	1035230W	1040000W
Branson SE	370730N	370000N	1034500W	1035230W
Brown Canyon	373730N	373000N	1031500W	1032230W
Brown Sheep Camp	373000N	372230N	1040000W	1040730W
Buck Canyon	373000N	372230N	1030730W	1031500W
Carrizo Mountain	371500N	370730N	1030000W	1030730W
Cherry Canyon	372230N	371500N	1032230W	1033000W
Cobert Mesa North	370730N	370000N	1033000W	1033730W
Culebra Peak	370730N	370000N	1050730W	1051500W
Dalerose Mesa	371500N	370730N	1032230W	1033000W
Delagua	372230N	371500N	1043730W	1044500W
Dennis Canyon	370730N	370000N	1031500W	1032230W
Doss Canyon North	373000N	372230N	1034500W	1035230W
Doss Canyon South	372230N	371500N	1034500W	1035230W
Earl	372230N	371500N	1041500W	1042230W
El Valle Creek	371500N	370730N	1050730W	1051500W
Fishers Peak	370730N	370000N	1042230W	1043000W

Las Animas County

Gulnare	372230N	371500N	1044500W	1045230W
Hidden Valley Ranch	373730N	373000N	1041500W	1042230W
Hoehne	372230N	371500N	1042230W	1043000W
Humbar Spring	372230N	371500N	1033730W	1034500W
Icehouse Canyon	373000N	372230N	1032230W	1033000W
Jesus Canyon	370730N	370000N	1032230W	1033000W
Johnson Canyon	373000N	372230N	1033730W	1034500W
Jones Lake Spring	374500N	373730N	1041500W	1042230W
Kim North	372230N	371500N	1031500W	1032230W
Kim South	371500N	370730N	1031500W	1032230W
Lambing Spring	372230N	371500N	1040000W	1040730W
Little Dome	373730N	373000N	1042230W	1043000W
Little Pine Canyon	370730N	370000N	1044500W	1045230W
Lockwood Arroyo	373730N	373000N	1035230W	1040000W
Lost Canyon	373730N	373000N	1032230W	1033000W
Ludlow	372230N	371500N	1043000W	1043730W
Madrid	371500N	370730N	1043730W	1044500W
Miners Peak	371500N	370730N	1033730W	1034500W
Model	372230N	371500N	1040730W	1041500W
Mooney Hills	371500N	370730N	1041500W	1042230W
O V Mesa	373730N	373000N	1033730W	1034500W
Painted Canyon	372230N	371500N	1035230W	1040000W
Patterson Crossing	371500N	370730N	1040730W	1041500W
Pine Canyon	370730N	370000N	1033730W	1034500W
Plug Hat Ranch	373730N	373000N	1030730W	1031500W
Plum Canyon	373000N	372230N	1033000W	1033730W
Robbers Roost Canyon	373000N	372230N	1031500W	1032230W
Rock Crossing	373000N	372230N	1035230W	1040000W
Seven Lakes Reservoir	373000N	372230N	1041500W	1042230W
Stage Canyon	373730N	373000N	1034500W	1035230W
Starkville	370730N	370000N	1043000W	1043730W
Stonewall	371500N	370730N	1050000W	1050730W
Sun Valley Ranch	374500N	373730N	1040730W	1041500W
Table Mesa	373000N	372230N	1030000W	1030730W
Tercio	370730N	370000N	1045230W	1050000W
Thatcher	373730N	373000N	1040000W	1040730W
The Hogback	373000N	372230N	1043000W	1043730W
Tobe	371500N	370730N	1033000W	1033730W
Torres	370730N	370000N	1050000W	1050730W
Trementina Canyon	371500N	370730N	1035230W	1040000W
Trinchera	370730N	370000N	1040000W	1040730W
Trinidad East	371500N	370730N	1042230W	1043000W
Trinidad West	371500N	370730N	1043000W	1043730W

Historical Assets Colorado

Tyrone	373000N	372230N	1040730W	1041500W
Utleyville	372230N	371500N	1030000W	1030730W
Valdez	370730N	370000N	1043730W	1044500W
Vega Corral	373000N	372230N	1042230W	1043000W
Vigil	371500N	370730N	1045230W	1050000W
Villegreen	372230N	371500N	1033000W	1033730W
Walker Canyon	373730N	373000N	1030000W	1030730W
Weston	371500N	370730N	1044500W	1045230W

Suggsted Reading

Beshoar, Michael. *All about Trinidad and Las Animas County, Colorado*. Trinidad, CO: Trinidad Historical Society, 1990.

Clyne, Rick J. *Coal People: Life in Southern Colorado's Company Towns, 1890-1930*. Denver: History Colorado, 1999.

Donachy, Patrick L. *Echoes of Yesteryear: Las Animas County: Things You Should Know, Places You Should Go*. Trinidad, CO: Inkwell, 1983.

Murray, Robert A and Dale R Andrus, Frederic J Athearn. *Las Animas, Huerfano and Custer: Three Colorado Counties on a Cultural Frontier: A History of the Raton Basin*. Denver: Colorado Bureau of Land Management, 1979.

Sneed, F Dean. *Las Animas County Ghost Towns and Mining Camps*. Pueblo, CO: Schusters' Printing, 2000.

Vigil, Philip Arnold. *Reminders of a Forgotten Past: Weston, Las Animas County, Colorado, the Legends and Lifestiles of a Community*. NL: Las Placitas Publications, 2014.

Lincoln County

Introduction

Established: 1889   Population: 5,467

Formed from: Elbert, Bent

Adjacent Counties: Washington, Kit Carson, Cheyenne, Crowley, Kiowa, Elbert, El Paso, Arapahoe, Pueblo

County Seat: Hugo

Other Communities: Arriba, Genoa, Limon, Bovina, Karval, Punkin Center

Website, http://www.lincolncountyco.us

Area Codes: 719, 970

Zip Codes: 80804, 80818, 80821, 80823, 80826, 80828

Historical Assets Colorado

Lincoln County Courthouse

Lincoln County 19th Century Courthouse

Courthouses & County Government

Lincoln County
 http://lincolncountyco.us
Lincoln County Courthouse (18th Judicial District), 103 3rd Ave, Hugo, CO 80821, 719-743-2455; http://www.courts.state.co.us/Courts/County/Index.cfm?County_ID=60
Assessor, 103 3rd Ave, Hugo, CO 80821, 719-743-2358; http://www.lincolncountyco.us/assessor/assessor.html
Board of County Commissioners, P.O. Box 39, Hugo, CO 80821, 719-743-2842; https://www.colorado.gov/pacific/logan/logan-county-commissioners
Clerk & Recorder, 103 3rd Ave, Hugo, CO 80821, 719-743-2444; http://www.lincolncountyco.us/clerk_recorder/clerk_recorder.html
Coroner, 103 3rd Ave, Hugo, CO, 719-740-8935; http://lincolncountyco.us/coroner/coroner.html
Public Health, 326 8th St, Hugo, CO 80821, 719-743-2526; http://www.lincolncountyco.us/public_health/public_health.html
Transportation (Road & Bridge), 43326 CR 33, Hugo, CO 80821, 719-743-2411; http://lincolncountyco.us/road_bridge/road_bridge.html
Treasurer, 103 3rd Ave, Hugo, CO 80821, 719-743-2633; http://www.lincolncountyco.us/Treasurer/Treasurer.html

County Records

Birth Unk	Marriage 1889	Divorce 1889
Death Unk	Land 1889	Probate 1889
Court 1889		

Lincoln County

County & Municipal Records Held at the State Level

The Colorado State Archives

Physical Records
Clerk & Recorder
County Court
District Court
WPA Historical Records
WPA Religious Institutions
   Survey
WPA Hugo, Limon
Cities
Limon

Records on Film
Clerk & Recorder
County Court
District Court

Records on Master Film
Clerk & Recorder
District Court
Combined Courts
School Districts

The Denver Public Library
WWI Draft Registration Cards (microfilm)

School Districts

School Districts, http://www.adcogov.org/local-school-districts

Arriba-Flagler School District C-20, 421 Julian Ave, Flagler, CO 80815, 719-765-4684; https://www.colorado.gov/af20

Crowley County School District RE-1J, 1001 Main St, Ordway, CO 81063, 719-267-3117; http://www.cck12.net/

Edison School District No. 54 JT, 14550 Edison Rd, Yoder, CO 80864, 719-478-2125; https://www.edison54jt.org/

Genoa-Hugo School District C113, 220 W 7th St, Hugo, CO 80821, 719-743-2428; http://www.genoahugo.org/

Karval School District RE-23, 16232 CR 29, Karval, CO 80823, 719-446-5311; http://www.karvalschool.org/

Limon School District RE-4J, 912 Badger Wy, Limon, CO 80828, 719-775-2350; http://www.limonbadgers.com/

Historic School Districts

1. Hugo Grade
2. Hugh High
3. Sunny Slope
4. Limon Grade
5. Love Valley, Walks Camp
6. Schneider
7. Ramsey-Olson, Genoa
8. Boyero
9. Forder, Peace Valley
10. Arickaree, Pioneer, Prairie View
11. Union, Genoa, Shaw
12. [1920]
13. Genoa
14. Clifford
15. Green Valley
16. [1920]
17. Boyero, Aroya
18. Pattonsburg, Hugo
19. Fairview, Haswell
20. Walker, Mountain View, Longbranch
21. Green Knoll, Arlington, Karval, Sugar City
22. Pleasant View, Genoa
23. Karval
24. Lincoln Valley, Kendrick, Rush, Highland, Little White
25. Nebraska Center, Hugo, Limon
26. Pleasant Center, Blue Cliff, Karvel, Arlington, Sugar City
27. Lincoln
28. Kendrick, Ordway
29. Pleasant View, Arriba, Shaw
30. Rush
31. Arriba
32. Pleasant View
33. Sunnyside, Kendrick, Rush
34. Excelsior, Hugo, Karvel
35. Carr Crossing, Sugar City
36. Henry Center, Kendrick, Ordway

Historical Assets Colorado

37. Valley, Carr Crossing, Ordway, Forder
38. Pride of Prairie, Amy, Karval, Forder
39. Union Valley, Arriba
40. Community Center, Kendrick
41. Lone Tree, Kutch
42. Sandhill, Hugo
43. Prairie Grove, Karval, Boyero
44. Lower Lincoln, Haswell
45. Cockle Burr, Kendrick/Ordway
46. Union Hall, Kendrick, Tacony

C1. Bovina

UH1. Limon High [Joint]

Fraternal Organizations

Granges
Progressive Plains, No. 357, Lincoln, Limon, 9 Nov 1917

Masons

Ancient Free & Accepted Masons
Hugo, No. 139, Lincoln, Hugo, 19 Sept 1911
Lincoln, No. 146, Lincoln, Limon, 21 Sept 1915

Royal Arch Masons
None

Knights Templar
None

Eastern Star
Palestine, No. 92, Lincoln, Hugo
Mayflower, No. 118, Lincoln, Limon

Odd Fellows
Genoa, No. 162, Lincoln, Genoa
Limon, No. 179, Lincoln, Limon

Rebekahs
Limon, No. 35, Lincoln, Limon
Hugo, No. 131, Lincoln, Hugo

Knights of Pythias
Ranchero, No. 58, Lincoln, Hugo
Limon, No. 108, Lincoln, Limon

Pythian Sisters
Purity, No. 14, Lincoln, Limon
Gold Leaf, No. 15, Lincoln, Limon

Benevolent Protective Order of Elks
None

City & Town Halls

Hugo, 522 2nd Ave, Hugo, CO 80821, 719-743-2485, http://townhugo.com
Arriba, 711 Front St, Arriba, CO 80804, 719-768-3381, https://www.colorado.gov/arriba
Genoa, 305 Main St, Genoa, CO 80818, 719-763-2313, https://www.colorado.gov/townofgenoa
Limon, 100 Civic Center Dr, Limon, CO 80828, 719-775-2346, https://www.townoflimon.com

Lincoln County

Archives & Manuscript Collections
None

Historical & Genealogical Societies
Limon Heritage Society, Limon Heritage Museum & Railroad Park, 701 1st St, P.O. Box 341, Limon, CO 80828, (719) 740-0782, http://limonmuseum.com

Local Libraries
Limon Memorial Public Library, 205 E Ave, Limon, CO 80828, (719) 775-2163, https://lincolncounty.colibraries.org/limon_public_library/

Links
CO GenWeb
http://cogenweb.com/lincoln/

Cyndi's List
https://www.cyndislist.com/us/co/counties/lincoln/

FamilySearch Wiki
https://www.familysearch.org/wiki/en/Lincoln_County,_Colorado_Genealogy

Linkpendium
http://www.linkpendium.com/lincoln-co-genealogy/

RootsWeb Wiki
https://wiki.rootsweb.com/wiki/index.php/Lincoln_County,_Colorado

Wikipedia
https://en.wikipedia.org/wiki/Lincoln_County,_Colorado

Historic Hotels
None

Museums & Historic Sites
Arriba Museum, 711 Front St, Arriba, CO 80804, (719) 768-3371, https://www.colorado.com/history-museums/arriba-museum

Eastern Trails Museum and Cultural Arts Center, 635 4th St, Hugo, CO 80821, (719) 743-2332,

Hedlund House Museum, 617 3rd Ave, P.O. Box 353, Hugo, CO 80821, (719) 740-0106, https://www.facebook.com/Hedlund-House-Museum-136843136348282/

Limon Heritage Society, Limon Heritage Museum & Railroad Park, 701 1st St, P.O. Box 341, Limon, CO 80828, (719) 740-0782, http://limonmuseum.com

Special Events & Scenic Locations
The Lincoln County Fair & Rodeo is held in August most years, at the Lincoln County Fairgrounds, 33747 Cty Rd 2W, Hugo, CO 80821, 719-743-2534, https://www.facebook.com/lincolncountycofair/

Historical Assets Colorado

Lincoln County has an events calendar here: http://seelincolncounty.com/events/

Smoky Hill Trail

Ghost Towns & Other Sparsely Populated Places
Bagdad, Bovina, Boyero, Creech, Genoa, Lake, Limon Station, Mirage, Sanborn

Newspapers
Lincoln County Ledger. (Hugo, Colo.) 1889-1898
The Range Ledger. (Hugo, Colo.) 1899-1935
The Eastern Colorado Leader. (Limon, Lincoln County, Colo.) 19??-1939
The Arriba Record. (Arriba, Lincoln County, Colo.) 19??-19??
The Genoa Sentinel. (Genoa, Colo.) 1912-19??
The Hugo Times. (Hugo, Colo.) 1914-19??
Eastern Colorado Plainsman. (Hugo, Colo.) 1935-19??
The Eastern Colorado Leader and The Genoa Sentinel. (Limon, Lincoln County, Colo.) 1939-1947
The Limon Leader. (Limon, Lincoln County, Colo.) 1947-Current

Places on the National Register
Hugo, Hugo Municipal Pool, Jct. of US 287 and 6th Ave.
Limon, Limon Railroad Depot, 897 First St.

USGS Historic Places
Hugo, Hugo Municipal Airport, 39.1530445, -103.4874452
McKenzie Draw, Wezel, 38.7983292, -103.4546635
Walks Camp Park, Thompson Landing Strips, 39.4385979, -103.5649477

Grand Army of the Republic Posts
None

USGS Historic Military Places
None

Military Bases
None

Post Offices

Amy	1909 Feb 2	1937 Mar 31	
Arriba	1889 Feb 4		80804
Bovina	1899 Jan 8	1955 Nov 30	
Boyero	1902 Mar 3		
Cable	1893 July 19	1895 Jan 30	
Carr Crossing	1915 Mar 25	1930 Apr 15	
Cowans	1915 Nov 2	1929 July 31	

Lincoln County

Damascus	1914 June 6	1917 Feb 15	
Forder	1901 Mar 5	1944 Sept 30	
Genoa	1895 Jan 30	1895 June 29	
Genoa 2	1903 Mar 31		80818
Girard	1912 Mar 22	1917 Nov 30	
Green Knoll	1917 Mar 31	1933 July 31	
Hugo	1871 Dec 1		80821
Karval	1911 Mar 2		80823
Kendrick	1906 Jan 25	1956 Nov 30	
Kutch	1899 July 17	1971 Jan 31*	
Limon	1903 Nov 14		80828
Limon Station	1889 Aug 6	1903 Nov 14	
Luslo	1904 Aug 18	1904 Nov 30	
McCollin	1915 June 10	1917 Nov 30	
Owen	1908 Sept 26	1915 Dec 15	
Sanborn	1878 May 17	1905 June 3	
Saugus	1908 Jan 4	1914 Jan 31	
Shaw	1908 Feb 24	1955 Nov 30	
Swift	1910 Dec 17	1919 Dec 31	
Wellons	108 June 10	1916 June 30	
Wezel	1911 Feb 8	1919 July 15	
White	1901 Mar 6	1901 Nov 30	

Topo Quads

Aroya	385230N	384500N	1030730W	1031500W
Arriba	392230N	391500N	1031500W	1032230W
Arriba NE	393000N	392230N	1031500W	1032230W
Arriba NW	393000N	392230N	1032230W	1033000W
Barrel Springs Draw	384500N	383730N	1031500W	1032230W
Barron Creek	391500N	390730N	1033000W	1033730W
Beckman Lake	390000N	385230N	1033000W	1033730W
Bluff Spring	383730N	383000N	1031500W	1032230W
Boyero	390000N	385230N	1031500W	1032230W
Clifford	390730N	390000N	1031500W	1032230W
Cockleburr Springs	383730N	383000N	1035230W	1040000W
Forder	384500N	383730N	1033730W	1034500W
Galatea SW	383730N	383000N	1030730W	1031500W
Genoa East	392230N	391500N	1032230W	1033000W
Genoa West	392230N	391500N	1033000W	1033730W
Hubbard Lake	384500N	383730N	1032230W	1033000W
Hugo	391500N	390730N	1032230W	1033000W
Hugo SW	390730N	390000N	1032230W	1033000W
Karval	384500N	383730N	1033000W	1033730W
Kinney Lake	390000N	385230N	1032230W	1033000W
Lake SE	390730N	390000N	1033000W	1033730W
McKenzie Draw	385230N	384500N	1032230W	1033000W

Historical Assets Colorado

Metz Springs	383730N	383000N	1033000W	1033730W
Peace Valley	384500N	383730N	1034500W	1035230W
Rock Basin	385230N	384500N	1031500W	1032230W
Sanborn Reservoir	384500N	383730N	1035230W	1040000W
Schafer Reservoir	390000N	385230N	1030730W	1031500W
Scott Draw	383730N	383000N	1032230W	1033000W
Sevenmile Ranch	391500N	390730N	1031500W	1032230W
Sharp Lake	383730N	383000N	1033730W	1034500W
Stacy Lakes Draw	384500N	383730N	1030730W	1031500W
Stanley Gulch	385230N	384500N	1033000W	1033730W
Truckton NE	384500N	383730N	1040000W	1040730W
Truckton SE	383730N	383000N	1040000W	1040730W
Walker Point	383730N	383000N	1034500W	1035230W
Walks Camp Park	393000N	392230N	1033000W	1033730W

Suggested Reading

Clagett, Laura Solze. *History of Lincoln County, Colorado*. Dallas: Curtis Media Corp, 1987.

Cooley, Dale, Mary Liz Owen and B Compton. *Where the Wagons Rolled: the History of Lincoln County and the People Who Came Before 1925*. Limon, CO: Eastern Colorado Printery, 1985.

Gray, Jean. *Homesteading Haxtun and the High Plains: Northeastern Colorado History*. Charleston, SC: The History Press, 2013.

Lincoln County Historical Society. *Lincoln County: from the Beginning to 1940*. Marceline, MO: Walsworth Pub Co, 1980.

Logan County

Introduction

Established: 1887   Population: 22,709
Formed from: Weld
Adjacent Counties: Phillips, Sedgwick, Yuma, Washington, Morgan, Weld
County Seat: Sterling
  Other Communities: Crook, Fleming, Iliff, Merino, Peetz, Proctor, Atwood, Padroni
Website, https://www.colorado.gov/logan
Area Codes: 970
Zip Codes: 80722, 80726, 80728, 80736, 80741, 80745, 80747, 80751

Historical Assets Colorado

Logan County Courthouse

Courthouses & County Government

Logan County
https://colorado.gov/logan

Logan County Courthouse (13th Judicial District), 110 N Riverview Rd, Sterling, CO 80751, 970-522-6565; http://www.courts.state.co.us/Courts/County/Index.cfm?County_ID=39

Assessor, 110 N Riverview Rd, Sterling, CO 80751, 970-522-2462; https://colorado.gov/pacific/logan/logan-county-assessor-0

Board of County Commissioners, 315 Main St, Sterling, CO 80751, 970-522-0888, https://www.colorado.gov/pacific/logan/logan-county-commissioners

Clerk & Recorder, 315 Main St, Sterling, CO 80751, 970-522-1544; https://colorado.gov/pacific/logan/county-clerk-and-recorder

Coroner, 330 S 2nd St, Sterling, CO 80751, 970-521-4850; https://colorado.gov/pacific/logan/logan-county-coroner

Public Health, 700 Columbine St, Sterling, CO 80751, 970-522-3741; http://www.nchd.org/

Transportation (Road & Bridge, 12603 CR 33, Sterling, CO 80751, 970-522-3426; https://colorado.gov/pacific/logan/road-and-bridge-department

Treasurer, 315 Main St, Sterling, CO 80751, 970-522-2462; https://colorado.gov/pacific/logan/logan-county-treasurer

County Records

Birth 1894
Death 1894
Court 1887

Marriage 1887
Land 1887

Divorce 1887
Probate 1887

Logan County

County & Municipal Records Held at the State Level

The Colorado State Archives

Physical Records
Clerk & Recorder
Coroner
County Commissioners
WPA Historical Records
WPA Religious Institutions
  Survey
WPA Sterling
Cities
  Sterling

Records on Film
Clerk & Recorder

Records on Master Film
Clerk & Recorder
County Commissioners
County Court
District Court
School Districts
Sheriff

The Denver Public Library

Ed Reed Farm Records, 1904-1939
WPA Historical Records Survey
WWI Draft Registration Cards (microfilm)

School Districts

School Districts, http://www.adcogov.org/local-school-districts
Buffalo School District RE-4J, 315 Lee St, Merino, CO 80741, 970-522-7424; http://merino.k12.co.us/
Frenchman School District RE-3, 506 N Fremont, Fleming, CO 80728, 970-265-2111; https://www.flemingschools.org/
Haxtun School District RE-2J, 201 W Powell St, Haxtun, CO 80731, 970-774-6111; https://www.haxtunk12.org/
Plateau School District Re-5, 311 Coleman Ave, Peetz, CO 80747, 970-334-2361; https://www.peetzschool.org/Page/1
Valley School District RE-1, 301 Hagen St, Sterling, CO 80751, 970-522-0792; https://www.re1valleyschools.org/

Historic School Districts

1. Willard
2. Prairie View
3. High Plains
4. [1888]
5. Barber
6. [1888]
7. Kelly
8. [1888]
9. Peetz, Mercer
10. [1888]
11. [1888]
12. Sterling
13. Rockland
14. Good HOpe
15. Valley View
16. [1888]
17. [1888]
18. [1888]
19. Stony Buttes
20. [1888]
21. [1888]
22. Highland
23. [1888]
24. Highland
25. Fyffe
26. [1888]
27. [1888]
28. Springdale
29. Lakeside
30. Sanders
31. Minto Valley
32. [1888]
33. [1888]
34. Primrose
35. [1888]
36. [1888]
37. [1888]
38. Highway
39. [1888]
40. [1888]
41. [1888]
42. [1888]
43. St Peter's
44. [1888]
45. [1888]

Historical Assets Colorado

46. [1887]
47. [1888]
48. [1888]
49. [1888]
50. Proctor
51. [1888]
52. Pumpkin Vine
53. [1887]
54. Iliff
55. Leroy
56. Pioneer
57. [1888]
58.
59. [1888]
60. Atwood
61.
62. Crook
63.
65. [1889]
66.
67. [1889]
68. [1887]
69. Fleming
70. Armstrong
71. Franklin
72. Harding
73. Graylin
74. Mount Hope
75. Blackhawk
76. Liberty
77. Heth
78. Dillon-McGinley
79. [1887]
80. Concord
81. Riverside
82. [1920]
83. Columbine
84. Fairview
85. Springdale Valley
86. Matthews
87. Stephens
88. Happy Valley
89. New Haven
90. Gage
91. Padroni
92. Pawnee Valley
93. Pleasant Divide
94. Valentine
95. Benson
96. [1920]
97. Hill View
98. Red Lion
99. Dailey

Fraternal Organizations

Granges
West Plaines, No. 263, Logan, Westplaines, 1 Apr 1916
Happy Valley, No. 289, Logan, Willard, 24 May 1916
Pawnee, No. 347, Logan, Sterling, 2 June 1917
Cedar Valley, No. 365, Logan, Peetz, 5 Mar 1918

Masons
Ancient Free & Accepted Masons
Sterling, No. 54, Logan, Sterling, 18 Sept 1883

Royal Arch Masons
Sterling, No. 47, Logan, Sterling

Knights Templar
Sterling Commandery, No. 35, Logan, Sterling, 1916 Dec 15

Eastern Star
Sterling, No. 68, Logan, Sterling

Odd Fellows
Merino, No. 64, Logan, Merino
Logan, No. 69, Logan, Sterling

Rebekahs
Olive Branch, No. 27, Logan, Sterling
Merino, No. 60, Logan, Merino

Knights of Pythias
Franklin, No. 27, Logan, Sterling, 1885 Mar 27

Pythian Sisters
None

Benevolent Protective Order of Elks
Sterling, No. 1336, Logan, Sterling

Logan County

City & Town Halls
Sterling, 521 N 4th St, Sterling, CO 80751, 970-522-9700, https://www.sterlingcolo.com

Crook, 212 4th St, Crook, CO 80726, 970-886-2222, https://www.facebook.com/TownofCrook/?rf=167711003240038

Fleming, 114 N Logan Ave, Fleming, CO 80728, 970-265-2692, https://www.facebook.com/pages/Town-Hall/177305612963646

Iliff, 405 W 2nd Ave, Iliff, CO 80736, 970-522-2283

Merino, 206 Colorado Ave, Merino, CO 80741, 970-522-1036, https://town.merino.co.us

Peetz, 621 Main St, Peetz, CO 80747, 970-334-2473, https://www.sites.google.com/site/townofpeetz/

Archives & Manuscript Collections
None

Historical & Genealogical Societies
Crook Historical Society, Historical Museum, 4th St & 4th Ave, P.O. Box 194, Crook, CO 80726

Local Libraries
Sterling Public Library, 420 N 5th St, P.O. Box 4000, Sterling, CO 80751-4000, (970) 522-2023, http://sterling.polarislibrary.com

Monahan Library, Northeastern Junior College, 100 College Ave, Sterling, CO 80751-2399, (970) 521-6600, http://www.njc.edu/library/

Links
CO GenWeb
http://cogenweb.com/logan/

Cyndi's List
https://www.cyndislist.com/us/co/counties/logan/

FamilySearch Wiki
https://www.familysearch.org/wiki/en/Logan_County,_Colorado_Genealogy

Linkpendium
http://www.linkpendium.com/logan-co-genealogy/

RootsWeb Wiki
https://wiki.rootsweb.com/wiki/index.php/Logan_County,_Colorado

Wikipedia
https://en.wikipedia.org/wiki/Logan_County,_Colorado

Historic Hotels
None

Historical Assets Colorado

Museums & Historic Sites
Crook Historical Society, Historical Museum, 4th St & 4th Ave, P.O. Box 194, Crook, CO 80726
Fleming Museum, 400 W Weston St, Fleming, CO 80728, (970) 265-2591,
Overland Trail Museum, 110 Overland Trail, Sterling, CO 80751, (970) 522-3895, https://www.facebook.com/OverlandTrailMuseum

Special Events & Scenic Locations
The Logan County Fair & Rodeo is held in August most years at the Lincoln County Fairgrounds, 1120 Pawnee Ave, Sterling, CO 80751, 970-522-0888, http://www.lcfair.org.
The Logan County Chamber of Commerce has a calendar of annual events here: https://www.logancountychamber.com/local-events/
There is a calendar of events near Sterling here: https://www.colorado.com/co/sterling/festivals-events

American Discovery Trail
Pawnee Pioneer Trail
South Platte Trail

Ghost Towns & Other Sparsely Populated Places
Chenoa, Crook, Fleming, Galien, Iliff, Le Roy, Merino, Padroni, Peetz, Proctor, Red Lion, Rockland, Summit Springs (Battlefield), Willard

Newspapers
The Fleming Herald. (Fleming, Logan County, Colo.) 188?-1???
The Atwood Advocate. (Atwood, Weld County, Colo.) 1885-1???
The Logan County Advocate. (Sterling, Colo.) 1885-19??
Logan County News. (Holyoke, Logan County, Colo.) 1887-1???
The State Herald. (Holyoke, Logan County, Colo.) 1887-1921
Holyoke Tribune. (Holyoke, Colo.) 1887-1???
The Daily Democrat. (Sterling, Colo.) 189?-1???
The Sterling Daily Advocate. (Sterling, Colo.) 1894-1894
The Sterling Democrat. (Sterling, Colo.) 1895-19??
Sterling Farm Journal. (Sterling, Colo.) 19??-1952
The Republican-Advocate. (Sterling, Colo.) 1907-1934
The Merino Breeze. (Merino, Colo.) 1909-1937
The Sterling Advocate. (Sterling, Colo.) 1910-1953
The Morning Advocate. (Sterling, Colo.) 1910-1911
The Evening Advocate. (Sterling, Colo.) 1911-192?
Buckley's Store News. (Crook, Colo.) 1913-19??
Crook News. (Crook, Colo.) 1915-19??
The Peetz Gazette. (Peetz, (Best Part of Logan County), Colo.) 1916-19??
The Crook Index. (Crook, Colo.) 1919-19??
Sterling Advocate. (Sterling, Colo.) 192?-1953

Logan County

The Crook Progress Review. (Crook, Colo.) 1928-19??
Tri-County Herald. (Merino, Logan County, Colo.) 1937-1943
The High Plains Daily Journal. (Sterling, Colo.) 1952-1953
Colorado Rea News. (Sterling, Colo.) 1952-19??
High Plains Journal. (Sterling, Colo.) 1953-1953
High Plains Journal and The Sterling Farm Journal. (Sterling, Colo.) 1953-1953
Sterling Journal-Advocate. (Sterling, Colo.) 1953-1984
High Plains Farm Journal and The Sterling Farm Journal. (Sterling, Colo.) 1953-1955
The Business Farmer and The High Plains Farm Journal. (Sterling, Colo.) 1955-19??
The Peetz Bridge. ([Peetz, Colo.]) 1978-Current
Journal-Advocate. (Sterling, Colo.) 1984-Current
South Platte Sentinel. (Sterling, Colo.) 1988-Current

Places on the National Register

Proctor, Powell and Blair Stone Ranch, Approx. 1 mi. N of jct. of US 138 and 65 Rd.
Sterling, Downtown Sterling Historic District, Roughly bounded by Division Ave., Poplar, Front, Ash & 4th Sts.
Sterling, First United Presbyterian Church, 130 S. 4th St.
Sterling, Harris, W. C., House, 102 Taylor St.
Sterling, I and M Building, 223 Main St.
Sterling, Logan County Courthouse, Main St.
Sterling, Luft, Conrad, Sr., House, 1429 CO 14
Sterling, St. Anthony's Roman Catholic Church, 329 S. 3rd St.
Sterling, Sterling Public Library, 210 S. 4th St.
Sterling, Sterling Union Pacific Railroad Depot, 113 N. Front St.
Sterling, US Post Office, Federal Building, and Federal Courthouse—Sterling Main, Third and Popular Sts.

USGS Historic Places

None

Grand Army of the Republic Posts

Sterling, No. 44, Logan, Sterling
Fleming, No. 82, Logan, Fleming

USGS Historic Military Places

None

Military Bases

None

Post Offices

Amherst	1888 Feb 18		80721
Armstrong	1911 Oct 30	1917 June 15	

Historical Assets Colorado

Arnold	1897 Jan 26	1900 Mar 30	
Atwood	1885 Aug 10		80722
Bryant	1888 Mar 27	1916 Mar 31	
Calvert	1887 Dec 22	1888 Aug 8	
Chenoa	1886 Nov 19	1895 Nov 19	
Crook	1882 May 26		80726
Dailey	1915 June 28	1961 July 7	
Emerson	1888 Mar 27	1890 Sept 20	
Fleming	1888 Aug 8	1904 May 31	
Fleming 2	1904 Sept 16		80728
Graylin	1910 Sept 26	1917 Dec 15	
Haxtun	1888 Apr 25	1922 Jan 17	
Holyoke	1887 Nov 9		80734
Iliff	1882 Mar 21	1895 Nov 27	
Iliff	1896 Apr 23		80736
Julesburg 3	1886 May 26		80737
Kelly	1909 Aug 26	1915 Aug 15	
Laura	1908 Apr 16	1916 June 30	
Le Roy	1888 July 2	1895 Aug 2	
Leroy	1895 Aug 2	1918 June 30	
Merino	1874 June 24		80741
New Haven	1910 Dec 7	1916 June 30	
Padroni	1909 Nov 10		80745
Paoli	1888 June 8	1890 Feb 11	
Paoli 2	1910 Mar 9		80746
Peetz	1908 Nov 20		80474
Proctor	1908 Nov 21	1963 Dec 30	
Red Lion	1886 Nov 19	1935 Nov 30*	
Rockland	1888 Apr 23	1891 Feb 4	
Sedgwick	1885 Sept 10	1894 May 11	
Sedgwick 2	1896 Apr 30		80749
Sterling	1874 Feb 24		80751
Wakeman	1887 Sept 19	1897 May 15	
Westplains	1910 May 23	1949 Feb 15	
Willard	1888 Sept 26	1967 July 14*	
Winston	1902 May 18	1918 Dec 31*	

Topo Quads

Atwood	403730N	403000N	1031500W	1032230W
Atwood NE	404500N	403730N	1031500W	1032230W
Avalo SE	405230N	404500N	1033000W	1033730W
Buffalo Springs Ranch NE	403000N	402230N	1030000W	1030730W
Buffalo Springs Ranch NW	403000N	402230N	1030730W	1031500W
Chimney Canyons	410000N	405230N	1032230W	1033000W

Logan County

Clarkville	403000N	402230N	1023730W	1024500W
Crook	405230N	404500N	1024500W	1025230W
Dipper Spring	410000N	405230N	1033000W	1033730W
Fleming	404500N	403730N	1024500W	1025230W
Galien	404500N	403730N	1030000W	1030730W
Glacken Hill	403000N	402230N	1025230W	1030000W
Haystack Butte	410000N	405230N	1025230W	1030000W
Iliff	405230N	404500N	1030000W	1030730W
Kirchnavy Butte	410000N	405230N	1031500W	1032230W
Leroy	403730N	403000N	1025230W	1030000W
Merino	403000N	402230N	1031500W	1032230W
Messex	403000N	402230N	1032230W	1033000W
New Haven	403000N	402230N	1024500W	1025230W
North Sterling Reservoir	405230N	404500N	1031500W	1032230W
Padroni	405230N	404500N	1030730W	1031500W
Padroni NW	410000N	405230N	1030730W	1031500W
Peetz	410000N	405230N	1030000W	1030730W
Proctor	405230N	404500N	1025230W	1030000W
Reiradon Hill	403730N	403000N	1030000W	1030730W
Rockland	403730N	403000N	1023730W	1024500W
Saint Petersburg	403730N	403000N	1024500W	1025230W
Sterling North	404500N	403730N	1030730W	1031500W
Sterling South	403730N	403000N	1030730W	1031500W
Stoneham NE	404500N	403730N	1033000W	1033730W
Stoneham SE	403730N	403000N	1033000W	1033730W
Twin Buttes	410000N	405230N	1024500W	1025230W
Uhler Ranch	404500N	403730N	1025230W	1030000W
Westplains	405230N	404500N	1032230W	1033000W
Wild Horse Lake	404500N	403730N	1032230W	1033000W
Willard	403730N	403000N	1032230W	1033000W

Suggested Reading

Conklin, Emma Burke. *A Brief History of Logan County, Colorado: With Reminiscences by Pioneers*. Salem, MA: Higginson Book Co, 2007.

Inventory of the County Archives of Colorado, No. 38, Logan County (Sterling). Denver: Historical Records Survey, 1940.

Mains, Walter S. *Logan County, Colorado, Cemetery Survey*. NL: Logan County Genealogy Society, 1984.

Propst, Nell Brown. *Where the Buffalo Roamed: a Historical Pageant of Logan County, Colorado*. Thesis, University of Denver, 1949.

Richards, Ada Davis. *Homestead Days and Future Dreams: Northwest Logan County History, Heritage and Great Memories*. Sterling, CO: A D Richards, 1989.

Sterling Centennial: a Logan County Family History. Frisco, CO: Taylor Pub Co, 1984.

Wells, Bud. *Logan County: Better by 100 Years: a Centennial History of Logan County, Colorado*. Dallas: Curtis Media Corp, 1987.

Historical Assets Colorado

Mesa County

Introduction

Established: 1883   Population: 146,723

Formed from: Gunnison

Adjacent Counties: Garfield, Pitkin, Gunnison, Delta, Montrose

County Seat: Grand Junction

Other Communities: Fruita, Colbran, De Beque, Palisade, Clifton, Fruitvale, Loma, Orchard Mesa, Redlands, Carpenter, Gateway, Mack, Mesa, Molina, Plateau City, Whitewater

Website, https://www.mesacounty.us

Area Codes: 970

Zip Codes: 81501, 80502, 81503, 81504, 81505, 81506, 81507, 81520, 81521, 81522, 81523, 81524, 81515, 81526, 81527, 81624, 81630, 81643, 81646

Historical Assets Colorado

Mesa County Justice Center

Mesa County 19th Century Courthouse

Courthouses & County Government

Mesa County
https://www.mesacounty.us

Mesa County Courthouse (Justice Center) (21st Judicial District), 125 N Spruce St, Grand Junction, CO 81501, 970-257-3650; http://www.courts.state.co.us/Courts/County/Index.cfm?County_ID=64

Assessor, 544 Rood Ave, Grand Junction, CO 81501, 970-244-1610; http://assessor.mesacounty.us/

Board of County Commissioners, 544 Rood Ave, Grand Junction, CO 81501, 70-244-1605, https://www.mesacounty.us/commissioners/

Clerk & Recorder, 200 S Spruce St, Grand Junction, CO 81501, 970-244-1679; http://clerk.mesacounty.us/

Coroner, 544 Rood Ave, Grand Junction, CO 81501, 970-244-1898; https://coroner.mesacounty.us/

Public Health, 510 29 1/2 Rd, Grand Junction, CO 81504, 970-248-6900; http://health.mesacounty.us/

Transportation (Road & Bridge), 970-244-1895; https://www.mesacounty.us/public-works/road-and-bridge-department/

Treasurer, 544 Rood Ave, Rm 100, Grand Junction, CO 81501, 970-244-1824; http://Treasurer.mesacounty.us/

County Records

Birth 1890	Marriage 1883	Divorce 1884
Death 1890	Land 1883	Probate 1884
Court 1884		
CSA Burial Permits 1941		
CSA Pauper Ledger (birth) [nd]		

Mesa County

County & Municipal Records Held at the State Level

The Colorado State Archives

Physical Records
Clerk & Recorder
County Court
District Court
Justice Court
Public Welfare (CCC)
Treasurer
WPA Historical Records
WPA Religious Institutions Survey
WPA Grand Junction

Records on Film
1885 Census
District Court
Combined Courts
Cities
Grand Junction

Records on Master Film
Building
Clerk & Recorder
County Court
District Court
Combined Courts
School Districts
Sheriff
Cities
Grand Junction

The Denver Public Library
WWI Draft Registration Cards (microfilm)

School Districts

School Districts, http://www.adcogov.org/local-school-districts

De Beque School District 49JT, 730 Minter Ave, De Beque, CO 81630, 970-283-5596; https://www.dbschools.org/

Mesa County Valley School District 51, 2115 Grand Ave, Grand Junction, CO 81501, 970-254-5100; https://www.d51schools.org/

Montrose County School District RE-1J, 930 Colorado Ave, Montrose, CO 81402, 970-249-7726; http://www.mcsd.org/

Plateau Valley School District 50, 56600 Hwy 330, Collbran, CO 81624, 970-487-3547; https://www.pvsd50.org/

Historic School Districts

1. Grand Junction
2. Fruita
3. Whitewater
4. Purdy Mesa
5. Loback
6. Collbran
7. Rhone
8. Snipes, Molina
9. Mesa
10. DeBeque
11. Pride, Esalante, Dolores
12. Pleasant View
13. Allen
14. Vega, Heiberger
15. Grand River, Cameo
16. Columbus
17. Parker Basin
18. Pear Park
19. Palisade
20. Garfield
21. Clover
22. Eagalite
23. Loma Park, Longfellow
24. Little Creek
25. Hunter
26. Canon
27. Star
28. Fruitvale
29. Lincoln
30. Georgia Mesa, Mormon Mesa
31. [1897]
32. Pomona
33. Columbine
34. Little Book Cliff
35. Mount Lincoln
36. [1920]
37. New Liberty
38.
39. Appleton
40. Redlands
41. Glade Park
42. Salt Creek
43. Clifton
44. Mack
45. Divided Creek

Historical Assets Colorado

Fraternal Organizations

Granges
Fruita, No. 105, Mesa, Fruita, 21 Apr 1890
Grand River, No. 106, Mesa, Grand Junction, 25 Apr 1890
Plateau, No. 111, Mesa, Eaglelite/DeBeque, 14 Oct 1890
College, No. 123, Mesa, Grand Junction, 26 Jan 1891

Masons

Ancient Free & Accepted Masons
Mesa, No. 55, Mesa, Grand Junction, 18 Sept 1883
Plateau, No. 101, Mesa, Mesa, 16 Sept 1896
Hesperia, No. 120, Mesa, Fruita, 21 Sept 1904
Fruita, No. 120, Mesa, Fruita, 15 Jan 1999
Palisade, No. 125, Mesa, Palisade, 17 Sept 1907
Tuscan, No. 131, Mesa, Colbran, 22 Sept 1908
Grand Junction, No. 173, Mesa, Grand Junction, 23 Jan 1952
Amethyst, No. 55, Mesa, Grand Junction, 18 Sept 1883

Royal Arch Masons
Grand Junction, No. 24, Mesa, Grand Junction

Knights Templar
Temple Commandery, No. 23, Mesa, Grand Junction, 1892 June 8

Eastern Star
Sunshine, No. 53, Mesa, Grand Junction
Cedar Springs, No. 62, Mesa, Mesa
Carnation, No. 70, Mesa, Fruita
Palisade, No. 90, Mesa, Palisade
Collbran, No. 102, Mesa, Collbran
Grand Junction, No. 103, Mesa, Grand Junction

Odd Fellows
Fruita, No. 35, Mesa, Fruita
Mesa, No. 58, Mesa, Grand Junction
Collbran, No. 84, Mesa, Collbran
Plateau, No. 113, Mesa, Mesa
Roan Creek, No. 125, Mesa, DeBeque
Palisade, No. 147, Mesa, Palisade
Clifton, No. 180, Mesa, Clifton

Rebekahs
Grand Valley, No. 40, Mesa, Grand Junction
Plateau Valley, No. 74, Mesa, Collbran
Mount Garfield, No. 78, Mesa, Clifton
Ruby, No. 79, Mesa, De Beque
Peach, No. 81, Mesa, Palisade
Grand Mesa, No. 95, Mesa, Mesa
Silver Bell, No. 115, Mesa, Fruita

Mesa County

Knights of Pythias
Monarch, No. 23, Mesa, Junction City, 1883 May 28
Grand Junction, No. 55, Mesa, Grand Junction, 1890 Apr 15
Columbian, No. 87, Mesa, Amethyst
Junction, No. 124, Mesa, Grand Junction

Pythian Sisters
Cherry Blossom, No. 60, Mesa, Grand Junction

Benevolent Protective Order of Elks
Grand Junction, No. 575, Mesa, Grand Junction

City & Town Halls

Grand Junction, 250 N 5th St, Grand Junction, CO 81501, 970-244-1500, https://www.gjcity.org
Fruita, 325 E Aspen Ave, Fruita, CO 81521, 970-858-935, https://www.fruita.org
Colbran, 1010 High St, Colbran, CO 81624, 970-487-3751, https://www.colorado.gov/townofcollbran
De Beque, 381 Minter Ave, De Beque, CO 81630, 970-283-5475, https://www.colorado.gov/debeque
Palisade, 175 E 3rd St, Palisade, CO 81526, 970-464-5602, http://www.townofpalisade.org

Archives & Manuscript Collections

Museum of the West & Loyd Files Research Library, 462 Ute Ave, P.O. Box 20000, Grand Junction, CO 81502-5020, (970) 242-0971, https://museumofwesternco.com

Historical & Genealogical Societies

Mesa County Genealogical Society, P.O. Box 1506, Grand Junction, CO 81502-1506, (970)242-0971, http://www.mesacountygenealogy.org
Mesa County Historical Society, 462 Ute Ave, P.O. Box 841, Grand Junction, CO 81502, (970) 260-5226, https://www.facebook.com/mesacountyhistoricalsociety/
National Railway Historical Society, Rio Grand Chapter, P.O. Box 3381, Grand Junction, CO 81501-3381, (970) 242-0784, http://www.nrhs.com/chapters/rio-grande/

Local Libraries

Mesa County Public Library, 443 N 6th St, Grand Junction, CO 81501-2731, (970) 243-4442, http://mesacountylibraries.org
Loyd Files Research Library, 462 Ute Ave, P.O. Box 20000, Grand Junction, CO 81502-5020, (970) 242-0971, https://museumofwesternco.com
Tomlinson Library, Colorado Mesa University, 1100 North Ave, Grand Junction, CO 81501, (970) 248-1860, https://www.coloradomesa.edu/library/

Links

CO GenWeb
http://cogenweb.com/mesa/

Historical Assets Colorado

Cyndi's List
https://www.cyndislist.com/us/co/counties/mesa/
FamilySearch Wiki
https://www.familysearch.org/wiki/en/Mesa_County,_Colorado_Genealogy
Linkpendium
http://www.linkpendium.com/mesa-co-genealogy/
RootsWeb Wiki
https://wiki.rootsweb.com/wiki/index.php/Mesa_County,_Colorado
Wikipedia
https://en.wikipedia.org/wiki/Mesa_County,_Colorado

Historic Hotels

None

Museums & Historic Sites

Colorado National Monument Museum, Hwy 340, Fruita, CO 81521, (970) 858-3617, https://www.nps.gov/colm/index.htm

Colorado Welcome Center Museum, 340 Hwy 340, Fruita, CO 81521, (970) 858-9335, https://www.colorado.com/colorado-official-state-welcome-center/colorado-welcome-center-fruita

Cross Orchards Historic Farm Museum, 3073 F Road (Patterson Rd), Grand Junction, CO 81506, (970) 434-9814, https://museumofwesternco.com/visit/locations/

Gateway Colorado Auto Museum, 43200 Hwy 141, Gateway, CO 81522, (970) 931-2458, http://gatewayautomuseum.com

Museum of the West & Loyd Files Research Library, 462 Ute Ave, P.O. Box 20000, Grand Junction, CO 81502-5020, (970) 242-0971, https://museumofwesternco.com

Rocky Mountain Wing of the Commemorative Air Force, 780 Heritage Wy, P.O. Box 4125, Grand Junction, CO 81506, (970) 256-0693, http://www.rockymountainwingcaf.org

Special Events & Scenic Locations

The Mesa County Fair is held in July most years at the Mesa County Fairgrounds, 2785 Hwy 50, Grand Junction, CO 81503, 970-255-7101, https://mesacountyfair.com/mcfair/

Visit Grand Junction keeps a calendar of events here: https://www.visitgrandjunction.com/events-calendar

And a calendar of festivals and fairs here: https://www.visitgrandjunction.com/events/festivals-fairs

Black Ridge Canyons Wilderness
Colorado National Monument
Dominguez Canyon Wilderness
Dominguez-Escalante National Conservation Area
Grand Mesa National Forest

Mesa County

Manti-La Sal National Forest
McInnis Canyons National Conservation Area
Uncompahgre National Forest
White River National Forest
Highline Lake State Park
James M Robb-Colorado River State Park
Vega State Park
American Discovery Trail
Dinosaur Diamond Prehistoric Highway National Scenic Byway
Grand Mesa National Scenic and Historic Byway
Kokopelli Trail
Old Spanish National Historic Trail
Unaweep-Tabeguache Scenic and Historic Byway
Colorado Riverfront Trail

Ghost Towns & Other Sparsely Populated Places

Book Cliff, Bridgeport, Cabeza, Cameo, Carpenter, Crevasse, Deer Run, Eagalite, Harlow, Hawxhurst, Kahnah, Mesa, Orson, Pallisades, Roan, Ruby, Shale, Tunnel, Unaweep, Utah Line, Vega, Whitewater

Newspapers

The Plateau Voice. (Collbran, Colo.) 1???-19??
Western Colorado Reporter. (Grand Junction, Colo.) 1???-19??
The Plateau Valley Voice. (Collbran, Mesa County, Colo.) 1???-19??
The New Critic. (Grand Junction, Colo.) 1???-19??
The Colorado Organizer. (Grand Junction, Colo.) 1???-19??
The Clifton Success. (Clifton, Colo.) 1???-19??
The De Beque New Era and Bugle. (De Beque, Colo.) 1???-1910
Grand Junction Daily News. (Grand Junction, Colo.) 1???-1923
The Semi-Weekly Star. (Grand Junction, Colo.) 18??-1898
The Western Slope. (Grand Junction, Mesa County, Colo.) 18??-1???
The Daily Star-Times. (Grand Junction, Mesa County, Colo.) 18??-1???
Grand Junction Star. (Grand Junction, Colo.) 18??-1900
The Western Trail. ([Chicago, Ill.]) 1881-19??
Grand Junction News. (Grand Junction, Gunnison Co., Colo.) 1882-1914
The Daily News. (Grand Junction, Colo.) 1882-1???
Mesa County Democrat. (Grand Junction, Colo.) 1883-????
Grand Junction Democrat. (Grand Junction, Colo.) 1883-????
The Fruita Star. (Fruita, Mesa County, Colo.) 1889-1???
Grand Valley Star and Western Colorado Horticulturist. (Grand Junction, Colo.) 1889-1890
Grand Valley Star. (Grand Junction, Colo.) 1890-1893
The Grand Valley Sun. (Grand Junction, Colo.) 189?-19??
The Mesa County Mail. (Cleveland [Fruita], Colo.) 1892-19??
The Daily Sentinel. (Grand Junction, Colo.) 1893-Current
Grand Valley Star-Times. (Grand Junction, Colo.) 1893-1896

Historical Assets Colorado

The Weekly Sentinel. (Grand Junction, Colo.) 1893-19??
The Weekly Star-Times. (Grand Junction, Mesa County, Colo.) 1896-1???
The Wild West. (Debeque, Colo.) 1896-1???
The Weekly Star. (Grand Junction, Colo.) 1898-1???
The De Beque Bugle and Weekly Record. (De Beque, Colo.) 1898-19??
Collbran Oracle. (Collbran, Mesa County, Colo.) 1899-19??
The Fruita Times. (Fruita, Colo.) 19??-Current
Collbran Journal. (Collbran, Colo.) 19??-19??
The Evening Sun. (Grand Junction, Colo.) 1900-19??
The Revolutionist. (Grand Junction, Colo.) 1902-19??
The Palisade Tribune. (Palisade, Mesa County, Colo.) 1903-1987
The Daily Herald. (Grand Junction, Colo.) 1903-19??
The Herald. (Grand Junction, Colo.) 1904-1910
The Herald and Grand Valley Progress. (Grand Junction, Colo.) 1910-1910
The Western Slope Ranchman and Herald-Progress. ([Grand Junction, Colo.]) 1910-1910
The Herald and Western Slope Ranchman. (Grand Junction, Colo.) 1910-1910
The Herald. (Grand Junction, Colo) 1910-19??
The De Beque New Era. (De Beque, Colo.) 1910-1910
The New Era. (De Beque, Mesa County, Colo.) 1910-1920
Grand Junction Weekly News. (Grand Junction, Colo.) 1914-19??
De Beque New Era. (De Beque, Mesa County, Colo.) 1921-1921
De Beque Shale And Oil News. (De Beque, Mesa County, Colo.) 1921-1923
The De Beque News formerly The De Beque Shale and Oil News. (De Beque, Mesa County, Colo.) 1923-19??
The Grand Junction News. (Grand Junction, Colo.) 1923-19??
Morning Sun and The Morning Record. (Grand Junction, Colo.) 1957-19??
The Grand Junction Morning Record. (Grand Junction, Colo.) 1957-19??
The County Mail. (Grand Junction, Colo.) 1963-19??
The Leader. (Grand Junction, Colo.) 1965-196?
The Citizen Newspaper. (Clifton, Colo.) 1978-1979
Mesa County Mail. (Fruita, Colo.) 1978-1979
Valley Citizen. (Clifton, Colo.) 1979-19??
Westpeople. (Grand Junction, Colo.) 1984-19??
The Valley Voice. (Collbran, Colo.) 1985-19??
Senior Beacon. (Grand Junction, Colo.) 1987-19??
The Palisade Tribune & Valley Report. (Palisade, Colo.) 1987-Current
Grand Junction Free Press. (Grand Junction, Co) 2003-Current

Places on the National Register

Clifton, Clifton Community Center and Church, F and Main St.
Clifton, Kettle-Jens House, 498 32nd Rd.
De Beque, Colorado River Bridge, I-70 Frontage Rd. at milepost 62.90
De Beque, IOOF Hall, Jct. of 4th St. and Curtis Ave.
DeBeque, De Beque House, 233 Denver Ave.
Fruita, Colorado National Monument Visitor Center, Colorado National Monument

Mesa County

Fruita, Fruita Bridge, Cty. Rd. 17.50 over Colorado River
Fruita, Fruita Museum, 432 E. Aspen
Fruita, Phillips, Harry and Lilly, House, 798 N. Mesa St.
Gateway, Calamity Camp, Address Restricted
Glade Park, Coates Creek Schoolhouse, D S Rd. 16 mi. W of Glade Park
Glade Park, Pipe Line School, 101 16.5 S Rd.
Grand Junction, Cross Land and Fruit Company Orchards and Ranch, NE of Grand Junction at 3079 F Rd.
Grand Junction, Denver and Rio Grande Western Railroad Depot, 119 Pitkin Ave.
Grand Junction, Devils Kitchen Picnic Shelter, Colorado National Monument
Grand Junction, Handy Chapel, 202 White Ave.
Grand Junction, Hotel St. Regis, 359 Colorado Ave.
Grand Junction, Margery Building, 519—527 Main St.
Grand Junction, North Seventh Street Historic Residential District, 7th St. between Hill and White Aves.
Grand Junction, Rim Rock Drive Historic District, Colorado National Monument
Grand Junction, Saddlehorn Caretaker's House and Garage, Colorado National Monument
Grand Junction, Saddlehorn Comfort Station, Colorado National Monument
Grand Junction, Saddlehorn Utility Area Historic District, Colorado National Monument
Grand Junction, Serpents Trail, Colorado National Monument
Grand Junction, Stranges Grocery, 226 Pitkin Ave.
Grand Junction, U.S. Post Office, 400 Rood Ave.
Loma, Loma Community Hall, 1341 Co. Rd. 13
Molina, Convicts' Bread Oven, W of Molina on CO 65
Palisade, Crissey, Herbert and Edith, House, 218 W. 1st St.
Palisade, Grand Valley Diversion Dam, Across Colorado R. N of jct. with Plateau Cr., 8 mi. NE of Palisade
Silt, Cayton Guard Station, Forest Service Road 814.1
Whitewater, Bloomfield Site, Address Restricted
Whitewater, Land's End Observatory, Land's End Rd., 10 mi. W of CO 65

USGS Historic Places

Unknown, Skyway Post Office, 0, 0
Vega Reservoir, The Meadows, 39.2244243, -107.7836729

Grand Army of the Republic Posts

Phil Sheridan, No. 18, Mesa, Grand Junction
John A Logan, No. 21, Mesa, Grand Junction, 1883
Grand Junction, No. 35, Mesa, Grand Junction
Spanish Peak, No. 60 Mesa, Powell

USGS Historic Military Places

None

Historical Assets Colorado

Military Bases
None

Post Offices

Arlington	1883 May 25	1884 Aug 12	
Bernard	1896 Oct 24	1905 May 31	
Cameo	1907 Dec 14	1969 Feb 28	
Carpenter	1890 June 11	1891 Aug 3	
Clifton	1900 Aug 18		81520
Clover	1895 Feb 1	1902 Sept 30*	
Collbran	1892 Jan 9		81624
Copper	1898 May 9	1899 Mar 2	
De Beque	1888 Mar 23	1894 Apr 28	
De Beque 2	1902 May 27		81630
Debeque	1894 Apr 28	1902 May 27	
Eaglite	1885 Dec 3	1901 Aug 26	
Escalante	1903 Sept 9	1903 Dec 5	
Excelsior	1899 Feb 18	1890 Oct 16	
Fruita	1884 Apr 4		81521
Fruitvale	1948 July 1	1950 Aug 24	
Gary	1955?	1985 Aug 30	
Gateway	1903 Apr 25	1903 July 29	
Gateway 2	1904 July 16		81522
Gavin	1916 Sept 26	1917 July 31	
Gilsonite	1957 May 18	1974	
Glade Park	1910 Nov 11		81523
Grand Junction	1882 May 26		81524
Harlow	1890 May 17	1891 Apr 7	
Hawxhurst	1882 Aug 25	1892 Mar 3	
Heiberger	1908 Oct 30	1925 Feb 14	
Hope	1896 Apr 22	1900 Mar 3	
Ionia	1899 Mar 2	1899 Oct 1	
Jones	1883 Apr 3	1883 May 25	
Leon	1883 Apr 13	1883 Aug 3	
Loma	1905 Aug 2		81524
Mack	1904 Apr 21		81525
Mainard	1901 May 24	1905 Aug 2*	
Mesa	1883 Apr 12	1884 Mar 4	
Mesa 2	1887 Apr 29		
Molina	1895 Apr 25	1896 Sept 1	
Molina 2	1906 May 3		81646
Mountainvale	1884 Sept 14	1903 Aug 31	
Orson	1882 Oct 3	1894 June 20*	
Palisade	1924 Nov 1		81526
Palisades	1891 Jan 26	1924 Nov 1	
Palisades 2	1895 July 15	1926 Mar 12*	

Mesa County

Pine Bluff	1913 June 6	1914 Dec 31
Plateau	1883 Nov 23	1887 Oct 27
Plateau City	1901 Aug 26	1942 Dec 31
Ravens	1885 Feb 5	1886 May 21
Ravensbeque	1886 May 21	1888 Mar 23
Rhone	1894 Sept 11	1904 Dec 15
Roan	1893 Aug 9	1894 Sept 11
Rocky	1905 Aug 12	1905 Nov 25
Sinbad	1914 Dec 19	1933 Jan 14
Skyway	1927 June 4	1945 June 30
Snipes	1897 Jan 9	1906 May 3
Tunnel	1902 Oct 10	1903 Dec 31
Unaweep	1883 Aug 21	1898 Sept 22*
Vega	1891 May 23	1914 Apr 15
Whitewater	1884 Oct 9		81527

Topo Quads

Atkinson Creek	383000N	382230N	1083730W	1084500W
Battleship Rock	390730N	390000N	1084500W	1085230W
Bieser Creek	390000N	385230N	1085230W	1090000W
Calamity Mesa	383730N	383000N	1084500W	1085230W
Cameo	391500N	390730N	1081500W	1082230W
Casto Reservoir	384500N	383730N	1083730W	1084500W
Chalk Mountain	390730N	390000N	1073730W	1074500W
Clifton	390730N	390000N	1082230W	1083000W
Collbran	391500N	390730N	1075230W	1080000W
Colorado National Monument	390730N	390000N	1083730W	1084500W
Corcoran Point	391500N	390730N	1083000W	1083730W
Dolores Point North	384500N	383730N	1090000W	1090730W
Dolores Point South	383730N	383000N	1090000W	1090730W
Dominguez	385230N	384500N	1081500W	1082230W
Elk Knob	391500N	390730N	1072230W	1073000W
Escalante Forks	384500N	383730N	1082230W	1083000W
Fish Creek	385230N	384500N	1084500W	1085230W
Fruita	391500N	390730N	1083730W	1084500W
Gateway	384500N	383730N	1085230W	1090000W
Glade Park	390000N	385230N	1083730W	1084500W
Grand Junction	390730N	390000N	1083000W	1083730W
Grand Mesa	390730N	390000N	1075230W	1080000W
Hells Kitchen	390000N	385230N	1080000W	1080730W
Indian Point	390000N	385230N	1080730W	1081500W
Island Mesa	390000N	385230N	1083000W	1083730W
Jacks Canyon	385230N	384500N	1083000W	1083730W
Juanita Arch	383730N	383000N	1085230W	1090000W
Juniata Reservoir	390000N	385230N	1081500W	1082230W

Historical Assets Colorado

Keith Creek	384500N	383730N	1083000W	1083730W
Kelso Point	383730N	383000N	1082230W	1083000W
Lands End	390730N	390000N	1080730W	1081500W
Leon Peak	390730N	390000N	1074500W	1075230W
Mack	391500N	390730N	1084500W	1085230W
Mesa	391500N	390730N	1080730W	1081500W
Mesa Lakes	390730N	390000N	1080000W	1080730W
Molina	391500N	390730N	1080000W	1080730W
Palisade	390730N	390000N	1081500W	1082230W
Payne Wash	390000N	385230N	1084500W	1085230W
Pine Mountain	384500N	383730N	1084500W	1085230W
Point Creek	385230N	384500N	1080730W	1081500W
Porter Mountain	391500N	390730N	1073730W	1074500W
Round Bottom	403000N	402230N	1073730W	1074500W
Round Mountain	391500N	390730N	1082230W	1083000W
Ruby Canyon	391500N	390730N	1085230W	1090000W
Sieber Canyon	390730N	390000N	1085230W	1090000W
Snipe Mountain	383730N	383000N	1083000W	1083730W
Snyder Flats	385230N	384500N	1083730W	1084500W
Spruce Mountain	391500N	390730N	1073000W	1073730W
Starvation Point	383000N	382230N	1082230W	1083000W
Triangle Mesa	385230N	384500N	1082230W	1083000W
Two V Basin	385230N	384500N	1085230W	1090000W
Uncompahgre Butte	383730N	383000N	1083730W	1084500W
Vega Reservoir	391500N	390730N	1074500W	1075230W
Whitewater	390000N	385230N	1082230W	1083000W
Windy Point	383000N	382230N	1083000W	1083730W

Suggested Reading

Anderson, Carol M. *Kannah Creek: The People, Their Stories, and the History*. Montrose, CO: Western Reflections Pub, 2005.

Fay, Abbott. *Grand Mesa Country: Stories from Mesa and Delta Counties in Colorado*. Montrose, CO: Western Reflections Pub, 2005.

Haskell, Charles W. *History and Business Directory of Mesa County, Colorado*. Grand Junction, CO: Mesa County Democrat, 1886.

Mesa County, Colorado: its Pioneers Days and its Wonderful Development. Grand Junction, CO: Daily Sentinel, 1915.

McCreanor, Emma and Lani Duke. *Mesa County, Colorado: a 100 Year History (1883-1983)*. Grand Junction, CO: Museum of Western Colorado Press, 1986.

McCreanor, Emma. *Mesa County, Colorado: a 100 Year History Updated and Expanded with Timeline through 2002*. Grand Junction, CO: Museum of Western Colorado Press, 2002.

McLeod, Robert W. *A Valley so Grand ... the Pioneer Citizens and Early History of Mesa County, Colorado*. Arvada, CO: CreateSpace, 2015.

Mineral County

Introduction

Established: 1893   Population: 712

Formed from: Hinsdale, Rio Grande, Saguache

Adjacent Counties: Saguache, Rio Grande, Archuleta, Hinsdale

County Seat: Creede

  Other Communities: Spar City, Wagon Wheel Gap

Website, https://www.colorado.gov/mineralcountycolorado

Area Codes: 719

Zip Codes: 81130

Historical Assets Colorado

Mineral County Courthouse

Courthouses & County Government

Mineral County
> https://www.colorado.gov/mineralcountycolorado

Mineral County Courthouse (12th Judicial District), 1201 N Main, Creede, CO 81130, 719-658-2575; http://www.courts.state.co.us/Courts/County/Index.cfm?County_ID=35

Assessor, P.O. Box 70, Creede, CO 81130, 719-658-2669; http://www.mineralcounty-colorado.com/assessor.html

Board of County Commissioners, P.O. Box 70, Creede, 81130, 719-480-2660, https://www.colorado.gov/pacific/mineralcountycolorado/mineral-county-commissioners

Clerk & Recorder, P.O. Box 70, Creede, CO 81130, 719-658-2440; http://www.mineralcountycolorado.com/clerkrecorder.html

Coroner, 719-658-2600; https://www.colorado.gov/pacific/mineralcountycolorado/mineral-county-coroner

Public Health, 802 Rio Grande Ave, Creede, CO 81130, 719-658-2416; http://www.mineralcountycolorado.com/publichealth.html

Transportation (Road & Bridge), 719-658-2329; https://www.colorado.gov/pacific/mineralcountycolorado/road-and-bridge-1

Treasurer, 1201 N Main St, Creede, CO 81130, 719-658-2325; http://www.mineralcountycolorado.com/Treasurer.html

County Records

Birth Unk	Marriage 1893	Divorce 1894
Death Unk	Land 1893	Probate 1893
Court 1893		

Mineral County

County & Municipal Records Held at the State Level
The Colorado State Archives

Physical Records
Assessor
County Commissioners
County Court
District Court
Treasurer
WPA Religious Institutions
   Survey
Cities
   Creede

Records on Film
District Court

Records on Master Film
District Court
School Districts

The Denver Public Library
Mineral County Mining Companies Records, 1905
WWI Draft Registration Cards (microfilm)

School Districts
School Districts, http://www.adcogov.org/local-school-districts
Creede School District, 450 Corsair Dr, Creede, CO 81130, 719-658-2220; , https://www.creedek12.net/

Historic School Districts
1. Fremont
2, Up River
3. Creede
4. [1895]
5. [1895]
6. [1896]

Fraternal Organizations

Granges
None

Masons

Ancient Free & Accepted Masons
Yampa, No. 94, Mineral, Creede, 20 Sept 1893

Royal Arch Masons
None

Knights Templar
None

Eastern Star
Rio Grande, No. 35, Mineral, Creede

Odd Fellows
Creede, No. 55, Mineral, Creede

Rebekahs
Woodfern, No. 62, Mineral, Creede

Historical Assets Colorado

Knights of Pythias
None

Pythian Sisters
Pine Mountain, No. 58, Mineral, Creede

Benevolent Protective Order of Elks
Creede, No. 506, Mineral, Creede

City & Town Halls

Creede, 2223 N Main St, Creede, CO 81130, 719-658-2276, https://www.colorado.gov/creede

Archives & Manuscript Collections

Creede Historical Society, Historical Museum, Library & Archive, 17 Main St, P.O. Box 608, Creede, CO 81130, (719) 658-2303, http://creedehistoricalsociety.com

Historical & Genealogical Societies

Creede Historical Society, Historical Museum, Library & Archive, 17 Main St, P.O. Box 608, Creede, CO 81130, (719) 658-2303, http://creedehistoricalsociety.com

Local Libraries

Mineral County Regional Library, 308 La Garita Ave, PO Box 429, Creede, CO 81130, (719) 658-2220, https://www.colorado.gov/pacific/mineralcountycolorado/mineral-county-library

Links

CO GenWeb
http://cogenweb.com/mineral/

Cyndi's List
https://www.cyndislist.com/us/co/counties/mineral/

FamilySearch Wiki
https://www.familysearch.org/wiki/en/Mineral_County,_Colorado_Genealogy

Linkpendium
http://www.linkpendium.com/mineral-co-genealogy/

RootsWeb Wiki
https://wiki.rootsweb.com/wiki/index.php/Mineral_County,_Colorado

Wikipedia
https://en.wikipedia.org/wiki/Mineral_County,_Colorado

Historic Hotels

None

Mineral County

Museums & Historic Sites
Creede Underground Mining Museum, 503 W Willow Creek Rd, P.O. Box 432, Creede, CO 81130, (719) 658-0811, http://www.undergroundminingmuseum.com

Special Events & Scenic Locations
The Creede ChuteOut Rodeo is held in July most years at the Mineral County Fairgrounds, 210 Airport Rd, Creede, CO 81130, 719-658-2376, http://www.upperriogrande.org

Creede and Mineral County have a calnedar of events here: https://www.creede.com/events.html

Rio Grande National Forest
San Juan National Forest
La Garita Wilderness
Weminuche Wilderness
Colorado Trail
Continental Divide National Scenic Trail
Lake Fork National Recreation Trail
Silver Thread Scenic Byway

Ghost Towns & Other Sparsely Populated Places
Bachelor City (Teller), Spar City, Sunnyside, Weaver

Newspapers
The Creede Miner. ([Creede, Colo.) 189?-1???
The Wason Miner. (Wason And Creede, Colo.) 1891-1???
The Teller Topics. (Bachelor, Teller P.o., Hinsdale County, Colo.) 1892-1???
The Creede News. (Creede, Saguache County, Colo.) 1892-1???
The Creede Amethyst. (Amethyst And Creede, Colo.) 1892-1892
Creede Daily Herald. (Amethyst, Colo.) 1892-1???
The Daily Creede Candle. (Creede, Amethyst Postoffice, Colo.) 1892-1???
The Creede Candle. (Creede, Colo.) 1892-1930
The Creede Chronicle. (Creede, Colo.) 1892-1895
Spar City Spark. (Spar City, Colo.) 1892-1895
The Daily Miner. (City Of Creede (Amethyst P.o.), Colo.) 1898-1???
Mineral County Miner and South Fork Tines. (Creede (Mineral County), Colo.) 1975-1983
The Mineral County Miner. (Creede, Colo.) 1983-Current

Places on the National Register
Creede, Sevenmile Bridge, County Rd. 6 miles SW of Creede
Creede, Wagon Wheel Gap Railroad Station, SE of Creede at Wagon Wheel Gap off CO 149

Historical Assets Colorado

USGS Historic Places
San Luis Peak, Weaver, 37.8839, -106.9312
Unknown, San Juan Post Office, 0, 0
Wagon Wheel Gap, Wagon Wheel Gap Post Office, 37.7700021, -106.7978212

Grand Army of the Republic Posts
Jim Bowie, No. 92, Mineral, Amethyst/Creede

USGS Historic Military Places
None

Military Bases
None

Post Offices
Amethyst	1892 Jan 25	1909 Feb 2	
Antelope Springs	1876 May 5	1903 May 30	
Creede	1891 July 1	1908 Nov 28	
Creede 2	1909 Feb 9		81130
North Creede	1908 Nov 28	1919 Apr 15	
San Juan	1874 June 24	1923 Mar 8*	
Spar	1892 Aug 16	1895 Aug 23	
Teller	1892 Apr 29	1912 Mar 15	
Thornton	1895 June 24	1901 Mar 26	
Wagon Wheel Gap	1875 Aug 27	1957 Sept 30*	
Wason	1891 Dec 26	1904 Apr 30	

Topo Quads
Beaver Creek Reservoir	373730N	373000N	1063730W	1064500W
Bristol Head	375230N	374500N	1070000W	1070730W
Creede	375230N	374500N	1065230W	1070000W
Elwood Pass	373000N	372230N	1063730W	1064500W
Lake Humphreys	374500N	373730N	1064500W	1065230W
Mount Hope	373730N	373000N	1064500W	1065230W
Pagosa Peak	373000N	372230N	1070000W	1070730W
Saddle Mountain	373000N	372230N	1065230W	1070000W
South Fork West	374500N	373730N	1063730W	1064500W
South River Peak	373730N	373000N	1065230W	1070000W
Spar City	374500N	373730N	1065230W	1070000W
Wagon Wheel Gap	375230N	374500N	1064500W	1065230W
Wolf Creek Pass	373000N	372230N	1064500W	1065230W

Mineral County

Suggested Reading

Bennett, Edwin Lewis. *Boom Town Boy in Old Creede, Colorado.* Chicago: Sage Books, 1966.

Jacobs, Janis. *Ribs of Silver, Hearts of Gold: the Story of Homesteading and Dude Ranching in Mineral County and the Upper Rio Grande.* Creede, CO: Creede Historical Society, 1994.

Van Horn, Beverly. *Early History of Mineral and Rio Grande Counties, Colorado.* NL: NP, 2000.

Historical Assets Colorado

Moffat County

Introduction

Established: 1911   Population: 13,795

Formed from: Routt

Adjacent Counties: Routt, Rio Blanco

County Seat: Craig

Other Communities: Dinosaur, Maybell, Elk Springs, Greystone, Hamilton, Massadona, Lay, Sunbeam

Website, https://www.colorado.gov/moffatcounty

Area Codes: 970

Zip Codes: 81610, 81625, 81626, 81633, 81638, 81640, 81653

Historical Assets Colorado

Moffatt County Courthouse

Moffatt County 19th Century Courthouse

Courthouses & County Government

Moffat County
   https://www.colorado.gov/moffatcounty
Moffatt County Courthouse (14th Judicial District), 221 W Victory Wy, Craig, CO 81625, 970-824-8254; http://www.courts.state.co.us/Courts/County/Index.cfm?County_ID=46
Assessor, 221 W Victory Wy, Craig, CO 81625, 970-824-9102; http://www.colorado.gov/cs/Satellite/CNTY-Moffat/CBON/1251574651254
Board of County Commissioners, 221 W Victory Wy, Craig, CO 81625, 970-824-5517, https://www.colorado.gov/pacific/moffatcounty/county-commissioners
Clerk & Recorder, 221 W Victory Wy, Craig, CO 81625, 970-824-9104; http://www.colorado.gov/cs/Satellite/CNTY-Moffat/CBON/1251574651173
Coroner, 970-824-9109; https://www.colorado.gov/pacific/moffatcounty/county-coroner
Public Health, 940 Central Park Dr, Ste 101, Steamboat Springs, CO 80487, 970-879-1632; http://www.nwcovna.org/
Transportation (Road & Bridge), 822 E 1st St, Craig, CO 81625, 970-824-3211 x 1014
Treasurer, 221 W Victory Wy, Ste 230, Craig, CO 81625, 970-824-9111; http://www.colorado.gov/cs/Satellite/CNTY-Moffat/CBON/1251574651183

County Records

Birth 1900	Marriage 1911	Divorce 1911
Death 1900	Land 1911	Probate 1911
Court 1911		

Moffat County

County & Municipal Records Held at the State Level
The Colorado State Archives
Physical Records
Clerk & Recorder
County Court
District Court
WPA Historical Records
WPA Religious Institutions
    Survey
WPA Craig
Cities
    Craig
    Robinson

Records on Film
Clerk & Recorder
District Court
Cities
    Craig

Records on Master Film
Clerk & Recorder
Associate Court
County Court
District Court
Combined Courts
School Districts
Cities
    Craig

The Denver Public Library
Water Works Records, 1915-1925
WWI Draft Registration Cards (microfilm)

School Districts
School Districts, http://www.adcogov.org/local-school-districts
Moffat County School District RE NO 1, 775 Yampa Ave, Craig, CO 81625, 970-824-3268; https://www.moffatsd.org/

Historic School Districts

1. Ladore
2. Wyocolo
3. Slater
4. Fairview
5. Craig
6. Maybell
7. Beal
8. Breeze Basin
9. Waddle Creek
10. Hamilton
11. Axial
12. Twin Wash
13. Round Bottom
14. Lower Big Gulch
15. Lower Fortification
16. Great Divide
17. Williams
18. Upper Fortification
19. Moraysos
20. Lay
21. Dry Fork
22. Antelope
23. Grandview
24. Greasewood
25. Timberlake
26. Spring Creek
27. Elk Springs
28. Dowden Bridge
29. Hiawatha
30. Price Creek
31. Wild Rose
32. Castle Park
33. Upper Big Gulch
34. Cedar Mountain
35. Sunbeam
36. Central Fortification
37. Scandinavian Gulch
38. Loyd

Fraternal Organizations
Granges
Big Gulch, No. 353, Moffat, Craig, 1 Oct 1917
Fortification, No. 358, Moffat, Craig, 8 Dec 1917
Dry Farmer, No. 359, Moffat, Craig, 17 Dec 1917
Rock Valley, No. 360, Moffat, Craig, 18 Dec 1917
Skyeline, No. 361, Moffat, Craig, 19 Nov 1917
High Mesa, No. 362, Moffat, Craig, 22 Feb 1918
Resolute, No. 366, Moffat, Craig, 28 Mar 1918

Historical Assets Colorado

Wheatland, No. 367, Moffat, Stayden, 4 Apr 1918
Cedar Mountain, No. 369, Moffat, Craig, 18 Apr 1918
Divide, No. 370, Moffat, Great Divide/Craig, 15 May 1918
Maybee, No. 371, Moffat, Maybee, 14 May 1918
Cross Mountain, No. 372, Moffat, Sunbeam, 15 May 1918
Sugar Loaf, No. 374, Moffat, Lay, 15 May 1918
Marapos, No. 375, Moffat, Marapos, 12 June 1918
Spring Creek, No. 377, Moffat, Great Divide, 13 May 1918
Black Mountain, No. 378, Moffat, Craig, 28 June 1918
Cedar Springs, No. 379, Moffat, Cedar Springs, 9 Aug 1918
Dry Lane, No. 380, Moffat, Maybee, 22 Aug 1918
Iron Springs, No. 381, Moffat, Craig/Iron Springs, 18 Sept 1918
Price Creek, No. 384, Moffat, Price Creek, 19 May 1919
Primrose, No. 386, Moffat, Craig, 15 Aug 1919
Highway, No. 390, Moffat, Craig, 21 Nov 1919

Masons
   Ancient Free & Accepted Masons
   Cortez, No. 88, Moffat, Craig, 16 Sept 1891

   Royal Arch Masons
   None

   Knights Templar
   None

   Eastern Star
   Anita, No. 41, Moffat, Craig

Odd Fellows
   Cedar Mountain, No. 104, Moffat, Craig

   Rebekahs
   Craig, No. 138, Moffat, Craig

Knights of Pythias
   None

   Pythian Sisters
   None

Benevolent Protective Order of Elks
   Craig, No. 1577, Moffat, Craig

City & Town Halls
Craig, 300 W 4th St, Craig, CO 81625, 970-826-2000, https://www.ci.craig.co.us
Dinosaur, 317 Stegasaurus Fwy, Dinosaur, CO 81610, 970-374-2286, https://www.colorado.gov/townofdinosaur

Archives & Manuscript Collections
None

Moffat County

Historical & Genealogical Societies
None

Local Libraries
Moffat County Libraries, 570 Green St, Craig, CO 81625-3027, (970) 824-5116, https://www.colorado.gov/pacific/moffatcounty/search-our-catalog

Links
CO GenWeb
http://cogenweb.com/moffat/

Cyndi's List
https://www.cyndislist.com/us/co/counties/moffat/

FamilySearch Wiki
https://www.familysearch.org/wiki/en/Moffat_County,_Colorado_Genealogy

Linkpendium
http://www.linkpendium.com/moffat-co-genealogy/

RootsWeb Wiki
https://wiki.rootsweb.com/wiki/index.php/Moffat_County,_Colorado

Wikipedia
https://en.wikipedia.org/wiki/Moffat_County,_Colorado

Historic Hotels
None

Museums & Historic Sites
Colorado Welcome Center Museum, 101 E Stegosaurus, P.O. Box 207, Dinosaur, CO 81610, (970) 374-2205, https://www.colorado.com/colorado-official-state-welcome-center/colorado-welcome-center-dinosaur

Museum of Northwest Colorado, 590 Yampa Ave, Craig, CO 81625, (970) 824-6360, http://www.museumnwco.org

Wyman Living History Ranch and Museum, 94350 E Hwy 40, P.O. Box 339, Craig, CO 81626, (970) 824-6346, https://www.thewymanmuseum.com

Special Events & Scenic Locations
The Moffat County Fair is held in July most years at the Moffat County Fairgrounds, 640 E Victory Way, Craig, CO 81625, 970-824-5708, https://www.moffatcountyfair.com

Visit Moffat County has a calendar of events here: https://www.visitmoffatcounty.com/signature-events.php

The city of Craig keeps a calendar of events here: https://www.colorado.com/co/craig/festivals-events

The Craig Chamber of Commerce keeps a calendar of events here: https://www.craig-chamber.com/events

Historical Assets Colorado

Browns Park National Wildlife Refuge
Dinosaur National Monument
Routt National Forest
White River National Forest
Yampa River State Park
Dinosaur Diamond Prehistoric Highway National Scenic Byway

Ghost Towns & Other Sparsely Populated Places
Dinosaur, Maybell, Elk Springs, Greystone, Hamilton, Massadona, Lay, Sunbeam

Newspapers
The Pantagraph. (Craig, Routt County, Colo.) 1891-1895
Craig Courier. (Craig, Moffat County, Colo.) 1895-1902
The Daily N.W. Colorado Press. (Craig, Colo.) 19??-1966
Yampa Valley Flashes. (Craig, Colo.) 19??-19??
Routt County Courier. (Craig, Routt County, Colo.) 1902-1911
Moffat County Courier. (Craig, Routt [Moffat] County, Colo.) 1911-1929
The Craig Empire. (Craig, Routt County, Colo.) 1911-1929
The Moffat County Bell. (Maybell, Moffat County, Colo.) 1916-19??
The Craig Empire-Courier. (Craig, Colo.) 1929-1960
The Moffat County Mirror. (Craig, Moffat County, Colo.) 1942-19??
The N.W. Colorado Daily Press. (Craig, Colo.) 1966-1968
The Daily Press. (Craig, Colo.) 1968-1970
The Northwest Colorado Daily Press. (Craig, Colo.) 1970-Current
The Craig Empire-Courier. (Craig, Colo.) 1981-198?

Places on the National Register
Brown's Park, Old Ladore School, By Green River on SR 318
Craig, First National Bank Building, 502-506 Yampa Ave.
Craig, Marcia (pullman car), 341 E. Victory Way
Craig, State Armory, 590 Yampa Ave.
Craig, Vanatta Apartments, 660 Yampa Ave.
Dinosaur, Castle Park Archeological District, Address Restricted
Dinosaur, Chew, Rial, Ranch Complex, US 40
Dinosaur, Julien, Denis, Inscription, US 40
Dinosaur, Mantle's Cave, Dinosaur NM
Dinosaur, Upper Wade and Curtis Cabin, US 40
Greystone, Bromide Charcoal Kilns, Off Cty. Rd. 10
Lay, Lay School, 7 Eddy Ave.
Maybell, Two-Bar Ranch, W of Maybell off CO 318
Sparks, White-Indian Contact Site, Address Restricted

USGS Historic Places
Greystone, Greystone Post Office, 40.6094097, -108.6739967

Moffat County

Grand Army of the Republic Posts
None

USGS Historic Military Places
None

Military Bases
None

Post Offices

Artesia	1946 Mar 20	1966 Jan 1	
Axial	1893 Mar 6	1958 Apr 30*	
Blue Mountain	1949 Sept 1	1957 Jan 31	
Caisson	1920 Sept 3	1937 Dec 31	
Craig	1883 Jan 12		81625
Cross Mountain	1919 July 16	1943 Nov 15	
Deep Channel	19022 June 28	1926 Aug 31	
Dinosaur	1946 Mar 20		81610
Elk Springs	1924 June 9	1944 Mar 18	
Elk Springs 2	1948 July 16		
Elkhead	1927 Jan 17	1929 Jan 31	
Fortification	1883 Jan 15	1922 June 30*	
Great Divide	1917 Jan 30	1954 July 31	
Greystone	1921 June 20	1975 Dec 5	
Hamilton	1896 July 7	1917 Aug 15	
Hamilton	1910 Sept 2		81638
Jack Rabbit	1916 Dec 20	1923 May 31	
Juniper	1906 Feb 9	1919 Sept 4	
Juniper Springs	1919 Sept 4	1946 Sept 30	
Ladore	1889 June 3	1924 Mar 25	
Lay	1881 Aug 15	1976 June 30*	
Lily	1889 Sept 17	1937 May 15*	
Lodore	1924 Mar 24	1933 Nov 30	
Loyd	1929 Feb 12	1955 Feb 28	
Massadona	1917 July 10	1932 Oct 15	
Maybell	1884 Oct 14		81640
Morapos	1912 Oct 14	1931 Sept 30	
Mount Streeter	1919 Dec 26	1921 Nov 15	
Price Creek	1912 May 28	1942 June 30	
Rivas	1924 July 26	1925 Sept 30	
Routt	1930 Feb 14	1953 Mar 31	
Skull Creek	1929 Feb 8	1949 Sept 1	
Slater	1888 Dec 24		81653
Sparks	1913 Nov 26	1914 Aug 15	
Sunbeam	1912 Oct 14	1942 June 15	
Youghal	1919 July 16	1934 June 15	

Historical Assets Colorado

Topo Quads

Adobe Springs	404500N	403730N	1075230W	1080000W
Axial	402230N	401500N	1074500W	1075230W
Bakers Peak	410000N	405230N	1072230W	1073000W
Bald Mountain	404500N	403730N	1080000W	1080730W
Beaver Basin	410000N	405230N	1085230W	1090000W
Big Joe Basin	405230N	404500N	1084500W	1085230W
Bighole Butte	410000N	405230N	1075230W	1080000W
Cactus Reservoir	401500N	400730N	1083730W	1084500W
Canyon of Lodore South	403730N	403000N	1085230W	1090000W
Castor Gulch	403000N	402230N	1073000W	1073730W
Cedar Knob	403000N	402230N	1080730W	1081500W
Citadel Plateau	402230N	401500N	1080730W	1081500W
Clay Buttes	404500N	403730N	1082230W	1083000W
Coffeepot Spring	410000N	405230N	1082230W	1083000W
Craig	403730N	403000N	1073000W	1073730W
Craig NE	404500N	403730N	1073000W	1073730W
Craig NW	404500N	403730N	1073730W	1074500W
Cross Mountain Canyon	403000N	402230N	1081500W	1082230W
Devils Hole Gulch	401500N	400730N	1075230W	1080000W
Diamond Peak	410000N	405230N	1053000W	1053730W
Dinosaur	401500N	400730N	1090000W	1090730W
Divide Creek	401500N	400730N	1083000W	1083730W
East Timberlake Creek	405230N	404500N	1073730W	1074500W
Easton Gulch	402230N	401500N	1075230W	1080000W
Elk Springs	402230N	401500N	1082230W	1083000W
Fortification	405230N	404500N	1073000W	1073730W
Fortification NE	410000N	405230N	1073000W	1073730W
Freeman Reservoir	405230N	404500N	1072230W	1073000W
G Spring	405230N	404500N	1083000W	1083730W
Great Divide	405230N	404500N	1074500W	1075230W
Greystone	403730N	403000N	1083730W	1084500W
Hamilton	402230N	401500N	1073000W	1073730W
Haystack Rock	403000N	402230N	1083730W	1084500W
Hells Canyon	403000N	402230N	1085230W	1090000W
Hiawatha	410000N	405230N	1083000W	1083730W
Horse Gulch	403000N	402230N	1074500W	1075230W
Indian Valley	401500N	400730N	1080730W	1081500W
Indian Water Canyon	403000N	402230N	1083000W	1083730W
Irish Canyon	405230N	404500N	1083730W	1084500W
Iron Springs	404500N	403730N	1074500W	1075230W
Jack Springs	404500N	403730N	1084500W	1085230W

Moffat County

Name				
Juniper Hot Springs	403000N	402230N	1075230W	1080000W
Juniper Mountain	403000N	402230N	1080000W	1080730W
Lang Spring	405230N	404500N	1081500W	1082230W
Lay	403730N	403000N	1075230W	1080000W
Lay SE	403730N	403000N	1074500W	1075230W
Lazy Y Point	402230N	401500N	1084500W	1085230W
Limestone Hill	403730N	403000N	1083000W	1083730W
Lodore School	405230N	404500N	1085230W	1090000W
Lone Mountain	403730N	403000N	1082230W	1083000W
M F Mountain	402230N	401500N	1083000W	1083730W
Maybell	403730N	403000N	1080000W	1080730W
Mayberry Spring	405230N	404500N	1075230W	1080000W
McInturf Mesa	404500N	403730N	1072230W	1073000W
Mellen Hill	401500N	400730N	1085230W	1090000W
Monument Butte	402230N	401500N	1073730W	1074500W
Ninemile Gap	401500N	400730N	1074500W	1075230W
Ninemile Hill	404500N	403730N	1080730W	1081500W
Ninemile Spring	383000N	382230N	1035230W	1040000W
Peck Mesa	403730N	403000N	1081500W	1082230W
Pine Ridge	403730N	403000N	1073730W	1074500W
Plug Hat Rock	402230N	401500N	1085230W	1090000W
Pole Gulch	410000N	405230N	1073730W	1074500W
Powder Wash	410000N	405230N	1081500W	1082230W
Price Creek	402230N	401500N	1080000W	1080730W
Rangely NE	401500N	400730N	1084500W	1085230W
Reservoir Draw	410000N	405230N	1080730W	1081500W
Rough Gulch	401500N	400730N	1082230W	1083000W
Sevenmile Draw	404500N	403730N	1081500W	1082230W
Sheephead Basin	404500N	403730N	1083000W	1083730W
Sheepherder Spgs	405230N	404500N	1082230W	1083000W
Skull Creek	402230N	401500N	1083730W	1084500W
Sleepy Cat Peak	401500N	400730N	1073000W	1073730W
Smizer Gulch	401500N	400730N	1081500W	1082230W
Sparks	410000N	405230N	1084500W	1085230W
Sunbeam	403730N	403000N	1080730W	1081500W
Tanks Peak	403000N	402230N	1084500W	1085230W
The Nipple	405230N	404500N	1080730W	1081500W
The Nipple NE	410000N	405230N	1080000W	1080730W
The Nipple SE	405230N	404500N	1080000W	1080730W
Thornburgh	401500N	400730N	1073730W	1074500W
Thornburgh Gulch	410000N	405230N	1074500W	1075230W
Twelvemile Mesa	403000N	402230N	1082230W	1083000W
Vermillion Mesa	404500N	403730N	1083730W	1084500W
Wapiti Peak	402230N	401500N	1081500W	1082230W
White Rock	401500N	400730N	1080000W	1080730W
Zenobia Peak	403730N	403000N	1084500W	1085230W

Historical Assets Colorado

Suggested Reading

Babcock, Harold R. *Historic Highlights of Moffat County and Surrounding Areas.* NL: H R Babcock, 1996.

Craig-Moffat Golden Jubilee: *Fifty Years of Progress, 1908-1958.* Craig, CO: Craif-Moffat Golden Jubilee Committee, 1958.

Craig, Diamond in the Rough: Craig Diamond Jubilee, 1908-1983. Craig, CO: NP, 1983.

Davidson, Daniel K. *Images: a Pictorial History of Moffat County, Colorado.* Craig, CO: The Print Shop, 1986.

Stoddard, C A, Dan Davidson, Janet Gerber and Shannan Koucherik. *Tales of the Old West Retold: Early Stories of Northwestern Colorado.* Montrose, CO: Lifetime Chronicle Press, 2007.

Montezuma County

Introduction

Established: 1889   Population: 25,535

Formed from: La Plata

Adjacent Counties: Dolores, San Juan, La Plata

County Seat: Cortez

Other Communities: Dolores, Mancos, Lewis, Towaoc, Arriola, Pleasant View, Yellow Jacket

Website, http://montezumacounty.org/web/

Area Codes: 970

Zip Codes: 81321, 81323, 81327, 81328, 81330, 81331, 81334, 81335

Historical Assets Colorado

Montezuma County Courthouse

Montezuma County 20th Century Courthouse

Courthouses & County Government

Montezuma County
http://montezumacounty.org/web/

Montezuma County Courthouse (District Court) (22nd Judicial District), 109 W Main, Cortez, CO 81321, 970-565-1111; http://www.courts.state.co.us/Courts/County/Index.cfm?County_ID=66

Montezuma County Courthouse (County Court), 601 N Mildred Rd, Cortez, CO 81321, 970-565-7580; ; http://www.courts.state.co.us/Courts/County/Index.cfm?County_ID=66

Assessor, 140 W Main St, Cortez, CO 81321, 970-565-3428; http://www.co.montezuma.co.us/newsite/assessorhome.html

Board of County Commissioners, 109 W Main St, Cortez, CO 81321, 970-749-5514, http://montezumacounty.org/web/departments/contact-commissioner-cortez/

Clerk & Recorder, 140 W Main St, Cortez, CO 81321, 970-565-3728; http://www.co.montezuma.co.us/newsite/clerkhome.html

Coroner, 970-749-1771; http://montezumacounty.org/web/services/coroner/

Public Health, 106 W North St, Cortez, CO 81321, 970-565-3056; http://www.co.montezuma.co.us/newsite/healthhome.html

Transportation (Road & Bridge), 1680 N Dolores Rd, Cortez, CO 81321, 970-565-8666; http://montezumacounty.org/web/departments/road-bridge/

Treasurer, 140 W Main St, Ste 2, Cortez, CO 81321, 970-565-7550; http://www.co.montezuma.co.us/newsite/Treasurerhome.html

County Records

Birth 1879	Marriage 1889	Divorce 1889
Death 1892	Land 1879	Probate 1889
Court 1889		

Montezuma County

County & Municipal Records Held at the State Level

The Colorado State Archives

Physical Records
Coroner
County Court
District Court
Treasurer
WPA Historical Records
WPA Religious Institutions Survey
Cities
Mancos

Records on Film
None

Records on Master Film
County Court
District Court
School Districts
Sheriff
Cities
Cortez

The Denver Public Library
Montezuma & La Plata County Mining Companies Records, 1907
WWI Draft Registration Cards (microfilm)

School Districts

School Districts, http://www.adcogov.org/local-school-districts
Dolores School District RE-4A, 100 N 6th St, Dolores, CO 81323, 970-882-7255; https://doloresschools.org/
Mancos School District RE-6, 355 W Grand Ave, Mancos, CO 81328, 970-533-7437; https://www.mancosre6.edu/
Montezuma-Cortez School District RE-1, P.O. Box R, Cortez, CO 81321, 970-565-7522; https://www.cortez.k12.co.us/

Historic School Districts

1. Cortez
2. Beulah
3. Lakeview
4. Delores
5. Lebanon
6. Mancos
7. Blue Door
8. Arriola
9. Lewis
10. Pleasant View, Sunnyside
11. Battle Rock, McElmo
12. Aztec
13. Arbor
14. Stoner
15. Mildred
16. Bear Creek
17. Menefee
18. Dripping Springs
19. Goodman Point, Shiloh
20. Oak Hill, Thomas
21. Sylvan, Hovenweep
22. Independent, Walker
23. Rhyman
24. Granath Mesa
25. Mesa Verde
26. Four Corners
27. Towac
28. Ackman
29. McPhee
30. Old Prospect, Prospect
31. Fair View

Fraternal Organizations

Granges
Ute Mountain, No. 334, Montezuma, Cortez, 3 Apr 1917
Mesa Verde, No. 335, Montezuma, Cortez, 4 Apr 1917
Lake Vista, No. 336, Montezuma, Cortez, 5 Apr 1917
Ariola, No. 337, Montezuma, Dolores, 7 Apr 1917
Mount Lookout, No. 339, Montezuma, Mancos, 28 Apr 1917

Historical Assets Colorado

    Fairview, No. 364, Montezuma, Yellow Jacket, 23 Feb 1918
    Lewis, No. 406, Montezuma, Lewis, 18 Oct 1929
    Rainbelt, No. 464, Montezuma, Pleasant View, 7 May 1946
    Yellow Jacket, No. 475, Montezuma, Yellow Jacket, 19 May 1956

Masons

Ancient Free & Accepted Masons
- Olathe, No. 100, Montezuma, Mancos, 16 Sept 1896
- Montezuma, No. 133, Montezuma, Cortez, 21 Sept 1909
- Mancos, No. 145, Montezuma, Dolores, 15 Sept 1914

Royal Arch Masons
None

Knights Templar
None

Eastern Star
- Mesa Verde, No. 76, Montezuma, Mancos
- Cortez, No. 87, Montezuma, Cortez
- Montezuma, No. 130, Montezuma, Dolores

Odd Fellows
- McElmo, No. 21, Montezuma, Cortez
- Toltec, No. 73, Montezuma, Mancos

Rebekahs
- Chipeta, No. 101, Montezuma, Cortez

Knights of Pythias
- Aztec, No. 94, Montezuma, Mancos
- Silver Star, No. 105, Montezuma, Dolores
- Mesa Verde, No. 114, Montezuma, Cortez

Pythian Sisters
- Ramona, No. 20, Montezuma, Mancos
- Silver Plume, No. 32, Montezuma, Dolores

Benevolent Protective Order of Elks
- Cortez, No. 1789, Montezuma, Cortez

City & Town Halls

Cortez, 123 E Roger Smith Ave, Cortez, CO 81321, 970-565-3402, http://www.cityofcortez.com

Dolores, 420 Central Ave, Dolores, CO 81323, 970-882-7720, https://www.townofdolores.com

Mancos, 117 N Main St, Mancos, CO 81328, 970-533-7725, https://www.mancoscolorado.com

Archives & Manuscript Collections

None

Montezuma County

Historical & Genealogical Societies

Galloping Goose Historical Railway Society of Dolores, Historical Museum, 421 Railroad Ave, P.O. Box 443, Dolores, CO 81323, (970) 882-7082, http://www.gallopinggoose5.org

Mancos Valley Historical Society, P.O. Box 465, Mancos, CO 81328, (970) 946-2460, http://mancosvalleyhistoricalsociety.com

Montezuma County Historical Society, P.O. Box 218, Cortez, CO 81321, https://www.facebook.com/montezumamuseum/

Local Libraries

Cortez Public Library, 202 N Park St, Cortez, CO 81321-3300, (970) 565-8117, https://www.cityofcortez.com/141/Library

Dolores Library District, 1002 Railroad Ave, P.O. Box 847, Dolores, CO 81323-0847, (970) 882-4127, http://www.doloreslibrary.org

Ute Mountain Tribal Library, Education Ctr, 450 Sunset, P.O. Box CC, Towaoc, CO 81334-0048, (970) 564-5348, https://narf.org/nill/tribes/ute_mtn_ute.html

Links

CO GenWeb
http://cogenweb.com/montezuma/

Cyndi's List
https://www.cyndislist.com/us/co/counties/montezuma/

FamilySearch Wiki
https://www.familysearch.org/wiki/en/Montezuma_County,_Colorado_Genealogy

Linkpendium
http://www.linkpendium.com/montezuma-co-genealogy/

RootsWeb Wiki
https://wiki.rootsweb.com/wiki/index.php/Montezuma_County,_Colorado

Wikipedia
https://en.wikipedia.org/wiki/Montezuma_County,_Colorado

Historic Hotels

None

Museums & Historic Sites

Anasazi Heritage Center Museum, 27501 Hwy 184, Dolores, CO 81323, (970) 882-5600, https://www.blm.gov/visit/anasazi-heritage-center

Canyons of the Ancients National Monument, 27501 Hwy 184, Dolores, CO 81323, (970) 882-5600, https://www.blm.gov/learn/interpretive-centers/CANM-visitor-center-museum

Colorado Welcome Center Museum, 928 E Main St, Cortez, CO 81321, (970) 565-4048, https://www.mesaverdecountry.com/welcome-center/

Cortez Cultural Center, 25 N Market St, Cortez, CO 81321, (970) 565-1151, http://www.cortezculturalcenter.org

Historical Assets Colorado

Crow Canyon Archaeological Center, 23390 Road K, Cortez, CO 81321, (970) 565-8975, http://www.crowcanyon.org

Galloping Goose Historical Railway Society of Dolores, Historical Museum, 421 Railroad Ave, P.O. Box 443, Dolores, CO 81323, (970) 882-7082, http://www.gallopinggoose5.org

Mesa Verde National Park Museum, P.O. Box 8, Mesa Verde National Park, CO 81330, (970) 529-4465, http://www.nps.gov/meve; http://mesaverde.org

Montezuma Heritage Museum, 35 S Chestnut St, Cortez, CO 81321, (970) 570-7333, https://www.facebook.com/pg/montezumamuseum

Notah Dineh Trading Company Museum, 345 W Main St, Cortez, CO 81321, (800) 444-2024, http://www.notahdineh.com

Special Events & Scenic Locations

The Montezuma County Fair is held in July and August most years at the Montezuma County Fairgrounds, 30100 Hwy 160, Cortez, CO 81231, 970-565-1000, http://montezumacounty.org/web/services/countyfair/

Montezuma County keeps a calendar of events here, although it has not been updated recently: https://montezumacounty.org/web/events/

The local newspaper, The Journal, has a calendar of events in or around Cortez here: https://the-journal.com/calendar#/81321-cortez/all/today

Mesa Verde Country has calendar of regional events here: https://www.mesaverdecountry.com/calendar/

Calico National Recreation Trail
Canyons of the Ancients National Monument
Highline Loop National Recreation Trail
Hovenweep National Monument
Lowry Ruin National Historic Landmark
Mesa Verde National Park
Mesa Verde Wilderness
Old Spanish National Historic Trail
Petroglyph Point National Recreation Trail
San Juan National Forest
Yucca House National Monument
Mancos State Park
McPhee Reservoir
Great Parks Bicycle Route
San Juan Skyway
Trail of the Ancients
Western Express Bicycle Route

Ghost Towns & Other Sparsely Populated Places

Battista, Bear Creek, Corkscrew, Lost Dome, McPhee (under McPhee Reservoir), Morgan

Montezuma County

Newspapers
Montezuma Journal. (Cortez, Colo.) 1888-1919
The Mancos Times. (Mancos, Colo.) 1893-1905
The Silver Star. (Dolores, Colo.) 1897-1901
Echo. (Towaoc, Colo.) 19??-1988
The Dolores Star. (Dolores, Montezuma County, Colo.) 1901-Current
The Mancos Times-Tribune. (Mancos, Montezuma County, Colo.) 1905-Current
The Cortez Herald. (Cortez, Colo.) 1908-1919
The Montezuma Journal and The Cortez Herald. (Cortez, Montezuma County, Colo.) 1919-1919
Cortez Journal-Herald. (Cortez, Montezuma County, Colo.) 1919-1932
The Cortez Sentinel. (Cortez, Montezuma County, Colo.) 1928-1978
The Montezuma Valley Journal. (Cortez, Colo.) 1932-Current
Durango Herald-News. (Durango, Colo.) 1952-1960
The Durango Herald. (Durango, Colo.) 1960-Current
Monday Cortez Sentinel. (Cortez, Colo.) 1978-1985
The Cortez Sentinel. (Cortez, Colo.) 1985-Current
Ute Mountain Ute Echo. ([Towoac, Colo.]) 1989-Current
Four Corners Free Press. [Volume] (Cortez, Co) 2003-Current
The Journal : Cortez, Dolores, Mancos. [Volume] (Cortez, Co) 2015-Current

Places on the National Register
Cortez, Cannonball Ruins, Address Restricted
Cortez, Ertel Funeral Home, 42 N. Market St.
Cortez, Hovenweep National Monument, NW of Cortez
Cortez, Indian Camp Ranch Archeological District, Address Restricted
Cortez, Mesa Verde National Park, 10 mi. E of Cortez on U.S. 160
Cortez, Mitchell Springs Archeological Site, Address Restricted
Cortez, Montezuma Valley Irrigation Company Flume No. 6, Approx. 4 mi. E. of Cortez on US 160
Cortez, Montezuma Valley National Bank and Store Building, 2-8 Main St.
Cortez, Mud Springs Pueblo, Address Restricted
Cortez, Roy's Ruin, Address Restricted
Cortez, Sand Canyon Archaeological District, Address Restricted
Cortez, Wallace Ruin, Address Restricted
Cortez, Yucca House National Monument, 12 mi. S of Cortez via U.S. 666
Dolores, Anasazi Archeological District, Address Restricted
Dolores, Escalante Ruin, Address Restricted
Dolores, Lebanon School, 24925 Co. Rd. T
Dolores, Southern Hotel, 101 S. Fifth St.
Mancos, Bauer Bank Block, 107 W. Grand Ave.
Mancos, Lost Canyon Archeological District, Address Restricted
Mancos, Mancos High School, 350 Grand Ave.
Mancos, Mancos Opera House, 136 W. Grand Ave.
Mancos, Wrightsman House, 209 Bauer Ave.

Historical Assets Colorado

Mesa Verde National Park, Mesa Verde Administrative District, Area at head of Spruce Canyon off park service road
Pleasant View, Lancaster, James A., Site, Address Restricted
Pleasant View, Lowry Ruin, 30 mi. NW of Cortez via U.S. 160
Pleasant View, Painted Hand Pueblo, Address Restricted
Pleasant View, Pigge Site, Address Restricted
Yellow Jacket, Albert Porter Pueblo, Address Restricted
Yellow Jacket, Archeological Site no. 5MT4700, Address Restricted
Yellow Jacket, Bass Site, Address Restricted
Yellow Jacket, Joe Ben Wheat Site Complex, Address Restricted
Yellow Jacket, Seven Towers Pueblo, Address Restricted
Yellow Jacket, Woods Canyon Pueblo, Address Restricted
Yellow Jacket, Yellowjacket Pueblo (5-MT-5), Address Restricted

USGS Historic Places

Moccasin Mesa, Swallows Nest, 37.1572182, -108.4678652
Orphan Butte, King's Ranch, 37.5936064, -108.1200764
Orphan Butte, Snyders Ranch, 37.6124954, -108.0895197
Orphan Butte, Waechters Ranch, 37.6211066, -108.0628519
Rico, Montelores, 37.6391622, -108.0514625
Unknown, Mesa Verde National Park Post Office, 0, 0
Wallace Ranch, Bear Creek, 37.5749947, -108.2009129
Wallace Ranch, Quarry, 37.5722166, -108.2442478
Wallace Ranch, Rio Lado, 37.5936063, -108.1342437
Wetherill Mesa, Badger House Community, 37.1886065, -108.5345345
Wetherill Mesa, Echo House, 37.1677734, -108.5000886

Grand Army of the Republic Posts

Warren, No. 89, Montezuma, Cortez

USGS Historic Military Places

None

Military Bases

None

Post Offices

Ackmen	1917 Nov 5	1941 May 31	
Arloa	1903 Mar 12	1914 Apr 15	
Arriola	1894 Dec 18	1933 Aug 15*	
Bear Creek	1899 Mar 11	118 Dec 14*	
Cortez	1887 June 21		81321
Dolores	1878 Apr 5		81323
Formby	1895 May 11	1901 Feb 14	
Golconda	1894 Apr 26	1895 July 1	

Montezuma County

Gradens	1896 July 7	1903 Nov 30	
Hogg	1903 Mar 12	1906 Mar 15	
Lakevista	1914 July 27	1918 Feb 15	
Lebanon	1908 Sept 29	1939 Apr 15	
Lewis	1911 Sept 7		81327
Lone Dome	1883 Oct 25	1894 Dec 6	
Lonedome	1894 Dec 6	1907 Jan 2	
Mancos	1877 Feb 19		
Mancos Creek	1961 July 16	1962 June 16	
McElmo	1892 Mar 11	1932 Feb 29*	
McPhee	1924 Sept 17	1948 Mar 31	
Mesa Verde National Park		1924 May 19	81330
Mildred	1895 Mar 18	1903 May 30	
Millard	1907 Sept 17	1909 June 30	
Moqui	1900 June 18	1914 Apr 15	
Morgan	1887 Oct 24	1891 May 4	
Navaho Springs	1910 Dec 24	1915 Apr 1	
Paymaster	1900 Mar 20	1900 June 20	
Pleasant View	1939 June 23		81331
Point Lookout	1939 Apr 22	1951 June 30	
Quarry	1892 June 30	1912 Apr 30	
Renaraye	1915 July 10	1929 Jan 15	
Ruin Canyon	1920 Sept 3	1928 July 31	
Sago	1922 July 20	1925 Dec 15	
Spargo	1920 Nov 17	1924 Feb 29	
Stoner	1917 Apr 4	1954 Nov 30	
Towaoc	1915 Apr 1		81334
Westford	1903 Apr 18	1907 Apr 20*	
Yellow Jacket	1914 May 5		81335

Topo Quads

Arriola	373000N	372230N	1083730W	1084500W
Battle Rock	372230N	371500N	1084500W	1085230W
Boggy Draw	373730N	373000N	1082230W	1083000W
Bowdish Canyon	372230N	371500N	1085230W	1090000W
Cortez	372230N	371500N	1083000W	1083730W
Dolores East	373000N	372230N	1082230W	1083000W
Dolores West	373000N	372230N	1083000W	1083730W
Mancos	372230N	371500N	1081500W	1082230W
Mariano Wash East	371500N	370730N	1084500W	1085230W
Mariano Wash West	371500N	370730N	1085230W	1090000W
Millwood	373000N	372230N	1081500W	1082230W
Moccasin Mesa	371500N	370730N	1082230W	1083000W
Moqui Canyon	370730N	370000N	1083000W	1083730W
Mud Creek	372230N	371500N	1083730W	1084500W
Negro Canyon	373000N	372230N	1085230W	1090000W

Historical Assets Colorado

Pleasant View	373730N	373000N	1084500W	1085230W
Point Lookout	372230N	371500N	1082230W	1083000W
Rampart Hills	373000N	372230N	1080730W	1081500W
Sentinel Peak SE	370730N	370000N	1084500W	1085230W
Sentinel Peak SW	370730N	370000N	1085230W	1090000W
Stoner	373730N	373000N	1081500W	1082230W
Tanner Mesa	370730N	370000N	1083730W	1084500W
Towaoc	371500N	370730N	1083730W	1084500W
Trimble Point	373730N	373000N	1083000W	1083730W
Wallace Ranch	373730N	373000N	1080730W	1081500W
Wetherill Mesa	371500N	370730N	1083000W	1083730W
Woods Canyon	373000N	372230N	1084500W	1085230W
Yellow Jacket	373730N	373000N	1083730W	1084500W

Suggested Reading

Freeman, Ira S. *A History of Montezuma County, Colorado: Land of Promise and Fulfillment.* Boulder, CO: Johnson Pub Co, 1958.

Great Sage Plain to Timberline: Our Pioneer History. Cortez, CO: MOntezuma County Historical Socity, 2009.

Montezuma County, Colorado. NL: NP, 1926.

Wardrip, Molly K. *Montezuma's Trails of Time.* Cortez, CO: M K Wardrip, 1993.

Montrose County

Introduction
Established: 1883   Population: 41,276

Formed from: Gunnison

Adjacent Counties: Mesa, Delta, Gunnison, Ouray, San Miguel, San Juan

County Seat: Montrose

Other Communities: Naturita, Nucla, Olathe, Redvale, Bedrock, Cimarron, Coventry, Maher, Mountain View, Oak Grove, Paradox, Pinon, Uravan, Ute

Website, https://www.montrosecounty.net

Area Codes: 970

Zip Codes: 81220, 81401, 81402, 81403, 81411, 81422, 81424, 81425, 81429, 81431

Historical Assets Colorado

Montrose County Courthouse

Courthouses & County Government

Montrose County
   https://www.montrosecounty.net
Montrose County Courthouse (Justice Center) (7th Judicial District), 1200 N Grand Ave, Montrose, CO 81401, 970-252-4300; http://www.courts.state.co.us/Courts/County/Index.cfm?County_ID=18
Montrose County Courthouse (Nucla), 300 Main St, Nucla, CO 81424, 970-864-7373; http://www.courts.state.co.us/Courts/County/Index.cfm?County_ID=18
Assessor, 320 S 1st St, Montrose, CO 81401, 970-249-3753; http://www.co.montrose.co.us/index.aspx?nid=68
Board of County Commissioners, 317 S 2nd St, Montrose, CO 81401, 970-249-7755, https://www.montrosecounty.net/172/County-Commissioners
Clerk & Recorder, 320 S 1st St, Montrose, CO 81401, 970-249-3362; http://www.co.montrose.co.us/index.aspx?NID=72
Coroner, 1200 N Grand Ave, Bin F, Montrose, CO 81401, 970-249-7755; https://www.montrosecounty.net/183/Coroner
Elections, 320 S 1st St, Rm 103, Montrose, CO 81401, 970-249-3362; https://www.montrosecounty.net/73/Elections
Public Health, 1845 S Townsend, Montrose, CO 81401, 970-252-5000; http://www.co.montrose.co.us/index.aspx?nid=108
Transportation (Public Works), 63160 LaSalle Rd, Montrose, CO 81401, 970-252-7000; https://www.montrosecounty.net/151/Public-Works
Treasurer, 320 S 1st St, Rm 106, Montrose, CO 81401, 970-249-3565; http://www.co.montrose.co.us/index.aspx?nid=169

County Records

Birth 1910	Marriage 1883	Divorce 1883
Death 1907	Land 1883	Probate 1883
Court 1883		

Montrose County

County & Municipal Records Held at the State Level
The Colorado State Archives
Physical Records
Clerk & Recorder
County Court
District Court
Combined Courts
Justice Court
WPA Historical Records
WPA Religious Institutions Survey
WPA Montrose

Records on Film
County Court
District Court

Records on Master Film
Clerk & Recorder
County Court
District Court
Combined Courts
School Districts
Cities
Montrose

The Denver Public Library
History of Cimarron, Colorado, 1984
WWI Draft Registration Cards (microfilm)

School Districts
School Districts, http://www.adcogov.org/local-school-districts
Gunnison Watershed School District, No. RE-1J, 800 N Boulevard St, Gunnison, CO 81230, 970-641-7770; https://www.gunnisonschools.net/
Montrose County School District RE-1J, 930 Colorado Ave, Montrose, CO 81402, 970-249-7726; http://www.mcsd.org/

Historic School Districts
1. Montrose
2. Frost
3. Riverside
4. [1884]
5. Fairview
6. Cimarron
7. Maher
8. Highland
9. Paraox
10. Menaken
11. Pal Grpve
12. [1887]
13. Maple Grove
14. Pea Green
15. Olathe
16. Coal Creek
17. [1890]
18. Nucla
19. Sanborn Park
20. Clear Fork
21. [1898]
22. [1901]
23. [1901]
24. Stone
25. Naturita, Long Park, Uravan
26. [1920]
27. Bedrock
28. Crawford
29. Uncompahgre
30. Colona
31. Ute
32. [1920]
33. Kinikin Heights
34. Shenandoah

Fraternal Organizations
Granges
Riverside, No. 80, Montrose, Montrose, 5 Mar 1888
Uncompahgre, No. 87, Montrose, Uncompahgre, 2 Mar 1889
Spring Creek, No. 202, Montrose, Montrose, 28 Oct 1911
Riverside, No. 203, Montrose, Montrose, 22 Feb 1912
Menoken, No. 204, Montrose, Montrose, 21 Feb 1912
Montrose, No. 214, Montrose, Montrose, 17 Feb 1913
Naturita Valley, No. 218, Montrose, Redvale/Coventry, 7 Oct 1913

Historical Assets Colorado

    Olathe, No. 241, Montrose, Olathe, 20 Mar 1915
    Olathe, No. 243, Montrose, Montrose, 20 Mar 1915
    Fairview, No. 252, Montrose, Olathe, 6 May 1915
    Paradox, No. 301, Montrose, Paradox, 12 Aug 1916
    Pea Green, No. 489, Montrose, Montrose, 23 Apr 1959
    Hub City, No. 490, Montrose, Olathe, 13 Aug 1959

Masons

  Ancient Free & Accepted Masons
    Brush, No. 63, Montrose, Montrose, 16 Sept 1885
    Montrose, No. 157, Montrose, Olathe, 20 Sept 1922

  Royal Arch Masons
    Montrose, No. 25, Montrose, Montrose

  Knights Templar
    Montrose Commandery, No. 19, Montrose, Montrose, 1891 June 5

  Eastern Star
    Silver Star, No. 40, Montrose, Montrose
    Bethany, No. 148, Montrose, Nucla

Odd Fellows
    Uncompaghre, No. 65, Montrose, Montrose
    Olathe, No. 143, Montrose, Olathe

  Rebekahs
    Montrose, No. 31, Montrose, Montrose
    Olathe, No. 99, Montrose, Olathe

Knights of Pythias
    Cascade, No. 33, Montrose, Montrose

  Pythian Sisters
    Apple Blossom, No. 42, Montrose, Montrose

Benevolent Protective Order of Elks
    Montrose, No. 1053, Montrose, Montrose

City & Town Halls

Montrose, 433 S 1st St, Montrose, Co 81401, 970-420-1400, https://www.cityofmontrose.org
Nucla, 320 Main St, Nucla, CO 81424, 970-864-7351, https://www.colorado.gov/nucla
Olathe, 420 Horton Ave, Olathe, CO 81425, 970-323-5601, http://www.townofolathe.org

Archives & Manuscript Collections

None

Historical & Genealogical Societies

Fore-Kin Trails Genealogical Society, P.O. Box 802, Montrose, CO 81401-0802, (970) 249-8140, https://montrosecogenealogy.org

Montrose County

Montrose County Historical Society, Depot Museum, 21 N Rio Grand Ave, P.O. Box 1882, Montrose, CO 81401, (970) 249-2085, https://www.montrosehistory.org

Rimrocker Historical Society, P.O. Box 913, Nucla, CO 81424, (970) 865-2100, http://www.rimrocker.org

Rimrocker Historical Society of West Montrose County, Historical Museum, 411 W 2nd Ave, Naturita, CO 81424, (970) 865-2100, http://www.rimrocker.org

Local Libraries

Montrose Genealogy Center, 700 E Main St, Ste 10-3, Montrose, CO 81401, (970) 240-1755, https://montrosecogenealogy.org

Montrose Library District, 320 S 2nd Ave, Montrose, CO 81401-3909, (970) 249-9656, http://www.montroselibrary.org

Links

CO GenWeb
http://cogenweb.com/montrose/

Cyndi's List
https://www.cyndislist.com/us/co/counties/montrose/

FamilySearch Wiki
https://www.familysearch.org/wiki/en/Montrose_County,_Colorado_Genealogy

Linkpendium
http://www.linkpendium.com/montrose-co-genealogy/

RootsWeb Wiki
https://wiki.rootsweb.com/wiki/index.php/Montrose_County,_Colorado

Wikipedia
https://en.wikipedia.org/wiki/Montrose_County,_Colorado

Historic Hotels

None

Museums & Historic Sites

Montrose County Historical Society, Depot Museum, 21 N Rio Grand Ave, P.O. Box 1882, Montrose, CO 81401, (970) 249-2085, https://www.montrosehistory.org

Museum of the Mountain West, 68169 E Miami Rd, Montrose, CO 81401, (970) 240-3400, https://museumofthemountainwest.org

Rimrocker Historical Society of West Montrose County, Historical Museum, 411 W 2nd Ave, Naturita, CO 81424, (970) 865-2100, http://www.rimrocker.org

Ute Indian Museum, 17253 Chipeta Dr, P.O. Box 1736, Montrose, CO 81402, (970) 249-3098, https://www.historycolorado.org/ute-indian-museum

Special Events & Scenic Locations

The Montrose County Fair & Rodeo is helt in July most years at the Montrose County Fairgrounds, 1001 N 2nd St, Montrose, CO 81401, 970-252-4358, https://montrosecountyfairandrodeo.com

Historical Assets Colorado

Visit Montrose has a calendar of events here: https://www.visitmontrose.com/events/
The Montrose County Event Center has a calendar of their events here: https://www.montrosecountyeventcenter.com

Black Canyon of the Gunnison National Park
Black Canyon of the Gunnison Wilderness
Curecanti National Recreation Area
Dominguez-Escalante National Conservation Area
Gunnison Gorge National Conservation Area
Gunnison Gorge Wilderness
Gunnison National Forest
Manti-La Sal National Forest
Old Spanish National Historic Trail
Uncompahgre National Forest
Great Parks Bicycle Route
Unaweep-Tabeguache Scenic and Historic Byway
West Elk Loop Scenic Byway
Western Express Bicycle Route
Hanging Flume

Ghost Towns & Other Sparsely Populated Places

Bedrock, Brown, Cameville, Cedar Creek, Cerro Summit, Cimarron, Colona, Colorow, Crystal Creek, Fairview, Fort Crawford, Hydraulic, Maher, Menoken, Naturita, Ouray Junction, Paradox, Uncompahgre, Uravan

Newspapers

The Western Slope Democrat. (Montrose, Colo.) 1???-19??
The Daily Montrose Enterprise. (Montrose, Colo.) 18??-19??
The Messenger. (Montrose, Colo.) 1882-1882
Montrose Messenger. (Montrose, Colo.) 1882-1???
The Montrose Press. (Montrose, Montrose County, Colo.) 1883-1912
Montrose Enquirer. (Montrose, Colo.) 1884-1885
Montrose Register. (Montrose, Colo.) 1885-????
The Montrose Republican. (Montrose, Colo.) 1885-????
The Montrose Enterprise. (Montrose, Montrose County, Colo.) 1888-19??
The Altrurian. (Denver [Colo.]) 1894-1901
The Naturita Valley Record. (Redvale, Montrose County, Colo.) 19??-19??
San Miguel Forum. (Telluride and Nucla, Colo.) 19??-19??
The Western Empire. (Montrose, Montrose County, Colo.) 19??-1912
Equality. (Denver, Colo.) 1900-19??
The Western Slope Criterion. (Olathe, Colo.) 1905-1919
Montrose Daily Press. (Montrose, Colo.) 1908-1912
Montrose Press. (Montrose, Colo.) 1908-1908
Daily Western Empire. (Montrose, Colo.) 1910-1912
Montrose Daily Press and Daily Western Empire. (Montrose, Colo.) 1912-1914
The Montrose Press and The Western Empire. (Montrose, Colo.) 1912-1914

Montrose County

The Nucla Independent. (Nucla, Colo.) 1913-19??
Montrose Daily Press. (Montrose, Colo.) 1914-Current
The Montrose Press. (Montrose, Colo.) 1914-1923
The Olathe Criterion. (Olathe, Montrose County, Colo.) 1919-19??
The Colorado Service Star. (Montrose, Colo.) 1921-19??
The Nucla News. (Nucla, Colo.) 1941-19??
The San Miguel Basin News. (Nucla, Colo.) 1942-19??
Nucla Forum. (Nucla, Colo.) 1953-1954
The Forum. (Nucla, Colo.) 1954-1971
The San Miguel Basin Forum. (Nucla and Norwood, Colo.) 1971-Current

Places on the National Register

Cimarron, D & RG Narrow Gauge Trestle, NE of Cimarron
Cimarron, Denver & Rio Grande Railroad Box Outfit Car No. 04414, 82800Q 83rd Rd., Cimarron Visitor Center, Curecanti National Recreation Center (CURE)
Cimarron, Denver & Rio Grande Western Railroad Boxcar No. 3132, Approx. 1 mi. N. by NE. of US 50 at Cimarron, near Marrow Point Dam Rd., Curecanti National Recreation Center
Cimarron, Denver & Rio Grande Western Railroad Caboose No. 0577, Approximately 1 mi. N. by NE of US 50 at cimarron, adjacent to Morrow Point Dam Rd., Curecanti National Recreation Ctr.
Cimarron, Denver & Rio Grande Western Railroad Locomotive No. 278 and Tender, Approximately 1 mi. N. by NE. of US 50 at Cimarron, near Marrow Point Dam Rd., Curecanti National Recreation Center
Cimarron, Denver & Rio Grande Western Railroad Stock Car No. 5620, 82800Q 83rd Rd., Cimarron Visitor Center, Curecanti National Recreation Area
Cimarron, Denver & Rio Grande Western Railroad Stock Car No. 5679D, 82800Q 83rd Rd., Cimarron Visitor Center, Curecanti National Recreation Area
Cimarron, Rio Grande Southern Railroad Derrick Car, 82800Q 83rd Rd, Cimarron Visitor Center, Curecanti National Recreation Area
Crawford, North Rim Road, Black Canyon of the Gunnison National Park, Black Canyon of the Gunnison National Park
Grand Mesa, Silesca Ranger Station, Grand Mesa, Uncompahgre and Gunnison National Forest
Montrose, Benevolent and Protective Order of Elks Lodge, 107 S. Cascade Ave.
Montrose, Denver and Rio Grande Depot, 20 N. Rio Grande Ave.
Montrose, Gunnison Tunnel, E of Montrose
Montrose, Lathrop, J. V., House, 718 Main St.
Montrose, Methodist Episcopal Church of Montrose, 19 S. Park Ave.
Montrose, Montrose City Hall, 433 S. 1st St.
Montrose, Montrose County Courthouse, 320 S. 1st St.
Montrose, Montrose Masonic Temple, Lodge No. 63, 509-513 E. Main St.
Montrose, Shavano Valley Rock Art Site, Address Restricted
Montrose, Shavano Valley Rock Art Site (Boundary Increase), Address Restricted
Montrose, Sherman and Ross Block Building, 232-236 Main St.
Montrose, Townsend, Thomas B., House, 222 S. 5th St.

Historical Assets Colorado

Montrose, US Bureau of Reclamation Project Office Building, 601 N. Park Ave.
Montrose, US Post Office—Montrose Main, 321 S. First St.
Montrose, Ute Memorial Site, 2 mi. S of Montrose on U.S. 550
Uravan, Hanging Flume, 5.7 mi. NW of Uravan on CO 141

USGS Historic Places
Cerro Summit, Portal, 38.483896, -107.743564
Cottonwood Basin, Little Monitor Reservoir, 38.528048, -108.3229412
Davis Mesa, Corral Number 1, 38.3049898, -108.8556573
Delta, Pea Green School, 38.6499851, -108.0956263
Hoovers Corner, Fairview School, 38.6213742, -108.0622917
Montrose East, Woods Stolport, 38.3885985, -107.823672
Montrose West, Happy Canyon Aero Ranch Airport, 38.4163761, -107.9011747
Roc Creek, Uranium, 38.4310996, -108.9048263

Grand Army of the Republic Posts
Jeff C Davis/Montrose, No. 38, Montrose, Montrose, 1885

USGS Historic Military Places
None

Military Bases
None

Post Offices

Barnes	1901 Nov 15	1903 Apr 15	
Bedrock	1883 Nov 8		81411
Brown	1883 Apr 2	1896 June 4*	
Cameville	1882 Nov 7	1890 Aug 20	
Cashin	1898 Sept 14	1905 Apr 29*	
Cedar Creek	1904 Oct 19	1924 Jan 15*	
Cimarron	1883 Aug 28		81220
Coventry	1894 Dec 26	1917 Dec 15	
Eva	1889 June 14	1889 Nov 20	
Horsefly	1886 May 1	1915 Dec 31*	
Hydraulic	1888 July 25	1905 May 31*	
Jojunior	1914 Dec 16		
Lujane	1905 Sept 1	1910 July 15	
Maher	1884 Apr 7	2003 Aug 30*	
Menoken	1891 Oct 1	1892 June 2	
Micheols	1919 Dec 27		
Montrose	1882 Feb 14		81401
Naturita	1882 Sept 15		81422
Nucla	1904 Dec 12		81424
Olathe	1896 June 4		81425

Montrose County

Paradox	1882 Jan 9		81429	
Paxton	1905 Nov 3	1907 Apr 15		
Pinon	1896 Feb 21	1905 June 15		
Redvale	1909 Dec 1		81431	
River Portal	1906 Jan 9	1910 May 14		
Rudolph	1886 Jan 27	1886 June 23		
Sams	1903 Apr 18	1903 May 5		
Sapinero	1882 Nov 23	1988 Nov 24		
Shenandoah	1892 Apr 29	1896 July 17		
Sinbad	1914 Dec 19	1933 Jan 14		
Uncompaghre	1880 Oct 14	1906 Nov 30		
Uranium	1900 Aug 29	1922 Feb 15		
Uravan	1936 Aug 27	1988 July 15		
Ute	1912 May 24	1951 Mar 31		

Topo Quads

Anderson Mesa	381500N	380730N	1085230W	1090000W
Antone Spring	382230N	381500N	1080730W	1081500W
Big Bucktail Creek	382230N	381500N	1082230W	1083000W
Buckeye Reservoir	383000N	382230N	1090000W	1090730W
Bull Canyon	381500N	380730N	1084500W	1085230W
Camel Back	383730N	383000N	1080730W	1081500W
Cerro Summit	383000N	382230N	1073730W	1074500W
Cimarron	383000N	382230N	1073000W	1073730W
Colona	382230N	381500N	1074500W	1075230W
Cottonwood Basin	383730N	383000N	1081500W	1082230W
Davis Mesa	382230N	381500N	1084500W	1085230W
Davis Point	383000N	382230N	1080730W	1081500W
Dry Creek Basin	383000N	382230N	1080000W	1080730W
Government Springs	382230N	381500N	1075230W	1080000W
Grizzly Ridge	383730N	383000N	1073730W	1074500W
Hoovers Corner	383730N	383000N	1080000W	1080730W
Horsefly Peak	381500N	380730N	1075230W	1080000W
Hotchkiss Reservoir	381500N	380730N	1080000W	1080730W
Montrose East	383000N	382230N	1074500W	1075230W
Montrose West	383000N	382230N	1075230W	1080000W
Moore Mesa	383000N	382230N	1081500W	1082230W
Naturita	381500N	380730N	1083000W	1083730W
Naturita NW	381500N	380730N	1083730W	1084500W
Norwood	381500N	380730N	1081500W	1082230W
Nucla	382230N	381500N	1083000W	1083730W
Olathe	383730N	383000N	1075230W	1080000W
Paradox	382230N	381500N	1085230W	1090000W
Pryor	373730N	373000N	1043730W	1044500W
Pryor Creek	382230N	381500N	1080000W	1080730W
Red Canyon	383000N	382230N	1084500W	1085230W

Historical Assets Colorado

Red Rock Canyon	383730N	383000N	1074500W	1075230W
Redvale	381500N	380730N	1082230W	1083000W
Roc Creek	383000N	382230N	1085230W	1090000W
Sanborn Park	381500N	380730N	1080730W	1081500W
Uravan	382230N	381500N	1083730W	1084500W
Ute	382230N	381500N	1081500W	1082230W

Suggested Reading

Brown, Evelyn Joan. *Early History of Montrose County, Colorado and its Settlement Years, 1880-1910*. Thesis Western State College of Colorado, 1987.

Hamrick, John S, Diane E Kocis and Sue E Shepard. *Uravan, Colorado: One Hundred Years of History*. Grand Junction, CO: Umetco Minerals Corp, 2002.

Hardcastle, John A. *Halfway Between Nobody Knows Where and Somebody's Starting Point: a History of the West End of Montrose County, Colorado*. Thesis, Utah State University, 1998.

Montrose County Historical Society & Museum. *Montrose*. Charleston, SC: Arcadia Publishing, 2017.

Templeton, Marie. *Naturita, Colorado: Where the Past Meets the Future*. Nucla, CO: Rimrocker Historical Society, 2002.

Morgan County

Introduction

Established: 1889   Population: 25,159

Formed from: Weld

Adjacent Counties: Logan, Washington, Adams, Weld

County Seat: Fort Morgan

Other Communities: Brush, Hillrose, Log Lane Village, Wiggins, Blue Sky, Jackson Lake, Morgan Heights, Orchard, Saddle Ridge, Snyder, Trail Side, Weldona, Goodrich, Hoyt

Website, https://www.colorado.gov/morgancounty

Area Codes: 303, 970

Zip Codes: 80649, 80653, 80654, 80701, 80705, 80723, 80733, 80750

Historical Assets Colorado

Morgan County Courthouse

Courthouses & County Government

Morgan County
https://www.colorado.gov/morgancounty

Morgan County Courthouse (13th Judicial District), 400 Warner St, Fort Morgan, CO 80701, 970-542-3435; http://www.courts.state.co.us/Courts/County/Index.cfm?County_ID=40

Assessor, 231 Ensign St, Fort Morgan, CO 80701, 970-542-3512; http://www.co.morgan.co.us/assessor/web/

Board of County Commissioners, 218 W Kiowa Ave, Fort Morgan, CO 80701, 970-542-3500, https://www.colorado.gov/pacific/morgancounty/commissioners-3

Clerk & Recorder, 231 Ensign St, Fort Morgan, CO 80701, 970-542-3521; http://www.co.morgan.co.us/CountyClerk.html

Coroner, 512 Edmunds, Brush, CO 80723, 970-842-4955; https://www.colorado.gov/pacific/morgancounty/coroner-6

Elections, 231 Ensign St, Fort Morgan, CO 80701, 970-542-3521; https://www.colorado.gov/pacific/morgancounty/elections-department

Public Health, 700 Columbine St, Sterling, CO 80751, 970-522-3741; http://www.nchd.org/

Transportation (Road & Bridge), 17303 CR S, Fort Morgan, CO 80701, 970-542-3560; https://www.colorado.gov/pacific/morgancounty/road-and-bridge-3

Treasurer, 231 Ensign St, Fort Morgan, CO 80701, 970-542-3518; http://mctre.org/

County Records

Birth 1906	Marriage 1898	Divorce 1889
Death 1900	Land 1898	Probate 1889
Court 1889		

Morgan County

County & Municipal Records Held at the State Level

The Colorado State Archives

Physical Records
Clerk & Recorder
County Court
District Court
Probate Court
Treasurer
WPA Historical Records
WPA Religious Institutions Survey
WPA Brush, Fort Morgan
Cities
  Brush
  Fort Morgan

Records on Film
Clerk & Recorder
Cities
  Brush

Records on Master Film
Clerk & Recorder
County Court
District Court
School Districts
Sheriff
Treasurer
Cities
  Brush
  Fort Morgan

The Denver Public Library

WPA Historical Records Survey
WWI Draft Registration Cards (microfilm)

School Districts

School Districts, http://www.adcogov.org/local-school-districts
Brush School District RE-2J, 527 Induistrial Park Rd, Brush, CO 80723, 970-842-5176; https://www.brushschools.org/
Buffalo School District RE-4J, 315 Lee St, Merino, CO 80741, 970-522-7424; http://merino.k12.co.us/
Fort Morgan School District RE-3, 715 W Platte Ave, Fort Morgan, CO 80701, 970-867-5633; https://www.morgan.k12.co.us/
Weldon Valley School District RE-20J, 911 N Ave, Weldona, CO 80653, 970-645-2411; http://weldonvalley.org/
Wiggins School District RE-50J, 320 Chapman St, Wiggins, CO 80654, 970-483-7762; http://wiggins50.k12.co.us/

Historic School Districts

1. Snyder
2. Brush
3. Fort Morgan
4. Weldona
5. Hoyt, Hillrose, Emerson
6. South of Gary, Colwell, Fairview
7. Gary, South Gary, Northeast Gary, Southeast Gary
8. Goodrich
9. Hoyt, Morey, Wildcat, Missouri Valley, Hunter's Hill, Wandel
10. Glencoe, Paul, Union, Hellrose
11. Orchard
12. North of Wiggins
13. OK-Adena, Centerville, Pleasant Ridge, Bijou View, Valley View
14. Pleasant Prairie
15. Sunnyside
16. Riverside, North Star, Gilliland, Cross
17. Plainsview
18. Union, Sandburg, Brammer
19. Antelope Springs, Valley View, Welcome Hollow
20. Weldon Valley

42. Hoyt, Old Trail, Long Meadow, Rock Creek, Antelope Valley

Jt71. Orchard
Jt124. Wiggins

Historical Assets Colorado

Fraternal Organizations
Granges
Homestead, No. 215, Morgan, Roggen, 21 June 1913
Orchard, No. 285, Morgan, Orchard, 10 May 1916
Goodrich, No. 290, Morgan, Weldona, 27 May 1916
Rock Creek, No. 300, Morgan, Wiggins, 2 Sept 1916
Wiggins, No. 467, Morgan, Wiggins, 7 Mar 1947
Beaver Valley, No. 472, Morgan, Brush, 13 Apr 1950

Masons
Ancient Free & Accepted Masons
Helena City, No. 67, Morgan, Fort Morgan, 21 Sept 1887
Oasis, No. 123, Morgan, Brush, 18 Sept 1906

Royal Arch Masons
Fort Morgan, No. 31, Morgan, Fort Morgan

Knights Templar
Fort Morgan Commandery, No. 28, Morgan, Fort Morgan, 1903 June 30

Eastern Star
Fort Morgan, No. 54, Morgan, Fort Morgan
Brush, No. 93, Morgan, Brush

Odd Fellows
Fort Morgan, No. 72, Morgan, Fort Morgan
Platte Valley, No. 92, Morgan, Brush
Orchard, No. 166, Morgan, Orchard
Weldona, No. 181, Morgan, Weldona

Rebekahs
Riverside, No. 6, Morgan, Orchard
Platte Valley, No. 61, Morgan, Fort Morgan
Golden Links, No. 69, Morgan, Snyder
Brush, No. 118, Morgan, Brush

Knights of Pythias
Silver, No. 60, Morgan, Fort Morgan
Brush, No. 69, Morgan, Brush

Pythian Sisters
Friendship, No. 46, Morgan, Brush

Benevolent Protective Order of Elks
Fort Morgan, No. 1143, Morgan, Fort Morgan

City & Town Halls
Fort Morgan, 110 Main St, Fort Morgan, CO 80701, 970-542-3960, https://www.cityoffortmorgan.com
Brush, 600 Edison St, Brush, CO 80723, 970-842-5001, http://www.brushcolo.com
Hillrose, 315B Co Rd W 5/10, Hillrose, CO 80733, 970-847-3761, http://www.hillrosecolorado.org

Morgan County

Log Lane Village, 109 Maine St, Log Lane Village, CO 80705, 970-867-8027
Wiggins, 304 Central Ave, Wiggins, CO 80654, 970-483-6161, http://www.wigginsco.com

Archives & Manuscript Collections
None

Historical & Genealogical Societies
Fort Morgan Museum and Heritage Foundation, Bledorn Research Ctr & Museum, 414 Main St, P.O. Box 184, Fort Morgan, CO 80701, (970) 542-4010, https://www.cityoffortmorgan.com/238/Museum

Local Libraries
Fort Morgan Public Library, 414 Main St, Fort Morgan, CO 80701-2209, (970) 867-9456, https://cityoffortmorgan.com/99/Library
East Morgan County Library District, 500 Clayton St, Brush, CO 80723-2016, (970) 842-4596, https://emcld.org

Links
CO GenWeb
http://cogenweb.com/morgan/
Cyndi's List
https://www.cyndislist.com/us/co/counties/morgan/
FamilySearch Wiki
https://www.familysearch.org/wiki/en/Morgan_County,_Colorado_Genealogy
Linkpendium
http://www.linkpendium.com/morgan-co-genealogy/
RootsWeb Wiki
https://wiki.rootsweb.com/wiki/index.php/Morgan_County,_Colorado
Wikipedia
https://en.wikipedia.org/wiki/Morgan_County,_Colorado

Historic Hotels
None

Museums & Historic Sites
Brush Area Museum and Cultural Center, 314 S Clayton, P.O. Box 341, Brush, CO 80723, (970) 842-9879
Fort Morgan Museum and Heritage Foundation, Bledorn Research Ctr & Museum, 414 Main St, P.O. Box 184, Fort Morgan, CO 80701, (970) 542-4010, https://www.cityoffortmorgan.com/238/Museum
Oasis on the Plains Museum, 18881 Morgan Cty Rd 1, Fort Morgan, CO 80701, (970) 867-3191

Historical Assets Colorado

Special Events & Scenic Locations

The Morgan County Fair is held in July and August most years at the Morgan County Fairgrounds, 750 Ellsworth St, Brush, CO 80723.

Morgan County Tourism has a calendar of events here: https://www.morgancountytourism.com/events/

The City of Fort Morgan has a calendar of events here: https://www.cityoffortmorgan.com/69/Annual-Events

Jackson Lake State Park
American Discovery Trail
Pawnee Pioneer Trails
South Platte Trail

Ghost Towns & Other Sparsely Populated Places

Deuel, Goodrich, Saddle Ridge, Snyder, Trail Side, Weldon

Newspapers

Fort Morgan Herald. (Fort Morgan, Colo.) 1???-1950
The Fort Morgan Times. (Fort Morgan, Weld County, Colo.) 1884-1926
The Lariat. (Brush, Colo.) 1884-1885
The Brush Lariat. (Brush, Weld Co., Colo.) 1884-1884
Morgan County Herald. (Fort Morgan, Colo.) 1888-19??
Brush Mirror. (Brush, Morgan County, Colo.) 189?-19??
The Brush Tribune. (Brush, Morgan County, Colo.) 1899-1925
Brush Tribune. (Brush, Colo.) 19??-1943
The Brush News. (Brush, Colo.) 19??-1943
The Brush News-Tribune. (Brush, Colo.) 19??-1982
The Wiggins Courier. (Wiggins, Morgan County, Colo.) 19??-Current
Morgan County Republican. (Brush, Colo.) 1901-19??
The Weldon Valley News. (Weldona, Colo.) 1907-19??
The Evening Times. (Fort Morgan, Colo.) 1908-1928
The Hillrose Enterprise. (Hillrose, Colo.) 1910-????
The Twice-a-Week Brush Tribune. (Brush, Colo.) 1925-19??
The Fort Morgan Times and The Evening Times. (Fort Morgan, Morgan County, Colo.) 1927-1931
The Fort Morgan Times. (Fort Morgan, Morgan County, Colo.) 1931-Current
Morgan County Herald. (Fort Morgan, Colo.) 1950-19??
Brush Country. (Brush, Colo.) 1979-Current
Brush-Morgan County News-Tribune. (Brush, Colo.) 1982-Current

Places on the National Register

Brush, All Saints Church of Eben Ezer, 120 Hospital Rd.
Brush, Central Platoon School, 411 Clayton St.
Brush, German Evangelical Immanuel Congregational Church, 209 Everett St.
Brush, Knearl School, 314 S. Clayton St.

Morgan County

Brush, Rankin Presbyterian Church, 420 Clayton St.
Fort Morgan, Farmers State Bank Building, 300 Main St.
Fort Morgan, Fort Morgan City Hall, 110 Main St.
Fort Morgan, Fort Morgan Power Plant Building, N. Main St. E side, N of jct. with US 6
Fort Morgan, Fort Morgan State Armory, 528 State St.
Fort Morgan, Lincoln School, 914 State St.
Fort Morgan, Morgan County Courthouse and Jail, 225 Ensign and 218 West Kiowa
Fort Morgan, Rainbow Arch Bridge, CO 52
Fort Morgan, Sherman Street Historic Residential District, 400 and 500 blks. of Sherman St.
Fort Morgan, US Post Office—Fort Morgan Main, 300 State St.
Snyder, Antelope Springs Methodist Episcopal Church, Address Restricted
Wiggins, Trail School, Old, 421 High St.

USGS Historic Places
Miller Ranch, Brush Golf Course, 40.2388686, -103.5955026

Grand Army of the Republic Posts
R A Cameron, No. 95, Morgan, Fort Morgan, 1882

USGS Historic Military Places
None

Military Bases
None

Post Offices

Adena	1910 Nov 8	1940 Sept 15	
Antelope Springs	1911 Mar 27	1917 Aug 15	
Bijou View	1921 June 10	1925 Nov 16	
Bijouview	1914 Apr 3	1921 June 10	
Brush	1882 Sept 19		80723
Corona	1882 Nov 10	1896 Dec 2	
Deuel	1883 Feb 15	1907 July 18	
Dodd	1904 Apr 7	1907 Dec 31	
Dublin Bay	1916 July 18		
Fort Morgan 2	1884 May 28		80701
Gary	1899 Feb 7	1954 May 31	
Goodrich	1908 Dec 14	1974 Aug 30	
Hillrose	1900 Nov 26		80733
Hoyt	1906 June 9		80641
Orchard	1882 Mar 6		80649
Pawnee	1903 Oct 26	1944 Jan 31	
Snyder	1882 June 16		80750

Historical Assets Colorado

Vallery	1907 Dec 21	1919 Aug 15*	
Weldona	1907 June 18		
Wiggins	1896 Dec 28		80654

Topo Quads

Adena	400730N	400000N	1035230W	1040000W
Antelope Springs	403000N	402230N	1033000W	1033730W
Brush East	402230N	401500N	1033000W	1033730W
Brush West	402230N	401500N	1033730W	1034500W
Dead Horse Springs	403000N	402230N	1033730W	1034500W
Fort Morgan	402230N	401500N	1034500W	1035230W
Gary	400730N	400000N	1033000W	1033730W
Hoyt	400730N	400000N	1040000W	1040730W
Huey Ranch	400730N	400000N	1033730W	1034500W
Judson Hills	403000N	402230N	1035230W	1040000W
Lamb	401500N	400730N	1034500W	1035230W
Merino SW	402230N	401500N	1032230W	1033000W
Miller Ranch	401500N	400730N	1033000W	1033730W
Orchard	402230N	401500N	1040000W	1040730W
Peace Valley School	403000N	402230N	1034500W	1035230W
Pinneo	401500N	400730N	1032230W	1033000W
Rago	400730N	400000N	1032230W	1033000W
Round Top	401500N	400730N	1033730W	1034500W
Sunken Lake	403000N	402230N	1040000W	1040730W
Vallery	401500N	400730N	1035230W	1040000W
Vallery SE	400730N	400000N	1034500W	1035230W
Weldona	402230N	401500N	1035230W	1040000W
Wiggins	401500N	400730N	1040000W	1040730W

Suggested Reading

Baer, Robert A and Anna C Baer. *History of Morgan County, Wiggins, Hoyt and Surrounding Areas.* NL: NP, 1966.

Gilliland, Shirley L. *World War II and the People and Events of Morgan County, Colorado.* Dallas: Curtis media, 1995.

History of East Morgan County, Colorado: a Project of the Friends of East Morgan County Library. Dallas: Curtis Media Corp, 1987.

Inventory of the County Archives of Colorado, No. 44, Morgan County (Fort Morgan). Denver: Historical Records Survey, 1939.

Mack, Brian and Linda Midcap. *Morgan County.* Charleston, SC: Arcadia Publishing, 2016.

Otero County

Introduction

Established: 1889　　　　　　　　　　Population: 18,831

Formed from: Bent

Adjacent Counties: Crowley, Kiowa, Bent, Las Animas, Pueblo

County Seat: La Junta

Other Communities: Rocky Ford, Cheraw, Fowler, Manzanola, Swink, La Junta Gardens, North La Junta

Website, https://www.oterogov.com

Area Codes: 719

Zip Codes: 81030, 81039, 81050, 81058, 81067, 81077

Historical Assets Colorado

Otero County Courthouse

Otero County 19th Century Courthouse

Courthouses & County Government

Otero County
https://www.oterogov.com

Otero County Courthouse (16th Judicial District), 13 W 3rd St, La Junta, CO 81050, 719-384-4951; http://www.courts.state.co.us/Courts/County/Index.cfm?County_ID=54

Assessor, P.O. Box 511, La Junta, CO 81050, 719-383-3010; http://www.qpublic.net/co/otero/

Board of County Commissioners, 13 W 3rd, La Junta, CO 81050, 719-383-3000; https://www.oterogov.com/elected-officials/commissioners

Clerk & Recorder, 13 W 3rd St, La Junta, CO 81050, 719-383-3020; http://www.oterogov.com/index.php?option=com_content&view=section&id=6&layout=blog&Itemid=140

Coroner, 323 Santa Fe, La Junta, CO 81050; https://www.oterogov.com/elected-officials/coroner

Elections, 719-383-3024; https://www.oterogov.com/elected-officials/clerk-and-recorder/elections

Public Health, 13 W 3rd St, La Junta, CO 81050, 719-383-3040; http://www.oterogov.com

Public Health, 811 S 13th St, Rocky Ford, CO 81067, 719-254-5300; http://www.oterogov.com

Public Health, 603 Main St, Ordway, CO 81063, 719-267-5245; http://www.oterogov.com

Transportation (Road & Bridge), 814 W 3rd, La Junta, CO 81050, 719-383-3091; https://www.oterogov.com/departments/road-and-bridge

Treasurer, 603 Main St, Rm 213, Ordway, CO 81063, 719-383-3030; http://www.oterogov.com

County Records

Birth 1900	Marriage 1889	Divorce 1889
Death 1900	Land 1889	Probate 1889
Court 1889		

Otero County

County & Municipal Records Held at the State Level

The Colorado State Archives

Physical Records
Clerk & Recorder
County Commissioners
County Court
District Court
Treasurer
WPA Historical Records
WPA Religious Institutions Survey
WPA La Junta, Rocky Ford
Cities
La Junta
Rocky Ford

Records on Film
Clerk & Recorder
County Commissioners
District Court
Cities
La Junta

Records on Master Film
Assessor
Clerk & Recorder
County Commissioners
County Court
District Court
School Districts
Cities
La Junta

The Denver Public Library
History of Swink, 1943
La Junta Community Records, 1965-1966
Rocky Ford Canal, Reservoir, Land, Loan & Trust Company Records, 1886-1908
WWI Draft Registration Cards (microfilm)

School Districts

School Districts, http://www.adcogov.org/local-school-districts
Cheraw School District 31, 110 Lakeview Ave, Cheraw, CO 81030, 719-853-6655; https://www.cheraw.k12.co.us/
East Otero School District R-1, 1014 E 6th St, La Junta, CO 81050, 719-384-6900; https://www.lajuntaschools.org/
Fowler School District 4J, 600 W Eugene, Fowler, CO 81039, 719-263-4224; http://www.fowler.k12.co.us/
Manzanola School District 3J, 200 S Canal St, Manzanola, CO 81058, 719-462-5528; http://www.manzanola.k12.co.us
Rocky Ford School District R-2, 601 S 8th St, Rocky Ford, CO 81067, 719-254-7423; http://www.rockyfordk12.org/
Swink School District 33, 610 Columbia Ave, Swink, CO 81077, 719-384-8103; http://www.swinkk12.net/

Historic School Districts

1. Timpas
2. Fort Bent
3. Manzanola
4. Rocky Ford
5. Cheraw
6. Elder
7. [1891]
8. La Junta
9. Newdale
10. Plaza
11. La Junta
12. [1892]
13. Swink
14. Muddy Vally, Salt Arroyo
15. Fairmount
16. [1892]
17. [1892]
18. Vroman
19. Patterson Valley
20. [1895]
21. [1897]
22. Star Valley, Mindeman
23. Fairview, Benton Valley, Packer's Gap
24. [1899]
25. [1900]

Historical Assets Colorado

26. Fowler
27. [1903]
28. Bloom
29. Grand Valley
30. Higbee
31. Cheraw
32. Timpas
33. Swink

Fraternal Organizations
Granges
Fairmount, No. 92, Otero, La Junta, 15 Jan 1890
Holbrook Valley, No. 142, Otero, La Junta, 14 Mar 1900
Grand Valley, No. 144, Otero, La Junta, 19 Feb 1901
Wide Awake, No. 268, Otero, La Junta, 10 Mar 1916
Live Wire, No. 287, Otero, La Junta, 15 May 1916
Rocky Ford, No. 314, Otero, Rocky Ford, 29 Dec 1916
Holbrook, No. 355, Otero, La Junta, 15 Sept 1917
Holbrook, No. 416, Otero, La Junta, 19 July 1935

Masons
Ancient Free & Accepted Masons
Ouray, No. 75, Otero, Rocky Ford, 18 Sept 1889
Manzanola, No. 115, Otero, Fowler, 16 Sept 1902
Saint John's, No. 124, Otero, Manzanola, 17 Sept 1907

Royal Arch Masons
La Junta, No. 20, Otero, La Junta
Rocky Ford, No. 36, Otero, Rocky Ford

Knights Templar
Palestine Commandery, No. 22, Otero, La Junta, 1891 Dec 24

Eastern Star
Chivington, No. 32, Otero, La Junta
Acacia, No. 38, Otero, Rocky Ford
Clear Water, No. 64, Otero, Fowler
Manzanola, No. 75, Otero, Manzanola

Prince Hall Masons
Morning Star Lodge, No. 11, Otero, La Junta

Odd Fellows
Manzanola, No. 66, Otero, Manzanola
La Junta, No. 74, Otero, La Junta
Rocky Ford, No. 87, Otero, Rocky Ford
Oxford, No. 129, Otero, Fowler

Rebekahs
Violet, No. 3, Otero, Rocky Ford
Lorena, No. 33, Otero, La Junta
Hyacinth, No. 80, Otero, Fowler

Knights of Pythias
La Junta, No. 28, Otero, La Junta
Valley, No. 98, Otero, Rocky Ford

Otero County

Orchard, No. 107, Otero, Manzanola
Otero, No. 121, Otero, Fowler

Pythian Sisters
La Junta, No. 28, Otero, La Junta
Otero, No. 67, Otero, Rocky Ford
Apple Blossom, No. 71, Otero, Manzanola

Benevolent Protective Order of Elks
La Junta, No. 701, Otero, La Junta
Rocky Ford, No. 1147, Otero, Rocky Ford

City & Town Halls

La Junta, 601 Colorado Ave, La Junta, CO 81050, 719-384-5991, https://lajunta-colorado.org

Rocky Ford, 203 S Main St, Rocky Ford, CO 81067, 719-254-7414, http://rockyfordco.com

Cheraw, 220 Railroad Ave, Cheraw, CO 81030, 719-853-6013

Fowler, 317 S Main St, Fowler, CO 81039, 719-263-4461, https://www.fowlercolorado.com

Manzanola, 301 N Park St, Manzanola, CO 81058, 719-462-5544

Swink, 301 Columbia Ave, Swink, CO 81077, 719-384-7155, http://townofswinkco.ourlocalview.com//HomeTown/

Archives & Manuscript Collections

None

Historical & Genealogical Societies

Fowler Historical Society, Historical Museum, 114 N Main St, Fowler, CO 81039, (719) 263-4046, https://www.fowlercolorado.com/historicalsociety.html

Local Libraries

Woodruff Memorial Library, 522 Colorado Ave, P.O. Box 479, La Junta, CO 81050-0479, (719) 384-4612, http://lajunta.colibraries.org

Links

CO GenWeb
http://cogenweb.com/otero/

Cyndi's List
https://www.cyndislist.com/us/co/counties/otero/

FamilySearch Wiki
https://www.familysearch.org/wiki/en/Otero_County,_Colorado_Genealogy

Linkpendium
http://www.linkpendium.com/otero-co-genealogy/

RootsWeb Wiki
https://wiki.rootsweb.com/wiki/index.php/Otero_County,_Colorado

Historical Assets Colorado

Wikipedia
https://en.wikipedia.org/wiki/Otero_County,_Colorado

Historic Hotels
None

Museums & Historic Sites
Bent's Old Fort National Historic Site Museum, 35110 Hwy 194 E, La Junta, CO 81050, (719) 383-5010, http://www.nps.gov/beol/
Fowler Historical Society, Historical Museum, 114 N Main St, Fowler, CO 81039, (719) 263-4046, https://www.fowlercolorado.com/historicalsociety.html
Koshare Indian Museum & Trading Post, 115 W 18th St, P.O. Box 580, La Junta, CO 81050-0580, (719) 384-4411, http://koshares.com
Otero Museum, 706 W 3rd St, P.O. Box 223, La Junta, CO 81050, (719) 384-7500, https://www.oteromuseum.org
Rocky Ford Historical Museum, 1005 Sycamore Ave, P.O. Box 835, Rocky Ford, CO 81067, (719) 254-6737, http://rockyfordco.com/museum-2/

Special Events & Scenic Locations
The Arkansas Valley Fair is held in August most years at the Arkansas Valley Fairgrounds, 800 N 9th St, Rocky Ford, CO 81067, 719-254-7723, https://www.arkvalleyfair.com
Included in the Arkansas Valley Fair is the fabulous Watermelon Days!

Bent's Old Fort National Historic Site
Comanche National Grassland
Santa Fe National Historic Trail
American Discovery Trail
Santa Fe Trail National Scenic Byway

Ghost Towns & Other Sparsely Populated Places
Angora, Benton, Bent's Old Fort, Bent's Stockade, Catlin, Higbee, Iron Springs, La Junta Gardens, Lolita, Numa, Olney, Sybl, Timpas

Newspapers
The Rocky Ford Gazette successor to The Times and The Republican. (Rocky Ford, Otero County, Colo.) 1???-1904
The Rocky Ford Daily Gazette Topic. (Rocky Ford, Otero County, Colo.) 1???-19??
La Junta Tribune. (La Junta, Bent County, Colo.) 1881-1939
Rocky Ford Enterprise. (Rocky Ford, Colo.) 1887-1950
The Otero County Eagle. (Lajunta, Colo.) 1889-1890
The Otero County Republican. (Lajunta, Colo.) 1890-????
The Daily Advertiser-Forum. (La Junta, Colo.) 1893-18??
Rocky Ford Republican. (Rocky Ford, Colo.) 1896-1898
The Ordway News. (Ordway, Otero County, Colo.) 1896-1???

Otero County

Daily Democrat. (La Junta, Colo.) 1897-1938
The Fowler Tribune. (Fowler, Colo.) 1897-1900
The Times-Republican. (Rocky Ford, Colo.) 1898-1900
The Saccharine Gazette. (Sugar City, Otero County, Colo.) 1900-1915
The Manzanola Sun. (Manzanola, Colo.) 1900-19??
Rocky Ford Tribune. (Rocky Ford, Colo.) 1900-19??
Rocky Ford Republican. (Rocky Ford, Otero County, Colo.) 1900-19??
Rocky Ford Tribune successor to Fowler Tribune. (Rocky Ford, Colo.) 1900-1900
The Ordway New Era. (Ordway, Colo.) 1902-1927
The Fowler Tribune. (Fowler, Colo.) 1902-Current
Rocky Ford Gazette. (Rocky Ford, Otero County, Colo.) 1904-1909
The Rocky Ford Gazette and Topic. (Rocky Ford, Otero County, Colo.) 1909-19??
La Junta Daily Democrat. (La Junta, Colo.) 1938-1944
La Junta Daily Tribune. (La Junta, Colo.) 1939-1944
The Pilot. (La Junta, Colo.) 1942-194?
La Junta Tribune-Democrat. (La Junta, Colo.) 1944-Current
Arkansas Valley Journal, Farm and Ranch. (Rocky Ford, Colo.) 1949-1952
The Rocky Ford Daily Gazette Topic and Enterprise. (Rocky Ford, Otero County, Colo.) 1950-19??
Arkansas Valley Journal. (La Junta, Colo.) 1952-Current
The Rocky Ford Daily Gazette. (Rocky Ford, Colo.) 1954-Current

Places on the National Register

La Junta, Bent's Old Fort National Historic Site, CO 194
La Junta, Finney, Dr. Frank, House, 608 Belleview Ave.
La Junta, Hart, Wilson A., House, 802 Raton Ave.
La Junta, La Junta City Park, Bounded by Colorado and Park Aves. and 10th and 14th Sts.
La Junta, Lincoln School, 300 block W. 3rd St.
La Junta, North La Junta School, Jct. of CO 109 and CO 194
La Junta, Rourke, Eugene, House, 619 Carson St.
La Junta, San Juan Avenue Historic District, San Juan Ave.
La Junta, Sciumbato, Daniel, Grocery Store, 706 2nd St.
La Junta, U.S. Post Office, 4th and Colorado Ave.
Manzanola, Santa Fe Railway Manzanola Depot, 212 N. Grand Ave.
Rocky Ford, Adobe Stables, Arkansas Valley Fairgrounds, 800 N 9th St.
Rocky Ford, Art Building, Arkansas Valley Fairgrounds, near jct. of Main St. and US 50
Rocky Ford, Carnegie Public Library, 1005 Sycamore Ave.
Rocky Ford, Rocky Ford Post Office, 401 9th St.

USGS Historic Places

Cheraw, La Junta Army Air Field, 38.0466667, -103.5125
Hadley, Old Fort Bent, 38.0405635, -103.4293827
La Junta, Atchinson, Topeka and Santa Fe Railroad Hospital, 37.985, -103.5377778
Rocky Ford, First Methodist Episcopal Church, 38.0541667, -103.7202778

Historical Assets Colorado

Rocky Ford, Physicians Hospital, 38.0522222, -103.7225
Rocky Ford, Todd Airport, 38.0238974, -103.743562

Grand Army of the Republic Posts
Kilpatrick, No. 41, Otero, La Junta
Wadsworth, No. 93, Otero, Rocky Ford

USGS Historic Military Places
Cheraw, La Junta Army Air Field, 38.0466667, -103.5125

Military Bases
None

Post Offices

Alexander	1900 Mar 20	1900 Mar 31	
Angora	1891 June 18	1894 July 7	
Ayer	1811 Oct 18	1941 Aug 31	
Bloom	1899 Apr 18	1938 May 31*	
Catlin	1879 Nov 6	1895 Nov 4	
Cheraw	1910 Aug 13		81030
Fairmount	1900 Jan 19	1906 Feb 7	
Fowler	1890 Sept 6	1900 Mar 20	
Fowler 2			81039
Hester	1905 June 16	1912 Nov 30	
Higbee	1872 Apr 25	1925 Feb 28	
Holbrook	1906 June 6	1907 Feb 27	
La Junta	1878 Sept 20		81050
Manzanola	1895 Nov 4		81058
Meredith	1889 Nov 29	1890 June 25	
Mindeman	1917 June 9	1934 Dec 31	
Olney	1890 June 28	1909 Mar 24	
Olney Springs	1909 Mar 24		81062
Omer	1900 Aug 30	1909 July 31	
Ordway	1890 June 25		81063
Oxford	1882 Apr 27	1890 Sept 6	
Pultney	1890 May 19	1890 June 11	
Rene	1912 Feb 16	1921 Sept 30	
Rocky Ford	1871 Dec 1		81067
Sugar City	1900 Mar 27		81076
Swink	1906 Feb 7		81077
Timpas	1891 May 27	1970 Oct 23	
Village	1943 Nov 1	1956 Mar 31	
Vroman	1918 July 22	1954 Dec 31	
Wait	1900 Feb 26	1900 Mar 27	
Weitzer	1908 June 27	1918 July 22	

Otero County

Topo Quads

Bloom	374500N	373730N	1035230W	1040000W
Hawley	380000N	375230N	1033730W	1034500W
La Junta	380000N	375230N	1033000W	1033730W
La Junta SE	375230N	374500N	1033000W	1033730W
La Junta SW	375230N	374500N	1033730W	1034500W
Packers Gap	374500N	373730N	1033730W	1034500W
Purgatoire Canyon	371500N	370730N	1040000W	1040730W
Riley Canyon	374500N	373730N	1033000W	1033730W
Rocky Ford	380730N	380000N	1033730W	1034500W
Sheep Canyon	374500N	373730N	1034500W	1035230W
Timpas	375230N	374500N	1034500W	1035230W
Timpas NE	380000N	375230N	1034500W	1035230W
Timpas NW	380000N	375230N	1035230W	1040000W
Timpas SW	375230N	374500N	1035230W	1040000W

Suggested Reading

Birmingham, Ahlrich. *Essays and Poems of Colorado: Including a Reminiscence of Twenty Years on an Otero County Homestead*. La Junta, CO: West Side Print Co, 1938.

Hewitt, Dorothy and Barbara Hanzas. *Otery County 1889*. La Junta, CO: Rocky Ford Daily Gazette, 1989.

Keck, Frances Bollacker. *Conquistadors to the 21st Century: a History of Otero and Crowley Counties, Colorado*. La Junta, CO: Otero Press, 1999.

La Junta Centennial Picture Book. La Junta, CO: La Junta Print Co, 1981.

Muth, David J. *Rocky Ford, Colorado—A Walk Past Local Doors: Businesses and Residences from the Fairgrounds to Reservoir Hill, US 50 Curve to Curve*. Niwot, CO: Iron Gate Publishing, 2016.

Historical Assets Colorado

Ouray County

Introduction

Established: 1877   Population: 4,436

Formed from: Hinsdale, Lake

Adjacent Counties: Montrose, Gunnison, Hinsdale, San Juan, San Miguel

County Seat: Ouray

Other Communities: Ridgway, Loghill Village, Portland, Colona, Eldredge, Camp Bird, Thistledown, Dallas, Ironton, Sneffels

Website, https://ouraycountyco.gov

Area Codes: 970

Zip Codes: 81427, 81432

Historical Assets Colorado

Ouray County Courthouse

Courthouses & County Government
Ouray County
    https://ouraycountyco.gov
Ouray County Courthouse (7th Judicial District), 541 S 4th St, Ouray, CO 81427, 970-325-4405; http://www.courts.state.co.us/Courts/County/Index.cfm?County_ID=19
Assessor, 421 6th Ave, Ouray, CO 81427, 970-325-4371; http://ouraycountyco.gov/assessor.html
Board of County Commissioners, 112 Village Square W, Ridgway, CO 81432, 970-325-7320, https://ouraycountyco.gov/122/Board-of-County-Commissioners
Clerk & Recorder, 541 S 4th St, Ouray, CO 81427, 970-325-4961; http://ouraycountyco.gov/clerk.html
Coroner, P.O. Box 833, Ouray, CO 81427, 970-765-1618; https://ouraycountyco.gov/337/Coroner
Public Health, 302 2nd St, Ouray, CO 81427, 970-325-4670; http://ouraycountyco.gov/publichealth.html
Transportation (Road & Bridge), 115 Mall Rd, Ridgway, CO 81432, 970-626-5391; https://ouraycountyco.gov/151/Road-Bridge
Treasurer, 541 4th St, Ouray, CO 81427, 970-325-4487; http://ouraycountyco.gov/Treasurer.html

County Records
Birth 1880　　　　　　　　　Marriage 1881　　　　　　　　Divorce 1878
Death 1894　　　　　　　　　Land 1881　　　　　　　　　　Probate 1878
Court 1878
CSA Birth 1880
CSA Death 1894

Ouray County

County & Municipal Records Held at the State Level

The Colorado State Archives

Physical Records
Assessor
Clerk & Recorder
County Court
District Court
Sheriff
Surveyor
Treasurer
WPA Historical Records
WPA Religious Institutions
   Survey

Records on Film
Clerk & Recorder

Records on Master Film
Clerk & Recorder
Coroner
District Court
Combined Courts
School Districts

The Denver Public Library
Ouray County Land Deeds, 1887-1980
Ouray County Mining Company Records, 1957-1959
Western Hotel Records, 1891-1929
WWI Draft Registration Cards (microfilm)

School Districts

School Districts, http://www.adcogov.org/local-school-districts
Montrose County School District RE-1J, 930 Colorado Ave, Montrose, CO 81402, 970-249-7726; http://www.mcsd.org/
Ouray School District R-1, 400 7th Ave, Ouray, CO 81427, 970-325-7343; https://ouray.k12.co.us/
Ridgeway School District R-2, 1115 W Clinton St, Ridgway, CO 81432, 970-626-4320; https://www.ridgway.k12.co.us/

Historic School Districts

1. Ouray
2. Dallas Mesa
3. Piedmont
4. [1879]
5. Old Dallas
6. [1887]
7. Upper Log Hill
8. [1886]
9. Cow Creek
10. Mayfield
11. Ridgway
12. [1898]
13. [1898]
14. Lower Log Hill

Jt30. Colona

Fraternal Organizations

Granges
Dallas, No. 86, Ouray, Dallas, 20 Jan 1889
Colona, No. 259, Ouray, Colona/Montrose, 17 Sept 1915
Ridgway, No. 438, Ouray, Ridgway, 11 Aug 1936

Masons

Ancient Free & Accepted Masons
Doric, No. 37, Ouray, Ouray, 17 Sept 1879

Historical Assets Colorado

Royal Arch Masons
Kilwinning, No. 21, Ouray, Ouray

Knights Templar
Ouray Commandery, No. 16, Ouray, Ouray, 1889 May 8

Eastern Star
Chipeta, No. 13, Ouray, Ouray

Odd Fellows
Crystal Fount, No. 30, Ouray, Ouray
Colona, No. 148, Ouray, Colona
Ridgeway, No. 158, Ouray, Ridgeway

Rebekahs
Ridgway, No. 12, Ouray, Ridgway
Mount Hayden, No. 54, Ouray, Ouray

Knights of Pythias
Rainbow, No. 62, Ouray, Red Mountain, 1890 Nov 14
Mount Hayden, No. 78, Ouray, Ouray
Centurion, No. 100, Ouray, Ridgway

Pythian Sisters
Snow Banner, No. 38, Ouray, Ouray
Mayflower, No. 40, Ouray, Ridgway

Benevolent Protective Order of Elks
Ouray, No. 492, Ouray, Ouray

City & Town Halls

Ouray, 320 6th Ave, Ouray, CO 81427, 970-325-7211, http://www.ci.ouray.co.us
Ridgway, 201 N Railroad St, Ridgway, CO 81432, 970-626-5308, https://www.colorado.gov/ridgway

Archives & Manuscript Collections

Ouray County Archive Center (digital); https://ouraycountyco.gov/Archive.aspx

Historical & Genealogical Societies

Ouray County Historical Society, Historical Museum, 420 6th Ave, P.O. Box 151, Ouray, CO 81427, (970) 325-4576, http://www.ouraycountyhistoricalsociety.org

Local Libraries

Ouray Public Library, 320 6th Ave, P.O. Box 625, Ouray, CO 81427, (970) 325-4616, https://ouray.colibraries.org
Ridgway Public Library, 300 Charles St, Ridgway, CO 81432, (970) 626-5252, https://ridgway.colibraries.org

Links

CO GenWeb
http://cogenweb.com/ouray/

Ouray County

Cyndi's List
https://www.cyndislist.com/us/co/counties/ouray/

FamilySearch Wiki
https://www.familysearch.org/wiki/en/Ouray_County,_Colorado_Genealogy

Linkpendium
http://www.linkpendium.com/ouray-co-genealogy/

RootsWeb Wiki
https://wiki.rootsweb.com/wiki/index.php/Ouray_County,_Colorado

Wikipedia
https://en.wikipedia.org/wiki/Ouray_County,_Colorado

Historic Hotels

1887 Beaumont Hotel & Spa, 505 Main St, Ouray, CO 81427, 970-325-7000, http://www.beaumonthotel.com

1891 Historic Western Hotel, 210 7th Ave, Ouray, CO 81427, 970-325-4645, http://www.historicwesternhotel.com

1893 Hotel Ouray, 303 6th Ave, Ouray, CO 81427, 970-325-0500, https://hotelouray.com

Museums & Historic Sites

Ouray Alchemist Pharmaceutical Museum, 533 Main St, Ouray, CO 81427, (970) 325-4003, https://www.ouraycolorado.com/directory/artsculture/history/207-ouray-alchemist-penthouse-suite

Ouray County Ranch History Museum, 321 Sherman St, P.O. Box 190, Ridgway, CO 81432, (970) 316-1085, https://www.ocrhm.org

Ridgway Railroad Museum, 150 Racecourse Rd, Ridgway, CO 81432, (970) 626-5458, http://www.ridgewayrailroadmuseum.org

Special Events & Scenic Locations

The Ouray County Fair is held at the Ouray County 4-H Events Center & Fairgrounds, 22739 Hwy 550, Ridgway, CO 81432, 970-626-3304, http://ouraycountyco.gov/349/Ouray-County-Fair

A Ouray Events calendar courtesy of several local Chambers of Commerce is here: https://www.ouraycolorado.com/events

Ridgway State Park
Ridgway Reservoir
Uncompahgre National Forest
Mount Sneffels Wilderness
Uncompahgre Wilderness
Bear Creek National Recreation Trail
Alpine Loop National Scenic Back Country Byway
San Juan Skyway National Scenic Byway
Great Parks Bicycle Route
Western Express Bicycle Route

Historical Assets Colorado

Ghost Towns & Other Sparsely Populated Places
Black Lake, Camp Bird, Colma, Corkscrew Gulch, Dallas, Eldredge, Engineer City, Guston, Hagen, Hillside Spur, Ironton (Copper Glen), Lake Hughes, Mount Sneffels, Paymaster, Piedmont, Portland, Red Mountain Town, Ruby City, Sneffels, Summit, Upper Camp Bird, Vanderbilt, Virginius, Yankee Girl

Newspapers
The Ridgway Reporter. (Ridgway, Colo.) 18??-19??
The Daily Budget. (Ouray, Colo.) 18??-1???
Ouray Times. (Ouray, Colo.) 1877-18??
Dolores News. (Rico, Ouray Co., Colo.) 1879-1886
The Solid Muldoon. (Ouray, Colo.) 1879-1892
San Miguel Journal. (San Miguel, Colo.) 1881-188?
The Daily Muldoon. (Ouray, Colo.) 1882-1882
Red Mountain Review. (Red Mountain, Colo.) 1883-1884
Red Mountain Pilot. (Red Mountain City, San Juan Co., Colo.) 1883-1???
The Morning Budget. (Ouray, Colo.) 1886-????
The Ouray Plaindealer. (Ouray, Colo.) 1888-1???
The Red Mountain Journal. (Red Mountain, Ouray County, Colo.) 1889-1893
The Western Slope. (Dallas, Ouray County, Colo.) 1889-1890
The Ridgway Herald. (Ridgway, Ouray County, Colo.) 1891-1???
Ouray Argus. (Ouray, Colo.) 1891-1???
The San Juan Silverite. (Ouray, Colo.) 1892-189?
The Populist. (Ridgway, Colo.) 1894-1904
The Silverite-Plaindealer. (Ouray, Colo.) 1894-1901
The Ouray Herald. (Ouray, Ouray County, Colo.) 1894-1920
Ouray Evening Herald. (Ouray, Colo.) 1898-1898
The Daily Plaindealer. (Ouray, Colo.) 1898-1???
The Plaindealer. (Ouray, Colo.) 1901-19??
The Ridgway Sun. (Ridgway, Ouray County, Colo.) 1908-19??
Arps Right Price Store Idea-O-Graph. (Ouray, Colo.) 1915-19??
The Ouray Herald and The Plaindealer. (Ouray, Ouray County, Colo.) 1921-1936
The Ouray Herald. (Ouray, Ouray County, Colo.) 1936-1939
The Ouray County Herald. (Ouray, Ouray County, Colo.) 1939-1969
Ouray County Plaindealer and Ouray Herald. (Ouray, Colo.) 1969-1980
Ouray County Plaindealer. (Ouray, Colo.) 1980-Current
The Ridgway Sun. ([Ridgway, Colo.]) 1980-Current

Places on the National Register
Ouray, Beaumont Hotel, US 550
Ouray, Ouray City Hall and Walsh Library, 6th Ave. between 3rd and 4th Sts.
Ouray, Ouray Historic District, US 550
Ridgway, Jackson, George, House, 129 Citadel Dr.

Ouray County

USGS Historic Places
Ironton, Guston, 37.916384, -107.6903386
Ironton, Sneffels, 37.9752716, -107.7497831
Ridgway, Ridgway Fire Department, 38.1519351, -107.7567261

Grand Army of the Republic Posts
F P Blair, No. 52, Ouray, Ouray

USGS Historic Military Places
None

Military Bases
None

Post Offices

Alder Creek	1878 Dec 31	1880 Sept 6	
Ames	1880 Dec 20	1922 June 3*	
Ash	1899 Oct 11	1905 Dec 31	
Aurora	1880 May 10	1884 Feb 19	
Campbird	1898 Apr 28	1918 Mar 15	
Colona	1891 Oct 19	1943 Mar 31	
Dallas	1884 Feb 11	1899 Oct 31	
Dallas Divide	1894 Mar 24	1909 July 23	
Dallasville	1877 Dec 21	1879 July 9	
Folsom	1880 Aug 17	1880 Dec 13	
Gabbert	1898 Apr 22	1903 Oct 14	
Guston	1892 Jan 26	1898 Nov 16	
Hot Springs	1877 May 4	1879 Aug 28	
ironton	1883 May 23	1920 Aug 7*	
Lawrence	1883 Feb 5	1884 Feb 11	
Mount Sneffels	1879 Oct 31	1895 Apr 3	
Ophir	1878 May 17	1921 Jan 31*	
Ouray 2	1876 May 9		81427
Pandora	1881 Aug 5	1902 Oct 15*	
Placerville	1878 Apr 22		81430
Plumer	1900 May 28	1901 Dec 14	
Portland	1878 Jan 11	1896 Apr 24*	
Red Mountain	1883 Jan 29	1913 Feb 28	
Rico	1879 Aug 25		81332
Ridgway	1890 Oct 1		81432
Rogersville	1883 Mar 19	1883 June 15	
Ruby City	1878 May 17	1879 July 31	
San Miguel	1877 July 16	1895 Sept 19	
Sneffels	1895 Apr 3	1930 Oct 6	
Telluride	1880 July 26	1880 Aug 17	

Historical Assets Colorado

Telluride 2	1880 Dec 13		81435
Trout	1881 June 9	1882 Mar 21	
Trout Lake	1882 June 14	1892 June 29*	
Virginius	1887 Aug 15	1894 Apr 24	
Wareville	1877 May 16	1877 July 17	
Windham	1878 Dec 9	1881 June 20	

Topo Quads

Dallas	381500N	380730N	1073730W	1074500W
Handies Peak	380000N	375230N	1073000W	1073730W
Ironton	380000N	375230N	1073730W	1074500W
Mount Sneffels	380730N	380000N	1074500W	1075230W
Ouray	380730N	380000N	1073730W	1074500W
Ridgway	381500N	380730N	1074500W	1075230W
Sams	380730N	380000N	1075230W	1080000W
Telluride	380000N	375230N	1074500W	1075230W
Wetterhorn Peak	380730N	380000N	1073000W	1073730W

Suggested Reading

Bachman, David C and Tod Bacigalupi. *The Way it Was: Historical Narrative of Ouray County.* Ouray, CO: Wayfinder Press, 1990.

Crum, Josie Moore. *Ouray County, Colorado.* Durango, CO: San Juan History, Inc., 1962.

Griffiths, Karen and Roger Henn. *Reflections on Lake Lenore: Historical Glimpses Covering 150 Years of a Noteworthy Locale in Ouray County, Colorado.* Lake City, CO: Western Reflections Publishing Co, 2008.

Ranching History of Ouray County. Ridgway, CO: County Graphics, 2004.

Rice, Frank A and Jack Luther Benham. *The Mines of Ouray County.* Ouray, CO: Bear Creek Pub Co, 1980.

Saunders, Gail Zanett and Maria Jones. *Ouray.* Charleston, SC: Arcadia Publishing, 2010.

Smith, P David. *A Quick History of Ouray.* Ouray, CO: Western Reflections, 2003.

Turner, Carol. *Notorious San Juans: Wicked Tales from Ouray, San Juan and La Plata Counties.* Charleston, SC: History Press, 2011.

Park County

Introduction

Established: 1861 Population: 16,206

Formed from: Original

Adjacent Counties: Clear Creek, Jefferson, Teller, Fremont, Chaffee, Lake, Summit

County Seat: Fairplay

Other Communities: Alma, Guffey, Bailey, Como, Grant, Hartsel, Jefferson, Lake George, Shawnee, Tarryall, Antero Junction, Buckskin Joe, Laurette, Garo, Howbert, Trump

Website, https://www.parkco.us

Area Codes: 719

Zip Codes: 80420, 80421, 80432, 80440, 80448, 80449, 80456, 80475, 80820, 80827

Historical Assets Colorado

Park County Courthouse

Courthouses & County Government

Park County
https://www.parkco.us

Park County Courthouse (11th Judicial District), 300 4th St, Fairplay, CO 80440, 719-836-2940; http://www.courts.state.co.us/Courts/County/Index.cfm?County_ID=31

Assessor, 501 Main St, Fairplay, CO 80440, 719-836-4331; http://www.parkco.us/index.aspx?NID=73

Board of County Commissioners, 856 Catello Ave, Fairplay, CO 80440, 719-836-2771, https://parkco.us/174/County-Commissioners

Clerk & Recorder, 501 Main St, Fairplay, CO 80440, 719-836-4333; http://www.parkco.us/index.aspx?nid=72

Clerk & Recorder, 59865 Hwy 285, Bailey, CO 80421, 303-816-5920; http://www.parkco.us/index.aspx?nid=72

Coroner, 911 Clark St, Fairplay, CO 80440, 719-836-4340; https://www.parkco.us/76/Coroner

Public Health, 200 6th St, Fairplay, CO 80440, 719-836-4161; http://www.parkco.us/index.aspx?nid=86

Transportation (Public Works), 1246 CR 16, Fairplay, CO 80440, 719-836-4277; https://www.parkco.us/87/Public-Works

Treasurer, 501 Main St, Fairplay, CO 80440, 719-836-2771; http://www.parkco.us/index.aspx?nid=91

County Records

Birth 1875	Marriage 1881	Divorce 1861
Death 1903	Land 1861	Probate 1861
Court 1861		
CSA Delayed Birth Certificates 1941		

Park County

County & Municipal Records Held at the State Level

The Colorado State Archives

Physical Records	Records on Film	Records on Master Film
Assessor	1885 Census	Clerk & Recorder
Clerk & Recorder	Clerk & Recorder	County Hospital
County Court	District Court	District Court
District Court		School Districts
Justice Court		
Probate Court		
County Jail		
Sheriff		
Treasurer		
WPA Historical Records		
WPA Religious Institutions Survey		

Cities
Como
Fairplay

The Denver Public Library

Colorado Deeds, 1868-1911
Colorado Bureau of Mines Records, 1897-1915
London-Butte Gold Mines Company Records, 1938-1943
Park County Mining Companies Records, 1932
WWI Draft Registration Cards (microfilm)

School Districts

School Districts, http://www.adcogov.org/local-school-districts
Park County School District RE-2, 640 Hathaway St, Fairplay, CO 80440, 719-836-3111; https://www.parkcountyre2.org/
Platte Canyon School District 1, 57393 US Hwy 285, Bailey, CO 80421, 303-838-7666; http://www.plattecanyonschools.org/

Historic School Districts

1. Long Meadow, Platte Canon
2. Bordenville, Elkhorn, Lost Park
3. Fairplay
4. Alma, Park City
5. Trump, Pleasant Valley, Badger Creek, Indian Springs
6. Howbert, Lone Chimney, Glentivar
7. Jefferson
8. Hartsel
9. Como
10. Doran
11. Garo
12. Rocky
13. Jefferson
14. Lake George
15. Buffalo Springs
16. Estabrook
17. West Four Mile, Slater Creek
18. Jefferson
19. Shawnee
20. Grant, Olava
21. Tarryall, Hayman
22. Bailey, Deer Creek
23. Balfour, Guffey
24. [1897]
25.
26.
27.
28. [1878]

49. Guffey

Jt25. [1890]
Jt28. [1891]

565

Historical Assets Colorado

Fraternal Organizations
Granges
Avoca, No. 118, Park, Sleights, 10 Nov 1890
Deer Valley, No. 119, Park, Bailey, 11 Nov 1890
Entriken Meadow, No. 235, Park, Bailey, 27 Feb 1915
Tarryall, No. 431, Park, Lake George, 7 Apr 1936
Trump, No 432, Park, Hartsel, 30 Apr 1936
Elkhorn, No. 433, Park, Hartsel, 30 Apr 1936
Jefferson, No. 435, Park, Jefferson, 21 May 1936
Glentivar, No. 436, Park, Hartsel, 25 May 1936
Blue Mountain, No. 453, Park, Lake George, 11 June 1942
Rocky Mountain, No. 468, Park, Lake George, 26 Apr 1947

Masons
Ancient Free & Accepted Masons
Haxtun, No. 25, Park, Fairplan, 30 Sept 1874

Royal Arch Masons
None

Knights Templar
None

Eastern Star
Liberty, No. 108, Park, Fairplay

Odd Fellows
South Park, No. 10, Park, Fairplay, 1870 Mar 16
Tarryall, No. 64, Park, Como

Rebekahs
South Park, No. 21, Park, Fairplay

Knights of Pythias
South Park, No. 71, Park, Como, 1891 June 18
Alma, No. 75, Park, Alma

Pythian Sisters
None

Benevolent Protective Order of Elks
None

City & Town Halls
Fairplay, 901 9th St, Fairplay, CO 80440, 719-836-2622, http://fairplayco.us
Alma, 59 Buckskin St, Alma, CO 80420, 719-836-2712, http://townofalma.com/wordpress/
Guffey, https://www.guffeycolorado.com

Archives & Manuscript Collections
Park County Local History Archives, 856 Castello Ave, P.O. Box 99, Fairplay, CO 80440, (719) 836-2771, http://www.parkcoarchives.org

Park County

Historical & Genealogical Societies
Park County Historical Society, P.O. Box 43, Bailey, CO 80421, (303) 838-9511, http://www.parkcountyhistory.com

South Park Historical Foundation, South Park City Museum, 100 4th St, P.O. Box 634, Fairplay, CO 80440, (719) 836-2387, http://www.southparkcity.org

Local Libraries
Fairplay Library, 400 Front St, Fairplay, CO 80440, (719) 836-4297

Park County Public Library, Old Park County Court House, 418 Main St, PO Box 592, Fairplay, CO 80440, (719) 836-4297, https://parkcounty.colibraries.org/fairplay/

Park County Public Library, 350 Bulldogger Rd, P.O. Box 282, Bailey, CO 80421-0282, (303) 838-5539, http://parkcounty.colibraries.org

Links
CO GenWeb
http://cogenweb.com/park/

Cyndi's List
https://www.cyndislist.com/us/co/counties/park/

FamilySearch Wiki
https://www.familysearch.org/wiki/en/Park_County,_Colorado_Genealogy

Linkpendium
http://www.linkpendium.com/park-co-genealogy/

RootsWeb Wiki
https://wiki.rootsweb.com/wiki/index.php/Park_County,_Colorado

Wikipedia
https://en.wikipedia.org/wiki/Park_County,_Colorado

Historic Hotels
**1897 South Park Hotel (Como Eating House), 17 6th St, Como, CO 80432, 720-386-1700, https://www.facebook.com/pages/category/Hotel/Como-Hotel-historically-known-as-the-Como-Eating-House-221049395852/ **I am unsure whether or not this place is still open.

Museums & Historic Sites
South Park Historical Foundation, South Park City Museum, 100 4th St, P.O. Box 634, Fairplay, CO 80440, (719) 836-2387, http://www.southparkcity.org

Special Events & Scenic Locations
The Park County Fair is held in July most years at the Park County Fairgrounds, 880 Bogue St, Fairplay, CO 80440, http://parkcofair.com

Explore Park County has a calendar of events here: https://www.exploreparkcounty.com/events-festivals

Historical Assets Colorado

Buffalo Peaks Wilderness
Los Creek Wilderness
Pike National Forest
San Isabel National Forest
Eleven Mile State Park
Spinney Mountain State Park
Staunton State Park
American Discovery Trail
Colorado Trail
Continental Divide National Scenic Trail
Great Parks Bicycle Route
Guanella Pass Scenic Byway
TransAmerica Trail Bicycle Route

Ghost Towns & Other Sparsely Populated Places

Alma, Antero Junction, Arthurs, Balfour, Bath, Bordenville, Boyer, Buckskin Joe, Buffalo Springs, Burrows, Cassells, Coal Branch Junction, Coals Spur, Como, Cortrite, Dake, Dudley, Estabrook, Garo, Geneva City, Geneva Gulch, Glen Isle, Glentivar, Grant, Guffey, Gulch, Halfway, Hall Valley, Hamilton, Handcart, Harris Park, Haver, Hay Ranch, Hoosier, Horseshoe (Doran, East Leadville), Howbert, Idlewild, Jefferson, Kenosha, Kester, King, Lake George, Laurette, Leavick, London Junction (Alma Station), London Mines, Meadows, Metcalf, Michigan, Montgomery, Mountaindale, Park City (Mosquito), Peabodys, Platte River, Platte Station, Puma City, Quarzville, Red Hill, Revelleville, Rocky, Rouarks, Sacramento, Salt Works, Saxonia, Selkirk, Shawnee, Slaghts, South Park City (Platte City, Fairplay Diggings), Spinney, Tarryall, Trump, Truro, Webster

Newspapers

Park County Bulletin. (Alma, Colo.) 18??-1913
The Como Record. (Como [Colo.]) 18??-1???
Miners' Record. (Tarryall Mines, South Park, C.t. [Colo.]) 1861-1861
The Fairplay Sentinel. (Fairplay, Park County, Colo.) 1874-1878
The Mount Lincoln News. (Alma, Colo.) 1875-1878
The Fairplay Flume. (Fairplay, Park County, Colo.) 1879-1913
Como Head Light. (Como, Colo.) 1883-1???
The Balfour News. (Balfour, Park County, Colo.) 1894-1???
The Park County News. (Fairplay, Park County, Colo.) 19??-19??
The Park County Republican and Fairplay Flume. (Fairplay, Colo.) 19??-Current
The Park County Bulletin and Fairplay Flume. (Fairplay, Colo.) 1913-1913
Fairplay Flume and Park County Bulletin. (Fairplay, Colo.) 1913-1914
Fairplay Flume. (Fairplay, Colo.) 1914-19??
The Alma Mining Record. (Alma, Park County, Colo.) 1934-19??
The Park County News & Alma Bulletin. (Alma, Park County, Colo.) 1935-19??
The Mountain Independent. (Jefferson And Park Counties, Colo.) 1975-19??
South Park Times. (Fairplay, Colo.) 1982-1985
Park County Times. (Fairplay, Colo.) 1985-1985

Park County

Places on the National Register
Alma, Paris Mill, Address Restricted
Bailey, Estabrook Historic District, NE of Bailey
Bailey, Glenisle, Off US Hwy 285
Como, Boreas Railroad Station Site, Boreas Pass Rd. NW of Como, Pike NF
Como, Como Roundhouse, Railroad Depot and Hotel Complex, Off U.S. 285
Como, Como School, Spruce St.
Fairplay, Fairplay Hotel, 500 Main St.
Fairplay, Park County Courthouse and Jail, 418 Main St.
Fairplay, South Park City Museum, 100 4th St.
Fairplay, South Park Community Church, 6th and Hathaway Sts.
Fairplay, South Park Lager Beer Brewery, 3rd and Front Sts.
Fairplay, Summer Saloon, 3rd and Front Sts.
Fairplay, Trout Creek—Annex—Settele Ranch, 3242 Co.Rd. 7
Hartsel, Buckley Ranch, Co. Rd. 59
Hartsel, Colorado Salt Works, 3858 US 285
Hartsel, EM Ranch, Cty Rd. 439
Hartsel, Salt Works Ranch, 3858 US 285
Hartsel, Threemile Gulch, Address Restricted
Jefferson, Jefferson Denver South Park and Pacific Railroad Depot, Jct. of US 285 and Cty. Rd. 35
Jefferson, Wahl Ranch, US 285 and Lost Park Rd.
Shawnee, Shawnee, 56016-56114 Frontage Rd; 55919-56278 Hwy 285; 31-36 W. Shawnee Rd; 54-152 Waterworks Rd
Tarryall, Tarryall School, 31000 County Rd.

USGS Historic Places
Alma, Dudley, 39.2969337, -106.0716858
Alma, Park City, 39.2783228, -106.0930751
Alma, Quartzville, 39.3449887, -106.0772416
Bailey, Insmont Post Office, 39.3919337, -105.4530545
Fairplay West, Horseshoe, 39.2038796, -106.0852966
Jefferson, Heckendorf Ranches-Georgia Pass Ranch Airport, 39.4080433, -105.8372339
Jefferson, South Park Historical Monument, 39.4035987, -105.7541754
Mount Sherman, Leavick, 39.1949909, -106.1375199
Tarryall, Badger Flats Airstrip, 39.0586026, -105.4630544
Unknown, Cassels Post Office, 0, 0
Unknown, Grousemont Post Office, 0, 0
Unknown, Kaiserheim Post Office, 0, 0
Unknown, Pine Grove School, 0, 0
Witcher Mountain, Dave Nash Ranch Airport, 38.7551225, -105.3832853

Grand Army of the Republic Posts
J Marshall Paul, No. 45, Park, Alma, 1883

Historical Assets Colorado

USGS Historic Military Places
None

Military Bases
None

Post Offices

Alma	1873 Mar 7		80420
Bailey	1878 Nov 20		80421
Balfour	1894 Feb 6	1907 Jan 31	
Black Mountain	1899 June 20	1911 Oct 14	
Bordenville	1879 Sept 29	1884 Nov 28	
Buckskin	1865 Dec 21	1873 Jan 24	
Buffalo Springs	1875 May 28	1912 May 15	
Cassels	1899 June 19	1929 Sept 30	
Chase	1892 July 15	1911 Oct 31	
Como	1879 July 23		
Conrad	1897 July 7	1905 Oct 14	
Contrite	1889 Nov 22	1892 Mar 29	
Dake	1883 May 23	1892 Oct 8	
Deer Valley	1871 Aug 25	1878 Nov 20	
Devine	1898 Feb 17	1899 June 20	
Doran	1901 Nov 1	1907 Jan 2	
Dudley	1872 Oct 31	1880 Oct 22	
Estabrook	1880 Aug 9	1937 Nov 15*	
Fair Play	1861 Aug 2	1924 Oct 1	
Fairplay	1924 Oct 1		80440
Fairville	1878 Sept 13	1882 Feb 23*	
Florissant	1872 Nov 20		80816
Garo	1880 June 29	1955 Feb 28	
Glentivar	1921 Apr 13	1955 Feb 28*	
Granite Vale	1861 Dec 19	1870 Jan 31	
Grant	1871 May 16	1925 Jan 14*	
Grant 2	1948 Jan 1		80448
Grousemont	1918 Feb 4	1919 Jan 15	
Guffey	1895 Apr 12		80820
Hall Valley	1874 Aug 10	1894 Nov 5*	
Hallvale	1894 Nov 5	1898 Mar 4	
Hamilton	1860 July 26	1881 Nov 10	
Hammond	1896 Apr 10	1903 May 15	
Hartsel	1875 Mar 16		80449
Hayman	1904 Aug 13	1918 Aug 10	
Holland	1874 Feb 24	1874 Dec 23	
Horse Shoe	1880 Aug 23	1886 July 8	
Horseshoe	1890 Apr 4	1894 July 2	
Howbert	1887 Dec 22	1933 June 30	

Park County

Idaville	1895 Apr 12	1896 May 23	
Insmont	1902 June 5	1917 Dec 15	
Jefferson	1861 Sept 3	1863 Apr 4	
Jefferson 2	1879 Oct 3		
Kaiserheim	1914 Apr 2	1918 Feb 4	
Kenosha	1891 May 16	1893 Oct 2	
Kester	1874 Aug 10	1891 Dec 21	
King	1884 Apr 14	1896 Oct 24	
Lake George	1891 May 15	1905 Sept 30	
Lake George 2	1910 Sept 27		80827
Laurette	1861 Nov 14	1865 Dec 21	
Leavick	1896 Dec 29	1899 Aug 31	
London	1883 June 25	1886 Aug 27	
Montgomery	1882 June 7	1888 May 3	
Montgomery Park	1862 July 21	1872 Oct 31	
Mountaindale	1880 Jan 5	1899 Oct 11	
Mullenville	1880 June 28	1882 Jan 31	
Olava	1936 Aug 27	1948 Jan 1	
Park	1879 Nov 26	1891 Apr 14	
Platte	1894 Nov 5	1894 Dec 12	
Platte Station	1878 Sept 27	1894 Dec 18*	
Rocky	1874 Dec 23	1898 Oct 31	
Shawnee	1900 Apr 19		80475
Slaughts	1882 Feb 23	1900 Apr 19	
South Park	1874 June 18	1879 June 24	
Spinney	1889 Feb 14	1908 Sept 1	
Springer	1901 Aug 23	1902 Oct 15*	
Sterling	1862 Dec 23	1865 Nov 17	
Sulphur Springs	1873 Feb 7	1874 Dec 23	
Tarryall	1860 Jan 4	1863 Sept 29	
Tarryall 2	1896 Sept 19	1933 Mar 31*	
Timberton	1898 May 25	1898 Oct 27	
Trump	1928 May 1	1931 Nov 30	
Truro	1887 Aug 11	1895 Sept 11	
Wadleigh	1895 June 24	1895 Nov 11	
Webster	1877 May 7	1909 Sept 30*	
Weston	1879 Nov 4	1880 Feb 24	

Topo Quads

Agate Mountain	385230N	384500N	1054500W	1055230W
Antero Reservoir	390000N	385230N	1055230W	1060000W
Antero Reservoir NE	390000N	385230N	1054500W	1055230W
Black Mountain	384500N	383730N	1053730W	1054500W
Cameron Mountain	384500N	383730N	1055230W	1060000W
Castle Rock Gulch	385230N	384500N	1055230W	1060000W
Como	392230N	391500N	1055230W	1060000W

Historical Assets Colorado

Cover Mountain	384500N	383730N	1052230W	1053000W
Dicks Peak	385230N	384500N	1053730W	1054500W
Eagle Rock	391500N	390730N	1053730W	1054500W
Elevenmile Canyon	390000N	385230N	1052230W	1053000W
Elkhorn	391500N	390730N	1054500W	1055230W
Fairplay East	391500N	390730N	1055230W	1060000W
Fairplay West	391500N	390730N	1060000W	1060730W
Farnum Peak	391500N	390730N	1053000W	1053730W
Garo	390730N	390000N	1055230W	1060000W
Glentivar	390730N	390000N	1053000W	1053730W
Gribbles Park	384500N	383730N	1054500W	1055230W
Guffey NW	390000N	385230N	1053730W	1054500W
Hackett Mountain	390730N	390000N	1051500W	1052230W
Hartsel	390730N	390000N	1054500W	1055230W
Harvard Lakes	390000N	385230N	1060730W	1061500W
High Park	384500N	383730N	1051500W	1052230W
Jones Hill	390730N	390000N	1060000W	1060730W
Lake George	390000N	385230N	1051500W	1052230W
Marmot Peak	390000N	385230N	1060000W	1060730W
Milligan Lakes	392230N	391500N	1054500W	1055230W
Mount Logan	393000N	392230N	1053730W	1054500W
Mount Sherman	391500N	390730N	1060730W	1061500W
Observatory Rock	392230N	391500N	1053730W	1054500W
Shawnee	393000N	392230N	1053000W	1053730W
South Peak	390730N	390000N	1060730W	1061500W
Spinney Mountain	390000N	385230N	1053000W	1053730W
Sulphur Mountain	390730N	390000N	1053730W	1054500W
Tarryall	390730N	390000N	1052230W	1053000W
Thirtynine Mile Mtn	385230N	384500N	1053000W	1053730W
Thirtyone Mile Mtn	384500N	383730N	1053000W	1053730W
Topaz Mountain	392230N	391500N	1053000W	1053730W
Witcher Mountain	385230N	384500N	1052230W	1053000W
Wrights Reservoir	385230N	384500N	1051500W	1052230W

Suggested Reading

Aldrich, John K. *Ghosts of Park County: A Guide to the Ghost Towns and Mining Camps of Park County, Colorado.* Lakewood, CO: Centennial Graphics, 2000.

Balough, Linda. *Park County, Colorado: Where History is Still Alive.* Alma, CO: Park County Vision, 2004.

Historic Stories and Legends of Park County. Bailey, CO: Park County Historical Society, 1988.

Park County Local History Archives. *Park County.* Charleston, SC: Arcadia Publishing, 2015.

Van Dusen, Laura. *Historic Tales from Park County: Parked in the Past.* Charleston, SC: The History Press, 2013.

Wright, Christie. *South Park Perils: Short Ropes & True Tales of Historic Park County, Colorado.* Palmer Lake, CO: Fitter Press, 2013.

Phillips County

Introduction

Established: 1889 Population: 4,442
Formed from: Logan
Adjacent Counties: Sedgwick, Yuma, Logan
County Seat: Holyoke
  Other Communities: Haxtun, Paoli, Amherst
Website, https://www.colorado.gov/phillipscounty
Area Codes: 970
Zip Codes: 80721, 80731, 80734, 80746

Historical Assets Colorado

Phillips County Courthouse

Courthouses & County Government

Phillips County
https://www.colorado.gov/phillipscounty
Phillips County Courthouse (13th Judicial District), 221 S Interocean Ave, Holyoke, CO 80734, 970-854-3279; http://www.courts.state.co.us/Courts/County/Index.cfm?County_ID=41
Assessor, 221 S Interocean Ave, Holyoke, CO 80734, 970-854-3151; http://www.colorado.gov/cs/Satellite/CNTY-Phillips/CBON/1251611091618
Board of County Commissioners, 221 S Interocean Ave, Holyoke, CO 80734, https://www.colorado.gov/pacific/phillipscounty/county-commissioners-0
Clerk & Recorder, 221 S Interocean Ave, Holyoke, CO 80734, 970-854-3131; http://www.colorado.gov/cs/Satellite/CNTY-Phillips/CBON/1251611091883
Coroner, 1001 E Johnson St, Holyoke, CO 80734, 970-854-2241; https://www.colorado.gov/pacific/phillipscounty/coroner-0
Public Health, 700 Columbine St, Sterling, CO 80751, 970-522-3741; http://www.nchd.org/
Transportation (Road & Bridge), 433 E Fletcher, Haxtun, CO 80731, 970-466-0482
Treasurer, P.O. Box 267, Holyoke, CO 80734, 970-854-2822; http://www.colorado.gov/cs/Satellite/CNTY-Phillips/CBON/1251611092276

County Records

Birth Unk	Marriage 1892	Divorce 1889
Death Unk	Land 1892	Probate 1889
Court 1889		

Phillips County

County & Municipal Records Held at the State Level

The Colorado State Archives

Physical Records	Records on Film	Records on Master Film
Clerk & Recorder	Clerk & Recorder	Clerk & Recorder
County Court	District Court	County Commissioners
District Court		County Court
WPA Historical Records		District Court
WPA Religious Institutions Survey		Combined Courts
		School Districts
WPA Holyoke		

The Denver Public Library
North Eastern Colorado Ministerial Association Minute Book, 1925-1942
WPA Historical Records Survey
WWI Draft Registration Cards (microfilm)

School Districts

School Districts, http://www.adcogov.org/local-school-districts
Haxtun School District Re-2J, 201 W Powell St, Haxtun, CO 80731, 970-774-6111; https://www.haxtunk12.org/
Holyoke School District RE-1J, 435 S Morlan Ave, Holyoke, CO 80734, 970-854-3634; https://www.hcosd.org/

Historic School Districts

1. Fairview
2. Amherst
3. Sunnyside
4. Green Prairie
5. Pleasant Valley
6. Highland Center
7. Prairie Star
8. Evergreen
9. Hilltop
10. Sunbeam
11. Plainsview
12. McKelvey
13.
14. Pleasant Prairie
15. Pleasant View
16. Silver Beam
17. Sunny Dale
18. Beachville
19. Grand View
20.
21.
22.
23. [1889]
24.
25.
26. Harmony
27. Prairie Gem
28.
29.
30.
31. Bryant
32.
33. [1889]
34.
35.
36. Highlands, Highline
37. [1889]
38.
39. Holyoke Grade
40. [1895]
41. Liberty
42.
43.
44. [1889]
45. [1889]
46.
47. Fairfield
48. Morning View
49. [1889]
50.
51. Fairy Dell
52. [1889]
53.
54.
55.
56.
57. Philarado
58. Glenwood
59.
60.
61. Morning Star
62.
63. Amitie
64. [1889]
65.
66. Paoli Grade
67.
68.
69.
70.
70. [1889]
71. Community Center

Historical Assets Colorado

72. [1889]
73.
74.
75.
76.
77. Broadway
78. Lone Star
79. [1889]
80.
81. Lakeside
82. [1889]
83.
84. Haxton Grade
85.
86.
87.
88.
89.
90.
91. North Star

Fraternal Organizations

Granges
Amity, No. 209, Phillips, Holyoke, 20 Apr 1912
Unity, No. 217, Phillips, Weatherly/Holyoke, 10 Oct 1913
Lakeside, No. 220, Phillips, Holyoke, 18 Nov 1913
Frenchman Valley, No. 222, Phillips, Paoli/Holyoke, 18 Nov 1913
Epworth, No. 275, Phillips, Holyoke, 24 Mar 1916

Masons

Ancient Free & Accepted Masons
Spar, No. 81, Phillips, Holyoke, 16 Sept 1890
Holyoke, No. 164, Phillips, Haxtun, 16 Sept 1925

Royal Arch Masons
None

Knights Templar
None

Eastern Star
Holyoke, No. 105, Phillips, Holyoke
Frida Wilson, No. 136, Phillips, Haxtun

Odd Fellows
Holyoke, No. 76, Phillips, Holyoke
Haxtun, No. 159, Phillips, Haxtun

Rebekahs
Neri, No. 122, Phillips, Haxtun

Knights of Pythias
Crescent, No. 38, Phillips, Holyoke

Pythian Sisters
Progressive, No. 66, Phillips, Holyoke

Benevolent Protective Order of Elks
None

City & Town Halls

Holyoke, 407 E Denver St, Holyoke, CO 80734, 970-854-2266, http://www.cityof-holyoke-co.gov
Haxtun, 145 S Colorado Ave, Haxtun, CO 80731, 970-774-6104

Phillips County

Archives & Manuscript Collections
None

Historical & Genealogical Societies
Phillips County Historical Society, Phillips County Museum, 109 S Campbell Ave, Holyoke, CO 80734-1501, (970) 854-2129, http://phillipscountymuseum.com

Local Libraries
Heginbotham Library, 539 S Baxter St, Holyoke, CO 80734, (970) 854-2597

Links
CO GenWeb
http://cogenweb.com/phillips/

Cyndi's List
https://www.cyndislist.com/us/co/counties/phillips/

FamilySearch Wiki
https://www.familysearch.org/wiki/en/Phillips_County,_Colorado_Genealogy

Linkpendium
http://www.linkpendium.com/phillips-co-genealogy/

RootsWeb Wiki
https://wiki.rootsweb.com/wiki/index.php/Phillips_County,_Colorado

Wikipedia
https://en.wikipedia.org/wiki/Phillips_County,_Colorado

Historic Hotels
None

Museums & Historic Sites
Phillips County Historical Society, Phillips County Museum, 109 S Campbell Ave, Holyoke, CO 80734-1501, (970) 854-2129, http://phillipscountymuseum.com

Special Events & Scenic Locations
The Phillips County Fair is held in July most years at the Phillips County Fairgrounds, 22505 Hwy 385, Holyoke, CO 80734, 970-854-3616, https://www.phillipscofair.com

Phillips County maintains a calendar of events here: https://www.colorado.gov/pacific/phillipscountyed/activites-and-events

The Holyoke Chamber of Commerce has a calendar of events here: http://www.holyokechamber.org/home/events

Ghost Towns & Other Sparsely Populated Places
Amherst, Bryant, Emerson, Paoli, Wakeman

Historical Assets Colorado

Newspapers
Logan County News. (Holyoke, Logan County, Colo.) 1887-1???
The State Herald. (Holyoke, Logan County, Colo.) 1887-1921
Holyoke Tribune. (Holyoke, Colo.) 1887-1???
Phillips County Republican. (Holyoke, Colo.) 1901-1910
Holyoke Enterprise formerly Phillips County Republican. (Holyoke, Colo.) 1911-1913
The Haxtun Herald. (Haxtun, Colo.) 1911-19??
The Holyoke Enterprise. (Holyoke, Colo.) 1913-19??
The Haxtun Harvest. (Haxtun, Colo.) 1919-1975
Phillips County Herald. (Holyoke, Colo.) 1921-1927
The Haxtun Herald. (Haxtun, Colo.) 1975-Current

Places on the National Register
Haxtun, Evergreen Corner Rural Historic District, Jct. of Cty. Rds. 30 & 17
Haxtun, First National Bank of Haxtun, 145 S. Colorado Ave.
Haxtun, Shirley Hotel, 101 S. Colorado Ave.
Holyoke, Hargreaves Homestead Rural Historic District, US 385 between Cty. Rds. 10 & 12
Holyoke, Heginbotham, W. E., House, 539 S. Baxter
Holyoke, Millage Farm Rural Historic District, Cty. Rd. 18 between Cty. Rd. 37 & US 385
Holyoke, Phillips County Courthouse, 221 Interocean Ave.
Holyoke, Reimer—Smith Oil Station, 109 S. Campbell Ave

USGS Historic Places
None

Grand Army of the Republic Posts
Holyoke, No. 51, Phillips, Holyoke

USGS Historic Military Places
None

Military Bases
None

Post Offices
Amherst	1888 Feb 18		80721
Armstrong	1911 Oct 30	1917 June 15	
Bryant	1888 Mar 27	1916 Mar 31	
Emerson	1888 Mar 27	1890 Sept 20	
Haxtun	1888 Apr 25	1922 Jan 17	
Haxtun	1922 Jan 17		80731
Holyoke	1887 Nov 9		80734
Paoli	1888 June 8	1890 Feb 11	

Phillips County

Paoli 2	1910 Mar 9		80746
Starr	1907 Feb 21	1907 June 11	
Wakeman	1887 Sept 19	1897 May 15	
Westplains	1910 May 23	1949 Feb 15	
Willard	1888 Sept 26	1967 July 14*	
Winston	1902 May 18	1918 Dec 31*	

Topo Quads

Alvin NW	403000N	402230N	1020730W	1021500W
Amherst SW	403730N	403000N	1020730W	1021500W
Clarkville NE	403000N	402230N	1023000W	1023730W
Fiddler Peak	403000N	402230N	1022230W	1023000W
Haxtun SE	403730N	403000N	1023000W	1023730W
Holyoke	403730N	403000N	1021500W	1022230W
Paoli	403730N	403000N	1022230W	1023000W
Wauneta NE	403000N	402230N	1021500W	1022230W

Suggested Reading

Gray, Jean. *Homesteading Haxtun and the High Plains: Northeastern Colorado History*. Charleston, SC: The History Press, 2013.

Inventory of the County Archives of Colorado, No. 48, Phillips County (Holyoke). Denver: Historical Records Survey, 1941.

Those Were the Days ... Reminiscences of Early Days by Early Settlers. Holyoke, CO: Phillips County Historical Society, 1973.

Historical Assets Colorado

Pitkin County

Introduction

Established: 1881 Population: 17,148

Formed from: Gunnison

Adjacent Counties: Eagle, Lake, Chaffee, Gunnison, Mesa, Garfield

County Seat: Aspen

Other Communities: Basalt, Snowmass Village, Norrie, Redstone, Woody Creek, Ashcroft, Buttermilk, Meredith, Snowmass

Website, https://www.pitkincounty.com

Area Codes: 970

Zip Codes: 80611, 80612, 80615, 80642, 80654, 80656

Historical Assets Colorado

Pitkin County Courthouse

Courthouses & County Government

Pitkin County
https://www.pitkincounty.com
Pitkin County Courthouse (9th Judicial District), 530 E Main St, Aspen, CO 81611, 970-925-7635; http://www.courts.state.co.us/Courts/County/Index.cfm?County_ID=25
Assessor, 530 E Main St, Aspen, CO 81611, 970-920-5160; http://www.aspenpitkin.com/Departments/Assessor
Board of County Commissioners, 530 E Main St, Aspen, CO 81661, 970-9200-5200, https://pitkincounty.com/342/Board-of-County-Commissioners
Clerk & Recorder, 530 E Main St, Aspen, CO 81611, 970-920-5180; http://www.aspenpitkin.com/Departments/Clerk-Recorder/
Coroner & Medical Examiner, 506 E Main St, Aspen, CO 81611, 970-920-5310; https://www.pitkincounty.com/899/Coroner
Elections, 530 E Main St, Ste 104, Aspen, CO 81611, 970-429-2732; https://www.pitkinvotes.com/
Public Health, 405 Castle Creek Rd, Ste 6, Aspen, CO 81611, 970-920-5420; http://www.aspencommunityhealth.org/
Transportation (Public Works), 76 Service Center Rd, Aspen, CO 81611, 970-920-5390; https://www.pitkincounty.com/304/Public-Works
Treasurer, 506 E Main St, Ste 201, Aspen, CO 81611, 970-920-5170; http://www.pitkinassessor.org/Treasurer/

County Records

Birth Unk	Marriage 1890	Divorce Unk
Death Unk	Land 1890	Probate Unk
Court Unk		

Pitkin County

County & Municipal Records Held at the State Level

The Colorado State Archives

Physical Records
Assessor
Clerk & Recorder
County Court
District Court
Justice Court
Treasurer
WPA Historical Records
WPA Religious Institutions
 Survey
Cities
 Aspen

Records on Film
Clerk & Recorder
Cities
 Aspen

Records on Master Film
Clerk & Recorder
County Commissioners
County Court
District Court
Combined Courts
Planning
Public Trustee
School Districts
Sheriff
Treasurer
Cities
 Aspen
 Snowmass Village

The Denver Public Library

Hope Mining, Milling & Leasing Company Records, 1912-1922
Pitkin County Mining Companies Records, 1880
WWI Draft Registration Cards (microfilm)

School Districts

School Districts, http://www.adcogov.org/local-school-districts
Aspen School District 1, 235 High School Rd, Aspen, CO 81611, 970-925-3760; https://www.aspenk12.net/
Roaring Fork School District RE-1, 400 Sopris Ave, Carbondale, CO 81623, 970-384-6000; http://www.rfsd.k12.co.us/

Historic School Districts

1. Washington
2. Castle View
3. Emma
4. [1887]
5. Woody Creek
6. Lower Capitol Creek
7. Rock Creek
8. [1890]
9. Redstone
10. Spring Gulch
11. Thomasville
12. Owl Creek
13. Brush Creek
14. West Sopris
15. Oak Grove
16. [1895]
17. Upper Snowmass

J1. Basalt Joint One
J5. [1890]

Fraternal Organizations

Granges
Mt Sopris, No. 239, Pitkin, Snowmass, 13 Mar 1915

Masons

Ancient Free & Accepted Masons
Hiram, No. 60, Pitkin, Aspen, 17 Sept 1884
East Gate, No. 98, Pitkin, Aspen, 18 Sept 1895

Royal Arch Masons
Keystone, No. 19, Pitkin, Aspen

Historical Assets Colorado

Knights Templar
Aspen Mountain Commandery, No. 14, Pitkin, Aspen, 1886 July 18

Eastern Star
Mizpah, No. 22, Pitkin, Aspen

Odd Fellows
Aspen, No. 59, Pitkin, Aspen
Mount Basalt, No. 83, Pitkin, Basalt
Silver City, No. 92, Pitkin, Aspen

Rebekahs
None

Knights of Pythias
Roaring Fork, No. 40, Pitkin, Aspen

Pythian Sisters
Calla Lily, No. 9, Pitkin, Basalt
Primrose, No. 16, Pitkin, Aspen

Benevolent Protective Order of Elks
Aspen, No. 224, Pitkin, Aspen

City & Town Halls

Aspen, 130 S Galena St, Aspen, CO 81611, 970-920-5000, https://www.cityofaspen.com
Basalt, 101 Midland Ave, Basalt, CO 81621, 970-927-4701, https://www.basalt.net
Snowmass Village, 130 Kearns Rd, Snowmass Village, Co 81615, 970-923-3777, https://www.tosv.com

Archives & Manuscript Collections

Aspen Historical Society Archives, Wheeler Stallard House Museum, 620 W Bleeker St, Aspen, CO 81611, (970) 925-3721, http://www.aspenhistory.org; http://www.aspenhistoricalsociety.com; https://archiveaspen.org

Historical & Genealogical Societies

Aspen Historical Society, Wheeler Stallard House Museum, 620 W Bleeker St, Aspen, CO 81611, (970) 925-3721, http://www.aspenhistory.org; http://www.aspenhistoricalsociety.com; https://archiveaspen.org

Local Libraries

Pitkin County Library, 120 N Mill St, Aspen, CO 81611, (970) 429-1900, http://www.pitcolib.org

Links

CO GenWeb
http://cogenweb.com/pitkin/

Cyndi's List
https://www.cyndislist.com/us/co/counties/pitkin/

Pitkin County

FamilySearch Wiki
https://www.familysearch.org/wiki/en/Pitkin_County,_Colorado_Genealogy

Linkpendium
http://www.linkpendium.com/pitkin-co-genealogy/

RootsWeb Wiki
https://wiki.rootsweb.com/wiki/index.php/Pitkin_County,_Colorado

Wikipedia
https://en.wikipedia.org/wiki/Pitkin_County,_Colorado

Historic Hotels

1889 Hotel Jerome, 330 E Main St, Aspen, CO 81611, 970-429-5028, https://aubergeresorts.com/hoteljerome/

Museums & Historic Sites

Aspen Historical Society, Wheeler Stallard House Museum, 620 W Bleeker St, Aspen, CO 81611, (970) 925-3721, http://www.aspenhistory.org; http://www.aspenhistoricalsociety.com; https://archiveaspen.org

Holden Marolt Mining & Ranching Museum, 40180 Hwy 82, Aspen, CO 81611, (970) 925-3721, https://aspenhistory.org

Special Events & Scenic Locations

The Snowmass Rodeo is held during the summer at the Snowmass Rodeo Arena, 2735 Brush Creek Rd, Snowmass Village, CO 81615, 970-923-8898, https://www.snowmassrodeo.org

There is a calendar of Aspen Fairs & Festivals here: https://www.colorado.com/co/aspen/festivals-events/fairfestival

White River National Forest
Collegiate Peaks Wilderness
Holy Cross Wilderness
Hunter-Fryingpan Wilderness
Maroon Bells-Snowmass Wilderness
American Discovery Trail
Continental Divide National Scenic Trail
West Elk Loop Scenic Byway

Ghost Towns & Other Sparsely Populated Places

Ashcroft, Concentrator, Douglass City, Emma, Hagerman, Independence, Ivanhoe, Janeway, Jerome Park, Lenado, Lime Creek, Massive City, Miller Creek, Nast, Norrie, Rathbone, Redstone, Ruby, Sellar, Sparkill, Spring Gulch, Tourtelotte, Tunnel Spur, Watson, Woody Creek

Newspapers

Aspen Daily Democrat. (Aspen, Colo.) 188?-????
Ashcroft Herald. (Ashcroft, Colo.) 1880-1???

Historical Assets Colorado

Rocky Mountain Sun. (Aspen, Colo.) 1881-1903
The Aspen Times. (Aspen, Colo.) 1881-1885
The Aspen Weekly Press. (Aspen, Colo.) 1883-18??
The Aspen Daily Press. (Aspen, Colo.) 1885-????
Aspen Democrat. (Aspen, Colo.) 1885-1???
Aspen Daily Times. (Aspen, Colo.) 1885-1909
The Aspen Weekly Times. (Aspen, Colo.) 1885-1???
The Aspen Evening Chronicle. (Aspen, Colo.) 1888-1888
The Aspen Chronicle. (Aspen, Colo.) 1888-1888
The Aspen Morning Chronicle. (Aspen, Colo.) 1888-1889
The Daily Chronicle. (Aspen, Colo.) 1889-1893
Aspen Weekly Chronicle. (Aspen, Colo.) 1889-1???
The Aspen Union Era. (Aspen, Colo.) 1891-1892
Aspen Daily Leader. (Aspen, Colo.) 1892-18??
The Aspen Morning Sun. (Aspen, Pitkin County, Colo.) 1895-1895
The Aspen Tribune. (Aspen, Pitkin County, Colo.) 1895-1901
The Bryan Democrat. (Aspen, Colo.) 1897-1897
The Aspen Democrat. (Aspen, Colo.) 1900-1909
Aspen Daily News. (Aspen, Colo.) 19??-Current
The Aspen Democrat-Times. (Aspen, Pitkin County, Colo.) 1909-1926
The Aspen Daily Times. (Aspen, Pitkin County, Colo.) 1926-1926
The Aspen Times. (Aspen, Pitkin County, Colo.) 1927-Current
The Aspen Flyer. ([Aspen, Colo.]) 1959-????
Aspen Illustrated News. (Aspen, Colo.) 1964-1970
The Snowmass Villager. (Aspen, Colo.) 1967-19??
Aspen Today. (Aspen, Colo.) 1971-19??
Snowmass Sun. (Snowmass Village, Colo.) 1979-Current

Places on the National Register

Aspen, Armory Hall, Fraternal Hall, 130 S. Galena St.
Aspen, Ashcroft, Colorado, 12 mi. S of Aspen in White River National Forest
Aspen, Aspen Community Church, 200 N. Aspen St.
Aspen, Boat Tow, 700 S. Aspen St.
Aspen, Bowles—Cooley House, 201 W. Francis St.
Aspen, Callahan, Matthew, Log Cabin, 205 S. Third St.
Aspen, Collins Block—Aspen Lumber and Supply, 204 S. Mill St.
Aspen, Dixon—Markle House, 135 E. Cooper Ave.
Aspen, Frantz, D. E., House, 333 W. Bleeker St.
Aspen, Hallett, Samuel I., House, 432 W. Francis St.
Aspen, Holden Mining and Smelting Co., 1000 Block W. Hwy. 82
Aspen, Hotel Jerome, 330 E. Main St.
Aspen, Hyman-Brand Building, 203 S. Galena St.
Aspen, Hynes, Thomas, House, 303 E. Main St.
Aspen, La Fave Block, 405 S. Hunter St.
Aspen, Maroon Creek Bridge, CO 82
Aspen, New Brick—The Brick Saloon, 420 E. Cooper Ave.

Pitkin County

Aspen, Newberry House, 206 Lake Ave.
Aspen, Pitkin County Courthouse, 506 E. Main St.
Aspen, Riede's City Bakery, 413 E. Hyman Ave.
Aspen, Sheely Bridge, Mill Street Park
Aspen, Shilling—Lamb House, 525 N. Fifth St.
Aspen, Smith—Elisha House, 320 W. Main St.
Aspen, Smuggler Mine, Smuggler Mountain
Aspen, Ute Cemetery, Ute Ave.
Aspen, Waite, Davis, House, 234 W. Francis St.
Aspen, Webber, Henry, House—Pioneer Park, 442 W. Bleeker St.
Aspen, Wheeler Opera House, 330 E. Hyman Ave.
Aspen, Wheeler-Stallard House, 620 W. Bleeker St.
Ghost Town, Independence and Independence Mill Site, On CO 82, in White River National Forest
Redstone, Osgood Castle, About 1 mi. S of Redstone on CO 133
Redstone, Osgood Gamekeeper's Lodge, 18679 CO 133
Redstone, Osgood-Kuhnhausen House, 0642 Redstone Blvd.
Redstone, Redstone Coke Oven Historic District, CO 133 and Chair Mountain Stables Rd.
Redstone, Redstone Historic District, Roughly along the Crystal River from Hawk Creek to 226 Redstone Blvd.
Redstone, Redstone Inn, 0082 Redstone Blvd.

USGS Historic Places

Independence Pass, Independence, 39.1072124, -106.6058652
Independence Pass, Ruby, 39.0208251, -106.6091984
Meredith, Meredith Post Office, 39.3630413, -106.7300359
Unknown, Coalbasin Post Office, 0, 0
Unknown, Columbine Post Office, 0, 0

Grand Army of the Republic Posts

Winfield Scott, No. 49, Pitkin, Aspen
Aspen, No. 87, Pitkin, Aspen
Roaring Fork, No. 113, Pitkin, Aspen

USGS Historic Military Places

None

Military Bases

None

Post Offices

Ashcroft	1880 Aug 12	1912 Nov 30*	
Aspen	1880 June 7		81611
Aspen-Gerbaz	1967 Dec 4		

Historical Assets Colorado

Calcium	1888 Mar 10	1890 Mar 31	
Carey	1883 Aug 21	1884 Jan 7	
Chipeta	1899 Apr 20	1899 Oct 17	
Chloride	1881 Aug 5	1882 Jan 3	
Coalbasin	1901 Dec 14	1909 Sept 15	
Davies	1895 Jan 7	1895 Oct 11	
Emma	1883 Nov 23	1949 May 31*	
Farwell	1881 July 14	1882 July 3	
Gerbazdale	1918 June 14	1918 Aug 10	
Gulch	1895 Apr 19	1916 Dec 15	
Ivanhoe	1888 Apr 26	1918 Aug 10*	
Janeway	1887 Aug 16	1900 Nov 30	
Lenado	1891 Feb 4	1907 Jan 2*	
Meredith	1893 Jan 25		81642
Nast	1909 May 4	1918 Aug 10	
Norrie	1894 Nov 16	1918 Aug 10*	
Placita	1899 Oct 25	1934 Oct 31	
Redstone	1898 May 19	1962 Aug 1*	
Satank	1882 June 27	1904 July 14	
Sellar	1888 Apr 12	1918 Aug 10*	
Sidney	1881 Jan 4	1887 Mar 20	
Snowmass	1901 Feb 19	1914 Jan 31	
Snowmass 2	1914 Apr 8		81654
Sparkill	1882 Feb 1	1887 Oct 18	
Spring Gulch	1891 Sept 10	1895 Apr 19	
Thomasville	1890 Mar 31	1918 Aug 10	
Tourtelotte	1889 Mar 19	1894 Nov 5	
Watson	1889 May 31	1918 June 14	
Woody Creek	1920 Sept 4		81656

Topo Quads

Aspen	391500N	390730N	1064500W	1065230W
Capitol Peak	391500N	390730N	1070000W	1070730W
Chair Mountain	390730N	390000N	1071500W	1072230W
Gothic	390000N	385230N	1065230W	1070000W
Hayden Peak	390730N	390000N	1064500W	1065230W
Highland Peak	391500N	390730N	1065230W	1070000W
Marble	390730N	390000N	1070730W	1071500W
Maroon Bells	390730N	390000N	1065230W	1070000W
New York Peak	390730N	390000N	1063730W	1064500W
Pearl Pass	390000N	385230N	1064500W	1065230W
Pieplant	390000N	385230N	1063000W	1063730W
Placita	391500N	390730N	1071500W	1072230W
Redstone	391500N	390730N	1070730W	1071500W
Snowmass Mountain	390730N	390000N	1070000W	1070730W
Thimble Rock	391500N	390730N	1063730W	1064500W

Pitkin County

Suggested Reading

Aldrich, John K. *Ghosts of Pitkin County: a Guide to the Ghost Towns and Mining Camps of Pitkin and Northern Gunnison Counties, Colorado.* Lakewood, CO: Centennial Graphics, 1992.

Arkell, MacMillan & Stewart. *Aspen, Pitkin County, Colorado: Her Mines and Mineral Resources.* Aspen, CO: Aspen Daily Leader, 1892.

Gates, Lisle J. *Redstone, Colorado: the Impossible Dream.* Gunnison, CO: NP, 1969.

Hart, Charles D. *History of Capitol & Snowmass Creeks.* NL: NP, 1999.

Knoll, Charlene Kay. *Memories Worth Saving: the Story of Ashcroft, Colorado.* Thesis, Western State College of Colorado, 1977.

Lansdowne, James Edward. *A Pioneer History of Aspen, Colorado.* Thesis, Wichita State University, 1948.

Rohrbough, Malcolm J. *Aspen, Colorado: the History of a Silver Mining Town, 1879-1893.* New York: Oxford University Press, 1986.

Historical Assets Colorado

Prowers County

Introduction

Established: 1889   Population: 12,551

Formed from: Bent

Adjacent Counties: Kiowa, Baca, Bent

County Seat: Lamar

   Other Communities: Granada, Hartman, Holly, Wiley, Bristol

Website, https://www.prowerscounty.net

Area Codes: 719

Zip Codes: 81401, 81043, 81047, 81052, 81092

Historical Assets Colorado

Prowers County Courthouse

Prowers County 19th Century Courthouse

Courthouses & County Government

Prowers County
   https://www.prowerscounty.net
Prowers County Courthouse (15th Judicial District), 301 S Main St, Lamar, CO 81052, 719-336-7424; http://www.courts.state.co.us/Courts/County/Index.cfm?County_ID=51
Assessor, 301 S Main St, Lamar, CO 81052, 719-336-8000; http://www.prowerscounty.net/
Board of County Commissioners, 301 S Main St, Lamar, CO 81052, 719-336-8025, https://www.prowerscounty.net/government/administration/commissioners/index.php
Clerk & Recorder, 301 S Main St, Lamar, CO 81052, 719-336-5306; http://www.prowerscounty.net/
Coroner, 223 S Main St, Lamar, CO 81052, 719-336-4917; https://www.prowerscounty.net/government/coroner/index.php
Elections, 301 S Main, Ste 210, Lamar, CO 81052, 719-336-8011; https://www.prowerscounty.net/departments/elections.php
Public Health, 1001 S Main St, Lamar, CO 81052, 719-336-8721; http://www.prowerscounty.net/
Transportation (Road & Bridge), 109 E Sherman, Lamar, CO 81052, 719-336-5536; https://www.prowerscounty.net/departments/road_and_bridge/index.php
Treasurer, 301 S Main St, Ste 200, Lamar, CO 81052, 719-336-8081; http://www.prowerscounty.net/

County Records

Birth 1908	Marriage 1889	Divorce 1889
Death 1908	Land 1889	Probate 1889
Court 1889		

Prowers County

County & Municipal Records Held at the State Level

The Colorado State Archives

Physical Records
Clerk & Recorder
County Court
District Court
WPA Historical Records
WPA Religious Institutions Survey
WPA Lamar
Cities
Lamar

Records on Film
District Court

Records on Master Film
County Court
District Court
School Districts

The Denver Public Library
WPA Historical Records Survey
WWI Draft Registration Cards (microfilm)

School Districts

School Districts, http://www.adcogov.org/local-school-districts
Granada School District RE-1, 201 S Hoisington Ave, Granada, CO 81041, 719-734-5492; https://www.granadaschools.org/
Holly School District RE-3, 206 N 3rd, Holly, CO 81047, 719-537-6616; http://www.hollyschool.org/
Lamar School District RE-2, 210 W Pearl St, Lamar, CO 81052; https://sites.google.com/lamarschools.org/district/home
Wiley School District RE-13 JT, 510 W Ward St, Wiley, CO 81092, 719-829-4806; http://www.wileyschool.org/

Historic School Districts

1. Liberty
2. Hopewell
3. May Valley
4. South Webb
5. Pleasant Heights, Mountain View
6. Holly
7. Sand Creek, Pleasant Valley
8. Granada, Koen
9. Carlton
10. North Webb
11. Upper Dry Creek
12. Clay Creek
13. Wiley
14. Lamar
15. Paradox
16. Cactus View
17. Riley
18. Plum Creek
19. Columbine
20. Webb
21. Progressive
22. Clearview
23. Clover Meadow
24. Alta Vista
25. East Riverview [Joint with Bent]
26. Sunny Slope, Mt Zion, High Plains
27. Channing
28. [1900]
29. Lone Star
30. Valley Center
31. Western Bell
32. [1900]
33. Dry Creek
34. Roosevelt
35. Bristol
36. Goodale
37. [1902]
38. Lakeview
39. Victory
40. Ridgeview
41. Hartman
42. Ridge View, Coulson
43. Plainview
44. Enterprise
45. Amerine
46. Star
47. Eagle Hill
48. Independence
49. Barrel Springs
50. Prairie Queen
51. Plains
53. Union
54. Bell
55. Butte Ridge, Two Buttes

Historical Assets Colorado

Fraternal Organizations
Granges
Liberty, No. 93, Prowers, Lamar, 3 Feb 1890
Pleasant Valley, No. 138, Prowers, Lamar, 20 Mar 1899
Sunflower, No. 139, Prowers, Lamar, 20 Mar 1899
Fair View, No. 141, Prowers, Lamar, 5 Mar 1900
Amityville, No. 143, Prowers, Holly, 31 Dec 1900
Pleasant Valley, No. 229, Prowers, Lamar, 4 Sept 1914
Big Bend, No. 234, Prowers, Wiley, 9 Feb 1915
Dry Creek, No. 242, Prowers, Lamar, 10 Mar 1915
May Valley, No. 251, Prowers, Lamar, 28 May 1915
Enterprise, No. 258, Prowers, Holly, 14 Sept 1915
Booster, No. 303, Prowers, Webb, 27 Sept 1916
Valley Center, No. 304, Prowers, Holly, 29 Sept 1916
Plum Valley, No. 328, Prowers, Granada, 10 Mar 1917
Bell, No. 330, Prowers, Plains, 26 Mar 1917
Prairie Queen, No. 332, Prowers, Holly, 18 Mar 1917
West River View, No. 345, Prowers, Lamar, 21 May 1917

Masons
Ancient Free & Accepted Masons
Lamar, No. 72, Prowers, Granada, 18 Sept 1888
Pueblo, No. 90, Prowers, Lamar, 20 Sept 1892
Granada, No. 113, Prowers, Holly, 17 Sept 1901

Royal Arch Masons
Orient, No. 32, Prowers, Lamar

Knights Templar
Malta Commandery, No. 32, Prowers, Lamar, 1912 Apr 30

Eastern Star
Holly, No. 50, Prowers, Holly
Lamar, No. 112, Prowers, Lamar

Odd Fellows
Granada, No. 78, Prowers, Granada
Lamar, No. 80, Prowers, Lamar
Holly, No. 144, Prowers, Holly
Wiley, No. 155, Prowers, Wiley
Hartman, No. 165, Prowers, Hartman

Rebekahs
Lamar, No. 55, Prowers, Lamar
Mizpah, No. 97, Prowers, Holly

Knights of Pythias
Holly, No. 117, Prowers, Holly
Lamar, No. 125, Prowers, Lamar

Pythian Sisters
Lily of the Valley, No. 47, Prowers, Holly

Prowers County

Benevolent Protective Order of Elks
Lamar, No. 1319, Prowers, Lamar

City & Town Halls
Lamar, 102 E Parmenter St, Lamar, CO 81052, 719-336-4376, https://www.ci.lamar.co.us
Granada, 103 S Main St, Granada, Co 81041, 719-734-5411, https://www.facebook.com/pages/category/Government-Organization/Town-Of-Granada-1272433709519327/
Holly, 100 Tony Garcia Dr, Holly, CO 81047, 719-537-6622, http://www.townofholly.com
Wiley, 304 Main St, Wiley, CO 81092, 719-829-4974, http://www.townofwiley.com

Archives & Manuscript Collections
None

Historical & Genealogical Societies
Prowers County Genealogical Society, 407 E Olive St, Lamar, CO 81052, (719) 336-4072, https://prowerscountygenealogicalsociety.weebly.com
Prowers County Historical Society, Big Timbers Museum, 7515 US Hwy 50, P.O. Box 362, Lamar, CO 81052, (719) 336-2472, http://www.bigtimbersmuseum.org

Local Libraries
Lamar Public Library, 104 E Parmenter St, Lamar, CO 81052-3239, (719) 336-4632, https://lamarlibrary.colibraries.org
Lamar Community College Library, Bowman Bldg, 2401 S Main St, Lamar, CO 81052-3999, (719) 336-1540, https://www.lamarcc.edu/academics/library/

Links
CO GenWeb
http://cogenweb.com/prowers/

Cyndi's List
https://www.cyndislist.com/us/co/counties/prowers/

FamilySearch Wiki
https://www.familysearch.org/wiki/en/Prowers_County,_Colorado_Genealogy

Linkpendium
http://www.linkpendium.com/prowers-co-genealogy/

RootsWeb Wiki
https://wiki.rootsweb.com/wiki/index.php/Prowers_County,_Colorado

Wikipedia
https://en.wikipedia.org/wiki/Prowers_County,_Colorado

Historic Hotels
None

Historical Assets Colorado

Museums & Historic Sites

Amache Museum, 109 E Goff Ave, Granada, CO 81041, (719) 734-5411, https://amache.org/amache-museum/

Prowers County Historical Society, Big Timbers Museum, 7515 US Hwy 50, P.O. Box 362, Lamar, CO 81052, (719) 336-2472, http://www.bigtimbersmuseum.org

Special Events & Scenic Locations

The Prowers Sand & Sage Roundup is held in Augst most years at the Prowers County Fairgrounds, 2206 Saddle Club Dr, Lamar, CO 81052, https://www.sandandsageroundup.com

The Holly Gateway Fair is held in September most years, https://www.facebook.com/hollycofair/

The local newspaper, The Prowers Journal, keeps a community calendar here: https://theprowersjournal.com/calendar/

American Discovery Trail
Santa Fe Trail National Scenic Byway
Granada Relocation Center National Historic District
Camp Amache WWII Internment Camp

Ghost Towns & Other Sparsely Populated Places

Adana, Albany, Amache, Ayr, Carlton, Granada, Hartman, Mulvane, State Line, Swift, Wilde, Zuck

Newspapers

The Lamar Daily News. (Lamar, Colo.) 1907-1961
The Sentinel. (Granada, Colo.) 1888-????
Arkansas Valley Call. (Holly, Colo.) 1909-????
The Granada Times. (Granada, Colo.) 1898-19??
The Holly Chieftain. (Holly, Colo.) 1897-1987
The Lamar Sparks. (Lamar, Prowers County, Colo.) 18??-19??
The Lamar Daily Register. (Lamar, Colo.) 1908-19??
The Lamar-Tri-State Daily News. (Lamar, Colo.) 1961-1982
The Lamar Daily News. (Lamar, Colo.) 1982-1987
The Lamar Daily News and Holly Chieftain. (Lamar, Colo.) 1987-Current
Wiley's New Baby. (Wiley, Colo.) 1940-1940
The Wiley Booster. (Wiley, Colo.) 1940-19??
The Granada Journal. (Granada, Colo.) 19??-19??
The Daily Sparks. (Lamar, Prowers County, Colo.) 19??-19??
Lamar Leader. (Lamar, Bent County, Colo.) 1886-1???
The Prowers County News. (Lamar, Colo.) 1901-1920
Amache Hi It. (None) 1943-1943
Bulletin. (Granada, Colo.) 1942-1942 | Languages: English, Japanese
Granada Pioneer. (Amache, Colo.) 1942-1945 | Languages: English, Japanese

Prowers County

The Lamar Register. (Lamar, Colo.) 1889-1952
Bent County Register. (Lamar, Colo.) 1886-1889

Places on the National Register
Granada, Douglas Crossing Bridge, Cty. Rd. 28
Granada, Granada Bridge, US 385 at milepost 97.32
Granada, Granada Relocation Ctr, 23900 Co. Rd. FF, Approx. 1 mi. SW of Granada
Holly, Holly City Hall, 119 E. Cheyenne St.
Holly, Holly Gymnasium, N. Main St.
Holly, Holly Santa Fe Depot, 302 S. Main St.
Holly, Holly SS Ranch Barn, 407 West Vinson
Lamar, Davies Hotel, 122 N. Main
Lamar, Paulsen Farm, 39035 Rd. 7
Lamar, Petticrew Stage Stop, Address Restricted
Lamar, Prowers Country Welfare Housing, 800 E. Maple St.
Lamar, Prowers County Building, 301 S. Main St.
Lamar, US Post Office—Lamar Main, 300 S. Fifth St.
Lamar, Willow Creek Park, Roughly bounded by Memorial Dr., Parkview Ave., Willow Balley Rd.
Wiley, Wiley Rock Schoolhouse, 603 Main St.

USGS Historic Places
Cat Creek, Springfield Landing Strip, 37.7536202, -102.7449193
Granada, Granada Relocation Center, 38.0486203, -102.3282454

Grand Army of the Republic Posts
Proctor, No. 43, Prowers, Grenada
Kit Carson, No. 59, Prowers, Lamar

USGS Historic Military Places
None

Military Bases
None

Post Offices
Albany	1887 July 21	1905 Sept 30*	
Amity	1898 July 18	1937 Feb 27	
Ayr	1888 July 25	1893 Sept 4	
Barton	1895 Mar 29	1917 Oct 15	
Bristol	1908 July 1		81028
Carlton	1891 Jan 14	1960 Mar 5	
Cheneycenter	1917 Feb 24	1936 June 30	
Duer	1916 Mar 25	1920 May 31	
Granada	1873 July 10		81041

Historical Assets Colorado

Hartman	1908 Mar 2		81043
Holly	1880 Nov 26		81047
Lamar	1886 July 16		81052
Martynia	1892 May 27	1893 July 25	
Mulvane	1888 June 8	1893 Feb 20	
Northway	1916 May 29	1919 Aug 30	
Plains	1908 Jan 11	1921 Mar 15*	
Rowe	1898 Nov 30	1900 Sept 29	
Toledo	1887 Apr 16	1889 Sept 16	
Verdun	1920 Feb 2	1920 June 15	
Webb	1910 May 31	1919 Nov 29	
Wilde	1887 Aug 6	1893 June 10	
Wiley	1907 Apr 22		81092
Zuck	1891 Dec 26	1895 Mar 20	

Topo Quads

Barrel Spring	375230N	374500N	1022230W	1023000W
Carlton	380730N	380000N	1022230W	1023000W
Cat Creek	375230N	374500N	1023730W	1024500W
Cat Creek NE	380000N	375230N	1023000W	1023730W
Cat Creek NW	380000N	375230N	1023730W	1024500W
Durkee Creek NW	380000N	375230N	1020730W	1021500W
Gobblers Knob	375230N	374500N	1023000W	1023730W
Granada	380730N	380000N	1021500W	1022230W
Granada NE	381500N	380730N	1021500W	1022230W
Granada NW	381500N	380730N	1022230W	1023000W
Hasser Ranch	374500N	373730N	1023730W	1024500W
Holly East	380730N	380000N	1020000W	1020730W
Holly NE	381500N	380730N	1020000W	1020730W
Holly NW	381500N	380730N	1020730W	1021500W
Holly West	380730N	380000N	1020730W	1021500W
Lamar East	380730N	380000N	1023000W	1023730W
Lamar West	380730N	380000N	1023730W	1024500W
May Valley	381500N	380730N	1023000W	1023730W
North Plum Creek NE	380000N	375230N	1021500W	1022230W
North Plum Creek NW	380000N	375230N	1022230W	1023000W
North Plum Creek SE	375230N	374500N	1021500W	1022230W
Plains Community	374500N	373730N	1021500W	1022230W
Two Butte Springs	375230N	374500N	1020730W	1021500W
Two Buttes NW	374500N	373730N	1022230W	1023000W
Two Buttes Reservoir	374500N	373730N	1023000W	1023730W

Prowers County

Webb	374500N	373730N	1020730W	1021500W
Wiley	381500N	380730N	1023730W	1024500W

Suggested Reading

Betz, Ava, Virginia Downing, Dixie Munro and Florence Dolsen. *A Prowers County History*. Lamar, CO: Prowers County Historical Society, 1986.

Inventory of the County Archives of Colorado, No. 50, Prowers County (Lamar). Denver: Historical Records Survey, 1939.

Millican, Valorie. *The Homestead Years: Prowers County, Colorado*. Pritchett, CO: V Millican, 1999.

Prowers County Centennial Bicentennial Committee. *Historical Sites: Prowers County, Colorado*. Holly, CO: Holly Publishing Co, 1976.

Prowers County, Colorado: the Home of the Prosperous and Contented Farmer. Denver: Williamson-Haffner Engraving Co, 1910.

Historical Assets Colorado

Pueblo County

Introduction

Established: 1861   Population: 159,063

Formed from: Original

Adjacent Counties: El Paso, Lincoln, Crowley, Otero, Las Animas, Huerfano, Custer, Fremont

County Seat: Pueblo

Other Cmmunities: Boone, Rye, Avondale, Beulah Valley, Blende, Colorado City, Pueblo West, Salt Creek, Vineland

Website, http://county.pueblo.org

Area Codes: 719

Zip Codes: 81001, 81002, 81003, 81004, 81005, 81006, 81007, 81008, 81009, 81010, 81011, 81012, 81019, 81022, 81023, 81025, 81069

Historical Assets Colorado

Pueblo County Courthouse

Courthouses & County Government

Pueblo County
   http://county.pueblo.org
Pueblo County Courthouse (10th Judicial District), 320 W 10th St, Pueblo, CO 81003, 719-583-7000; http://www.courts.state.co.us/Courts/County/Index.cfm?County_ID=27
Assessor, 215 W 10th St, Pueblo, CO 81003, 719-583-6597; http://county.pueblo.org/government/county/assessor
Board of County Commissioners, 215 W 10th St, Pueblo, CO 81003, 719-583-6537, https://county.pueblo.org/board-county-commissioners/board-county-commissioners
Clerk & Recorder, 215 W 10th St, Pueblo, CO 81003, 719-583-6507; http://county.pueblo.org/government/county/elected-office/clerk-and-recorder
Coroner, 480 Midtown Cr, Pueblo, CO 81003; http://county.pueblo.org/government/county/department/coroner/coroner
Public Health, 101 W 9th St, Pueblo, CO 81003, 719-583-4300; http://county.pueblo.org/government/county/pueblo-city-county-health
Transportation (Public Works), 33601 United Ave, Pueblo, CO 81001, 719-583-6040; http://county.pueblo.org/government/county/department/public-works/road-and-bridge
Treasurer, 215 W 10th St, Rm 110, Pueblo, CO 81003, 719-583-6015; http://county.pueblo.org/government/county/Treasurer

County Records

Birth 1887	Marriage 1865	Divorce 1876
Death 1887	Land 1865	Probate 1876
Court 1876		
CSA County Physicians Report 1883		
CSA Pauper Burials 1856		

Pueblo County

County & Municipal Records Held at the State Level

The Colorado State Archives

Physical Records
Clerk & Recorder
Coroner
County Commissioners
County Court
District Court
Sheriff
WPA Historical Records
WPA Religious Institutions
  Survey
WPA Pueblo
Cities
  Beulah
  Pueblo

Records on Film
Clerk & Recorder
District Court
Cities
  Pueblo

Records on Master Film
Clerk & Recorder
County Court
District Court
School Districts
Treasurer
Cities
  Pueblo

The Denver Public Library
Fremont & Pueblo County Mining Companies Records, 1894
WWI Draft Registration Cards (microfilm)

School Districts

School Districts, http://www.adcogov.org/local-school-districts
Edison School District No. 54 JT, 14550 Edison Rd, Yoder, CO 80864, 719-478-2125; https://www.edison54jt.org/
Fowler School District 4J, 600 W Eugene, Fowler, CO 81039, 719-263-4224; http://www.fowler.k12.co.us/
Pueblo City School District 60, 315 W 11th St, Pueblo, CO 81003, 719-549-7100; http://www.pueblocityschools.us/
Pueblo County School District 70, 301 28th St, Pueblo, CO 81001, 719-542-0220; https://www.district70.org/

Historic School Districts

1. City, District No. 1
2. Excelsior
3. Cedarwood
4. Pinon
5. Park, Fairview
6. Cedarview, Doyle
7. Hooker
8. Lime
9. Graneros
10. Abbey, Red Creek
11. Eden
12. Pleasant View
13. Rye
14. Beulah
15. North Creek
16. Swallows
17. Greenhorn Creek, Verde
18. Avondale
19. Baxter
20. City, District No. 20
21. [1883]
22. Whittier
23. Couzzen Springs
24. White Rock, Prairie View
25. Siloam
26. Hardin
27. Unity
28. Livesey, Lees, Rush Creek
29. Boone
30. Swallows, Carlile
31. Nicholson
32. Mountain View
33. [1883]
34. Kemah Lodge, Rock Creek
35. [1886]
36. Banner
37. Goodpasture, Cedar Grove

Historical Assets Colorado

38. Myrtle, Stone City
39. Sitton
40. Boone
41. Hamilton
42. [1889]
43. [1889]
44. Burnt Mill
45. Belle Plain
46. Overton
47. Lakeside Vineland
48. [1891]
49. Goodnight
50. Wilson
51. Undercliff
52. Napesta
53. Highlands, Prairie Hill, Lakeview
54. Drinkard-Emmert
56. Devine
57. K.Y.

Fraternal Organizations

Granges
Evergreen, No. 39, Pueblo, Mace's Hole, 21 Jan 1874
Greenwood Farm, No. 41, Pueblo, Greenwood, 23 Jan 1874
Unity, No. 45, Pueblo, Pueblo, 11 Feb 1874
Turkey Creek, No. 46, Pueblo, Pueblo, 19 Feb 1874
Wood Valley, No. 47, Pueblo, Pueblo, 28 Feb 1874
Greenhorn, No. 54, Pueblo, Muddy Creek, 20 Mar 1874
Green Valley, No. 68, Pueblo, Greenhorn, 30 Nov 1874
Gardiner, No. 69, Pueblo, Gardner, 7 Dec 1874
Orchard Park, No. 260, Pueblo, Pueblo, 18 Dec 1915
Pinon, No. 262, Pueblo, Pinon, 22 Jan 1916
Mountain View, No. 272, Pueblo, Boone, 22 Mar 1916
Unity, No. 316, Pueblo, Fowler, 6 Jan 1917
Nepesta, No. 329, Pueblo, Nepesta, 24 Mar 1917
Steel City, No. 491, Pueblo, Pueblo, 24 Jan 1960

Masons

Ancient Free & Accepted Masons
Greenhorn Valley, No. 17, Pueblo, Pueblo, 6 Oct 1868
Silver State, No. 31, Pueblo, Pueblo, 20 Sept 1876
Rangely, No. 95, Pueblo, Pueblo, 20 Sept 1893
South Pueblo, No. 196, Pueblo, Colorado City, 22 Jan 1983

Royal Arch Masons
Pueblo, No. 3, Pueblo, Pueblo
South Pueblo, No. 12, Pueblo, Pueblo
Euclid, No. 45, Pueblo, Colorado City

Knights Templar
Pueblo Commandery, No. 3, Pueblo, Pueblo, 1874 Aug 17

Eastern Star
Pueblo, No. 7, Pueblo, Pueblo
Pueblo, No. 9, Pueblo, Pueblo
Adah, No. 34, Pueblo, Pueblo

Prince Hall Masons
Ashby Lodge No. 2, Pueblo, Pueblo, before 1926
Eureka Lodge No. 2, Pueblo, Pueblo, 1967
Rising Sun Lodge No. 3, Pueblo, Pueblo, before 1926

Pueblo County

Prince Hall Order of the Eastern Star
  Star of Pueblo Chapter No. 5, Pueblo, Pueblo
  Bathsheba Chapter, No. 45, Pueblo, Pueblo

Odd Fellows
  Pueblo, No. 8, Pueblo, Pueblo, 1869 Jan 5
  Ark, No. 28, Pueblo, Pueblo
  Minnequa, No. 53, Pueblo, Bessemer
  Ark, No. 53, Pueblo, Pueblo
  Nolen, No. 114, Pueblo, Pueblo

Rebekahs
  Social Star, No. 2, Pueblo, Pueblo
  Silver Star, No. 2, Pueblo, Pueblo
  Cactus, No. 24, Pueblo, Pueblo

Knights of Pythias
  Pueblo, No. 15, Pueblo, Pueblo, 1881 Jan 26
  Ivanhoe, No. 24, Pueblo, Pueblo, 1883 May 20
  Triangle, No. 30, Pueblo, Pueblo, 1885 Nov 25
  Pueblo, No. 52, Pueblo, Pueblo
  Bessemer, No. 115, Pueblo, Pueblo

Pythian Sisters
  Most Worthy, No. 48, Pueblo, Pueblo
  Pueblo, No. 52, Pueblo, Pueblo

Benevolent Protective Order of Elks
  Pueblo, No. 90, Pueblo, Pueblo

City & Town Halls

Pueblo, 1 City Hall Pl, Pueblo, CO 81003, 719-533-2489, https://www.pueblo.us
Boone, 421 E 1st St, Boone, CO 81025, 719-947-3311
Rye, 2067 Main St, Rye, CO 81069, 719-489-2011, https://www.pueblo.us

Archives & Manuscript Collections

Robert Hoag Rawlings Library Special Collections, 100 E Abriendo Ave, Pueblo, CO 81004-4290, (719) 562-5601, http://www.pueblolibrary.org
Steelworks Center of the West and CF&I Archives, 215 Canal St, Pueblo, CO 81004, (719) 564-9086, http://www.steelworks.us
University Library Archives & Special Collections, CSU Pueblo, 2200 Bonforte Blvd, Pueblo, CO 81001-4901, (719) 549-2475, https://www.csupueblo.edu/library/archives/index.html
University of Southern Colorado Library, Special Collections, 2200 Bonforte Blvd, Pueblo, CO 81001-4901, (719) 549-2361, https://www.csupueblo.edu/library/archives/index.html

Historical & Genealogical Societies

Bessemer Historical Society, Steelworks Center of the West and CF&I Archives, 215 Canal St, Pueblo, CO 81004, (719) 564-9086, http://www.steelworks.us

Historical Assets Colorado

Beulah Historical Society, Beulah History Center, 8882 Grand Ave, P.O. Box 76, Beulah, CO 81023, (719) 485-3937, https://www.facebook.com/Beulah-Historical-Society-290678254398000/

Genealogical Society of Hispanic America, P.O. Box 81005, Pueblo, CO 81005, https://www.gshaa.org

Pueblo County Historical Society, Edward H Broadhead Library, 201 West B Street, Pueblo, CO 81003, (719) 543-6772, http://www.pueblohistory.org

Southeastern Colorado Genealogical Society, c/o Pueblo City County Library, 100 E Abriendo, P.O. Box 1407, Pueblo, CO 81002, (719) 564-7815, http://www.seco-gensoc.org

Local Libraries

Robert Hoag Rawlings Library, 100 E Abriendo Ave, Pueblo, CO 81004-4290, (719) 562-5601, http://www.pueblolibrary.org

Links

CO GenWeb
http://cogenweb.com/pueblo/

Cyndi's List
https://www.cyndislist.com/us/co/counties/pueblo/

FamilySearch Wiki
https://www.familysearch.org/wiki/en/Pueblo_County,_Colorado_Genealogy

Linkpendium
http://www.linkpendium.com/pueblo-co-genealogy/

RootsWeb Wiki
https://wiki.rootsweb.com/wiki/index.php/Pueblo_County,_Colorado

Wikipedia
https://en.wikipedia.org/wiki/Pueblo_County,_Colorado

Historic Hotels

None

Museums & Historic Sites

Beulah Historical Society, Beulah History Center, 8882 Grand Ave, P.O. Box 76, Beulah, CO 81023, (719) 485-3937, https://www.facebook.com/Beulah-Historical-Society-290678254398000/

Colorado Mental Health Institute at Pueblo Museum, 1600 W 24th St, Pueblo, CO 81005, (719) 543-2012, http://www.cmhipmuseum.org

Dr Martin Luther King Jr Cultural Center, 2713-15 N Grand Ave, Pueblo, CO 81005, (719) 253-1015, https://www.facebook.com/pages/Martin-Luther-King-Jr-Cultural-Center/397750423595038

El Pueblo History Museum, 301 N Union Ave, Pueblo, CO 81003, (719) 583-0453, https://www.historycolorado.org/el-pueblo-history-museum

Pueblo County

Hose Company No. 3 - Pueblo's Fire Museum, 116 Broadway Ave, Pueblo, CO 81004, (719) 553-2830, http://www.hosecono3.com

Infozone News Museum, 100 E Abriendo Ave, Pueblo, CO 81004, (719) 562-5604, http://www.infozonenewsmuseum.com

Pueblo Heritage Museum, 201 West B Street, Pueblo, CO 81003, (719) 295-1517, http://www.theheritagecenter.us

Pueblo Railway Museum, 132 West B Street, Pueblo, CO 81003, (719) 544-1773, http://www.puebloreilway.org

Pueblo Weisbrod Aircraft Museum, 31001 Magnuson Ave, Pueblo, CO 81001, (719) 748-9219, http://www.pwam.org

Rosemount Museum, 419 W 14th St, P.O. Box 5259, Pueblo, CO 81002, (719) 545-5290, http://www.rosemount.org

Slovenian Genealogy Center-Gornick Library & Museum, Saint Mary's Church, 211 E Mesa Ave, Pueblo, CO 81006, (719) 542-6323

Special Events & Scenic Locations

Pueblo is the location of Colorado's State Fair & Rodeo held in August and September every year at the Colorado State Fairgrounds, 1001 Beulah Ave, Pueblo, CO 81004, 719-561-8484, https://www.coloradostatefair.com

The Pueblo County Fair is held in July most years, also at the Colorado State Fairgrounds, https://www.pueblocountyfair.com

Pueblo Events hosts a calendar here: https://www.puebloevents.net

Pueblo has a calendar of festivals and events here: https://www.colorado.com/co/pueblo/festivals-events

San Isabel National Forest
Greenhorn Mountain Wilderness
American Discovery Trail
Frontier Pathways National Scenic and Historic Byway
TransAmerica Trail Bicycle Route
Western Express Bicycle Route
Lake Pueblo State Park
Pueblo City Park Carousel
Historic Arkansas Riverwalk

Ghost Towns & Other Sparsely Populated Places

Abbey, Armour, Baxter, Bessemer Junction, Carlisle, Carter's, Chico, Chilcott, Crow, Dawkins, Dundee, Eden, Goodnight, Graneros, Greenhorn, Gulf Junction, Herrick, Juniata, Larimer, Levisy, Meadows, Mesa, Nepesta, Nyburg, Pinon, Pultney, Rye, Salt Creek, San Carlos, Seven Lakes, Siloam, Swallows, Taylors, Taylorville, Undercliffe, Vegas, Verde

Newspapers

The Labor Advocate. (Pueblo, Colo.) 1???-19??
Mir Katolišk Tednik. (Pueblo, Colo.) 1???-19?? | Languages: English, Slovenian
The Pueblo Evening Star. (Pueblo, Colo.) 18??-18??

Historical Assets Colorado

The Pueblo Courier. (Pueblo, Colo.) 18??-1903
Daily Colorado News. (South Pueblo, Colo.) 18??-1???
The Bessemer Indicator. (Bessemer, Colo.) 18??-1894
Pueblo Review and Standard. (Pueblo, Colo.) 18??-1???
The Colorado Chieftain. (Pueblo, Colo.) 1868-1875
The Great West. (Pueblo, Colo.) 1870-1???
The People. (Pueblo, Colo.) 1871-1875
The Daily Chieftain. (Pueblo, Colo.) 1872-1874
The Anvil. (South Pueblo, Colo.) 1873-1???
The Daily People. (Pueblo, Colo.) 1873-1873
Pueblo Daily Chieftain. (Pueblo, Colo.) 1874-1875
The Daily Pueblo Chieftain. (Pueblo, Colo.) 1875-1875
Colorado Weekly Chieftain. (Pueblo, Colo.) 1875-1881
The Pueblo Republican. (Pueblo, Colo.) 1875-1876
Colorado Daily Chieftain. (Pueblo, Colo.) 1875-1881
Daily Republican. (South Pueblo, Colo.) 188?-????
Daily Evening News. (South Pueblo, Colo.) 1880-1???
Pueblo Welcome. (South Pueblo, Colo.) 188?-1???
Pueblo Daily Chieftain. (Pueblo, Colo.) 1881-1883
The Daily Vox Populi. (South Pueblo, Colo.) 1881-1???
Pueblo Daily News. (Pueblo [Colo.]) 1881-1???
Colorado Chieftain. (Pueblo, Colo.) 1881-1???
Pueblo Sunday Opinion. (South Pueblo, Colo.) 1882-1???
Pueblo Weekly Commercial Standard. (Pueblo, Colo.) 1882-1883
Pueblo Commercial Standard. (Pueblo, Colo.) 1882-1882
Daily News. (South Pueblo, Colo.) 1883-1???
Pueblo Chieftain. (Pueblo, Colo.) 1883-1887
Commercial Standard. (Pueblo, Colo.) 1883-1885
Colorado Live Stock Review and Commercial Standard. (Pueblo, Colo.) 1885-1???
Double-Header. (South Pueblo, Colo.) 1886-????
The Daily Pueblo Press. (Pueblo, Colo.) 1886-????
The Pueblo World. (Pueblo, Colo.) 1887-????
Pueblo Daily Chieftain. (Pueblo, Colo.) 1887-1889
Pueblo Chieftain. (Pueblo, Colo.) 1889-Current
La Hermandad. (Pueblo, Colo.) 1889-1907 | Languages: Spanish
The Thinkograph. (Pueblo, Colo.) 1891-????
The Coming Crisis. (Pueblo, Colo.) 1891-1???
Pueblo Labor. (St. Louis, Mo.) 1893-189?
The Indicator. (Pueblo, Colo.) 1894-1911
Independent Reform Press. (Pueblo, Colo.) 1895-????
The Individual. (Pueblo, Colo.) 1896-1898
L'unione. (Pueblo, Colo.) 1897-1947 | Languages: English, Italian
Catholic Crosswinds. (Pueblo, Colo.) 19??-198?
Mir. (Pueblo, Colo.) 19??-19?? | Languages: English, Slovenian
Colorado Sun. (Pueblo, Colo.) 19??-19??
El Coloradeño. (Pueblo, Colo.) 19??-???? | Languages: Spanish

Pueblo County

The Western Ideal. (Pueblo, Colo.) 19??-????
Arkansas Valley Review. (Pueblo, Colo.) 1901-19??
Glas Svobode. (Pueblo, Colo.) 1901-19?? | Languages: English, Slovenian
Srbin. (Pueblo, Colo.) 1901-19?? | Languages: English, Serbian
Pueblo Star-Journal. (Pueblo, Colo.) 1901-1984
Servian Echo - Srpki Odjek. (Pueblo, Colo.) 1902-19?? | Languages: English, Serbian
Pueblo Labor Advocate. (Pueblo, Colo.) 1903-1904
The Pueblo County Democrat. (Pueblo, Colo.) 1903-19??
The Pueblo Sun. (Pueblo, Colo.) 1906-1910
Il Vindice. (Pueblo, Colo.) 1908-???? | Languages: Italian
The Breeze. (Beulah, Colo.) 1909-19??
The Pueblo Indicator. (Pueblo, Colo.) 1911-1921
The Pueblo Leader. (Pueblo, Colo.) 1911-19??
Western Weekly Leader. (Pueblo, Colo.) 1913-19??
Il Co-operatore. [Volume] (Pueblo, Colo.) 1918-19?? | Languages: English, Italian
Marsica Nuova. (Pueblo, Colo.) 1918-1923 | Languages: Italian
The Indicator. (Pueblo, Colo.) 1921-1925
Abruzzo-Molise. (Pueblo, Colo.) 1924-1926 | Languages: English, Italian
The Pueblo Indicator. (Pueblo, Colo.) 1925-19??
The Pueblo Times. (Pueblo, Colo.) 1925-1949
La Voce Del Popolo = The Voice Of The People. [Volume] (Pueblo, Colo.) 1926-1937 | Languages: English, Italian
The Colorado Tribune. (Pueblo, Colo.) 193?-Current
The Air-Scoop. (Army Air Base, Pueblo, Colo.) 1942-1945
L'unione combined with "Il Risveglio." (Pueblo, Colo.) 1949-1949 | Languages: Italian
Beulah Bugle. (Beulah, Colo.) 1951-19??
The Colorado City Sun. (Colorado City, Colo.) 1963-19??
Colorado City Call. (Colorado City, Colo.) 1963-19??
Pueblo West Colorado News (Pueblo West, Colo.) 1969-19??
The Greenhorn Valley News. (Colorado City, Colo.) 1973-19??
La Cucaracha. (Pueblo, Colo.) 1976-198? | Languages: English, Spanish
Tierra Libertad. (El Valle De San Luis, Chama, Colo. [New Mex.]) 1979-19?? | Languages: English, Spanish

Places on the National Register

Avondale, Avondale Bridge, Cty. Rd. 327
Beulah, Pueblo Mountain Park, 1 mi. S of Co. Rd. 220 on S. Pine Dr. (CO 78) in the San Isabel NF
Beulah, Squirrel Creek Recreational Unit, San Isabel National Forest
Boone, Boone Santa Fe Railroad Depot, 100 Baker Ave.
Boone, Huerfano Bridge, U.S. Hwy 50
Devine, St. Charles River Bridge, I-50 at milepost 7.77
Penrose, Indian Petroglyphs and Pictographs, Address Restricted
Pueblo, Barndollar—Gann House, 1906 Court St.
Pueblo, Baxter House, 325 W. 15th St.

Historical Assets Colorado

Pueblo, Beaumont, Allen, J., House, 425 W. 15th St.
Pueblo, Black, Dr. John A., House Complex, 102 W. Pitkin Ave.
Pueblo, Bowen Mansion, 229 W. 12th St.
Pueblo, Butler House, 6916 Broadacre Rd.
Pueblo, Carlile, James N., House, 44 Carlile Pl.
Pueblo, Central High School, 431 E. Pitkin Ave.
Pueblo, City Park Carousel, City Park
Pueblo, Colorado Building, 401—411 N. Main St.
Pueblo, Colorado State Hospital Superintendent's House, 13th & Francisco Sts.
Pueblo, Doyle Settlement, SE of Pueblo on Doyle Rd.
Pueblo, Duke, Nathaniel W., House, 1409 Craig St.
Pueblo, Edison School, 900 W. Mesa
Pueblo, El Pueblo, Jct. of 1st St. and Union Ave.
Pueblo, First Congregational Church, 225 W. Evans
Pueblo, First Methodist Episcopal Church, 400 Broadway St.
Pueblo, First Methodist Episcopal Church, 310 W. 11th St.
Pueblo, Fitch Terrace, 401, 403, 405, 407, 409, and 411 W. Eleventh St.
Pueblo, Frazier, R. T., House, 2121 N. Elizabeth St.
Pueblo, Galligan House, 501 Colorado Ave.
Pueblo, Gast Mansion, 1801 Greenwood St.
Pueblo, Goodnight Barn, W of Pueblo at CO 96W and Siloam Rd.
Pueblo, Hazelhurst, 905 Berkley Ave.
Pueblo, Henkel-Duke Mercantile Company Warehouse, 212-222 W. 3rd Ave.
Pueblo, King, Dr. Alexander T., House and Carriage House, 229 Quincy St. and 215 W. Routt Ave.
Pueblo, McClelland Orphanage, 415 E. Abriendo Ave.
Pueblo, Mechanics Building/Masonic Building, 207-211 N. Main St.
Pueblo, Minnequa Steel Works Office Building and Dispensary, Colorado Fuel and Iron Company, 215 and 225 Canal St.
Pueblo, Montgomery Ward Building, 225 N. Main St.
Pueblo, Orman-Adams House, 102 W. Orman Ave.
Pueblo, Pitkin Place Historic District, S side of 300 block W. Pitkin Pl.
Pueblo, Pryor, Frank, House, 1325 Greenwood St.
Pueblo, Pueblo Christopher Columbus Monument, Median in 100 Blk. of E. Abriendo Ave.
Pueblo, Pueblo City Park Zoo, 3455 Nuckolls Ave.
Pueblo, Pueblo County Courthouse, 10th and Main Sts.
Pueblo, Pueblo Federal Building, 421 N. Main St.
Pueblo, Quaker Flour Mill, 102 S. Oneida St.
Pueblo, Rice, Ward, House, 1825 Grand Ave.
Pueblo, Rood Candy Company Building, 408-416 W. 7th St.
Pueblo, Rosemount, 419 W. 14th St.
Pueblo, Sacred Heart Church, 1025 N. Grand Ave.
Pueblo, Sacred Heart Orphanage, 2316 Sprague St.
Pueblo, Santa Fe Avenue Bridge, US-50 at milepost 1.33
Pueblo, St. Charles Bridge, Cty. Rd. 65

Pueblo County

Pueblo, St. John's Greek Orthodox Church, 1000-1010 Spruce St.
Pueblo, Star Journal Model Home, 2920 High St.
Pueblo, Stickney, Charles H., House, 101 E. Orman Ave.
Pueblo, Streit, J. L., House, 2201 Grand Ave.
Pueblo, Temple Emanuel, 1425 N. Grand Ave.
Pueblo, Tooke—Nuckolls House, 38 Carlile Pl.
Pueblo, Tutt Building, 421 Central Plaza
Pueblo, Union Avenue Historic Commercial District, Roughly bounded by RR tracks, Main St., Grand and Victoria Aves.
Pueblo, Union Depot, Victoria and B Sts.
Pueblo, Vail Hotel, 217 S. Grand Ave.
Pueblo, Walter, Martin, House, 300 W. Abriendo Ave.
Pueblo, White, Asbury, House, 417 W. 11th St.
Pueblo, Young Women's Christian Association, 801 N. Santa Fe Ave.

USGS Historic Places

Beulah, Good Pasture Airport, 38.0972281, -104.9105411
Colorado City, Greenhorn Valley Airport, 37.9597304, -104.7841498
Devine, Pueblo Army Air Base, 38.2938889, -104.4991667
Doyle Bridge, Undercliffe, 38.1044495, -104.387748
Hobson, Siloam Post Office, 38.2513924, -104.975819
Northwest Edenway Airport, 38.3452508, -104.6324213

Grand Army of the Republic Posts

E T Upton, No. 8, Pueblo, Pueblo, 1881
Colorado City, No. 48, Pueblo, Colorado City, 1887
B F Butler, No. 91, Pueblo, Pueblo
James A Shields, No. ?, Pueblo, South Pueblo

USGS Historic Military Places

Devine, Pueblo Army Air Base, 38.2938889, -104.4991667
North Avondale, Pueblo Chemical Depot, 38.3142959, -104.3313425

Military Bases

Pueblo Chemical Depot Army Base
45825 CO 96, Pueblo, CO 81006, (14 miles east of Pueblo), 719-549-4111
Some areas are restricted

Post Offices

Abbey	1891 May 29	1914 Dec 31
Agate	1880 Apr 7	1881 Apr 15
Airport	1953 Dec 1	1955 Aug 31
Andersonville	1868 Dec 1	1869 Aug 19
Arland	1895 Jan 7	rescinded
Armour	1886 May 6	1892 Feb 3

Historical Assets Colorado

Artman	1892 Aug 31	1901 Feb 14	
Avondale	1892 Mar 22		81022
Bents Fort	1863 June 4	1873 Dec 2	
Beulah	1876 Oct 25		81023
Boone	1891 Dec 5		81025
Booneville	1863 Dec 5	1891 Dec 5	
Bronquist	1917 Aug 30	1925 June 30	
Burnt Mill	1911 Oct 17	1921 Sept 30	
Cedarwood	1912 Mar 22	1943 Mar 15	
Chilcott	1884 Mar 24	1890 Oct 21	
Colorado City	1964 Sept 1		
Cousin Springs	1914 Oct 8	1920 Nov 30	
Crow	1885 Oct 30	1907 Nov 30*	
Dawkins	1885 Feb 5	1907 Feb 21	
Duke	1908 May 5	1908 Aug 4	
Eden	1890 Jan 14	1914 Mar 31	
Excelsior	1866 Feb 16	1871 Apr 24*	
Fisher	1895 Feb 11	1908 July 31	
Foothills	1921 Aug 10	1927 Feb 5	
Fort Lyon	1862 Aug 2	1889 Dec 26	
Fort Reynolds	1869 June 15	1870 Feb 25	
Goodpasture	895 May 25	1923 May 31	
Graneros	1889 Aug 17	1925 Apr 15	
Greenhorn	1866 Dec 10	1911 Dec 15*	
Grimaldi	1913 Aug 22	1920 Nov 30	
Haynes Ranch	1861 July 31	1863 Mar 3	
Hermosilla	1867 Mar 21	1872 Jan 15	
Holden	1892 Jan 15	1893 June 13	
Huerfano	1882 Nov 10	1929 Apr 15*	
Jackson	1873 Mar 21		
Juniata	1869 June 16	1893 Aug 31	
Keble	1899 Apr 25	1899 July 29	
Kinkel	1907 Dec 19	1911 Oct 7	
Lamar	1885 Aug 12	1886 July 9	
Lebanon	1875 Apr 16	1876 June 6	
Lees	1897 Aug 3	1904 May 14	
Lime	1898 Apr 13	1943 June 30	
Maces Hole	1873 Apr 23	1876 Oct 25	
Marnel	1917 Sept 24	1923 Nov 30	
Mercier	1906 Sept 22	1913 Nov 30	
Mercier	1906 Sept 22	1913 Nov 30	
Muddy Creek	1870 Dec 8	1886 Nov 19	
Myrtle	1906 Feb 23	1913 July 13	
Nepesta	1876 June 7	1929 Dec 31	
North Avondale	1917 Aug 17	1976 May 31	
Nyburg	1889 Aug 6	1918 July 31	

Pueblo County

Osage	1884 Apr 4	1888 Oct 24		
Osage Avenue	1873 Apr 16	1882 Jan 31		
Overton	1892 Apr 9	1900 Dec 15		
Pinon	1907 Feb 21	1921 June 30		
Pueblo	1860 Dec 13			
Pueblo West	1969 Oct 20			
Rock Creek	1909 May 11	1915 Apr 30		
Rye	1881 Mar 7		81069	
Saint Charles	1866 May 28	1881 Jan 3*		
Salt Creek	1880 Oct 5	1908 May 31*		
Siloam	1891 Mar 31	1943 Apr 30		
Sitton	1906 Dec 22	1917 Aug 31		
South Pueblo	1874 Aug 26	1887 June 4		
South Side	1869 Feb 22	1877 Sept 12		
Sparrow	1883 Oct 18	1885 Dec 23		
Sperryvale	1901 Jan 5	1901 Apr 15		
Stone City	1912 Oct 14	1957 June 30		
Swallows	1892 Nov 12	1947 Aug 6*		
Table Mountain	1879 Sept 12	1880 Oct 4		
Tacony	1915 Mar 25	1942 July 31		
Taylorville	1878 June 17	1892 Nov 12		
Undercliffe	1879 Jan 20	1925 Sept 30		
Verde	1903 Apr 9	1912 Oct 31		
Waremont	1916 June 13	1922 Apr 15		
White Rock	1909 May 17	1927 Aug 31		
Wilson	1911 June 24	1913 Sept 15		
Wood Valley	1862 June 12	1869 Dec 15*		

Topo Quads

Apishapa Bridge	380000N	375230N	1040000W	1040730W
Avondale	381500N	380730N	1041500W	1042230W
Bar J H Ranch	383000N	382230N	1042230W	1043000W
Beulah	380730N	380000N	1045230W	1050000W
Beulah NE	381500N	380730N	1044500W	1045230W
Boone Hill	382230N	381500N	1040730W	1041500W
Capps Springs	375230N	374500N	1043000W	1043730W
Cedarwood	380000N	375230N	1043000W	1043730W
Chicos Well	380730N	380000N	1041500W	1042230W
Colorado City	380000N	375230N	1044500W	1045230W
Delhi	374500N	373730N	1040000W	1040730W
Devine	382230N	381500N	1042230W	1043000W
Doyle Bridge	380730N	380000N	1042230W	1043000W
Flying A Ranch	380730N	380000N	1040730W	1041500W
Goat Butte	380730N	380000N	1043000W	1043730W
Graneros Flats	380000N	375230N	1043730W	1044500W
Hardesty Reservoir	380730N	380000N	1040000W	1040730W

Historical Assets Colorado

Highlands Church	383000N	382230N	1040730W	1041500W
Hog Ranch Canyon	380000N	375230N	1042230W	1043000W
Muldoon Hill	380730N	380000N	1044500W	1045230W
Myers Canyon	375230N	374500N	1041500W	1042230W
Nepesta	381500N	380730N	1040730W	1041500W
North Avondale	382230N	381500N	1041500W	1042230W
North Avondale NE	383000N	382230N	1041500W	1042230W
North Rattlesnake Butte	375230N	374500N	1042230W	1043000W
Northeast Pueblo	382230N	381500N	1043000W	1043730W
Northwest Pueblo	382230N	381500N	1043730W	1044500W
Owl Canyon	381500N	380730N	1045230W	1050000W
Pinon	383000N	382230N	1043000W	1043730W
Red Top Ranch	380000N	375230N	1041500W	1042230W
Rye	380000N	375230N	1045230W	1050000W
Saint Charles Peak	380730N	380000N	1050000W	1050730W
San Isabel	380000N	375230N	1050000W	1050730W
Sanford Hills	375230N	374500N	1040730W	1041500W
Snowden Lake	375230N	374500N	1040000W	1040730W
Southeast Pueblo	381500N	380730N	1043000W	1043730W
Southwest Pueblo	381500N	380730N	1043730W	1044500W
Steele Hollow	383000N	382230N	1043730W	1044500W
Stone City	383000N	382230N	1044500W	1045230W
Swallows	382230N	381500N	1044500W	1045230W
Verde School	380730N	380000N	1043730W	1044500W
Vineland	381500N	380730N	1042230W	1043000W
Wetmore	381500N	380730N	1050000W	1050730W
Yellowbank Creek	380000N	375230N	1040730W	1041500W

Suggested Reading

Aschermann, Arla. *Winds in the Cornfields Pueblo County, Colorado: Ghost Towns and Settlements, 1787-1872*. Pueblo, CO: Pueblo County Historical Society, 1994.

Macy, Guy E. *A History of Pueblo County, Colorado*. Thesis, Colorado State Teachers College, 1933.

Pueblo Board of Trade. *Sketch of the Pueblos and Pueblo County, Colorado*. Pueblo, CO: Chieftain Steam Print, 1883.

Pueblo County History. Pueblo, CO: Pueblo DAR, 1939.

Simms, Charlene Garcia et al. *Pueblo*. Charleston, SC: Arcadia Publishing, 2017.

US National Youth Administration. *History of Pueblo County*. Pueblo, CO: NP, 1938.

Vickers, W B and O L Baskin & Co. *History of the Arkansas Valley, Colorado; Illustrated*. Chicago: O L Baskin Historical Publishers, 1881.

Rio Blanco County

Introduction

Established: 1889   Population: 6,666

Formed from: Summit

Adjacent Counties: Moffat, Routt, Garfield

County Seat: Meeker

  Other Communities: Rangely, Buford, Rio Blanco

Website, http://www.co.rio-blanco.co.us

Area Codes: 970

Zip Codes: 81641, 81648

Historical Assets Colorado

Rio Blanco County Courthouse

Courthouses & County Government

Rio Blanco County
   http://www.co.rio-blanco.co.us
Rio Blanco County Courthouse (9th Judicial District), 555 Main St, Meeker, CO 81641, 970-878-5622; http://www.courts.state.co.us/Courts/County/Index.cfm?County_ID=26
Rio Blanco County Courthouse (Rangely), 209 E Main, Rangely, CO 81648, 970-675-2342; http://www.courts.state.co.us/Courts/County/Index.cfm?County_ID=26
Assessor, 555 Main St, Meeker, CO 81641, 970-878-9410; http://www.co.rio-blanco.co.us/assessor/
Board of County Commissioners, 555 Main St, Meeker, CO 81641, 970-878-5731, https://www.rbc.us/186/Board-of-County-Commissioners
Clerk & Recorder, 17497 Hwy 64, Rangely, CO 81648, 970-878-9465; http://www.co.rio-blanco.co.us/clerkandrecorder/
Clerk & Recorder, 555 Main St, Meeker, CO 81641, 970-878-9460; http://www.co.rio-blanco.co.us/clerkandrecorder/
Coroner, 970-274-0850; http://www.co.rio-blanco.co.us/203/Coroner
Elections, 555 Main St, Meeker, CO 81641, 970-878-9460; http://www.co.rio-blanco.co.us/177/Elections
Public Health, 209 E Main, #103, Rangely, CO 81648, 970-878-9525; http://www.co.rio-blanco.co.us/healthnurse/
Transportation (Road & Bridge), 570 2nd St, Meeker, CO 81641, 970-878-9590; http://www.co.rio-blanco.co.us/293/Road-Bridge
Treasurer, 555 Main St, Meeker, CO 81641, 970-878-9660; http://www.co.rio-blanco.co.us/Treasurer/

County Records

Birth 1902	Marriage 1889	Divorce 1889
Death 1902	Land 1889	Probate 1889
Court 1889		
CSA Birth 1896		

Rio Blanco County

CSA Deaths 1896
CSA Burials 1893
CSA Disinterments 1908

County & Municipal Records Held at the State Level

The Colorado State Archives

Physical Records
Clerk & Recorder
District Court
WPA Historical Records
WPA Religious Institutions
  Survey
Cities
  Rangely

Records on Film
County Court
Cities
  Rangely

Records on Master Film
County Court
District Court
Combined Courts
School Districts
Cities
  Rangely

The Denver Public Library
WWI Draft Registration Cards (microfilm)

School Districts

School Districts, http://www.adcogov.org/local-school-districts
Meeker School District Re-1, 555 Garland, Meeker, CO 81641, 970-878-9040; https://www.meeker.k12.co.us/
Rangely School District RE-4, 402 W Main, Rangely, CO 81648, 970-675-2207; https://www.rangelyk12.org/

Historic School Districts

1. Meeker Grade
2. Thornburg
3. Mesa
4. Rangely
5. Strawberry
6. Piceance
7. Buford
8. Miller Creek
9. Angora
10. [1920]
11. Pyramid
12. [1920]
13. Powell Park
14. Coal Creek
15. White Rock

Jt1. [1897]
Jt5. Pine Grove
Jt21. Rio Blanco

Fraternal Organizations

Granges
Powel Park, No. 101, Rio Blanco, Powel Park/Meeker, 1 Apr 1890
Highland, No. 102, Rio Blanco, Meeker, 4 Apr 1890
Buford, No. 103, Rio Blanco, Meeker, 7 Apr 1890
Rio Blanco, No. 385, Rio Blanco, Meeker, 11 Aug 1919
Petrolite, No. 388, Rio Blanco, Meeker, 11 Oct 1919
Elk Head, No. 389, Rio Blanco, Colerade/Elk Head, 15 Nov 1919
White Rock, No. 394, Rio Blanco, Meeker, 24 July 1920
White River, No. 395, Rio Blanco, Meeker, 15 June 1922

Historical Assets Colorado

Masons
Ancient Free & Accepted Masons
Del Norte, No. 80, Rio Blanco, Meeker, 16 Sept 1890
Rio Blanco, No. 175, Rio Blanco, Rangely, 23 Jan 1952
Royal Arch Masons
Meeker, No. 37, Rio Blanco, Meeker
Knights Templar
Meeker Commandery, No. 33, Rio Blanco, Meeker, 1913 May 27
Eastern Star
Meeker, No. 100, Rio Blanco, Meeker
Rangely, No. 143, Rio Blanco, Rangely
Odd Fellows
Valentine, No. 47, Rio Blanco, Meeker
Rebekahs
Josephine, No. 86, Rio Blanco, Meeker
Knights of Pythias
None
Pythian Sisters
None
Benevolent Protective Order of Elks
Rangely, No. 1907, Rio Blanco, Rangely

City & Town Halls
Meeker, 345 Market St, Meeker, CO 81641, 970-878-5344, https://www.townofmeeker.org
Rangely, 1624 E Main St, Rangely, CO 81648, 970-675-2221, https://www.colorado.gov/townofrangely

Archives & Manuscript Collections
None

Historical & Genealogical Societies
Rio Blanco County Historical Society, White River Museum, 565 Park St, P.O. Box 413, Meeker, CO 81641, (970) 878-9982, https://www.facebook.com/preserveringourpast/

Local Libraries
Meeker Public Library, 490 Main St, Meeker, CO 81641, (970) 878-5911, https://meekerlibrary.booksys.net
Colorado Northwestern Community College Library, 500 Kennedy Dr, Rangely, CO 81648, (970) 675-3334, https://www.cncc.edu/library

Rio Blanco County

Links
CO GenWeb
http://cogenweb.com/rioblanco/
Cyndi's List
https://www.cyndislist.com/us/co/counties/rio-blanco/
FamilySearch Wiki
https://www.familysearch.org/wiki/en/Rio_Blanco_County,_Colorado_Genealogy
Linkpendium
http://www.linkpendium.com/rio_blanco-co-genealogy/
RootsWeb Wiki
https://wiki.rootsweb.com/wiki/index.php/Rio_Blanco_County,_Colorado
Wikipedia
https://en.wikipedia.org/wiki/Rio_Blanco_County,_Colorado

Historic Hotels
1896 Meeker Hotel, 560 Main St, Meeker, CO 81641, 970-878-5255, http://www.meekerhotel.com

Museums & Historic Sites
Rangely Outdoor Museum, 200 Kennedy Dr, P.O. Box 740, Rangely, CO 81648, (970) 675-2612, https://www.rangelyoutdoormuseum.org

Rio Blanco County Historical Society, White River Museum, 565 Park St, P.O. Box 413, Meeker, CO 81641, (970) 878-9982, https://www.facebook.com/preserveringourpast/

Special Events & Scenic Locations
The Rio Blanco County Fair is held at the Rio Blanco County Fairgrounds, 835 Sulphur Creek Rd, Meeker, CO 81641, https://www.rbc.us/466/Rio-Blanco-County-Fair

Rio Blanco County has a calendar of events here: https://www.colorado.com/co/rio-blanco/festivals-events

Routt National Forest
White River National Forest
Flat Tops Wilderness
Dinosaur Diamond Prehistoric Highway National Scenic Byway
Flat Tops Trail Scenic Byway
Colorow Mountain State Wildlife Area

Ghost Towns & Other Sparsely Populated Places
None

Historical Assets Colorado

Newspapers
The Meeker Herald. (Meeker, Colo.) 1885-Current
Rio Blanco News. (Meeker, Colo.) 1889-1892
Rangely Driller. (Rangely, Colo.) 19??-1955
White River Review. (Meeker, Rio Blanco County, Colo.) 1902-1934
The Rangely News. (Rangely, Colo.) 1945-19??
The Rangely Times. (Rangely, Colo.) 1956-????
The White River Press. (Meeker, Colo.) 1964-1966

Places on the National Register
Meeker, Battle of Milk River Site, Address Restricted
Meeker, Coal Creek School, 617 Cty. Rd. 6
Meeker, Duck Creek Wickiup Village, Address Restricted
Meeker, Hay's Ranch Bridge, Cty. Rd. 127
Meeker, Hotel Meeker, 560 Main St.
Meeker, Meeker I.O.O.F. Lodge—Valentine Lodge No. 47, 400 Main St.
Meeker, St. James Episcopal Church, 368 4th St.
Rangely, Canon Pintado, Address Restricted
Rangely, Carrot Men Pictograph Site, Address Restricted
Rangely, Collage Shelter Site, Address Restricted
Rangely, Fremont Lookout Fortification Site, Address Restricted

USGS Historic Places
Wolf Ridge, Tract C-A-84 Mesa Airstrip, 39.9469166, -108.4395374

Grand Army of the Republic Posts
Meeker, No. 109, Rio Blanco, Meeker

USGS Historic Military Places
None

Military Bases
None

Post Offices

Angora	1896 Oct 24	1912 Sept 30	
Buford	1890 Mar 19	1961 Dec 15*	
Farwell	1892 Feb 5	1894 May 10	
Little Beaver	1919 Sept 13	1925 July 15	
Marvine	1895 May 14	1934 Jan 15*	
Meeker	1871 Sept 29		81641
Morapos	1912 Oct 14	1931 Sept 30	
Piceance	1892 June 25	1926 Apr 15*	
Pyramid	1896 Apr 24	1932 Dec 15*	
Rangely	1885 Sept 10		81648

Rio Blanco County

Rio Blanco	1950 July 1	1975 May 23		
Rioblanco	1899 May 6	1950 July 1		
Sulphur	1902 July 2	1926 Jan 15		
Thornburg	1900 Oct 10	1937 Oct 30		
White River	1888 Aug 15	1908 Mar 15		

Topo Quads

Banta Ridge	400000N	395230N	1085230W	1090000W
Banty Point	400730N	400000N	1085230W	1090000W
Barcus Creek	400730N	400000N	1082230W	1083000W
Barcus Creek SE	400730N	400000N	1081500W	1082230W
Big Beaver Reservoir	400000N	395230N	1073730W	1074500W
Big Foundation Creek	394500N	393730N	1084500W	1085230W
Big Marvine Peak	400000N	395230N	1071500W	1072230W
Black Cabin Gulch	395230N	394500N	1083000W	1083730W
Blair Mountain	395230N	394500N	1072230W	1073000W
Brushy Point	394500N	393730N	1083730W	1084500W
Buckskin Point	400730N	400000N	1080000W	1080730W
Buford	400000N	395230N	1073000W	1073730W
Bull Fork	394500N	393730N	1081500W	1082230W
Calamity Ridge	400730N	400000N	1083000W	1083730W
Cutoff Gulch	394500N	393730N	1080730W	1081500W
Del Norte Peak	373730N	373000N	1063000W	1063730W
Devils Causeway	400730N	400000N	1070730W	1071500W
East Evacuation Creek	394500N	393730N	1085230W	1090000W
Fawn Creek	400730N	400000N	1073000W	1073730W
Figure Four Spring	394500N	393730N	1082230W	1083000W
Gillam Draw	400730N	400000N	1083730W	1084500W
Greasewood Gulch	400000N	395230N	1080730W	1081500W
Jessup Gulch	395230N	394500N	1080730W	1081500W
LO 7 Hill	400000N	395230N	1075230W	1080000W
Lost Park	400730N	400000N	1072230W	1073000W
McCarthy Gulch	394500N	393730N	1080000W	1080730W
Meadow Creek Lake	395230N	394500N	1073000W	1073730W
Meeker	400730N	400000N	1075230W	1080000W
No Name Ridge	395230N	394500N	1080000W	1080730W
Oyster Lake	400000N	395230N	1072230W	1073000W
Philadelphia Creek	400000N	395230N	1083730W	1084500W
Rangely	400730N	400000N	1084500W	1085230W
Rattlesnake Mesa	400730N	400000N	1074500W	1075230W
Razorback Ridge	394500N	393730N	1083000W	1083730W
Red Elephant Point	395230N	394500N	1074500W	1075230W
Rio Blanco	394500N	393730N	1075230W	1080000W

Historical Assets Colorado

Ripple Creek	400730N	400000N	1071500W	1072230W
Rock School	395230N	394500N	1081500W	1082230W
Sagebrush Hill	400000N	395230N	1083000W	1083730W
Sawmill Mountain	400730N	400000N	1073730W	1074500W
Segar Mountain	400000N	395230N	1080000W	1080730W
Square S Ranch	400000N	395230N	1081500W	1082230W
Texas Creek	395230N	394500N	1085230W	1090000W
Texas Mountain	395230N	394500N	1084500W	1085230W
Thirteenmile Creek	395230N	394500N	1075230W	1080000W
Triangle Park	395230N	394500N	1073730W	1074500W
Veatch Gulch	400000N	395230N	1074500W	1075230W
Water Canyon	400000N	395230N	1084500W	1085230W
White Coyote Draw	395230N	394500N	1083730W	1084500W
White River City	400730N	400000N	1080730W	1081500W
Wolf Ridge	400000N	395230N	1082230W	1083000W
Yankee Gulch	395230N	394500N	1082230W	1083000W

Suggested Reading

Ball, W O. *Rio Blanco County*. Denver: Civil Works Administration, 1934.

Buckles, Ricki. *A History of Buford, Colorado*. NL: Ricki Buckles, 2005.

Buckles, Ricki. *A History of the Upper White River Country*, Meeker, Colorado. NL: NP, 2006.

Bury, Susan et al. *This is What I Remember*. Meeker, CO: Rio Blanco County Historical Society, 1972.

Gray, Forrest N. *Thornburgh, Rio Blanco County, Colorado*. NL: Banner Printing Center, 1991.

Hurt, Kathy and John Hurt. *Between the Bookcliffs and the Blue*. Grand Junction, CO: NP, 1987.

Rio Grande County

Introduction

Established: 1874   Population: 11,982

Formed from: Conejos, Costilla

Adjacent Counties: Saguache, Alamosa, Conejos, Archuleta, Mineral

County Seat: Del Norte

  Other Communities: Monte Vista, Center, South Fork, Homelake, Parma, Alpine, Gerrard

Website, https://www.riograndecounty.org

Area Codes: 719

Zip Codes: 81125, 81132, 81135, 81144, 81154

Historical Assets Colorado

Rio Grande County Courthouse

Rio Grande County 19th Century Courthouse

Courthouses & County Government

Rio Grande County
https://www.riograndecounty.org

Rio Grande County Courthouse (12th Judicial District), 925 6th St, Del Norte, CO 81132, 719-657-3394; http://www.courts.state.co.us/Courts/County/Index.cfm?County_ID=36

Assessor, 925 6th St, Del Norte, CO 81132, 719-657-3326; https://www.riograndecounty.org/departments/elected-officials/assessor

Board of County Commissioners, 925 6th St, Del Norte, CO 81132, 719-657-2744, https://www.riograndecounty.org/commissioners

Clerk & Recorder, 965 6th St, Del Norte, CO 81132, 719-657-3334; https://www.riograndecounty.org/departments/elected-officials/clerk

Coroner, 404 Morris Ave, Monte Vista, CO 81144, 719-588-1289; https://www.riograndecounty.org/departments/elected-officials/coroner

Public Health, 925 6th St, Rm 101, Del Norte, CO 81132, 719-657-3352; https://www.riograndecounty.org/departments/business-offices/public-health

Transportation (Road & Bridge), 168 Washington St, Monte Vista, CO 81144, 719-852-4781; https://www.riograndecounty.org/departments/business-offices/road-a-bridge

Treasurer, 925 6th St, Rm 103, Del Norte, CO 81132, 719-657-2747; https://www.riograndecounty.org/departments/elected-officials/treasurer

County Records

Birth Unk
Death Unk
Court 1876
Marriage 1876
Land 1874
Divorce 1876
Probate 1876

Rio Grande County

County & Municipal Records Held at the State Level

The Colorado State Archives

Physical Records
Clerk & Recorder
County Court
District Court
WPA Historical Records
WPA Religious Institutions Survey
Cities
Monte Vista

Records on Film
1885 Census
County Court
District Court
School Districts

Records on Master Film
District Court
Combined Courts
School Districts

The Denver Public Library
WWI Draft Registration Cards (microfilm)

School Districts

School Districts, http://www.adcogov.org/local-school-districts
Center School District 25 JT, 550 S Sylvester Ave, Center, CO 81125; https://www.center.k12.co.us/
Montevista School District C-8, 345 E Prospect Ave, Monte Vista, CO 81144, 719-852-5996; https://ww2.monte.k12.co.us/
Sargent School District RE-33J, 7090 N Road 2 E, Monte Vista, CO 81144, 719-852-4025; http://www.sargent.k12.co.us/
Upper Rio Grande School District C-7, 770 11th St, Del Norte, CO 81132, 719-657-4040; https://www.dncsd.org/

Historic School Districts

1. Rock Creek
2. Del Norte
3. Aydelotte, Sargent
4. North Farm
5. Plaza
6. Swede Lane
7. Upper Pinos Creek, Del Norte
8. Mathias, Monte Vista
9. Monte Vista
10. [1885]
11. [1885]
12. Francisco Creek
13. Granger
14. South Fork
15. Fair View
16. Weyand
17. Martinez
18. Bowen
19. Bronson
20. Schulz
21. Warr
22. Ydren
23. Robb
24. Milner
25. Levin Mt
26. [1891]
27. Eureka
28. West Farm
Jt26. Center

Fraternal Organizations

Granges
Del Norte, No. 71, Rio Grande, Del Norte, 27 Nov 1875
San Juan, No. 74, Rio Grande, Del Norte, 24 Mar 1879
Rock Creek, No. 79, Rio Grande, Monte Vista, 27 Feb 1888

Historical Assets Colorado

Masons
Ancient Free & Accepted Masons
Monte Vista, No. 29, Rio Grande, Del Norte, 20 Sept 1876
Temple Gate, No. 73, Rio Grande, Monte Vista, 18 Sept 1888
Del Norte, No. 105, Rio Grande, Del Norte, 20 Sept 1899
Egeria, No. 128, Rio Grande, Center, 17 Sept 1907
Royal Arch Masons
Del Norte, No. 43, Rio Grande, Del Norte
Knights Templar
None
Eastern Star
Del Norte, No. 49, Rio Grande, Del Norte
Bethlehem, No. 56, Rio Grande, Monte Vista
Odd Fellows
Del Norte, No. 26, Rio Grande, Del Norte, 1876 Feb 3
Monte Vista, No. 73, Rio Grande, Monte Vista
Monte Vista, No. 128, Rio Grande, Monte Vista
Center, No. 161, Rio Grande, Center
Rebekahs
Mountain View, No. 132, Rio Grande, Monte Vista
Harvest Home, No. 136, Rio Grande, Center
Knights of Pythias
Coronado, No. 25, Rio Grande, Del Norte
Solon, No. 46, Rio Grande, Monte Vista
Pythian Sisters
None
Benevolent Protective Order of Elks
Monte Vista, No. 2456, Rio Grande, Monte Vista

City & Town Halls
Del Norte, 140 Spruce St, Del Norte, CO 81132 719-657-2708, http://www.delnortecolorado.com
Monte Vista, 95 W 1st Ave, Monte Vista, CO 81144, 719-852-2692, https://cityofmontevista.colorado.gov
Center, 294 Worth St, Center, CO 81125, 719-754-3497, https://www.colorado.gov/townofcenter
South Fork, 28 Silver Thread Ln, South Fork, CO 81154, 719-873-0152, https://www.southfork.org

Archives & Manuscript Collections
None

Rio Grande County

Historical & Genealogical Societies
Lookout Mountain Observatory Association, P.O. Box 432, Del Norte, CO 81132,
Monte Vista Historical Society, Historical Museum, 110 Jefferson St, P.O. Box 323, Monte Vista, CO 81144, (719) 849-0974, https://www.museumtrail.org/monte-vista-historical-society-museum.html
Rio Grande County Historical Society, Historical Museum, 580 Oak St, Del Norte, CO 81132-2210, (719) 657-2847, https://www.riograndecounty.org/museum

Local Libraries
Del Norte Public Library, 790 Grand Ave, Del Norte, CO 81132, (719) 657-2633, http://www.delnortecountylibrary.org
Carnegie Public Library, 120 Jefferson St, Monte Vista, CO 81144-1797, (719) 852-3931, http://www.montevistalibrary.org

Links
CO GenWeb
http://cogenweb.com/riogrande/

Cyndi's List
https://www.cyndislist.com/us/co/counties/rio-grande/

FamilySearch Wiki
https://www.familysearch.org/wiki/en/Rio_Grande_County,_Colorado_Genealogy

Linkpendium
http://www.linkpendium.com/rio_grande-co-genealogy/

RootsWeb Wiki
https://wiki.rootsweb.com/wiki/index.php/Rio_Grande_County,_Colorado

Wikipedia
https://en.wikipedia.org/wiki/Rio_Grande,_Colorado

Historic Hotels
1874 Windsor Hotel, 605 Grand Ave, Del Norte, CO 81132, 719-657-9031, https://www.windsorhoteldelnorte.com
1926 Spruce Lodge, 29431 US 160, South Fork, CO 81154, 719-480-1858, https://www.sprucelodges.com

Museums & Historic Sites
Homelake Veterans' History Museum, 3749 Sherman Ave, P.O. Box 97, Homelake, CO 81135, (719) 852-8235, http://www.homelakeveteransmuseum.org
Monte Vista Historical Society, Historical Museum, 110 Jefferson St, P.O. Box 323, Monte Vista, CO 81144, (719) 849-0974, https://www.museumtrail.org/monte-vista-historical-society-museum.html
Rio Grande County Historical Society, Historical Museum, 580 Oak St, Del Norte, CO 81132-2210, (719) 657-2847, https://www.riograndecounty.org/museum
Transportation of the West Museum, 916 1st Ave, Monte Vista, CO 81144, (719) 849-9320, https://www.museumtrail.org/transportation-of-the-west-museum.html

Historical Assets Colorado

Special Events & Scenic Locations

The San Luis Valley Fair (Alamosa, Rio Grande, Costilla, Conejos, Mineral & Saguache Counties) is held in August most years at the Ski Hi Park, 2255 Sherman Ave, Monte Vista, CO 81144, 719-298-1185, https://www.facebook.com/slvfair/

Rio Grande County has a calendar of events here: https://www.riograndecounty.org/events

Monte Vista National Wildlife Refuge
Rio Grande National Forest
Continental Divide National Scenic Trail
Old Spanish National Historic Trail
Silver Thread Scenic Byway

Ghost Towns & Other Sparsely Populated Places

Bowen, Cornwall, Jasper, Parma, South Fork, Summitville, Wagon Wheel Gap, White River

Newspapers

The San Juan Prospector. (Del Norte, Colo.) 1874-1929
The San Juan Mining Reporter. (Del Norte, Colo.) 1877-1???
Summitville Nugget. (Summitville, Colo.) 1883-????
The Little Presbyterian. (Del Norte, Colo.) 1883-1???
San Luis Valley Graphic. (Henry, Rio Grande County, Colo.) 1884-1900
San Luis Valley Gazette. (Henry, Rio Grande County, Colo.) 1884-1???
The Monte Vista Journal. (Monte Vista, Rio Grande County, Colo.) 1888-1921
San Luis Valley Graphic. (Monte Vista, Rio Grande County, Colo.) 1889-189?
Del Norte Daily Enquirer. (Del Norte, Colo.) 189?-1???
Del Norte Enquirer. (Del Norte, Colo.) 1892-189?
Daily Del Norte Inquirer. (Del Norte, Colo.) 1892-1???
The Monte Vista Reporter. (Monte Vista, Rio Grande County, Colo.) 1899-1900
The Monte Vista Reporter and The San Luis Valley Graphic. (Monte Vista, Rio Grande County, Colo.) 1900-19??
San Luis Valley Graphic and Monte Vista Reporter. (Monte Vista, Rio Grande County, Colo.) 19??-19??
Monte Vista Tribune. (Monte Vista, Rio Grande County, Colo.) 1915-19??
Monte Vista Journal and Monte Vista Graphic-Reporter. (Monte Vista, Colo.) 1921-1925
Monte Vista Journal. (Monte Vista, Colo.) 1925-Current
The Del Norte Prospector (continuing The San Juan Prospector). (Del Norte, Colo.) 1929-1932
The Monte Vista Journal. (Monte Vista, Colo.) 1932-Current
The Monte Vista Journal with which is consolidated The Monte Vista Tribune. (Monte Vista, Colo.) 1932-19??
The Del Norte Prospector. (Del Norte, Colo.) 1932-1934

Rio Grande County

The Del Norte Prospector with which is combined The Creede Candle. (Del Norte, Colo.) 1934-1972

The Valley Courier. (Alamosa, Colo.) 1955-Current

The Del Norte Prospector and Creede (Mineral County) Candle. (Del Norte, Colo.) 1972-1982

Mineral County Miner and South Fork Times. (Creede (Mineral County), Colo.) 1975-1983

The South Fork Times. (South Fork, Colo.) 1981-Current

The Del Norte Prospector. (Del Norte, Colo.) 1982-Current

Valley Voice. (Monte Vista, Colo.) 1991-Current

Places on the National Register

Del Norte, Keck Homestead, 12888 Cty. Rd. 15
Del Norte, Sutherland Bridge, Off U.S. 160
Del Norte, Wheeler Bridge, Off U.S. 160
Monte Vista, Carnegie Library, 120 Jefferson St.
Monte Vista, Central School Auditorium and Gymnasium, 612 First Ave.
Monte Vista, El Monte Hotel, 925 First Ave.
Monte Vista, First Methodist Episcopal Church, 215 Washington St.
Monte Vista, Monte Vista Downtown Historic District, Jct. of First Ave. and Washington St.
Monte Vista, Monte Vista Library, 110 Jefferson St.
Monte Vista, US Post Office and Federal Building—Monte Vista Main, Washington and Second Ave.
South Fork, Creede Branch, Denver and Rio Grande Railroad, Along the D&RGW right-of-way bet. South Fork and Creede
South Fork, Denver & Rio Grande Railroad South Fork Water Tank, US-160
South Fork, Spruce Lodge, 29431 W. US Hwy. 160

USGS Historic Places

Monte Vista, Movie Manor Landing Area, 37.5825032, -106.2008636
Summitville, Summitville, 37.4305621, -106.592261
Unknown, Elwood Post Office, 0, 0

Grand Army of the Republic Posts

Joe Hooker, No. 16, Rio Grande, Monte Vista, 1917
Putnam, No. 27, Rio Grande, Del Norte
Soldiers' Welcome, No. 106, Rio Grande, Monte Vista

USGS Historic Military Places

None

Military Bases

None

Historical Assets Colorado

Post Offices

Blainvale	1882 June 20	1884 Sept 18*	
Bowen	1883 May 25	1901 Sept 30	
Bowenton	1881 Aug 10	1884 Aug 21	
Cornwall	1879 Oct 31	1882 Nov 20	
Del Norte	1883 Jan 28		81132
Elwood	1882 Sept 18	1899 Aug 16*	
Granger	1902 Oct 14	1903 Jan 12	
Henry	1884 Apr 16	1886 Feb 18	
Homelake	1919 Feb 11	1965 Dec 3	
Jasper	1882 Nov 20	1927 Feb 15*	
Lariat	1881 Aug 5	1884 Apr 16	
Liberty	1887 Oct 11	1898 Apr 30	
Loyton	1884 Sept 10	1884 Oct 2	
Monte Vista	1886 Feb 18		81144
Nichols	1903 Dec 22	1904 Apr 2	
Norma	1896 Dec 16	1899 Dec 15	
Parma	1886 Mar 20	1910 June 15*	
Piedra	1875 Jan 27	1878 Mar 24	
South Fork	1876 Feb 10	1909 Sept 9	
South Fork 2	1910 Nov 9		81154
Summitville	1880 Nov 17	1947 Nov 25*	
Wagon Wheel Gap	1875 Aug 27	1957 Sept 30*	
Wason	1891 Dec 26	1904 Apr 30	

Topo Quads

Dog Mountain	373730N	373000N	1061500W	1062230W
Fulcher Gulch	373000N	372230N	1060730W	1061500W
Greenie Mountain	373000N	372230N	1061500W	1062230W
Homelake	373730N	373000N	1060000W	1060730W
Horseshoe Mtn	373730N	373000N	1062230W	1063000W
Jasper	373000N	372230N	1062230W	1063000W
Monte Vista	373730N	373000N	1060730W	1061500W
Summitville	373000N	372230N	1063000W	1063730W
Waverly	373000N	372230N	1060000W	1060730W

Suggested Reading

Huston, Richard C. *A Gold Camp Called Summitville*. Lake City, CO: Western Reflections, 2012.

Van Horn, Beverly. *Early History of Mineral and Rio Grande Counties, Colorado*. NL: NP, 2000.

Routt County

Introduction

Established: 1877   Population: 23,509

Formed from: Grand

Adjacent Counties: Jackson, Grand, Eagle, Garfield, Rio Blanco, Moffat

County Seat: Steamboat Springs

Other Communities: Hayden, Oak Creek, Yampa, Phippsburg, Clark, Hahns Peak Village, Toponas, Milner

Website, http://www.co.routt.co.us

Area Codes: 970

Zip Codes: 80428, 80467, 80469, 80477, 80479, 80483, 80487, 80488, 81639

Historical Assets Colorado

Routt County Courthouse

Courthouses & County Government

Routt County
> http://www.co.routt.co.us

Routt County Courthouse (14th Judicial District), 1955 Shield Dr, Steamboat Springs, CO 80477, 970-879-5020; http://www.courts.state.co.us/Courts/County/Index.cfm?County_ID=47

Assessor, 522 Lincoln Ave, Steamboat Springs, CO 80477, 970-870-5544; http://www.co.routt.co.us/115/Assessor

Board of County Commissioners, 522 Lincoln Ave, Steamboat Springs, CO 80487, 970-879-0108, http://www.co.routt.co.us/103/County-Commissioners

Clerk & Recorder, 522 Lincoln Ave, Steamboat Springs, CO 80477, 970-870-5556; http://www.co.routt.co.us/133/Clerk-Recorder

Coroner, 136 6th St, Steamboat Springs, CO 80477, 970-870-5405; http://www.co.routt.co.us/147/Coroner

Public Health, 940 Central Park Dr, Ste 101, Steamboat Springs, CO 80487, 970-879-1632; http://www.co.routt.co.us/641/Public-Health-Services

Transportation (Public Works), 136 6th St, 1st Fl, Steamboat Springs, CO 80477, 970-870-5552; http://www.co.routt.co.us/198/Public-Works

Treasurer, 522 Lincoln Ave, Steamboat Springs, CO 80477, 970-870-5555; http://www.co.routt.co.us/211/Treasurer

County Records

Birth Unk	Marriage 1877	Divorce 1877
Death Unk	Land 1877	Probate 1877
Court 1877		

Routt County

County & Municipal Records Held at the State Level

The Colorado State Archives

Physical Records
Assessor
Clerk & Recorder
County Court
District Court
Justice Court
Public Trustee
Treasurer
WPA Historical Records
WPA Religious Institutions Survey
Cities
Oak Creek
Yampa

Records on Film
District Court
Combined Courts
School Districts
Cities
Oak Creek

Records on Master Film
County Court
District Court
Combined Courts
School Districts
Cities
Oak Creek
Steamboat Springs

The Denver Public Library
Routt County Mining Companies Records, 1907
WWI Draft Registration Cards (microfilm)

School Districts

School Districts, http://www.adcogov.org/local-school-districts
Eagle County School District RE 50, 948 Chambers Ave, Eagle, CO 81631, 970-328-6321; https://www.eagleschools.net/
Hayden School District Re-1, 495 W Jefferson Ave, Hayden, CO 81639, 970-276-3864; http://haydenschools.org/
South Routt School District RE-3, 305 S Grant St, Oak Creek, CO 80467, 970-736-2313; https://www.southroutt.k12.co.us/
Steamboat Springs School District RE-2, 325 7th St, Steamboat Springs, CO 80487, 970-871-3199; http://www.sssd.k12.co.us/

Historic School Districts

1. Battle Creek
2. Edson, Hayden
3. Mt Harris
4. Steamboat Springs
5. Sidney
6. Phippsburg, Crosho, Hunt Creek
7. Deep Creek
8. Toponas, Eugeria Park
9. Fly Gulch, Fairplay School
10. Moon Hill, Clark, Deep Creek
11. Elkhead, Hayden
12. Haybro
13. Mesa
14. Dunkley
15. Pagoda, SW of Hayden
16. Southside, 20 Mile
17. Morrison Creek
18. Pleasant Valley, Sidney
19. Clark
20. Lancaster, Around Yampa
21. Beardsley, Bradley, Pagoda, Dunkley
22. Long Gulch, Clark
23. Dunston, SW of Hayden
24. Windy Point, Clark
25. Milner, MacGregor
26. Hilton Gulch, Cow Creek
27. Foidl Canyon, Twenty Mile, Pinnacle
28. Mystic, Elk Mt, Upper Deep Creek
29. Pleasant View, Hayden
30. Cobb, Lower MOrrison Creek
31. Tow Creek, Bear River
32. Yampa
33. Middle Elk
34. Hahn's Peak, Pine Grove
35. Lower Oak Creek, Deer Park
36. Lone Springs, Terhune Basin, Seyfang Ranch

Historical Assets Colorado

37. Trout Creek
38. Oak Creek
39. Yellow Jacket
40. Fairplay
41. Red Dirt
42. Eddy
43. Milner
44. Slater Falls
Jt1. [1896]
Jt4. Eagle County
Jt5. Rio Blanco

Fraternal Organizations

Granges
Elk Mountain, No. 195, Routt, Trull/Steamboat Springs, 14 Apr 1911
Pleasant Valley, No. 201, Routt, Steamboat Springs, 17 June 1911
Community, No. 376, Routt, Steamboat Springs, 18 June 1918

Masons

Ancient Free & Accepted Masons
Elk Mountain, No. 106, Routt, Yampa, 20 Sept 1899
Hayden Valley, No. 118, Routt, Steamoat Springs, 21 Sept 1904
Oak Creek, No. 126, Routt, Hayden, 17 Sept 1907
Egeria, No. 167, Routt, Oak Creek, 22 Sept 1926
Crestone, No. 167, Routt, Yampa, 26 Jan 1996

Royal Arch Masons
Steamboat, No. 34, Routt, Steamboat Springs

Knights Templar
Red Cross Commandery, No. 37, Routt, Steamboat Springs

Eastern Star
Edith, No. 61, Routt, Yampa
Steamboat Springs, No. 95, Routt, Steamboat Springs
Hayden, No. 99, Routt, Hayden
Wild Rose, No. 132, Routt, Oak Creek

Prince Hall Masons
Mount Harris Lodge No. 7, Routt, Mount Harris, before 1926

Odd Fellows
Hayden, No. 111, Routt, Hayden
Finger Rock, No. 130, Routt, Yampa
Steamboat Springs, No. 131, Routt, Steamboat Springs
Oak Creek, No. 171, Routt, Oak Creek

Rebekahs
Hayden, No. 75, Routt, Hayden
Fern Leaf, No. 84, Routt, Oak Creek
Evergreen, No. 93, Routt, Steamboat Springs

Knights of Pythias
Onyx, No. 116, Routt, Steamboat Springs, 1901 June 19

Pythian Sisters
Oak Leaf, No. 3, Routt, Oak Creek
Blue Spruce, No. 3, Routt, Oak Creek

Benevolent Protective Order of Elks
None

Routt County

City & Town Halls
Steamboat Springs, 137 10th St, Steamboat Springs, CO 80477, 970-879-2060, https://steamboatsprings.net
Hayden, 178 W Jefferson Ave, Hayden, CO 81639, 970-276-3741, https://haydencolorado.org
Oak Creek, 129 Nancy Crawford Blvd, Oak Creek, CO 80467, 970-736-2422, https://townofoakcreek.com
Yampa, 56 Lincoln St, Yampa, CO 80483, 970-638-4511, https://www.townofyampa.com

Archives & Manuscript Collections
Routt County Public Records Archive (digital); http://www.co.routt.co.us/140/Recorded-Documents

Historical & Genealogical Societies
Bud Werner Memorial Library Genealogy Club, c/o Bud Werner Memorial Library, 1289 Lincoln Ave, Steamboat Springs, CO 80487, (970) 879-0240 x331, http://www.steamboatlibrary.org/genealogy-club
Hahns Peak Area Historical Society, Hahns Peak Village Museum, RCR 129 & Main St, P.O. Box 803, Clark, CO 80428, (970) 879-6781, http://www.hahnspeakhistoric.com
Historic Routt County, 141 9th St, P.O. Box 775717, Steamboat Springs, CO 80477, (970) 875-1305, http://www.historicrouttcounty.org
Historical Society of Oak Creek and Phippsburg, Tracks & Trails Museum, 129 E Main St, P.O. Box 1, Oak Creek, CO 80467, (970) 736-8245, http://www.tracksandtrailsmuseum.com

Local Libraries
Bud Werner Memorial Library & Digital Archive, 1289 Lincoln Ave, Steamboat Springs, CO 80487, (970) 879-0240, http://www.steamboatlibrary.org
Hayden Public Library, 201 E Jefferson, P.O. Box 1813, Hayden, CO 81639-1813, (970) 276-3777, http://www.haydenpubliclibrary.org
Toponas Public Library, 33650 Hwy 131, P.O. Box C, Toponas, CO 80479-0249, (970) 638-4436
Yampa Public Library, 310 Main St, P.O. Box 10, Yampa, CO 80483-0010, (970) 638-4654, https://southroutt.colibraries.org

Links
CO GenWeb
http://cogenweb.com/routt/
Cyndi's List
https://www.cyndislist.com/us/co/counties/routt/
FamilySearch Wiki
https://www.familysearch.org/wiki/en/Routt_County,_Colorado_Genealogy

Historical Assets Colorado

Linkpendium
http://www.linkpendium.com/routt-co-genealogy/

RootsWeb Wiki
https://wiki.rootsweb.com/wiki/index.php/Routt_County,_Colorado

Wikipedia
https://en.wikipedia.org/wiki/Routt_County,_Colorado

Historic Hotels

1948 Hotel Bristol, 917 Lincoln Ave, Steamboat Springs, CO 80487, 970-879-3083, https://steamboathotelbristol.com

Museums & Historic Sites

Hahns Peak Area Historical Society, Hahns Peak Village Museum, RCR 129 & Main St, P.O. Box 803, Clark, CO 80428, (970) 879-6781, http://www.hahnspeakhistoric.com

Hayden Heritage Center, 300 W Pearl St, P.O. Box 543, Hayden, CO 81639, (970) 276-4380, https://www.haydenheritagecenter.org

Historical Society of Oak Creek and Phippsburg, Tracks & Trails Museum, 129 E Main St, P.O. Box 1, Oak Creek, CO 80467, (970) 736-8245, http://www.tracksandtrailsmuseum.com

Tread of Pioneers Museum, 800 Oak St, P.O. Box 772372, Steamboat Springs, CO 80477, (970) 879-2214, http://www.treadofpioneers.org

Yampa-Egeria Historical Museum, 100 Main, Yampa, CO 80483, (970) 638-4480, http://nwcoloradoheritagetravel.org/yampa-colorado/

Special Events & Scenic Locations

The Routt County Fair is held in August most years at the Routt County Fairgrounds, 398 S Poplar St, Hayden, CO 81639, 970-276-3068, https://www.routtcountyfair.org

Routt County has a calendar of events here: http://www.co.routt.co.us/Calendar.aspx

The Steamboat Springs Chamber of Commers has a calendar of annual events here: https://www.steamboatchamber.com/events/annual-events/

Mount Zirkel Wilderness
Routt National Forest
Sarvis Creek Wilderness
White River National Forest
Peal Lake State Park
Stagecoach State Park
Steamboat Lake State Park
Yampa River State Park
Continental Divide National Scenic Trail
Fish Creek Falls National Recreation Trail
Swamp Park National Recreation Trail

Routt County

Flat Tops Trail Scenic Byway
Great Parks Bicycle Route

Ghost Towns & Other Sparsely Populated Places

Axial, Clark, Dunckley, Eddy, Egeria, Escalante, Hahn's Peak, Honnold, Ladore, Lay, Lily, Maybell, Pagoda, Routt, Sidney, Slater, Toponas, Trull, Yampa

Newspapers

The Steamboat Pilot. (Steamboat Springs, Routt County, Colo.) 1885-1927
The Inter Mountain. (Steamboat Springs, Routt County, Colo.) 1889-1???
The Pantagraph. (Craig, Routt County, Colo.) 1891-1895
The Routt County Sentinel. (Steamboat Springs, Colo.) 19??-19??
Routt County Republican. (Hayden, Routt County, Colo.) 19??-1954
Routt County Courier. (Craig, Routt County, Colo.) 1902-1911
The Yampa Leader. (Yampa, Colo.) 1903-1926
The Oak Creek Times. (Oak Creek, Colo.) 1908-1920
The Craig Empire. (Craig, Routt County, Colo.) 1911-1929
The Oak Creek Times and The Oak Creek Herald. (Oak Creek, Routt County, Colo.) 1921-1925
The Oak Creek Times. (Oak Creek, Routt County, Colo.) 1925-1926
The Oak Creek Times and The Yampa Leader. (Oak Creek, Routt County, Colo.) 1926-1942
The Steamboat Pilot and The Routt County Sentinel. (Steamboat Springs, Colo.) 1927-1928
The Steamboat Pilot with which is combined The Routt County Sentinel. (Steamboat Springs, Colo.) 1928-1944
Southern Routt County Oak Creek-Yampa Times-Leader. (Oak Creek, Routt County, Colo.) 1942-1944
The Steamboat Pilot with which is combined The Routt County Sentinel and Oak Creek Times-Leader. (Steamboat Springs, Colo.) 1944-1946
The Steamboat Pilot. (Steamboat Springs, Colo.) 1946-Current
The Hayden Valley Press. (Hayden, Colo.) 1965-Current
The Rustler. (Oak Creek, Co) 1988-1989
The Yampa Valley Rustler. ([Oak Creek, Colo.]) 1989-Current

Places on the National Register

Clark, Columbine, 645 Routt County Rd. 129
Columbine, Summit Creek Ranger Station, Cty Rd. 129
Hahns Peak, Hahns Peak Schoolhouse, Main St.
Hayden, Dawson—Carpenter Ranch, 13250 W. US 40
Hayden, Hayden Depot, 300 W. Pearl St.
Hayden, Hayden Rooming House, 295 S. Poplar St.
Hayden, Kimsey—Bolten Ranch Rural Historic Landscape, 41090 Cty. Rd. 80
Hayden, Solandt Memorial Hospital, 150 W. Jackson St.
Oak Creek, Bell Mercantile, 101—111 Moffat Ave.

Historical Assets Colorado

Oak Creek, Foidel Canyon School, NW of Oak Creek
Steamboat Springs, Chamber of Commerce Building, 1201 Lincoln Ave.
Steamboat Springs, Christian Science Society Building, 641 Oak St.
Steamboat Springs, Crawford House, 1184 Crawford Ave.
Steamboat Springs, First National Bank Building, 803-807 Lincoln Ave., and 57 1/2 8th St.
Steamboat Springs, Maxwell Building, 840 Lincoln Ave.
Steamboat Springs, Mesa Schoolhouse, 33985 S. US 40.
Steamboat Springs, Perry—Mansfield School of Theatre and Dance, 40755 Routt Co. Rd. 36
Steamboat Springs, Routt County National Bank Building, 802-806 Lincoln Ave.
Steamboat Springs, Steamboat Apartments, 302 11th St.
Steamboat Springs, Steamboat Laundry Building, 127 and 131 11th St.
Steamboat Springs, Steamboat Springs Depot, 39265 Routt County Rd. 33B
Steamboat Springs, Steamboat Springs Downtown Historic District, Lincoln Ave. roughly bounded by 5th to 11th Sts.
Toponas, Rock Creek Stage Station, E of Toponas off CO 84
Yampa, Antlers Cafe and Bar, 40 & 46 Moffat Ave.
Yampa, Bell and Canant Mercantile—Crossan's M and A Market, 101 Main St.
Yampa, Pyramid Guard Station, Cty. Rd. 8

USGS Historic Places
Milner, Bear River, 40.4838637, -107.1172774
Rattlesnake Butte, Foidel School, 40.3569224, -107.055608
Unknown, Dawson Post Office, 0, 0

Grand Army of the Republic Posts
Jim Laird, No. 77, Routt, Steamboat Springs

USGS Historic Military Places
None

Military Bases
None

Post Offices

Anthracite	1905 Feb 11	1906 July 17
Axial	1893 Mar 6	1958 Apr 30*
Barbee	1906 Jan 13	1909 Aug 14
Battle Creek	1911 Mar 3	1938 Feb 3
Bear River	1914 Nov 10	1940 Sept 20
Bison	1898 Feb 18	Never in operation
Brookston	1914 Mar 25	1930 Apr 15
Cary Ranch	1914 Mar 25	1930 Nov 29

Routt County

Clark	1889 Sept 16		80428
Coalview	1916 Dec 12	1921 Nov 30	
Columbine	1896 June 5	1967 May 19	
Conger	1894 Mar 27	1895 July 15	
Craig	1883 Jan 12		81625
Dawson	1917 Nov 27	1919 Nov 15	
Deepcreek	1900 Jan 30	1936 Jan 15	
Drygulch	1896 July 2	1898 June 2	
Dunkley	1892 Dec 16	1942 Dec 31	
Eddy	1890 Mar 19	1913 Aug 31	
Edith	1883 Feb 21	1885 July 9	
Egeria	1883 Apr 2	1900 Mar 15	
Elkhead	1884 June 24	1924 Sept 15*	
Escalante	1889 Sept 18	1893 Aug 31	
Eula	1900 June 23	1902 Apr 15	
Fortification	1883 Jan 15	1922 June 30*	
Fourmile	1895 Mar 16	1899 July 24	
Hahns Peak	1877 May 3	1941 Nov 26	
Hamilton	1896 July 7	1917 Aug 15	
Hardscrabble	1925 Feb 12	1925 Nov 15	
Harrison	1901 Mar 27	1908 Jan 15	
Haybro	1918 Mar 15	1951 July 15	
Hayden	1875 Nov 15	1881 Aug 1*	
Hayden	1881 Oct 24		81639
Honnold	1890 Apr 26	1904 Apr 30	
Huggins	1906 Mar 23	1908 Sept 15	
Hydrate	1920 June 17	1937 Sept 15	
Junction City	1912 May 13	1916 Dec 12	
Juniper	1906 Feb 9	1919 Sept 4	
Ladore	1889 June 3	1924 Mar 25	
Lay	1881 Aug 15	1976 June 30*	
Lily	1889 Sept 17	1937 May 15*	
Maybell	1884 Oct 14		81640
McGregor	1915 July 1	1942 Oct 31	
Milner	1920 Jan 22	1988 Oct 31*	
Mobley	1906 Mar 17	1907 Jan 2	
Mount Harris	1915 Apr 12	1958 May 30	
Mystic	1910 June 17	1942 Nov 30	
Oak Creek	1907 Feb 5		80467
Oneco	1900 July 12	1901 Dec 14	
Pagoda	1890 Feb 15	1947 Mar 31	
Pershing	1918 June 17	1942 Dec 31	
Phippsburg	1909 Mar 3		80469
Pool	1900 Mar 17	1920 Jan 22	
Puma	1896 Apr 17	1897 Aug 10	
Pyramid	1896 Apr 24	1932 Dec 15*	

639

Historical Assets Colorado

Routt	1884 Oct 3	1892 Mar 22*		
Sidney	1888 Aug 10	1941 Dec 4*		
Slater	1888 Dec 24		81653	
Steamboat Springs	1878 May 20		80487	
Thiesen	1909 June 3	1911 Dec 31		
Toponas	1888 July 25		80479	
Tosh	1915 Oct 8	1917 Jan 15		
Trout Creek	1926 Mar 13	1935 Feb 15		
Trull	1888 June 16	1922 Nov 15*		
Wallrock	1902 July 29	1903 June 30		
Willow Creek	1923 Feb 12	1943 Sept 30*		
Windsor	1877 Apr 26	1880 July 19		
Yampa	1883 Jan 12	1889 Aug 28		
Yampa 2	1894 Oct 30		80483	
Yarmony	1908 Jan 6	1908 Jan 27		

Topo Quads

Bears Ears Peaks	405230N	404500N	1070730W	1071500W
Blacktail Mountain	402230N	401500N	1064500W	1065230W
Blue Hill	400000N	395230N	1064500W	1065230W
Breeze Mountain	403000N	402230N	1072230W	1073000W
Buck Point	405230N	404500N	1071500W	1072230W
Buffalo Pass	403730N	403000N	1063730W	1064500W
Burns North	400000N	395230N	1065230W	1070000W
Clark	404500N	403730N	1065230W	1070000W
Cow Creek	403000N	402230N	1065230W	1070000W
Davis Peak	410000N	405230N	1063730W	1064500W
Deadman Park	405230N	404500N	1054500W	1055230W
Dome Peak	400000N	395230N	1070000W	1070730W
Dunckley	402230N	401500N	1070730W	1071500W
Dunckley Pass	401500N	400730N	1070730W	1071500W
Elkhorn Mountain	410000N	405230N	1065230W	1070000W
Farwell Mountain	405230N	404500N	1064500W	1065230W
Floyd Peak	404500N	403730N	1064500W	1065230W
Fly Creek	410000N	405230N	1071500W	1072230W
Gore Mountain	401500N	400730N	1063730W	1064500W
Green Ridge	401500N	400730N	1064500W	1065230W
Hahns Peak	405230N	404500N	1065230W	1070000W
Hayden	403000N	402230N	1071500W	1072230W
Hayden Gulch	402230N	401500N	1071500W	1072230W
Hooker Mountain	403730N	403000N	1070730W	1071500W
Lynx Pass	400730N	400000N	1063730W	1064500W
Mad Creek	403730N	403000N	1065230W	1070000W
McCoy	400000N	395230N	1063730W	1064500W
Meaden Peak	405230N	404500N	1070000W	1070730W
Milner	403000N	402230N	1070000W	1070730W

Routt County

Mount Ethel	404500N	403730N	1063730W	1064500W
Mount Harris	403000N	402230N	1070730W	1071500W
Mount Werner	403000N	402230N	1063730W	1064500W
Mount Zirkel	405230N	404500N	1063730W	1064500W
Oak Creek	402230N	401500N	1065230W	1070000W
Orno Peak	400730N	400000N	1070000W	1070730W
Pagoda	402230N	401500N	1072230W	1073000W
Pagoda Peak	401500N	400730N	1071500W	1072230W
Pilot Knob	404500N	403730N	1070000W	1070730W
Quaker Mountain	404500N	403730N	1070730W	1071500W
Ralph White Lake	403730N	403000N	1072230W	1073000W
Rattlesnake Butte	402230N	401500N	1070000W	1070730W
Rock Spring Gulch	403730N	403000N	1071500W	1072230W
Rocky Peak	403730N	403000N	1064500W	1065230W
Sand Point	401500N	400730N	1070000W	1070730W
Shield Mountain	410000N	405230N	1070000W	1070730W
Slide Creek	401500N	400730N	1072230W	1073000W
Slide Mountain	404500N	403730N	1071500W	1072230W
Steamboat Springs	403000N	402230N	1064500W	1065230W
Toponas	400730N	400000N	1064500W	1065230W
Trapper	400730N	400000N	1065230W	1070000W
Tumble Mountain	410000N	405230N	1070730W	1071500W
Walton Peak	402230N	401500N	1063730W	1064500W
West Fork Lake	410000N	405230N	1064500W	1065230W
Wolf Mountain	403730N	403000N	1070000W	1070730W
Yampa	401500N	400730N	1065230W	1070000W

Suggested Reading

Aldrich, John K. *Ghosts of Eagle and Grand Counties: Stories from the Ghost Towns and Mining Camps of Eagle, Grand, Jackson, Larimer and Routt Counties*, Colorado. Denver: Columbine Ink, 2009.

Gay, Elaine. *How Pleasant is the Valley: Routt County, Colorado, a Historical Perspective*. NL: NP, 1995.

History of Routt County, Colorado. Hurst, TX: Curtis Media, 1995.

History of West Routt County, Colorado. Hurst, TX: Curtis Media, 1995.

Leckenby, Charles H. *The Tread of Pioneers: Some Highlights in the Dramatic and Colorful History of Northwestern Colorado*. Steamboat Springs, CO: Steam Boat Pilot, 1945.

Metcalf, F A. *Developing an Empire: Steamboat Springs and Routt County, Colorado*. Steamboat Springs, CO: Steamboat Pilot Print, 1911.

Stanko, Jim et al. *The Historical Guide to Routt County*. Steamboat Springs, CO: Treat of Pioneers Museum, 2010.

Stoddard, C A, Dan Davidson, Janet Gerber and Shannan Koucherik. *Tales of the Old West Retold: Early Stories of Northwestern Colorado*. Montrose, CO: Lifetime Chronicle Press, 2007

Historical Assets Colorado

Saguache County

Introduction

Established: 1866   Population: 6,108

Formed from: Costilla, Lake

Adjacent Counties: Chaffee, Fremont, Custer, Huerfano, Rio Grande, Alamosa, Mineral, Hinsdale, Gunnison

County Seat: Saguache

Other Communities: Bonanza, Center, Crestone, Moffat, Alder, Bonita, Chester, Duncan, Iris, Kerper, La Garita, Liberty, Mineral Hot Springs, Parkville, Sargents, Spook City, Villa Grove

Website, https://www.saguachecounty.net

Area Codes: 719

Zip Codes: 81131, 81143, 81149, 81155, 81248

Historical Assets Colorado

Saguache County Courthouse

Courthouses & County Government

Saguache County
https://www.saguachecounty.net

Saguache County Courthouse (12th Judicial District), 501 Christy Ave, Saguache, CO 81149, 719-655-2522; http://www.courts.state.co.us/Courts/County/Index.cfm?County_ID=37

Assessor, P.O. Box 38, Saguache, CO 81149, 719-655-2521; http://www.saguachecounty.net/index.php/departments/assessor-home

Board of County Commissioners, P.O. Box 100, Saguache, CO 81149, 719-655-2231, https://www.saguachecounty.net/index.php/commissioners-home

Clerk & Recorder, 501 4th St, Saguache, CO 81149, 719-655-2512; http://www.saguachecounty.net/index.php/departments/clerk-a-recorder-home

Coroner, P.O. Box 353, Center, CO, 719-850-2219; https://www.saguachecounty.net/index.php/departments/coroner

Public Health, 505 3rd St, Saguache, CO 81149, 719-655-2533; http://www.saguachecounty.net/index.php/public-health-home

Transportation (Road & Bridge), 305 3rd St, Saguaqche, CO 81149, 719-655-2554; https://www.saguachecounty.net/index.php/departments/road-and-bridge

Treasurer, P.O. Box 177, Saguache, CO 81149, 719-655-2656; http://www.saguachecounty.net/departments/Treasurerpublic-trustee

County Records

Birth Unk
Death Unk
Court 1900
CSA Board of Health Records 1882

Marriage 1885
Land 1885

Divorce 1900
Probate 1900

Saguache County

County & Municipal Records Held at the State Level

The Colorado State Archives

Physical Records
Board of Health
Clerk & Recorder
Coroner
County Court
District Court
WPA Historical Records
WPA Religious Institutions Survey
Cities
  Saguache

Records on Film
1885 Census
Clerk & Recorder
County Court

Records on Master Film
County Court
District Court
Combined Courts
School Districts
Cities
  Sargent

The Denver Public Library

Saguache County Mining Companies Records, 1892
WWI Draft Registration Cards (microfilm)

School Districts

School Districts, http://www.adcogov.org/local-school-districts
Center School District 25 JT, 550 S Sylvester Ave, Center, CO 81125; https://www.center.k12.co.us/
Gunnison Watershed School District, No. RE-1J, 800 N Boulevard St, Gunnison, CO 81230, 970-641-7770; https://www.gunnisonschools.net/
Moffat School District 2, 501 Garfield Ave, Moffat, CO 81143, 719-745-0500; https://www.moffatschools.org/
Mountain Valley School District RE-1, 403 Pitkin Ave, Saguache, CO 81149, 719-655-2578; http://mountainvalleyschool.org/
Sangre de Christo School District 22J, 8751 Lane 7 N, Mosca, CO 81146, 719-378-2321; http://sdc.schooldesk.net/

Historic School Districts

1. Lawrence, Saguache
2. Moffat, Scandrett
3. Cotton Creek, Mirage
4. Gay, La Garita
5. Alder
6. Saguache
7. Craig
8. Crestone, Moffat
9. Goodwin
10. [1881]
11. Higgins
12. Bonanza
13. Villa Grove
14. Parkville, Claytonia
15. Werner
16. MacFarland
17. Veteran
18. Lockett
19. Sargents
20. White
21. Richards
22. Foster
23. Bordow, Hooper [Joint with Alamosa]
24. Bulen
25. Mattern, Upper La Garita
26. Myers Creek, Center
27. Hodding, Dome Lake, Jack's Creek
28. Hodding, Wills
29. Duncan
30. Crookston
31. Moffat
32. [1898]
33. Embargo

Historical Assets Colorado

Fraternal Organizations
Granges
Center, No. 403, Saguache, Center, 11 Jan 1927
San Luis Valley, No. 422, Saguache, Villa Grove, 30 Sept 1935
Moffat, No. 423, Saguache, Moffat, 2 Oct 1935
Saguache, No. 424, Saguache, Saguache, 13 Nov 1935
Center, No. 425, Saguache, Center, 19 Nov 1935

Masons
Ancient Free & Accepted Masons
San Juan, No. 32, Saguache, Saguache, 18 Sept 1877
Olive Branch, No. 112, Saguache, Crestone, 17 Sept 1901

Royal Arch Masons
None

Knights Templar
None

Eastern Star
Minnehaha, No. 48, Saguache, Saguache
Golden Grain, No. 80, Saguache, Center

Odd Fellows
Centennial, No. 23, Saguache, Moffat
Centennial, No. 23, Saguache, Saguache
Bonanza, No. 44, Saguache, Bonanza, 1882 Jan 21

Rebekahs
None

Knights of Pythias
None

Pythian Sisters
None

Benevolent Protective Order of Elks
None

City & Town Halls
Saguache, 504 San Juan Ave, Saguache, CO 81149, 719-655-2232, http://www.townofsaguache.org
Center, 294 Worth St, Center, Co 81125, 719-754-3497, https://www.colorado.gov/townofcenter
Crestone, 199 Alder St, Crestone, CO 81131, 719-256-4313, https://www.colorado.gov/pacific/townofcrestone/
Moffat, 401 Lincoln Ave, Moffat, CO 81143, 719-588-2391, https://www.colorado.gov/townofmoffat

Archives & Manuscript Collections
None

Saguache County

Historical & Genealogical Societies
None

Local Libraries
Saguache County Public Library, 702 Pitkin Ave, P.O. Box 448, Saguache, CO 81149-0448, (719) 655-2551, http://nscld.colibraries.org

Links
CO GenWeb
http://cogenweb.com/saguache/

Cyndi's List
https://www.cyndislist.com/us/co/counties/saguache/

FamilySearch Wiki
https://www.familysearch.org/wiki/en/Saguache_County,_Colorado_Genealogy

Linkpendium
http://www.linkpendium.com/saguache-co-genealogy/

RootsWeb Wiki
https://wiki.rootsweb.com/wiki/index.php/Saguache_County,_Colorado

Wikipedia
https://en.wikipedia.org/wiki/Saguache_County,_Colorado

Historic Hotels
None

Museums & Historic Sites
Crestone Historical Museum, 222 Cottonwood St, P.O. Box 64, Crestone, CO 81131, (719) 588-4279, https://www.museumtrail.org/crestone-historical-museum.html

Hazard House Museum, 807 Pitkin Ave, Saguache, CO 81149, (719) 655-2557, https://www.museumtrail.org/hazard-house-museum.html

Saguache County Museum, 405 8th St, P.O. Box 569, Saguache, CO 81149, (719) 655-2557, https://www.museumtrail.org/saguache-county-museum.html

Special Events & Scenic Locations
The Saguache County Annual Fall Festival is held in September each year, https://saguachechamber.org/saguache-colorado-annual-fall-festival/#

Saguache County keeps a printable calendar of upcoming events here: https://saguachechamber.org

Great Sand Dunes National Park and Preserve
Great Sand Dunes Wilderness
Gunnison National Forest
Rio Grande National Forest
La Garita Wilderness
Sangre de Christo Wilderness

Historical Assets Colorado

Colorado Trail
Continental Divide National Scenic Trail
Great Parks Bicycle Route
Liberty Road Historic Mail Route
Medano Pass Primitive Road
Montville Nature Trail
Mosca Pass Trail
Old Spanish National Historic Trail
Sand Ramp Trail
Western Express Bicycle Route

Ghost Towns & Other Sparsely Populated Places

Alder, Biedell, Bonanza (Bonanza City), Buxton, Carnero, Chester, Claytonia, Cotton Creek, Crestone, Cuenin, Davenport, Duncan, Dune, Elko, Grays, Hilldon, Hot Springs, Iris, LaGarita, Liberty, Lockett, Los Magotes, Marshall Pass, Mirage, Moffat, Orient, Pocono, Poncho Pass, Rio Alto, Round Hill, Saguache, San Isabel, Sargents, Shawano, Veteran, Villa Grove

Newspapers

The Crestone Miner. (Crestone, Saguache County, Colo.) 1???-19??
Sentinel. (Saguache, Saguache County, Colo.) 18??-1???
Saguache Chronicle. (Saguache, Colo.) 1874-1886
The Colorado Herald. (Saguache, Saguache County, Colo.) 188?-1???
The Daily Enterprise. (Bonanza, Colo.) 1881-1882
Saguache Advance. (Saguache, Colo.) 1882-1885
Crystal Hill Pilot. (Bellevue, Colo.) 1883-1883
Saguache Democrat. (Saguache, Colo.) 1885-1889
Saguache Crescent. (Saguache, Colo.) 1889-Current
The Creede News. (Creede, Saguache County, Colo.) 1892-1???
Cochetopa Gold Belt. (Iris, Colo.) 1895-1???
The Centerview Reporter. (Centerview, Saguache County, Colo.) 1898-1899
The Center Reporter. (Center, Saguache County, Colo.) 1899-1???
Moffat Home and Farm with which has been consolidated, The Moffat Times. (Moffat, Colo.) 19??-19??
The Moffat Times. (Moffat, Saguache County, Colo.) 19??-19??
Moffat Home and Garden. (Moffat, Colo.) 19??-19??
The Center Star. (Center, Colo.) 1900-19??
The Bonanza Bee. (Bonanza, Colo.) 1901-1902
The Center Dispatch. (Center, Saguache County, Colo.) 1901-1911
The Center Post. (Center, Colo.) 1910-1911
The Center Post-Dispatch. (Center, Saguache County, Colo.) 1911-Current
The Farmers' Exchange Bulletin. (San Luis Valley [Colo.]) 1916-19??
The Needles. (Crestone, Colo.) 1990-1990

Saguache County

Places on the National Register
Crestone, Crestone School, Cottonwood St. and Carbonate Ave.
La Garita, Capilla de San Juan Bautista, NW of La Garita
La Garita, Carnero Creek Pictographs, Address Restricted
Moffat, First Baptist Church of Moffat, 401 Lincoln Ave.
Mosca, Indian Grove, Address Restricted
Saguache, Saguache Downtown Historic District, Roughly 300 & 400 blks. of 4th St.
Saguache, Saguache Flour Mill,
Saguache, Saguache School and Jail Buildings, U.S. 285 and San Juan Ave.
Sargents, Sargents Water Tank, Denver & Rio Grande Railroad, Western Line, 45 Front St

USGS Historic Places
Bonanza, Sedgewick, 38.2791663, -106.1477983
Center North, Finley Airport, 37.7666675, -106.1228047
Mirage, Mirage, 38.1027769, -105.8644574

Grand Army of the Republic Posts
Bonanza, No. ?, Saguache, Bonanza

USGS Historic Military Places
None

Military Bases
None

Post Offices

Alder	1881 Aug 29	1910 Aug 31	
Alder	1911 Nov 11	1927 Nov 30	
Amethyst	1892 Jan 25	1909 Feb 2	
Barnum	1876 Mar 20	1881 June 7	
Biedell	1883 June 26	1884 Spr 28	
Bismarck	1872 Feb 7	1879 Oct 10	
Bonanza	1880 Aug 12	1938 May 14*	
Bonito	1881 Mar 7	1883 Aug 28	
Carnero	1870 June 16	1884 Mar 18*	
Carnero 2	1884 Apr 28	1911 Aug 31	
Center	1899 July 1		81125
Centerview	1898 Apr 22	1899 July 1	
Claytonia	1881 Mar 11	1892 Mar 10	
Cochetopa	1877 Feb 23	1916 Apr 15	
Cotton Creek	1875 Aug 9	1895 Feb 13	
Creede	1891 July 1	1908 Nov 28	
Crestone	1880 Nov 16		81131
Cristonie	1872 Feb 7	1873 Oct 29	

649

Historical Assets Colorado

Crookstown	1904 May 25	1906 Feb 28	
Cuenin	1884 Feb 4	1892 May 21	
Duncan	1892 Nov 21	1900 Sept 15	
Dune	1891 Apr 24	1895 June 10	
Embargo	1903 Sept 23	1905 Mar 15	
Exchequer	1881 July 22	1883 June 6	
Garibaldi	1870 June 13	1872 Jan 19	
Gibson	1911 Dec 1	1923 Aug 14	
Green	1884 Mar 18	1884 Sept 30	
Haumann	1882 Jan 19	1885 Aug 25	
Herard	1905 Nov 13	1912 Dec 15	
Iris	1894 Oct 30	1902 Mar 15*	
Kimbrell	1881 Mar 11	1881 Oct 14	
La Garita	1874 June 24	1972 Nov 11*	
Lanark	1898 Mar 29	1898 Dec 27	
Liberty	1900 Nov 1	1921 Mar 31*	
Lockett	1889 May 22	1905 Jan 14	
Loma	1867 Apr 1	1875 July 22*	
Los Mogotes	1888 July 28	1890 Jan 8	
Los Pinos	1872 Nov 20	1877 Feb 23	
Marshall Pass	1919 Mar 6	1952 Sept 30*	
Marshaltown	1880 July 13	1882 Jan 26	
Mineral Hot Springs	1911 May 9	1947 Dec 15	
Mirage	1895 Feb 13	1927 Jan 31	
Moffat	1890 Aug 20		81149
Orient	1894 Oct 15	1905 May 15	
Oriental	1881 Mar 25	1884 Feb 25	
Parkville	1885 Jan 12	1886 Mar 2	
Perry	1896 Dec 16	1898 Nov 16	
Pruden	1895 Mar 5	1900 Dec 31	
Pyke	1900 Nov 8	1902 Sept 15	
Rito Alto	1872 Feb 7	1884 Feb 18	
Rock Cliff	1874 Aug 10	1880 July 29	
Saguache	1867 Apr 1		81149
San Isabel	1872 Feb 7	1912 May 15	
Sangre de Christo	18767 Apr 19	1884 Feb 28	
Sargents	1880 July 13		81248
Schistos	1894 Oct 30	1895 May 7	
Sedgwick	1880 Aug 23	1885 Jan 12	
Shirley	1881 May 31	1882 May 11	
Spanish	1898 May 25	1898 Nov 21	
Tetons	1880 Aug 30	1881 June 7	
Veteran	1888 May 17	1894 Apr 16	
Villa Grove	1872 Jan 19	1894 Oct 12	
Villa Grove 2	1950 July 1		81155
Villagrove	1894 Oct 12	1950 July 1	

Saguache County

Wabash	1911 May 9	1911 Dec 1
Wagon Wheel Gap	1875 Aug 27	1957 Sept 30*
Watonga	1910 June 6	1911 Oct 31
White Earth	1876 Jan 24	1880 June 24
Willow	1891 May 12	1891 July 1

Topo Quads

Baldy Cinco	380000N	375230N	1070000W	1070730W
Beck Mountain	380000N	375230N	1052230W	1053000W
Bonanza	382230N	381500N	1060730W	1061500W
Bowers Peak	380000N	375230N	1063000W	1063730W
Center North	375230N	374500N	1060000W	1060730W
Center South	374500N	373730N	1060000W	1060730W
Chester	382230N	381500N	1061500W	1062230W
Cochetopa Park	381500N	380730N	1063730W	1064500W
Cold Spring Park	381500N	380730N	1064500W	1065230W
Crestone	380000N	375230N	1053730W	1054500W
Crestone Peak	380000N	375230N	1053000W	1053730W
Deadman Camp	375230N	374500N	1054500W	1055230W
Deadman Camp SW	375230N	374500N	1055230W	1060000W
Del Norte	374500N	373730N	1061500W	1062230W
Electric Peak	381500N	380730N	1053730W	1054500W
Elk Park	380730N	380000N	1064500W	1065230W
Graveyard Gulch	381500N	380730N	1060000W	1060730W
Grouse Creek	380730N	380000N	1063000W	1063730W
Halfmoon Pass	380000N	375230N	1064500W	1065230W
Harrence Lake	380000N	375230N	1060000W	1060730W
Hickey Bridge	380730N	380000N	1060000W	1060730W
Hooper East	374500N	373730N	1054500W	1055230W
Hooper West	374500N	373730N	1055230W	1060000W
Horn Peak	380730N	380000N	1053000W	1053730W
Indian Head	374500N	373730N	1062230W	1063000W
Klondike Mine	381500N	380730N	1060730W	1061500W
La Garita	375230N	374500N	1060730W	1061500W
Lake Mountain	380730N	380000N	1062230W	1063000W
Lake Mountain NE	381500N	380730N	1061500W	1062230W
Laughlin Gulch	380730N	380000N	1061500W	1062230W
Liberty	375230N	374500N	1053000W	1053730W
Lime Creek	380000N	375230N	1061500W	1062230W
Lookout Mountain	380000N	375230N	1062230W	1063000W
Medano Pass	375230N	374500N	1052230W	1053000W
Mesa Mountain	380000N	375230N	1063730W	1064500W
Mineral Mountain	380730N	380000N	1070000W	1070730W
Mirage	380730N	380000N	1054500W	1055230W
Moffat North	380730N	380000N	1055230W	1060000W
Moffat South	380000N	375230N	1055230W	1060000W

Historical Assets Colorado

North Pass	381500N	380730N	1063000W	1063730W
Pine Cone Knob	375230N	374500N	1063000W	1063730W
Pool Table Mountain	375230N	374500N	1063730W	1064500W
Razor Creek Dome	382230N	381500N	1063730W	1064500W
Rito Alto Peak	380730N	380000N	1053730W	1054500W
Rock Creek Park	381500N	380730N	1065230W	1070000W
Saguache	380730N	380000N	1060730W	1061500W
Saguache Park	380730N	380000N	1063730W	1064500W
San Luis Peak	380000N	375230N	1065230W	1070000W
Sand Camp	375230N	374500N	1053730W	1054500W
Sargents Mesa	382230N	381500N	1062230W	1063000W
Sawtooth Mountain	382230N	381500N	1064500W	1065230W
Sevenmile Plaza	374500N	373730N	1060730W	1061500W
Sheds Camp	380000N	375230N	1054500W	1055230W
South Fork East	374500N	373730N	1063000W	1063730W
Stewart Peak	380730N	380000N	1065230W	1070000W
Swede Corners	380000N	375230N	1060730W	1061500W
Trickle Mountain	381500N	380730N	1062230W	1063000W
Twin Mountains	375230N	374500N	1062230W	1063000W
Twin Mountains SE	375230N	374500N	1061500W	1062230W
Valley View Hot Springs	381500N	380730N	1054500W	1055230W
Villa Grove	381500N	380730N	1055230W	1060000W
West Baldy	382230N	381500N	1063000W	1063730W
Whale Hill	382230N	381500N	1060000W	1060730W

Suggested Reading

Dwire, John Franklin and Patricia Ann Webster. *A Brief History of Sargents, Colorado*. Gunnison, CO: NP, 1969.

Hoyt, Louise. *The Forgotten Road*. Gunnison, CO: NP, 1968.

Huffman, Walter. *Saguache County Military During the Ute Uprising, Saguache County, Colorado, 1875-1881*. Denver: Colorado State DAR, 1989.

Kempner, Helen Ashley Anderson. *Bonanza! A Pictoral History of Colorado's Kerber Creek Country*. Colorado Springs, CO: Little london Press, 1978.

Lawrence, John and Bernice Martin. *Frontier Eyewitness: a Diary of John Lawrence, 1867-1908*. NL: NP, 1990.

Saguache County Museum's Images of the Past: Places, People, Events. Saguache, CO: Saguache County Museum, 1998.

San Juan County

Introduction

Established: 1876   Population: 699

Formed from: Lake

Adjacent Counties: Ouray, Hinsdale, La Plata, Montezyma, Dolores, San Miguel

County Seat: Silverton

  Other Communities: Howardsville, Middleton, Needleton, Animas Forks, Eureka

Website, https://www.colorado.gov/sanjuan

Area Codes: 970

Zip Codes: 81433

Historical Assets Colorado

San Juan County Courthouse

Courthouses & County Government

San Juan County
http://www.sanjuancountycolorado.us
San Juan County Courthouse (6th Judicial District), 1557 Greene St, Silverton, CO 81433, 970-387-5790; http://www.courts.state.co.us/Courts/County/Index.cfm?County_ID=14
Assessor, 1557 Greene St, Silverton, CO 81433, 970-387-5632; http://www.sanjuancountycolorado.us/assessor.html
Board of County Commissioners, 1557 Greene St, Silverton, CO 81433, https://www.colorado.gov/sanjuan
Clerk & Recorder, 1557 Greene St, Silverton, CO 81433, 970-387-5671; http://www.sanjuancountycolorado.us/clerk—recorder.html
Coroner, 1557 Greene St, Silverton, CO 81433, 970-903-7952; http://www.sanjuancountycolorado.us/coroner.html
Public Health, 1315 Snowden St, Silverton, CO 81433, 970-387-0242; http://sjchealth.org/
Transportation (Road & Bridge), 1127 Animas St, Silverton, CO 81433, 970-387-9932; http://www.sanjuancountycolorado.us/road—bridge.html
Treasurer, 1557 Greene St, Silverton, CO 81433, 970-387-5488; http://www.sanjuancountycolorado.us/Treasurer.html

County Records

Birth 1880	Marriage 1880	Divorce 1876
Death 1901	Land 1880	Probate 1876
Court 1876		

San Juan County

County & Municipal Records Held at the State Level

The Colorado State Archives

Physical Records
Clerk & Recorder
County Commissioners
County Court
District Court
WPA Historical Records
WPA Religious Institutions Survey

Records on Film
County Court

Records on Master Film
School Districts

The Denver Public Library
Big Five Mining Companies Records, 1892-1921
San Juan County Mining Companies Records, 1879-1881
WWI Draft Registration Cards (microfilm)

School Districts
School Districts, http://www.adcogov.org/local-school-districts
Silverton School District 1, 1160 Snowden St, Silverton, CO 81433, 970-387-5543; http://www.silvertonschool.org/

Historic School Districts
1. San Juan, Silverton
2. [1883]

Fraternal Organizations

Granges
None

Masons

Ancient Free & Accepted Masons
Norwood, No. 33, San Juan, Silverton, 18 Sept 1878

Royal Arch Masons
Silverton, No. 41, San Juan, Silverton

Knights Templar
None

Eastern Star
Gem, No. 15, San Juan, Silverton

Odd Fellows
Silverton, No. 51, San Juan, Silverton

Rebekahs
None

Knights of Pythias
Snow Flake, No. 61, San Juan, Silverton

Historical Assets Colorado

Pythian Sisters
Baker Park, No. 19, San Juan, Silverton

Benevolent Protective Order of Elks
None

City & Town Halls
Silverton, 1360 Greene St, Silverton, CO 81433, 970-387-5522, https://www.colorado.gov/townofsilverton

Archives & Manuscript Collections
San Juan County Historical Society, Mining Heritage Center & Archives, 1567 Greene St, P.O. Box 154, Silverton, CO 81433, (970) 387-5838, https://sanjuancountyhistoricalsociety.org

Historical & Genealogical Societies
San Juan County Historical Society, Mining Heritage Center & Archives, 1567 Greene St, P.O. Box 154, Silverton, CO 81433, (970) 387-5838, https://sanjuancountyhistoricalsociety.org

Local Libraries
Silverton Public Library, 1111 Reese, P.O. Box 68, Silverton, CO 81433-0068, (970) 387-5770, http://silverton.colibraries.org

Links
CO GenWeb
http://cogenweb.com/sanjuan/

Cyndi's List
https://www.cyndislist.com/us/co/counties/san-juan/

FamilySearch Wiki
https://www.familysearch.org/wiki/en/San_Juan_County,_Colorado_Genealogy

Linkpendium
http://www.linkpendium.com/san_juan-co-genealogy/

RootsWeb Wiki
https://wiki.rootsweb.com/wiki/index.php/San_Juan_County,_Colorado

Wikipedia
https://en.wikipedia.org/wiki/San_Juan_County,_Colorado

Historic Hotels
1893 Grand Imperial Hotel, 1219 Greene St, Silverton, CO 81433, 970-387-5527, https://www.grandimperialhotel.com

1896 Teller House, 1250 Greene St, Silverton, CO 81433, 970-387-5423, http://www.meekerhotel.com

San Juan County

Museums & Historic Sites

San Juan County Historical Society, Mining Heritage Center & Archives, 1567 Greene St, P.O. Box 154, Silverton, CO 81433, (970) 387-5838, https://sanjuancountyhistoricalsociety.org

Special Events & Scenic Locations

A calendar of events & festivals in and around Silverton is here: https://www.colorado.com/co/silverton/festivals-events

Durango-Silverton Narrow-Gauge Railroad National Historic District
Rio Grande National Forest
San Juan National Forest
Shenandoah-Dives (Mayflower) Mill
Silverton National Historic District
Uncompahgre National Forest
Weminuche Wilderness
Alpine Loop National Back Country Byway
Colorado Trail
Continental Divide National Scenic Trail
San Juan Skyway National Scenic Byway

Ghost Towns & Other Sparsely Populated Places

Animas Forks, Bandora, Buffalo Boy, Bullion City (Howardsville), Burro Bridge, Chattanooga, Elk Park, Eureka, Gladstone, Highland Mary, Howardsville, Middleton, Mineral Point (Mineral City), Niegoldstown, Old Hundred, Red Mountain City, Summit

Newspapers

Silverton Industry. (Silverton, Colo.) 18??-1???
Silverton Weekly Miner and San Juan Democrat. (Silverton, San Juan County, Colo.) 18??-1890
La Plata Miner. (Silverton, Colo.) 1875-1886
The San Juan Expositor. (Eureka, San Juan County, Colo.) 1880-1???
The San Juan Herald. (Silverton, San Juan County, Colo.) 1881-1885
Animas Forks Pioneer. (Animas Forks, Colo.) 1882-1???
Red Mountain Review. (Red Mountain, Colo.) 1883-1884
The Silverton Democrat. (Silverton, Colo.) 1883-1885
The Daily Herald. (Silverton, San Juan County, Colo.) 1883-1???
Red Mountain Pilot. (Red Mountain City, San Juan Co., Colo.) 1883-1???
The Democrat-Herald. (Silverton, Colo.) 1885-1885
The Silverton Democrat-Herald. (Silverton, Colo.) 1885-1885
The Silverton Democrat. (Silverton, Colo.) 1885-1888
The San Juan. (Silverton, San Juan County, Colo.) 1886-1888
San Juan-Democrat. (Silverton, San Juan County, Colo.) 1888-18??
Silverton Standard. (Silverton, Colo.) 1889-1934

Historical Assets Colorado

Silverton Weekly Miner. (Silverton, Colo.) 1890-189?
Silverton Weekly Miner and Red Mountain Journal. (Silverton and Red Mountain, Colo.) 189?-1896
The San Juan Silverite. (Ouray, Colo.) 1892-189?
Gold Run Silvertip. (Gold Run, Bear Creek Camp, San Juan County, Colo.) 1893-1???
The Daily Standard. (Silverton, Colo.) 1894-1894
The San Juan Herald. (Silverton, San Juan County, Colo.) 1895-1???
Silverton Weekly Miner. (Silverton, Colo.) 1897-1919
Silverton Miner. (Silverton, Colo.) 1919-1920
The Silverton Standard and The Miner. (Silverton, Colo.) 1934-Current

Places on the National Register
Durango, Cascade Boy Scout Camp, Adjacent to Lime Creek Rd., San Juan National Forest
San Juan, Placer Gulch Boarding House, Address Restricted
Silverton, Animas Forks, Address Restricted
Silverton, Gold Prince Mine, Mill and Aerial Tramway, Address Restricted
Silverton, Martin Mining Complex, 6350 Cty Rd. # 2
Silverton, Minnie Gulch Cabins, Address Restricted
Silverton, Shenandoah—Dives Mill, CO 110, 2 mi. NE of Silverton
Silverton, Silverton Historic District, US 550
Silverton, Silverton Historic District (Boundary Increase), Roughly, along CO 110 and aerial tramway from Lodore Mine to Mayflower Mine
Silverton, Sound Democrat Mill and Mine & Silver Queen Mine, Address Restricted

USGS Historic Places
Handies Peak, Animas Forks, 37.931107, -107.5714483
Ironton, Gladstone, 37.8902735, -107.6503383
Silverton, Chattanooga, 37.8736064, -107.7253394
Storm King Peak, Beartown, 37.7227765, -107.5039473

Grand Army of the Republic Posts
McCrae, No. 43, San Juan, Silverton

USGS Historic Military Places
None

Military Bases
None

Post Offices
Animas Forks	1875 Feb 8	1915 Nov 30*
Arastra	1895 June 15	1919 Mar 31
Chattanooga	1883 Apr 4	1894 June 4
Congress	1883 Apr 2	1884 Jan 7

San Juan County

Del Mine	1883 June 22	1884 May 19	
Eureka	1875 Aug 9	1942 Apr 30	
Gladstone	1878 Jan 24	1912 Jan 15*	
Grassy Hill	1879 Jan 30	1880 July 15	
Highland Mary	1878 Mar 26	1885 June 29	
Howardsville	1874 June 24	1939 Oct 31*	
Mineral Point	1875 Oct 29	1897 Jan 28*	
Needleton	1882 May 26	1910 Jan 31*	
Niccora	1877 July 16	1877 Nov 26	
Niegoldstown	1878 Jan 10	1881 Aug 15	
Ouray	1875 Oct 28	1876 Mar 20	
Ouray 2	1876 May 9		81427
Poughkeepsie	1880 Jan 12	1881 Aug 15	
Silverton	1875 Feb 1		81433
Sylvanite	1893 Sept 20	1894 Oct 26	
Uncompaghre	1876 Mar 20	1877 Feb 23	

Topo Quads

Engineer Mountain	374500N	373730N	1074500W	1075230W
Hermosa Peak	374500N	373730N	1075230W	1080000W
Silverton	375230N	374500N	1073730W	1074500W
Snowdon Peak	374500N	373730N	1073730W	1074500W
Storm King Peak	374500N	373730N	1073000W	1073730W

Suggested Reading

Dalla, Fury. *The History of Mining in San Juan County, Colorado.* Thesis, Colorado State Teachers College, 1934.

Pioneers of the San Juan County. Durango, CO: Sarah Platt Decker Chapter, DAR. 1952.

Remembrances: the Silver San Juan: the Bride of the Silver San Juan. Pagosa Springs, CO: San Juan County Historical Society, 1997.

San Juan County in the 1890s. NL: Standard and the San Juan County Book Co, 1969.

Turner, Carol. *Notorious San Juans: Wicked Tales from Ouray, San Juan and La Plata Counties.* Charleston, SC: History Press, 2011.

Historical Assets Colorado

San Miguel County

Introduction

Established: 1883   Population: 7,359

Formed from: San Juan

Adjacent Counties: Montrose, Ouray, San Juan, Dolores

County Seat: Telluride

Other Communities: Mountain Village, Norwood, Ophir, Sawpit, Ames, Egnar, Pandora, Placerville, Sams, Slick Rock, Tomboy

Website: https://www.sanmiguelcountyco.gov

Area Codes: 970

Zip Codes: 81325, 81423, 81426, 81430, 81435

Historical Assets Colorado

San Miguel County Courthouse

Courthouses & County Government
San Miguel County
   https://www.sanmiguelcountyco.gov
San Miguel County Courthouse (7th Judicial District), 305 W Colorado Ave, Telluride, CO 81435, 970-369-3300; http://www.courts.state.co.us/Courts/County/Index.cfm?County_ID=20
Assessor, 333 W Colorado Ave, Telluride, CO 81435, 970-728-3174; http://www.sanmiguelcounty.org/departments/assessor/index.html
Board of County Commissioners, 333 W Colorado Ave, Telluride, CO 81435, 970-728-3844, https://www.sanmiguelcountyco.gov/Directory.aspx?did=34
Clerk & Recorder, 305 W Colorado Ave, Telluride, CO 81435, 970-728-3954; http://www.sanmiguelcounty.org/departments/clerk/index.html
Coroner, 333 W Colorado Ave, Telluride, CO 81435, 970-369-5480; https://www.sanmiguelcountyco.gov/170/Coroner
Elections, 305 W Colorado Ave, 1st Fl, Telluride, CO 81435, 970-728-3954; https://www.sanmiguelcountyco.gov/164/Elections
Public Health, 333 W Colorado Ave, Ste 315, Telluride, CO 81435, 970-728-4289; http://www.sanmiguelcounty.org/departments/publichealth/index.html
Transportation (Road & Bridge), 120 Summit St, Norwood, CO 81423, 970-327-4835; https://www.sanmiguelcountyco.gov/200/Road-Bridge
Treasurer, 305 W Colorado Ave, Telluride, CO 81435, 970-728-4451; http://www.sanmiguelcounty.org/departments/Treasurer/index.html

County Records

Birth 1897	Marriage 1900	Divorce 1883
Death 1906	Land 1890	Probate 1883
Court 1883		

San Miguel County

County & Municipal Records Held at the State Level

The Colorado State Archives

Physical Records	Records on Film	Records on Master Film
Clerk & Recorder	None	County Court
Coroner		District Court
County Commissioners		Combined Courts
County Court		Probate Court
Justice Court		School Districts
WPA Historical Records		
WPA Religious Institutions Survey		

The Denver Public Library
San Miguel County Mining Companies Records, 1934-1935
San Miguel Gold Placers COmpany Records, 1889-1890
WPA Historical Records Survey
WWI Draft Registration Cards (microfilm)

School Districts
School Districts, http://www.adcogov.org/local-school-districts
Dolores County School District RE-2J, 425 N Main St, Dove Creek, CO 81324, 970-677-2522; https://www.dc2j.org
Norwood School District R-2J, 1225 W Summit Ave, Norwood, CO 81423, 970-327-4336; https://www.norwoodk12.org/
Telluride School District R-1, 725 W Colorado Ave, Telluride, CO 81435; http://tellurideschool.org/

Historic School Districts

1. Telluride
2. San Miguel
3. Alta, Ophir
4. Wilson Mesa
5. Hastings Mesa, Washburn
6. Norwood
7. Cedar
8. Sawpit, Vanadium, Specie Mesa
9. Placerville
10. Leopard Creek, Howard Springs, Sams
11. Iron Springs
12. Cone, Lone Cone, Dry Creek Basin
13. Egnar
14. Peel [Joint with Dolores]
15. Burns, Northdale
16. Dolores River
17. Norwood
18. Egnar, Burn

Fraternal Organizations

Granges
Circle N, No. 486, San Miguel, Norwood, 23 Sept 1958

Masons
Ancient Free & Accepted Masons
Logan, No. 56, San Miguel, Telluride, 17 Sept 1884
Telluride, No. 111, San Miguel, Norwood, 19 Sept 1900

Historical Assets Colorado

Royal Arch Masons
Telluride, No. 28, San Miguel, Telluride

Knights Templar
Telluride Commandery, No. 27, San Miguel, Telluride, 1899 Oct 23

Eastern Star
Miriam, No. 20, San Miguel, Telluride
Sunset, No. 138, San Miguel, Norwood

Odd Fellows
Telluride, No. 103, San Miguel, Telluride
Norwood, No. 136, San Miguel, Norwood

Rebekahs
Crescent, No. 39, San Miguel, Telluride
Lone Cone, No. 94, San Miguel, Norwood

Knights of Pythias
Bridal Veil, No. 80, San Miguel, Telluride

Pythian Sisters
Bethany, No. 25, San Miguel, Telluride
Bridal Veil, No. 59, San Miguel, Telluride

Benevolent Protective Order of Elks
Telluride, No. 692, San Miguel, Telluride

City & Town Halls

Telluride, 113 W Columbia Ave, Telluride, CO 81435, https://www.telluride-co.gov
Mountain Village, 455 Mountain Village Blvd, Mountain Village, CO 81435, 970-728-8000, https://townofmountainvillage.com
Norwood, 1670 Naturita St, Norwood, CO 81423, 970-327-4288, http://www.norwoodtown.com

Archives & Manuscript Collections

None

Historical & Genealogical Societies

Telluride Historical Society, Historical Museum, 201 W Gregory Ave, P.O. Box 1597, Telluride, CO 81435, (970) 728-3344, http://www.telluridemuseum.com

Local Libraries

Wilkinson Public Library, 100 W Pacific Ave, P.O. Box 2189, Telluride, CO 81435, (970) 728-4519, https://www.telluridelibrary.org

Links

CO GenWeb
http://cogenweb.com/sanmiguel/

Cyndi's List

San Miguel County

https://www.cyndislist.com/us/co/counties/san-miguel/
FamilySearch Wiki
https://www.familysearch.org/wiki/en/San_Miguel_County,_Colorado_Genealogy
Linkpendium
http://www.linkpendium.com/san_miguel-co-genealogy/
RootsWeb Wiki
https://wiki.rootsweb.com/wiki/index.php/San_Miguel_County,_Colorado
Wikipedia
https://en.wikipedia.org/wiki/San_Miguel_County,_Colorado

Historic Hotels
1891 New Sheridan Hotel, 231 W Colorado Ave, Telluride, CO 81435, 970-728-4351, https://www.newsheridan.com

Museums & Historic Sites
Telluride Historical Society, Historical Museum, 201 W Gregory Ave, P.O. Box 1597, Telluride, CO 81435, (970) 728-3344, http://www.telluridemuseum.com

Special Events & Scenic Locations
The San Miguel Basin Fair & Rodeo is held in July most years at the San Miguel Basin Fairgrounds, 1165 Summit St, Norwood, CO 81423, 970-327-4321, https://www.sanmiguelcountyco.gov/491/San-Miguel-Basin-Fair-and-Rodeo
Telluride keeps a calendar of local festivals & events here: https://www.telluride.com/festivals-and-events

Lizard Head Wilderness
Mount Sneffels Wilderness
Old Spanish National Historic Trail
Telluride National Historic District
Uncompahgre National Forest
Great Parks Bicycle Route
San Juan Skyway National Scenic Byway
Unaweep-Tabeguache Scenic and Historic Byway
Western Express Bicycle Route

Ghost Towns & Other Sparsely Populated Places
Alta, Ames, Black Bear, Brown, Columbia, Dallas Divide, Deep Creek, Fall Creek, Haskill, Illium, Iron Springs, Keystone, Leopard, Leopard Creek, Marshall Basin, Matterhorn, Norwood, Ophir, Pandora (Newport), Placerville, San Miguel, Sawpit, Smuggler, South Fork, Tomboy (Savage Basin Camp), Trout Lake, Vance Junction

Newspapers
The Post-Independent. (Norwood, San Miguel County, Colo.) 1???-19??
The Telluride Tribune. (Telluride, San Miguel County, Colo.) 1???-19??

Historical Assets Colorado

The Telluride Journal. (Telluride, Colo.) 18??-19??
Telluride News. (Telluride, Colo.) 188?-????
San Miguel Journal. (San Miguel, Colo.) 1881-188?
The San Miguel Examiner. (Telluride, San Miguel County, Colo.) 1881-1929
The Evening News. (Telluride, Colo.) 1884-1884
Mining News. (Telluride, Colo.) 1884-????
Telluride Republican. (Telluride, San Miguel County, Colo.) 1886-1???
The Daily Journal. (Telluride, Colo.) 1894-1927
The Saw Pit Hummer. (Saw Pit, San Miguel County, Colo.) 1896-1???
The Ophir Mail. (Ophir, San Miguel County, Colo.) 1897-1???
The Norwood Star. (Norwood, Colo.) 19??-19??
San Miguel Forum. (Telluride And Nucla, Colo.) 19??-19??
The Norwood Post. (Norwood, San Miguel County, Colo.) 1912-19??
Telluride Daily Journal. (Telluride, Colo.) 1927-1929
Telluride Journal. (Telluride, San Miguel County, Colo.) 1929-1938
The San Miguel County Journal. (Telluride, Colo.) 1938-1942
The Daily Tribune. (Telluride, Colo.) 1941-19??
The Telluride Journal. (Telluride, San Miguel County, Colo.) 1942-19??
The Forum. (Nucla, Colo.) 1954-1971
The Telluride Times. (Telluride, San Miguel County, Colo.) 1962-1988
The San Miguel Basin Forum. (Nucla And Norwood, Colo.) 1971-Current
Deep Creek Review. ([Telluride, Colo.) 1974-1975
Wright's Mesa Review. (Norwood, Colo.) 1982-19??
The Telluride Times-Journal. (Telluride, Co.) 1988-1998

Places on the National Register

Ophir, Rio Grande Southern Railroad Trout Lake Water Tank, along North Trout Lake Rd.
Ophir, Valley View Leasing and Mining Company Mill, CO 145, 2.8 mi. S. of Ophir
Telluride, Fort Peabody, Uncompahgre National Forest
Telluride, Lewis Mill, 3.5 mi. SE of Telluride at the head of Bridal Veil Basin
Telluride, Smuggler-Union Hydroelectric Power Plant, SE of Telluride at Bridal Veil Falls
Telluride, Telluride Historic District, Rt. 145

USGS Historic Places

Norwood, Norwood Airport, 38.151379, -108.2534132
Placerville, Leonard, 38.0638803, -108.0270129
Placerville, Placerville School, 38.0180476, -108.0559032
Telluride, Alta, 37.8863832, -107.8528424
Telluride, Tomboy, 37.936661, -107.7545058

Grand Army of the Republic Posts

Steadman, No. 54, San Miguel, Telluride

San Miguel County

USGS Historic Military Places
None

Military Bases
None

Post Offices

Ames	1880 Dec 20	1922 June 3*	
Bulkley	1895 Mar 7	1895 Mar 29	
Cedar	1892 Apr 7	1943 Nov 15*	
Cornell	1903 Mar 11	1903 July 10	
Dallas Divide	1894 Mar 24	1909 July 23	
Dinan	1929 Oct 9		
Egnar	1917 May 28		81325
Fall Creek	1933 June 22	1943 Nov 13	
Gladel	1922 Dec 14	1929 May 31	
Haskill	1888 Feb 10	1907 Feb 28	
Illium	1891 Feb 10	1917 Nov 30*	
Leonard	1900 Mar 23	1940 Dec 31	
Leopard	1890 Oct 6	1892 Apr 6	
Lizard Head	1898 Mar 19	1898 Nov 3*	
Newmire	1895 Apr 4	1913 May 17	
Noel	1909 July 23	1923 June 30	
Norwood	1887 Dec 22		81423
Ophir	1878 May 17	1921 Jan 31*	
Ophir 2	1922 June 3		81436
Pandora	1881 Aug 5	1902 Oct 15*	
Placerville	1878 Apr 22		81430
Sams	1903 May 7	1950 Aug 24*	
San Bernardo	1892 June 29	1907 Apr 7*	
San Miguel	1877 July 16	1895 Sept 19	
Sawpit	1896 Feb 21	1926 Mar 31	
Seymour	1892 July 13	1896 Feb 21	
Slick Rock	1941 May 1	1946 June 30	
Slick Rock 2	1957 Aug 10		81333
Smuggler	1895 Apr 6	1928 Dec 5	
Sultana	1899 Jan 25	1903 Oct 14	
Telluride	1880 July 26	1880 Aug 17	
Telluride 2	1880 Dec 13		81435
Trout Lake	1882 June 14	1892 June 29*	
Vanadium	1913 May 17	1942 July 31	
Vance	1894 Oct 26	1909 Sept 30	
Wilson	1895 Feb 7	1901 Nov 15	

Historical Assets Colorado

Topo Quads

Barkelew Draw	380730N	380000N	1082230W	1083000W
Basin	380730N	380000N	1083000W	1083730W
Beaver Park	380000N	375230N	1080730W	1081500W
Dawson Draw	380000N	375230N	1083730W	1084500W
Dolores Peak	375230N	374500N	1080000W	1080730W
Egnar	380000N	375230N	1085230W	1090000W
Gray Head	380000N	375230N	1075230W	1080000W
Groundhog Mtn	375230N	374500N	1080730W	1081500W
Gurley Canyon	380730N	380000N	1080730W	1081500W
Gypsum Gap	380730N	380000N	1083730W	1084500W
Hamm Canyon	380730N	380000N	1084500W	1085230W
Horse Range Mesa	380730N	380000N	1085230W	1090000W
Joe Davis Hill	380000N	375230N	1084500W	1085230W
Little Cone	380000N	375230N	1080000W	1080730W
Lone Cone	380000N	375230N	1081500W	1082230W
McKenna Peak	380000N	375230N	1083000W	1083730W
Mount Wilson	375230N	374500N	1075230W	1080000W
North Mountain	380000N	375230N	1082230W	1083000W
Oak Hill	380730N	380000N	1081500W	1082230W
Ophir	375230N	374500N	1074500W	1075230W
Placerville	380730N	380000N	1080000W	1080730W

Suggested Reading

Barry, Glenn. *Hastings Mesa: at the Foot of Mount Hayden*. Grand Junction, CO: Glenn Berry, 1984.

Freeman, Dona, Rafael Rutson and Larry Lindahl. *Last Dollar Ranch: Hastings Mesa, San Miguel County, Colorado*. Montrose, CO: Double Shoe Publishing, 2005.

Inventory of the County Archives of Colorado, No. 57, San Miguel County (Telluride). Denver: Historical Records Survey, 1941.

Turner, Carol. *Notorious Telluride: Tales from San Miguel County*. Charleston, SC: History Press, 2010.

Sedgwick County

Introduction

Established: 1889   Population: 2,379

Formed from: Logan

Adjacent Counties: Phillips, Logan

County Seat: Julesburg

  Other Communities: Ovid, Sedgwick

Website, https://www.colorado.gov/sedgwickcounty

Area Codes: 970

Zip Codes: 80737, 80744, 80749

Historical Assets Colorado

Sedgwick County Courthouse

Sedgwick County 19th Century Courthouse

Courthouses & County Government

Sedgwick County
  https://www.colorado.gov/sedgwickcounty
Sedgwick County Courthouse (13th Judicial District), 3rd & Pine, Julesburg, CO 80737, 970-474-3627; http://www.courts.state.co.us/Courts/County/Index.cfm?County_ID=42
Assessor, 315 Cedar St, Julesburg, CO 80737, 970-474-2531; https://www.colorado.gov/pacific/sedgwickcounty/assessor-7
Board of County Commissioners, 315 Cedar St, Julesburg, CO 80737, 970-474-2485, https://www.colorado.gov/pacific/sedgwickcounty/commissioners-4
Clerk & Recorder, 315 Cedar St, Julesburg, CO 80737, 970-474-3346; https://www.colorado.gov/pacific/sedgwickcounty/clerk-recorder-2
Coroner, 315 Cedar St, Julesburg, CO 80737, 970-580-9981; https://www.colorado.gov/pacific/sedgwickcounty/coroner-7
Public Health, 118 W 3rd St, Julesburg, CO 80737, 970-474-3397; https://www.colorado.gov/pacific/sedgwickcounty/human-services-4
Transportation (Road & Bridge), 223 S Cedar St, Julesburg, CO 80737, 970-474-3576; https://www.colorado.gov/pacific/sedgwickcounty/road-bridge-2
Treasurer, 315 Cedar St, Ste 210, Julesburg, CO 80737, 970-474-3473; https://www.colorado.gov/pacific/sedgwickcounty/treasurerpublic-trustee-1

County Records

Birth Unk	Marriage 1889	Divorce 1889
Death Unk	Land 1889	Probate 1888
Court 1888		

Sedgwick County

County & Municipal Records Held at the State Level

The Colorado State Archives

Physical Records
Clerk & Recorder
Justice Court
WPA Historical Records
WPA Religious Institutions Survey
WPA Julesburg
Cities
Julesburg

Records on Film
Clerk & Recorder

Records on Master Film
County Court
District Court
Combined Courts
School Districts

The Denver Public Library
County Superintendent of Schools Certification, 1907
WWI Draft Registration Cards (microfilm)

School Districts

School Districts, http://www.adcogov.org/local-school-districts
Haxtun School District Re-2J, 201 W Powell St, Haxtun, CO 80731, 970-774-6111; https://www.haxtunk12.org/
Julesburg School District RE-1, 102 W 6th St, Julesburg, CO 80737, 970-474-3365; https://www.neboces.org/o/ne-colorado-boces/page/julesburg-re-1—2
Revere School District, 500 Main St, Ovid, CO 80744, 970-463-5477; https://sites.google.com/a/revereschool.com/revere-school-district/

Historic School Districts

1. Rolling Prairie
2. [1889]
3. Miller
4. Green Prairie
5. [1890]
6. Columbia
7. North Prairieview
8. Riverside, Highland
9. West Fairview
10. East Fairview
11. South Plainview
12. [1896]
13. Prairie View
14.
15.
16.
17. Sunny Dale
18.
19.
20. Liberty

35. Ovid
36. High Line
37.
38.
39. [1920]
40.
41.
42. [1904]
43.
44.
45.
46. Sedgwick Grade
47. Fairfield
48.
49.
50.
51. Fairydale
52. [1889]
53. Julesburg Grade
54.
55.

56.
57.
58. [1889]
59. [1889]

68. Middle 68, South 68
69.
70.
71.
72
73. Plainview
74. Prairie Center
75. East Prairie View
76. East Prairie View
77.
78.
79.
80. [1889]
81.
82.
83. Never Fail

Historical Assets Colorado

Fraternal Organizations
Granges
Oregon Trail, No. 445, Sedgwick, Ovid, 13 Apr 1938
Masons
Ancient Free & Accepted Masons
Summit, No. 70, Sedgwick, Julesburg, 18 Sept 1888
Royal Arch Masons
None
Knights Templar
None
Eastern Star
Mistletoe, No. 82, Sedgwick, Julesburg
Odd Fellows
Sedgwick, No. 22, Sedgwick, Sedgwick
Julesburg, No. 67, Sedgwick, Julesburg
Rebekahs
Courage, No. 32, Sedgwick, Sedgwick
Jewel, No. 125, Sedgwick, Julesburg
Knights of Pythias
None
Pythian Sisters
None
Benevolent Protective Order of Elks
None

City & Town Halls
Julesburg, 100 W 2nd St, Julesburg, CO 80737, 970-474-3344, https://townofjulesburg.com
Ovid, 211 Main St, Ovid, CO 80744, 970-463-5446, https://www.facebook.com/Ovid-Colorado/
Sedgwick, 29 Main Ave, Sedgwick, CO 80749, 970-463-8814, https://www.sedgwick-colorado.com

Archives & Manuscript Collections
None

Historical & Genealogical Societies
Fort Sedgwick Historical Society, Depot Museum, 201 W 1st St, P.O. Box 69, Julesburg, CO 80737, (970) 474-2264, https://www.colorado.com/history-museums/fort-sedgwick-museum-and-depot-museum
Sedgewick County Genealogical Society, c/o Julesburg Public Library, 320 Cedar St, P.O. Box 86, Julesburg, CO 80737, (970) 474-2608, http://www.rootsweb.com/~cosedgwi/society.htm

Sedgwick County

Local Libraries
Julesburg Public Library, 320 Cedar St, Julesburg, CO 80737, (970) 474-2608, https://julesburg.colibraries.org

Links
CO GenWeb
http://cogenweb.com/sedgwick/

Cyndi's List
https://www.cyndislist.com/us/co/counties/sedgwick/

FamilySearch Wiki
https://www.familysearch.org/wiki/en/Sedgwick_County,_Colorado_Genealogy

Linkpendium
http://www.linkpendium.com/sedgwick-co-genealogy/

RootsWeb Wiki
https://wiki.rootsweb.com/wiki/index.php/Sedgwick_County,_Colorado

Wikipedia
https://en.wikipedia.org/wiki/Sedgwick_County,_Colorado

Historic Hotels
None

Museums & Historic Sites
Colorado Welcome Center Museum, 20934 Cty Rd 28, Julesburg, CO 80737, (970) 474-2054

Fort Sedgwick Historical Society, Depot Museum, 201 W 1st St, P.O. Box 69, Julesburg, CO 80737, (970) 474-2264, https://www.colorado.com/history-museums/fort-sedgwick-museum-and-depot-museum

Fort Sedgwick Museum, 114 E 1st St, Julesburg, CO 80737, (970) 474-2061, https://www.colorado.com/history-museums/fort-sedgwick-museum-and-depot-museum

Special Events & Scenic Locations
The Sedgwick County Fair is held at the Sedgwick County Fairgrounds, 17000 Cty Rd 41, Julesburg, CO 80737, https://www.facebook.com/pg/Sedgwick-County-Fair-and-Rodeo-286715194522/events/

Sedgwick County has a calendar of events here: https://sedgwickcounty.colorado.gov

American Discovery Trail
First Transcontinental Railroad
Pony Express National Historic Trail
South Platte River Trail Scenic and Historic Byway
South Platte Trail
Upper Crossing of the California Trail

Historical Assets Colorado

Ghost Towns & Other Sparsely Populated Places
Flora, Sedgwick, Wier

Newspapers
Julesburg Grit. (Julesburg, Colo.) 1894-1899
The Julesburg Advocate. (Julesburg, Colo.) 1896-1899
The Grit-Advocate. (Julesburg, Colo.) 1899-1907
The Sedgwick Independent. (Sedgwick, Sedgwick County, Colo.) 19??-1942
The Julesburg Grit-Advocate. (Julesburg, Colo.) 1907-1972
The Ovid Record. (Ovid, Sedgwick County, Colo.) 1926-1950
The Independent. (Sedgwick, Sedgwick County, Colo.) 1942-1950
The Platte Valley News. (Ovid, Colo.) 1950-19??
Julesburg Advocate. (Julesburg, Colo.) 1972-Current

Places on the National Register
Julesburg, Sedgwick County Courthouse, 315 Cedar St.
Julesburg, Union Pacific Railroad Julesburg Depot, 210 W. First St.

USGS Historic Places
Julesburg, Fort Julesburg, 40.9430478, -102.3582421
Ovid, Fort Sedgwick, 40.9430477, -102.3804646

Grand Army of the Republic Posts
John A Logan, No. 21, Sedgwick, Julesburg

USGS Historic Military Places
None

Military Bases
None

Post Offices
Flora	1889 Nov 4	1894 July 30	
Julesburg 3	1886 May 26		80737
Ovid	1907 Dec 12		80744
Sedgwick	1885 Sept 10	1894 May 11	
Sedgwick 2	1896 Apr 30		80749
Weir	1889 June 21	1890 Dec 22	

Topo Quads
Haxtun East	404500N	403730N	1023000W	1023730W
Haxtun West	404500N	403730N	1023730W	1024500W
Holyoke NE	404500N	403730N	1021500W	1022230W
Holyoke NW	404500N	403730N	1022230W	1023000W

Sedgwick County

Julesburg	410000N	405230N	1021500W	1022230W
Julesburg Reservoir	410000N	405230N	1023730W	1024500W
Julesburg SE	405230N	404500N	1021500W	1022230W
Julesburg SW	405230N	404500N	1022230W	1023000W
Marks Butte	405230N	404500N	1023000W	1023730W
Ovid	410000N	405230N	1022230W	1023000W
Sedgwick	410000N	405230N	1023000W	1023730W
Tamarack Ranch	405230N	404500N	1023730W	1024500W
Venango NW	410000N	405230N	1020730W	1021500W
Venango SW	405230N	404500N	1020730W	1021500W

Suggested Reading

Cavender, Mabel. *History of the Town of Ovid*. Julesburg, CO: NP, 1957.

Fort Sedgwick Historical Society. *The History of Sedgwick County, Colorado*. Dallas: Curtis Media Corp, 1985.

Hargrove, V V. *Ovid*. Denver: Federal Civil Works Administration, 1934.

Historic Julesburg. Denver: Civil Works Administration, 1934.

Julesburg, Colorado: Gateway Colorado. Julesburg, CO: Julesburg Business Men's Association, 1910.

Historical Assets Colorado

Summit County

Introduction

Established: 1861   Population: 27,994

Formed from: Original

Adjacent Counties: Grand, Clear Creek, Park, Lake, Eagle

County Seat: Breckenridge

Other Communities: Blue River, Dillon, Frisco, Montezuma, Silverthorne, Copper Mountain, Heeney, Keystone, Parkville

Website, http://www.co.summit.co.us/

Area Codes: 970

Zip Codes: 80424, 80435, 80443, 80497, 80498

Historical Assets Colorado

Summit County Courthouse

Courthouses & County Government
Summit County
    http://www.co.summit.co.us
Summit County Courthouse (Justice Center) (5th Judicial District), 501 N Park Ave, Breckenridge, CO 80424, 970-453-2272; http://www.courts.state.co.us/Courts/County/Index.cfm?County_ID=11
Assessor, 208 E Lincoln Ave, Breckenridge, CO 80424, 970-453-3480; http://www.co.summit.co.us/86/Assessor
Board of County Commissioners, 208 E Lincoln Ave, Breckenridge, CO 80424, 970-453-3413, http://www.co.summit.co.us/91/County-Commissioners
Clerk & Recorder, 208 E Lincoln Ave, Breckenridge, CO 80424, 970-453-3470; http://www.co.summit.co.us/index.aspx?NID=90
Coroner, P.O. Box 4923, Frisco, CO 80443, 970-668-2964; http://www.co.summit.co.us/95/Coroner
Public Health, 360 Peak One Dr, Ste 230, Frisco, CO 80443, 970-668-9161; http://www.co.summit.co.us/107/Public-Health
Transportation (Public Works), 0037 Peak One Dr, CR 1005, Frisco, CO 80443, 970-668-4202; http://www.co.summit.co.us/108/Road-Bridge
Treasurer, 208 Lincoln Ave, Breckenridge, CO 80424, 970-453-3440; http://www.co.summit.co.us/113/Treasurer-Public-Trustee

County Records
Birth Unk   Marriage 1900   Divorce 1900
Death Unk   Land 1861   Probate 1900
Court 1900

Summit County

County & Municipal Records Held at the State Level

The Colorado State Archives

Physical Records
County Court
District Court
Justice Court
WPA Historical Records
WPA Religious Institutions
  Survey
Cities
  Breckenridge
  Dillon
  Frisco

Records on Film
District Court
Combined Courts
Cities
  Breckenridge
  Dillon
  Frisco

Records on Master Film
County Court
District Court
Combined Courts
School Districts
Cities
  Dillon
  Frisco

The Denver Public Library

Blue Flag Gold Mining Company Records, 1906-1910
Breckenridge Electric Company Records, 1891-1906
Honky Dory Mine Records, 1887-1888
Summit County Mining Companies Records, 1880-1921
WWI Draft Registration Cards (microfilm)

School Districts

School Districts, http://www.adcogov.org/local-school-districts
Summit School District RE-1, 150 School Rd, Frisco, CO 80443, 970-368-1000; http://www.summit.k12.co.us/
West Grand School District 1-JT, 715 Kinsey Ave, Kremmling, CO 80459, 970-724-3217; https://www.wgsd.us/

Historic School Districts

1. Breckenridge
2. Montezuma
3. Kokomo
4. Tiger
5. [1881]
6. Lakeside
7. Slate Creek
8. Dillon
9. Frisco
10. Hillcrest [Joint with Grand]
11. [1884]
12. [1902]

Fraternal Organizations

Granges
None

Masons

Ancient Free & Accepted Masons
Corinthian, No. 2, Summit, Parkville, 2 Aug 1861
Breckenridge, No. 42, Summit, Kokomo, 21 Sept 1881
Goldfield, No. 47, Summit, Breckenridge, 20 Sept 1882

Royal Arch Masons
None

Historical Assets Colorado

Knights Templar
None

Eastern Star
Breckenridge, No. 78, Summit, Breckenridge

Odd Fellows
Summit, No. 37, Summit, Kokomo
Blue River, No. 49, Summit, Breckenridge
Dillon, No. 164, Summit, Dillon

Rebekahs
Three Rivers, No. 135, Summit, Dillon

Knights of Pythias
Gold Nugget, No. 89, Summit, Breckenridge
Elk Mountain, No. 90, Summit, Kokomo, 1893 July 20

Pythian Sisters
None

Benevolent Protective Order of Elks
Summit County, No. 2561, Summit, Silverthorne

City & Town Halls

Breckenridge, 150 Ski Hill Rd, Breckenridge, CO 80424, 970-453-2251, https://www.townofbreckenridge.com

Blue River, 110 Whispering Pines Cr, Blue River, Co 80424, 970-547-0545, https://www.colorado.gov/townofblueriver

Dillon, 275 Lake Dillon Dr, Dillon, CO 80435, 970-468-5100, https://www.townofdillon.com

Frisco, 1 E Main St, Frisco, CO 80443, 970-668-5276, https://www.friscogov.com

Montezuma, 5465 Hardwick St, Montezuma, CO 80435

Silverthorne, 601 Center Cr, Silverthorne, CO 80498, 970-262-7300, https://www.silverthorne.org

Archives & Manuscript Collections

Breckenridge Heritage Alliance, Dr Sandra F Mathew Archives, 309 N Main St, P.O. Box 2460, Breckenridge, CO 80424, (970) 453-9767, http://www.breckheritage.com

Historical & Genealogical Societies

Breckenridge Heritage Alliance, Dr Sandra F Mathew Archives, 309 N Main St, P.O. Box 2460, Breckenridge, CO 80424, (970) 453-9767, http://www.breckheritage.com

Frisco Historical Society, Frisco Historic Park & Museum, 120 Main St, P.O. Box 820, Frisco, CO 80433, (970) 668-3428, https://www.townoffrisco.com/play/historic-park-and-museum/general-info/

Saddle Rock Society, 111 E Washington, P.O. Box 4195, Breckenridge, CO 80424, (970) 453-5761,

Summit County

Summit Historical Society, Dillon School House Museum, 403 La Bonte St, P.O. Box 143, Dillon, CO 80435, (970) 468-2207, https://summithistorical.org

Local Libraries

Summit County Library-South Branch, 103 S Harris St, PO Box 96, Breckenridge, CO 80424, (970) 453-3544, https://summitcountylibraries.org

Summit County Public Library, 37 Peak One Dr, P.O. Box 770, Frisco, CO 80443-0770, (970) 668-5555, http://summitcountylibraries.org

Links

CO GenWe
http://cogenweb.com/summit/

Cyndi's List
https://www.cyndislist.com/us/co/counties/summit/

FamilySearch Wiki
https://www.familysearch.org/wiki/en/Summit_County,_Colorado_Genealogy

Linkpendium
http://www.linkpendium.com/summit-co-genealogy/

RootsWeb Wiki
https://wiki.rootsweb.com/wiki/index.php/Summit_County,_Colorado

Wikipedia
https://en.wikipedia.org/wiki/Summit_County,_Colorado

Historic Hotels

None

Museums & Historic Sites

Alice G Milne House & Memorial Park, 102 N Harris St, Breckenridge, CO 80424, (970) 453-9767, https://www.townofbreckenridge.com/live/heritage-history/alice-g-milne-memorial-park

Barney Ford House Museum, 111 E Washington Ave, Breckenridge, CO 80424, (970) 453-5761, https://www.breckheritage.com/barney-ford-victorian-home

Breckenridge Mining Camp Museum, 115 N Main St, Breckenridge, CO 80424, (970) 453-2342,

Breckenridge Sawmill Museum, Boreas Pass & Munroe Rd, Breckenridge, CO 80424, https://www.breckheritage.com/breckenridge-sawmill-museum

Breckenridge Welcome Center Museum, 203 S Main St, Breckenridge, CO 80424, (970) 453-9767, https://www.breckheritage.com/breckenridge-welcome-center-museum

Edwin Carter Discovery Center, 111 N Ridge St, P.O. Box 745, Breckenridge, CO 80424, (970) 453-9022, https://www.breckheritage.com/edwin-carter-discovery-center

Historical Assets Colorado

Frisco Historical Society, Frisco Historic Park & Museum, 120 Main St, P.O. Box 820, Frisco, CO 80433, (970) 668-3428, https://www.townoffrisco.com/play/historic-park-and-museum/general-info/

High Line Railroad Park & Museum, 189 Boreas Pass Rd, Breckenridge, CO 80424, https://www.breckheritage.com/high-line-railroad-park-and-museum

Summit Historical Society, Dillon School House Museum, 403 La Bonte St, P.O. Box 143, Dillon, CO 80435, (970) 468-2207, https://summithistorical.org

Summit Ski Museum, 305B S Main St, Breckenridge, CO 80424, (970) 453-9767, https://www.breckheritage.com/museums

William H Briggle House Museum, 104 N Harris St, Breckenridge, CO 80424, (970) 453-9767, https://www.breckheritage.com/briggle-house-museum

Special Events & Scenic Locations

Everything Summit County has a calendar of events here: https://everythingsummit.com/annual-events

Events in Colorado has a calendar of events in Summit County here: https://eventsincolorado.com/ecategory/summit-county

American Discovery Trail
Colorado Trail
Vail Pass National Recreation Trail
Wheeler Ten Mile National Recreation Trail
Continental Divide National Scenic Trail
Top of the Rockies National Scenic Byway
Great Parks Bicycle Route
TransAmerica Trail Bicycle Route

Ghost Towns & Other Sparsely Populated Places

Adrian, Argentine (Decatur, Rathbone), Baker's Summit, Bartholomews, Boreas, Braddock, Carbonateville, Chihuahua, Colleyville, Conger (Conger Camp), Curtin, Decatur, Delaware Flats (Delaware City, Preston, Braddock), Dickey, Dwyer, Dyersville, Farnham Spur, Hathaways, Kokomo, Lincoln City (Paige City), Little Mountain, Masontown, Mayflower Gulch, Mayo, Montezuma, Parkville (Park City), Preston, Rathbone, Recen, Rexford, Robinson (Camp Robinson, Ten Mile), Rock Creek, Saints John (Saint John, Coleyville), Santiago, Suttons, Swan, Swandyke, Swanville, Tiger, Wheeler, Wild Irishman, Wilders

Newspapers

The Ten-Mile News with which are incorporated The Summit County and Leadville Circulars. (Kokomo-Recen, Colo.) 18??-188?

Eagle River Shaft. (Red Cliff, Summit County, Colo.) 18??-1???

The Summit County Times. (Kokomo, Colo.) 1879-1???

Robinson Tribune. (Robinson, Colo.) 1880-????

The Summit County Circular. (Kokomo-Recine, Colo.) 188?-1???

Daily Journal. (Breckenridge, Colo.) 1880-1???

Summit County

The Summit County Leader. (Breckenridge, Colo.) 1880-1???
The Breckenridge Daily Journal. (Breckenridge [Colo.]) 1880-1???
The Ten-Mile News. (Kokomo-Recene, Colo.) 188?-188?
The Dillon Enterprise. (Dillon, Colo.) 1882-1???
Montezuma Mill Run. (Montezuma, Colo.) 1882-1???
The Summit County Journal. (Breckenridge, Colo.) 1883-1909
The Whooper. (Kokomo, Colo.) 189?-1???
The Bi-Metallic. (Breckenridge, Colo.) 1893-1???
Breckenridge Bulletin. (Breckenridge, Summit County, Colo.) 1899-1909
Sentinel Altitudes. (Fresco, Colo.) 19??-Current
Montezuma Prospector. (Montezuma, Summit County, Colo.) 1906-19??
Summit County Journal and Breckenridge Bulletin. (Breckenridge, Colo.) 1909-1914
The Blue Valley Times. (Dillon, Colo.) 191?-19??
Summit County Journal. (Breckenridge, Colo.) 1914-19??
The Breckenridge Herald. (Breckenridge, Colo.) 1917-19??
The Summit County Star. (Breckenridge, Colo.) 1918-19??
The Summit Gazette. (Breckenridge, Summit County, Colo.) 1926-19??
The Summit Sentinel. (Dillon, Colo.) 1968-1976
The Summit County Sentinel. (Dillon, Colo.) 1976-1977
The Summit County Sentinel and The Frisco News. (Dillon, Colo.) 1977-1977
The Summit Sentinel and The Frisco News. (Dillon, Colo.) 1977-1977
The Summit Sentinel's Frisco News. (Frisco, Colo.) 1977-1977
The Summit Sentinel. (Dillon, Colo.) 1977-199?
The Ten Mile Times. (Frisco, Summit County, Colo.) 1984-19??
Keystone News. (Breckenridge, Colo.) 1985-????
The Quandary Times of Breckenridge. ([Breckenridge, Colo.]) 1988-1988
The Quandary Times. (Breckenridge, Colo.) 1988-1989
Timberline. (Frisco, Colo.) 1989-19??

Places on the National Register
Breckenridge, Breckenridge Historic District, Roughly bounded by Jefferson Ave., Wellington Rd., High and Main St.
Breckinridge, Masonic Placer Cemetery—Valley Brook Cemetery, 905 Airport Rd.
Dillon, Porcupine Peak Site, Address Restricted
Frisco, Frisco Schoolhouse, 120 Main St.
Frisco, Wildhack's Grocery Store-Post Office, 510 Main St.
Keystone, Soda Creek Ranch, Off Keystone Ranch Rd. and Co. Rd. 351
Montezuma, Montezuma Schoolhouse, 5375 Webster St.
Slate Creek, Slate Creek Bridge, Cty. Rd. 1450 over Blue River

USGS Historic Places
Boreas Pass, Dyersville, 39.4205434, -105.9839056
Breckenridge, Preston, 39.4958202, -106.021129
Copper Mountain, Kokomo, 39.4241542, -106.1897452
Frisco, Breckenridge Airport, 39.5069311, -106.0497411
Keystone, Rexford, 39.5338757, -105.8958462

Historical Assets Colorado

    Keystone, Saints John, 39.5716535, -105.8816788
    Keystone, Swandyke, 39.5083202, -105.8922351
    Keystone, Swandyke Post Office, 39.5083202, -105.8922351
    Keystone, Tiger, 39.522833, -105.962117
    Toner Reservoir, Parkville, 39.4988727, -106.9500441
    Unknown, Swan City, 0, 0

Grand Army of the Republic Posts
Joseph A Mower, No. 31, Summit, Breckenridge, 1883

USGS Historic Military Places
None

Military Bases
None

Post Offices

Adrian	1882 Apr 12	1882 Aug 31	
Argentine	1881 Jan 31	1883 Oct 22	
Argentine 2	1901 Nov 18	1907 Feb 28	
Boreas	1896 Jan 2	1905 Jan 31	
Braddock	1884 Jan 18	1890 Dec 27	
Breckenridge	1860 Jan 18		
Breckenridge	1861		80424
Buffer	1917 Dec 5	1921 Oct 15	
Carbonateville	1879 Feb 2	1881 Jan 27	
Chihuahua	1880 Jan 23	1892 May 9	
Cleveland	1883 Mar 21	1884 Aug 14	
Climax	1917 Dec 5		
Conger	1880 July 8	1881 Jan 3	
Cooper	1881 June 15	1882 Sept 28	
Copper Mountain	1977 Sept 8		
Crocker	1880 Feb 18	1882 Sept 13*	
Decatur	1879 Oct 31	1885 Jan 28	
Delaware City	1861 Nov 13	1875 July 13*	
Dickey	1892 Feb 19	1893 Sept 13	
Dillon	1879 Oct 24	1881 Jan 5	
Dillon 2	1881 June 28		80435
Eagle	1880 Oct 4	1882 Mar 6	
Farnham	1881 Dec 2	1895 Nov 2	
Frawley	1916 July 29	1918 July 31	
Frisco	1879 Aug 29		80443
Gold Park	1881 Mar 31	1883 Oct 5	
Haywood	1879 Aug 14	1882 Oct 2	
Heeney	1939 June 20	1974 Apr 26*	
Holy Cross	1882 Jan 23	1905 Aug 7*	

Summit County

Josie	1882 July 21	1883 Jan 4	
Kokomo	1879 May 5	1965 Oct 8	
Lakeside	1882 Sept 14	1886 Sept 20	
Laurium	1895 May 6	1899 Apr 1	
Lincoln City	1861 Aug 13	1894 July 10	
Meeker	1871 Sept 29		81641
Montezuma	1871 June 15	1972 June 30	
Naomi	1883 Jan 4	1888 Apr 3	
Paige City	1861 June 28	1861 Aug 1	
Parkville	1861 Dec 13	1866 Oct 22	
Plain	1898 Jan 21	1899 Aug 31	
Preston	1875 July 13	1889 Dec 26*	
Rathbone	1891 Sept 19	1895 July 11	
Red Cliff	1880 Feb 4	1895 Feb 7	
Rexford	1882 Jan 9	1883 Nov 10	
Robinson	1881 Feb 17	1911 Feb 28*	
Roudebush	1880 Dec 15	1883 Apr 2	
Saints John	18776 Aug 8	1881 Feb 1	
Silver Lake	1862 Nov 22	1864 Jan 15	
Silverthorne	1962 Jan 1		
Swan	1880 Aug 4	1898 Feb 23	
Swandyke	1898 Nov 30	1910 Sept 30	
Taylor	1882 Sept 28	1886 July 31	
Ten Mile	1879 May 16	1881 Feb 17	
Tiger	1919 Dec 26	1940 Oct 31	
Wapiti	1894 Mar 16	1903 Apr 15	
Wheeler	1880 Apr 13	1894 May 14	
White River	8171 Sept 29	1880 Aug 23	

Topo Quads

Alma	392230N	391500N	1060000W	1060730W
Boreas Pass	393000N	392230N	1055230W	1060000W
Breckenridge	393000N	392230N	1060000W	1060730W
Frisco	393730N	393000N	1060000W	1060730W
Grays Peak	394500N	393730N	1054500W	1055230W
Jefferson	393000N	392230N	1054500W	1055230W
Keystone	393730N	393000N	1055230W	1060000W
Montezuma	393730N	393000N	1054500W	1055230W

Suggested Reading

Aldrich, John K. *Ghosts of Summit County: a Guide to the Ghost Towns and Mining Camps of Summit County, Colorado*. Lakewood, CO: Centennial Graphics, 1997.

Gilliland, Mary Ellen. *Summit: a Gold Rush History of Summit County, Colorado*. Silverthorne, CO: Alpenrose Press, 2006.

Mather, Sandra F. *Behind Swinging Doors: the Saloons of Breckenridge and Summit County, Colorado 1859-1900*. Breckenridge, CO: Town of Breckenridge, 2003.

Historical Assets Colorado

Mather, Sandra F. *Men, Mining & Machines: Hardrock Mining in Summit County, Colorado*. Dillon, CO: Summit Historical Society, 1996.

Mather, Sandra F. *Summit County*. Charleston, SC: Arcadia Pub, 2008.

Sharp, Verna. *A History of Montezuma, Sts John and Argentine: Early Mining Camps of Summit County*. Montezuma, CO: Summit Historical Society, 1971.

That's Gold in Them Thar' Hills! an Authentic Story of Gold and Adventure in Summit County, Colorado. Breckenridge, CO: Summit County Journal, 1955.

Teller County

Introduction
Established: 1899   Population: 23,350
Formed from: El Paso
Adjacent Counties: Douglas, Jefferson, El Paso, Fremont, Park
County Seat: Cripple Creek
  Other Communities: Victor, Woodland Park, Divide, Florissant, Goldfield, Midland
Website, http://www.co.teller.co.us
Area Codes: 719
Zip Codes: 80813, 80814, 80816, 80860, 80863, 80866

Historical Assets Colorado

Teller County Courthouse

Courthouses & County Government

Teller County
  http://www.co.teller.co.us
Teller County Courthouse (4th Judicial District), 101 W Bennett Ave, Cripple Creek, CO 80813, 719-689-2574; http://www.courts.state.co.us/Courts/County/Index.cfm?County_ID=7
Assessor, 101 W Bennett Ave, Cripple Creek, CO 80813, 719-689-2941; http://www.co.teller.co.us/Assessor/default.aspx
Board of County Commissioners, 112 North A Street, Cripple Creek, CO 80813, 719-689-2988, http://www.co.teller.co.us/BOCC/default.aspx
Clerk & Recorder, 101 W Bennett Ave, Cripple Creek, CO 80813, 719-689-2951; http://www.co.teller.co.us/CR/ContactInfo.aspx
Coroner, P.O. Box 959, Cripple Creek, CO 80813, 719-689-2724; http://www.co.teller.co.us/coroner/default.aspx
Public Health, 11115 W Hwy 24, Unit 2C, Divide, CO 80814, 719-687-6416; http://www.tellercountypublichealth.org/
Transportation, 308 Weaverville Rd, Bldg A, Divide CO 80814, 719-687-8812; http://www.co.teller.co.us/PublicWorks/TDOT.aspx
Treasurer, 101 W Bennett Ave, Cripple Creek, CO 80813, 719-689-2985; http://www.co.teller.co.us/pt/

County Records

Birth 1876
Death 1899
Court 1899
CSA Maternity Record 1940
CSA Hospital Register 1902
CSA Hospital Record of Births 1941
CSA Physicians Record of Births 1930
CSA Death 1902

Marriage 1899
Land 1899

Divorce 1899
Probate 1899

Teller County

County & Municipal Records Held at the State Level
The Colorado State Archives

Physical Records
Clerk & Recorder
County Court
District Court
Combined Courts
Hospital District
WPA Historical Records
WPA Religious Institutions Survey
Cities
Cripple Creek
Gillett
Goldfield
Pemperton
West Creek
Woodland Park

Records on Film
Clerk & Recorder
School Districts
Cities
Arequa
Cripple Creek
Gillett
Victor
West Creek
West Cripple Creek
Woodland Park

Records on Master Film
District Court
Combined Courts
School Districts
Cities
Cripple Creek

The Denver Public Library
Cripple Creek Miner's Strike Records, 1903-1904
Nimrod Gold Mining Company Records, 1895-1900
Old Gold Mines Company Voucher Record Book, 904-1912
Teller County Mining Companies Records, 1896-1959
Victor, Colorado Collection, 1915
WWI Draft Registration Cards (microfilm)

School Districts
School Districts, http://www.adcogov.org/local-school-districts
Cripple Creek Victor School District RE-1, 410 North B Street, Cripple Creek, CO 80813, 719-689-2685; http://www.ccvschools.com/
Woodland Park School District RE-2, 155 Panther Wy, Woodland Park, CO 80863, 719-686-2000; https://wpsdk12.org/

Historic School Districts
1. Cripple Creek, Victor
2. Kittridge
3. Pinewood
4. Florissant
5. Marigold
6. Divide
7. Edlowe
8. Portland City
9. Midland, Tracy
10. Pine Grove
11. Spielman
12. Woodland Park
13. Clyde, Rosemont
14. [1920]

31. [1920]

35. [1901]

Fraternal Organizations
Granges
Florissant, No. 420, Teller, Florissant, 11 Sept 1935
Divide, No. 421, Teller, Divide, 25 Sept 1935

Historical Assets Colorado

Four Mile, No. 429, Teller, Guffey, 21 Mar 1936
Manitou Park, No. 430, Teller, Woodland Park, 3 Apr 1936
Guffey, No. 434, Teller, Guffey, 5 May 1936

Masons

Ancient Free & Accepted Masons
Cripple Creek, No. 96, Teller, Cripple Creek, 20 Sept 1893
Victor, No. 96, Teller, Cripple Creek, 27 Jan 1919
Argenta, No. 99, Teller, Victor, 18 Sept 1895
Cripple Creek, No. 108, Teller, Goldfield, 19 Sept 1900
Ute Pass, No. 110, Teller, Cripple Creek, 19 Sept 1900
Mount Pisgah, No. 188, Teller, Woodland Park, 25 Jan 1961

Royal Arch Masons
Cripple Creek, No. 33, Teller, Cripple Creek

Knights Templar
Cripple Creek Commandery, No. 26, Teller, Cripple Creek, 1897 Mar 12

Eastern Star
Victoria, No. 28, Teller, Victor
Gold Nugget, No. 30, Teller, Cripple Creek

Odd Fellows
Seth H Sawyer, No. 15, Teller, Woodland Park
Victor, No. 26, Teller, Victor
Florissant, No. 88, Teller, Florissant
Cripple Creek, No. 101, Teller, Cripple Creek, 1892 Sept 20
Mountain, No. 172, Teller, Cripple Creek

Rebekahs
None

Knights of Pythias
Sylvanite, No. 93, Teller, Cripple Creek
Victor, No. 95, Teller, Victor
Goldfield, No. 106, Teller, Goldfield, 1897 June 18
Cripple Creek, No. 110, Teller, Cripple Creek, 1900 Sept 28

Pythian Sisters
Gold Nugget, No. 23, Teller, Cripple Creek
Carnation, No. 31, Teller, Victor

Benevolent Protective Order of Elks
Cripple Creek, No. 316, Teller, Cripple Creek
Victor, No. 367, Teller, Victor

City & Town Halls

Cripple Creek, 337 E Bennett Ave, Cripple Creek, CO 80813, 719-689-2502, https://cityofcripplecreek.com
Victor, 500 Victor Ave, Victor, CO 80860, 719-689-2284, https://cityofvictor.com
Woodland Park, 220 W South Ave, Woodland Park, CO 80866, 719-687-9246, https://city-woodlandpark.org

Teller County

Archives & Manuscript Collections
None

Historical & Genealogical Societies
Pikes Peak Historical Society, Historical Museum, 18033 Teller Cty Rd 1, P.O. Box 823, Florissant, CO 80816, (719) 748-8259, http://www.pikespeakhsmuseum.org

Ute Pass Historical Society, Historical Museum, 231 E Henrietta Ave, P.O. Box 6875, Woodland Park, CO 80866-6875, (719) 686-7512, http://www.utepasshistoricalsociety.org

Local Libraries
Franklin Ferguson Memorial Library, 410 North B Street, P.O. Box 975, Cripple Creek, CO 80813, (719) 689-2800,

Rampart Regional Library District, 218 E Midland, P.O. Box 336, Woodland Park, CO 80866-0336, (719) 687-9281, http://rampartlibrarydistrict.org

Victor Public Library, 124 S 3rd St, P.O. Box 5, Victor, CO 80860-0005, (719) 689-2011

Links
CO GenWe
http://cogenweb.com/teller/

Cyndi's List
https://www.cyndislist.com/us/co/counties/teller/

FamilySearch Wiki
https://www.familysearch.org/wiki/en/Teller_County,_Colorado_Genealogy

Linkpendium
http://www.linkpendium.com/teller-co-genealogy/

RootsWeb Wiki
https://wiki.rootsweb.com/wiki/index.php/Teller_County,_Colorado

Wikipedia
https://en.wikipedia.org/wiki/Teller_County,_Colorado

Historic Hotels
1899 Victor Hotel, 321 Victor Ave, Victor, CO 80860, 719-689-3553, https://www.victorhotelcolorado.com

Museums & Historic Sites
Adeline Hornbeck Homestead, Florissant Fossil Bedds National Monument, 15806 County Rd 1, P.O. Box 185, Florissant, CO 80816, (719) 748-3253, https://www.nps.gov/flfo/learn/historyculture/adeline-hornbek.htm

Cripple Creek District Museum, 500 E Bennett Ave, P.O. Box 1210, Cripple Creek, CO 80813, (719) 689-2634, http://www.cripple-creek.com

Historical Assets Colorado

Cripple Creek Heritage Center, 9283 S Hwy 67, Cripple Creek, CO 80813, (719) 689-3315, https://visitcripplecreek.com/attractions/cripple-creek-heritage-information-center/

Florissant Schoolhouse Museum, 2009 Teller Cty Rd 31, Florissant, CO 80816, (719) 748-8257, http://www.pikespeakhsmuseum.org/museums/

Mollie Kathleen Mine Museum, 9388 Hwy 67, P.O. Box 339, Cripple Creek, CO 80813, (719) 689-2466, http://www.goldminetours.com

Old Homestead Parlour House Museum, 353 Myers Ave, P.O. Box 540, Cripple Creek, CO 80813, (719) 689-3090, https://www.oldhomesteadhouse.com

Outlaws & Law Men Jail Museum, 136 W Bennett Ave, Cripple Creek, CO 80813, (719) 689-6556, https://visitcripplecreek.com/attractions/cripple-creek-jail-museum/

Pikes Peak Historical Society, Historical Museum, 18033 Teller Cty Rd 1, P.O. Box 823, Florissant, CO 80816, (719) 748-8259, http://www.pikespeakhsmuseum.org

Ute Pass Historical Society, Historical Museum, 231 E Henrietta Ave, P.O. Box 6875, Woodland Park, CO 80866-6875, (719) 686-7512, http://www.utepasshistoricalsociety.org

Victor Lowell Thomas Museum, 298 Victor Ave, P.O. Box 238, Victor, CO 80860, (719) 689-5509, https://victormuseum.com

Special Events & Scenic Locations

The Teller County Fair is held at the Cripple Creek Fairgrounds, 421-433 Carr Ave, Cripple Creek, CO 80813, http://www.tcafas.org

Visit Cripple Creek has a calendar of events here: https://visitcripplecreek.com/events/

The Woodland Park Chamber of Commerce has a calendar of events here: https://www.chamberorganizer.com/members/calendar5.php?org_id=GWPC

Cripple Creek National Historic District
Florissant Fossil Beds National Monument
Pike National Forest
Mueller State Park
American Discovery Trail
Gold Belt Tour National Scenic and Historic Byway

Ghost Towns & Other Sparsely Populated Places

Altman (Midway), Anaconda (Mound City, Squaw Gulch, Barry), Cameron (Gassy, Grassy), Divide, Elkton (Beacon Hill, Eclipse, Arequa), Florissant, Gillett, Goldfield, Hornbek Homestead, Hull City, Independence, Pemberton (Ackerman, West Creek), Seven Lakes, Stratton, Victor

Newspapers

The Cripple Creek Times & The Victor Daily Record. (Cripple Creek, Colo.) 1???-19??
Daily Advertiser. (Cripple Creek [Colo.) 1???-1???
Cripple Creek Mining News. (Cripple Creek, Colo.) 1???-1???

Teller County

The Evangel. (Victor, Colo.) 1???-19??
The Weekly Miner. (Cripple Creek, Colo.) 18??-1???
The Gillett Forum and North Teller County Miner Vol. 1, No. 37. (Gillett, Teller County, Colo.) 18??-19??
The Florissant Eagle. (Florissant, Teller County, Colo.) 18??-19??
The Weekly Tribune and Advertiser. (Cripple Creek, Colo.) 18??-1???
Cripple Creek Crusher. (Cripple Creek, Colo.) 189?-1???
The Cripple Creek Prospector. (Fremont, El Paso County, Colo.) 1891-1???
The Morning Times. (Cripple Creek, El Paso County, Colo.) 1891-1900
The Weekly Journal. (Cripple Creek, Colo.) 1893-1???
Cripple Creek Crusher. (Cripple Creek, Colo.) 1893-1???
The Daily Crusher. (Cripple Creek, Colo.) 1893-1???
Cripple Creek Sunday Herald. (Cripple Creek, Colo.) 1893-1???
The Morning Journal. (Cripple Creek, Colo.) 1894-1895
Victor Daily News. (Victor, Colo.) 1894-1???
Victor Daily Record. (Victor, Colo.) 1895-1908
The Gillett Forum. (Gillett, El Paso County, Colo.) 1895-1???
The Cripple Creek Mail. (Cripple Creek, Colo.) 1895-1898
Anaconda Assayer. (Anaconda, Colo.) 1896-19??
The Cripple Creek Sun. (Cripple Creek, Colo.) 1896-1???
The Ledger. (West Cripple Creek, Colo.) 1896-1???
The Woodland Park Times The West Creek Times. (Woodland Park And West Creek, Colo.) 1896-1???
The Cripple Creek Times. (Cripple Creek, El Paso County, Colo.) 1896-1896
The Weekly Cripple Creek Times. (Cripple Creek, El Paso County, Colo.) 1896-1901
The Victor Weekly Record. ([Victor, Colo.]) 1897-1899
Victor Daily Times. (Victor, Colo.) 1897-19??
Cripple Creek Citizen. (Cripple Creek, Colo.) 1897-1???
The Cripple Creek Star. (Cripple Creek, Colo.) 1898-1900
The Golden Crescent. (Cameron, Touraine P.o., Colo.) 1899-19??
The Daily Press. (Victor, Colo.) 1899-1903
Victor Record. (Victor, Colo.) 1899-1904
The Cripple Creek Evening Star. (Cripple Creek, Colo.) 1900-190?
The Evening Star. (Cripple Creek, Colo.) 190?-19??
The Morning Times - Citizen. (Cripple Creek, Colo.) 1900-1902
The Cripple Creek Times. (Cripple Creek, Colo.) 1901-19??
The Cripple Creek Times. (Cripple Creek, Colo.) 1902-1913
Victor Weekly Record. (Victor, Colo.) 1904-1908
The Victor Record. (Victor, Colo.) 1908-19??
The Cripple Creek Times & The Victor Daily Record. (Cripple Creek, Colo.) 1913-1918
The Times-Record. (Cripple Creek, Colo.) 1918-1942
Cripple Creek Times-Victor Daily Record. (Cripple Creek, Colo.) 1942-1942
Cripple Creek Times-Victor Record. (Cripple Creek, Colo.) 1942-1951
Cripple Creek Gold Rush. (Cripple Creek, Colo.) 1952-1984
The Miner's Digest. (Cripple Creek, Colo.) 1961-19??

Historical Assets Colorado

The Eagle. (Woodland Park, Colo.) 1964-1964
The Ute Pass Courier. (Woodland Park, Colo.) 1964-Current
Teller County Sentinel. (Woodland Park, Colo.) 1981-1982
The Gold Rush. (Cripple Creek, Colo.) 1983-1984
Cripple Creek Gold Rush. (Cripple Creek, Colo.) 1984-1984
Cripple Creek Gold Rush's Teller County Times. (Cripple Creek, Colo.) 1984-1987
Gold Rush. (Woodland Park, Colo.) 1987-Current
High Mountain Sun. ([Woodland Park, Colo.) 1989-Current

Places on the National Register

Cripple Creek, Cripple Creek Historic District, Rt. 67
Florissant, Florissant School, 2009 Co. Rd. 31
Florissant, Hornbek House, CR 1
Florissant, Twin Creek Ranch, 1465 Teller Co. Rd. 31
Goldfield, Goldfield City Hall and Fire Station, Victor Ave. and 9th St.
Victor, Midland Terminal Railroad Depot, 230 N. 4th St.
Victor, Stratton's Independence Mine and Mill, Jct. of Rangeview Rd. and CO 67
Victor, Victor Downtown Historic District, Roughly bounded by Diamond Ave., Second, Portland and 5th Sts.
Victor, Victor Hotel, 4th St. and Victor Ave.
Woodland Park, Manitou Experimental Forest Station, 232 Cty Rd. 79

USGS Historic Places

Cripple Creek South, Altman, 38.7360995, -105.1338686
Cripple Creek South, Independence, 38.7322108, -105.1366466
Divide, Bethel School, 38.9627693, -105.2177673
Pikes Peak, Gillett, 38.7819327, -105.1227577
Pikes Peak, Seven Lakes, 38.7816533, -105.0085859
Roubideau, Anaconda, 38.731929, -105.163129
Unknown, Cameron, 0, 0
Unknown, Mound City, 0, 0

Grand Army of the Republic Posts

J W Anderson, No. 96, Teller, Cripple Creek
Victor, No. 100, Teller, Victor

USGS Historic Military Places

None

Military Bases

None

Post Offices

Altman	1895 Mar 21	1911 May 20
Anaconda	1893 Dec 7	1917 Nov 15*

Teller County

Cameron	1901 Apr 10	1909 Aug 31	
Clyde	1899 Oct 12	1909 Sept 30*	
Cripple Creek	1892 June 20		80813
Crystola	1911 Nov 24	1913 Dec 31	
Divide	1889 July 26		80814
Edlowe	1896 Jun 9	1899 June 16	
Elkton	1895 Apr 2	1926 Nov 15	
Florissant	1872 Nov 20		80816
Gillett	1894 Aug 29	1913 Mar 15*	
Goldfield	1895 May 5	1932 June 3	
Highpark	1896 June 2	1917 May 31*	
Hobart	1900 Feb 6	1902 Feb 15	
Independence	1899 May 12	1954 June 30	
Langdon	1907 Dec 21	1911 Nov 24	
Love	1894 Dec 29	1902 July 15	
Macon	1895 Feb 20	1899 May 12	
Marigold	1895 Oct 31	1902 June 30	
Midland	1892 June 27	1899 Aug 31*	
Rosemont	1903 Mar 31	1926 Nov 15	
Seward	1896 Aug 6	1899 Oct 12	
Torrington	1896 Sept 14	1903 Nov 14	
Touraine	1889 Nov 9	1901 Apr 10	
Victor	1894 June 7		80860
Woodland Park	1873 Sept 1		80863

Topo Quads

Big Bull Mountain	384500N	383730N	1050000W	1050730W
Cripple Creek North	385230N	384500N	1050730W	1051500W
Cripple Creek South	384500N	383730N	1050730W	1051500W
Divide	390000N	385230N	1050730W	1051500W
Signal Butte	390730N	390000N	1050730W	1051500W

Suggested Reading

Aldrich, John K. *Ghosts of Teller County: a Guide to the Ghost Towns and Mining Camps of Teller County, Colorado.* Lakewood, CO: Centennial Graphics, 1994.

Bowman, George. *The Fabulous Cripple Creek District.* Cripple Creek, CO: NP, 1958.

Collins, Jan MacKell. *Lost Ghost Towns of Teller County.* Charleston, SC: Arcadia Publishing, 2016.

Feitz, Leland. *A Quick History of Victor (Teller County): Colorado's City of Mines.* Colorado Springs, CO: Little London Press, 1969.

MacIver, Kathi. *Law and Order: Early Teller County Colorado.* Cripple Creek, CO: Columbine Press, 2008.

Pettit, Jan. *A Quick History of Ute Pass.* Colorado Springs, CO: Little London Press, 1979.

Historical Assets Colorado

Washington County

Introduction

Established: 1887   Population: 4,814

Formed from: Weld

Adjacent Counties: Logan, Yuma, Kit Carson, Lincoln, Adams, Arapahoe, Morgan

County Seat: Akron

Other Communities: Otis, Anton, Cope, Last Chance, Lindon, Platner, Rago, Thurman, Woodrow, Abbott, Arickaree, Burdett, Elba, Harrisburg, Messex, Pinneo, Simpson, Spence, Waitley, Xenia

Website: https://www.colorado.gov/washingtoncounty

Area Codes: 970

Zip Codes: 80720, 80740, 80743, 80757, 80801, 80812

Historical Assets Colorado

Washington County Courthouse

Courthouses & County Government
Washington County
https://www.colorado.gov/washingtoncounty
Washington County Courthouse (13th Judicial District), 26861 Hwy 34, Akron, CO 80720, 970-345-2756; http://www.courts.state.co.us/Courts/County/Index.cfm?County_ID=43
Assessor, 150 Ash Ave, Akron, CO 80720, 970-345-6662; https://www.colorado.gov/pacific/washingtoncounty/assessor-3
Board of County Commissioners, 150 Ash St, Akron, CO 80720, 970-345-2701, https://www.colorado.gov/pacific/washingtoncounty/board-county-commissioners-1
Clerk & Recorder, 150 Ash Ave, Akron, CO 80720, 970-345-6565; https://www.colorado.gov/pacific/washingtoncounty/clerk-0
Coroner, 150 Ash Ave, Akron, CO 80720, 970-345-2424; https://www.colorado.gov/pacific/washingtoncounty/coroner-3
Public Health, 700 Columbine St, Sterling, CO 80751, 970-522-3741; http://www.nchd.org/
Transportation (Road & Bridge), 551 W 2nd St, Akron, CO 80720, 970-345-2337; https://www.colorado.gov/pacific/washingtoncounty/road-and-bridge-0
Treasurer, 150 Ash Ave, Akron, CO 80720, 970-345-6601; https://www.colorado.gov/pacific/washingtoncounty/treasurer-1

County Records
Birth Unk
Death Unk
Court 1887
Marriage 1887
Land 1887
Divorce 1887
Probate 1887

Washington County

County & Municipal Records Held at the State Level

The Colorado State Archives

Physical Records
Clerk & Recorder
WPA Historical Records
WPA Religious Institutions
  Survey

Records on Film
Clerk & Recorder
School Districts

Records on Master Film
County Court
District Court
Combined Courts
School Districts
Cities
  Akron

The Denver Public Library
WPA Historical Records Survey
WWI Draft Registration Cards (microfilm)

School Districts

School Districts, http://www.adcogov.org/local-school-districts
Akron School District R-1, 600 Elm Ave, Akron, CO 80720, 970-345-2268; https://www.akronrams.net/
Arickaree School District R-2, 12155 CR NN, Anton, CO 80801, 970-383-2202; https://www.arickaree.org/
Brush School District RE-2J, 527 Induistrial Park Rd, Brush, CO 80723, 970-842-5176; https://www.brushschools.org/
Buffalo School District RE-4J, 315 Lee St, Merino, CO 80741, 970-522-7424; http://merino.k12.co.us/
Lone Star School District 101, 44940 CR 54, Otis, CO 80743, 970-848-2778; https://www.lonestarschool.net/
Otis School District R-3, 518 Dungan St, Otis, CO 80743, 970-246-3486; https://www.otisr3.com/
Woodlin School District R-104, 15400 CR L, Woodrow, CO 80757, 970-386-2223; https://www.woodlinschool.com/

Historic School Districts

1. Akron
2. Hyde (North, South, East, West, Center)
3. Otis
4. Sunnyvale, Iowa Valley
5. Prairie Vale
6. Antelope Springs
7. Pleasant Valley
8. Ashland
9. Rago, Pinneo 1, Pinneo 2, Lone Valley
10. Hillrose [Joint with Morgan]
11. Star
12. Missouri Valley
13. Valley View, Masters, Last Chance, Howard, Spence
14. Pleasant View
15. Pleasant
16. Platner
17. Sunnyside
18. West Point, Roosevelt
19. Liberty Hill, Fair View, West Point
20. Anton, Harrisburg
21. Center
22. Farley
23. Burdett
24. Capitol Hill
25. Columbine, Goldenrod
26. Hillside, Clark, Mizpah
27. Woodrow Center, East Prong, Lone Prairie
28. Lone Star
29. Roadside, Curtis, Lincoln
30. [1888]
31. East Abbott, West Abbott, Abbott
32. Rock Springs
33. Glen
34. Fremont
35. Sunny Dale
36. East Arickaree
37. Pleasant Hill

Historical Assets Colorado

38. Victory, Fight
39. Lincoln, Lindon
40. Thurman
41. Sunshine
42. Butte, West Butte
43. Prairie View, Bellevue
44. Cactus Hill
45. Elba, High Point
46. White
47. West Antelope
48. Meekton
49. Richmond
50. Sampson
51. Mountain View, Flat Lope, Pleasant Valley
52. High Prairie
53. Antioch, West Fairview
54. Harmony
55. White Rose, Yucca Center
56. Fairview
57. Cope
58. North Buena Vista, South Buena Vista
59.
60. Hurry Back Valley
61. Hillcrest
62. Union Center, Liberty
63. Happy Valley
64. Clay Center
65. White Springs, Ford Center
66. Edville
67. Pleasant Hill
68. Wiladel
69. Antelope Valley
70. Sunshine, Beaverdale
71. Highland
72. Home Valley
73. Welch
74. Rosalind
75. Victor
76. Lafayette
77. [1920]
78. Sunnyslope
79. Plumbush, Pride of the Prairie
80. Crystal Heights
81.
82. Hope
83. Charity
84. Zendner
85. Palmer Valley
86. East Antelope
87. West Arickaree
88. De Nova, Craig
89. Flat Top
90. South Buena Vista
91. Liberty

101.
102. Roosevelt
103.
104.

Fraternal Organizations

Granges
Guiding Star, No. 98, Washington, Akron, 6 Mar 1890
Livingston, No. 99, Washington, Akron, 14 Mar 1890
Superior, No. 349, Washington, Waitley, 8 June 1917
Union Center, No. 350, Washington, Waitley/Merino, 9 June 1917
Platner, No. 354, Washington, Platner, 7 Sept 1917
Buena Vista, No. 356, Washington, Akron, 14 Sept 1917

Masons

Ancient Free & Accepted Masons
Eaton/Abdallah, No. 74, Washington, Akron, 18 Sept 1889

Royal Arch Masons
Akron, No. 26, Washington, Akron

Knights Templar
Akron Commandery, No. 21, Washington, Akron, 1891 Nov 14

Eastern Star
Martha Washington, No. 47, Washington, Akron

Odd Fellows
Akron, No. 89, Washington, Akron

Rebekahs
Akron, No. 82, Washington, Akron

Knights of Pythias
None

Washington County

Pythian Sisters
None

Benevolent Protective Order of Elks
Akron, No. 2579, Washington, Akron

City & Town Halls
Akron, 245 Main Ave, Akron, CO 80720, 970-345-2624, https://www.colorado.gov/pacific/townofakron/

Otis, 102 S Washington St, Otis, CO 80743, 970-246-3235, https://www.colorado.gov/pacific/townofotis

Archives & Manuscript Collections
None

Historical & Genealogical Societies
None

Local Libraries
Akron Public Library, 302 Main Ave, Akron, CO 80720-1437, (970) 345-6818, http://akron.colibraries.org

Links
CO GenWeb
http://cogenweb.com/washington/

Cyndi's List
https://www.cyndislist.com/us/co/counties/washington/

FamilySearch Wiki
https://www.familysearch.org/wiki/en/Washington_County,_Colorado_Genealogy

Linkpendium
http://www.linkpendium.com/washington-co-genealogy/

RootsWeb Wiki
https://wiki.rootsweb.com/wiki/index.php/Washington_County,_Colorado

Wikipedia
https://en.wikipedia.org/wiki/Washington_County,_Colorado

Historic Hotels
None

Museums & Historic Sites
Washington County Museum, 201 E 1st St, Akron, CO 80720, (970) 345-6446

Historical Assets Colorado

Special Events & Scenic Locations
The Eastern Colorado Roundup is held at the Washington County Fairgrounds, 551 W 2nd, Akron, CO 80720, 970-554-0949, http://www.ecroundup.com

Washington County keeps a calendar of events here: https://washingtoncounty.colorado.gov

American Discovery Trail
South Platte Trail

Ghost Towns & Other Sparsely Populated Places
Burdett, Cody, Curtis, Harman, Hyde, Last Chance, Leslie, Millet, Otis, Pinneo

Newspapers
The Otis Independent. (Otis, Washington County, Colo.) 1???-19??
Thurman Times. (Thurman, Colo.) 18??-1???
The Colorado Topics. (Hyde, Weld County, Colo.) 1886-1889
Akron Pioneer Press. (Akron, Washington County, Colo.) 1886-19??
Colorado Clipper. (Otis, Colo.) 1887-1???
The Lindon Sun. (Lindon, Arapahoe County, Colo.) 1890-18??
Washington County Leader. (Akron, Colo.) 1897-19??
The Akron Reporter. (Akron, Washington County, Colo.) 19??-1929
Akron Weekly Pioneer Press. (Akron, Washington County, Colo.) 19??-1923
The News. (Akron, Washington County, Colo.) 1910-1912
The Akron News. (Akron, Washington County, Colo.) 1913-1928
The Akron Semi-Weekly News. (Akron, Colo.) 1928-1929
The Akron News-Reporter. (Akron, Washington County [Colo.]) 1929-1989
News-Reporter. (Akron, Colo.) 1989-Current

Places on the National Register
Akron, Akron Gymnasium, W. 4th St. & Custer Ave.
Last Chance, Plum Bush Creek Bridge, US 36 at milepost 138.16
Last Chance, West Plum Bush Creek Bridge, US 36 at milepost 134.59

USGS Historic Places
Buffalo Springs Ranch NW, Summit Springs Battlefield Historical Marker, 40.4338737, -103.1402133
De Nova, De Nova, 39.8588913, -102.9732656
Last Chance NW, Frasier Ranch Airport, 39.6413748, -103.6452271
Lindon NE, Decker Farms Airport, 39.7066516, -103.3518859
Otis, Otis Airport, 40.155261, -102.9674371
Otis, Stansfield Airport, 40.18165, -102.9224361
Woodlin School, Chenoweth Airport, 39.8330413, -103.5899462

Grand Army of the Republic Posts
Akron, No. 25, Washington, Akron

Washington County

USGS Historic Military Places
None

Military Bases
None

Post Offices

Abbott	1887 Aug 6	1926 Apr 15	
Akron	1883 Jan 30		80720
Anton	1916 July 18		80801
Arikaree	1888 June 9	1961 June 23	
Brunker	1907 Dec 28	1917 Jan 31	
Burdett	1888 Apr 4	1937 Apr 30	
Cope	1888 Apr 23		80812
Curtis	1888 Apr 27	1901 Apr 30	
De Nova	1916 Mar 20	1955 Mar 31	
Dillingham	1911 Jan 24	1920 July 1*	
Eckley	1883 Nov 15	1884 June 16	
Elba	1910 May 9	1958 Jan 10	
Flat Top	1915 Jan 30	1921 Jan 15	
Fremont	1908 Oct 28	1914 Feb 15	
Glen	1905 June 25	1920 May 31	
Harrisburg	1908 Oct 29	1955 Mar 31	
Henry	1907 Dec 26	1917 Nov 15	
Hyde	1882 Aug 1	1940 Feb 15*	
Laird	1887 July 12	1892 Feb 17	
Leslie	1888 June 6	1896 Mar 2	
Lindon	1888 Sept 21		80740
Meekton	1910 July 7	1918 Nov 30	
Messex	1907 June 18	1942 Nov 30	
Millett	1890 Apr 8	1890 Dec 27	
Otis	1886 Jan 11		80743
Pinnero	1883 Nov 15	1931 Dec 5*	
Platner	1892 June 15	1957 Mar 1	
Plum Bush	1910 Aug 16	1918 June 15	
Prairie	1910 July 7	1917 Mar 31	
Schlueter	1912 Sept 10	1913 July 31	
Simpson	1910 June 24	1943 Aug 31	
Spence	1910 Aug 20	1926 Jan 31	
Thurman	1888 July 6	1955 Mar 31	
Waitley	1915 June 15	1936 Jan 15	
Woodrow	1913 Sept 10		80757
Wray	1882 June 26		80758

Historical Assets Colorado

Topo Quads

Name				
Akron	401500N	400730N	1030730W	1031500W
Akron SE	400730N	400000N	1030000W	1030730W
Akron SW	400730N	400000N	1030730W	1031500W
Antelope Creek East	400000N	395230N	1031500W	1032230W
Antelope Creek SE	395230N	394500N	1031500W	1032230W
Antelope Creek West	400000N	395230N	1032230W	1033000W
Anton	394500N	393730N	1030730W	1031500W
Anton SE	393730N	393000N	1030000W	1030730W
Arickaree	394500N	393730N	1030000W	1030730W
Buffalo Springs Ranch	402230N	401500N	1030730W	1031500W
Buffalo Springs Ranch SE	402230N	401500N	1030000W	1030730W
Burdett	402230N	401500N	1025230W	1030000W
Cope NW	394500N	393730N	1025230W	1030000W
Cope SW	393730N	393000N	1025230W	1030000W
De Nova	395230N	394500N	1025230W	1030000W
De Nova NW	400000N	395230N	1025230W	1030000W
Dry Gulch	395230N	394500N	1032230W	1033000W
Elba	400000N	395230N	1030730W	1031500W
Elba NE	400000N	395230N	1030000W	1030730W
Elba SE	395230N	394500N	1030000W	1030730W
Elba SW	395230N	394500N	1030730W	1031500W
Fremont Butte	401500N	400730N	1031500W	1032230W
Last Chance	394500N	393730N	1033000W	1033730W
Last Chance NW	394500N	393730N	1033730W	1034500W
Last Chance SW	393730N	393000N	1033730W	1034500W
Lindon	394500N	393730N	1032230W	1033000W
Lindon NE	394500N	393730N	1031500W	1032230W
Lindon SW	393730N	393000N	1032230W	1033000W
Lusto Springs	393730N	393000N	1033000W	1033730W
Merino SE	402230N	401500N	1031500W	1032230W
Otis	401500N	400730N	1025230W	1030000W
Pinneo SE	400730N	400000N	1031500W	1032230W
Platner	401500N	400730N	1030000W	1030730W
Shaw	393730N	393000N	1031500W	1032230W
Snyder Lake	400730N	400000N	1025230W	1030000W
Thurman	393730N	393000N	1030730W	1031500W
Wetzel Creek	395230N	394500N	1033730W	1034500W
Woodlin School	395230N	394500N	1033000W	1033730W
Woodrow	400000N	395230N	1033000W	1033730W
Woodrow NW	400000N	395230N	1033730W	1034500W

Washington County

Suggested Reading

100 Years in Pictures: Akron, 1882-1982. Akron, CO: Washington County Museum Association, 1982.

Brown, Jane. *History of Washington County, Colorado*. Dallas: Curtis Media Corp, 1989.

Inventory of the County Archives of Colorado, No. 61, Washington County (Akron). Denver: Historical Records Survey, 1941.

Jesse, Frances and Billie Jesse. *The War Years and the People of Washington County*. Dallas: Curtis Media Corp, 1993.

Washington County Museum Association. *The Pioneer Book of Washington County, Colorado*. Salem, MA: Higginson Book Co, 2007.

Historical Assets Colorado

Weld County

Introduction

Established: 1861   Population: 252,825

Formed from: Original

Adjacent Counties: Greeley

County Seat: Logan, Morgan, Adams, Broomfield, Boulder, Larimer

Other Communities: Dacono, Evans, Fort Lupton, Ault, Eaton, Erie, Firestone, Frederick, Garden City, Gilcrest, Grover, Hudson, Keenesburg, Kersey, LaSalle, Lochbuie, Mead, Milliken, Nunn, Pierce, Platteville, Raymer, Severance, Windsor, Adna, Auburn, Avalo, Briggsdale, Carr, Dearfield, Galeton, Gill, Hereford, Highlandlake, Ione, Keota, Lucerne, Roggen, Stoneham, Tampa, Wattenburg

Website, https://www.weldgov.com

Area Codes: 303, 720, 970

Zip Codes: 80504, 80514, 80520, 80530, 80534, 80542, 80543, 80546, 80550, 80551, 80603, 80610, 80611, 80612, 80615, 80624, 80631, 80633, 80634, 80638, 80639, 80642, 80643, 80644, 80646, 80648, 80650, 80651, 80652, 80729, 80732, 80742, 80754

Historical Assets Colorado

Weld County Courthouse

Weld County 19th Century Courthouse

Courthouses & County Government
Weld County
https://www.weldgov.com
Weld County Courthouse (19th Judicial District), 901 9th Ave, Greeley, CO 80631, 970-475-2400; http://www.courts.state.co.us/Courts/County/Index.cfm?County_ID=61
Weld County Courthouse (Centennial), 915 10th St, Greeley, CO 80631, 970-475-2400; http://www.courts.state.co.us/Courts/County/Index.cfm?County_ID=61
Weld County Courthouse (Plaza West), 910 10th Ave, Greeley, CO 80631, 970-475-2400; http://www.courts.state.co.us/Courts/County/Index.cfm?County_ID=61
Assessor, 1400 N 17th Ave, Greeley, CO 80631, 970-652-4255; http://www.co.weld.co.us/Departments/Assessor/index.html
Board of County Commissioners, 1150 O Street, Greeley, CO 80632, 970-336-7204, https://www.weldgov.com/departments/commissioners
Clerk & Recorder, 1402 N 17th St, Greeley, CO 80631, 970-353-3840; http://www.co.weld.co.us/Departments/ClerkRecorder/index.html
Coroner, 915 10th St, Greeley, CO 80632, 970-400-4990; https://www.weldgov.com/departments/coroner
Public Health, 1555 N 17th Ave, Greeley, CO 80631, 970-304-6410; http://www.co.weld.co.us/Departments/HealthEnvironment/index.html
Transportation (Public Work), 1111 H Street, Greeley, CO 80632, 970-4000-3750; https://www.weldgov.com/departments/public_works
Treasurer, 1400 N 17th Ave, Greeley, CO 80632, 970-353-3845; http://www.co.weld.co.us/Departments/Treasurer/index.html

County Records
Birth 1908	Marriage 1861	Divorce 1876
Death 1900	Land 1861	Probate 1876
Court 1876		
CSA Applications for Burial 1912		
CSA Delayed or Corrected Birth Certificates 1941		

Weld County

County & Municipal Records Held at the State Level
The Colorado State Archives

Physical Records
Agricultural Extention Agent
Assessor
Clerk & Recorder
County Commissioners
County Court
District Court
Justice Court
Treasurer
WPA Historical Records
WPA Religious Institutions Survey
Cities
Fort Lupton
Greeley
Keota
Windsor

Records on Film
1885 Census
District Court
School Districts
Cities
Fort Lupton
Greeley
Keota

Records on Master Film
County Court
District Court
Combined Courts
District Attorney
Cities
Fort Lupton
Greeley
Keota
Platteville

The Denver Public Library
Colorado Deeds, 1868-1911
Colorado Theatre Program Collection, 1900-
German-Russians in Weld County, 1900-1920
Greeley Farmers' Club Records, 1870-1873
New Raymer Farmers' Educational and Co-operative Union Records, 1915-1934
Records Relating to Historical Development in Weld County, 1864-1963
Rough & Ready Irrigating Canal, 1885
St Vrain County (Jefferson Territory) Land Claim Association Records, 1859-1867
WWI Draft Registration Cards (microfilm)

School Districts
School Districts, http://www.adcogov.org/local-school-districts
Ault Highland School District RE-9, 210 W 1st St, Ault, CO 80610, 970-834-1345; https://www.weldre9.k12.co.us/
Briggsdale School District Re-10, 515 Leslie St, Briggsdale, CO 80611, 970-656-3417; http://briggsdaleschool.org/
Eaton School District RE-2, 211 1st St, Eaton, CO 80615, 970-454-3402; http://www.eaton.k12.co.us/
Greeley School District 6, 1025 9th Ave, Greeley, CO 80631, 970-348-6000; https://www.greeleyschools.org/
Johnstown-Milliken School District RE-5J, 110 S Centennial Dr, Ste A, Milliken, CO 80543, 970-587-6050; https://www.weldre5j.k12.co.us/
Pawnee School District RE-12, 19 Chatoga Ave, Grover, CO, 90729, 970-895-2222; http://www.pawneeschool.org/

Historical Assets Colorado

Platte Valley School District RE-7, 501 Clark St, Kersey, CO 80644, 970-336-8500; http://www.plattevalley.k12.co.us/home
Prairie School District RE-11, 42315 CR 133, New Raymer, CO 80742, 970-437-5351; https://www.prairieschool.org/
St Vrain Valley School District, 395 S Pratt Pkwy, Longmont, CO 80501, 303-776-6200; https://www.svvsd.org/
Weld County School District RE-1, 14827 CR 42, Gilcrest, CO 80623, 970-350-4201; https://www.weld-re1.k12.co.us/
Weld County School District RE-3J, 99 W Broadway St, Keensburg, CO 80643, 303-536-2000; https://re3j.com/
Weld County School District S/D RE 8, 200 S Fulton Ave, Fort Lupton, CO 80621, 303-857-3200; https://www.weld8.org/
Wiggins School District RE-50J, 320 Chapman St, Wiggins, CO 80654, 970-483-7762; http://wiggins50.k12.co.us/
Windsor School District RE-4, 1020 Main St, Windsor, CO 80550, 970-686-8000; https://weldre4.org/

Historic School Districts

1. Idaho Creek
2. St Vrain
3. Four Way
4. Windsor
5. Purcell, High Five
6. Greeley
7. Worley
8. Fort Lupton
9. Pawnee Center
10. Larkspur
11. Auburn
12. Keenesburg
13. Wheeler
14. Vim
15. Evans
16. Lone Star
17. Bracewell
18. Whipple
19. Wattenburg
20. Delta
21. Daniels
22. Oklahoma
23. Independence
24. Ashton
25. Coffin
26. Rockaway
27. La Grante
28. Pearl
29. Big Bend
30. Hilltop
31. Ione
32. Pleasant Hill
33. Degler
34. Ault
35. East Sunnyside
36. Sunnyside
37. Eaton
38. Twin Mounds
39. Lone Tree
40. Pierce
41. Sky View
42. Highland
43. Mountain View
44. Morning Star
45. Pleasant View
46. Carr
47. Cotton Creek
48. Johnstown
49. Sligo
50. Wiggins
51. Central, Casten
52. Severance
53. [1885]
54. Barnesville
55. Erkenbeck
56. Columbine
57. Lakeview
58. Pleasant Valley
59. Buell
60. Olin
61. South Victor
62. Olive Branch
63. Liberty
64. Milliken
65. La Salle
66. Smith
67. Nunn
68. [1886]
69. Dover
70. Springdale
71. Masters
72. Hardin
73. Kuner
74. Grout
75. Antelope Springs
76. Frederick
77. Union
78. Block
79. Plainview
80. Hudson
81. Valley View
82. Roggen
83. Hazelton
84. Beebe Draw
85. West Pawnee
86. Peter Brown
87. Gill
88. Kiowa
89. Grover
90. Wyatt
91. New Raymer
92. Keota
93. Midway

Weld County

94. Indian Cave
95. Prairie View
96. Prospect Valley
97. Gilcrest
98. Kersey
99. Wentz
100. Porter
101. Observation
102. Pleasant Valley, Brighton
103. Galeton
104. Vollmar
105. Osgood
106. Buckingham
107. Briggsdale
108. Lucas
109. Fosston
110. Stoneham
111. Fairview
112. Cornish
113. Tonville
114. Point of Rocks
115. Purcell
116. Prairie Dale
117. Mead
118. Platteville
119. Gerry Valley
120. Coleman
121. Erie
122. Sunnyridge
123. Glennada
124. Deerfield [Joint with Morgan]
125. Sunnydale
126. Judd-Eberson
127. Primrose
128. Willow Creek
129. Bluff
130. Silver Cliff
131. Mount Lookout
132. North Victor
133. Salem
134. Stone
135. Dailey
136. North Pawnee

Fraternal Organizations

Granges

Greeley, No. 3, Weld, Greeley, 5 Dec 1873
Lower Boulder, No. 15, Weld, Erie, 23 Dec 1873
Meadow Island, No. 17, Weld, Ft Lupton/St Vrain, 27 Dec 1873
Lower Thompson, No. 18, Weld, Evans, 29 Dec 1873
Fort Lupton, No. 20, Weld, Ft Lupton, 3 Jan 1873
Star, No. 21, Weld, Ft Lupton, 9 Jan 1874
Eureka, No. 35, Weld, Erie, 19 Jan 1874
Cache la Poudre, No. 43, Weld, Greeley, 23 Jan 1874
Pomona, No. 51, Weld, Greeley, 11 Mar 1874
Industry, No. 61, Weld, Evans, 17 June 1874
Centre, No. 84, Weld, Eaton, 5 May 1888
Pleasant Valley, No. 85, Weld, Greeley, 14 May 1888
Fairplay, No. 152, Weld, Eaton, 12 Mar 1906
Silver State, No. 171, Weld, Ft Lupton, 12 June 1909
Pleasant Valley, No. 191, Weld, Fort Lupton, 4 Oct 1910
Buckingham, No. 212, Weld, Buckingham, Jan 1913
Raymer, No. 224, Weld, New Raymer, 14 Mar 1914
Gerry Creek, No. 228, Weld, Gault, 11 July 1914
Elbert Center, No. 244, Weld, Hereford, 23 Mar 1915
Igo, No. 246, Weld, Keota, 30 Mar 1915
Keota, No. 247, Weld, Keota, 1 Apr 1915
Avalo, No. 249, Weld, Avalo, 5 May 1915
Hudson, No. 257, Weld, Hudson, 13 July 1915
Prairie View, No. 266, Weld, Purcell, 1 Apr 1916
Crow Valley, No. 267, Weld, Briggsdale, 1 Apr 1916
Sligo, No. 270, Weld, Sligo, 16 Mar 1916
Harmony, No. 279, Weld, Briggsdale, 5 May 1916
Valley, No. 286, Weld, Graham, 22 May 1916
Fairfield, No. 291, Weld, Gifford, 12 June 1916

Historical Assets Colorado

Rockaway, No. 292, Weld, Kauffman, 13 June 1916
Pleasant Valley, No. 296, Weld, Briggsdale, 1 July 1916
Liberty, No. 320, Weld, Orchard, 9 Feb 1917
Valley View, No. 326, Weld, Ft Lupton, 3 Mar 1917
Platte Valley, No. 455, Weld, Kersey, 23 Mar 1944
VE, No. 457, Weld, Hudson, 8 May 1945
Fort Vasquez, No. 483, Weld, Greeley, 21 Aug 1958
County Line, No. 484, Weld/Boulder, Longmont/Erie?, 28 Aug 1958

Masons
  Ancient Free & Accepted Masons
    Garfield, No. 20, Weld, Greeley, 26 Sept 1871
    Windsor, No. 50, Weld, Erie, 20 Sept 1882
    Cheyenne, No. 69, Weld, Windsor, 21 Sept 1887
    Lupton, No. 109, Weld, Eaton, 19 Sept 1900
    Hudson, No. 119, Weld, Fort Lupton, 21
    Century, No. 168, Weld, Hudson, 22 Sept 1926
    Occidental, No. 190, Weld, Greeley, 23 Jan 1962
  Royal Arch Masons
    Greeley, No. 13, Weld, Greeley
    Windsor, No. 40, Weld, Windsor
  Knights Templar
    Greeley Commandery, No. 10, Weld, Greeley, 1884 Jan 26
  Eastern Star
    Garden City, No. 3, Weld, Greeley
    Columbia, No. 16, Weld, Windsor
    Ruth, No. 19, Weld, Erie
    Eaton, No. 67, Weld, Eaton
    Bountiful, No. 72, Weld, Fort Lupton
    Johnstown, No. 114, Weld, Johnstown

Odd Fellows
  Poudre Valley, No. 12, Weld, Greeley, 1871 Apr 26
  Erie, No. 46, Weld, Erie
  Platteville, No. 81, Weld, Platteville
  Lakeside, No. 88, Weld, New Windsor
  Milliken, No. 97, Weld, Milliken
  Fort Lupton, No. 100, Weld, Fort Lupton
  Prosperity, No. 109, Weld, Evans
  Excelsior, No. 121, Weld, Eaton
  Weld, No. 151, Weld, Ault
  Grover, No. 167, Weld, Grover
  La Salle, No. 174, Weld, La Salle
  Pierce, No. 176, Weld, Pierce

Rebekahs
  Oasis, No. 13, Weld, Greeley
  Blue Bird, No. 28, Weld, Fort Lupton

Weld County

Rose of Sharon, No. 29, Weld, Erie
Loyal, No. 70, Weld, Eaton
Refulgent, No. 98, Weld, Milliken
Dorothy, No. 104, Weld, Ault

Knights of Pythias
Greeley, No. 31, Weld, Greeley
Erie, No. 35, Weld, Erie
I X L, No. 70, Weld, Fort Lupton
Damascus, No. 72, Weld, Platteville, 1891 July 23

Pythian Sisters
Easter Lily, No. 35, Weld, Erie
Greeley, No. 43, Weld, Greeley

Benevolent Protective Order of Elks
Greeley, No. 809, Weld, Greeley

City & Town Halls

Greeley, 1000 10th St, Greeley, CO 80631, 970-350-9741, https://greeleygov.com
Dacono, 512 Cherry St, Dacono, CO 80514, 303-833-2317, https://www.cityofdacono.com
Evans, 1100 37th St, Evans, CO 80620, 970-475-1170, https://www.evanscolorado.gov
Fort Lupton, 130 S McKinley Ave, Fort Lupton, CO 80621, 303-857-6694, https://www.fortlupton.org
Ault, 201 1st St, Ault, CO 80610, 970-834-2844, https://www.townofault.org
Eaton, 223 1st St, Eaton, CO 80615, 970-454-3338, https://www.colorado.gov/townofeaton
Erie, 645 Holbrook St, Erie, CO 80516, 303-926-2700, https://www.erieco.gov
Firestone, 151 Grant Ave, Firestone, CO 80520, 303-833-3291, https://www.firestoneco.gov
Frederick, 401 Locust St, Frederick, CO 80530, 720-382-5500, https://www.frederickco.gov
Garden City, 621 27th Street Rd, Garden City, CO 80631, 970-351-0041, https://townofgardencity.com
Gilcrest, 304 8th St, Gilcrest, CO 80623, 970-737-2426, http://townofgilcrest.org
Grover, 315 Chatoga Ave, Grover, CO 80729, 970-895-2213, https://www.facebook.com/pages/Town-of-Grover/139356669444907
Hudson, 50 Beech St, Hudson, CO 80642, 303-536-9311, https://hudsoncolorado.org
Keenesburg, 140 Main St, Keenesburg, CO 80643, 303-732-4281, https://www.townofkeenesburg.com
Kersey, 332 3rd St, Kersey, CO 80644, 970-353-1681, http://www.kerseygov.com
LaSalle, 128 N 2nd St, LaSalle, CO 80645, 970-284-6931, https://www.lasalletown.com
Lochbuie, 703 Co Rd 37, Lochbuie, CO 80603, 303-655-9308, https://www.lochbuie.org
Mead, 441 3rd St, Mead, CO 80542, 970-535-4477, https://www.townofmead.org

Historical Assets Colorado

Milliken, 1101 Broad St, Milliken, CO 80543, 970-587-4331, https://www.millikenco.gov

Nunn, 185 Lincoln Ave, Nunn, CO 80648, 970-897-2385, http://www.nunncolorado.com

Pierce, 144 Main Ave, Pierce, CO 80650, 970-834-2851, https://townofpierce.org

Platteville, 400 Grand Ave, Platteville, CO 80651, 970-785-2245, https://www.plattevillegov.org

Severance, 3 Timber Ridge Pkwy, Severance, CO 80550, 970-686-1218, https://townofseverance.org

Windsor, 301 Walnut St, Windsor, CO 80550, 970-674-2400, https://www.windsorgov.com

Archives & Manuscript Collections

James A Michener Library, Archives & Special Collections, Univ of Northern Colorado, 501 20th St, Greeley, CO 80639, (970) 351-2562, https://www.unco.edu/library/archives/

Historical & Genealogical Societies

American Historical Society of Germans from Russia, Northern Colorado Chapter, 6728 Cty Rd 3 1/4, Erie, CO 80516, (970) 674-3225, https://www.ahsgr.org/page/NorthernColo

Erie Historical Society, Wise Homestead Museum, 11611 Jasper Rd, P.O. Box 156, Erie, CO 80515, (303) 828-4561, http://www.eriehistoricalsociety.org

High Plains Historical Society, Northern Drylanders Museum, 755 3rd St, P.O. Box 122, Nunn, CO 80648, (970) 897-3125, http://www.highplainshistory.homestead.com

Johnstown Historical Society, Parish House & Museum, 701 Charlotte St, Johnstown, CO 80534-8611, (970) 587-0278, http://johnstownhistoricalsociety.org

Milliken Historical Society, Historical Museum, 1101 Broad St, P.O. Box 92, Milliken, CO 80543, (970) 587-4251, http://www.millikenhistoricalsociety.org

Pawnee Historical Society, Grover Depot Museum, P.O. Box 7, Grover, CO 80729, https://www.facebook.com/pawneehistoricalsociety/

Platteville Historical Society, Pioneer Museum, 502 Marion, P.O. Box 567, Platteville, CO 80651, (970) 785-2481, https://www.plattevillegov.org/2306/Platteville-Pioneer-Museum

South Platte Valley Historical Society, Fort Lupton Historic Park, 1875 Factory Dr, P.O. Box 633, Fort Lupton, CO 80621, (303) 847-1710, http://www.spvhs.org

Weld County Genealogical Society, P.O. Box 278, Greeley, CO 80632-0278, (970) 356-2568, http://www.weldgenerations.org

Local Libraries

Hazel E Johnson Genealogical Research Center, Greeley History Museum, 714 8th St, Greeley, CO 80631, (970) 350-9220, https://greeleymuseums.com/locations/greeley-history-museum/hazel-e-johnson-research-center/

Weld County Library District-Centennial Park, 2227 23rd Ave, Greeley, CO 80631, (970) 506-8600, https://www.mylibrary.us

Weld County

First Congregational Church Library, 2101 16th St, Greeley, CO 80631, 970-353-0828, https://www.firstconggreeley.com
Glenn A Jones Memorial Library, 400 S Parish Ave, P.O. Box 457, Johnstown, CO 80534, (970) 587-2459, https://www.mylibrary.us
High Plains Library District - Farr Regional Library, 1939 61st Ave, Greeley, CO 80634-7940, (970) 506-8500, http://www.mylibrary.us
High Plains Library District, Lincoln Park Branch, 1012 11th St, Greeley, CO 80631, (970) 350-9212, https://www.mylibrary.us
High Plains Library District-Hudson Public Library, 100 Beech St, Hudson, CO 80642, (303) 536-4550, https://www.mylibrary.us
Kiefer Library, Aims Community College, 5401 W 20th St, P.O. Box 69, Greeley, CO 80632-0069, (970) 330-8008, Ext 6237, https://www.aims.edu/kieferlibrary/index.php
Northern Plains Public Library, 216 2nd St, P.O. Box 147, Ault, CO 80610-0147, (970) 834-1259, http://northernplainspl.org
Platteville Public Library, 504 Marion Ave, P.O. Box 567, Platteville, CO 80651-0567, (970) 785-2231, http://www.coloradoplattevillelibrary.us
Windsor-Severance Library District, 720 3rd St, Windsor, CO 80550, (970) 686-5603, https://clearviewlibrary.org

Links

CO GenWeb
http://cogenweb.com/weld/

Cyndi's List
https://www.cyndislist.com/us/co/counties/weld/

FamilySearch Wiki
https://www.familysearch.org/wiki/en/Weld_County,_Colorado_Genealogy

Linkpendium
http://www.linkpendium.com/weld-co-genealogy/

RootsWeb Wiki
https://wiki.rootsweb.com/wiki/index.php/Weld_County,_Colorado

Wikipedia
https://en.wikipedia.org/wiki/Weld_County,_Colorado

Historic Hotels
None

Museums & Historic Sites

City of Evans Museum, 3720 Golden St, Evans, CO 80620, (970) 506-2721, http://www.cityofevans.org
Colorado Model Railroad Museum, 680 10th St, Greeley, CO 80631, (970) 392-2934, https://www.cmrm.org
Eaton House Museum, 207 Elm Ave, Eaton, CO 80615, (970) 454-3338, https://www.colorado.gov/pacific/townofeaton/eaton-house-museum

Historical Assets Colorado

Erie Historical Society, Wise Homestead Museum, 11611 Jasper Rd, P.O. Box 156, Erie, CO 80515, (303) 828-4561, http://www.eriehistoricalsociety.org

Fort Lupton Museum, 453 1st St, Fort Lupton, CO 80621, (303) 857-1634, https://www.fortlupton.org/157/Museum

Fort Vasquez Museum, 13412 US Hwy 85, Platteville, CO 80651, (970) 785-2832, https://www.historycolorado.org/fort-vasquez

High Plains Historical Society, Northern Drylanders Museum, 755 3rd St, P.O. Box 122, Nunn, CO 80648, (970) 897-3125, http://www.highplainshistory.homestead.com

Historic Centennial Village Museum, 1475 A Street, Greeley, CO 80631, (970) 350-9224, http://www.greeleymuseums.com

Johnstown Historical Society, Parish House & Museum, 701 Charlotte St, Johnstown, CO 80534-8611, (970) 587-0278, http://johnstownhistoricalsociety.org

Meeker Home Museum, 1324 9th Ave, Greeley, CO 80631, (970) 350-9220, https://greeleymuseums.com/locations/meeker-home/

Milliken Historical Society, Historical Museum, 1101 Broad St, P.O. Box 92, Milliken, CO 80543, (970) 587-4251, http://www.millikenhistoricalsociety.org

Pawnee Historical Society, Grover Depot Museum, P.O. Box 7, Grover, CO 80729, https://www.facebook.com/pawneehistoricalsociety/

Platteville Historical Society, Pioneer Museum, 502 Marion, P.O. Box 567, Platteville, CO 80651, (970) 785-2481, https://www.plattevillegov.org/2306/Platteville-Pioneer-Museum

South Platte Valley Historical Society, Fort Lupton Historic Park, 1875 Factory Dr, P.O. Box 633, Fort Lupton, CO 80621, (303) 847-1710, http://www.spvhs.org

Spirit of Flight Center, Erie Municipal Airport, 2650 S Main St, Erie, CO 80516-8155, (303) 460-1156, http://www.spiritofflight.com

Vintage Aero Flying Museum, Platte Valley Airpark, 7507 CR 39, Fort Lupton, CO 80621-8530, (303) 502-5347, http://www.vafm.org

White-Plumb Farm Learning Center, 955 39th Ave, Greeley, CO 80631, (970) 350-9220, http://www.greeleymuseums.com

Windsor Museum, 116 N 5th St, Windsor, CO 80550, (970) 686-7476, http://www.windsorgov.com

Special Events & Scenic Locations

The Weld County Fair is held in July and August most years in Island Grove Regional Park, 525 N 15th Ave, Greeley, CO 80631, 970-400-2066, https://www.weldcountyfair.com

The Greeley Stampede takes place in July most years also at Island Grove Regional Park, https://www.greeleystampede.org

Visit Greeley has a calendar of festivals and events here: https://www.visitgreeley.org/things-to-do/festivals-events/

Pawnee National Grassland
Fort Vasquez State History Museum
St Vrain State Park
American Discovery Trail

Weld County

Pawnee Pioneer Trails
Poudre River National Recreation Trail
South Platte Trail

Ghost Towns & Other Sparsely Populated Places

Agricola, Alden, Alfalfa, Athol, Boyds, Buckingham, Carbon Valley, Carr, Chapelton, Chenoa, Cherokee City, Cloverly, Coleman, Corona, Dearfield, Dick, Dover, Elwell, Farmers, Flemings Ranch, Fort St Vrain, Fort Vasquez, Fosston, Gault, Geary, Graham, Green City, Grover, Hardin, Hereford, Highland Lake, Hillsborough, Hiltonville, Hungerford, Kalous, Kauffman, Keene, Keota, Koenig, Lancaster, Latham, Liberty, Lupton, Masters, Mitchell, Nantes, New Liberty, Orchard, Orr, Osgood, Peckham, Pierce, Platte Valley, Plumbs, Purcell, Raymer, Rinn, Roggen, Rosedale, Saint Vrain(s), Serene, Sligo, Spanish Colony, Stoneham, Wentz, Zilar, Zita

Newspapers

The Greeley Coloradoan. (Greeley, Colo.) 1???-1935
The Kersey Midget. (Kersey, Weld County, Colo.) 1???-19??
The Kersey Courier. (Kersey, Colo.) 1???-19??
The Crow Valley News. (Grover, Weld County, Colo.) 1???-19??
The Fort Lupton Spirit. (Fort Lupton, Weld County, Colo.) 1???-19??
The Journal. (Evans, Colo.) 18??-1???
The Evans Courier. (Evans, Colo.) 18??-1915
The Greeley Tribune. (Greeley, Colo.) 1870-1913
The Evans Journal. (Evans, Weld County, Colo.) 1871-1889
The Colorado Sun. (Greeley, Weld County, Colo.) 1872-1882
The Colorado Farmer. (Evans, Colo.) 1873-1???
The Sterling Record. (Sterling, Colo.) 1882-????
Rocky Mountain Howitzer. (Greeley, Colo.) 1883-188?
The Fort Morgan Times. (Fort Morgan, Weld County, Colo.) 1884-1926
The Lariat. (Brush, Colo.) 1884-1885
The Brush Lariat. (Brush, Weld Co., Colo.) 1884-1884
The Atwood Advocate. (Atwood, Weld County, Colo.) 1885-1???
The Colorado Topics. (Hyde, Weld County, Colo.) 1886-1889
The Howitzer. (Greeley, Colo.) 1886-1889
The Times. (Greeley, Colo.) 189?-1897
The Greeley Sun. (Greeley, Colo.) 1892-1909
New Windsor Tribune. (Windsor, Colo.) 1893-1894
The Eaton Herald. (Eaton, Colo.) 1894-1979
The Weld County Republican. (Greeley, Colo.) 1897-1913
The Fort Lupton Press. (Fort Lupton, Weld County, Colo.) 1898-1980
The Greeley Home Journal. (Greeley, Colo.) 1900-19??
Town & Country News. (Greeley, Colo.) 19??-19??
Erie Herald. (Erie, Weld County, Colo.) 19??-19??
The Weld County News and The Weld County Democrat. (Greeley, Weld County, Colo.) 19??-1917
The Greeley Tribune. (Greeley, Colo.) 19??-1908

Historical Assets Colorado

The Milliken Mail. (Milliken, Weld County, Colo.) 19??-19??
The Primrose and Cattlemen's Gazette. (Hudson, Colo.) 19??-19??
The Poudre Valley. (New Windsor, Colo.) 1902-1947
The Ault Advertiser. (Ault, Weld County, Colo.) 1904-1904
The Ault Advertiser and The Ault Record. (Ault, Weld County, Colo.) 1904-1909
The Johnstown Breeze. (Johnstown, Weld County, Colo.) 1904-Current
The Windsor Optimist. (New Windsor, Colo.) 1904-19??
The Nunn News. (Nunn, Colo.) 1907-1942
The Mead Messenger. (Mead, Weld County, Colo.) 1907-1927
The Erie News. (Erie, Weld County, Colo.) 1907-1907
The Platteville Herald. (Platteville, Colo.) 1908-Current
The Pawnee Press. (Grover, Colo.) 1908-????
The Greeley Daily Tribune. (Greeley, Colo.) 1908-1913
The Greeley Daily Pioneer. (Greeley, Colo.) 1908-19??
The Ault Advertiser. (Ault, Weld County, Colo.) 1909-1926
The Raymer Enterprise. (New Raymer, Weld County, Colo.) 1910-19??
The Ft. Lupton Booster (and Farm Herald). (Fort Lupton, Weld County, Colo.) 191?-1920
The Keota News. (Keota, Weld County, Colo.) 1911-1922
The Weld County News. (Greeley, Weld County, Colo.) 1913-1933
The Greeley Tribune and The Weld County Republican. (Greeley, Colo.) 1913-19??
The Greeley Daily Tribune and The Greeley Republican. (Greeley, Colo.) 1913-1945
The Carbon Star. (Frederick, Weld County, Colo.) 1915-19??
The Evans Courier and The Messenger. (Evans, Weld County, Colo.) 1915-1916
The Evans Courier-Messenger. (Evans, Weld County, Colo.) 1916-19??
Greeley Morning Spokesman. (Greeley, Colo.) 1916-19??
The Movie Fan. (Greeley, Colo.) 1916-19??
Colorado Herold Greeley Edition. (Denver, Colo.) 1917-1918 | Languages: German
The Ft. Lupton Booster. (Fort Lupton, Weld County, Colo.) 1920-19??
The Pawnee Herald. (Keota, Weld County, Colo.) 1923-19??
Keene Valley Sun. (Keenesburg, Weld County, Colo.) 1925-Current
The Ault Booster (and The Ault Advertiser). (Ault, Weld County, Colo.) 1926-1927
The Ault Booster. (Ault, Weld County, Colo.) 1927-1935
The Mead Gazette. (Johnstown, Colo.) 1932-19??
Farmer and Miner. (Frederick, Colo.) 1932-1968
The Greeley Booster and The Weld County News. (Greeley, Weld County, Colo.) 1933-1935
The Greeley Ad-Journal. (Greeley, Colo.) 1935-1935
The Ault Progress. (Ault, Weld County, Colo.) 1935-1972
The Greeley Booster. (Greeley, Weld County, Colo.) 1935-1965
The Greeley Journal. (Greeley, Colo.) 1935-1978
The Greeley Daily Tribune and The Tribune Republican. (Greeley, Colo.) 1945-1947
Unsere Zeitung. (Kriegsgefangenenlager Greeley, Colo.) 1945-194? | Languages: German
The Windsor Beacon. (Windsor, Colo.) 1947-Current
The Greeley Daily Tribune and The Greeley Republican. (Greeley, Colo.) 1947-1972

Weld County

La Salle Leader. (La Salle, Colo.) 1948-Current
The Greeley Booster and The Weld County News. (Greeley, Colo.) 1965-1???
Farmer and Miner and The Erie Echo. (Frederick, Colo.) 1968-1978
Highland-Today. (Ault, Colo.) 1972-1979
Greeley Tribune and The Greeley Republican. (Greeley, Colo.) 1972-1978
Platte Valley News. (Fort Lupton, Colo.) 1976-1976
Adams-Weld Market Place. (Brighton, Colo.) 1978-1979
Greeley Tribune. (Greeley, Colo.) 1978-Current
Farmer and Miner. (Frederick, Colo.) 1978-1979
Platte Valley Voice. (Kersey, Colo.) 1979-Current
The North Weld Herald. (Eaton, Colo.) 1979-Current
The New Fort Lupton Press. (Fort Lupton, Colo.) 1980-1981
Farmer and Miner and The Erie Echo. (Frederick, Co.) 1980-1982
Fort Lupton Press. (Fort Lupton, Colo.) 1981-Current
Farmer And Miner. (Frederick, Co.) 1982-Current
Evans Star Press. (Evans, Colo.) 1983-1989
The News Of Colorado Centennial Country. (Greeley, Co.) 1985-198?

Places on the National Register

Berthoud, Little Thompson River Bridge, I-25 Service Rd. at mipepost 249.90
Briggsdale, Ball, Elmer and Etta, Ranch, Weld Co. Rd. 69 W of Briggsdale
Briggsdale, Land Utilization Program Headquarters, 44741 Weld Co. Rd. 77
Eaton, Alger, Amanda K., Memorial Methodist Episcopal Church, 303 Maple Ave.
Eaton, Eaton, Aaron James, House, 207 Elm St.
Erie, Lincoln School, 645 Holbrook St.
Fort Lupton, Ottesen Grain Company Feed Mill, 815 7th ST.
Greeley, Clubhouse—Student Union, Between 18th & 19th Sts., & 8th & 10th Aves.
Greeley, First Baptist Church, Tenth Ave. at Eleventh St., NW corner
Greeley, Glazier House, 1403 10th Ave.
Greeley, Greeley Downtown, Roughly bounded by 8th St., 8th Ave., 10th St., and 9th Ave.
Greeley, Greeley High School, 1515 14th Ave.
Greeley, Greeley High School and Grade School, 1015 8th St.
Greeley, Greeley Junior High School, 811 15th St.
Greeley, Greeley Masonic Temple, 829 10th Ave.
Greeley, Greeley Tribune Building, 714 8th St.
Greeley, Greeley Union Pacific Railroad Depot, Jct. of 7th Ave. and 9th St.
Greeley, Meeker Memorial Museum, 1324 9th Ave.
Greeley, Nettleton—Mead House, 1303 9th Ave.
Greeley, SLW Ranch, 27401 Weld Co. Rd. 58 1/2
Greeley, Von Gohren—Thompson Homestead—Gerry Farm Rural Historic Landscape, Address Restricted
Greeley, Von Trotha-Firestien Farm at Bracewell, Address Restricted
Greeley, Weld County Courthouse, 9th St. and 9th Ave.
Greeley, White—Plumb Farm, 955 39th Ave.
Greeley, Woodbury, Joseph A., House, 1124 7th St.

Historical Assets Colorado

Johnstown, Anderson Barn, 5255 CO 60
Johnstown, Brush, Jared L., Barn, 24308 Weld Co. Rd. 17
Johnstown, Parish, Harvey J., House, 701 Charlotte St.
Keota, Keota Stone Circles Archeological District, Address Restricted
Kersey, Jurgens Site, Address Restricted
Longmont, Sandstone Ranch, E of Longmont off CO 119
Lucerne, Milne Farm, 18457 CO 392
Mead, United Church of Christ of Highlandlake, 16896 Weld CR 5
Milliken, Daniels School, US 60 and Weld Cty Rd. 25
Platteville, Fort Vasquez, 13412 US 85
Stoneham, West Stoneham Archeological District, Address Restricted
Wiggins, Dearfield, Along CO 34, 11 mi. W of Wiggins
Windsor, First Methodist Episcopal Church, 503 Walnut St.
Windsor, Windsor Milling and Elevator Co. Building, 301 Main St.
Windsor, Windsor Town Hall, 116 5th St.

USGS Historic Places

Buckingham, Williams Ranch Airport, 40.6027053, -103.9403703
Fort Lupton, Delventhal Farm Airport, 40.0108169, -104.7902491
Gowanda, Carrera Airpark, 40.2163727, -104.9508103
Gowanda, Frontier Airstrip, 40.2122062, -104.982756
Greeley, Auburn School, 40.3777589, -104.6394071
Greeley, Buell School, 40.4738695, -104.7166323
Greeley, Lincoln School, 40.4216476, -104.6852422
Greeley, Olin School, 40.4788695, -104.6788527
Greeley, Uhrich Airport, 40.4602585, -104.6457957
Keenesburg, Hayes Airport, 40.0752607, -104.5888507
Keenesburg, Lindys Airpark, 40.0385943, -104.6244081
Kersey, Lone Tree School, 40.4866473, -104.6205165
Kersey, Peter Brown School, 40.449703, -104.5996825
Longmont, Cartwheel Airport, 40.2077418, -105.0128665
Masters, Yocam Ranch Airport, 40.3000844, -104.2300668
Milliken, Fort Saint Vrain, 40.2788717, -104.8549726
Platteville, Old Fort Vasquez, 40.1944273, -104.8210829
South Roggen, Reid Ranches Airport, 40.1163711, -104.317453

Grand Army of the Republic Posts

US Grant, No. 13, Weld, Greeley, 1883
Poudre Valley, No. 13, Weld, Greeley
Evans, No. 23, Weld, Evans
Phil Kearney, No. 73, Weld, Platteville
R B Hayes, No. 90, Weld, New Windsor

USGS Historic Military Places

None

Weld County

Military Bases
None

Post Offices

Akron	1883 Jan 30		80720
Alfalfa	1892 Feb 19	1892 Oct 29	
American Ranch	1863 Feb 9	1867 Nov 25*	
Atwood	1885 Aug 10		80722
Ault	1898 Mar 29		80610
Avalo	1898 July 1	1936 May 30	
Barnesville	1910 June 9	1935 Sept 14	
Black Wolf	1885 May 9	1885 Oct 30	
Briggsdale	1910 Aug 1		80611
Brush	1882 Sept 19		80723
Buckingham	1888 Dec 21	1966 July 1*	
Buffalo	1874 June 24	1883 Feb 21	
Camfield	1910 Apr 18	1921 Feb 15	
Carr	1872 Mar 26	1878 Nov 19	
Carr	1884 Oct 17		80612
Chapelton	1917 Jan 11	1922 June 15	
Chenoa	1886 Nov 19	1895 Nov 19	
Cherokee City	1862 Nov 25	1863 Nov 25	
Clearwater	1862 Sept 10	1864 Jan 20	
Coleman	1915 Apr 10	1919 Mar 31	
Cornish	1914 Nov 24	1967 Mar 31	
Corona	1874 Apr 14	1878 Dec 20	
Cotsworth	1882 Sept 28	1883 Jan 17	
Crest	1909 Mar 8	1923 June 30	
Crook	1882 May 26		80726
Dacono	1907 Dec 21		80514
Dover	1905 Dec 16	1931 Apr 30	
Eaton	1882 Sept 25		80615
Eatonton	1882 Sept 25	1883 Sept 28	
Eckley	1883 Nov 15	1884 June 16	
Erie	1871 Jan 24		80516
Evans	1862 Nov 25		80620
Firestone	1907 Aug 30		80520
Flemings Ranch	1863 Mar 23	1875 Sept 1	
Fort Junction	1866 Feb 5	1867 Mar 19	
Fort Lupton	1861 Jan 14	1869 Jan 18	
Fort Lupton 2	1869 Jan 18	1873 Apr 17	
Fort Lupton 3	1873 May 9		80621
Fort Moore	1866 Jan 15	1868 Jan 22	
Fort Morgan	1864 Dec 14	1868 June 26	
Fort Sedgwick	1866 May 3	1869 Apr 8	
Fosston	1910 Apr 5	1941 July 31	

Historical Assets Colorado

Frederick	1907 Dec 21		80530
Fremonts Orchard	1863 Aug 28	1877 Mar 2*	
Galeton	1910 Sept 16		80622
Gault	1900 July 13	1916 Oct 31	
Geary	1888 May 21	1894 June 30	
Gilcrest	1907 May 17		80623
Gill	1910 Dec 27		80624
Gowanda	1915 Aug 3	1930 Nov 15	
Graham	1911 Apr 1	1918 Feb 28	
Greeley	1870 Apr 21		80631
Green City	1871 June 15	1874 Apr 14	
Grover	1885 Mar 3		80729
Hardin	1881 Nov 2	1955 Feb 15*	
Henderson	1872 Aug 29		80640
Hereford	1888 Dec 21	1894 June 30	
Hereford 2	1909 May 8		80732
Highland Lake	1910 Jan 29	1913 Aug 9	
Highlandlake	1883 Nov 8	1910 Jan 29	
Hillsboro	1891 Apr 12	1903 Nov 14*	
Hillsborough	1871 June 15	1891 Apr 12	
Hiltonville	1873 Oct 10	1875 Sept 24	
Hudson	1883 Mar 27		80642
Hyde	1882 Aug 1	1940 Feb 15*	
Iliff	1882 Mar 21	1895 Nov 27	
Ione	1927 June 16	1958 Mar 21	
Johnstown	1903 Apr 17		80534
Julesburg	1860 May 29	1862 Sept 10	
Julesburg 2	1864 Jan 20	1886 Jan 7*	
Julesburg 3	1886 May 26		80737
Junction House	1864 Dec 14	1866 July 16	
Kalous	1915 Apr 12	1931 Apr 15	
Kauffman	1914 Sept 12	1934 Feb 28	
Keenesburg	1907 Apr 10		80643
Keota	1888 Sept 11	1973 Dec 21*	
Kersey	1894 Dec 20		80644
Koenig	1913 Jan 9	1930 Dec 31*	
Kuner	1908 July 22	1920 Sept 30	
La Salle	1886 May 6		80645
Latham	1863 Nov 25	1870 May 16*	
Levinson	1906 Apr 12	1906 June 29	
Lillian Springs	1863 July 23	1864 Apr 9	
Lucerne	1892 June 23		80646
Mamre	1886 June 4	1886 Sept 13	
Masters	1900 Feb 15	1967 Dec 29	
Mead	1907 Mar 1		80542
Merino	1874 June 24		80741

Weld County

Milliken	1909 Nov 10		80543
Morgan	1879 Nov 26	1883 Feb 15	
Nantes	1887 Aug 19	1888 Feb 9	
New Liberty	1876 July 17	1884 June 18	
New Raymer	1909 Nov 13		80742
New Wattenburg	1911 Mar 9	1916 Feb 29	
New Windsor	1884 Jan 18	1911 Aug 19	
Nunn	1905 Sept 28		80648
Omar	1915 Apr 17	1923 May 15*	
Orchard	1882 Mar 6		80649
Orr	1884 Mar 16	1894 Dec 20	
Osgood	1910 Sept 2	1928 June 30	
Otis	1886 Jan 11		80743
Peckham	1898 Aug 11	1931 Dec 31*	
Pierce	1903 Nov 4		80650
Pinnero	1883 Nov 15	1931 Dec 5*	
Platte Valley	1876 Jan 31	1881 Nov 2	
Platteville	1859 Jan 18		80651
Purcell	1911 Dec 23	1951 Apr 30	
Raymer	1888 June 27	1895 May 14	
Red Lion	1886 Nov 19	1935 Nov 30*	
Rinn	1901 June 22	1907 Jan 2	
Roggen	1883 Nov 15		80542
Saint Vrains	1915 Sept 30	1918 Mar 15	
Sarinda	1875 July 28	1882 Feb 7	
Sedgwick	1885 Sept 10	1894 May 11	
Sedgwick 2	1896 Apr 30		80749
Serene	1923 Jan 25	1942 Aug 31	
Severance	1894 Mar 8	1902 June 30*	
Severance 2	1907 Sept 18		80546
Sligo	1908 Oct 27	1941 Aug 31	
Snyder	1882 June 16		80750
South Platte	1873 June 20	1883 Jan 9	
Spurgin	1916 Dec 7	1927 Dec 16	
St Vrain	1859 Jan 18	1875 Feb 11	
Sterling	1874 Feb 24		80751
Stoneham	1888 Aug 2	1908 Oct 15*	
Stoneham 2	1910 June 8		80754
Tipperary	1915 July 14	1917 Jan 15	
Vim	1927 Dec 1	1944 Sept 30	
Vollmar	1910 Nov 2	1912 Oct 31	
Wachtel	1913 Mar 20	1916 Mar 15	
Weld	1861 Jan 14	1873 Dec 7	
Weld 2	1900 June 9	1900 Oct 27	
Weldon Valley	1880 Mar 8	1880 Nov 19	
Wentz	1891 Nov 24	1903 Mar 14	

Historical Assets Colorado

Wheatland	1875 Sept 24	1881 Feb 10	
Whitman	1882 Apr 4	1882 July 18	
Windsor	1911 Aug 19		80550
Wray	1882 June 26		80758
Yuma	1885 Nov 24		80759
Zilar	1892 May 5	1894 Oct 30	
Zita	1910 Feb 21	1910 Sept 16	

Topo Quads

Antelope Reservoir	404500N	403730N	1043730W	1044500W
Avalo	405230N	404500N	1033730W	1034500W
Baker Draw	404500N	403730N	1042230W	1043000W
Barnesville	403000N	402230N	1042230W	1043000W
Battle Canyon	410000N	405230N	1033730W	1034500W
Berthoud	402230N	401500N	1050000W	1050730W
Bracewell	403000N	402230N	1044500W	1045230W
Briggsdale	404500N	403730N	1041500W	1042230W
Buckingham	403730N	403000N	1035230W	1040000W
Carr SW	405230N	404500N	1045230W	1050000W
Chalk Bluffs East	410000N	405230N	1043000W	1043730W
Cobb Lake	404500N	403730N	1045230W	1050000W
Cornish	403730N	403000N	1042230W	1043000W
Dearfield	402230N	401500N	1041500W	1042230W
Dolan Spring	410000N	405230N	1035230W	1040000W
Dover	405230N	404500N	1044500W	1045230W
Dutch Girl Lake	403730N	403000N	1040730W	1041500W
Eastlake	400000N	395230N	1045230W	1050000W
Eastman Creek SE	405230N	404500N	1043000W	1043730W
Eastman Creek South	405230N	404500N	1043730W	1044500W
Eaton	403730N	403000N	1043730W	1044500W
Erie	400730N	400000N	1050000W	1050730W
Fort Lupton	400730N	400000N	1044500W	1045230W
Fosston	403730N	403000N	1041500W	1042230W
Frederick	400730N	400000N	1045230W	1050000W
Galeton	403730N	403000N	1043000W	1043730W
Gatehook Spring	405230N	404500N	1034500W	1035230W
Gowanda	401500N	400730N	1045230W	1050000W
Greasewood Lake	403000N	402230N	1040730W	1041500W
Greeley	403000N	402230N	1043730W	1044500W
Grover NE	410000N	405230N	1040000W	1040730W
Grover North	410000N	405230N	1040730W	1041500W
Grover SE	405230N	404500N	1040000W	1040730W
Grover South	405230N	404500N	1040730W	1041500W
Hardin	402230N	401500N	1042230W	1043000W
Hereford	410000N	405230N	1041500W	1042230W

Weld County

Hereford NW	410000N	405230N	1042230W	1043000W
Hereford SE	405230N	404500N	1041500W	1042230W
Hudson	400730N	400000N	1043730W	1044500W
Johnstown	402230N	401500N	1045230W	1050000W
Keenesburg	400730N	400000N	1043000W	1043730W
Keota	404500N	403730N	1040000W	1040730W
Keota NW	404500N	403730N	1040730W	1041500W
Keota SE	403730N	403000N	1040000W	1040730W
Kersey	403000N	402230N	1043000W	1043730W
Klug Ranch	401500N	400730N	1043000W	1043730W
La Salle	402230N	401500N	1043730W	1044500W
Masters	402230N	401500N	1040730W	1041500W
Milliken	402230N	401500N	1044500W	1045230W
Milton Reservoir	401500N	400730N	1043730W	1044500W
Nunn	404500N	403730N	1044500W	1045230W
Omar	401500N	400730N	1040730W	1041500W
Pawnee Buttes	405230N	404500N	1035230W	1040000W
Platteville	401500N	400730N	1044500W	1045230W
Point of Rocks	403000N	402230N	1041500W	1042230W
Prospect Valley	400730N	400000N	1042230W	1043000W
Purcell	404500N	403730N	1043000W	1043730W
Raymer	403730N	403000N	1034500W	1035230W
Raymer NE	404500N	403730N	1034500W	1035230W
Raymer NW	404500N	403730N	1035230W	1040000W
Reno Reservoir	405230N	404500N	1042230W	1043000W
Roggen	401500N	400730N	1041500W	1042230W
Severance	403730N	403000N	1044500W	1045230W
South Roggen	400730N	400000N	1041500W	1042230W
Stoneham	403730N	403000N	1033730W	1034500W
Stoneham NW	404500N	403730N	1033730W	1034500W
Tampa	401500N	400730N	1042230W	1043000W
Timnath	403730N	403000N	1045230W	1050000W
Valley View School	402230N	401500N	1043000W	1043730W
Vim School	410000N	405230N	1034500W	1035230W
Wiggins SW	400730N	400000N	1040730W	1041500W
Windsor	403000N	402230N	1045230W	1050000W

Suggested Reading

Ball, Wilbur P. *Early History of Crow Creek,* Eaton, CO: WP Ball, 1997.

Ball, Wilbur P. *The Last Roundup: a History of the Early Cattle Roundups in Northern Weld County, Colorado.* Eaton, CO: WP Ball, 1991.

Ball, Wilbur P and Katherine Halverson. *The Old Stone Corral: a Story of the Early Sheep Men in Northern Weld County, Colorado.* Eaton, CO: WP Ball, 1997.

Bell, Mary Ellen. *Weld County School District RE-3(J), 1859-1996.* NL: Weld County School District, 1997.

Historical Assets Colorado

Geffs, Mary L. *Under Ten Flags: a History of Weld County, Colorado*. Greeley, CO: NP, 1938.

Krakel, Dean. *South Platte Country: a History of Old Weld County, Colorado, 1739-1900*. Laramie, WY: Powder River Publishers, 1954.

Shwayder, Carol Rein. *Chronology of Weld County, Colorado, 1836-1983*. Greeley, CO: Unicorn Ventures, 1983.

Shwayder, Carol Rein. *People & Places: Historical Gazetteer, Dictionary of Place Names, Weld County, Colorado, Pre-historic Indians to 1992*. Greeley, CO: Unicorn Ventures, 1992.

Wells, Bud. *Homesteading the Dryland: a History of Northeast Weld County, Colorado*. Dallas: Curtis Media, 1986.

Yuma County

Introduction
Established: 1889   Population: 10,043
Formed from: Washington
Adjacent Counties: Phillips, Kit Carson, Washington, Logan
County Seat: Wray
  Other Communities: Yuma, Eckley, Idalia, Joes, Kirk, Laird, Vernon, Hale
Website, http://yumacounty.net
Area Codes: 970
Zip Codes: 80727, 80735, 80755, 80758, 80759, 80822, 80824

Historical Assets Colorado

Yuma County Courthouse

Yuma County 19th Century Courthouse

Courthouses & County Government
Yuma County
   http://yumacounty.net
Yuma County Courthouse (13th Judicial District), 310 Ash St, Wray, CO 80758, 970-332-4118; http://www.courts.state.co.us/Courts/County/Index.cfm?County_ID=44
Assessor, 310 Ash St, Wray, CO 80758, 970-332-5032; http://www.yumacounty.net/assessor.html#top
Board of County Commissioners, 310 Ash St, Wray, CO 80758, 970-332-5796, http://yumacounty.net/commissioners/
Clerk & Recorder, 310 Ash St, Wray, CO 80758, 970-332-5809; http://www.yumacounty.net/clerk_recorder.html
Coroner, 128 S Ash St, Yuma, CO 80759, 970-848-2101; http://yumacounty.net/elected-officials/
Public Health, 700 Columbine St, Sterling, CO 80751, 970-522-3741; http://www.nchd.org/
Transportation (Road & Bridge), 110 S Blake St, Wray, CO 80758, 970-332-5718; http://yumacounty.net/departments/road-and-bridge/
Treasurer, 310 Ash St, Ste C, Wray, CO 80758, 970-332-4965; http://www.yumacounty.net/Treasurer.html

County Records
Birth Unk	Marriage 1889	Divorce 1889
Death Unk	Land 1887	Probate 1889
Court 1889		

Yuma County

County & Municipal Records Held at the State Level

The Colorado State Archives

Physical Records
Clerk & Recorder
Treasurer
School Board
WPA Historical Records
WPA Religious Institutions
    Survey
WPA Wray
Cities
    Wray

Records on Film
Clerk & Recorder
Treasurer

Records on Master Film
County Court
District Court
School Districts
Cities
    Wray
    Yuma

The Denver Public Library
WPA Historical Records Survey
WWI Draft Registration Cards (microfilm)

School Districts

School Districts, http://www.adcogov.org/local-school-districts

Burlington School District RE-6J, 2600 Rose Ave, Burlington, CO 80807, 719-346-8737; https://www.burlingtonk12.org/

Idalia School District RJ-3, 26845 CR 9.2, Idalia, CO 80735, 970-354-7298; https://www.idaliaco.us/

Liberty School District J-4, 9332 Hwy 36, Joes, CO 80822, 970-358-4288; http://www.libertyschoolj4.com/

Wray School District RE-2, 30222 CR 35, Wray, CO 80758, 970-332-5764; http://www.wrayschools.org/

Yuma School District 1, 418 S Main St, Yuma, CO 80759, 970-848-5831; https://www.yumaschools.org/

Historic School Districts

1. Yuma Union
2. Wray
3. Bald Eagle
4. Pleasant View
5. Enterprise Union
6. South Star
7. Laird
8. Schram
9. Pleasant Valley
10. Graham
11. Union Ridge
12. Star
13. Sunnyside
14. Hill Top
15. Union Valley
16. Barnes
17. Pleasant View
18. Pleasant Valley
19. Brand
20. Sunnyside
21. Mt Cline Union
22. Pleasant Valley
23. Buffalo Grass
24. Eckley
25. Waverly
26. Bryant Union
27. North Independence
28. Prairie Valley
29. Plainview Union
30. West Valley Union
31. Model
32. Hillsdale
33. Robb
34. Morning Star
35. Black Union
36. Star
37. Pleasant Hill
38. Columbine
39. Harmon
40. Union
41. Mount HOpe
42. Prairie View Union
43. Vernon
44. Liberty
45. Lansing
46. Glendale
47. Friend
48. Hermes
49. Abarr Union
50. Champion Valley
51. Ells Union

Historical Assets Colorado

52. Happyville
53. Beecher Island
54. progressive
55. Center Union
56. Columbine
57. Cope
58. Sunnyside
59. Pleasant Valley Union
60. Pioneer
61. Golden Gate
62. North Logan
63. Clark
64. Wages
65. Prairie Ridge
66. Pleasant Hill
67. Star
68. Kayton
69. Pioneer
70. Fair View
71. Hope
72. Fair View
73. Liberty
74. Idalia
75. Fair View
76. Fox
77. Browning
78. Antelope
79. Cement
80. West Gurney
81. Progressive Valley
82. Kirk
83. Hale
84. White Eagle
85. Riverside
86. Cook
87. Mount Pleasant
88. Red Top
89. South Alvin
90. Joes
91. NOrth Star
92. Boden
93. Newton
94. Bunch Grass
95. Lincoln Valley
96.
97. South Willow
98. Weld County Union
99. Mount Hope
100. Mildred
101. Dewey Ridge
102. Bunker HIll
103. North Willow
104. Radnor
105. South Logan
106. South Valley
107. Fairview Union
108. Strawder
109. Sunny SLope
110. Ash Grove
111. Happy Valley
112. Sunnyside
113. South Independence
114.
115. Hill Top
116. Prairie View
117. Cement

125. Prairie View

Fraternal Organizations

Granges
Rainbelt, No. 97, Yuma, Yuma, 15 Feb 1890
Idonian, No. 170, Yuma, Kirk, 12 June 1909
Idalia, No. 174, Yuma, Idalia, 22 Aug 1909
Vernon, No. 175, Yuma, Vernon, 18 Sept 1909
Eureka Valley, No. 176, Yuma, Armel, 22 Aug 1909
Cope, No. 177, Yuma, Cope, 25 Aug 1909
Hale, No. 178, Yuma, Hale, 2 Sept 1909
Newton, No. 179, Yuma, Landsman/Newton, 17 Sept 1909
Corn Valley, No. 180, Yuma, Fox, 17 Sept 1909
Royal, No. 185, Yuma, Siebert, 10 Feb 1910
Fair Haven, No. 188, Yuma, Siebert, 1 Feb 1910
Eckley, No. 271, Yuma, Eckley, 23 Mar 1916
Starr, No. 277, Yuma, Laird, 22 Apr 1916
Laird, No. 321, Yuma, Laird, 15 Feb 1917
Sand Hill, No. 401, Yuma, Wray, 15 Apr 1926
Hill Top, No. 476, Yuma, Yuma, 22 Sept 1956
Red Willow, No. 477, Yuma, Yuma, 7 Nov 1956
Pioneer, No. 478, Yuma, Laird, 12 Dec 1956

Masons

Ancient Free & Accepted Masons
Yuma, No. 71, Yuma, Wray, 18 Sept 1888
Wray, No. 149, Yuma, Yuma, 1 Sept 1916

Yuma County

Royal Arch Masons
None

Knights Templar
None

Eastern Star
Wray, No. 65, Yuma, Wray
Yuma, No. 117, Yuma, Yuma

Odd Fellows
Wray, No. 123, Yuma, Wray
Yuma, No. 160, Yuma, Yuma

Rebekahs
Wray, No. 76, Yuma, Wray
Sunflower, No. 129, Yuma, Yuma

Knights of Pythias
Yuma Valley, No. 39, Yuma, Yuma, 1888 Mar 28

Pythian Sisters
None

Benevolent Protective Order of Elks
Wray, No. 2409, Yuma, Wray

City & Town Halls

Wray, 245 W 4th St, Wray, CO 80758, 970-332-4431, https://cityofwray.org
Yuma, 320 S Main St, Yuma, CO 80759, 970-848-3878, https://www.colorado.gov/pacific/cityofyuma
Eckley, 235 NW Morten St, Eckley, CO 80727, 970-359-2222, https://townofeckley.weebly.com

Archives & Manuscript Collections

None

Historical & Genealogical Societies

East Yuma County Historical Society, Wray Museum, 205 E 3rd St, P.O. Box 161, Wray, CO 80758-0161, (970) 332-5063, https://cityofwray.org/179/Wray-Museum

Local Libraries

Wray Public Library, 521 Blake St, Wray, CO 80758-1619, (970) 332-4744, https://cityofwray.org/161/Wray-Public-Library
Yuma City Library, 910 S Main St, Yuma, CO 80759-2402, (970) 848-2368, https://yuma.colibraries.org

Links

CO GenWeb
http://cogenweb.com/yuma/

Historical Assets Colorado

Cyndi's List
https://www.cyndislist.com/us/co/counties/yuma/

FamilySearch Wiki
https://www.familysearch.org/wiki/en/Yuma_County,_Colorado_Genealogy

Linkpendium
http://www.linkpendium.com/yuma-co-genealogy/

RootsWeb Wiki
https://wiki.rootsweb.com/wiki/index.php/Yuma_County,_Colorado

Wikipedia
https://en.wikipedia.org/wiki/Yuma_County,_Colorado

Historic Hotels

None

Museums & Historic Sites

East Yuma County Historical Society, Wray Museum, 205 E 3rd St, P.O. Box 161, Wray, CO 80758-0161, (970) 332-5063, https://cityofwray.org/179/Wray-Museum

Yuma Museum, 3rd & Detroit, P.O. Box 192, Yuma, CO 80759, (970) 858-5162, https://www.facebook.com/yumaCOmuseum/

Special Events & Scenic Locations

The Yuma County Fair is held at the Yuma County Fairgrounds, 410 W Hoag Ave, Yuma, CO 80759, 970-848-3333, http://yumacounty.net/county-fair/

Yuma County has a calendar of events here: http://yumacounty.net/county-fair/event-information/

Ghost Towns & Other Sparsely Populated Places

Abarr, Alvin, Arlene, Armel, Arnold, Avoca, Beecher, Bolton, Bryant, Clarkville, Condon, Ford, Fox, Friend, Gurney, Happyville, Heartstrong, Hermes, Hughes, Joes, Kirk, Ladlum, Laird, Lansing, Leslie, Logan, Ludlum, Mildred, Newton, Robb, Rogers, Schramm, Shields, Steffens, Wages, Wauneta, Waverly, Weld City, Witherbee

Newspapers

The Yuma Pioneer. (Yuma, Yuma County, Colo.) 1886-Current
The Wray Rattler. (Wray, Yuma County, Colo.) 1886-1949
The Wray Weekly Times. (Wray, Yuma County, Colo.) 1898-1901
The Spooktown Fixen. (Yuma, Yuma County, Colo.) 1899-1899
The Republican Mail. (Yuma, Yuma County, Colo.) 1899-19??
The Wray Gazette. (Wray, Yuma County, Colo.) 1903-Current
The Colorado Patriot. (Wray, Yuma County, Colo.) 1919-1927

Places on the National Register

Eckley, Boggs Lumber and Hardware Building, 125 N. Main St.
Idalia, Zion, Walter and Anna, Homestead, off Cty Rd. 15

Yuma County

Wray, Beecher Island Battleground, 16.5 mi. SE of Wray on Beecher Rd.
Wray, Cliff Theater, 420 Main St.
Yuma, Lett Hotel, 204 S. Ash

USGS Historic Places
Bonny Reservoir North, Bonny Dam Landing Strip, 39.6452711, -102.1826896
Bonny Reservoir North, M A and K A Dickson Airport, 39.6816599, -102.1715783
Joes SW, Hill Airport, 39.6205449, -102.7438192
Vernon NW, Dickson Landing Strip, 39.8983234, -102.4107549
Vernon NW, Lundvall Brothers Landing Field, 39.9547118, -102.4440897
Vernon NW, Stultz Landing Field, 39.9155457, -102.380754
Yuma North, Jackson Airfield, 40.1950979, -102.6976965

Grand Army of the Republic Posts
James A Lowrie, No. 50, Yuma, Yuma
Wray, No. 70, Yuma, Wray, 1906
McCowen, No. 71, Yuma, Idalia
H A Condon, No. 105, Yuma, Vernon

USGS Historic Military Places
None

Military Bases
None

Post Offices

Abarr	1923 Feb 26	1947 Nov 30	
Alvin	1910 Sept 12	1929 Feb 28	
Arlene	1916 Oct 30	1918 Aug 31	
Armel	1903 Oct 17	1958 May 31	
Arnold	1913 Nov 17	1914 Sept 15	
Beecher	1902 Aug 12	1905 Nov 3	
Beecher Island	1924 Nov 13	1958 May 31	
Bryant	1888 Mar 27	1916 Mar 31	
Clarkville	1938 May 18	1954 Apr 30	
Eckley	1885 Aug 14		80727
Ford	1909 June 4	1917 Mar 31	
Fox	1890 May 17	1912 Dec 15	
Glory	1924 Nov 13	1925 Feb 1	
Gurney	1907 Sept 17	1923 Sept 15	
Hale	1890 May 17	1984 June 1*	
Happyville	1910 July 26	1922 Feb 28	
Heartstrong	1921 May 31	1940 Jan 31	
Hermes	1908 Sept 11	1919 Nov 15	
Hughes	1913 Apr 11	1954 Oct 31	

Historical Assets Colorado

Hyde	1882 Aug 1	1940 Feb 15*	
Idalia	1888 Sept 18		80735
Joes	1912 Oct 22		80822
Kirk	1887 Nov 18		80824
Laird	1887 July 12	1892 Feb 17	
Landsman	1883 Mar 27	1918 May 31	
Lansing	1886 Sept 17	1910 Feb 28	
Ludlum	1889 Sept 16	1890 Dec 24	
Newton	1889 Aug 6	1918 Apr 15	
Robb	1889 Dec 21	1920 Nov 15*	
Schramm	1913 Apr 11	1925 Dec 31*	
Seebarsee	1892 Feb 17	1899 Jan 25	
Steffens	1915 Aug 25	1919 Nov 15	
Vernon	1888 June 26		80755
Wages	1917 Mar 31	1950 May 31	
Witherbee	1912 May 28	1918 Aug 31	
Wray	1882 June 26		80758

Topo Quads

Abarr	395230N	394500N	1023730W	1024500W
Abarr SE	395230N	394500N	1023000W	1023730W
Adler Creek	394500N	393730N	1023000W	1023730W
Alvin	402230N	401500N	1020000W	1020730W
Alvin NE	403000N	402230N	1020000W	1020730W
Alvin SW	402230N	401500N	1020730W	1021500W
Beecher Island	395230N	394500N	1020730W	1021500W
Beecher Island NW	400000N	395230N	1020730W	1021500W
Beverly Grove	400000N	395230N	1023730W	1024500W
Bonny Reservoir North	394500N	393730N	1020730W	1021500W
Bonny Reservoir South	393730N	393000N	1020730W	1021500W
Clarkville SE	402230N	401500N	1023000W	1023730W
Clarkville SW	402230N	401500N	1023730W	1024500W
Cope	394500N	393730N	1024500W	1025230W
Cope SE	393730N	393000N	1024500W	1025230W
De Nova NE	400000N	395230N	1024500W	1025230W
De Nova SE	395230N	394500N	1024500W	1025230W
Eckley	400730N	400000N	1022230W	1023000W
Eckley NE	401500N	400730N	1021500W	1022230W
Eckley NW	401500N	400730N	1022230W	1023000W
Hale Ponds	394500N	393730N	1020000W	1020730W
Heartstrong	400000N	395230N	1023000W	1023730W
Hyde	401500N	400730N	1024500W	1025230W
Idalia	394500N	393730N	1021500W	1022230W
Idalia SE	393730N	393000N	1021500W	1022230W

Yuma County

Idalia SW	393730N	393000N	1022230W	1023000W
Joes	394500N	393730N	1023730W	1024500W
Joes SW	393730N	393000N	1023730W	1024500W
Kirk	393730N	393000N	1023000W	1023730W
Laird	400730N	400000N	1020000W	1020730W
Lone Star	402230N	401500N	1024500W	1025230W
Old Baldy	402230N	401500N	1022230W	1023000W
Otis SE	400730N	400000N	1024500W	1025230W
Robb	400730N	400000N	1021500W	1022230W
Schramm	400730N	400000N	1023000W	1023730W
Spring Canyon	394500N	393730N	1022230W	1023000W
Vernon	400000N	395230N	1021500W	1022230W
Vernon NW	400000N	395230N	1022230W	1023000W
Vernon SW	395230N	394500N	1022230W	1023000W
Wauneta	402230N	401500N	1021500W	1022230W
Wildcat Canyon	395230N	394500N	1021500W	1022230W
Wray	400730N	400000N	1020730W	1021500W
Wray NE	401500N	400730N	1020000W	1020730W
Wray NW	401500N	400730N	1020730W	1021500W
Yuma NE	401500N	400730N	1023000W	1023730W
Yuma North	401500N	400730N	1023730W	1024500W
Yuma South	400730N	400000N	1023730W	1024500W

Suggested Reading

A *History of East Yuma County: a Collection of General History and Family Histories of East Yuma County from 1868 through 1978*. Wray, CO: East Yuma County Historical Society, 1978.

History of Wray, Colorado, 1886-1986. Dallas: Curtis Media Corp, 1986.

Inventory of the County Archives of Colorado, No. 63, Yuma County (Wray). Denver: Historical Records Survey, 1941.

Seedorf, Sylvia et al. *Histories of the Towns of Yuma County and Surrounding Area*. Yuma, CO: Yuma County Historical Society, 2000.

Starnes, Shirley M. *West Yuma County Colorado: a History of West Yuma County, 1886-1986*. Yuma, CO: Taylor Publishing, 1985.

Wells, Bud. *World War II and the People of Yuma County*. Dallas: Curtis Media Corp, 1993.

Yuma County: the Hundred Year Review: a Centennial History of Yuma County, Colorado, 1889-1989. Dallas: Curtis Media Corp, 1989.

Historical Assets Colorado

Cities & Towns Index

Abbey, Pueblo
Abbeyville, Gunnison
Abbott, Arapahoe
Abbott, Washington
Aberdeen, Gunnison
Aberdeen Junction, Gunnison
Able, Bent
Acequia, Douglas
Adair, Las Animas
Adams, Larimer
Adana, Prowers
Adelaide, Fremont
Adelaide City, Lake
Adna, Weld
Adobe, Fremont
Adrian, Summit
Aetna Estates, Arapahoe
Agate, Elbert
Aguilar, Las Animas
Akron, Washington
Alamo, Huerfano
Alamosa, Alamosa
Albany, Prowers
Alder, Saguache
Alexander, Lake
Alfalfa, Weld
Alford, Larimer
Alicante, Lake
Alice, Clear Creek
Allen, Garfield
Allen, Gunnison
Allenspark, Boulder
Allenton, Eagle
Allison, La Plata
Alma, Park
Almont, Gunnison
Alnwick, El Paso
Alpine, Chaffee
Alpine, Rio Grande
Alpine Tunnel, Chaffee
Alta, San Miguel
Alta Vista, El Paso
Altman, Teller
Altona, Boulder
Alvord, Larimer
Amache, Prowers
American City, Gilpin
Americus, Chaffee
Ames, San Miguel

Amherst, Phillips
Anaconda, Teller
Angora, Otero
Animas City, La Plata
Animas Forks, San Juan
Antelope Park, Hinsdale
Antelope Springs, Hinsdale
Antero Junction, Park
Anthracite, Gunnison
Antlers, Garfield
Anton, Washington
Antonito, Conejos
Apache, Huerfano
Apex, Gilpin
Apishapa, Las Animas
Applewood, Jefferson
Arapahoe, Cheyenne
Arapahoe, Jefferson
Arboles, Archuleta
Arbourville, Chaffee
Archer's, Jefferson
Arena, Chaffee
Arena, Cheyenne
Argentine, Summit
Argo, Arapahoe
Argo, Denver
Argo Junction, Arapahoe
Argo Park, Arapahoe
Arickaree, Arapahoe
Arickaree, Washington
Arkansas Junction, Lake
Arkins, Larimer
Arlington, Kiowa
Armour, Pueblo
Aroya, Cheyenne
Arriba, Lincoln
Arriola, Montezuma
Arrow, Grand
Arthurs, Park
Arvada, Jefferson
Ascalon, Cheyenne
Ashcroft, Pitkin
Ashland, Kit Carson
Aspen, Pitkin
Aspen Junction, Eagle
Aspen Park, Jefferson
Athol, Weld
Atlanta, Baca
Atlantic, Gunnison

Atwood, Logan
Auburn, Weld
Augusta, Custer
Ault, Weld
Auraria, Arapahoe
Auraria, Denver
Aurora, Adams
Aurora, Arapahoe
Austin, Delta
Austin, Garfield
Autobees, Huerfano
Avalo, Weld
Avendale, Kit Carson
Avoca, Arapahoe
Avon, Eagle
Avondale, Pueblo
Axial, Routt
Ayr, Prowers
Bachelor City, Mineral
Badger, Arapahoe
Badito, Huerfano
Bagdad, Lincoln
Bailey, Park
Baker's Summit, Summit
Bakerville, Clear Creek
Bald Mountain, Gilpin
Baldwin, Gunnison
Baldy, Costilla
Balfour, Park
Baltimore, Gilpin
Balzac, Garfield
Bandora, San Juan
Banker Mine, Chaffee
Barela, Las Animas
Bark Ranch, Boulder
Barnes, Las Animas
Barnum, Arapahoe
Barnum, Denver
Barr, Arapahoe
Bartholomews, Summit
Basalt, Eagle
Basalt, Pitkin
Bassick City (Querida), Custer
Bath, Park
Battista, Montezuma
Battlement Mesa, Garfield
Baxter, Pueblo
Bay City, La Plata
Bayfield, La Plata

Historical Assets Colorado

Bear Canon, Douglas
Bear Creek, Montezuma
Bear Town, Hinsdale
Beartown, Hinsdale
Beaumont, El Paso
Beaver Brook, Jefferson
Beaver City, Chaffee
Beaver Creek, Fremont
Bedrock, Montrose
Belden, Eagle
Belleview, Chaffee
Bellevue, El Paso
Bellevue, Larimer
Bellevue Junction, Larimer
Bellvue, Larimer
Beloit, Kit Carson
Bennett, Adams
Bennett, Arapahoe
Bent Canyon, Las Animas
Benton, Otero
Bent's Old Fort, Otero
Berkeley, Arapahoe
Berkeley, Denver
Berlin, Arapahoe
Berthoud, Larimer
Berwind, Las Animas
Beshoar, Las Animas
Bessemer Junction, Pueblo
Bethune, Kit Carson
Beulah, Pueblo
Beulah Valley, Pueblo
Biedell, Saguache
Bierstadt, El Paso
Big Hill, Jefferson
Big Sandy, El Paso
Bijou Basin, El Paso
Birdseye, Lake
Birmingham, Huerfano
Black Bear, San Miguel
Black Forest, El Paso
Black Hawk, Gilpin
Black Lake, Ouray
Blackburn, Custer
Blanca, Costilla
Bland, Elbert
Blende, Pueblo
Blue River, Summit
Blue Sky, Morgan
Boaz, Las Animas
Bocea, La Plata
Boggsville, Bent
Bonanza, Saguache

Bond, Eagle
Bondad, La Plata
Bonita, Gunnison
Bonita, Saguache
Bonvcarbo, Las Animas
Book Cliff, Mesa
Boone, Pueblo
Bordenville, Park
Boreas, Summit
Borst, El Paso
Boston, Baca
Boulder Junction, Boulder
Bovina, Lincoln
Bow Mar, Arapahoe
Bow Mar, Jefferson
Bowen, Rio Grande
Bowerman, Gunnison
Bowman, Gunnison
Box Elder, Larimer
Boyds, Weld
Boyer, Park
Boyero, Lincoln
Braddock, Summit
Bradford, Huerfano
Brandon, Kiowa
Branson, Las Animas
Breckenridge, Summit
Breen, La Plata
Brick Center, Arapahoe
Bridge Three, Fremont
Bridgeport, Mesa
Briggsdale, Weld
Brighton, Adams
Bristol, Larimer
Bristol, Prowers
Brodhead, Las Animas
Brookfield, Baca
Brookside, Fremont
Brookvale, Clear Creek
Broomfield, Broomfield
Brown, Montrose
Brown, San Miguel
Brownlee, Jackson
Brown's Canon, Chaffee
Brush, Morgan
Bryant, Phillips
Buckeye, Larimer
Buckingham, Weld
Buckskin Joe, Park
Buena Vista, Chaffee
Buffalo Boy, San Juan
Buffalo Creek, Jefferson

Buffalo Springs, Park
Buffalo Tank, Jefferson
Buford, Rio Blanco
Bullion City (Howardsville), San Juan
Burdett, Washington
Burlington, Kit Carson
Burnham, Arapahoe
Burnito, Fremont
Burns Junction, Boulder
Burro Bridge, San Juan
Burrows, Park
Burrows Park, Hinsdale
Busk, Lake
Butler, Larimer
Butte City, Las Animas
Butte Valley, Huerfano
Buttermilk, Pitkin
Butte's, El Paso
Buxton, Saguache
Byers, Arapahoe
Cabeza, Mesa
Cable Junction, El Paso
Caddoa, Bent
Calhan, El Paso
Calumet, Huerfano
Cameo, Mesa
Cameron, Elbert
Cameville, Montrose
Camp Bird, Ouray
Camp Hale, Eagle
Campion, Larimer
Campo, Baca
Canadian, Larimer
Canfield, Boulder
Canon City, Fremont
Canon Mine, Boulder
Capital/Capitol City, Hinsdale
Capulin, Conejos
Carbon Valley, Weld
Carbondale, Garfield
Cardiff, Garfield
Caribou, Boulder
Carlisle, Kit Carson
Carlisle, Pueblo
Carlton, Prowers
Carnero, Saguache
Carpenter, Mesa
Carr, Weld
Carracas, Archuleta
Carrizo City (Carriso), Baca
Carrizo Springs, Baca

Index

Carson, Hinsdale
Carter's, Pueblo
Cascade, Chaffee
Cascade-Chipita Park, El Paso
Cassells, Park
Castle Pines, Douglas
Castle Rock, Douglas
Castles, Eagle
Castleton, Gunnison
Castlewood, Arapahoe
Cathedral, Hinsdale
Catherin, Conejos
Catherine, Garfield
Catlin, Otero
Cattle Creek, Garfield
Cebolla, Gunnison
Cedar Creek, Montrose
Cedar Point, Elbert
Cedaredge, Delta
Centennial, Arapahoe
Center, Saguache
Centerville, Chaffee
Central City, Gilpin
Centreville, Chaffee
Cerro Summit, Montrose
Chacra, Garfield
Chama, Costilla
Chandler, Fremont
Chapin, Kit Carson
Chapman, Boulder
Chappell, Las Animas
Charcoal, Chaffee
Chattanooga, San Juan
Chemung, Cheyenne
Chenoa, Logan
Cheraw, Otero
Cherokee Park, Larimer
Cherry Creek, Arapahoe
Cherry Hills Village, Arapahoe
Chester, Saguache
Cheyenne Wells, Cheyenne
Chico, Pueblo
Chicosa Junction, Las Animas
Chihuahua, Summit
Chilcott, Pueblo
Chimney Gulch, Jefferson
Chimney Rock, Archuleta
Chipeta, Delta
Chivington, Kiowa
Chromo, Archuleta
Church's, Jefferson

Cimarron, Montrose
Cimarron Hills, El Paso
Circle Crossing, Arapahoe
Claremont, Kit Carson
Clark, Routt
Clay Spur, Jefferson
Claytonia, Saguache
Clelland, Fremont
Clemmons, Elbert
Cleora, Chaffee
Cliff, Jefferson
Cliff Junction, Fremont
Cliffs Spur, Larimer
Clifton, Mesa
Climax, Lake
Clohseys Lake, Chaffee
Coal Branch Junction, Park
Coal Creek, Boulder
Coal Creek, Fremont
Coal Creek, Gilpin
Coal Creek, Jefferson
Coal Mine, Garfield
Coal Park, Boulder
Coal Tank, Jefferson
Coaldale, Fremont
Coalmont, Jackson
Coalridge, Garfield
Coals Spur, Park
Cockrell, Conejos
Cody, Washington
Coke Oven, Las Animas
Cokedale, Las Animas
Colbran, Mesa
Cold Spring, Custer
Colfax, Arapahoe
Colfax, Custer
Colfax, Denver
Colleyville, Summit
Colma, Ouray
Colona, Montrose
Colona, Ouray
Colorado Central Cut Off, Arapahoe
Colorado City, El Paso
Colorado City, Pueblo
Colorado Springs, El Paso
Colorow, Grand
Colorow, Montrose
Columbia, San Miguel
Columbia City, Boulder
Columbine, Arapahoe
Columbine, Jefferson

Columbine Valley, Arapahoe
Comanche Creek, Arapahoe
Commerce City, Adams
Como, Park
Concentrator, Pitkin
Conchito Junction, Huerfano
Condon, Arapahoe
Conejos, Conejos
Conifer, Jefferson
Cooper, Eagle
Cope, Arapahoe
Cope, Washington
Copper City, Baca
Copper Mountain, Summit
Corcoran, Arapahoe
Corkscrew, Montezuma
Corkscrew Gulch, Ouray
Corona, Grand
Corona, Weld
Coronado, Arapahoe
Cortez, Montezuma
Cortrite, Park
Cory, Delta
Coryell, Garfield
Cosden, Gunnison
Cotopaxi, Fremont
Cotton Creek, Saguache
Cottonwood, Gilpin
Cottonwood Springs, Chaffee
Coulter, Grand
Coventry, Montrose
Cowdrey, Jackson
Craig, Moffat
Crane Park, Lake
Crawford, Delta
Creech, Lincoln
Creede, Mineral
Crescent, Grand
Crested Butte, Gunnison
Crestone, Saguache
Creswell, Jefferson
Crevasse, Mesa
Cripple Creek, Teller
Crisman, Boulder
Crook, Logan
Crooks, Gunnison
Crookton, Gunnison
Crossons, Jefferson
Crow, Pueblo
Crowley, Crowley
Crystal, Gunnison
Crystal Creek, Montrose

Historical Assets Colorado

Crystal Lake, Jefferson
Crystal Lake, Lake
Crystola, El Paso
Cucharas, Huerfano
Cuenin, Saguache
Culver Siding, El Paso
Cumbres, Conejos
Currant Creek, Fremont
Currecanti, Gunnison
Curtin, Summit
Curtis, Washington
Custer City, Custer
Dacono, Weld
Dakan, Douglas
Dake, Park
Dakota Ridge, Jefferson
Dallas, Ouray
Dallas Divide, San Miguel
Davenport, Saguache
Dawkins, Pueblo
Dawson's, Jefferson
De Beque, Mesa
Deansbury, Douglas
Deansbury, Jefferson
Dearfield, Weld
Decatur, Baca
Decatur, Summit
Deckers, Douglas
Deep Creek, San Miguel
Deer Run, Mesa
Deer Trail, Arapahoe
Del Norte, Rio Grande
Delagua, Las Animas
Delhi, Las Animas
Delta, Delta
Denver, Denver
Denver Mills, Arapahoe
Deora, Baca
Derby, Arapahoe
Deuel, Las Animas
Deuel, Morgan
Dick, Weld
Dickey, Summit
Dillon, Summit
Dinosaur, Moffat
Diston, Kiowa
Divide, Chaffee
Divide, Teller
Dix, La Plata
Dixon, Larimer
Dixon's Mill, Boulder
Dolores, Montezuma
Dome Rock, Jefferson
Dominguez, Delta
Dorchester, Gunnison
Dotsero, Eagle
Douglass City, Douglas
Douglass City, Pitkin
Dove Creek, Dolores
Dove Valley, Arapahoe
Dover, Weld
Downieville, Clear Creek
Downing, Las Animas
Doyleville, Gunnison
Drake, Larimer
Dudley, Park
Duff, Arapahoe
Dumont, Clear Creek
Duncan, Delta
Duncan, Saguache
Dunckley, Routt
Dundee, Pueblo
Dune, Saguache
Dunton, Dolores
Durango, La Plata
Dwyer, Summit
Dyersville, El Paso
Dyersville, Summit
Eads, Kiowa
Eagalite, Mesa
Eagle, Eagle
Eagle-Vail, Eagle
Earl, Las Animas
East Idaho Springs, Clear Creek
East Pleasant View, Jefferson
Eastonville, El Paso
Eastonville, Elbert
Eaton, Weld
Ebert, Arapahoe
Echo, Fremont
Eckert, Delta
Eckley, Yuma
Eddy, Routt
Eden, Pueblo
Edgerton, El Paso
Edgewater, Jefferson
Edwards, Eagle
Egeria, Routt
Egnar, San Miguel
Eilers, Lake
El Jebel, Eagle
El Moro, Las Animas
El Paso, El Paso
Elba, Washington
Elbert, Elbert
Eldora, Boulder
Eldorato Springs, Boulder
Eldredge, Ouray
Elizabeth, Elbert
Elk Creek, Jefferson
Elk Park, San Juan
Elk Springs, Moffat
Elko, Saguache
Elkton, Gunnison
Ellicott, El Paso
Elsmere, El Paso
Elyria, Arapahoe
Elyria, Denver
Emerson, Phillips
Emma, Pitkin
Empire, Clear Creek
Engineer City, Ouray
Engle, Las Animas
Engleville Junction, Las Animas
English Gulch, Lake
Erie, Weld
Escalante, Delta
Escalante, Routt
Estabrook, Park
Estes Park, Larimer
Eureka, San Juan
Evans, Weld
Evergreen, Jefferson
Fair Grounds, Las Animas
Fairmount, Jefferson
Fairplay, Park
Fairview, Custer
Fairview, Custer
Fairview, Montrose
Fairy Glen, Fremont
Falcon, El Paso
Falfa, La Plata
Fall Creek, San Miguel
Fall River, Clear Creek
Farisita, Huerfano
Farmers, Weld
Farnham Spur, Summit
Federal Heights, Adams
Fergus, Kiowa
Ferguson, Garfield
Finntown, Lake
Firestone, Weld
First View, Cheyenne
Fisher, Chaffee

Index

Flagler, Kit Carson
Fleming, Logan
Flora, Sedgwick
Florbes, Las Animas
Florence, Fremont
Floresta, Gunnison
Florida, La Plata
Florissant, Teller
Florrisant, El Paso
Floyd Hill, Clear Creek
Fondis, Elbert
Forbes Junction, Las Animas
Forbes Mine, Las Animas
Forest Hill, Gunnison
Forks Creek, Jefferson
Fort Collins, Larimer
Fort Crawford, Montrose
Fort Garland, Costilla
Fort Logan, Arapahoe
Fort Lupton, Weld
Fort Lyon, Bent
Fort Morgan, Morgan
Fort Vasquez, Weld
Fountain, El Paso
Fowler, Otero
Fowler, Otero
Fox, Arapahoe
Foxfield, Arapahoe
Foxton, Jefferson
Franceville, El Paso
Franceville Junction, El Paso
Franktown, Douglas
Fraser, Grand
Frederick, Weld
Freeland, Clear Creek
Fremont Pass, Lake
French Gulch, Lake
Friend, Arapahoe
Frisco, Summit
Fruita, Mesa
Fruitvale, Mesa
Frying Pan, Eagle
Fulford, Eagle
Futurity, Chaffee
Galatea, Kiowa
Galena, Custer
Galena City, Hinsdale
Galeton, Weld
Galien, Logan
Garcia, Costilla
Garden City, Weld
Garden of the Gods, El Paso

Gardner, Huerfano
Garfield, Chaffee
Garnett, Costilla
Garo, Park
Garrison, Costilla
Gate View, Gunnison
Gateway, Mesa
Gaylor's Spur, Jefferson
Gem Village, La Plata
Genesee, Jefferson
Geneva City, Park
Geneva Gulch, Park
Genoa, Lincoln
Genoa, Lincoln
George, Fremont
Gerrard, Rio Grande
Gilcrest, Weld
Gill, Weld
Gillespie, Jefferson
Gillett, Teller
Gilman, Eagle
Gilman, Eagle
Gilman, Jefferson
Gilson Gulch, Clear Creek
Glaciers, Gunnison
Glade, Douglas
Gladstone, San Juan
Glen Haven, Larimer
Glen Isle, Park
Glencoe, Jefferson
Glendale, Arapahoe
Glendale, Boulder
Glendale, Fremont
Glendevey, Larimer
Gleneagle, El Paso
Glentivar, Park
Glenwood, Garfield
Glenwood Springs, Garfield
Globeville, Arapahoe
Globeville, Denver
Godfrey, Elbert
Goff, Kit Carson
Gold Hill, Boulder
Gold Hill Station, Boulder
Gold Park, Eagle
Golden, Jefferson
Goldfield, Teller
Gomers Mills, Elbert
Gooding, Boulder
Goodnight, Pueblo
Goodrich, Morgan
Gothic, Gunnison

Gould, Jackson
Govetown, Custer
Grabiola, Gunnison
Granada, Prowers
Granby, Grand
Grand Junction, Mesa
Grand Lake, Grand
Graneros, Pueblo
Granite, Chaffee
Granite Spur, Jefferson
Granity, Chaffee
Grant, Park
Graymount, Clear Creek
Grays, Saguache
Greeley, Weld
Green Mountain Falls, El Paso
Greenhorn, Pueblo
Greenland, Douglas
Greenwood, Custer
Greenwood Village, Arapahoe
Greysill Mines, La Plata
Greystone, Moffat
Grover, Weld
Guffey, Park
Guinare, Las Animas
Gulch, Park
Gulf Junction, Pueblo
Gunnison, Gunnison
Gunnison Smelter, Gunnison
Guston, Ouray
Guy Gulch, Jefferson
Gwillimville, El Paso
Gypsum, Eagle
Hagen, Ouray
Hagerman, Pitkin
Hahn's Peak, Routt
Hahn's Peak Village, Routt
Hale, Arapahoe
Hale, Yuma
Half Way House, El Paso
Halfway, Park
Hall Valley, Park
Hall's, Clear Creek
Hamilton, Chaffee
Hamilton, Moffat
Hamilton, Park
Hancock, Chaffee
Handcart, Park
Hanging Bridge, Fremont
Hardin, Weld
Harlow, Mesa
Harman, Arapahoe

Historical Assets Colorado

Harman, Denver
Harman, Washington
Harris, Arapahoe
Harris, Jefferson
Harris Park, Park
Harrisburg, Arapahoe
Harrisburg, Washington
Hartman, Prowers
Hartsel, Park
Hartsville, Chaffee
Harvard City, Chaffee
Haskell, Kiowa
Haskill, San Miguel
Hastings, Las Animas
Hasty, Bent
Haswell, Kiowa
Hatchery, Arapahoe
Hathaways, Summit
Haver, Park
Haworth, Larimer
Hawxhurst, Mesa
Haxtun, Phillips
Hay Ranch, Park
Hayden, Routt
Hayes, Costilla
Haywood Springs, Chaffee
Hebron, Jackson
Hebron, Larimer
Hecla Junction, Chaffee
Heeney, Summit
Henderson, Arapahoe
Henry, Conejos
Henson, Hinsdale
Hereford, Weld
Hereford, Weld
Hermosa, La Plata
Herrick, Pueblo
Hesperus, La Plata
Hidden Lake, Boulder
Hierro, Gunnison
Higbee, Otero
Higgins, Chaffee
Highland, Boulder
Highland Lake, Weld
Highland Mary, San Juan
Highlandlake, Weld
Highlands, Arapahoe
Highlands, Denver
Highlands Ranch, Douglas
Highmore, Garfield
Higho, Larimer
Hill Top, Douglas

Hilldon, Saguache
Hillerton, Gunnison
Hillrose, Morgan
Hillsboro, Weld
Hillside, Fremont
Hillside Spur, Ouray
Hilton, Bent
Hinkles, Gunnison
Hoehne, Las Animas
Holly, Prowers
Holly Hills, Arapahoe
Holtwold, Elbert
Holy Cross City, Eagle
Holyoke, Phillips
Home, Larimer
Home Ranch, La Plata
Homelake, Rio Grande
Homestead Meadows, Larimer
Honnold, Routt
Hooper, Alamosa
Hoosier, Park
Hopkins, Eagle
Hornbek Homestead, Teller
Horseshoe, Park
Hortense, Chaffee
Hot Springs, Saguache
Hot Sulphur Springs, Garfield
Hot Sulphur Springs, Grand
Hotchkiss, Delta
Hotchkiss, Weld
Howard, Fremont
Howardsville, San Juan
Howbert, Park
Hoyt, Elbert
Hoyt, Morgan
Hudson, Weld
Huerfano, Huerfano
Hugo, Lincoln
Hulbert, El Paso
Hull City, Teller
Husted, El Paso
Hutchinson, Jefferson
Hyde, Washington
Hydraulic, Montrose
Hygiene, Boulder
Idaho Creek, Boulder
Idalia, Arapahoe
Idalia, Yuma
Idledale, Jefferson
Idlewild, Park
Ignacio, La Plata
Iliff, Logan

Illium, San Miguel
Ilse, Custer
Independence, Arapahoe
Independence, Pitkin
Independence, Teller
Indian Hills, Jefferson
Interlaken, Chaffee
Interlaken, Lake
Inverness, Arapahoe
Iola (under Blue Mesa Reservoir), Gunnison
Ione, Weld
Iris, Saguache
Iron City, Chaffee
Iron Springs, Otero
Iron Springs, San Miguel
Irondale, Arapahoe
Ironton, Ouray
Irwin, Gunnison
Island Station, Arapahoe
Ivanhoe, Pitkin
Ivywild, El Paso
Jack's Cabin, Gunnison
Jackson, Gunnison
Jackson Lake, Morgan
Jamestown, Boulder
Janeway, Pitkin
Jansen, Las Animas
Jaroso, Las Animas
Jasper, Rio Grande
Jefferson, Park
Jerome Park, Pitkin
Jersey, Arapahoe
Jimmy's Camp, El Paso
Joes, Yuma
Johnson Village, Chaffee
Johnstown, Larimer
Johnstown, Weld
Juanita, Archuleta
Julesburg, Sedgwick
Juniata, Pueblo
Kahnah, Mesa
Kanorado, Cheyenne
Karval, Lincoln
Kebler, Gunnison
Keeldar, Lake
Keene, Weld
Keenesburg, Weld
Kelker, El Paso
Ken Caryl, Jefferson
Kenmuir, El Paso
Kenosha, Park

Index

Kenwood, Arapahoe
Keota, Weld
Kerper, Saguache
Kersey, Weld
Kester, Park
Keystone, San Miguel
Keystone, Summit
Kezar, Gunnison
Kilburn, Kiowa
Kim, Las Animas
King, Park
King's Canyon, Jackson
Kinikinik, Larimer
Kiowa, Elbert
Kirk, Yuma
Kit Carson, Cheyenne
Kittredge, Jefferson
Kline, La Plata
Kohinoor, Clear Creek
Kokomo, Summit
Kraft, Chaffee
Kremmling, Grand
Kuhn's Crossing, Elbert
La Boca, La Plata
La Foret, El Paso
La Garita, Saguache
La Jara, Conejos
La Junta, Otero
La Junta Gardens, Otero
La Plata, La Plata
La Plata Junction, La Plata
La Porte, Larimer
La Salle, Weld
La Sauses, Conejos
La Veta, Huerfano
Ladore, Routt
Lady Murphy, Chaffee
Lafayette, Boulder
LaGarita, Saguache
Laird, Yuma
Lake, Lincoln
Lake City, Hinsdale
Lake George, Park
Lake Hughes, Ouray
Lake Junction, Gunnison
Lakeshore, Hinsdale
Lakeside, Jefferson
Lakewood, Jefferson
Lamar, Prowers
Lamartine, Clear Creek
Lamb, Jefferson
Landsman, Kit Carson

Langford, Boulder
Lansing, Arapahoe
LaPorte, Larimer
Larimer, Pueblo
Larkspur, Douglas
Las Animas, Bent
LaSalle, Weld
Last Chance, Washington
Laurette, Park
Laurette, Park
Lavender, Dolores
Lawson, Clear Creek
Lay, Moffat
Lay, Routt
Lazear, Delta
Le Roy, Logan
Leadville, Lake
Leadville Junction, Lake
Leadville North, Lake
Leavick, Park
Lebanon, Clear Creek
Lee Siding, Jefferson
Lehigh Coal Mine, Douglas
Lenado, Pitkin
Leon, Garfield
Leopard, San Miguel
Leopard Creek, San Miguel
Leschers, Larimer
Leslie, Washington
Levisy, Pueblo
Lewis, Montezuma
Leyner, Boulder
Liberty, Saguache
Lidderdale, Jefferson
Liggett, Boulder
Lily, Routt
Lime Creek, Pitkin
Limon, Lincoln
Limon Station, Lincoln
Lincoln City, Summit
Lincoln Park, Fremont
Lindon, Arapahoe
Lindon, Washington
Little Buttes, El Paso
Little Mountain, Summit
Littleton, Arapahoe
Littleton, Jefferson
Livermore, Larimer
Lizard Head, Dolores
Lochbuie, Weld
Lockett, Saguache
Log Lane Village, Morgan

Logan, Arapahoe
Loghill Village, Ouray
Lolita, Otero
Loma, Mesa
London Mines, Park
Lone Tree, Douglas
Longmont, Boulder
Long's Junction, Las Animas
Lord's Ranch, Lake
Lord's Spur, Larimer
Loretto, Arapahoe
Los Cerritos, Conejos
Los Magotes, Saguache
Los Pinos, La Plata
Los Sauches, Conejos
Lost Dome, Montezuma
Louisville, Boulder
Louviers, Douglas
Loveland, Larimer
Lowland, Elbert
Lucerne, Weld
Ludlow, Las Animas
Ludlum, Yuma
Lulu City, Grand
Lupton, Weld
Lycan, Baca
Lyman, Arapahoe
Lynn, Las Animas
Lyons, Boulder
Lytle, El Paso
Mack, Mesa
Macon, Fremont
Madrid, Las Animas
Magnolia, Arapahoe
Magnolia, Boulder
Maher, Montrose
Malaby's, Larimer
Malachite, Huerfano
Malta, Lake
Manassas, Conejos
Manassas Station, Conejos
Mancos, Montezuma
Manhattan, Larimer
Manhattan, Larimer
Manitou Iron Springs, El Paso
Manitou Junction, El Paso
Manitou Springs, El Paso
Manzanola, Otero
Marble, Gunnison
Marion, Garfield
Marion, Gunnison
Marlman, Bent

Historical Assets Colorado

Marsh, Fremont
Marshall, Boulder
Marshall Basin, San Miguel
Marshall Junction, Boulder
Marshall Pass, Saguache
Martinsen, Las Animas
Marvel, La Plata
Mary Murphy, Chaffee
Masonville, Larimer
Massadona, Moffat
Massive City, Pitkin
Masters, Weld
Matheson, Elbert
Matterhorn, San Miguel
Mattison, Elbert
Maxey, Baca
Maxwell, Las Animas
Maybell, Moffat
Maybell, Routt
Mayday, La Plata
Mayfield, Jefferson
Mayflower Gulch, Summit
Mayo, Summit
Maysville, Chaffee
McClave, Bent
McConnellsville, El Paso
McCoy, Eagle
McFerran, El Paso
McGee's, Chaffee
McGinty, Costilla
McKenzie Junction, Custer
McPhee (under McPhee Reservoir), Montezuma
Mead, Weld
Meadows, Park
Meadows, Pueblo
Mears Junction, Chaffee
Meeker, Rio Blanco
Melina, Bent
Melvin, Arapahoe
Menger, Las Animas
Menoken, Montrose
Meredith, Eagle
Meredith, Pitkin
Meridian, Douglas
Merino, Logan
Mesa, Mesa
Mesa, Pueblo
Messex, Washington
Metcalf, Park
Michigan, Park
Middleton, San Juan
Midland, Teller
Midway, Chaffee
Midway, Gunnison
Military Junction, Arapahoe
Military Post, Arapahoe
Mill Gulch, Jefferson
Mill Pond, Eagle
Miller Creek, Pitkin
Millet, Washington
Milliken, Weld
Milner, Routt
Minaret, Gunnison
Miner, Larimer
Mineral Hot Springs, Saguache
Mineral Point, San Juan
Minneapolis, Baca
Minnehaha, El Paso
Minturn, Eagle
Mirage, Lincoln
Mirage, Saguache
Missouri City, Gilpin
Mitchell, Eagle
Mitchell, Weld
Model, Las Animas
Moffat, Saguache
Molina, Mesa
Monarch, Chaffee
Montana City, Arapahoe
Montana City, Denver
Montclair, Arapahoe
Montclair, Denver
Monte Vista, Rio Grande
Montelores, Dolores
Montezuma, Summit
Montgomery, Park
Montrose, Montrose
Montville, Costilla
Monument, El Paso
Mooreville, Arapahoe
Moraine, Larimer
Morey, Boulder
Morgan, Montezuma
Morgan Heights, Morgan
Morland, El Paso
Morley, Las Animas
Morris, Garfield
Morrison, Jefferson
Mosca, Alamosa
Mosca, Costilla
Mound, Gunnison
Mount Carbon, Gunnison
Mount Carbon, Jefferson
Mount Crested Butte, Gunnison
Mount Princeton, Chaffee
Mount Sneffels, Ouray
Mount Vernon, Jefferson
Mountain City, Gilpin
Mountain Meadows, Boulder
Mountain View, El Paso
Mountain View, Jefferson
Mountain View, Montrose
Mountain Village, San Miguel
Mountaindale, Park
Mule Shoe, Huerfano
Mulford, Garfield
Mulvane, Prowers
Namouna, Cheyenne
Nantes, Weld
Nast, Pitkin
Nathrop, Chaffee
Nathrop, Montrose
Naturita, Montrose
Navajo Ranch, Huerfano
Nederland, Boulder
Needleton, La Plata
Needleton, San Juan
Nepesta, Pueblo
Nevadaville, Gilpin
New Castle, Garfield
New Windsor, Weld
Newett, Chaffee
Newton, Arapahoe
Ni Wot [Niwot], Boulder
Niegoldstown, San Juan
Nighthawk, Douglas
Ninaview, Bent
No Name, Garfield
Noland, Boulder
Norrie, Pitkin
North Denver, Arapahoe
North Denver, Denver
North Empire, Clear Creek
North La Junta, Otero
North Star, Gunnison
Northglenn, Adams
Northrup, Boulder
Norwood, San Miguel
Nucla, Montrose
Numa, Otero
Nunn, Weld
Nyburg, Pueblo
Oak Creek, Fremont

Index

Oak Creek, Routt
Oak Creek Junction, Fremont
Oak Grove, Montrose
Oakes, Arapahoe
Ogle, Eagle
Ohio City, Gunnison
Ojo, Huerfano
Olathe, Montrose
Old Carson, Hinsdale
Old Homestead, Jackson
Old Hundred, San Juan
Old Roach, Larimer
Old Zounds, El Paso
Olney, Otero
Olney Springs, Crowley
Ophir, San Miguel
Orchard, Morgan
Orchard, Weld
Orchard City, Delta
Orchard Mesa, Mesa
Ordway, Crowley
Ordway, Otero
Oredel [Oradel], Boulder
Orient, Saguache
Oro City, Lake
Orr, Weld
Orsburn, Elbert
Orson, Mesa
Ortiz, Conejos
Osier, Conejos
Otis, Washington
Otto, Chaffee
Ouray, Ouray
Ouray Junction, Montrose
Overland Park, Arapahoe
Oversteg, Gunnison
Ovid, Sedgwick
Owl, Jackson
Oxford, La Plata
Padroni, Logan
Pagoda, Routt
Pagosa Junction, Archuleta
Pagosa Springs, Archuleta
Palisade, Mesa
Palmer Lake, El Paso
Pando, Eagle
Pandora, San Miguel
Paoli, Phillips
Paonia, Delta
Parachute, Garfield
Paradox, Montrose
Park City, Jackson

Park City, Park
Park Siding, Jefferson
Parkdale, Fremont
Parker, Douglas
Parker, Douglas
Parkville, Saguache
Parkville, Summit
Parlin, Gunnison
Parma, Rio Grande
Parrot City, La Plata
Parshall, Grand
Patterson, El Paso
Paymaster, Ouray
Peabodys, Park
Peachblow, Eagle
Pearl, Jackson
Pearl, Larimer
Peetz, Logan
Penrose, Fremont
Peoria, Arapahoe
Perry Park, Douglas
Petersburgh, Arapahoe
Peyton, El Paso
Phippsburg, Routt
Pictou, Huerfano
Pie Plant, Gunnison
Piedmont, Ouray
Piedra, Archuleta
Piedra, Hinsdale
Pierce, Weld
Pike View, El Paso
Pine, Jefferson
Pine Creek, Lake
Pine Grove, Jefferson
Pine Junction, Jefferson
Pine River, La Plata
Pinewood, Larimer
Pinewood Springs, Larimer
Pingree Park, Larimer
Pinkhampton, Larimer
Pinneo, Washington
Pinon, Montrose
Pinon, Pueblo
Pitkin, Gunnison
Pittsburg, Gunnison
Placer, Costilla
Placerville, San Miguel
Plateau, Douglas
Plateau City, Mesa
Platner, Washington
Platoro, Conejos
Platte Canon, Jefferson

Platte River, Park
Platte Station, Park
Platteville, Weld
Pleasant View, Montezuma
Pleasant View Ridge, Boulder
Plumbs, Weld
Pocono, Saguache
Poncha Springs, Chaffee
Poncho Pass, Saguache
Ponderosa Park, Elbert
Porter, La Plata
Portland, Fremont
Portland, Ouray
Poudre City, Larimer
Poudre Park, Larimer
Powderhorn, Gunnison
Powell, Las Animas
Preston, Summit
Princeton, Chaffee
Pring, El Paso
Pritchett, Baca
Proctor, Logan
Progress, Baca
Prospect, Gunnison
Prowers, Bent
Pryor, Huerfano
Pueblo, Pueblo
Pueblo West, Pueblo
Pullen, Larimer
Pultney, Pueblo
Puma City, Park
Punkin Center, Lincoln
Purcell, Weld
Quartz, Gunnison
Quarzville, Park
Querida, Custer
Radium, Grand
Rago, Washington
Ralston, Jefferson
Ramah, El Paso
Rand, Jackson
Rand, Larimer
Rangely, Rio Blanco
Raspberry, Chaffee
Rathbone, Pitkin
Rathbone, Summit
Raymer, Weld
Recen, Summit
Red Cliff, Eagle
Red Elephant, Clear Creek
Red Feather Lakes, Larimer
Red Hill, Park

Historical Assets Colorado

Red Lion, Logan
Red Mesa, La Plata
Red Mountain, Gunnison
Red Mountain City, San Juan
Red Mountain Town, Ouray
Red Wing, Huerfano
Redlands, Mesa
Redstone, Pitkin
Redvale, Montrose
Reno, Fremont
Resolis, Elbert
Revelleville, Park
Rexford, Summit
Richan, Larimer
Rico, Dolores
Ridgway, Ouray
Rifle, Garfield
Rio Alto, Saguache
Rio Aquilla, Eagle
Rio Blanco, Rio Blanco
River Bend, Elbert
Riverside, Chaffee
Riverside, Jefferson
Roan, Mesa
Robb, Yuma
Robinson, Bent
Robinson, Summit
Rock Creek, Eagle
Rock Creek, Summit
Rock Creek Park, El Paso
Rock Ridge, Douglas
Rock Spur, Jefferson
Rockdale, Chaffee
Rockford, Garfield
Rockland, Logan
Rockvale, Fremont
Rockwood, La Plata
Rocky, Park
Rocky Ford, Otero
Roggen, Weld
Rollinsville, Gilpin
Romeo, Conejos
Romley, Chaffee
Rosalias, Elbert
Roses Cabin, Hinsdale
Rosita, Custer
Roswell, El Paso
Rouarks, Park
Roubideau, Delta
Round Hill, Saguache
Rouse, Huerfano
Rouse's Junction, Huerfano
Routt, Routt
Roxborough, Douglas
Roxborough Park, Douglas
Ruby, Mesa
Ruby, Pitkin
Ruby City, Ouray
Ruedi, Eagle
Ruff, Baca
Rush, El Paso
Russell, Costilla
Russell Gulch, Gilpin
Rustic, Larimer
Rye, Pueblo
Ryssby, Boulder
Sacramento, Park
Saddle Horse, El Paso
Saddle Ridge, Morgan
Saguache, Saguache
Saint Cloud, Larimer
Saint Elmo, Chaffee
Saint Kevin, Lake
Saint Mary's, Huerfano
Saint Vrains, Weld
Saints John [Saint John's], Summit
Salida, Chaffee
Salina, Boulder
Salt Creek, Pueblo
Salt Works, Park
Sams, San Miguel
San Acacio, Costilla
San Carlos, Pueblo
San Isabel, Custer
San Isabel, Saguache
San Juan, Hinsdale
San Luis, Costilla
San Miguel, San Miguel
San Pedro, Costilla
San Rafael, Conejos
Sanborn, Lincoln
Sands, Garfield
Sanford, Conejos
Santa Clara, Huerfano
Santa Clara Junction, Huerfano
Sapinero, Gunnison
Sargents, Saguache
Satank, Garfield
Sawpit, San Miguel
Saxonia, Park
Schofield, Gunnison
Schwanders, Chaffee
Scissors, Huerfano
Scranton, Arapahoe
Secor, Boulder
Security-Widefield, El Paso
Sedalia, Douglas
Sedgwick, Sedgwick
Segundo, Las Animas
Seibert, Kit Carson
Selak, Grand
Selkirk, Park
Sellar, Pitkin
Semper, Jefferson
Seven Hills, Boulder
Seven Lakes, Pueblo
Seven Lakes, Teller
Severance, Weld
Shale, Mesa
Sharpsdale, Huerfano
Shavano, Chaffee
Shawano, Saguache
Shawnee, Park
Sheridan, Arapahoe
Sheridan Junction, Arapahoe
Sheridan Lake, Kiowa
Sherman, Eagle
Sherman, Hinsdale
Sherrod, Gunnison
Sherwood, Eagle
Shields, Arapahoe
Shirley, Chaffee
Shoshone, Garfield
Siding, Kit Carson
Sidney, Elbert
Sidney, Routt
Siebert, Kit Carson
Siloam, Fremont
Siloam, Pueblo
Siloam Springs, Garfield
Silt, Garfield
Silver Cliff, Custer
Silver Cliff, Garfield
Silver Creek, Clear Creek
Silver Dale, Clear Creek
Silver Lake, Huerfano
Silver Plume, Clear Creek
Silverdale, Chaffee
Silverthorne, Summit
Silverton, San Juan
Silvia, Las Animas
Simla, Elbert
Simpson, Washington
Slaghts, Park

Index

Slater, Routt
Slick Rock, San Miguel
Sligo, Weld
Sloane, Eagle
Smeltertown, Chaffee
Smith Hill, Gilpin
Smuggler, San Miguel
Sneffels, Ouray
Snowden, Lake
Snowmass, Pitkin
Snowmass Village, Pitkin
Snyder, Morgan
Soda Springs, Fremont
Soda Springs, Lake
Somerset, Gunnison
Sopris, Las Animas
Sorrento, Cheyenne
South Canon, Garfield
South Denver, Arapahoe
South Denver, Denver
South Fork, Rio Grande
South Fork, San Miguel
South Platte, Jefferson
South Pueblo, Jefferson
Southern Ute, La Plata
Southglenn, Arapahoe
Spar City, Mineral
Sparkill, Pitkin
Spence, Washington
Spicer, Jackson
Spicer, Larimer
Spike Buck, Fremont
Spinney, Park
Spook City, Saguache
Spring Gulch, Pitkin
Springdale, Boulder
Springfield, Baca
St Elmo, Chaffee
St Mary's, Clear Creek
Stamford, Las Animas
Stanley, Costilla
Starkville, Las Animas
State Line, Prowers
Steamboat Springs, Routt
Sterling, Hinsdale
Sterling, Logan
Stevens Gulch, Jefferson
Stewart, Kiowa
Stone Spur, Jefferson
Stoneham, Weld
Stonewall, Chaffee
Stonewall, Las Animas

Stonewall Gap, Las Animas
Stonington, Baca
Stonwall Gap, Las Animas
Stout (under Horsetooth Reservoir), Larimer
Strasburg, Arapahoe
Stratmoor, El Paso
Stratton, Kit Carson
Streator, Costilla
Struby, Douglas
Stuart, Kiowa
Stumptown, Lake
Stunner, Conejos
Sublette, Conejos
Sugar City, Crowley
Sugarloaf, Boulder
Summit, El Paso
Summit, Ouray
Summit, San Juan
Summit Park, El Paso
Summit Springs (Battlefield), Logan
Summitville, Rio Grande
Sunbeam, Moffat
Sunflower, Conejos
Sunnyside, Hinsdale
Sunset, Boulder
Sunshine, Boulder
Sunshine, Garfield
Sunview, El Paso
Superior, Boulder
Suttons, Summit
Swallows, Pueblo
Swan, Summit
Swandyke, Summit
Sweetwater, Eagle
Swift, Prowers
Swink, Otero
Swiss Boy, Chaffee
Swissvale, Fremont
Sybl, Otero
Symes, Jefferson
Tabaco, Las Animas
Tabernash, Grand
Table Rock, El Paso
Tabor, Boulder
Talpa, Huerfano
Tampa, Weld
Tanglewood Acres, Custer
Tarryall, Park
Tasmania, Chaffee
Taylors, Pueblo

Taylorville, Pueblo
Teachout, Gunnison
Teds Place, Larimer
Teller City, Jackson
Telluride, San Miguel
Tellurium, Hinsdale
Tennessee Pass, Eagle
Texas Creek, Fremont
Thatcher, Las Animas
Thistledown, Ouray
Thomasville, Eagle
Thompson's, Las Animas
Three Mile Tank, Lake
Thurman, Arapahoe
Thurman, Washington
Tiffany, La Plata
Timnath, Larimer
Timpas, Otero
Tinball, Jefferson
Tincup, Gunnison
Tindale, Jefferson
Tioga, Huerfano
Tip Top, El Paso
Tiptop, Gilpin
Toll Gate, Fremont
Tolland, Gilpin
Toluca, Douglas
Tomah, Douglas
Tomboy, San Miguel
Tomichi, Chaffee
Toonerville, Bent
Toponas, Routt
Tourtelotte, Pitkin
Towaoc, Montezuma
Tower Junction, Boulder
Towner, Kiowa
Townsend, Arapahoe
Trail City, Bent
Trail Side, Morgan
Trimble, La Plata
Trimble Stage Stop, Gunnison
Trinchera, Costilla
Trinchera, Las Animas
Trinidad, Las Animas
Troublesome, Grand
Trout Lake, San Miguel
Troy, Las Animas
Tructon, El Paso
Trull, Routt
Trump, Park
Truro, Park
Tuna, Huerfano

Historical Assets Colorado

Tungsten, Boulder
Tunnel, Mesa
Tunnel Spur, Pitkin
Turret, Chaffee
Tuttle, Kit Carson
Twin Lakes, Lake
Two Buttes, Baca
Tyrone, Las Animas
Ula, Custer
Una, Garfield
Unaweep, Mesa
Uncompahgre, Montrose
Undercliffe, Pueblo
University Park, Arapahoe
Upper Bear Creek, Clear Creek
Upper Camp Bird, Ouray
Uptop (Old La Veta Pass), Huerfano
Uravan, Montrose
Urmston, Jefferson
Utah Junction, Arapahoe
Utah Line, Mesa
Ute, Huerfano
Ute, Montrose
Ute Park, El Paso
Utleyville, Baca
Vail, Eagle
Valdal, Larimer
Valdez, Las Animas
Valentine Spur, Larimer
Vallejo, La Plata
Valley Spur, Gunnison
Vallie, Fremont
Valmont, Boulder
Valverde, Arapahoe
Valverde, Denver
Vance Junction, San Miguel
Vanderbilt, Ouray
Vega, Mesa
Vegas, Pueblo
Venice, Chaffee
Verde, Pueblo
Vermillion, Jefferson
Vernon, Yuma
Veta Pass, Huerfano
Veteran, Saguache
Viceto, La Plata
Vicksburg, Chaffee
Victor, Teller
Vidals Spur, Gunnison
Vilas, Baca
Villa Grove, Saguache
Villa Park, Arapahoe
Villegreen, Las Animas
Vineland, Pueblo
Virginia Dale, Larimer
Virginius, Ouray
Vona, Kit Carson
Vulcan, Gunnison
Wagon Wheel Gap, Mineral
Wagon Wheel Gap, Rio Grande
Wahotoya, Huerfano
Waitley, Washington
Wakeman, Phillips
Walden, Jackson
Walden, Larimer
Waldorf, Clear Creek
Wallet, Kit Carson
Walsenburg, Huerfano
Walsh, Baca
Ward, Boulder
Washburn, Arapahoe
Water Valley, Kiowa
Watervale, Las Animas
Watkins, Arapahoe
Watson, Pitkin
Wattenburg, Weld
Waunita Hot Springs, Gunnison
Waverly, Alamosa
Waverly, Larimer
Weaver, Mineral
Webster, Park
Weir, Sedgwick
Weldon, Morgan
Weldona, Morgan
Wellington, Larimer
Wellsville, Fremont
Wentz, Weld
West Denver, Arapahoe
West Glenwood, Garfield
West Pleasant View, Jefferson
Westcliffe, Custer
Westminster, Adams
Westminster, Jefferson
Weston, Las Animas
Wests, Las Animas
Westwood, Arapahoe
Westwood, Denver
Wetmore, Custer
Wheat Ridge, Jefferson
Wheatland, Jefferson
Wheeler, Garfield
Wheeler, Summit
White Cross, Hinsdale
White Pine, Gunnison
White River, Rio Grande
White Rock, Boulder
Whitehorn, Fremont
Whitewater, Mesa
Whitford, Las Animas
Whitney, Kiowa
Widefield, El Paso
Wiggins, Morgan
Wigwam, El Paso
Wild Horse, Chaffee
Wild Horse, Cheyenne
Wild Irishman, Summit
Wilde, Prowers
Wilders, Summit
Wilde's Spur, Larimer
Wiley, Prowers
Willard, Logan
Williamsburg, Fremont
Williamsville, El Paso
Windsor, Larimer
Windsor, Weld
Winfield, Chaffee
Winona, Larimer
Winter Park, Grand
Wohlhurst, Douglas
Wolcott, Eagle
Wondervu, Boulder
Woodland Park, El Paso
Woodland Park, Teller
Woodmoor, El Paso
Woodrow, Washington
Woodruff, Fremont
Woodstock, Gunnison
Woody Creek, Pitkin
Wootton, Las Animas
Wray, Yuma
Wynetka, Arapahoe
Xenia, Washington
Yale, Kit Carson
Yampa, Routt
Yankee Girl, Ouray
Yellow Jacket, Montezuma
Yoder, El Paso
Yorkville, Fremont
Youman, Gunnison
Yuma, Yuma
Zangs Spur, Boulder
Zapato, Costilla
Zirkel, Jackson
Zuck, Prowers

Archives & Museums Index

Symbols

4th Infantry Division Museum-Mountain Post Historical Center 265

A

Adams County Historical Society, Historical Museum 34
Adeline Hornbeck Homestead 691
Agricultural Heritage Center 107
Alice G Milne House & Memorial Park , 681
Amache Museum 596
American Nimismatic Association, Money Museum 265
Anasazi Heritage Center Museum 521
Anderson Academic Commons, Special Collections 202
Animas Museum & Research Library 417, 418
Animas School Museum 418
Arapahoe County Colorado Archive Center (digital) 57
Archives of the Archdiocese of Denver 202
Archives of the Episcopal Diocese of Colorado 202
Archuleta County Archive (digital) 74
Argo Gold Mine & Mill Museum 150
Arriba Museum 473
Arthur Lakes Library & Special Collections 382
Aspen Historical Society Archives 584
Auraria Library, Special & Digital Collections 202
Aurora History Museum 57

B

Baca House, Trinidad History Museum 458
Bailey Library & Archives 202
Bailey Saddleland Museum 286
Baker Schneider Archives Vestig 440
Barco Library & Cable Center Museum 204
Barney Ford House Museum 681
Bent's Old Fort National Historic Site Museum 550
Beulah History Center 606
Big Timbers Museum 596
Black American West Museum and Heritage Center 204

Blair Caldwell African American Research Library 202
Bledorn Research Ctr & Museum 541
Bloom House Museum 458
Boettcher Mansion Museum 204
Boulder County Records Archive (digital) 105
Bowles House Museum 34
Bowman White House Museum 150
Breckenridge Mining Camp Museum 681
Breckenridge Sawmill Museum 681
Breckenridge Welcome Center Museum 681
Brighton City Museum & Research Room 34
Brush Area Museum and Cultural Center, 541
Buckhorn Exchange Restaurant and Museum 204
Buena Vista Depot Museum 129
Buena Vista Heritage Association, Courthouse Museum 129

C

Callahan House & Garden 107
Canyons of the Ancients National Monument 521
Carnegie Library for Local History 105
Catholic Diocese of Colorado Springs Archives 263
Center for Southwest Studies 417
Central City Opera House Association, Historical Museum 320
Charles Leaming Tutt Library & Special Collections 263
City of Boulder Records Archive (digital) 105
City of Evans Museum 715
Clear Creek County Archives 149
Clear Creek Historic Mining & Milling Museum 150
Coeur d'Alene Mine Shaft House Museum 320
Colorado Chautauqua Association, Archive and History Room 105
Colorado Division of State Archives and Public Records 202
Colorado Heritage Center 204
Colorado Mental Health Institute at Pueblo Museum 606
Colorado Model Railroad Museum 715
Colorado National Monument Museum 492
Colorado Snow Sports Museum Hall of Fame 251

Historical Assets Colorado

Colorado Sports Hall of Fame 204
Colorado Springs Pioneer Museum & Archives 263, 265
Colorado Territorial Prison Museum 296
Colorado Welcome Center Museum 408, 458, 492, 511, 521, 673
Comanche Crossing Historical Society, Historical Museum 34
Conejos County Museum 159
Cortez Cultural Center 521
Cottage Camp Museum 329
Cozens Ranch Museum 329
Creede Historical Society, Historical Museum, Library & Archive 502
Creede Underground Mining Museum 503
Crested Butte Mountain Heritage Museum 340
Crestone Historical Museum 647
Cripple Creek District Museum 691
Cripple Creek Heritage Center 692
Crook Historical Society, Historical Museum 482
Cross Orchards Historic Farm Museum 492
Crow Canyon Archaeological Center 522
Crowley County Heritage Center 175
CU Heritage Center Museum 107
Custer County Historical & Genealogical Society 180

D

Dayton Memorial Library, Archives & Special Collections 33
Deer Trail Pioneer Museum 240
Delaney Farm Museum 204
Delta County Museum 190
Denver Firefighters Museum 204
Denver Museum of Nature & Science 204
Denver Public Library-Western History & Genealogy 202
Denver & Rio Grande RR Station Museum 240
Dillon School House Museum 682
Dougherty Museum 107
Douglas County Library & History Research Center 239
Dr Martin Luther King Jr Cultural Center 606
Dr Sandra F Mathew Archives 680
Dr Verity Museum 83
Durango & Silver Narrow Gauge Railroad Museum 418

E

Eagle Valley Library District & Local History Archive 250
Eastern Colorado Historical Society, Old Jail Museum 141
Eastern Trails Museum and Cultural Arts Center 473
Eaton House Museum 715
Edwin Carter Discovery Center 681
Elbert County Historical Society, Historical Museum 286
El Pueblo History Museum 606
Emily Warner Field Aviation Museum 329
Englewood Public Library & City Archive 57

F

Flagler Hospital Museum & Hal Borland Room 408
Fleming Museum 482
Florissant Fossil Bedds National Monument 691
Florissant Schoolhouse Museum 692
Forney Museum of Transportation 204
Fort Collins Museum of Discovery Local History Archive 440
Fort Francisco Museum 363
Fort Garland Museum 167
Fort Lupton Historic Park 716
Fort Lupton Museum 716
Fort Sedgwick Historical Society, Depot Museum 673
Fort Sedgwick Museum 673
Fort Uncompahgre Living History Museum 190
Fort Vasquez Museum 716
Four Mile Historic Park Museum 204
Fowler Historical Society, Historical Museum 550
Francisco Fort Museum 363
Frisco Historic Park & Museum 682
Frontier Historical Society, Historical Museum 308

G

Galloping Goose Historical Railway Society of Dolores, Historical Museum 522
Gateway Colorado Auto Museum 492
George Rowe Museum at the Schoolhouse 150
Georgetown Energy Museum 150

Index

Georgetown Loop Historic Mining & Railroad Museum 150
Ghost Town Museum 265
Gilpin County Museum 320
Golconda Boarding House Museum 355
Gold Hill Museum 107
Grand County Archive Center (digital) 328
Grand County Museum & Pioneer Village 329
Grand Lodge A.F. & A.M. of Colorado 263
Grant-Humphreys Mansion Museum 204
Grover Depot Museum 716
Gunnison County Archive (digital) 339
Gunnison County Historic Preservation Commission 339
Gunnison County Pioneer and Historical Society 339

H

Hahns Peak Village Museum 636
Hard Tack Mine Museum 355
Hart Research Center 202
Hayden Heritage Center 636
Hazard House Museum 647
Healy House-Dexter Cabin Museum 429
Hedlund House Museum 473
Heritage Park Museum 329
High Line Railroad Park & Museum 682
Historical Society of Oak Creek and Phippsburg, Tracks & Trails Museum 636
Historic Centennial Village Museum 716
Historic Fort Logan 204
Historic Georgetown, Hamill House Museum 150
Historic Hover Home & Farmstead 107
History Colorado, Colorado Heritage Center, 204
Holden Marolt Mining & Ranching Museum 585
Homelake Veterans' History Museum 627
Hose Company No. 3 - Pueblo's Fire Museum 607
Hotchkiss-Crawford Historical Society, Historical Museum 190
Hotel de Paris Museum 150
House with the Eye Museum 429
Huerfano Heritage Center 363

I

Infozone News Museum 607
IOOF Grand Lodge of Colorado 295

Ira J Taylor Library & Margaret E Scheve Archives 202
Ira M Beck Memorial Collection of Rocky Mountain Jewish History 202

J

Jack Dempsey Museum 159
James A Michener Library, Archives & Special Collections 714
James F Bailey Assay Office Museum 107
James Underhill Museum & Victorian Garden 150
Jefferson County Archives 382
John W Rawlins Heritage Center 93

K

Kaufman House Museum 329
Kiowa County Museum 399
Kit Carson County Carousel & Museum 408
Kit Carson Historical Society, Historical Museum 141
Koshare Indian Museum & Trading Post 550

L

Lace House Museum, 320
Lafayette Historical Society, Miner's Museum 107
Lake City (Hinsdale County) Museum 355
Lake County Public Library Digital Collection 428
Leslie J Savage Library Archives & Special Collections 339
Limon Heritage Museum & Railroad Park 473
Littleton Historical Society, Historical Museum 57
Longmont Museum and Cultural Center 105, 107
Louisville Historical Commission, Historical Museum 108
Loyd Files Research Library 491
Lucretia Vaile Museum 266
Luther Bean Museum 45
Lyons Redstone Museum 108

M

Manitou Cliff Dwellings Museum 265
Manitou Springs Heritage Center 265
Manitou Springs Historical Society, Miramont Castle 265

Historical Assets Colorado

Marble Historical Society, Historical Museum 308
Marcetta Luz Historical Library & Archives 382
Marin Museum of Bicycling and Mountain Bike Hall of Fame Museum 340
Matchless Mine Museum 429
McAllister House Museum 266
McDermott Library & Clark Special Collections Branch 263
Meeker Home Museum 716
Melvin Schoolhouse Museum & Library 57
Mesa Verde National Park Museum 522
Michener Library, Archives & Special Collections 714
Milliken Historical Society, Historical Museum 716
Miramont Castle 265
Mizel Museum 204
Mollie Kathleen Mine Museum 692
Molly Brown House Museum 204
Molly Brown Summer House Museum 204
Monte Vista Historical Society, Historical Museum 627
Montezuma Heritage Museum 522
Montrose County Historical Society, Depot Museum 531
Mountain States Telephone & Telegraph Museum 141
Museo de las Americas 204
Museum of Boulder , 108
Museum of Northwest Colorado 511
Museum of the Mountain West 531
Museum of the West 492
Museum of the West & Loyd Files Research Library 491

N

National Archives at Denver 121
National Mining Hall of Fame Museum 429
National Museum of World War II Aviation 265
New Castle Historical Society, Historical Museum 308
Niwot Historical Society, Firehouse Museum 108
Norlin Library, Archives & Special Collections 105
Northern Drylanders Museum 716
North Park Pioneer Association, Historical Museum 372
Notah Dineh Trading Company Museum 522

O

Oasis on the Plains Museum 541
Old Colorado City Historical Society, Historical Museum 266
Old Fort Garland Museum 167
Old Homestead Parlour House Museum 692
Old St Stephen's 1881 Church 108
Old Town Museum 408
Otero Museum 550
Ouray Alchemist Pharmaceutical Museum 559
Ouray County Archive Center (digital) 558
Ouray County Ranch History Museum 559
Outlaws & Law Men Jail Museum 692
Overland Trail Museum 482

P

Pagosa Springs History Museum 74
Parish House & Museum 716
Park County Local History Archives , 567
Park County Public Library 567
Parker Area Historical Society, Schoolhouse Museum 240
Penrose Heritage Museum 266
Peterson Air & Space Museum 266
Phillips County Museum 577
Pikes Peak Auto Hill Climb Museum 266
Pikes Peak Historical Society, Historical Museum 692
Pikes Peak Historic Street Railway Museum 266
Pikes Peak Radio & Electronics Museum 266
Pine River Valley Heritage Society, Historical Museum 418
Pioneer Museum 340, 716
Pioneer Town Museum 190
Price Pioneer Museum 296
Pro Rodeo Hall of Fame Museum 266
Prospect Heights Jail Museum 296
Pueblo Heritage Museum 607
Pueblo Railway Museum 607
Pueblo Weisbrod Aircraft Museum 607

R

Rambler Ranch Museum 286
Rangely Outdoor Museum 619
Rawlins Heritage Center 93
Rico Historical Society, Historical Museum 231
Ridgway Railroad Museum 559
Rifle Heritage Center 309

Index

Rimrocker Historical Society of West Montrose County, Historical Museum 531
Rio Grande County Historical Society, Historical Museum 627
Robert Hoag Rawlings Library Special Collections 605
Rock Ledge Ranch Historic Site Museum 266
Rocky Ford Historical Museum 550
Rocky Mountain Motorcycle Museum 266
Rocky Mountain Wing of the Commemorative Air Force 492
Rosemount Museum 607
Routt County Public Records Archive (digital) 635
Royal Gorge Dinosaur Experience 296
Royal Gorge Regional Museum and History Center 296

S

Saguache County Museum 647
Saint Vrain Historical Society, Old Mill Park 108
Salida Archive (digital) 129
Salida Museum Association, Historical Museum 129
Sand Creek Massacre National Historic Site 399
Sanford Colorado History Museum 159
Sangre de Cristo Heritage Center 167
San Juan County Historical Society, Mining Heritage Center & Archives 656
San Luis Valley History Museum 45
Santa Fe Trail Museum 458
Second Central School Museum 408
Sidney Heitman Germans from Russia Collection 440
Silt Historical Society, Historical Museum 309
Silver Cliff Museum 181
Slovenian Genealogy Center-Gornick Library & Museum 607
Southern Ute Cultural Center 418
South Park City Museum 567
Spirit of Flight Center 716
Springfield Museum , 83
Starsmore Center for Local History, 263
Steelworks Center of the West and CF&I Archives 605
Stephen H Hart Research Center 202
Stiles African American Heritage Center 204
Summit Ski Museum 682

Surface Creek Historical Society, Pioneer Town Museum 190

T

Tabor Historic Home Museum 429
Tabor Opera House Museum 429
Telluride Historical Society, Historical Museum 665
Temple Israel Synagogue and Museum 429
Thomas House Museum 320
Thompson House Museum 308
Transportation of the West Museum 627
Tread of Pioneers Museum 636
Trinidad History Museum 458
Turin Shroud Center of Colorado 266
Turner Farm and Apple Orchard Museum 129
Two Buttes-Dr Verity Museum 83

U

Underhill Museum & Victorian Garden 150
United States Mint Museum 205
United States Space Foundation Headquarters & Discovery Center 266
University Library Archives & Special Collections 605
University of Southern Colorado Library, Special Collections 605
US Air Force Academy Visitor Center 266
US Geological Survey Photographic Library 382
Ute Indian Museum 531
Ute Pass Historical Society, Historical Museum 692

V

Vaile Museum 266
Victor Lowell Thomas Museum 692
Vintage Aero Flying Museum 716
Vintage Ski World Museum 309

W

Walsenburg Mining Museum 363
Washington County Museum 701
Washington Hall Museum 320
Western Museum of Mining & Industry 266
Westminster History Center 34
Wheeler Stallard House Museum 585
White-Plumb Farm Learning Center 716
White River Museum 619

Historical Assets Colorado

William E Morgan Library, Colorado State Univ, Special Collections & Archives 440
William H Briggle House Museum , 682
Will Rogers Shrine of the Sun 266
Windsor Museum 716
Wings Over the Rockies Air & Space Museum 205
Wise Homestead Museum 716
World Figure Skating Museum 266
Wray Museum 732
Wyman Living History Ranch and Museum 511

Y

Yampa-Egeria Historical Museum 636
Yuma Museum 732